Critical acclaim for the Berkeley Guides

"[The Berkeley Guides are] brimming with useful information for the low-budget traveler—material delivered in a fresh, funny, and often irreverent way."   —*The Philadelphia Inquirer*

"The [Berkeley Guides] are deservedly popular because of their extensive coverage, entertaining style of writing, and heavy emphasis on budget travel...If you are looking for tips on hostels, vegetarian food, and hitchhiking, there are no books finer."
                    —*San Diego Union-Tribune*

"Straight dirt on everything from hostels to look for and beaches to avoid to museums least likely to attract your parents... they're fresher than Harvard's Let's Go series."   —*Seventeen*

"The [Berkeley Guides] give a rare glimpse into the real cultures of Europe, Canada, Mexico, and the United States...with in-depth historical backgrounds on each place and a creative, often poetical style of prose."   —*Eugene Weekly*

"More comprehensive, informative and witty than Let's Go."
                    —*Glamour*

"The Berkeley Guides have more and better maps, and on average, the nuts and bolts descriptions of such things as hotels and restaurants tend to be more illuminating than the often terse and sometimes vague entries in the Let's Go guides."
                    —*San Jose Mercury News*

"These well-organized guides list can't-miss sights, offbeat attractions and cheap thrills, such as festivals and walks. And they're fun to read."   —*New York Newsday*

"Written for the young and young at heart...you'll find this thick, fact-filled guide makes entertaining reading."
                    —*St. Louis Dispatch*

"Bright articulate guidebooks. The irreverent yet straight-forward prose is easy to read and offers a sense of the adventures awaiting travelers off the beaten path."   —*Portland Oregonian*

On the Loose
On the Cheap
Off the Beaten Path

THE BERKELEY GUIDES

California '97
Central America (2nd Edition)
Eastern Europe (3rd Edition)
Europe '97
France (4th Edition)
Germany & Austria (4th Edition)
Great Britain & Ireland '97
Italy '97
London '97
Mexico '97
New York City '97
Pacific Northwest & Alaska (3rd Edition)
Paris (3rd Edition)
San Francisco '97

THE BERKELEY GUIDE TO SAN FRANCISCO

Editor: Kathleen Dodge
Managing Editors: Tara Duggan, Kristina Malsberger, Sora Song
Executive Editor: Sharron Wood
Creative Director: Fabrizio La Rocca
Cartographer: David Lindroth, Inc.; Eureka Cartography
Text Design: Tigist Getachew
Cover Design: Fabrizio La Rocca
Cover Art: Poul Lange (3-D art), Robert Holmes (photo in frame), Paul D'Innocenzo (still life)

SPECIAL SALES

Fodor's **BERKELEY** budget guides

san francisco '97

On the Loose
On the Cheap
Off the Beaten Path

WRITTEN BY BERKELEY STUDENTS IN COOPERATION WITH
THE ASSOCIATED STUDENTS OF THE UNIVERSITY OF CALIFORNIA

Contents

THANKS TO YOU *vii*
BERKELEY BIOS *viii*
MAP OF THE BAY AREA *xi*

1 BASICS *1*
Getting In, Out, and Around *1*
By Car *1*
By Bus *3*
By BART *5*
By Bike *5*
By Train *6*
By Taxi *6*
By Ferry *7*
By Plane *7*
Bay Area Directory *8*

Low-Cost Medical Aid *8*
Phones and Mail *10*
Media *10*
Resources for Gays and Lesbians *12*
Resources for People of Color *14*
Resources for Women *15*
Resources for People with Disabilities *15*
Festivals *16*
Climate *20*
Visitor Information *21*

2 EXPLORING THE BAY AREA *23*
San Francisco *23*
Map of San Francisco 24–25
Map of Golden Gate Park 29
Map of Downtown San Francisco 32–33
Map of the Haight, Castro, and Mission
  Districts 48–49

East Bay *59*
Map of Berkeley 61
Map of Oakland 69
Marin County *73*
Map of Marin County 74
South Bay *81*

3 SHOPPING *91*
New Clothes *91*
Secondhand Clothing *93*
Books *95*
Records, Tapes, and CDs *97*

Household Furnishings *99*
Flea Markets *100*
Specialty Items *101*

4 FOOD *105*
San Francisco *106*
East Bay *123*
Marin County *130*

South Bay *132*
Markets and Specialty Stores *134*
Reference Listings *136*

5 CAFÉ CULTURE *141*

6 AFTER DARK *149*
Bars *149*
Live Music *157*
Clubs *161*
Movie Houses *164*
Theater *166*

Multimedia Performance
  Spaces *168*
Classical Music *169*
Dance *171*

7 WHERE TO SLEEP *173*
San Francisco *173*
Map of Downtown San Francisco
  Lodging 178–179
Map of Haight, Castro, and Mission
  Lodging 181

East Bay *186*
Marin County *189*
South Bay *192*

8 THE GREAT OUTDOORS 195

League Sports and
  Pickup Games 196
Hiking and Biking 199
In-Line Skating 209
Rock Climbing 210

Sailing 211
Sea Kayaking 211
Surfing 212
Windsurfing 213
Spectator Sports 215

9 DAY AND WEEKEND TRIPS 217

The Wine Country 217
Map of the Wine Country 218
Lake Tahoe 229
Map of Lake Tahoe 230
Yosemite National Park 240

Map of Yosemite National Park 241
Santa Cruz 250
Map of Santa Cruz 251
Monterey 259
Big Sur 262

INDEX 265

Thanks to You

Lots of people helped us put together the *Berkeley Guide to San Francisco*. Some are listed below, but many others, whom our writers met briefly on buses, in cafés, and in clubs, also helped out. We would like you to help us update this book and give us feedback. Drop us a line—a postcard, a scrawled note on some toilet paper, whatever—and we'll be sure to pass on your tips to future writers. Our address is 515 Eshleman Hall, University of California, Berkeley, CA 94720.

Special thanks go to The AAA guy who fixed Charlene Pinzon's flat (Cotati), Julie Anderson (SF), John Arnold and the entire CA State Parks staff (Sacramento), Katharine Bancroft (SF), Michele Back (SF), CJ Blankenship (San Jose), Thomas Day (SF), Melissa de la Rosa (Oakland), Nancy Dito (SF), Dodge Family (CA), Carlos Duarte (New York), Dina Fayer (Richmond), John Fisher (SF), Kayce Garcia (SF), Gina Gatta of Damron Co. (SF), Elizabeth Gray (Fairyland), Anthony Grealy (SF), Professor Paul Groth (Berkeley), Gabe and Alex (Reno), Hal Hartley (NYC), Alison Harvey and Tom (Reno), The Jack London Lodge (Glen Ellen), Julie Jares (SF), Connie Ko (Lake Tahoe), Michael Kloster (Oakland), Robby Kramer (Oakland), Liz Lazich (Richmond), Irina Leimbacher(SF), Gregory Lenczycki (SF), Richard Littlejohn (Oakland), Pink Man (Berkeley), Kristin Madison (Palo Alto), Karen Meltzer (La Honda), Peter Merholtz (SF), Rachael Myrow (LA), Kenny Ng (SF), Michele Posner (SF), Quazar (NYC), Mary Reilly (UK), John Rother (Oakland), Shana Samuels (SF), Elisabeth Schriber (SF), Brent Searcy (Blacksburg), Michael Somaza (Albany), Simon Trainer (SF), Vegan Cookie Co. (Berkeley), Rebecca Wall (Sheffield), Richard Wallen (NYC), James Wang (SF), Jennifer Wedel (AZ), Todd, Judi, and Karl Weisgraber (Walnut Creek), Sharron Wood (SF).

Back home in the Berkeley office, a glass should be raised to the EEN with an M who provided innumerable laughs, office calisthenics, and that all-important theme song, "Cut, Cut, Cut . . . It Out!" Additionally, the invaluable Suzanne Stein provided keen insight into every aspect of the San Francisco guide from beginning to end. We'd also like to thank the Random House folks who helped us with cartography, page design, and production: Steven Amsterdam, Bob Blake, Denise DeGennaro, Tigist Getachew, Laura Kidder, Fabrizio La Rocca, and Linda Schmidt.

Berkeley Bios

Behind every restaurant blurb, lodging review, and introduction in this book lurks a hard-working writer. After years of living in San Francisco and the East Bay, the writers had plenty of ideas about how to have a great time here for next to nothing. They spent the spring and summer sizing up all their favorite places and dozens of unknown, out-of-the-way joints to bring you the very best ways to live in and explore the Bay Area on a budget (though they may have kept one or two secrets to themselves).

The Writers

After living three years near the Powell Street cable car line atop the "tender-nob" district of San Francisco, **Simon Dang** couldn't help but feel somewhat overwhelmed watching hordes of ignorant tourists rush like lemmings towards commonplace attractions like Pier 39 and the Hard Rock Café. So, he decided to save a few souls by writing about hip, alternative sites such as the newly discovered San Simone Park. Along the way, he realized it was possible to exhaust the poetic implications of S.F. lexicons such as *Victorian* and *bay-view* after having to use them over two dozen times.

A breached birth from the womb of university, the spawn of a thousand lectures, **Mylah de la Rosa** went forth into the cold hard world with a Bachelor's degree in feigning intelligence as her only tool of survival. After experiencing the entire continuum of her era within a period of six months—from Generation X to the dreaded malaise known as Corporate America—she settled with the notion that she is a writer with a day job. Whether she was born to write the After Dark and Great Outdoors chapters or this was merely a product of gentle environmental influences remains in question. In the meantime, she resides in an Oakland warehouse raising the rabbits that will keep her company while she studies the analytical reasoning section of the GRE.

Super falafels, crêpes Nutella, greasy slices, ducks confit, salsas verdes, imperial rolls, saffron polentas, garden burgers, raw oysters, penne arrabiata, pork buns, blackened catfish, prawn burritos, California rolls . . . oh, the memories. Persevering through indigestion and fatigue, **Tara Duggan** persuaded friends and relatives to follow her to all corners of the city to eat and comment on dishes they may not have chosen, but liked anyway. She soon discovered the limits of the English language when it comes to expressing the inner taste bud in you (though the Simpsons were a big help), but she never found a limit to the wonders of San Francisco food.

Maureen Klier has enjoyed many a jaunt through Oakland and wishes it all the best.

After trampling through Southeast Asia and the South Pacific for six months, **Charlene Pinzon** opted for a domestic assignment with *The Berkeley Guides* (Marin County, South Bay and the Wine Country). This way, Mom and Dad wouldn't worry again about her venturing through countries deemed "ill-advised for travelers." And, besides, she thought it would be easier and less stressful. That was *far* from the truth as she racked up mileage on her Paseo, dealt with crusty hotel managers, and rushed back from her excursions to teach step aerobics classes. Her AAA membership (thanks Dad!) came in handy more than once as she got a flat on U.S. 101 on the way to San Rafael, and locked her keys in the car in Palo Alto. Would Charlene do it all again? Probably. But for now, she's content beating on her Tahitian drum. How's that for someone with a geophysics degree?!

Several dozen cups of coffee, newly-found bookstores, and a few mocha-splattered Internet terminals have shown **Stephan von Pohl** what he—currently on assignment 8,000 miles away—has felt for some time: There's no place like home.

A self-proclaimed adventure journalist, **Michelle Kaye** has traveled around the world almost as many times as her luggage. She has covered more miles of ball-busting dirt road than the U.S. mail, has fled valiantly (and quickly we might add) from bears, mountain lions, and tarantulas, not to mention Burmese pythons. A desert rat at heart, Michelle has traversed hundreds of miles of badlands just to get a good Wicki Wacker (on an expired learner's permit, no less). For *The Berkeley Guides,* she tracked more than 4,000 miles on a bullet-ridden, duct tape-encrusted, un-air-conditioned Ford in 120° heat to ferret out some of California's most solemn, untamed, and truly beautiful spots. With any luck she is still lost in Titus Canyon.

Owning a bike, and legs too short to go that far, it took a rental and a writing job to get transplanted New Mexican **Irene J. Nexica** out to the eastern wilds of the state. Lucky enough to visit Lake Tahoe in the off (yet springlike) season, she found that, at least for now, the water is nearly as blue as in the postcards. Reno contains excellent fruit pies, though the casino odds will never be so great. In her free time, Irene is a graduate student of popular musics, listening to teenage girl and queer audience subcultures.

Jeff Stark is a free-lance writer living in San Francisco.

The Editor

Sadly, **Kathleen Dodge** worked with a fantastic group of writers. Sad, because she couldn't justify her desire to eat a burrito at every taquería in the Mission, have a glass (or three) of red at every North Beach bar, and groove in every club south of Market—all in the name of research, of course. But, hell, getting a second opinion never hurt. Proud to have edited the Haight chapters without acquiring a tattoo, tongue pierce, or drug habit, Kathleen will not rest until she's written bad poetry in every San Francisco café.

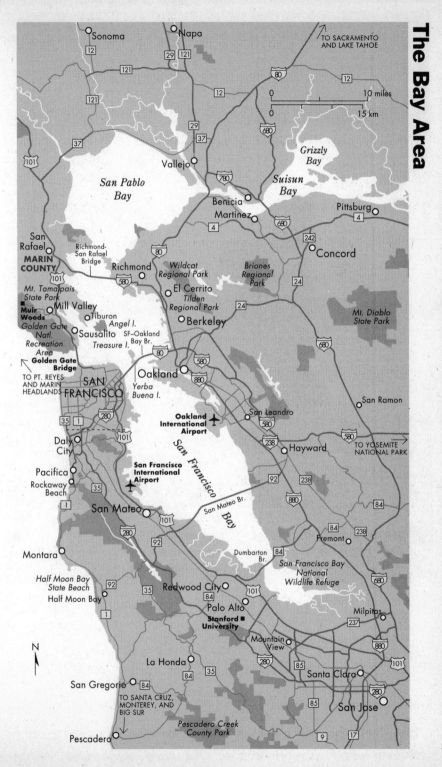

The Bay Area

Sonoma

Napa

TO SACRAMENTO
AND LAKE TAHOE

12

29 121

121

12

80

12

10 miles

121

15 km

37

29

37

101

Vallejo

780

*San Pablo
Bay*

*Grizzly
Bay*

680

*Suisun
Bay*

Benicia

Pittsburg

San
Rafael

**MARIN
COUNTY**

Martinez

4

680

4

Richmond-
San Rafael
Bridge

80

242

Concord

101

Richmond

580

*Wildcat
Regional
Park*

*Briones
Regional
Park*

*Mt. Tamalpais
State Park*

**Muir
Woods**

Mill Valley

El Cerrito

24

*Tilden
Regional
Park*

24

*Mt. Diablo
State Park*

Tiburon

Angel I.

Berkeley

680

*Golden Gate
Natl.
Recreation
Area*

Sausalito

Treasure I.

SF–Oakland
Bay Br.

80

**Golden Gate
Bridge**

580

TO PT. REYES
AND MARIN
HEADLANDS

**SAN
FRANCISCO**

Oakland

880

*Yerba
Buena I.*

San Ramon

35 1

280

**Oakland
International
Airport**

San Leandro

580

580

101

Daly
City

238

Hayward

TO YOSEMITE
NATIONAL PARK

Pacifica

**San Francisco
International
Airport**

*San Francisco
Bay*

92

238

880

Rockaway
Beach

1

35

San Mateo Br.

84

238

Montara

San Mateo

101

280

92

84

*Half Moon Bay
State Beach*

92

Dumbarton
Br.

84

Fremont

238

Half Moon Bay

35

Redwood City

*San Francisco Bay
National
Wildlife Refuge*

680

1

84

101

Palo Alto

Milpitas

**Stanford
University**

237

880

Mountain
View

La Honda

84

35

280

85

Santa Clara

101

San Gregorio

84

280

TO SANTA CRUZ,
MONTEREY, AND
BIG SUR

85

San Jose

*Pescadero Creek
County Park*

9

17

Pescadera

N

xi

BASICS

By Stephan von Pohl

Sometimes it's wonderful to drift through the city without thinking, letting Zen adventures come your way. But there are other times when you need to have a clue about things, whether it's how to get from San Francisco's Sunset district to downtown Oakland, where to look for this weekend's live music line-up, when next year's San Francisco Book Festival will take place, or what organizations exist to help women in trouble. Below are some basic facts to help you survive and keep your sanity in the Bay Area. For more comprehensive listings, let your fingers do the walking through the **Pacific Bell Yellow Pages;** the Local Access pages, in the front of the book, can help you with everything from choosing seats for a concert to finding the nearest park with a swimming pool.

Getting In, Out, and Around

The San Francisco Bay Area has one of the most comprehensive public transportation systems of any U.S. region, making it easy for commuters and travelers to get around without contributing to traffic jams. For the lowdown on public transit, get your hands on the *Regional Transit Guide* ($3.95), an excellent resource listing transportation agencies, lines, and frequency. Pick one up at a bookstore, the San Francisco Visitor Center (*see* Visitor Information, *below*) or at the **Berkeley TRiP Commute Store** (2033 Center St., one block west of Berkeley BART, tel. 510/644–7665). You can buy passes for the whole Bay Area at the latter. Or send a check for $3.50 to MTC/Regional Transit Guide, 101 8th St., Oakland 94607. For information on how to maneuver through the city and its public transit system with a bicycle, *see* By Bike, *below*.

You wouldn't be the first to shudder as you sit at a stoplight on a steep San Francisco hill in a temperamental stick shift, staring in the rearview mirror at the car you expect to cream as soon as you lift your foot off the brake.

BY CAR

It's not Los Angeles, but no one's going to mistake Bay Area driving for a relaxing spin down a country road. Common frustrations include high tolls on the Golden Gate Bridge, traffic jams at any time, and a notable lack of places to leave the damn car once you've arrived at your destination. For degree-of-difficulty bonus points, go straight to San Francisco: If you learned to drive just about anywhere else, the combination of hills and traffic should present a formidable challenge to your driving skills—not to mention your car's brakes and transmission.

From San Francisco, **I-80** heads east over the Bay Bridge to Oakland and Berkeley, then continues toward Sacramento and Lake Tahoe. Heading north across the Golden Gate are **Highway 1** (19th Ave. and Park Presidio Blvd.) and **U.S. 101** (Van Ness Ave. and Lombard St.). Hwy. 1 then splits off for a beautiful drive (complete with stunning views and treacherous curves) to Stinson Beach and north along the coast. U.S. 101 continues through Marin County toward the wine country. South along the Peninsula, U.S. 101 (known here as the Bayshore Freeway) passes the airport on the way to San Jose. **I-280** heads south further inland. This route is a bit longer mile-wise, but sees less traffic and is fairly accurately called "The World's Most Beautiful Freeway." Hwy. 1 hugs the coastline south to Half Moon Bay and beyond. In the East Bay, **I-880** links San Jose with Oakland, where it connects with I-80 to San Francisco or Berkeley and Sacramento. AAA's "Bay and River Area" road map will keep you on track.

RENTAL CARS Because of the dearth of parking, the extensive public transportation systems, and high insurance rates in much of the Bay Area, many residents choose to forgo car ownership entirely. Still, for those times when you're seized by the urge to meander up the coast, a rental car can be a great convenience. Your best bet is always to rent at one of the region's airports. Although the cheapest rates are available only to those who can present a plane ticket, even residents can save as much as $15 a day over the rates at downtown rental franchises. If you absolutely can't make it to the airport, almost all rental car agencies have pick-up and drop-off spots in downtown San Francisco within five or six blocks of Union Square. No matter where you pick up your car, you'll always pay a heavy surcharge (starting at about $25) if you don't return it to the same spot.

Small, independent agencies generally have cheaper daily rates than the national chains but usually impose mileage charges. A typical weekday price for a subcompact at an independent company is $18–$30, with a limit of 50–100 miles a day. **Flat Rate Rent-A-Car** (830 Huntington Ave., San Bruno, tel. 415/583–9232), near San Francisco International Airport, rents cars for a rock-bottom $20 ($25 if you're age 21–24) a day with 150 free miles, and 20¢ for each additional mile. The national companies (Avis, Hertz, Budget, etc.) usually offer unlimited mileage, so if you're planning on going far, they may end up being cheaper. If you call around, you should be able to find a subcompact car for about $40 a day on weekdays, $25 on weekends (Thursday–Monday). At press time, **Enterprise** (tel. 800/325–8007) was the cheapest of the lot ($26 per day on weekends). They're also the only major company that will rent to the 21–24 set, for an extra $8 a day.

All Bay Area companies require a credit card for deposit purposes. Some cards—American Express, for example—provide liability and damage insurance, so check with your credit card company before paying for the rental agency's insurance policy. Some final notes: You'll usually pay less if you reserve in advance, and always ask about specials and discounts—some rental agencies, for example, offer 10%–20% discounts if you have AAA or frequent-flier miles on certain airlines.

PARKING If you actually find a parking space in San Francisco, it may be on the side of a sheer precipice. Should you succeed in the hideous task of parallel parking on this 90° angle, remember to curb your wheels. Here's how: Turn the wheels so they point toward the curb (to the left when facing uphill, to the right when facing downhill), set the emergency brake, and if you're in a stick shift, leave the car in gear. Not only does this keep you from rolling into other cars, it also keeps you from being stuck with a $23 ticket from the S.F. Police Department.

Circled North Beach for half an hour? Ready to dump your car any place it fits? Think again. The city issues 2.4 million parking tickets a year—and the number is only expected to increase.

The large **Sutter-Stockton Garage** (444 Stockton St., tel. 415/982–7275) is within walking distance of Union Square, Chinatown, and North Beach, and charges a graduated rate—$3 for 3 hours, $8 for 5 hours, and $18 for 24 hours. The cheapest lot near Fisherman's Wharf ($2 an hour) is the **Wharf Garage** (350 Beach St., btw Taylor and Mason Sts.). Parking in the East Bay is less difficult, though finding a spot near the U.C. Berkeley campus is no easy task. At **Sather Gate Garage** (2450 Durant Ave., just west of Telegraph Ave.), the rate is $1 an hour for the first 2 hours, $1.50 for each hour thereafter. The daily rate is $10. The garage is open weekdays 7 AM–1 AM,

Saturday 7 AM–2 AM, and Sunday 8 AM–10 PM. For all-day parking, the lot next to **Berkeley Arts** (2590 Durant Ave.) is a better deal; $6 lets you park from 8 AM to 7 PM.

BRIDGE TOLLS The toll on the **Golden Gate Bridge** (tel. 415/921–5858) is $3, collected when you travel south into San Francisco. Discount ticket books are available at the toll office next to the bridge, Westamerica banks, Safeway stores, and some gas stations. For $16 you get six crossings (available at the bridge tollbooth only); $40 gets you 15 crossings. Carpoolers (three people per car) pay no toll 5–9 AM and 4–6 PM weekdays. All the state bridges, including the **Bay Bridge, San Mateo Bridge, Dumbarton Bridge,** and **Richmond/San Rafael Bridge,** have the same toll ($1), collected in the westbound direction. A discount book, good for four months from purchase, is available at Safeway and Lucky stores as well as at the bridges. For $34 you get 40 crossings. Carpoolers cross free 5 AM–10 AM and 3 PM–6 PM weekdays in the far left lane.

Since carpoolers don't pay tolls and often get to ride in special lanes on Bay Area bridges, commuters are grateful for the chance to pick up a couple of passengers for the drive over the bridge. Savvy types who lack cars can head to **Park and Ride** locations—or to the Emeryville bus nexus (cnr Yerba Buena and San Pablo Aves.) or the North Berkeley BART station in the East Bay—and hitch a ride into the city. **Rides for Bay Area Commuters** (tel. 800/755–POOL), **Berkeley TRiP** (tel. 510/644–POOL), and **Solano Commuter Information** (tel. 800/53–KMUTE) can hook you up with fellow carpoolers for free. Tell them your commute info, and within a few days you'll get a list of commuters who live and work near you and want to share a ride.

BY BUS

Despite all the griping about graffiti and rising fares, most Bay Area bus systems are pretty darn good. **Bus passes** and discount tickets are available at most grocery stores and check-cashing places. The only regional pass available is **BART Plus** (see By BART, below). The companies listed below have wheelchair-accessible buses for almost all routes; call for specifics.

SAN FRANCISCO MUNI's (tel. 415/673–MUNI or 415/923–6168 for lost and found) bus and streetcar service can put you within 3 blocks of anywhere you want to go. Buses are scheduled to run as often as every 5 minutes in certain well-traveled parts of town. However, regular MUNI users will attest to chronically late bus lines. Frequent breakdowns, disgruntled drivers, and belligerent passengers may also show you a side of the city you didn't plan on seeing. Between 1 AM and 5 AM, the **Owl Service** offers just nine lines that run every 30 minutes.

The adult fare is $1; the youth (5–17), senior (65+), and disabled fare is 35¢. Your fare gets you a free transfer good for at least an hour. **Passport** passes allow unlimited access to MUNI (including cable cars) for one day ($6), three days ($10), or one week ($15). Passes are available at the Powell Street Visitor Information Center (see Visitor Information, below). The monthly **Fast Pass** ($35) allows unlimited travel on MUNI buses, streetcars, and cable cars, as well as on BART and CalTrain within San Francisco. The $8 youth, senior, and disabled pass can be purchased at City Hall.

➤ **CABLE CARS** • San Francisco's cable cars were the world's first large-scale mechanized street transportation: Developer Andrew Hallidie drove the first run on August 2, 1873. In 1964, the cable cars were declared a National Historic Landmark, the first moving entity to receive that honor (also see box Hallidie's San Francisco Treat, in Chapter 2). If you can handle hordes of tourists, the cable cars are actually pretty groovy; you should take the ride at least once, if only to feel like you're in a Rice-A-Roni commercial. They run at a pace straight out of the early 1900s (the cables that propel the cars move at 9½ mph), so if you're Type A, take the bus. For great views, take the **Hyde and Powell** line, which travels from Fisherman's Wharf to Powell and Market streets downtown. Along the way, you'll get a gander at Alcatraz and pass right by Lombard Street, the crookedest street in the world. The line to get on at the Hyde Street turnaround can last more than an hour, so take the less scenic **California** line from Embarcadero BART if you don't want to wait. Fare is $2, and all passes except the weekly pass are accepted.

EAST BAY With more than 100 lines, **AC Transit** (1600 Franklin St., Oakland, tel. 510/839–2882, or 800/559–INFO) covers the East Bay from north of Richmond to south of Fremont. The adult and youth fare is $1.25; seniors and disabled 60¢. Transfers (25¢) are good for 90 minutes. Monthly passes run $45 for adults, $25 for youth, and $11 for seniors and the disabled. Books of 10 tickets cost $10 for adults and $5 for youth, seniors, and the disabled.

AC Transit lines designated by letters rather than numbers cross the Bay Bridge to San Francisco's **Transbay Terminal** (1st and Mission Sts.). Most only run from dawn to dusk; exceptions include the F (Berkeley) and T (Oakland, connecting to Berkeley on Bus 40), which operate until 2 AM, and the 24-hour N line. Transbay fare is $2.20 for adults ($1.10 youth, seniors, and disabled). Monthly transbay passes cost $75.

NORTH BAY Golden Gate Transit (tel. 415/455–2000 in Marin County, 415/923–2000 in S.F., 707/541–2000 in Sonoma County) provides service almost everywhere in the North Bay. Buses connect San Francisco with Sausalito, Mill Valley, Tiburon, San Rafael, Novato, Rohnert Park, and Santa Rosa every half hour during the week. Many buses run weekdays only, from dawn to dusk, but some routes (including the 20 and 50) run on weekends and go as late as 4 AM. Within San Francisco, buses leave from the **Transbay Terminal** (1st and Mission Sts.), and make stops throughout the city. Rates range $2–$4.50 depending on the length of your trip. Books of 20 tickets at a 25% discount can be purchased at the **San Rafael Transit Center** (Hetherton and 3rd Sts., San Rafael); at the **Larkspur Ferry Terminal** (101 E. Sir Francis Drake Blvd., Larkspur); and at many bookstores, gas stations, and grocery stores.

SOUTH BAY South of the city, **SamTrans** (tel. 800/660–4BUS) runs buses regularly throughout San Mateo County. They leave from the Daly City BART station, downtown San Francisco, and San Francisco International Airport (see By Plane, below), and go as far as Año Nuevo State Reserve at the southern end of the county (see South Bay, in Chapter 2). Bus 1L travels from Daly City BART along the coast to Half Moon Bay ($1) about five times daily on weekends. Most other buses run weekdays only, though some heavily trafficked routes are covered all week; call SamTrans for help planning your trip. Fares are $1–$2 for adults, 50¢–$1 for youth, and 35¢–$2 for seniors and the disabled. No transfers are issued. Monthly passes cost $36 for adults ($72 for an express route pass), $18 for youth, and $13 for seniors and people with disabilities.

Santa Clara County Transportation Agency operates buses and one light rail line throughout San Jose and the Silicon Valley. Basic fares are $1.10, 55¢ for youth age 5–17, and 35¢ for seniors or disabled persons (express buses cost $1.75–$2.25). The information center (4 N. Second St., tel. 408/321-2300 or 800/894–9908) sells day passes (double regular fare) and month passes ($6–$55).

GREYHOUND Greyhound (tel. 800/231–2222) travels to and from Bay Area cities all day, every day, but it's more useful for long distances than for local jaunts. They're the folks to call if you're sans auto and need to get to Tahoe (5–6 hrs, $20 one-way), Santa Cruz (2–4 hrs, $15 one-way), L.A. (11–12 hrs, $29 one-way), or Seattle (20–26 hrs, $48 one-way). In San Francisco, Greyhound operates out of the **Transbay Terminal** (1st and Mission Sts., tel. 415/495–1569), where many MUNI lines (see above) begin. Plan your arrival for daytime, as this terminal is dicey at night. You'll find Greyhound on the terminal's third floor. In the East Bay, the Greyhound office is in **Oakland** (2103 San Pablo Ave., at 20th St., tel. 510/834–3213); in the South Bay in **San Jose** (70 Almaden Ave., at Santa Clara St., tel. 408/295–4151); and in Marin County in downtown **San Rafael** (850 Tamalpais St., at 3rd St., tel. 415/453–0795).

GREEN TORTOISE Green Tortoise Adventure Travel (494 Broadway, San Francisco 94133, tel. 415/285–2441) is the cheap, fun alternative to humdrum bus travel. Only on Green Tortoise does your journey to Seattle (24 hrs, $49 one-way) feature a cookout ($3) and skinny-dipping. Buses come equipped with sleeping pads, kitchens, and stereos to make the ride enjoyable. Regularly scheduled runs also go from the Bay Area to L.A. (12 hrs, $30), Eugene

(17 hrs, $39), and Portland (20 hrs, $39) with select stops along the way. For an additional $10 you can be dropped off at several points along I–5. Make reservations before you show up at their pick-up point in San Francisco (1st and Natoma Sts.) or Berkeley (Berkeley Marina, across from the bait shop). Bring cash because you can't pay with plastic.

BY BART

Relatively clean and quiet, **Bay Area Rapid Transit** (tel. 415/992–2278 or 510/465–BART; lost and found 510/464–7090) is a smooth subway and commuter rail system that's better at moving you from one town to another than getting you around town. Its four lines serve San Francisco, Daly City/Colma, and the East Bay from Richmond to Fremont and out to North Concord. A BART extension to San Francisco International Airport is also being planned, but the project has yet to get off the ground. All BART stations and trains are wheelchair accessible. Trains run every 10–20 minutes until around midnight; you may be able to catch trains from some stations as late as 1 AM, but don't bank on it. Service starts up again at 4 AM weekdays, 6 AM Saturdays, and 8 AM Sundays. Evenings, Sundays, and holidays only the North Concord–Colma and Richmond–Fremont lines operate. Transfer at 12th Street or MacArthur stations.

➤ **FARES AND DISCOUNTS** • The cost of a BART ticket ranges from $1 to $4 depending on the length of the journey. Machines at each station allow you to buy tickets worth anywhere between $1–$40. The fare gates automatically deduct the fare from your ticket. For example, a 15-minute ride from San Francisco's Embarcadero station to Oakland's MacArthur station costs $2.10; from downtown San Francisco to Berkeley (20–25 min) you'll pay $2.35. Insert your ticket into the fare gate, then hold onto it when it pops out the top—you'll need it to exit. Any amount left unused can be used on your next ride, as you can add fare to old tickets.

BART is seriously lacking in discount fares. Adults can purchase a "discount" ticket that gets them $32 worth of rides for $30—big whoop. Seniors, children under 12, and the disabled get a much better deal: A $16 ticket for $4. A bus transfer to MUNI or AC Transit is available from the white machines near the BART gate. The two-part ticket gets you on the bus and is also good for a ride back to the same station within three days. In S.F., put four quarters in the machine—both bus rides are then free. In the East Bay, the transfer reduces the fare to $1 for each trip. The **BART Plus** ticket gives a discount on local bus systems. A $24–$61 ticket entitles you to $15–$50 worth of BART rides plus unlimited rides on any Bay Area bus system for either the first or last two weeks of the month.

BY BIKE

"Flat" streets in S.F.: Stockton, Polk, Broadway Tunnel, Geary/Post, Market, and Valencia.

Spend some time pedaling San Francisco's hills, and you will come out with legs and nerves of steel and infinitely more respect for bike messengers. All told, biking in the Bay Area is easier than you might think. Even San Francisco has bicycle routes that keep you away from traffic and get you around the larger hills. **Berkeley TRiP** (*see above*) has great biking maps, including the *San Francisco Biking/Walking Guide* ($3), which shows street grades and bike routes. Steep hills aside, traffic is no joke here, and you should always keep your eyes peeled for the opening doors of parked cars. *See* Biking, in Chapter 8, for suggested cycling routes around San Francisco and the Bay Area.

Professional bike thieves can unburden you of your $500 bike faster than you can say, "Welcome to the big city." Buy used, buy cheap, and *always* use U-shaped locks to secure both wheels and the frame to a sturdy post. You can get a good bicycle for around $50 at any flea market or police bike auction, where unclaimed bikes are sold.

BIKES ON PUBLIC TRANSIT You can take your bicycle on almost all Bay Area transit systems with varying degrees of hassle. **CalTrain** allows bikes on all trains, save some express trains. All **ferries,** except the Blue and Gold Fleet's Bay cruises, take on bicycles anytime.

➤ **BIKES ON BART** • As of October 1996, bicyclists no longer need a permit to bring their bikes on BART. To make BART more bike-friendly, officials also decided to no longer mandate that bike riders enter the last car. You are not, however, allowed to bring bikes on the escalator; they must be lugged up the stairs, or you'll receive a tongue lashing. During rush hour, 6:30 AM–9 AM and 3:30 PM–6:30 PM, you cannot take your bike in the commute direction (toward downtown S.F. in the morning, away in the evening). During these hours, a bike shuttle ($1) operates every 30–45 minutes between MacArthur BART station and the Transbay Terminal (1st and Mission Sts.). Call 415/923–4444 for more information. Most S.F. stations have bike lockers.

➤ **BIKES ON BUSES** • Taking your bike on Bay Area buses isn't easy. Often it depends solely on the discretion of the driver, and no more than two bikes are allowed at once. In the East Bay, **AC Transit** allows bikes on all lines midnight–5:30 AM and on Buses 65 (weekdays) and 67 (weekends) in summertime for transit to Tilden Park. **Golden Gate Transit** has one bike bus, Bus 40, that allows two bikes during non-commute hours, and occasionally Bus 80 allows bikes. Sadly, **S.F. MUNI** has no bike program, so get those legs pumping.

BY TRAIN

CALTRAIN CalTrain (tel. 800/660–4BUS) offers regular service from San Francisco (4th and Townsend Sts.) to downtown San Jose (65 Cahill St.). A one-way trip costs $4.50 and takes 1½ hours; trains leave hourly between 5 AM and 10 PM, more frequently during commute times. Along the way, the trains stop at a number of Peninsula cities, including Burlingame (30 min, $2.25), Palo Alto (1 hr, $3.50), Mountain View (1 hr 10 min, $3.50), and Santa Clara (1 hr 20 min, $4). Not all trains stop at all stations, so check schedules carefully.

AMTRAK Several Amtrak (tel. 800/USA–RAIL) lines stop at the five Bay Area stations: **Richmond** (16th St. and MacDonald Ave., adjoining Richmond BART), **Berkeley** (3rd St. and University Ave.; you can board, but you can't buy tickets here), **Oakland** (245 2nd St., at Jack London Square), **Emeryville** (5885 Landregan St.), and **San Jose** (65 Cahill St.). From the Emeryville station, you can catch a connecting Amtrak bus that will drop you off at the Ferry Building in San Francisco. Fares vary according to the time of year and other factors; a Bay Area–Seattle round-trip (24 hrs each way) runs $88–$176, while Bay Area–Los Angeles round-trips (12 hrs each way) are $78–$146.

BY TAXI

You can occasionally hail a cab in San Francisco, but this ain't New York. Most residents phone. All taxis are metered, but you may be able to negotiate a flat rate to the airport. Both

Critical Mass

Every month, an incredible human-powered movement takes place in the Bay Area. Hundreds of recreational riders, cycling-rights activists, and bike messengers gather in downtown San Francisco and take off on a 1½-hour ride through the city. The group, called Critical Mass, is responding to the predominance of cars in the city by encouraging bicycles as an alternative means of transport. They meet around 5:30 PM on the last Friday of each month at Justin Herman Plaza to tie up traffic, piss off motorists, aggravate police officers, and generally have a good ol' time. The East Bay's Critical Mass gathers at the same time on the second-to-last Friday of the month at the downtown Berkeley BART station. The East Bay group tends to be smaller and more politically active, as demonstrated by their procycling chanting, antidriving pamphlets, and occasional obstruction of I-80. Police on bikes sometimes escort the San Francisco and East Bay groups in an effort to "prevent" problems and direct traffic.

Veteran's Cab (tel. 415/552–1300) and Yellow Cab (tel. 415/626–2345) in San Francisco charge a base fee of $1.70, 30¢ every ⅕-mile, and 30¢ for every minute of waiting time or traffic delay. In the East Bay, both Friendly Cab (tel. 510/536–3000) and Yellow Cab (tel. 510/841–8294) offer competitively priced service ($2 base fee, $2 a mile). Fares to San Francisco are $25–$30. Don't forget to tip the driver (15% is typical).

BY FERRY

If you're sick of Bay Area traffic or in the mood for a change of pace, pack a thermos of coffee and a warm jacket and hop on one of the Bay Area's commuter ferries. The ferries are comparable to other forms of transport in speed (though not in price), and you can drink your morning java in peace while taking in a lovely view. Your ferry ticket acts as a free transfer to buses on both sides of the bay.

GOLDEN GATE FERRY Golden Gate Ferry (tel. 415/923–2000) crosses the bay between the San Francisco Ferry Building (on the Embarcadero, at the foot of Market St.) and Larkspur (45–55 min, $2.50 weekdays, $4.25 weekends) or Sausalito (30 min, $4.25). Ferries depart roughly every hour from about 7 AM to 8 PM.

RED AND WHITE FLEET The fleet (tel. 415/546–BOAT or 800/229–2784) leaves from Pier 43½ at Fisherman's Wharf for Sausalito and Tiburon. Fare is $5.50 ($2.75 children), the trip takes 20–30 minutes, and ferries leave every 1–2 hours (last ferry to S.F., 7:30 or 8 PM). The fleet also runs excursion trips to Angel Island ($10) and Alcatraz ($10).

BLUE AND GOLD FLEET The Oakland/Alameda Ferry (tel. 510/522–3300 or 415/705–5555) leaves from Jack London Square (Embarcadero and Broadway) in Oakland or the Alameda Ferry Dock (2990 Main St., Alameda) for the San Francisco Ferry Building (30 min) or Pier 39 (40 min). Ferries run every 1–2 hours from 6 AM on weekdays, 10 AM on weekends and holidays, until 8:50 PM. You'll find free parking at the Alameda and Oakland terminals. Of all the ferry rides, this is the best, with great views of Oakland's harbor and the Bay Bridge. Fare is $3.75.

The Blue and Gold Fleet's Vallejo Ferry (tel. 415/705–5444) has a commuter run ($7.50) and an excursion fare to Marine World/Africa U.S.A. ($39 round-trip; includes park admission and shuttle to and from the park). The ferries leave from the Ferry Building and Pier 39 in San Francisco. Call for current schedule.

BY PLANE

SAN FRANCISCO INTERNATIONAL AIRPORT San Francisco International (tel. 415/876–7809), the big cheese of Northern California airports, lies about 10 miles south of San Francisco on U.S. 101. All major domestic airlines and many international ones fly into SFO, as it's called; contact individual carriers for specific information. The airport has two currency exchange offices, both in the International Terminal. Baggage storage (tel. 415/877–0422; open 7 AM–11 PM), in the walkway between the international terminal and South Terminal, charges according to luggage size; an average bag runs $3.50 per day. There are also lockers inside each terminal near the gates: Small lockers run $2 for 4 hours ($4 for 24 hrs), medium-size ones go for $5 the first day ($2 for every day after that).

➤ AIRPORT TRANSIT AND PARKING • Until BART finally extends its service to the airport (sometime around 2002); you can take either SamTrans Buses 7B (55 min, $2) or 7F (35 min, $2.50) to San Francisco's Transbay Terminal (1st and Mission Sts.); or Bus 3X (20 min, $1) to the Colma BART station. From here you can catch a train to downtown San Francisco (20 min, $1.80) or Berkeley (45 min, $2.40). The buses run every half hour: Bus 3X from 7 AM to 11:30 PM, Buses 7B and 7F from about 4:45 AM to 12:45 AM. Bus 7F restricts you to one small carry-on bag. Bus 7F will also tote you to Palo Alto, near the Stanford Shopping Center. Locals tend to rely on private shuttles for their convenience and reliability (see Airport Shuttles, below). Long-term parking (tel. 415/877–0227) is $11 a day, but the lot tends to fill up during peak travel times, especially three-day weekends. Call the above number and listen to their recording on availability before you set out, and plan for extra time to take the shuttle from the lot to the terminal.

OAKLAND INTERNATIONAL AIRPORT Oakland International (1 Airport Dr., off Hegenberger Rd., tel. 510/577–4000), off I–880, is a smallish airport, easily accessible by public transportation and less hectic and crowded than SFO. It's often much cheaper to arrive here, particularly on **Southwest** (tel. 800/435–9792), which has more than 80 flights in and out of Oakland, many of which go to Los Angeles. With Southwest's Companion Fare program, two people can fly round-trip to Los Angeles for a total of $144 on selected flights; reservations for these fares should be made well in advance.

➤ **AIRPORT TRANSIT AND PARKING** • The **Air-Bart Shuttle** (tel. 510/562–7700; $2) and AC Transit **Bus 58** ($1.25) run every 15–20 minutes to the Coliseum BART station. The bus continues on to downtown Oakland (50 min). Another cheap—though not as cheap as the bus—and easy option is a van company (*see* Airport Shuttles, *below*). A taxi to downtown Berkeley from Oakland International costs about $30–$35. **Long-term parking** (tel. 510/633–2571) is $8.25 for 24 hours or $6.60 in the economy lot next to Terminal 1. A free shuttle will take you to the terminals.

SAN JOSE INTERNATIONAL AIRPORT Fourteen carriers, most notably **American Airlines** (tel. 800/433–7300), fly into San Jose International Airport (1661 Airport Blvd., off I–880 near U.S. 101, tel. 408/277–4759). **Bus 65** (direction: Almaden) heads downtown every 30–60 minutes. For S.F. or the East Bay, take a private shuttle (*see* Airport Shuttles, *below*). Short-term parking runs 75¢ per half hour and $15 per day; long-term is $8 per day.

AIRPORT SHUTTLES Can't find a friend to take you to the airport for that 5 AM flight? No worries—just call an airport shuttle, one of the Bay Area's favorite ways to ride (and the biggest thing to happen to vans since the 1970s). Shuttles will pick you up at your doorstep at any time, day or night, and whisk you to the airport. Fare from San Francisco to SFO runs a mere $10–$11; expect to pay roughly $20 from Oakland to SFO, and about the same from downtown San Francisco to the Oakland airport. There's often a reduced rate for a pickup of two or more people. You can save a couple bucks (up to $10) by getting on the shuttle at a major hotel rather than at your home.

The king of airport service is **Super Shuttle** (tel. 415/558–8500), serving SFO from San Francisco and the Peninsula. If big companies turn you off, try reliable, employee-owned **Quake City** (tel. 415/255–4899): It costs a dollar less than Super Shuttle and its friendly drivers can be counted on for chitchat during the trip. In addition, **Yellow Shuttle Service** (tel. 415/282–7433) and **Airport Connection** (tel. 510/841–0150) run from most Bay Area cities to SFO, Oakland International, and San Jose International. The **BayPorter Express** (tel. 415/467–1800) runs from the East Bay and South Bay to SFO, Oakland, and San Jose; and from San Francisco to Oakland. The **Marin Airporter** (tel. 415/461–4222) will take you from Marin County to SFO.

Bay Area Directory

LOW-COST MEDICAL AID

We all like to hope that we'll never require medical attention. Still, if you've been living in a drafty room feeding on coffee and Powerbars, chances are good something's going to go. But don't despair—even if you're one of the millions of Americans without health coverage, many community clinics offer services on a sliding scale, depending on your income. County hospitals cannot turn you away, but thanks to the Republicans (and one hell of a lot of Democrats), funding is drying up, services are shrinking, and the wait can be a nightmare (bring a book). Oakland's **Highland Hospital** (1411 E. 31st St., tel. 510/437–4800) and **San Francisco General Hospital** (1001 Potrero Ave., tel. 415/206–8000) handle all kinds of medical problems, including emergencies, and use a sliding scale.

Alta Bates Medical Center's 24-hour **Audio Health Library** (tel. 800/606–2582) gives information on over 400 health-related topics and can refer you to a private practitioner or clinic in your area, should you need one. The **San Francisco AIDS Hotline** (tel. 415/863–AIDS) has the most up-to-date information on programs to help those who are infected, as well as comprehensive listings of free or low-cost HIV testing sites in every city. For affordable family planning services, **Planned Parenthood** administers pregnancy tests and gynecological exams; prescribes birth control; performs abortions; treats sexually transmitted diseases (STDs); and offers free, anonymous AIDS tests. Check the phone book for an office near you.

Clinics don't always make you prove how much money you make, which helps when you're truly strapped for cash; but try to be a good socialist and give according to your ability.

The following codes are used below to indicate services provided: DEN—dentistry; EYE—optometry; GM—general medicine; GYN—gynecology and family planning; OB—perinatal care; PED—pediatrics; STD—sexually transmitted disease treatment. Some clinics cater towards specific ethnic groups, but all accept those in need.

SAN FRANCISCO San Francisco Department of Public Health. Cost: sliding. Services: GM, GYN, PED, STD; HIV testing and referrals. Call to see which of its eight health centers is nearest you. *Main office: tel. 415/554–2500.*

Buena Vista Women's Services. Cost: $75 first exam, $55 each subsequent. Services: GYN, STD. *1801 Bush St., at Octavia St., tel. 415/771–5000.*

Haight-Ashbury Free Medical Clinic. Cost: free, donations requested. Services: GM, GYN, STD; HIV programs. *558 Clayton St., at Haight St., tel. 415/487–5632.*

Mission Neighborhood Health Center. Cost: sliding. Services: DEN, GM, GYN, PED. *240 Shotwell St., at 16th St., tel. 415/552–3870.*

Native American Health Center. Cost: free. Services: DEN, GM, GYN, PED, STD. *56 Julian Ave., btw 14th and 15th Sts., tel. 415/621–8051.*

San Francisco City Clinic. Cost: sliding. Services: GYN, STD. *356 7th St., btw Folsom and Harrison Sts., tel. 415/487–5500.*

South of Market Health Center. Cost: sliding. Services: DEN, GM, GYN, OB, PED, STD. *551 Minna St., btw 6th and 7th Sts., tel. 415/626–2951.*

UCSF Eye Clinic. Cost: sliding. Services: EYE. *400 Parnassus Ave., near 3rd Ave., tel. 415/476–3700.*

BERKELEY Berkeley Free Clinic. Cost: free. Services: DEN, GM, GYN, STD; free, anonymous HIV testing. *2339 Durant Ave., at Dana St., tel. 510/548–2570.*

Berkeley Women's Health Center. Cost: sliding. Services: GM, GYN, OB, STD. *2908 Ellsworth St., tel. 510/843–6194. 1 block from Ashby Ave. near Howe St.*

City of Berkeley Health Clinic. Cost: sliding. Services: GYN, STD; free, anonymous HIV testing. *830 University Ave., at 6th St., tel. 510/644–8571.*

OAKLAND Asian Health Services. Cost: sliding. Services: GM, GYN, PED, STD; HIV services. *310 8th St. #200, at Harrison St., tel. 510/763–4411.*

Central Health Center. Cost: sliding. Services: GM, GYN, PED, STD. *470 27th St., near Telegraph Ave., tel. 510/271–4263.*

La Clinica de la Raza. Cost: free with $25 annual family membership. Services: DEN, EYE, GM, GYN, OB, PED, STD; there's a special "teen clinic," too. *1515 Fruitvale Ave., at E. 14th St., tel. 510/535–4000.*

Native American Health Center. Cost: sliding. Services: GM, GYN, OB, PED, STD; HIV services. *3124 E. 14th St., near Fruitvale Ave., tel. 510/261–1962.*

West Oakland Health Center. Cost: sliding. Services: DEN, EYE, GM, GYN, OB, PED, STD. *700 Adeline St., 3 blocks south of West Oakland BART, tel. 510/835–9610.*

Women's Choice Clinic. Cost: sliding. Services: GYN, STD. The clinic also gives referrals for Chinese medicine and acupuncture. *2930 McClure Ave., btw 29th and 30th Sts., tel. 510/444–5676.*

MARIN COUNTY **Marin Community Clinic.** Cost: sliding. Services: GM, GYN, PED. *250 Bon Air Rd., on the grounds of Marin General Hospital, Greenbrae, tel. 415/461–7400.*

Marin County STD Clinic. Cost: $20 for adults, free to those under 18. Services: STD. *920 Grand Ave., San Rafael, tel. 415/499–6944.*

SOUTH BAY **Drew Health Foundation Community Medical Clinic.** Cost: sliding. Services: DEN, EYE, GM, GYN, PED, STD. *2111 University Ave., East Palo Alto, tel. 415/328–5060.*

Seton Medical Center Family Health Care Program. Cost: free. Services: GM, GYN, PED, STD. *1900 Sullivan Ave., Daly City, tel. 415/992–4000.*

PHONES AND MAIL

The area code for Oakland, Berkeley, and the East Bay is **510**; for San Francisco, Marin County, Palo Alto, and San Mateo County, it's **415**; and for San Jose and Santa Cruz, it's **408**. Calling home? Pre-paid phone cards are good for long-distance and international calls, can be used at any time and from any phone, and offer rates slightly cheaper than regular long-distance companies. Buy them at any convenience store in denominations of $6, $11, and $21. San Francisco's Civic Center post office (101 Hyde St., at Golden Gate Ave., tel. 415/441–8329) will hold letters sent to general delivery for 10 days (send to: Your name, General Delivery, San Francisco, CA 94142) and usually has post office boxes available at $22 for six months. A passport or valid ID is required to pick up mail. The **Postal Answer Line** (tel. 415/695–8760) is a 24-hour automated service that provides post office hours, postal rates, and more. In Berkeley, the main post office (200 Allston Way, Berkeley, CA 94704, tel. 510/649–3100) holds mail for 10 days.

MEDIA

DAILY PAPERS The Bay Area's two big dailies, the *San Francisco Chronicle* (morning) and the *San Francisco Examiner* (afternoon), are equally unremarkable. The "Chron" does have some great columns, and it has strangely endeared itself to local readers despite its lightweight coverage. The combined *Chronicle-Examiner* Sunday paper comes with the "Pink Section," useful for its extensive movie reviews and listings of all sorts of upcoming events.

The *Oakland Tribune*, formerly one of the country's premier African-American–owned dailies, is part of a newspaper chain that has reduced it to a small-town rag. Many Berkeleyans read the student-produced *Daily Californian*, but it, too, wavers in the quality department. The *Marin Independent Journal* focuses mostly on Marin County, but also tackles some more general issues. The big surprise in Bay Area dailies is the *San Jose Mercury News*, a paper that's well read throughout the area and highly respected in the journalism community. It's stronger on national and international news than any other Bay Area paper.

Written from a gay male's perspective, SF Weekly's sex-advice column "Savage Love" is fun, raunchy, and useful (for nipple tattooing advice, that is), but the Guardian's "Ask Isadora" Alman has described the competition as "monumentally offensive."

WEEKLY PAPERS You'll find better local coverage (and often better writing) in the Bay Area's many free weekly newspapers. The *San Francisco Bay Guardian* has run daring investigative pieces that the dailies don't dare print. Look for the *Guardian*'s "Best of the Bay Area" special every August and the "Insider's guide" issue in February. The *SF Weekly* occasionally comes up with an excellent cover story, but spends the rest of the time diddling with fonts and layout. Both papers are an excellent source for cultural events and listings. You'll find a lot of good information in the Bay Area's many gay and lesbian publications (*see* Resources for Gays and Lesbians, *below*).

The **East Bay Express** comes in two parts: The front section has the East Bay's best local coverage of politics and issues, and the varied front-page articles (which may discuss Oakland history, highlight current issues, or showcase active locals) are always well-written and researched. The "Billboard" section has the best events listings in the East Bay as well as a huge classified section. The ads for real estate and children's day camps in Marin County's **Pacific Sun** contrast sharply with the *Guardian*'s sex chat lines and leather boutiques, but you'll also find an events calendar and decent (if scant) local news. The much better Santa Clara **Metro** covers the whole South Bay with high-quality feature articles and events listings.

ON-LINE RESOURCES Is the Internet all it's cracked up to be or is it the 8-track of the '90s? While that remains to be seen, it *is* possible to find a breadth of helpful and downright freaky San Francisco sites on the net. Your first stop for Bay Area information should be the **San Francisco Bay Resource Net** (http://www.slip.net/~scmetro/sfbayr.html), which has links to over a hundred websites for government, media, music, job and housing listings, sights, and community groups. **Yahoo** has a whole subsection devoted to San Francisco (http://sfbay.yahoo.com) chock-full of links to entertainment, art, housing, travel, you name it. **Guardian Online** (http://www.sfbayguardian.com) offers free e-mail service and displays past articles of the *Bay Guardian* (*see* Weekly Papers, *above*), as well as their most recent Insider's Guide and Best of the Bay picks. **KUSF** (*see* Radio Stations, *below*) runs a website (http://www.usfca.edu/usf/kusf) with local information and a program guide. Check out "Radio Segue" for info on music, arts, and culture. A good gay resource is **The Gay Guys Guide to San Francisco** (http://www.coming-n-going.com), a good, funny guide to gay life.

What about when you're in town without a laptop? Most public libraries have terminals with Internet access, so you can check your mail or make new friends. The new **San Francisco Main Library** (100 Larkin St., tel. 415/557–4400) has an on-line catalog (http://sfpl.lib.ca.us) and many text-only terminals for net and web access. (For on-line access in cafés, *see* box Plug In, Tune In, Drink Up, in Chapter 5).

RADIO STATIONS The Bay Area radio scene isn't as bleak as you might think after hearing all those Top 40, classic rock, and soft-rock mega-stations as you twirl the dial. Browse the left end of the FM range to find some less conventional programming. Because of the many hills, you may have trouble tuning in some of these stations. U.C. Berkeley's **KALX** (90.7 FM), a typically cool, alternative college station run by an all-volunteer staff, can be counted on for the eclectic, the avant garde, and the noisy. They have some excellent regular programs: "Women Hold Up Half the Sky" (Sat. 11–noon) features interviews with fierce and fabulous women from around the country; and "Straightjackets" (Mon. noon–12:30) deals with issues of gender and (homo)sexuality. **KUSF** (90.3 FM) comes out of the University of San Francisco, playing new music, ethnic music, and specialty shows. "Spotlight" (Sun. 4 PM–6 PM) is a 2-hour tribute to a particular musical artist, label, or genre; "Shoestring Radio Theatre" (Thurs. 9:30 PM–10 PM) takes you back to pre-TV days with original comedy or mystery radio plays.

Much-loved, listener-supported **KPFA** (94.1 FM) broadcasts all over central and Northern California. You can listen to classical, reggae, rap, soul, folk, blues, and national news all in one

Who to Call When Nobody Else Is Home

No need to spend money on a 900 line just because you're sitting by the phone feeling bored. The Bay Area offers plenty of information lines to amuse you at any hour of the day or night. For starters, try the Public Library's Dial-a-Story (tel. 415/437–4880), where the tale changes once a week. Then move on to the U.C. Berkeley Seismographic Station (tel. 510/642–2160) for the latest on any recent earthquakes. The Northern California Bird Box (tel. 510/524–5592) lets local bird-watchers leave messages and hear about the latest unusual sightings. The Hearing Society Dial-a-Test (tel. 415/834–1620) lets you know if the old eardrums are still in working order.

place. Also tune in for interviews with artists and members of special-interest groups you didn't know even existed. At **KPOO** (89.5 FM) tunes range from Coltrane to salsa with great DJs spinning all day. As locals know, "it's the shit." In the South Bay, Foothill Junior College's **KFJC** (89.7 FM) beams out all kinds of music, plus some outstanding shows. The award-winning "Norman Bates Memorial Soundtrack Hour," plays your favorite TV and movie themes Saturday 9–noon; "Phil's Garage," features grungy garage-band music Saturday 7–10 PM; and you'll find the news show "One Step Beyond" on Sunday 7–11 PM. Again, listeners in San Francisco are subject to the whims of atmospheric conditions when tuning in.

News junkies have a few different options. On the AM dial, **KCBS** (740 AM) has rapid-fire news bites around the clock. They may not have the most in-depth coverage, but they certainly have the fastest. For higher-quality reporting, try **KQED** (88.5 FM), which broadcasts a lot of National Public Radio programming. "All Things Considered" starts at 4:30 PM weekdays and is repeated at 11 PM. The BBC News Hour airs at 9 PM and is repeated at 1 AM. **KALW** (91.7 FM) also plays NPR and BBC throughout the day.

RESOURCES FOR GAYS AND LESBIANS

San Francisco's gay community, particularly in the Castro district, is extremely supportive and close-knit. If you're trying to find your niche (be it a support group or a political organization), some friendly asking around at one of the Castro cafés or diners should get you helpful advice, if not a pal. **Café Flore** (see Chapter 5), despite all the winking and butt-wagging going on, is actually a great spot to get information from those in the know.

Generally, lesbian resources are much harder to ferret out. The Castro is definitely slanted toward gay men; women should head to Valencia Street in San Francisco's Mission District, home to several women's bookstores and organizations. **Red Dora's Bearded Lady** (see Mission District, in Chapter 5) is a café and performance space frequented by young women, primarily in their twenties. Berkeley is another good spot for lesbian resources and hangouts. In particular, the bookstore and coffeehouse **Mama Bears** (see Books, in Chapter 3) offers readings and

Pump Up the Volume

Pirate radio operators are busting out all over the Bay Area, whiling away the hours with political back-and-forths, eclectic music playlists, and chitchat. Broadcasting from undisclosed (sometimes mobile) locations on unoccupied frequencies, their philosophy is that requiring low-wattage stations to pay the same $3000 licensing fee that commercial stations pay shuts out community voices and lets big money tell us what we should listen to. The Free Communications Coalition—the People's FCC (tel. 510/464–3041)—and Radio Free Berkeley won a historic ruling in January, 1994, when the Oakland Federal District Court denied the real FCC's request for an injunction to silence Free Radio Berkeley and its operator, Stephen Dunifer. However, the court (and political) battle rages on, with the government still seeking to shut down alternative broadcasters.

Due to low power, you need to be nearby to pick up the following stations' broadcasts. Radio Libre (103.3 FM) is heard in the Mission, parts of Noe Valley, and in the SoMa area; San Francisco Liberation Radio (93.7 FM) can be picked up in the Richmond and Sunset districts; North Beach Radio (88.1 FM) transmits in the area between Columbus Avenue and Pier 39 in San Francisco; and Free Radio Berkeley (104.1 FM) can be heard in North Oakland and Berkeley.

social events in a warm, supportive environment. The lesbian-owned and -operated café **Ann Kong's Bleach Bottle Pig Farm** (2072 San Pablo Ave., Berkeley, tel. 510/848–7376) is another happening spot—look in the papers for readings and other evening activities. For action of a more direct nature, check out the **Lesbian Avengers,** a group of lesbian, bisexual, and transgendered women. Call 415/267–6195 for the lowdown on meetings and events.

GAY AND LESBIAN PUBLICATIONS The weekly *Bay Area Reporter* and the bi-weekly *Bay Times* are the two main gay and lesbian papers. Both have excellent news (local, national, international), though the B.A.R. is heavier on news coverage and lighter on events and listings. For a more conservative gay perspective, pick up *The Sentinel*, which emphasizes national gay news and has an interesting column called "This Week in Leather." The section "168 Hours" is an excellent listing of arts, films, literary events, and social goings-on. The biweekly *Out Now!* is a thin San Jose–based forum for gay and lesbian news and community happenings, and comes out in South Bay and East Bay editions. All of these papers are free.

On Our Backs and *Curve* are two popular lesbian pseudo-porn mags, both based in San Francisco. Pick them up at **A Different Light** (*see* Books, in Chapter 3), the Bay Area's best gay bookstore. Among the store's wide selection of queerzines published by special-interest groups are *Bear*, the magazine for big, hairy, husky men, and the men who love them; *Girljock*, the tongue-in-cheek magazine for girls who like sports; *Girlfriend*, aimed at drag queens; and *Raw Vulva*, for the bike-riding dyke.

The 200-page *Gaybook* ($9.95), published by Rainbow Ventures Publishing (584 Castro St., Suite 632, tel. 415/928–1859) contains a resource guide listing organizations that cater to gays and lesbians, as well as a classified advertising section. If you're traveling, pick up *Bob Damron's Address Book* ($13.95 plus $5 shipping), which lists services and entertainment options for gay men, or *The Women's Traveler* ($10.95 plus $5 shipping), with resources for lesbians and women in general. Both are available through the **Damron Company** (tel. 415/255–0404).

SAN FRANCISCO The **Lavender Youth Recreation and Information Center** (127 Collingwood St., at 18th St., tel. 415/703–6150, hotline 415/863–3636 or 800/246–7743) is a social and support organization for gays, lesbians, and transgenders 23 years old and younger. If you call the hotline Monday–Wednesday 4 PM–9 PM or Thursday–Sunday 6:30 PM–9 PM, you can talk to other young gays and lesbians, or a counselor (at off hours, you get recorded info). **Communities United Against Violence** (973 Market St., Suite 500, tel. 415/777–5500, 24-hour emergency hotline 415/333–HELP) provides crisis counseling and referrals for gays and lesbians who are victims of anti-gay violence.

➤ **AIDS SUPPORT GROUPS AND ACTIVISM** • If you or a loved one has AIDS, or you just want to learn more about it, head to the **San Francisco AIDS Foundation** (25 Van Ness Ave., at Market St., tel. 415/864–5855, AIDS hotline 415/863–2437), an umbrella organization that can direct people to whichever AIDS-related group best suits them. **Shanti Project** (1546 Market St., at Van Ness Ave., tel. 415/864–2273) provides emotional support and has housing and activities programs for people living with AIDS. For late-night counseling or information, call the **AIDS/HIV Nightline** (tel. 415/434–AIDS, 800/273–AIDS in Northern California) 5 PM–5 AM seven nights a week. If you're pissed about the AIDS crisis and want to do something about it, call **ACT-UP SF** (tel. 415/252–9200). Making headlines with its confrontational tactics, ACT-UP rallies for increased AIDS research and an end to discrimination against those living with AIDS. You can attend meetings every Tuesday at 7:30 PM at 592 Castro Street, Suite B.

BERKELEY The **Pacific Center for Human Growth** (2712 Telegraph Ave., at Derby St., tel. 510/548–8283) is a well-known gay and lesbian gathering place. The organization offers counseling, social gatherings, rap sessions, and support groups (covering topics like coming out, jealousy in relationships, parents, etc.). Also check out the bulletin boards, littered with everything from apartment rentals to social invitations. You can drop in weekdays 10–10, Saturday noon–4 and 6–10, or Sunday 6 PM–10 PM to see what's going on and to use any services. The **Pacific Center's Gay, Lesbian, and Bisexual Switchboard** (tel. 510/841–6224) doles out information and referrals. The East Bay chapter of **ACT-UP** (*see above*) meets monthly at different locations; call (tel. 510/568–1680) for specifics.

PALO ALTO The **Stanford Lesbian/Gay/Bisexual Community Center** (Fire Truck House, Stanford Campus, tel. 415/725–4222 or 415/723–1488 for event information) knows all about gay and lesbian happenings around campus and can refer you to a vast number of support groups and resources. During the school year the center is generally open weekdays noon–5; hours vary during summer. The place is staffed by volunteers, so it's best to call ahead to see if anyone will be there.

RESOURCES FOR PEOPLE OF COLOR

Northern California has a rich mix of ethnicities, but the melting pot is more often like a tossed salad, with everyone maintaining strong individual cultural identities. A wealth of resources support, educate, celebrate, and bring together people of color in the Bay Area. In addition to community organizations, look into student services and groups at the universities.

AFRICAN-AMERICAN RESOURCES Oakland's **Black Women's Resource Center** (518 17th St., Suite 202, tel. 510/763–9501) works to establish, improve, and maintain support systems that empower African-American women, especially those with low incomes. They offer information and referrals and publish a newsletter for women in the community. The **Northern California Center for African-American History and Life** (5606 San Pablo Ave., Oakland, tel. 510/658–3158) is an extensive museum, archive, and research center. The preeminent local African-American bookstore is **Marcus Books** (*see* Books, in Chapter 3).

Check out "Historic Black Landmarks: A Traveler's Guide" (Gale Research Inc.; $18), or "African American Historic Places" (National Park Service, Preservation Press; $26), two solid travel books that include information on African-American landmarks in California.

The **Center for African and African-American Art and Culture** (762 Fulton St., San Francisco, tel. 415/928–8546) provides a home for six different African-American groups that sponsor poetry readings, speakers, and storytelling in the African tradition. The center also has research materials and will refer you to other Bay Area African-American events and organizations. The **Oakland History Room** (tel. 510/238–3222) in the main branch of the Oakland Public Library (125 14th St., btw Oak and Madison Sts.) has an extensive archive of past African-American life in Oakland. Bill Sturm, who runs the room, is reputed to know everything.

ASIAN-PACIFIC RESOURCES In Oakland, **Asian Immigrant Women Advocates** (310 8th St., Suite 301, tel. 510/268–0192) works to empower immigrant Asian women through leadership development and education. The **East Bay Vietnamese Association** (1218 Miller Ave., Oakland, tel. 510/533–4219) provides employment services and other assistance for the Vietnamese community. In San Jose, **Korean American Community Services** (2750 Westfield Ave., tel. 408/248–5227) helps recently arrived Koreans with English skills and other issues. Oakland's **Filipinos for Affirmative Action** (310 8th St., Suite 308, tel. 510/465–9876), a nonprofit social agency, works with the community on employment issues, AIDS and substance abuse education, and activism. Also in Oakland, the **Japan Pacific Resource Network** (310 8th St., Suite 305B, tel. 510/891–9045) can point you to all sorts of resources for the Japanese community in the Bay Area. In San Francisco, the **Chinese Cultural Center** (750 Kearny St., 3rd Floor, tel. 415/986–1822) is dedicated to the preservation of Chinese culture and community. Stop by and talk to the helpful staff for information on Chinese community events.

CHICANO/LATINO RESOURCES San Francisco's entire Mission District is a resource for Chicanos and Latinos, with theater groups, cultural centers, and zillions of Latino-owned restaurants and bookstores. One important meeting place is the **Mission Cultural Center** (2868 Mission St., btw 24th and 25th Sts., tel. 415/821–1155), site of an art gallery and dance, music, and theater classes. In the East Bay, **La Peña Cultural Center** (3105 Shattuck Ave., Berkeley, tel. 510/849–2568) has concerts and dances, workshops, a store with Latino books and music, and a café. In the South Bay, the **Centro Cultural Latino** (tel. 415/343–7476) has after-school and summer programs for Latino youth and sponsors cultural activities.

NATIVE AMERICAN RESOURCES The **International Indian Treaty Council** (54 Mint St., Suite 400, San Francisco, tel. 415/512–1501) is an information center that works with indigenous people both locally and around the world, promoting sovereignty, human rights, and indigenous prisoners' rights. They work as a consultant to the United Nations. The **American Indian Center of Santa Clara Valley, Inc.** (919 Alameda, San Jose, tel. 408/971–9622) has support services and a reference library (tel. 408/971–0772). For medical help, the **Native American Health Center** has free clinics in the Bay Area (*see* Low-Cost Medical Aid, *above*).

RESOURCES FOR WOMEN

The most comprehensive resource center in the Bay Area is the **Women's Building** (3543 18th St., San Francisco, tel. 415/431–1180), which houses nine women's organizations, including the **National Organization for Women (NOW), San Francisco Women Against Rape (SF WAR),** and **Mujeres Unidas y Activas.** The Women's Building staff can also help you find housing, health care, employment, or just about anything else. Regular meetings at the Women's Building include NOW (call 415/861–8880) and **Women Embracing Life** (call 415/668–3675), a support group for women living with HIV. The **Equal Rights Advocates** (1663 Mission St., Suite 550) offer legal counseling for low-income and minority women through their Spanish/English advice hotline (tel. 800/839–4ERA). The **Young Women's Christian Association (YWCA)** (620 Sutter St., San Francisco, tel. 415/775–6502) offers social-service programs, employment listings, and lodging referrals for women. The San Francisco office can refer you to the six other YWCAs in Marin and the East Bay.

In the East Bay, one of the best resources is the **Women's Resource Center** (250 Golden Bear Center, U.C. Berkeley, tel. 510/642–4786). Come here to get referrals for other organizations. Only U.C. students and staff can borrow materials from the book and audiovisual collections, but anyone can dig through the community resources files, which have info on support groups, internships, grant opportunities, and more.

➤ **EMERGENCIES AND MEDICAL AID** • An important women's health resource is **Planned Parenthood,** a pro-choice family-planning clinic (*see* Low-Cost Medical Aid, *above*). The **Women's Needs Center** (1825 Haight St., San Francisco, tel. 415/487–5607) also offers pro-choice gynecological services for low-income women and anonymous HIV testing for men and women. San Francisco Women Against Rape (*see above*) runs a 24-hour crisis hotline (tel. 415/647–7273 or 510/845–RAPE). Female victims of domestic violence can call **A Safe Place** (tel. 510/536–7233), a shelter for battered women, 24 hours a day.

➤ **PUBLICATIONS** • **Mama Bears** (*see* Books, in Chapter 3) stocks female-oriented literature, sponsors readings, and can refer you to other bookstores around California if they don't have what you want. The **Women of Color Resource Center** (2288 Fulton St., Suite 103, Berkeley, tel. 510/848–9272) publishes the excellent book *Women of Color, Organizations and Projects: A National Directory* ($8.95 plus shipping), which points you to hundreds of organizations dedicated to women of almost every ethnicity.

RESOURCES FOR
PEOPLE WITH DISABILITIES

The Bay Area is an important national center for resources for the disabled, thanks mostly to Berkeley's **Center for Independent Living,** started in the early '70s by a group of people with disabilities who fought for their right to be accepted at U.C. Berkeley. There are now more than 300 independent living centers nationwide, working for rights for the disabled, helping people with disabilities discover their potential, and giving referrals. You'll find several in the Bay Area: in Berkeley (2539 Telegraph Ave., tel. 510/841–4776); in Hayward (439 A St., tel. 510/881–5743); in San Rafael (710 4th St., tel. 415/459–6245); in Santa Clara (1601 Civic Dr., Suite 100, tel. 408/985–1243); and in San Francisco (70 10th St., tel. 415/863–0581).

GETTING AROUND Transit organizations in the Bay Area have joined ranks to create an ID card that gives people with disabilities discounts on travel throughout nine Bay Area counties;

each transit company decides what kind of a discount to give (*see* Getting In, Out, and Around, *above*). You can get the pass at any transit office by filling out a form and getting proof from your doctor.

➢ **BY CAR** • Some major car-rental companies are able to supply hand-controlled vehicles with a minimum of 24-hours advance notice. **Avis** (tel. 800/331–1212) will install hand-control mechanisms at no extra charge if given a day's notice. **Hertz** (tel. 800/654–3131, TDD 800/654–2280) asks for 48-hour notice (except at San Francisco International Airport, where a day will suffice). Rental companies often can't install hand controls on economy cars.

➢ **BY PUBLIC TRANSIT** • BART **Customer Service Office** (800 Madison St., at the Lake Merritt BART Station, tel. 510/464–7133, TDD 510/839–2220) can tell you where to buy a $16 ticket for a mere $4. All BART stations have elevators. Call 510/834–LIFT for a list of possible out-of-service elevators. Contact San Francisco MUNI's **Elderly and Handicapped Discount ID Office** (tel. 415/923–6070) for discount pass and access information for that system. Most buses are wheelchair accessible, and you'll pay 35¢ instead of $1. Monthly passes for the disabled are $8. **AC Transit** (tel. 510/891–4777) issues a disabled ID card allowing the bearer to pay 60¢ instead of $1.25 to ride the bus. To find out which bus routes are wheelchair accessible (most are), contact their bus information line (tel. 510/839–2882). All **Golden Gate Transit** (tel. 415/332–6600) buses are wheelchair accessible and you get 50% off the bus fare.

➢ **WHEELCHAIRS** • In the East Bay, **Grand Mar** (1311 63rd St., at Doyle St., Emeryville, tel. 510/428–0441) rents and repairs wheelchairs. Manual wheelchairs rent for $10 the first day, $5 each subsequent day, or $45–$97 a month; power wheelchairs are $20 a day, $348–$500 a month. In San Francisco, **Abbey Home and Healthcare** (390 9th St., tel. 415/864–6999) rents manual wheelchairs for $80 a month.

SERVICES FOR THE DEAF AND BLIND American Foundation for the Blind (111 Pine St. #725, San Francisco, tel. 415/392–4845) has brochures and catalogues to help people access resources. Call before stopping by. **Lighthouse for the Blind and Visually Disabled** (214 Van Ness Ave., at Grove St., San Francisco, tel. 415/431–1481) has assistant devices (canes, talking watches) and can direct people to support groups. **Lion's Blind Center** in Oakland (3834 Opal St., at 38th St., tel. 510/450–1580) or San Jose (101 North Bascon Ave., tel. 408/295–4016) also has resources for blind people. **Peninsula Center for the Blind** (2470 El Camino Real, Suite 107, Palo Alto, tel. 415/858–0202) has orientation and mobility specialists, social workers, and short-term counseling. For the hearing-impaired, **Hearing Society for the Bay Area** (870 Market St., Suite 330, tel. 415/693–5870, TDD 415/834–1005) provides social services, interpreting, vocational rehab, and referrals.

THE GREAT OUTDOORS ACCESS/ABILITIES (Box 458, Mill Valley 94942, tel. 415/388–3250, fax 415/383–8718) provides travel info on accessible tours and customizes itineraries for both the Bay Area and other places in the country. In San Francisco, the nonprofit **Environmental Traveling Companions** (Fort Mason Center, Bldg. C, tel. 415/474–7662) organizes cross-country skiing, kayaking, and rafting trips for the physically disabled and other people with special needs—cancer survivors, the developmentally disabled, etc.—as well as the population at large. Their prices are very reasonable (one-day trips start at about $38 per person), and they're willing to negotiate if you're truly unable to pay. In the East Bay, **Bay Area Outreach and Recreation Program** (tel. 510/849–4663) organizes sports events and outdoor activities for the disabled, with programs for youth, adults, and seniors. **California State Parks** offers a discount pass ($3.50) that gets you 50% off all parking and camping fees (provided the fees are over $3). To apply for a pass write to: California State Parks, Disabled Discount Pass Program, P.O. Box 942896, Sacramento, CA 94296–0001.

FESTIVALS

JANUARY In addition to the kick-off of the ballet and chamber orchestra seasons, January is a big month in the California **whale-watching** season, which runs through April. Patient watchers bundle up and pull out their binoculars at Point Reyes (*see* Chapter 8). The rangers at the

Point Reyes lighthouse (tel. 415/669–1534) can tell you how many beasties have swum past in the past few days.

Tet Festival. This one-day street fair is held on the Saturday nearest the Vietnamese New Year (the first new moon after January 20). The streets around Civic Center come alive with performances by Vietnamese, Cambodian, and Laotian singers and dancers, and numerous booths sell Southeast Asian delicacies. The festival is not just a celebration of the New Year but also of the diverse neighborhood in which it takes place. *Tel. 415/885–2743.*

FEBRUARY **Chinese New Year.** Celebrate the dawn of the Year of the Ox (year 4695 on the lunar calendar) with North America's oldest Chinese community. Cultural events and festivities start February 7, 1997, and culminate February 22 at 5:30 PM with the fireworks and colorful costumes of the Golden Dragon Parade in S.F.'s Chinatown. *Tel. 415/982–3000.*

MARCH During **Tulipmania** (March 4–18), more than 35,000 tulips bloom around Pier 39 at Fisherman's Wharf. You can walk around on your own, or show up at the Entrance Plaza any morning at 10 for a free guided tour. *Tel. 415/705–5512.*

St. Patrick's Day Parade. Boasting shamrocks, Guinness stout, and enough green to make even Mother Nature envious, this parade (March 16 at 12:30 PM) is a party in motion. Despite the recent politicization of the parade, with "Gaylic Pride" and "IRA All the Way" banners popping up, the emphasis for San Francisco's Irish community is still firmly on green beer and folk tunes. *Tel. 415/661–2700.*

APRIL **Cherry Blossom Festival.** This cultural festival in Japantown features nearly 400 Japanese performers who come to dance along with numerous exhibits of Japanese art. Perhaps the most popular attraction is the taiko drum performance on Saturday night. For a schedule of events, send a self-addressed, stamped envelope to Cherry Blossom Festival, Box 15147, San Francisco 94115. The festivities conclude with a 2½-hour parade. *Tel. 415/ 563–2313.*

San Francisco International Film Festival. The nation's oldest film festival features two full weeks of seminars and films ranging from the almost-mainstream (Pedro Almódovar, Wayne Wang) to the truly obscure. Screenings take place near the end of April at the Kabuki 8 and the Castro Theatre in San Francisco, the Pacific Film Archive in Berkeley, and other locations in the South Bay and Marin. *Tel. 415/929–5000. Admission: $7.50 per program, $5.50 students, seniors, and the disabled.*

Whole Life Expo. If your energy needs to be rechanneled, come to this New Age fest, held at San Francisco's Fashion Design Center (8th and Brannan Sts.). During the last weekend in April (April 25–27 in 1997), more than 250 booths display energy pyramids, massage tools, and sprout-growing paraphernalia. Another exposition is held the third week in October, when the emphasis is on food and health. *Tel. 415/721–2484. Admission: $7 Fri., $12 Sat. or Sun.*

MAY **Cinco de Mayo.** Vibrant mariachi bands and colorful Mexican folklórico dancers congregate in the Mission district the weekend nearest May 5 to celebrate the anniversary of Mexico's defeat of the French at the Battle of Puebla. On Sunday, floats, bands, and salsa dancers wearing little more than feathers parade through the Mission, starting at 24th and Bryant Streets and ending with a festival at Civic Center. *Tel. 415/826–1401.*

Festival of Greece. On May 19–21, the emphasis is on food—moussaka, dolmas, baklava—and wine, though music and Greek crafts also make an appearance. Costume-clad dancers perform for the crowds, but when the bands pull out their bouzoukis, everyone gets in on the action. Festivities take place from 11–11 Friday and Saturday and noon–9 on Sunday. *Greek Orthodox Cathedral, 4700 Lincoln Ave., at Hwy 13, Oakland, tel. 510/531–3710. Admission: about $5.*

Bay to Breakers. Listed in the *Guinness Book of World Records* as the world's largest foot race, this zany 100,000-person event pits world-class runners against costumed human centipedes and huge safe-sex condom caravans in a 7½-mile race from the Financial District to Ocean Beach. The race takes place the third Sunday of every May (May 18 in 1997). Entry forms start appearing in the *San Francisco Examiner* (*see* Media, *above*) March 1. If you like crowds and silly fun, this is the event for you, but be warned that you could spend 45 minutes just jostling your way across the starting line. *Tel. 415/777-7770.*

Carnaval. On Memorial Day Weekend, long after Carnaval celebrations in New Orleans and Rio are over, the Mission District revives the party. Dozens of Latin American musical groups, including the Caribbean All-Stars and Xiuhcoatc Danza Azteka, keep the energy at top levels. The parade along 24th and Mission streets starts at 10 AM on Sunday and terminates at the fair on Harrison Street (btw 16th and 22nd Sts.), which features food, craft booths, and performances. *Tel. 415/826-1401.*

JUNE Summer brings out the neighborhood festivals. On the first weekend in June, the **Union Street Spring Festival** (tel. 415/346-4561) highlights this upscale Marina District street with big bands and swing. The following weekend, the **Haight-Ashbury Street Fair** (tel. 415/661-8025) has two stages, featuring mostly local bands playing rap, jazz, rock, or just about anything. Come see the "Worlds Biggest Salami" at the **North Beach Festival** (tel. 415/403-0666), the country's oldest urban street fair, held in mid-June. There's chalk street painting, small-press booksellers, and music (flamenco, jazz, tarantella).

Free Folk Festival. It's surprising that more Bay Area residents haven't been turned on to the free, feel-good festival that takes place for two days every June at the John Adams Campus of City College (1860 Hayes St., at Masonic Ave., San Francisco). Bring your guitar, harmonica, or whatever you can carry a tune on to the workshops and impromptu jam sessions that spring up between concerts of folk, blues, and international music. It's a very loosely organized event, and participants change yearly, but if you check entertainment listings in the newspapers you should be able to track it down.

Festival at the Lake. The East Bay's largest urban fair has gotten so big it has expanded from its Lakeside Park home to include sites at Laney College and the Henry J. Kaiser Convention Center across Lake Merritt (ferries and trams shuttle you between different sites). The fair takes place the first weekend in June and features crafts, international food, storytelling, and world music. *Tel. 510/286-1061. Admission: $2-$7.*

Juneteenth. The day Lincoln's Emancipation Proclamation was read in Texas is celebrated in nearly every city in the Bay Area. One of the larger events is the **Oakland Juneteenth Celebration,** held at Lakeside Park at Lake Merritt, which emphasizes cultural enrichment and African-American history. Show up at the park June 16 noon-6 for big-name blues and R&B acts, ethnic food booths, arts and crafts, and lots of activities for the kids. *Tel. 510/238-7765.*

Making Waves. On June 21st, the longest day of the year, the streets vibrate with the sounds of over 250 bands (everything from local funk to Zydeco to jazz to African indigenous music) playing for free (!) in downtown San Francisco on 25 stage sites. A bacchanalian celebration of summer solstice and International Music Day, Making Waves is presented by the Alliance Française and the Goethe-Institut. *Tel. 415/775-7755.*

Stern Grove Music Festival. Come see free music (classical, jazz, world music, and more) in a beautiful park setting. Stern Grove (19th St. at Sloat Blvd.) is found in the southwest corner of San Francisco. *Tel. 415/252-6252.*

San Francisco Lesbian, Gay, Bisexual, Transgender Pride Celebration. Known as San Francisco Pride for short (and formerly known as the Gay and Lesbian Freedom Day Parade), this is San Francisco at its queer best. The parade traditionally attracts huge names in the gay community; one of 1995's grand marshals was Candice Gingrich, Newt's out half-sister. Check local newspapers or call for location and date. June also brings the much-loved **International Lesbian and Gay Film Festival** (*see* Movie Houses, in Chapter 6). *Tel. 415/864-3733.*

JULY Summer heat keeps the festivals coming. In mid-July, you can groove your way down Polk Street between Jackson and Bush streets thanks to the festival of **Blues and Art on Polk** (tel. 415/346-4561).

Fourth of July Waterfront Festival. The biggest Independence Day celebration in the Bay Area takes place along the waterfront between Aquatic Park and Pier 39 with music in the afternoon and fireworks at night. The show is even impressive when the waterfront is fogged in. *Tel. 415/777–8498.*

Jazz and All That Art on Fillmore. In the 1940s, '50s, and '60s, the Fillmore area was famous for its happening jazz and blues clubs, but the slash-and-burn redevelopment of the '70s erased all that. Old-time musicians (and younger ones, too) revive those heady days on the first weekend of every July on Fillmore Street between Post and Jackson streets, when arts-and-crafts booths peddle their wares, and outdoor cafés serve everything from barbecue ribs to knishes. Admission to all shows is free. *Tel. 415/346–4446.*

KQED International Beer and Food Festival. If you're looking to acquire a beer belly, join 5,000 San Franciscans at the Concourse Exhibition Center (Brannan and 8th Sts.) in early July to sample 250 different beers at the largest international beer festival in the nation. There's live music on two stages, and food booths hand out everything from Thai cuisine to pizza. Free cable car shuttles run from Civic Center BART station. Get tickets in advance by calling the number below; KQED members get a 15% discount on advance tickets and profits support public TV. *Tel. 415/553–2200. Admission: about $35.*

Jewish Film Festival. Taking place during the last two weeks of July, the festival is the largest of its kind in the world. Films are shown at theaters in Berkeley and San Francisco. Call for admission prices. *Tel. 510/ 548–0556.*

Oakland Chinatown Streetfest. Oakland's large Chinatown celebrates its diversity on the fourth weekend in August with food and cultural activities representing all East Asian cultures. *Tel. 510/893–8979.*

AUGUST Ahoy, maties! The **Festival of the Sea** celebrates San Francisco's maritime tradition with sailmaking and rope making demonstrations, sea-faring music, and a parade of tall ships and yachts along the San Francisco waterfront. The free festival takes place at San Francisco's Hyde Street Pier, usually late in the month. *Tel. 415/929–0202.*

SEPTEMBER **Shakespeare in the Park.** Free outdoor performances of a selected Shakespeare play begin Labor Day weekend in San Francisco's Golden Gate Park and continue in October at Lakeside Park in Oakland and St. James Park in San Jose. Shows take place at 1:30 PM Saturday and Sunday. *Tel. 415/666–2221.*

Opera in the Park. The San Francisco Opera kicks off the opera season with a free concert in Golden Gate Park's Sharon Meadow the Sunday after the first performance of the season, usually the week after Labor Day. *Tel. 415/861–4008.*

Folsom Street Fair. Even in San Francisco, this fest has created controversy with its past displays of leather and bondage. People crowd the blocks of Folsom Street between 7th and 12th Streets strutting their latest leatherware, often connected to one another by a leather or metal-link strap. Look for the fair the last or next-to-last Sunday in September. *Tel. 415/861–FAIR.*

Festival de las Americas. This Mission District festival, celebrating the independence of Mexico and seven other Latin American countries, attracts more than 80,000 people to 24th Street between Mission and Hampshire streets. The socially responsible, alcohol-free, family-oriented event promotes pride in the Latino community. Latino musicians, ethnic food, and booths selling original crafts will crowd the streets Sunday, September 17, from 11 to 6. *Tel. 415/826–1401.*

San Francisco Blues Festival. Big-name musicians perform at the country's oldest blues festival, usually the last weekend of the month at Fort Mason's scenic Great Meadow (cnr Marina Blvd. and Laguna St.). Past performers have included B.B. King and Robert Cray. One-day tickets are $16.50 in advance, $20 at the door; two-day tickets are $28, advance purchase only. Performances take place 11–5:30 each day, and all seating is on the lawn. A free kick-off concert happens at Justin Herman Plaza on September 21. *Tel. 415/826–6837 or 415/979–5588 for recorded info.*

Berkeley Beer and Music Festival. Taste home-brewed beer at Berkeley's Civic Center Park the first or second weekend in September, and you may never drink anything else. A $15 tasting kit includes a beer mug and ten drink coupons. *Tel. 510/THE–ROCK.*

OCTOBER **Castro Street Fair.** On the first Sunday of the month, the Castro Street Fair brings out crafts vendors; booths run by community, health, and social organizations; and musical entertainment. *Tel. 415/467–3354.*

The Black Cowboys Parade (tel. 510/531-7583) takes place the first Saturday in October and honors the role of minorities in the Old West.

Halloween. Traditionally, this huge, raucous, queers-only party has taken place on the closed-off streets of the Castro District, but at press time, a change of venue was being considered due to overcrowding and the recent influx of gawking "breeders." Call CUAV (Community United Against Violence), tel. 415/777–5500, for the latest. And if you aren't dressed to the nines, don't even bother.

San Francisco International Accordion Festival. Held the third weekend in October, this wacky festival features food, dancing, and booths (pick up an "I Play the Accordion and I Vote" bumper sticker). Perennial faves Zydeco Flames and Those Darn Accordions should be there to compete in the "I'm San Francisco's Main Squeeze" contest, which chooses the accordionist with the wildest costume to be next year's poster child. *Anchorage Shopping Center, Fisherman's Wharf, tel. 415/775–6000.*

NOVEMBER **San Francisco Book Festival.** Bibliophiles eagerly await this big festival held the first weekend in November. Over 300 booths representing big publishers and small alternative presses show off their books, often selling them at a discount. About 250 authors show up to read and sign their books; Isabel Allende, Tony Hillerman, and June Jordan are just a few who have appeared in recent years. *Concourse Exhibition Center, 8th and Brannan Sts., tel. 415/908–2833. Admission: $2.*

Día de los Muertos. The Day of the Dead is held on November 2 in San Francisco. Derived from Aztec rituals and the Catholic All Souls' Day, the holiday is celebrated in the Mission with art exhibitions and a parade starting from the Mission Cultural Center (2868 Mission St., tel. 415/821–1155).

Run to the Far Side. More than 13,000 people dress like their favorite Gary Larson characters to compete in a 5-kilometer walk and a 10-kilometer run through Golden Gate Park on the Sunday after Thanksgiving. The cost is about $18 if you preregister, $22 on the day of the race; the event benefits the California Academy of Sciences' environmental education programs. *Tel. 415/564–0532.*

DECEMBER In celebration of the season, the San Francisco Ballet (tel. 415/865–2000) presents *The Nutcracker* every year. In Oakland, the Mormon Temple (4766 Lincoln Ave., tel. 510/531–0704) holds a **tree-lighting ceremony** early in the month and offers musical entertainment during the evenings until Christmas Eve.

Celebration of Craftswomen. This fair, held during the first two weekends of December at Fort Mason, features leather work, wearable art, and glasswork along with gourmet food and live entertainment. Admission is $6 ($4 for seniors). *Tel. 415/821–6480.*

CLIMATE

The Bay Area is home to something called "micro-climates." In lay terms, this means that while you're burning furniture to stay warm in San Francisco's Sunset District, your friend is talking to you cordless and poolside in 80°F Palo Alto, a mere 45 miles away. And when you call the **National Weather Service** (tel. 415/364–7974) to figure out what to wear, they tell you something helpful about "highs from the upper 50s to the low 90s." At least if you call between 10 and 6 you can talk to a live meteorologist, who might be able to narrow things down. For ski conditions in Northern California, Tahoe, or the Sierras, call the **California State Automobile Association's Ski Report** (tel. 415/864–6440).

SAN FRANCISCO A local writer in the *East Bay Express* put it best: When it comes to San Francisco weather, "summer is winter, winter is spring, and fall is summer." In sum, it never snows here, but it's cold and windy a lot of the time—except in September and October, the Indian summer months, and May, which is usually beautiful. Late fall gets really cold, it rains

Your vacation.

Your vacation after losing your hard-earned vacation money.

 Lose your cash and it's lost forever. Lose American Express®
Travelers Cheques and you can get them quickly replaced.
They can mean the difference between the vacation of
your dreams and your worst nightmare. And, they are
accepted virtually anywhere in the world. Available at participating banks, credit
unions, AAA offices and American Express Travel locations. *Don't take chances.
Take American Express Travelers Cheques.*

do more

**Travelers
Cheques**

All the best trips start with **Fodor's**.

EXPLORING GUIDES
Like the best of all possible travel magazines

"As stylish and attractive as any guide published." —*The New York Times*

"Worth reading before, during, and after a trip." —*The Philadelphia Inquirer*

More than 30 destinations available worldwide. $19.95 - $21.00 ($27.95 - 28.95 Canada)

BERKELEY GUIDES

The hippest, freshest and most exciting budget-minded travel books on the market.

"Berkeley's scribes put the funk back in travel." —*Time*

"Fresh, funny, and funky as well as useful." —*The Boston Globe*

"Well-organized, clear and very easy to read." —*America Online*

14 destinations worldwide. Priced between $13.00 - $19.50. ($17.95 - $27.00 Canada)

AFFORDABLES

"All the maps and itinerary ideas of Fodor's established Gold Guides with a bonus—shortcuts to savings." —*USA Today*

"Travelers with champagne tastes and beer budgets will welcome this series from Fodor's." —*Hartford Courant*

"It's obvious these Fodor's folks have secrets we civilians don't." —*New York Daily News*

Also available: Florida, Europe, France, London, Paris. Priced between $11.00 - $18.00 ($14.50 - $24.00 Canada)

At bookstores, or call **1-800-533-6478**

Fodor's
The name that means smart travel.™

pretty often in winter, and July is notoriously blustery and foggy. The average high temperature is 69°F, the average low 46°F.

EAST BAY The East Bay tends to be a few degrees warmer than San Francisco. Summer is mild, fall hot, winter unpredictable but usually rainy, and spring mild again. Overall, the climate here is pretty fabulous, especially if you enjoy mellow, overcast days or cool but sunny afternoons. It's smart to layer your clothing, because there's no guarantee that the morning's foggy turtleneck weather won't betray you and become an afternoon tank-top heat wave. Highs average 72°F, lows 43°F.

MARIN COUNTY In a region of micro-climates, Marin goes one better: Even within the county, the weather differs from town to town. The coast is usually fogged in, the bayside towns of Tiburon and Sausalito get a cool breeze, and San Rafael checks in at a solid few degrees warmer than most of the Bay Area (with an average summer high of 82°F).

SOUTH BAY Don't move to the South Bay if you thrive on unpredictability. Spring and fall are sunny and warm, and summer is sunny and hot (average summer highs, both on the coast and inland, hover in the 80s). In the winter, things cool down to a medium rare, with lows dipping to 40°F.

VISITOR INFORMATION

SAN FRANCISCO If you're into pre-trip planning, write or call the **San Francisco Convention and Visitors Bureau** for free info about hotels, restaurants, festivals, and shopping. *201 3rd St., Suite 900, 94103, tel. 415/974–6900. Open weekdays 8:30–5.*

Visitors can stop in for maps, brochures, and MUNI Passports at the city's **Visitor Information Center** in the lower level of Hallidie Plaza, next to the Powell Street BART station. Come in the afternoons to avoid long lines. The info booth upstairs at the cable car turnaround sells Pass-

Walk This Way

Have a laugh at all the bus-riding, pastel-clad, camera-toting tourists that infiltrate Fisherman's Wharf if you like, but don't let them turn you off tours entirely. Even longtime residents can learn something from enthusiastic guides, who know the city's neighborhoods inside out. Wok Wiz Chinatown Tours and Cooking Company (tel. 415/981–5588) leads daily culinary/historic tours and the popular "I Can't Believe I Ate My Way Through Chinatown" tour ($55). Though the name is pure fromage, this is a great way to single out some great restaurants and learn about Chinese cuisine from cookbook author Shirley Fong-Torres. Tours usually start on Saturday mornings at 10 and end, according to Shirley, "when the first person explodes." Trevor Hailey (375 Lexington St., tel. 415/550–8110), a prominent member of the San Francisco lesbian community, leads a highly recommended tour of the city's famous gay neighborhood called "Cruisin' the Castro" ($30). The 3½-hour tour includes brunch; call for reservations. Finally, to be led around San Francisco for free, call City Guides (tel. 415/557–4266), whose guided walks are sponsored by the San Francisco Public Library. Tours, which cover almost every corner of town, include Roof Gardens and Open Spaces, the Telegraph Hill Hike, Art Deco Marina, History of Haight-Ashbury, and the Mission Murals. Quality varies according to the skills of the library volunteer, but it's hard to beat being shown around the city for free by a knowledgeable local.

ports only. *Tel. 415/391–2000, or 415/391–2001 for 24-hour recorded information. Open weekdays 9–5:30, Sat. 9–3, Sun. 10–2.*

EAST BAY **Berkeley Convention and Visitors Bureau.** Stop by for a decent selection of pamphlets and listings of Berkeley events. *1834 University Ave., at Martin Luther King Jr. Way, tel. 510/549–7040 or 510/549–8710 for recorded info. Open weekdays 9–5.*

The **East Bay Regional Parks District** has maps and information about the 46 parks and 13 regional trails in the Oakland hills. *2950 Peralta Oaks Ct., at 106th St., Oakland, tel. 510/635–0135. Open weekdays 8:30–5.*

The **Oakland Convention and Visitors Bureau** is geared toward convention-goers, but the staff is happy to answer all inquiries. Pick up a copy of their small pamphlet, "The Official Visitors Guide," which lists dozens of museums, historical attractions, and community events. *1000 Broadway, Suite 200, tel. 510/839–9000. From 12th St. BART, walk down Broadway to 11th Street. Open weekdays 8:30–5.*

MARIN COUNTY The **Marin County Convention and Visitors Bureau** distributes the free *Weekender Magazine,* which lists live music and cultural events in the area. *Marin Center, on Avenue of the Flags, San Rafael, tel. 415/472–7470. Open weekdays 9–5.*

The **West Marin Chamber of Commerce** (Box 1045, Point Reyes Station 94956, tel. 415/663–9232) has a free pamphlet, "The Coastal Traveler," with great information on out-of-the-way beaches, bike rides, and backpacking trips. You can also visit the **West Marin Network** to get a lodging guide and information on activities in the region. *Mesa Rd., at Hwy. 1, Point Reyes Station, tel. 415/663–9543. Open Mon.–Sat. 9–7.*

SOUTH BAY The **Palo Alto Chamber of Commerce** (325 Forest Ave., at Bryant St., tel. 415/324–3121) has maps of the city, as well as limited information on sights, restaurants, and lodging. *Open weekdays 9–5.*

The **San Jose Convention and Visitors Bureau** (150 W. San Carlos St., San Jose, tel. 408/283–8833) is open weekdays 8–5:30, weekends 11–5. You can call the **San Jose Events Hotline** (tel. 408/295–2265) for listings of community events and after-dark diversions.

The **Pacifica Chamber of Commerce** has info on Pacifica and Montara as well as limited materials about Half Moon Bay and points south. *450 Dondee Way #2, Pacifica, tel. 415/355–4122. Near Rockaway Beach. Open weekdays 9–noon and 1–5, weekends 10–4:30.*

The friendly staff at the **Half Moon Bay Chamber of Commerce** will give you more info than you ever wanted on Half Moon Bay and the surrounding area, as well as a smattering of maps and brochures for the entire San Mateo County coast. *520 Kelly Ave., at Hwy. 1, Half Moon Bay, tel. 415/726–8380. Open weekdays 10–4.*

EXPLORING THE BAY AREA

2

By Simon Dang, Maureen Klier, and Charlene Pinzon

You'll never run out of opportunities for adventure in the Bay Area, no matter how long you stay. San Francisco is a dense, cosmopolitan city, yet its historic Victorian homes, wide open parks, and jaw-dropping views render it anything but claustrophobic. The best way to explore is by walking its dozen distinct neighborhoods; along the way, you'll encounter shops, parks, and cafés that invite you to stop and soak up the atmosphere. On days when you feel more rugged, head for Marin County's stunning cliffs, forests, and beaches—an impressive backdrop to the multimillion-dollar homes that dot the landscape. The East Bay offers acres of hilly parks with incredible views of the city and the bay beyond. The East Bay's two major cities are Berkeley, known for its university, its radical politics, and its wacky street people; and Oakland, a sprawling, unpretentious city with a strong African-American identity. If you miss the bland suburban flavor that pervades much of the rest of the United States, check out the South Bay. Hidden in the 70 or so miles of sprawl is one of the better-kept of the Bay Area's myriad secrets: the striking, wind-swept San Mateo County Coast.

San Francisco

No matter how well you think you know San Francisco, the dense, eclectic city will surprise you. Whatever's hit the streets, from the drinking and whoring of the gold prospectors to the living and loving of the country's largest lesbian and gay population, has left reminders of its presence in nooks and crannies all over this eminently explorable city. Weathered brick and iron warehouses of the Barbary Coast are now the sites of antique shops in the financial district, while huge Victorian mansions that survived the 1906 quake are still standing proud in the Mission. One minute you're marveling at the frenetic pace of Financial District workers and the next you're strolling through Chinese herb shops and produce markets. You down a cappuccino and biscotti at a noisy Italian café, and 10 minutes later you're gazing at the Golden Gate Bridge from the water's edge. Bored? You should be ashamed of yourself.

You can spend endless days—and no money at all—just kicking around the hilly streets. Expound upon the latest artistic trend as you gallery-hop; get your exercise climbing through other people's backyards on hidden stairway streets; gawk at the mansions that dominate the peaks of Pacific Heights and the Presidio; or get lost for a day in Golden Gate Park. When your dogs get tired, as they inevitably will on the dizzying hills in some parts of the city, hop a bus for a higher-speed version of the San Francisco scene. You can get a MUNI transportation map at most liquor and grocery stores for $2.50; carry it with you, and when you're all tuckered out you should be able to find a bus to take you someplace interesting. If you want enthusiastic

San Francisco

Golden Gate Bridge

Fort Point National Historic Site

101

Golden Gate National Recreation Area

The Presidio

PACIFIC OCEAN

W. Pacific Ave.

Baker Beach

Phelan Beach

Lands End

Lincoln Park

Palace of the Legion of Honor

SEACLIFF

Lake St.

Lincoln Blvd.

Park Presidio Blvd.

8th Ave.

Arguello Blvd.

Geary Expr

Point Lobos

Cliff House

Clement St.

Geary Blvd.

43rd Ave.

34th Ave.

25th Ave.

19th Ave.

Balboa St.

Turk

Masonic

RICHMOND

Fulton St.

Golden Gate Park

HAI ASH

Kennedy Dr.

Middle Dr.

Luther

Martin

King

Jr.

Dr.

Stanyan St.

Clayton

COLE VALLEY

Lincoln Way

Judah St.

28th Ave.

Funston Ave.

7th Ave.

Clarendon Ave.

Ocean Beach

Great Highway

Lawton St.

1

Noriega St.

Ortega St.

SUNSET

Quintara St.

41st Ave.

Sunset Blvd.

19th Ave.

14th Ave.

Dewey Blvd.

T P.

McCoppin Square

Taraval St.

Larsen Park

Vicente St.

Dr.

Mt. Davidson

Stern Grove

Portola

Yerba Buena Ave.

Monterey Blvd.

Miramar Ave.

Mont

San Francisco Zoo

Sloat Blvd.

STONESTOWN

Juniper Serra Blvd.

Ocean Ave.

Harding Park

San Francisco State Univ.

Holloway Ave.

Garfield St.

Plymouth Ave.

Skyline Blvd.

Lake Merced

Lake Merced Blvd.

Font Blvd.

280

Fort Funston

Brotherhood Way

N

0   1 mile

0   1 km

35

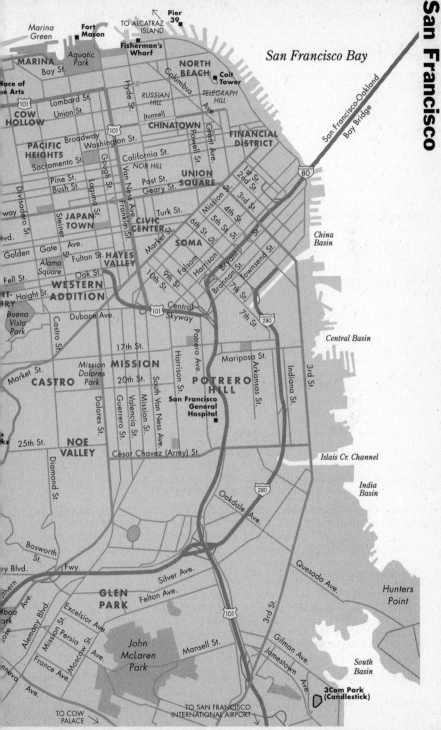

San Francisco

San Francisco Bay

Marina Green

Fort Mason

Pier 39

TO ALCATRAZ ISLAND

Fisherman's Wharf

MARINA

Bay St.

Aquatic Park

NORTH BEACH

Coit Tower

lace of e Arts

COW HOLLOW

Lombard St.

Union St.

Columbus Ave.

RUSSIAN Hill

TELEGRAPH HILL

101

Hyde St.

(tunnel)

CHINATOWN

PACIFIC HEIGHTS

Broadway

Washington St.

101

Powell St.

Grant Ave.

FINANCIAL DISTRICT

San Francisco-Oakland Bay Bridge

Sacramento St.

California St.

NOB HILL

Gough St.

Pine St.

Bush St.

Post St.

Geary St.

UNION SQUARE

1st St.

2nd St.

Divisadero St.

Laguna St.

Van Ness Ave.

Franklin St.

Steiner

JAPAN-TOWN

Turk St.

CIVIC CENTER

3rd St.

4th St.

5th St.

6th St.

80

China Basin

way

Golden Gate Ave.

Fulton St.

HAYES VALLEY

Market St.

SOMA

Mission St.

Fell St.

Alamo Square

Oak St.

Folsom St.

Harrison

Bryant St.

Brannan St.

Townsend St.

Central Basin

IT- RY

Haight St.

WESTERN ADDITION

Duboce Ave.

101

Central Skyway

9th St.

10th St.

7th St.

280

Buena Vista Park

Castro St.

17th St.

Potrero Ave.

Mariposa St.

Arkansas St.

Indiana St.

3rd St.

Market St.

CASTRO

Mission Dolores Park

MISSION

20th St.

Harrison St.

South Van Ness Ave.

POTRERO HILL

San Francisco General Hospital

Dolores St.

Guerrero St.

Valencia St.

Mission St.

Islais Cr. Channel

25th St.

NOE VALLEY

Cesar Chavez (Army) St.

280

Oakdale Ave.

India Basin

Diamond St.

Bosworth St.

y Blvd.

Fwy.

Silver Ave.

Felton Ave.

Quesada Ave.

Hunters Point

southern

boa ork

jose

Ave.

Alemany Blvd.

Excelsior Ave.

GLEN PARK

Mission St.

Persia Ave.

Moscow St.

Ave.

Mansell St.

101

3rd St.

Gilman Ave.

Jamestown Ave.

France Ave.

eneva Ave.

John McLaren Park

South Basin

3Com Park (Candlestick)

TO COW PALACE

TO SAN FRANCISCO INTERNATIONAL AIRPORT

25

locals to show you their fair city, tag along on one of San Francisco's quirky tours (for more info, *see box* Walk this Way, in Chapter 1).

Major Sights

With the exception of Fisherman's Wharf, which bludgeons visitors with its banality, San Francisco's major sights are considered major for a reason. Even the most jaded natives can't help but inhale a reverent breath at the sight of the Golden Gate Bridge looming overhead. The Alcatraz tour explores such a fascinating place—on such a genuinely stark, scary island—that, for all the hype, it is utterly compelling. Despite the best efforts of merchants selling tourist schlock, the spirit of San Francisco refuses to yield.

GOLDEN GATE BRIDGE

The bridge to end all bridges has come to symbolize San Francisco more than any other monument. This masterpiece of design and engineering, which links San Francisco to its wealthy neighbor, Marin County, has endured wind, fog, the daily load of 100,000 cars, the ignominy of over 1,000 suicides, and the weight of the more than 200,000 people who showed up to celebrate its 50th birthday in 1987. More than a mile long, the bridge is painted International Orange for visibility in fog (so the seagulls don't crash into it). Engineer Joseph Strauss designed the bridge to withstand winds of more than 100 miles per hour and to swing nearly 27 feet in its center. The cables that support it are more than 3 feet in diameter, and the combined lengths of the individual strands would wrap around the earth three times.

To catch a glimpse of the bridge, you'll have to scale a hill or two or head to the waterfront near Fisherman's Wharf. Bus 28 will drop you at the toll plaza, at the northern tip of the Presidio (*see* Neighborhoods, *below*), from which point you can hoof it or hitch. And of course, you'll want to cross the bridge. To walk across and back takes about an hour and the wind can be freezing. Bicycling across the bridge is a thrill; Lincoln Boulevard in the Presidio is a gorgeous way to get there. (To reach Lincoln, take a gentle ride west down Lombard Street, or go for the screaming downhill adventure by approaching from the south on Presidio Boulevard.) The pedestrian walkway and the bicycle path are both open 5 AM–9 PM.

ALCATRAZ ISLAND

Known as the Rock, Alcatraz Island served for 59 years as the nation's most notorious federal penitentiary, holding high-risk prisoners in its isolated maw. Al Capone, Robert "The Birdman" Stroud, and Machine Gun Kelly were among the more famous bad guys who got "Rock fever" gazing out day after day at the bittersweet sight of San Francisco.

Of course, ever since the prison closed in 1963, people have been trying to get onto Alcatraz Island rather than off it. In 1969, a group of Native Americans attempted to reclaim the land, saying that an 1868 federal treaty allowed Native Americans to use all federal territory that the government wasn't actively using. After almost two years of occupation, the U.S. government forced them off, none too gently. The bloody incident is recounted in the island's small museum, and graffiti still reminds visitors that "This is Native American Land."

Today the island is part of the national park system, and tourists visit the grounds in hordes—though even heavy weekend crowds don't affect the lonely, somber, abandoned feel of the place. Rangers on Alcatraz offer a variety of free talks—subjects include escape attempts, the island's history as a 19th-century military fort, the Native American occupation, and Alcatraz's unique properties as part of an island chain in San Francisco Bay. Check for schedules at the ranger station at the ferry landing when you arrive or call the dock office at 415/705–1042.

The **Red and White Fleet** (tel. 415/546–2896 for info or 415/546–2700 for tickets) ferries you to the island from San Francisco's Pier 41. The price ($10) includes the ferry ride and an audiocassette tour of the prison itself; tapes are available in several languages, and the average tour takes about 2½ hours. You can skip the cassette tour and pay only $6.75, but the tape, which features former inmates and guards talking about their experiences on Alcatraz, is one of the best parts of the experience. Ferries leave Pier 41 9:30 AM–2:15 PM year-round and until 4:15 PM June–August. You'll need a Visa, American Express, or MasterCard to reserve tickets by phone and you'll pay a $2 service charge. If you're buying tickets in person, go to the ferry ticket office (open 8:30–5) at Pier 41. You should reserve or purchase tickets *several* days in advance. Bus 32 will get you to Pier 41 from the Ferry Building downtown. All tours are wheelchair accessible, although the paths are often steep.

FISHERMAN'S WHARF

Once the domain of Italian fishermen, the wharf is now San Francisco's prize tourist trap, whose sole purpose is to get you to spend money. (Finding an ATM has never been easier.) You won't see many fishermen here unless you arrive in the misty early morning hours (around 5 AM) to watch the fishing boats unload. Otherwise, it's schlock city. Jefferson Street, the wharf's main drag, is packed with expensive seafood restaurants, tacky souvenir shops, and rip-off "museums" like the **Wax Museum, Ripley's Believe It or Not!,** the **Guinness Museum of World Records, The Haunted Gold Mine,** and the **Medieval Dungeon** (featuring graphic re-creations of torture devices from the Middle Ages). Each can be yours for the low admission price of $6–$10. The only thing that remains fairly authentic (albeit rather pricey) is the array of seafood stands along Jefferson Street. Buy clam chowder ($3–$4) or a half-pound of shrimp ($7) from one of the sidewalk vendors and a loaf of sourdough bread ($2.50–$3) from **Boudin Bakery** (156 Jefferson St., tel. 415/928–1849), and eat on one of the piers, watching cruise ships and fishing boats glide in and out of the harbor. Then hightail it out of there to catch a ferry to Alcatraz (*see above*) or Angel Island (*see* Tiburon and Angel Island, in Marin County, *below*) or walk over to Fort Mason to check out the museums.

If you must stick around the wharf, check out the **U.S.S. *Pampanito* Submarine** ($5, Pier 45, tel. 415/929–0202) or the **Maritime Museum** (Beach St., at foot of Polk St., tel. 415/929–0202), housed in an art deco building that features all sorts of artifacts from the maritime history of San Francisco. The museum is free, but if you have $2 to spare, you might have more fun walking around on one of the old ships at Hyde Street Pier, between the Cannery and Ghirardelli Square. Among the ships docked there are the *Balclutha*, a 100-year-old square-rigged ship, and the *Eureka* (Hyde St., at Jefferson, tel. 415/556–3002), an old ferry that now holds a classic car collection and was being restored at press time. Comedian Jonathan Winters was once briefly institutionalized after he climbed the mast of the *Balclutha* and hung from it, shouting "I am the man in the moon!" Closer to the wharf, and recently opened in April 1996, **UnderWater World** (tel. 415/623–5300) is a 707,000-gallon "diver's-eye view" aquarium, where visitors listen to a taped 30-minute tour as they glide through a 300-foot-long transparent tunnel. Though the two main tanks are full of sharks, rays, anemones, and thousands of fish, many visitors seem more amused by the scuba divers who scrub the tanks each morning. It's entertaining in a surreal sort of way, but the $12.95 admission price is mighty steep for an attraction that you can breeze through in under an hour.

Pier 39's one redeeming quality is the swarm of sea lions that took over several of the marina docks a few years ago and have refused to leave. The owners wanted them removed (killed if necessary) until they realized the barking sea mammals were attracting more tourists.

Three shopping complexes girdle the wharf: **Pier 39,** the **Cannery,** and **Ghirardelli Square.** Owned by the billionaire Bass brothers of Texas, Pier 39 is a bland imitation of a turn-of-the-century New England seaport village—the shopping mall of your worst nightmares. A former Del Monte peach-canning factory, the **Cannery** (Jefferson, Leavenworth, Beach, and Hyde Sts., tel. 415/771–3112) is now a gallery of chic boutiques. Chocolate is no longer made on-site at **Ghirardelli Square** (900 North Point St., tel. 415/775–5500), but you can buy it here in bars or atop a huge, tasty ice cream sundae ($5.50). To reach Fisherman's Wharf, take Bus 32 from the Ferry Building downtown. Or fulfill your other tourist obligation by taking a cable car from Powell Street (*see* Getting In, Out, and Around, in Chapter 1) to the end of the line (a nice metaphor for Fisherman's Wharf).

COIT TOWER

Built to memorialize San Francisco's volunteer firefighters, the 210-foot concrete observation tower atop Telegraph Hill is named for the colorful woman who left the funds to build it, Lillie Hitchcock Coit (1843–1929). Heiress Coit was a cross-dresser (she could gain access to the city's more interesting realms in men's clothes) who literally chased fire engines around town. Most people agree the building resembles a fire nozzle—supposedly, that's not intentional. It's also been nicknamed "Coit-us" tower since it's a popular spot to park and . . . you know.

The walls inside the lobby are covered with Depression-era murals in the style of Diego Rivera, painted by local artists on the government dole. **City Guides** (tel. 415/557–4266) offers free descriptive tours of the murals every Saturday at 11 AM, including the second-floor works normally closed to the public. For $3, the elevator inside the tower will take you to the top for a drop-dead, 360° view of Golden Gate Bridge, the Bay Bridge, and Alcatraz.

One of the best (albeit tiring) ways to reach Coit Tower is via two old-fashioned stairways: The historic **Filbert Steps** wind through gardens on narrow wooden walkways, while the concrete **Greenwich Stairs** offer stunning scenery. It's best to tackle the Filbert Steps on the way up, and marvel at magnificent views as you head down the Greenwich Stairs. To start, take Bus 42 from Market Street north to Filbert Street. At the base of the cliff, you will see a set of concrete steps; take a deep breath and start climbing. The concrete will eventually yield to a rickety wooden path. When the path meets Montgomery Street, look to your left and check out Lauren Bacall's apartment from the 1947 Humphrey Bogart classic *Dark Passage*. Cross the street and continue up the steps to Coit Tower. Start your descent under the GREENWICH STREET sign near the parking lot. Brick steps will lead you back down to Montgomery Street, head south about half a block, and on your left you'll find the second half of the stairway. The stairs bottom out at the site of a 1966 Janis Joplin concert hosted by a nearby drug halfway house—now a trendy health club. *Tel. 415/362–0808. From Market and 3rd Sts. downtown, Bus 30 or 45 to Washington Sq.; walk 2 blocks east on Union St., left on Kearny St. Or Bus 39 from Fisherman's Wharf to top of Telegraph Hill. Tower open daily 10–6:30.*

GOLDEN GATE PARK

The western keyhole to San Francisco is Golden Gate Park—1,000 acres of plant life, museums, Dutch windmills, sporting events, open-air performances, and even a herd of bison. Packed into an area that is 4 miles long and less than a mile wide are zillions of varieties of vegetation, wooded areas, wide swaths of grass, and tiny gardens. And, as a bonus, if you make it all the way to the western end of the park, you'll hit blustery Ocean Beach and the Pacific Ocean. Lying close to Haight Street, the park has always been a natural hangout for the countercultural denizens of that neighborhood: Hippie historians should note that Ken Kesey and friends celebrated the first **Human Be-In** here on January 14, 1966. Fittingly, a devotional shrine was erected in tribute to Jerry Garcia's death in 1995. The park has hosted rock concerts ranging from the Grateful Dead and Jefferson Airplane to Pearl Jam and the Beastie Boy's Tibetan Freedom benefit.

On Sundays, John F. Kennedy Drive, the park's main thoroughfare, is closed to car traffic between Stanyan Street and 19th Avenue, when flocks of bicyclists, in-line skaters, and skateboarders take over.

Once a collection of sand dunes, Golden Gate Park was designed in 1868 by William Hammond Hall, a 24-year-old civil engineer with no prior experience (his bid was lowest), and landscaped by John MacLaren. The park is the largest of its kind and is much prettier than New York's Central Park, debunking the claim of that park's designer, Frederick Law Olmsted (who also designed the Stanford University campus), that "beautiful trees could not be made to grow in San Francisco." Today, blue gum eucalyptus, Monterey pine, and Monterey cypress, not to mention one of the world's foremost horticultural displays, are peppered throughout the park. Bordered by Stanyan Street, the Great Highway, Lincoln Way, and Fulton Street, several places near the park rent bikes and in-line skates: **Park Cyclery** (1749 Waller St., at Stanyan St., tel. 415/752–8383) rents mountain bikes for $5 an hour or $30 a day (for skate rental, *see* In-Line Skating, in Chapter 8).

Golden Gate Park

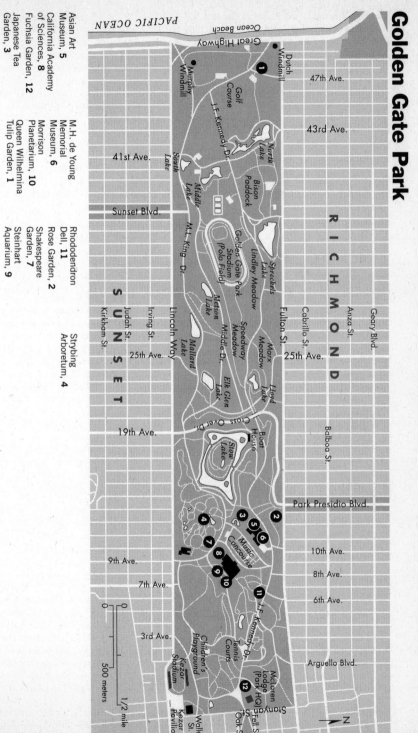

Asian Art
Museum, **5**
California Academy
of Sciences, **8**
Fuchsia Garden, **12**
Japanese Tea
Garden, **3**

M.H. de Young
Memorial
Museum, **6**
Morrison
Planetarium, **10**
Queen Wilhelmina
Tulip Garden, **1**

Rhododendron
Dell, **11**
Rose Garden, **2**
Shakespeare
Garden, **7**
Steinhart
Aquarium, **9**

Stryking
Arboretum, **4**

PACIFIC OCEAN

Ocean Beach

Great Highway

Dutch
Windmill

47th Ave.

43rd Ave.

Murphy
Windmill

Golf
Course

J.F. Kennedy Dr.

North
Lake

41st Ave.

South
Lake

Bison
Paddock

Middle
Lake

Sunset Blvd.

M.L. King Dr.

Golden Gate Park
Stadium
(Polo Field)

Lindley Meadow

Spreckels
Lake

R I C H M O N D

Geary Blvd.

Anza St.

Cabrillo St.

Fulton St.

Marx
Meadow

Metson
Lake

Speedway
Meadow

Middle Dr.

S
U
N
S
E
T

Judah St.

Irving St.

Lincoln Way

25th Ave.

19th Ave.

Kirkham St.

Mallard
Lake

Elk Glen
Lake

Cross Over Dr.

Lloyd
Lake

25th Ave.

Balboa St.

Boat
House

Stow
Lake

Park Presidio Blvd.

9th Ave.

7th Ave.

3rd Ave.

Music Concourse

4

3
5
6
2

7
8
9
10

11

J.F. Kennedy Dr.

10th Ave.

8th Ave.

6th Ave.

Children's
Playground

Tennis
Courts

McLaren
Lodge
(Park HQ)

Kezar
Stadium

Kezar
Pavilion

12

Waller St.

Stanyan St.

Oak St.

Fell St.

Arguello Blvd.

0

500 meters

1/2 mile

N

29

Strybing Arboretum and Botanical Gardens (tel. 415/661–1316), off Martin Luther King Jr. Drive near the museum complex, has a dazzling display of 70 acres of plants, featuring some 5,000 specimens arranged by country of origin, genus, and fragrance. Admission is free. One of the park's star attractions is the **Japanese Tea Garden** (tel. 415/752–4227), originally built for the 1894 Mid-Winter Fair, San Francisco's first world's fair. During the week or on a rainy

The "Chinese" fortune cookie was invented by the Hagiwara family who managed the Japanese Tea Garden from 1895–1942.

day, the garden is well worth the $2.50 admission (free before 9:30 AM, after 5:30 PM); at other times, crowds spoil any chance at serenity. The meticulously designed garden, open daily 9–6:30, features an exquisite 18th-century Buddha and a scant number of koi in the fish ponds—survivors of raids by local raccoons and hawks. The Hagiwara family took care of the garden until World War II when they, along with other Japanese Americans, were removed to internment camps. In 1994, on the garden's 100th-year anniversary, a cherry blossom tree was planted in their memory. While you're there, treat yourself to a pot of green tea and cookies ($2.50) to complete the experience.

The park's many free gardens include the **Shakespeare Garden,** which features all the types of plants that are mentioned in Shakespeare's works—don't eat the nightshade—comfortable benches, and quotations engraved in bronze. The **Rose Garden,** especially in early June, is too noisy to be peaceful. There's also **Rhododendron Dell, Fuchsia Garden,** and the **Queen Wilhelmina Tulip Garden,** with its two nearby Dutch windmills. A herd of bison lives near the park's northwest end, though it usually takes some effort to see them in the large paddock.

The park's fixtures also include three world-class museums: the **Asian Art Museum**; the **M. H. de Young Memorial Museum,** notable for its collection of American art; and the **California Academy of Sciences** (*see* Museums, *below*). Or head to the **Laserium** (in the California Academy of Sciences, tel. 415/750–7138), where high-tech music and light shows are projected onto the planetarium's dome; Pink Floyd's *Dark Side of the Moon* is a standard favorite. Shows are held three or four times daily Thursday–Sunday, and admission is $7 (matinee $6). To reach the park from Downtown or Civic Center, take Bus 5, 71, or 73.

Neighborhoods

Though the city of San Francisco is only 49 square miles, its neighborhoods often seem worlds apart. Each district is a distinct entity culturally, socially, and often politically, and they are all fascinating grounds for urban exploration. The best way to experience the city's neighborhoods is to walk until you drop, preferably into a chair on some café patio. Plan your walk with a map, or just start off in an interesting spot and surrender to the whims of the streets. Certain parts of the city lend themselves especially well to the second type of exploration. One such area is the Mission–Noe Valley–Castro region. Get off BART at 16th and Mission streets, and head west on 16th or south on Mission or Valencia, or do a little bit of both. In either direction, you'll find a unique community: funky shops, galleries, cafés, and restaurants aplenty when it's time to refuel.

DOWNTOWN

For better or worse, Downtown is grand old San Francisco—that of tea dances, cocktail hours, piano bars, fedoras, and big winter overcoats. Looking up at the beautiful architectural details, you can forget what decade it is. Noteworthy architectural stops include the 1930 art deco **Shell Building** (100 Bush St., btw Battery and Sansome Sts.) and the 1926 châteauesque-and-Romanesque-style **Hunter-Dulin Building** (111 Sutter St., btw Montgomery and Kearny Sts.). Today, the downtown area has become the major concentration of money-making businesses; the modern face is still big, though maybe not so grand. It's typical cosmopolitan walking territory, with all of the ensuing fascinating and horrifying elements of urban American life.

UNION SQUARE Union Square is the physical heart—though not the soul—of the city, especially for tourists who come to shop, browse the galleries, attend the theater, and then sleep in the finer hotels. The square, bordered by Powell, Post, Stockton, and Geary streets, was named in honor of rallies held prior to the Civil War in support of the Union. Some San Franciscans will tell you the name more appropriately refers to the huge demonstrations held here in the 1930s by labor organizations, which at one point effectively shut down the city for a week.

Today, Union Square consists of a park (graced with a few palm trees to remind you that you're still in California) encircled by a ring—make that a solid gold band—of the city's ritziest stores and boutiques, including Neiman-Marcus, Saks, Chanel, Tiffany, Cartier, Hermès, and Gump's. The park can be a relaxing place to rest your weary feet after a hard day's window-shopping, if you don't mind pigeons and homeless folks for company. At Christmas time, merchants haul in some snow and dump it in the park to satisfy all those who have dreamed in vain for a "White Christmas" in California. By nightfall it starts to get a little seedy, so it may be time to hop a bus out of here.

Does the wealth of Union Square have you longing for a cheap thrill? Hop on the glass "Tower" elevator in the St. Francis Hotel (335 Powell St.) and ride it up to the Oz restaurant for an excellent view of the City.

Heading south on Powell Street from Union Square, you'll come to the intersection of Market and Powell streets. Everyone passes through here: proselytizers, street musicians, artists, punks, young professionals, vendors, protesters, dogs, pigeons, and tourists in matching jogging suits. All converge around the cable-car turnaround, the Powell Street BART station, and the **San Francisco Visitor Information Center** (900 Market St., tel. 415/391–2000), tucked below the street in the underground Hallidie Plaza.

➤ **MAIDEN LANE** • This short alley off the east side of Union Square was home to the "cribs" (brothels) that formed the center of a notoriously rowdy red-light district. Now it's a shopping arcade for the thick-walleted and the site of San Francisco's only Frank Lloyd Wright building, the **Circle Gallery** (140 Maiden Ln., tel. 415/989–2100), which served as the prototype for the Guggenheim Museum in New York. Wright also designed the gallery's gorgeous Philippine mahogany cabinets and chairs. The gallery sells paintings by artists as incongruous as *Love to Love You Baby* diva Donna Summer, Yaacov Agam, and fashion illustrator René Gruau.

FINANCIAL DISTRICT San Francisco is the financial capital of the West Coast. The center of San Francisco's Financial District is **Montgomery Street,** the "Wall Street of the West," where the towers of wealth block out the sun at street level. This part of town is built on landfill comprised of the remains of hundreds of abandoned ships and docks; on the corner of Sacramento and Clay streets you'll find a plaque dedicated to the Niantic—a trading ship buried at this site. Nowadays, it's a monument to the Type A personality, where traffic lights stop vehicles in all four directions to allow harried office workers to cross diagonally and kamikaze bicycle messengers to cheat death.

Since you're in the Financial District, you may as well see what those monstrously large California banks are doing with your savings. You'll find the glowering **Bank of America World**

Tour Bus of a Different Breed

For a quick tour of some of the city's most varied neighborhoods that only costs a buck, hop on MUNI's 30 Stockton Bus. From the Montgomery Street BART station, the bus transports you through the thick of downtown up to Broadway, then west on Columbus Avenue past North Beach. Skirting the Victorian homes of San Francisco's upper crust on Russian Hill, the bus continues along Chestnut Street to the Palace of Fine Arts, the Exploratorium, and reaches the eastern edge of the Presidio at the end of the line. The route then returns through the picturesque Marina and touristy Ghirardelli Square, back up Columbus, and then plows through the heart of Chinatown on Stockton Street before depositing you back on Market Street at the Powell Street BART station.

MARINA

Chestnut St.

Lombard St.

COW
HOLLOW

Octavia St.

Gough St.

Franklin St.

Van Ness Ave.

Polk St.

Larkin St.

Hyde St.

Leavenworth St.

Greenwi

Filbert S

Union St

Macondray Ln.

Russell St.

Green St.

RUSSIAN
HILL

Vallejo St.

Broadway

Broadway Tunnel

PACIFIC
HEIGHTS

Pacific St.

Jackson St.

Taylor St.

Alta
Plaza

Lafayette
Park

Washington St.

Clay St.

Sacramento St.

California St.

NO
HI

Pierce St.

Steiner St.

Fillmore St.

Webster St.

Buchanan St.

Laguna St.

Gough St.

Franklin St.

Van Ness Ave.

Pine St.

Bush St.

POLK
GULCH

Sutter St.

Larkin St.

Polk St.

Hyde St.

Jones St.

Leavenworth St.

JAPANTOWN

Geary Expressway

Post St.

Geary St.

O'Farrell St.

TENDERLOIN

Ellis St.

Eddy St.

Turk St.

WESTERN
ADDITION

Golden Gate Ave.

McAllister St.

Market St.

Fulton St.

Alamo
Square

CIVIC
CENTER

Grove St.

Civic Center
BART Station

ba

HAYES
VALLEY

Hayes St.

8th St.

7th St.

Ansel Adams
Center, 50

Bank of America
World
Headquarters, 48

Bella Union
Building, 35

Belli Building, 43

Cable Car
Museum, 22

Capp Street
Project, 64

Center for the
Arts, 52

Chinatown Gate, 40

Chinese Historical
Society of
America, 46

Chinese Telephone
Exchange, 36

Circle Gallery, 39

City Lights
Bookstore, 33

City Hall, 17

Coit Tower, 24

Coleman House, 7

Embarcadero
Center, 57

Fairmont Hotel, 28

Ferry Building, 58

Glide Memorial
Methodist
Church, 26

Golden Gate Fortune
Cookie Factory, 31

Grace Cathedral, 21

Haas-Lilienthal
House, 6

Hallidie Plaza, 55

Herbst Theatre, 16

Hunter-Dulin
Building, 54

Jackson Square, 42

Japan Center, 8

Jewish Community
Museum, 60

Justin Herman
Plaza, 59

Kabuki 8
Theatres, 10

Kabuki Hot
Springs, 11

Kong Chow
Temple, 30

Little Fox
Theatre, 34

Lombard Street, 18

0   1/2 mile

0   500 meters

KEY

----- Cable Car

𝑖 Tourist Information

San Francisco Bay

N

Chestnut St.

Lombard St.

NORTH BEACH

TELEGRAPH HILL

St.

Columbus Ave.

Grant Ave.

Mason St.

Powell St.

Stockton St.

Waverly Pl.

CHINATOWN

Kearny St.

Montgomery St.

Sansome St.

Battery St.

Front St.

Davis St.

The Embarcadero

Drumm St.

Davis St.

FINANCIAL DISTRICT

Halleck St.

Embarcadero BART Station ᗷᗩ

Montgomery St. BART Station ᗷᗩ

UNION SQUARE

Union Square

Maiden Ln.

Market St.

SOMA

New Montgomery St.

Hawthorne St.

2nd St.

1st St.

Fremont St.

Beale St.

Main St.

Spear St.

Steuart St.

Powell St. BART Station 𝑖 ᗷᗩ

Mission St.

4th St.

3rd St.

Moscone Center

Folsom St.

Harrison St.

Bryant St.

Brannan St.

Townsend St.

The Embarcadero

5th St.

4th St.

Howard St.

80

Louise M. Davies Symphony Hall, **13**	Palace of Fine Arts, **1**	South Park, **65**	War Memorial Opera House, **14**
Main Library, **19**	Peace Plaza, **9**	Spreckels Mansion, **5**	Washington Square, **23**
Mark Hopkins Hotel, **27**	Portsmouth Square, **41**	Stanford Court Hotel, **29**	Wave Organ, **2**
North Beach Museum, **25**	Rincon Center, **61**	Tin Hou Temple, **31**	Wedding Houses, **4**
Old Temple, **3**	St. Francis Hotel, **38**	Transamerica Pyramid, **44**	Wells Fargo History Museum, **47**
Pacific Heritage Museum, **45**	San Francisco Centre, **37**	Transbay Terminal, **63**	Yerba Buena Gardens, **51**
Pacific Stock Exchange, **56**	San Francisco Museum of Modern Art, **53**	United Nations Plaza, **20**	
Painted Ladies, **12**	Shell Building, **62**	Veterans Building, **15**	

Headquarters at the corner of California and Kearny streets. Its north plaza is graced with a black granite shard of public art officially called *Transcendence,* but popularly known as "The Banker's Heart." Up on the 52nd story in the elegant **Carnelian Room** (tel. 415/433–7500), you can nurse a $6.50 cocktail and gaze in wonder at the city below. Bank of America's arch-rival, Wells Fargo Bank, lures you in with the free **Wells Fargo History Museum** (420 Montgomery St., tel. 415/396–2619), detailing the history of California's oldest bank and interminably celebrating the short-lived but picturesque Pony Express.

➤ **TRANSAMERICA PYRAMID** • The Pyramid (600 Montgomery St., btw Clay and Washington Sts.) is *the* distinguishing feature of the San Francisco skyline. If you can get past the security guards (business attire would probably do the trick), you can ride the elevator to the 27th-floor observation area for a bird's-eye view of Coit Tower and Columbus Avenue, but the building itself seems much less impressive once you're in it. Adjacent to the Pyramid, a little redwood park (open weekdays 8–6), complete with fountain, provides a peaceful retreat from the frenzied commercial pace—the perfect setting for an urban picnic.

➤ **BARBARY COAST** • In the 1850s, San Francisco was home to the Barbary Coast, one of the most infamous red-light districts ever to exist. It was not uncommon to enter a bar, get drugged, clubbed, or fall through a trap door, and find yourself a prisoner sailor heading for the Orient the next morning. Sorry pal—you just got shanghaied. The strip of Pacific Street, between Sansome Street and Columbus Avenue, once called "Terrific Pacific," was the heart of the action: Every building along this street was once a saloon, gambling hall, or brothel. Many of the bars and dance halls featured nightly shows of women dancers engaged in acts of bestiality. Today, you can still visit the remains of the Barbary Coast at the **Jackson Square Historical District** just north of the Financial District. To the chagrin of Bible-thumping reformists, many of the buildings survived the 1906 earthquake and fire. One of the most notable structures in the area is the **Belli Building** (722 Montgomery St.), which once served as a musical saloon, and was the famed office of notorious San Francisco attorney Melvin Belli, the "King of Torts" (who represented the likes of the Rolling Stones, Mae West, and Jim and Tammy Baker). Belli, who died in July of 1996, used to shoot cannons off the roof of the building after winning big cases. Also worth a look-see are the nude nymphs carved on the entrance gateway to the **Bella Union** building (555 Pacific St.), and the **Little Fox Theatre** (535 Pacific St.), which was once a saloon and went on to illegally house a 60-foot distillery tank during Prohibition.

Bar owner Shanghai Kelly was one of the most ruthless shanghaiers along the Barbary Coast. He was famed for serving the deadly "Mickey Finn," a whiskey, gin, brandy, and opium concoction named for the chemist who invented it.

EMBARCADERO The Embarcadero, Spanish for "wharf," looks more like a string of office buildings than anything vaguely maritime. One exception is the **Ferry Building** at the end of Market Street. The 230-foot clock tower, modeled after Venice's Campanile, is an attractive landmark that can be seen along much of Market Street. Ferries still depart from here for Sausalito or Larkspur (*see* Getting In, Out, and Around, in Chapter 1).

Embarcadero Center is a set of neatly stacked concrete buildings along Sacramento Street between Battery and Drumm streets. Its monolithic architectural style is no draw, but it *is* one of the few shopping malls that boasts free parking on weekends for buying customers. The center is a conglomeration of four nearly identical towers connected to each other by bridges housing offices, restaurants, boutiques that cater to the corporate crowd, and the **Embarcadero Center Cinema,** which features foreign and independent films (*see* Movie Houses, in Chapter 6). The fifth tower you'll see is the **Hyatt Regency Hotel,** which offers incredible views of the city from the rooftop bar that revolves 360°, and happy-hour specials in the lobby bar.

➤ **JUSTIN HERMAN PLAZA** • Between Embarcadero Center and the Ferry Building stretches Justin Herman Plaza, a favorite haunt of the office bag-lunch crowd and young skateboarders who favor long expanses of brick and concrete. Around the winter holidays, you can take a moonlit spin on the ice rink they set up in the middle of the plaza. Here, Jean Dubuffet's mammoth stainless-steel sculpture *La Chiffonière* poses like a Napoleonic Pillsbury doughboy. Nearby, Armand Vaillancourt's huge building-block fountain looks a little too much like prehistoric plumbing, but you can gambol among its girders even when the water is streaming through. The plaza hosts sporadic free concerts and shows, usually Wednesdays or Fridays at noon when the weather is nice. During a free, unannounced concert by the band U2 in the plaza in 1988, Bono spray-painted the fountain, earning the ire of city officials, who were waging a war against graffiti at the time. (Bono later apologized.) The "anarchist" gesture is recorded for posterity in the concert movie *Rattle and Hum*.

➤ **RINCON CENTER** • Another water adventure awaits nearby at the stately, restored Rincon Center, formerly the city's main post office. The outside of the building is unassuming—you'll recognize it by the raised blue dolphins on its sides—but inside there's a recently restored 1940s lobby and a stately atrium into which a tall, shimmering column of water descends. The socialist realist murals in the lobby depict the history of California, including the oppression of Native Americans and the exploitation of workers by capitalist overlords similar to those who own the building, which now houses shops, offices, and apartments. *101 Spear St., at Mission St., tel. 415/243–0473.*

CIVIC CENTER AREA

The Civic Center is the locus of San Francisco government and home of many of the city's cultural events, including dance, opera, and big-name theater. The area immediately surrounding the center is also where a good percentage of San Francisco's homeless have camped out since the 1940s. To reach the area, take BART to the Civic Center station, or catch any of a thousand buses down Market Street.

CITY HALL The offices of San Francisco's mayor and board of supervisors are in this building, built in classic beaux arts style with a prominent bronze rotunda that can be seen blocks away. City Hall has a fascinating history. Joe DiMaggio and Marilyn Monroe got married here on January 15, 1954. In 1960, civil rights and freedom of speech protesters were washed down City Hall's central stairway with giant fire hoses, while the hearings of the House Un-American Activities Committee went on inside—all of which is depicted in the amusing government propaganda effort (now a cult film) *Operation Abolition*. Mayor George Moscone and Supervisor Harvey Milk were murdered here on November 27, 1978. On February 14, 1991, scores of gay couples lined up to get "married" in celebration of the passage of San Francisco's Domestic Partners Act the previous November. Has this building seen some crazy times or what? *Btw Van Ness Ave. and Grove, McAllister, and Polk Sts.*

Surrounding City Hall are many of the city's cultural mainstays. On Van Ness Avenue the **Louise M. Davies Symphony Hall** and the more stately **War Memorial Opera House** offer San Franciscans their fill of high culture (*see* Classical Music, in Chapter 6). You can catch a variety of cultural events, including concerts, readings, and lectures at **Herbst Theatre,** just north of the Opera House. The Opera House will be closed for renovations until late 1997, but volunteers conduct 75-minute tours of the other two buildings every Monday on the hour and half hour from 10 AM to 2 PM, leaving from the Grove Street entrance of Davies Symphony Hall. Tickets are $3. Call 415/552–8338 for more info. The spanking new **San Francisco Main Library** (Larkin St., at Grove St., tel. 415/557–4400) is big, beautiful, and state-of-the-art—the most technologically advanced in the country. It houses a fine collection of books, records, CDs, and San Francisco memorabilia; as well as 300 computer terminals, many with free Web access and CD-ROM capability. Far from a mere place to browse books, there is also a café, a rooftop garden, an incredible children's library, an excellent video library, an African-American center, the nation's first Gay and Lesbian Archive Center, an Asian-American center, and more, more, more! If you're walking around the area, head to Hayes Street between Franklin and Webster streets; dubbed **Hayes Valley,** this area is loaded with specialty shops, art galleries, cafés, and restaurants (*see* Chapters 4 and 5).

Across from City Hall on the south side is the large plaza where protest marches usually culminate in rallies (including a few 200,000-people-plus ones during the Persian Gulf War) and an occasional riot. It is also home to farmers' markets on Sundays and Wednesdays. Leading away from City Hall toward Market Street is the **United Nations Plaza,** commemorating the founding of the U.N. in San Francisco in 1945. The plaza is presided over by a dramatic statue of revolutionary war hero Simón Bolívar.

POLK GULCH Once the gay heart of San Francisco, Polk Gulch is now the city's second most prominent gay area after the Castro. Polk Gulch is part yuppie neighborhood, part urban blight. In other words, it's is a good place to buy roasted coffee, browse a bookstore, and watch a drug bust. For the coffee purchase, try one of two **Royal Ground** locations (2216 Polk St., near Vallejo St., tel. 415/474–5957; 1605 Polk St., at Sacramento St., tel. 415/749–1731). Two of Polk's big growth industries are drug sales and prostitution. Rumor has it that the hustlers get more expensive by the block—the most expensive block is the stretch from Bush to Pine streets. The bargain basement is around Geary Street.

Once you get past the sleaze, Polk Street makes a nice 15-minute walk to Aquatic Park and Fisherman's Wharf. The street is lined with small businesses and cafés, including **Les Croissants** (1406 Polk St., btw Pine and California Sts., tel. 415/922–3286), a popular place to drink coffee, eat sandwiches, and loiter. On the more gentrified stretch of Polk Street, you'll find **Pure T** (2238 Polk St., at Green St., tel. 415/441–7878)—a full-service teahouse that features exotic teas from Asia such as monkey-picked Ti Kuan Yin blend ($3–$4 a pot), and 15 delicious homemade tea-flavored ice creams. Bus 19 from Civic Center BART runs up Polk Street on its way to Ghirardelli Square at Fisherman's Wharf.

THE TENDERLOIN The **Tenderloin** weaves through O'Farrell, Geary, Post, and Sutter streets—great places to check out the local bar and live music scene *and* get to know your neighborhood pimp, prostitute, and transvestite. Keep in mind that the area has the highest reported incidence of rape in the city—a particularly seedy triangle is formed by Larkin, Market, and Post streets. The Tenderloin has traditionally been a dangerous area. In the early days, policemen got higher wages for working these streets, whereby they were able to afford more tender cuts of meat. Hence the name. While the call of cheap beer, live music, and inexpensive Vietnamese and Thai food beckons, take a cab rather than wander around inebriated.

CHINATOWN

The best way to experience San Francisco's Chinatown—possibly the most famous immigrant community in the world—is to go in hungry and energetic. The shops are fine, but the real appeal of Chinatown is its street life. Chinatown steadfastly remains a residential area, where the largest Chinese community outside Asia has made its home for 140 years—despite tourist-oriented shops. The original immigrants were refugees from the Opium Wars who came to San Francisco to seek their fortune during the Gold Rush; most ended up working on the railroad—not what they'd expected, perhaps. To learn more about the history of Chinese immigration to San Francisco and the development of Chinatown, visit the **Chinese Historical Society of America** (*see* Museums, *below*).

Welcome All Ye Sinners

Ever been to church and come away humming, tapping your toes, and with the phone number of the stranger you sat next to? Enjoy all of the religion and none of the guilt at Glide Memorial United Methodist Church—presided over by a beaming Reverend Cecil Williams. Instead of organ music, a funky band and choir give parishioners reason to stand up and groove with the music when the spirit moves them. The Rev. Williams is also a famous community activist in San Francisco; among the many community programs offered at Glide are a daily free meal program, an HIV/AIDS project, a families in crisis center, recovery programs for men and women, and women's health services. Celebrations occur every Sunday morning at 9 and 11. It gets crowded and hot—try to arrive early. 330 Ellis St., at Taylor St., tel. 415/771–6300. From Powell St. BART/MUNI, walk 1 block on Powell St., left on Ellis St.

If Chinatown's pagoda-heavy architecture looks contrived, that's because it is. In the late 1800s, many right-wing groups blamed the shortage of jobs on the Chinese and wanted to completely destroy Chinatown. Indeed, after the natural destruction of the 1906 earthquake, it looked as if Chinatown wouldn't survive. Political groups put increasing pressure on the city government, and Chinatown's proximity to the Financial District attracted the attention of real-estate barons. Thanks to the persuasive powers of some local politicians, Chinatown was saved and rebuilt on the premise that it could attract tourists. Soon American and European architects were put to work, projecting their stereotypes of Asian building styles, on a Chinese theme park.

Don't miss the huge, week-long Chinese New Years festival held during the first new moon in February. Come early to get a spot for the final parade—a riotous celebration of Asian culture, featuring firecrackers, lion dancers, and painted dragons.

To reach Chinatown, take Bus 45 from Market and 3rd streets downtown. You'll know you're in the 16-block neighborhood when you see street signs in Chinese. The best way to enter is through the dragon-crowned **Chinatown Gate** on Grant Avenue at Bush Street. Or enter through **Portsmouth Square** (Washington St., at Kearny St.), where dozens of old Chinese men gather to gamble and shoot the breeze. If you are coming from the North Beach area, check out the **Imperial Tea Court** (1411 Powell St., at Broadway, tel. 415/788–6080), where you can relax and enjoy full tea service among wise old locals in an elegant Chinese tearoom.

During the late 1850s you could have witnessed public hangings at Portsmouth Square (cnr Kearny and Clay Sts.).

GRANT AVENUE The main tourist thoroughfare in Chinatown, Grant Avenue also reigns as the oldest street in San Francisco—dating back to 1834. The Chinese characters above Chinatown's Gate read "all under heaven is good for the people"; decide if that's the case as you wander by gimmicky souvenir shops, restaurants, and flocks of wide-eyed visitors clutching $1.50 bamboo back-scratchers. Formerly known as Dupont Street, Grant Avenue once swarmed with opium dens, bordellos, and gangs, especially in the sections near the Barbary Coast (*see above*). Today, the real Chinatown can be better found by exploring the numerous small alleys that branch off of Washington, Clay, and Sacramento streets, where you're more likely to see locals shopping for groceries and carrying grandchildren down the street on their backs. The old **Chinese Telephone Exchange** building, now the Bank of Canton, stands at 743 Washington Street, at Grant Avenue. It's both architecturally and historically interesting: Operators here had to memorize the names of all their customers and speak English and five Chinese dialects.

STOCKTON STREET Sick of tourist-infested, gimmicky Grant Avenue? The crowded shops and throngs of Stockton Street aren't far removed from the barter and trade sections of Hong Kong. In the stretch of Stockton Street between Sacramento and Green streets, you'll find

The Root of the Problem

Purchasing Chinese herbs for medicinal purposes is a tricky business. Unlike Western medications, which mainly treat generic symptoms of an ailment, like a stuffy nose or depression, herbs need to be chosen and combined with the individual in mind. Some ingredients, like ginger and ginseng, are widely used in teas; you can pick these up in one of the many stores along Stockton or Washington streets. Besides tasting good, ginger prevents motion sickness and may also help prevent blood clots that cause heart attacks. Ginseng stimulates the immune system, helps defend the liver against toxins, and acts as a stimulant. Some people believe it also increases sexual potency. If you're looking for teas, your first stop should be Tea Ren Tea Co. (949 Grant Ave., tel. 415/362–0656), which stocks a variety of teas for both enjoyment and medicinal purposes.

meat and produce shops letting it all hang out (vegetarians might wince at the pigs hanging from hooks). The friendly staff at **Ellison Enterprises Co. USA Ltd.** (805 Stockton St., tel. 415/982–3886) will happily explain the secrets and powers of herbal medicine—and may show you a dried human placenta. Also worth seeing is the **Kong Chow Temple** above the post office (835 Stockton St., tel. 415/434–2513)—a Taoist temple where you can light incense offerings to 17 gods sitting on the altar.

WAVERLY PLACE One of the most colorful streets is Waverly Place, off California and Clay streets, between Grant and Stockton streets. You may recognize the name from Amy Tan's *The Joy Luck Club*; it's also known as the "street of painted balconies." There are a number of Chinese temples along Waverly Place, including the **Tin Hou Temple** (125 Waverly Pl., top floor), purportedly the oldest in the city. Don't miss nearby **Ross Alley,** between Grant and Stockton and Jackson and Washington streets, the home of the **Golden Gate Fortune Cookie Factory** (56 Ross Alley), where you can watch old women fold cookies, some with risqué fortunes. Fun at parties. In the second half of the 1800s, this alley was full of brothel activity. One of its main attractions was Ah Toy, a young Chinese woman forced into prostitution by the Chinese gangs that operated in the area. At the end of Ross Alley is **Jackson Street,** where you'll find several Chinese herbal medicine shops with drawers that contain the therapeutic plants lined along the walls.

NORTH BEACH

Walk north on Columbus Avenue from the Columbus and Broadway intersection (long the site of one of San Francisco's best-known red-light districts) and you'll find yourself in the heart of the legendary Italian district where the Beat movement was born. Nowadays North Beach offers an incredible selection of restaurants, delis, and cafés. Poets and writers including Jack Kerouac, Lawrence Ferlinghetti, and Allen Ginsberg came to North Beach around 1953 to write, play music, and generally promote a lifestyle that emphasized Eastern religions, free love, drugs, and crazy new means of artistic expression. Ferlinghetti's **City Lights Bookstore** (261 Columbus Ave., tel. 415/362–8193) continues to publish and sell works by little-known alternative authors, as well as stuff by the Beats, who have been anthologized to high heaven and hardly qualify as alternative anymore. In the late 1980s Ferlinghetti led a movement to rename a number of small San Francisco streets after authors who had lived here; the recently renamed **Jack Kerouac Lane** is right next to the store. In 1994, Ferlinghetti received the same honor: An alley off Union Street near Stockton Street was renamed **Via Ferlinghetti,** though the short, dead-end street is barely longer than its new name.

Although the Beats reached their peak back in the late 1950s, and the number of Italian Americans living in North Beach is diminishing, the neighborhood remains one of San Francisco's most interesting. Some of the shops and watering holes here have been catering to the same clientele since North Beach's bohemian heyday. Those looking to immerse themselves in Beat history can poke around **Vesuvio** (*see* Chapter 6), a bar just across the alley from City Lights, where the boys undoubtedly consumed more than one glass of red. **Caffè Trieste** (*see* Chapter 5) fueled the Beats with their favorite legal amphetamine, espresso; the clientele, some 35 years later, still looks pretty beat.

Continue the pilgrimage by leaving a poem or a stick of incense in front of **29 Russell Street,** a hefty walk away on Russian Hill (btw Larkin and Hyde Sts. and Union and Green Sts.), where Kerouac crashed with Neal and Carolyn Cassady for a time in the early '50s. (His relationship with Neal is immortalized in his popular novel *On the Road*, though *The Subterraneans* better evokes Kerouac's North Beach days.) The **North Beach Museum,** on the mezzanine level of Eureka Federal Savings (1435 Stockton St., at Columbus Ave., tel. 415/391–6210), contains a handwritten manuscript of Ferlinghetti's "The Old Italians Dying," a poem about the old men of North Beach.

Some people choose to live in North Beach—and subject themselves to dealing with tourists on a daily basis—just for the food. Stop in at **Liguria Bakery** (1700 Stockton St., at Filbert St., tel. 415/421–3786) for focaccia right out of the oven. **Molinari Delicatessen** (*see* Markets and Specialty Stores, in Chapter 4) has an insane selection of salami, olive oils, cheeses, pastas, wines, chocolate, and bread to sate your need for a coma-inducing picnic at **Washington Square Park** (*see* Parks, *below*). Buses 30 or 45 will get you to North Beach from Market and 3rd streets.

NOB HILL AND RUSSIAN HILL

The most classically elitist of San Francisco's districts is **Nob Hill,** the locus of San Francisco high society for more than a century. Its borders are arguable among locals, but most agree that the area between California, Powell, Broadway, and Leavenworth streets forms the crux of the neighborhood. The hill has great views that even the downtrodden will enjoy, assuming they aren't too out of breath from the strenuous walk up the hill. North of Nob Hill lies **Russian Hill,** originally the burial ground for Russian seal hunters and traders, which today houses a combination of old Victorian homes, new high-rises, and even more of San Francisco's upper crust.

Fittingly, Nob Hill derives its nomenclature from the term nabob, which means anyone of great worth or wealth.

A steep walk (or $2 cable-car ride, if you get caught) north up Powell Street from Union Square brings you to what once were the hilltop estates of some of the city's biggest robber barons, er, entrepreneurs; this is where the original "Big Four" railroad kings—Leland Stanford, Mark Hopkins, Collis Huntington, and Charles Crocker—set up camp. Now the city's poshest hotels are here: Ignore the doormen's suspicious looks as you nose around the lobbies of the **Fairmont Hotel,** at California and Mason streets; the **Mark Hopkins,** across California Street from the Fairmont; and the **Stanford Court Hotel,** at California and Powell streets. The mansion belonging to silver magnate James Flood is one of the few that survived the '06 quake, and it now houses the Pacific Union Club (1000 California St.). See how many times you can ride up and down the glass elevator at the Fairmont before the management ever-so-politely suggests that you scram.

CABLE CAR MUSEUM On your way from Nob Hill to Russian Hill, check out this small museum, which has photographs, scale models, vintage cars, and other memorabilia—all devoted to the cable car's 121-year history. From the adjacent overlook you can gander at the brawny cables that haul the cars up and down the city's hills, or watch the cables turn from an underground room. *1201 Mason St., at Washington St., tel. 415/474–1887. Admission free. Open daily 10–5.*

GRACE CATHEDRAL Come to Grace Cathedral and repent for all the trouble you've caused the employees at Nob Hill's fancy hotels. The cathedral is a nouveau Gothic structure that took 53 years to build; it's essentially a poured-concrete replica of an old European-style cathedral. The gilded bronze doors at the east entrance were taken from casts of Ghiberti's *Gates of Paradise* on the Baptistery in Florence. For a truly sublime experience, come for the singing of **vespers** every Thursday at 3:30 PM; an all-male choir will lift you out of the muck of your petty little world and leave you feeling almost sanctified. If this doesn't do the trick, try meditating as you walk through the marble labyrinth to the right of the east entrance—it's a replica of the one at France's Chartres Cathedral. Guided tours of the cathedral are free, but donations are accepted. *1051 Taylor St., at California St., tel. 415/776–6611. From Embarcadero BART/MUNI, Bus 1 west to cnr Sacramento and Jones Sts.*

Hallidie's San Francisco Treat

One rainy evening in 1873, young engineer Andrew Hallidie witnessed a horrible sight: One of four horses drawing a streetcar slipped; when the car driver applied the brake, the brake chain broke and the streetcar went barreling down a steep hill, dragging the helpless horses behind it. This tragic incident, it is said, inspired Hallidie to devise the era's most complex and industrious transportation system: the cable car.

LOMBARD STREET AND ENVIRONS Since you've made it all the way up here, don't miss the chance to do some strenuous walking around Russian Hill's well-maintained streets. The most famous is undoubtedly **Lombard Street,** the block-long "crookedest street in the world." It descends the east side of Russian Hill in eight switchbacks between Hyde and Leavenworth streets.

The insanely steep Russian Hill has a number of funky little stairway streets that wind through the trees or lead up to miniature parks. Try the steps at Lombard and Larkin streets; you'll eventually reach a small rest spot with benches, plants, and an incredible view of the Golden Gate to help you recover from the climb. Another stairway adventure begins on the eastern side of Russian Hill on Vallejo Street at Mason Street. These steps will transport you to **Ina Coolbrith Park**—lined with trees, flowers, benches, and views of the East Bay and Bay Bridge. When you reach Taylor Street you have the choice of tackling an additional set of stairs across the street or a chance to relax and visit **Macondray Lane.** If you want to take the relaxation route, hang a right on Taylor Street, and stroll down 2 blocks to a set of wooden stairs between Green and Union streets (don't worry, this is an official path, not someone's private entrance). These steps will bring you to a tiny, cobblestone alley (Macondray Lane) lined with houses on one side and foliage on the other. This was the thinly veiled setting of Armistead Maupin's *Tales of the City.* Also look for the pre-1906 quake, dark, wood-shingled houses designed by Willis Polk. One lies on the **1000 block of Green Street,** which also contains one of the city's two remaining eight-sided houses, built in the 1850s, as well as a firehouse dating from 1907. If you want the more strenuous route, continue straight ahead through the intersection of Taylor and Vallejo streets. You will find yourself on a path lined with daisies, roses, and carnations, culminating at **San Simone Park** with amazing views of Alcatraz and the East Bay. Coming down Vallejo Street, you will pass by a few side alleys, notable are **Florence Place** and the beautiful English cottages of **Russian Hill Place.**

THE PRESIDIO AND MARINA

Stretching over a gorgeous strip of waterfront between Fort Mason and the Presidio and bordered to the south by **Union Street,** the Marina provides a home—actually a series of pricey, Mediterranean-style homes—for San Francisco's young professionals. Ironically, all these folk with stable incomes live on decidedly unstable property; the Marina is built on landfill and dangerously susceptible to the whims of Mother Earthquake. Freshly graduated members of the Greek system come to the Marina's main drag, **Chestnut Street,** from all over the city to chow down and drink up at innumerable restaurants and bars and engage in yuppie mating rituals at singles bars.

Even if it's not your scene, you'll probably find yourself wandering Chestnut Street at some point. It's the most convenient place to come for a bite to eat or a drink after visiting Fort Mason, and has lately been benefiting from an influx of new restaurants. A well-stocked **Safeway** (15 Marina Blvd., btw Laguna and Buchanan Sts.), right across the street from Fort Mason, provides cheap food for guests of the **Ft. Mason International Hostel** (*see* Hostels, in Chapter 7). This particular store is nicknamed 'Singles' Safeway—due to all of the "meet-market" opportunities; try the produce section for the best results. If you're in a picnicking mood, **Marina Green,** directly west of Fort Mason, provides the necessary lawn as well as stunning views of the bay and the Marin Headlands.

FORT MASON Fort Mason, a series of warehouses built on piers, forms the Marina's eastern border. Once an army command post, Fort Mason is now a nexus of artistic, cultural, and environmental organizations (*also see* Museums, *below*). Although it's fairly quiet most days (except for a trickle of people taking advantage of classes, lectures, and museums), Fort Mason is well worth a trip or two just for the views of the bay and the peaceful tourist-free solitude. While you're here, read through their newsletter to find out what's going on this month (you can pick one up at the museums).

Fill your belly at the renowned vegetarian restaurant **Greens** (*see* Chapter 4), also tucked into one of the warehouses. Or relax at the **Book Bay Bookstore** (Fort Mason Center, Bldg. C, tel. 415/771–1076), run by the Friends of the San Francisco Public Library, where you can still get a book for 33¢. From Fisherman's Wharf, it's about a 10-minute walk west to Fort Mason: Go down Beach Street past the Municipal Pier, climb the forested hill past the hostel; as you descend on the other side, you'll see it spread out on the waterfront. *Fort Mason general info: tel. 415/979–3010. Buses 22, 28, 30, 42, 47, and 49. Free parking.*

PALACE OF FINE ARTS At the far western edge of the Marina is the Palace of Fine Arts, which looks like a classic Roman temple, complete with columns and a pond in front. A bunch of similar structures were built for the 1915 Panama Pacific Expo, but this is the only one that remains. Inside, you'll find the **Exploratorium** (*see* Museums, *below*), a hands-on museum devoted to making science interesting for common folk. If you're visiting on Sunday, Bus 76 north from Montgomery Street BART/MUNI station takes you within a few blocks of Fort Mason, skirts the southern edge of the Marina, passes the Palace of Fine Arts, and goes all the way to Golden Gate Bridge. Otherwise, pick up Bus 30 from Montgomery Street BART/MUNI, which follows a similar route but stops short of the Presidio. *Baker and Beach Sts., tel. 415/563–6504.*

THE PRESIDIO The Presidio, a huge chunk of prime waterfront land stretching from the western end of the Marina all the way to the Golden Gate Bridge, was one of the oldest military installations in the United States. The land was officially turned over to the National Park Service on October 1, 1994, but the army will remain here for a while in a reduced capacity. Since it's some of the most desirable real estate in the city, profit-hungry developers are fighting with conservationists over its future.

While the original plan for the park was to include office space for nonprofit organizations, big businesses like Pacific Gas & Electric Co. threaten to take control of the park's facilities. It is yet to be determined how much of the park will remain open space and how much will be developed. Enjoy the park while you can: rolling hills crossed by plenty of trails and paths through cypress and eucalyptus forests (for specifics on hiking, *see* Chapter 8); historic military buildings; and terrific views of the bay. Check out the **Officer's Club** (Moraga Ave.), which contains one adobe wall reputed to date from 1776, the year the base was founded. Find out more about the Presidio's history at the free **Presidio Army Museum** (Funston Ave., at Lincoln Blvd., tel. 415/561–4331; open Wed.–Sun. 10–4).

The easiest way to get to the Presidio is to drive north toward the bay on Van Ness Avenue, turn left on Lombard Street, and then follow the signs. Otherwise, take Bus 38 from Montgomery Street BART/MUNI station to Geary Boulevard and Presidio Avenue, then switch to Bus 43, which travels into the Presidio.

UNION STREET While officially in **Cow Hollow** (so named because it used to house a dairy-farming community), Union Street competes with Chestnut Street for titles like "Cutest Boutique" and "Most Expensive Coffee." If you've come to San Francisco to shop and lounge about without such nasty distractions as homeless people or street life, Union Street is for you. Its rows of sparkling, refurbished Victorian houses are undoubtedly beautiful, but the area clobbers you on the cranium with quaintness.

If you do elect to come for some window shopping or a latte, stop in at **Carol Doda's Champagne and Lace Lingerie Boutique** (1850 Union St. No. 1, tel. 415/776–6900), owned by the woman who led the vanguard to legalize topless dancing in the 1960s, when she became the first woman to bare her breasts as part of a nightclub show. She never waitressed again. Other neighborhood landmarks include the **Wedding Houses** (1980 Union St., near Buchanan St.), two identical houses built side by side as wedding presents for two daughters who got married at the same time. The brides' father had the houses stationed next to each other so he could keep an eye on them. These days, all he'd see are two stunning Victorians filled with upscale shops. The Vedanta Society of Northern California's **Old Temple** (2963 Webster St., at Filbert St., tel. 415/922–2323), a Hindu Temple built in 1905 (closed to tourists), combines all the best elements of Victorian architecture and the Taj Mahal. No joke. Bus 41 from Embarcadero BART/MUNI station runs down Union Street.

THE WAVE ORGAN Truly a unique and peaceful experience, locals claim that the wave organ is one of the best spots to recover from a hangover. The organ is constructed of a set of pipes that extend underwater, beneath the tides of the bay. By placing your ear on the pipe, you will be treated to the soothing musical tones of lapping waves—acoustics are best at high tide. The project was built by artists with help from the Exploratorium and is decorated with recycled granite, old curbstones, and the headstones from an old cemetery. Some of the stone blocks were made into benches where you can sit and listen to the organ while gazing out at the bay. *From Exploratorium (see Museums, below), walk north on Baker St., cross Marina Blvd. and take Yacht Rd. (or Lyon St.), walk to end of jetty, past the St. Francis and Golden Gate Yacht clubs.*

PACIFIC HEIGHTS

Rising above the Marina and the Western Addition, Pacific Heights is the posh neighborhood of Victorian mansions that stretches up from Van Ness and over to the Presidio, between California and Union streets. The mostly residential area is bisected by Fillmore Street, separating the eastern and western halves with its upscale boutiques and trendy restaurants. The stretch of Fillmore from Bush Street to Jackson Street—known as **Upper Fillmore**—is a "cute" area in which to stroll, browse, and have a cup of espresso. Pacific Heights's defining characteristics, however, are the Victorian mansions, spared from the 1906 fire that ravaged the rest of the city east of Van Ness Avenue (houses along Van Ness were dynamited to create a firebreak). To get to Pacific Heights, take Bus 1 California from Embarcadero BART/MUNI station or Bus 22 Fillmore from the Marina.

HAAS-LILIENTHAL HOUSE A good place to start your tour of Victorian Pacific Heights is at the Haas-Lilienthal House, the only one that's open to the public. Modest in comparison to the mansions that once stood along Van Ness, the 1886 Queen Anne–style house is now the property of **The Foundation for San Francisco's Architectural Heritage,** headquartered here. The trick is, you'll have to join an hour-long, docent-led tour ($5) in order to step inside and see the original furnishings. These leave Wednesdays noon–3:15 and Sundays 11–4, whenever a small group is gathered. Meet here at 12:30 PM on Sundays for a $5 walking tour covering the surrounding blocks of Victorians and Edwardians—and learn once and for all that these terms refer to periods (1837–1901 and 1901–1910, respectively), not architectural styles. *2007 Franklin St., near Washington St., tel. 415/441–3000.*

LAFAYETTE PARK From the Haas-Lilienthal House, walk 1 block south to the corner of California Street, the location of the **Coleman House** (1701 Franklin St.), which is now filled with law offices and closed to the nonlitigious public. This a Queen Anne tower house—you'll see the aforementioned tower prominently displayed on the corner. Turn right on California Street and right again on Octavia Street to reach **Lafayette Park.** Visited by dog walkers, picnickers, and sunbathers, the park's expansive lawns slope to a wooded crest, just as a well-behaved English-style garden should. On the north side of the park, behold the **Spreckels Mansion** (2080 Washington St.), an imposing 1913 French baroque structure now owned by author Danielle Steele and her husband. You can see the effects of San Francisco's moist and salty air on the ill-chosen Utah limestone, which has noticeably eroded. Blame architect George Applegarth (who also designed the California Palace of the Legion of Honor).

JAPANTOWN

Modern Japantown, which spans the area north of Geary Expressway between Fillmore and Laguna streets, unfortunately consists mostly of the massive, somewhat depressing shopping complex called Nihonmachi, better known as **Japan Center.** The community was once much larger, until it was dispersed during World War II when California made a practice of "relocating" Japanese Americans to concentration camps. Today, there are several shops selling Japanese wares in the area, as well as a number of good restaurants (*see* Chapter 4).

The **Peace Plaza** and five-story **Pagoda** in the Japan Center were designed by architect Yoshiro Taniguchi as a gesture of goodwill from the people of Japan. The plaza is landscaped with traditional Japanese-style gardens and reflecting pools, and is the site of many traditional festivals throughout the year. The **Nihonmachi Street Fair** (tel. 415/771–9861), held in early

August, is a two-day festival celebrating the contributions of Asian Americans in the United States. The popular **Cherry Blossom Festival** (*see* Festivals, in Chapter 1), held in late April, features taiko drumming, martial arts, food, music, dance, and a parade.

To relax after a tough day, try a Japanese steam bath at the **Kabuki Hot Springs** (1750 Geary Expressway, tel. 415/922–6000 for appointments), where you can use the steam room, sauna, and hot and cold baths (all sex-segregated) for $10, or get a 25-minute shiatsu massage and unlimited bath use for $35. The bath is reserved for women on Sunday, Wednesday, and Friday; men get to use it the rest of the week. Also in the Japan Center, the **Kabuki 8** theaters (*see* Movie Houses, in Chapter 6) shows first-run films in a high-tech complex. On public transportation, Buses 2, 3, 4, and 38 will deposit you in Japantown from the Montgomery Street BART/MUNI station.

RICHMOND DISTRICT

The Richmond District, a sprawling, unassuming area north of Golden Gate Park, is full of quiet streets and rows of bland town houses that have attracted a lot of Southeast Asian and Chinese families who have moved away from the cramped conditions of Chinatown. The main shopping blocks on **Clement Street,** between Arguello Boulevard and 8th Avenue, contain a dizzying array of produce markets, Chinese herb shops, and Asian restaurants, as well as a smattering of Irish pubs and a couple of good used bookstores. Bus 2 from Montgomery Street BART/MUNI station downtown will get you here.

Clement Street can be a comforting place to hang out—show up here after a day in Golden Gate Park or at the beach for a stroll and some tasty, cheap food. **Haig's Delicacies** (642 Clement St., tel. 415/752–6283), a one-of-a-kind market and delicatessen, imports interesting food items from the Middle East, India, and Europe and is a great place to stock up on picnic goods. **New May Wah Supermarket** (547 Clement St., no phone) offers a huge number of special ingredients (sauces, tea, noodles, and much, much more) for Chinese, Vietnamese, Thai, or Japanese food. Also don't miss **Green Apple Books** (*see* Books, in Chapter 3) for a huge selection of new and used books—you could lose yourself in this store for days.

HAIGHT-ASHBURY

East of Golden Gate Park sits the Haight-Ashbury District, the name of which still strikes fear in the hearts of suburban parents everywhere. The Haight, nicknamed "Hashbury" by Hunter S. Thompson, began its career as a center for the counterculture in the late 1950s and early '60s, when some of the Beat writers, several more or less illustrious fathers of the drug culture, and bands like the Grateful Dead and Jefferson Airplane moved in. There went the neighborhood. Attracted by the experimental, liberal atmosphere, several hundred thousand blissed-out teenagers soon converged on the Haight to drop their body weight in acid, play music, sing renditions of "Uncle John's Band" for days at a time, and do things that they would still be reminiscing about with utopian exaggeration 20 years later. But like the '60s themselves, Haight-Ashbury's atmosphere of excitement and idealism was pretty much washed up by the mid-1970s. Nowadays, the Haight is a punky hangout where '90s kids do things that frighten their formerly hippie parents.

Since the 1970s, the stretch of Haight Street between Divisadero and Stanyan streets—often called the Upper Haight to distinguish it from the Lower Haight (*see below*)—has gone through various stages of increasing and decreasing seediness and gentrification. With no little irony, its countercultural spirit survives largely in terms of the goods you can buy—like bongs, leather harnesses, and rave wear. Neohippies still play guitar on the street corner, but the revolution is nowhere in sight. What *is* in sight is the gleaming Gap store taking residence on the famed corner of Haight-Ashbury—an undeniable testament to the changes that have taken place. The youthful slackers who live here now wear black, ride motorcycles, pierce body parts, and listen to dissonant music at bars like **The Thirsty Swede** (1821 Haight St.) or to live jazz and swing at **Club Deluxe** (*see* Bars, in Chapter 6). The attraction is probably less the neighborhood's historical legacy than its cheap apartments and its bars, cafés, and breakfast joints, like the **Pork**

HOME SWEET HOME:

- *Janis Joplin: 112 Lyon St., btw Page and Oak Sts.*

- *The Grateful Dead: 710 Ashbury St., at Waller St.*

- *The Manson Family: 636 Cole St., at Haight St.*

- *Jefferson Airplane: 2400 Fulton St., at Willard St.*

- *Sid Vicious: 26 Delmar St., at Frederick St.*

- *Jimi Hendrix: 142 Central Ave., at Haight St.*

- *Hunter S. Thompson: 318 Parnassus Ave., at Willard St.*

Store Café (*see* Chapter 4). You can still buy drugs at the intersection of Haight Street and Golden Gate Park; in fact, it's pretty rare to walk through the Haight *without* being offered 'shrooms, kind buds, or doses.

Haight-Ashbury doesn't have many real sights or attractions. It's more a place where people come to hang out or to shop the jewelry and clothing stores lining the blocks between Masonic and Clayton streets. It's also a great place to people-watch, though the arrogance of panhandlers in advanced stages of inebriation can get old. In addition to the used-clothing standbys **Wasteland** and **Buffalo Exchange** (*see* Secondhand Clothing, in Chapter 3), you'll find T-shirts on the Haight that you just can't get anywhere else. The Grateful Dead, Speed Racer, Alfred E. Newman, Bob Marley, and more of the Grateful Dead are all represented on the walls of **Haight-Ashbury T-Shirts** (1500 Haight St., at Ashbury St., tel. 415/863–4639). Down the street, the **Haight-Ashbury Free Medical Clinic** (558 Clayton St., at Haight St., tel. 415/487–5632) is one of the last vestiges of hippie idealism on the street—it's been offering free medical care ever since the '60s. Just east of Masonic Street, strategically located **Pipe Dreams** (1376 Haight St., tel. 415/431–3553) is a well-stocked head shop adjacent to a tattoo parlor. When the weather is warm, head down the street to **Buena Vista Park** (*see* Parks, *below*), which has become a hangout/meeting spot/home for skaters. Buses 6, 7, 66, 71, and 73 will get you to Haight-Ashbury from downtown Market Street.

LOWER HAIGHT AND THE WESTERN ADDITION

Despite everything you've heard, the hip, alternative Haight of the '60s isn't dead, it's just relocated. You'll find the sleazy-yet-trendy new digs of young urban nihilists in the Lower Haight—between **Divisadero** and **Webster streets.** Like the Upper Haight, consumerism and counterculture go hand-in-hand here; the street is full of head shops, record stores, underground cafés, and nightclubs. This colorful haven of new subcultures is itself subverted, however, by the very real poverty of its neighboring district to the north, the Western Addition.

LOWER HAIGHT Full of disaffected youths and bedraggled Victorian houses, the Lower Haight is a new breeding ground for a community of angry youth, eccentrics of all ages, mental cases, and—perhaps an amalgam of all three—aspiring artists and writers. Take a stroll down the dirty sidewalks and you're bound to see an American flag hanging upside down from an iron window grate and folks hawking a variety of stolen goods. At night, the street is loud with the din of '70s funk or '90s hip-hop blaring from the doorway of **Nickie's BBQ** (*see* Clubs, in Chapter 6), which overflows with sweaty, dancing youth of all races. If you're looking for a more laid-back scene, skirt the ornery drunks and drug dealers and head for **Tornado** or **Mad Dog in the Fog,** an English-style pub (*see* Bars, in Chapter 6). During daylight, the **Horse Shoe Coffee House** (*see* Chapter 5) is a meeting place for neo-psychedelic artists and trust-fund poets, while **Café International** (*see* Chapter 5) plays those old Donovan songs you thought you'd finally escaped. Join the neo-beatniks and punks for brunch at **Spaghetti Western** (*see* Chapter 4), or head to **Naked Eye News and Video** (*see* Chapter 3) for underground magazines and avant-garde videos.

WESTERN ADDITION Best explored during daylight hours, the Western Addition is a community struggling with a legacy of poverty and discrimination. During World War II, African Americans migrated here in droves to fill vacated factory jobs; after the war, most lost their jobs to returning whites and the neighborhood became a nest of brothels and gambling joints. Later, many of the older buildings were torn down as part of the "urban renewal" program in the 1960s. The main commercial drag is Fillmore Street between Oak Street and Geary Expressway. If you're interested in African–American literature or history, make a beeline for the outstandingly comprehensive **Marcus Books** (*see* Books, in Chapter 3). If you couldn't find the material you want (or didn't want to pay for it), check it out at the **African American Historical Society Library and Archives** (762 Fulton St., at Webster St., tel. 415/292–6172). Along with a modest library dedicated to African-American books and magazines, it also features Internet and computer databases and an archive room full of rare pamphlets, magazines, and publications. Call ahead for events such as poetry workshops. Nearby, at the corner of Octavia and Bush streets, a half-dozen eucalyptus trees and a memorial plaque mark the former residence of Mary Ellen Pleasant (1816–1904), the heroine of the Western Addition. Rumored to be a madam, a murderer, a witch, or some combination thereof, Pleasant was most renowned for her business savvy, profits from which financed the western leg of the Underground Railroad.

➤ **PAINTED LADIES** • The most famous row of houses in San Francisco is situated across from **Alamo Square,** a block west of Fillmore Street. Featured on hundreds of postcards and the opening credits of several TV shows set in San Francisco, the Painted Ladies—six beautifully restored, brightly painted Victorians—sit side by side on a steep street with the downtown skyline looming majestically behind. To snap the obligatory picture, take Bus 6, 7, 66, or 71 from downtown to Haight and Steiner streets, and walk north on Steiner to Hayes Street.

CASTRO DISTRICT

To get to the Castro, just follow the trail of rainbow flags adorning businesses and homes and the pink triangle bumper stickers on the back of many of the cars. Since the early 1970s, the area around Castro Street has been attracting queer men and women from around the world. Before the AIDS epidemic, it was known as a spot for open revelry, with disco music pumping 24 hours a day. Today, the community is less carefree than since the first days of open gay

Gay and Lesbian San Francisco

San Francisco promotes the fact that it is a gay city, the gayest in the world, even. Some neighborhood populations are as much as 95% gay, and it is feasible here for lesbian women and gay men to go about their lives dealing almost exclusively with other gays and lesbians, both in business and in pleasure. And while gay bashing is still a reality, at least here many such cases are fully prosecuted.

San Francisco's most concentrated gay neighborhood is the Castro district, followed closely by Polk Gulch. Although there isn't a lesbian neighborhood per se, many young lesbians gravitate to the Mission. Bernal Heights seems to attract slightly older women-loving women, while the more upwardly mobile lesbian set heads to Noe Valley. Valencia Street in the Mission is home to the greatest concentration of women-oriented shops, though it is not nearly the dyke enclave it was in the 1980s.

Until the early 1970s, the Castro was a neighborhood of middle-class heterosexual families. But when the countercultural fervor in nearby Haight-Ashbury came too close for comfort, whole blocks of families fled for more suburban digs. Houses stood vacant, rents plummeted, and young single men moved in. By 1967, the first gay bars opened on Castro Street and in the '70s the scene exploded. Lured by national publicity, gay men and lesbian women from all over the country migrated to the Castro and Polk Street and the community became a real political force in the city. Gays and lesbians are the city's most prominent special-interest group and many hold public office, ranging from the Board of Supervisors to the Police Commission to the judges on the Municipal Court.

pride, but, on weekends, it still bustles with people socializing on the streets, in the bars, and at the gyms.

The heart of the district is **Castro Street,** between Market and 19th streets. At the southwest corner of Market and Castro, where the K, L, and M MUNI streetcar lines stop, is **Harvey Milk Plaza,** named in honor of California's first openly gay elected official. On November 27, 1978, Milk and then-Mayor George Moscone were assassinated by Dan White, a disgruntled former supervisor. White proceeded to use the "Twinkie defense"—claiming that his junk food diet, and subsequent sugar high, altered his mental state—and was convicted of voluntary manslaughter by reason of "diminished capacity." That night, 40,000 San Franciscans gathered at the plaza and proceeded to City Hall, where the murder took place, in a candlelight march. The procession is repeated every year on the anniversary of the event.

One block away, 18th and Castro streets meet at the gayest four corners in the world. On weekends, people hand out advertisements and discounts for clubs and upcoming queer events and canvas for political causes. All of the shops, bars, and cafés in the neighborhood cater to the gay community. Travel agencies bill themselves as gay and lesbian vacation experts and card shops have names such as **Does Your Mother Know . . .** (4079 18th St., tel. 415/864–3160). The **Castro Theatre** (see Movie Houses, in Chapter 6) is an impressive art deco repertory house that hosts the much-loved International Lesbian and Gay Film Festival each summer. The Castro is also a good area to pick up information on gay and, to a lesser extent, lesbian resources—try **A Different Light** bookstore (see Books, in Chapter 3), with its extensive collection of lesbian and gay literature.

Don't leave the Castro without catching a film at the art deco Castro Theatre, complete with a live organist and trippy ceiling decorations.

The Castro is filled with unique gift shops and boutiques, especially those selling men's clothing. At **Man Line** (516 Castro St., tel. 415/863–7811), you can buy Keith Haring earrings and a rainbow-striped robe for yourself, and a decorative wine bottle holder and an American flag in a red, white, and Roy G. Biv rainbow motif for your home. **Under One Roof** (see Charitable Causes, in Chapter 3), adjacent to the NAMES Project Foundation (see below), gives 100% of its profits to AIDS organizations. The shop carries license plate holders bearing pink triangles, red ribbon pins, and a good selection of soaps, lotions, books, cards, and wind chimes. Don't step into **Jaguar** (4057 18th St., tel. 415/863–4777) unless you're prepared to be confronted with a foot-long silicon fist and other *objets d'art* and books on how to use them. Not for the faint of heart. Visit **Gauntlet** (see Body Decorations, in Chapter 3), the friendly neighborhood piercing studio, to see photos of piercing possibilities and to chat with the knowledgeable staff.

The social hub of the neighborhood is east of Harvey Milk Plaza at **Café Flore** (see Chapter 5), where the eyes turn and the gossip mills churn. Closer to Castro Street, **The Café** (see Bars, in Chapter 6) is the only bar in the area where women represent a majority of the clientele, although even The Café has shifted toward a more mixed and male crowd in recent years. At the intersection of Castro and Market streets, **Twin Peaks** (see Bars, in Chapter 6) has the distinction of being the first gay bar in the city with clear glass windows, a celebration of the fact that gay bars no longer risked arbitrary and frequent police raids.

If you're in the city around the end of June, come to the Castro to witness one of San Francisco's craziest parties—the **San Francisco Lesbian, Gay, Bisexual, Transgender Pride Celebration** (tel. 415/864–3733), which attracts tens of thousands of participants. The Castro is also home to another big bash—**Halloween,** an extravagant, queer-dominated street party. At press time, however, a change of venue was being considered due to overcrowding and the recent influx of gawking "breeders" (*also see* Festivals, in Chapter 1).

NAMES PROJECT FOUNDATION For a sobering reminder of the continuing crisis facing the gay community, drop by the NAMES Project Foundation's **Visitor Center and Panelmaking Workshop,** where panels from the now famous NAMES Quilt—a tribute to those who have died of AIDS—are displayed. The project started in 1987 when gay rights activist Cleve Jones organized a meeting with several others who had lost friends or lovers to AIDS, in hopes that they could create a memorial. They decided on a quilt, each panel to be created by loved ones of individuals who have succumbed to the disease. The idea caught on big and people from all over the country sent in quilt panels. To date, the entire quilt (more than 30,000 panels) has been displayed in front of the White House four times. There are always some panels on display in the San Francisco office, as well as in other offices all over the world. For those who are interested in creating a panel, the foundation provides sewing machines, fabric, company, and support, as well as a weekly quilting bee (Wed. 7–10 PM) if you need to brush up on your sewing skills. *2362A Market St., tel. 415/863–1966. Visitor center open daily noon–5.*

TWIN PEAKS Looming high above the Castro, Twin Peaks is one of the few places in the city where you can see both the bay and the ocean, and everything in between. Naturally, it's one of the prime make-out spots in San Francisco. If you surface long enough to look at the view, you'll have to admit it's truly spectacular—definitely worth the hassle of getting here on public transportation. Bring a picnic, and budget at least 30 minutes to walk up and around this twin-peaked mountain. When the Spanish came to this area in the 18th century, they named the peaks *Los Pechos de la Choca* (the Breasts of the Indian Maiden). Just another example of missionaries hard at work converting the heathens. To reach Twin Peaks, take Bus 37 west from Castro and Market streets.

One of San Francisco's most beautiful staircases, Pemberton Place, lies off Clayton Street in Twin Peaks. Take Bus 33 to Corbett Avenue, and start climbing the stairs off Clayton Street. You will be rewarded with incredible views of the city, bay, and beautiful homes—and a workout to boot!

NOE VALLEY

Lying one major hill away from the hectic Mission and Castro districts, Noe Valley seems like their sedate older sister—you know the type, the one who traded the glitz and glamour and hard edges of city life for a more settled arrangement. Home to large numbers of babies and dogs and those who love them, Noe Valley provides a sunny, neighborly venue for the eco-conscious set to convene and exchange child-care advice. Noe Valley was once an enclave of Irish and German immigrants. These days, you can still find grandmotherly types gabbing in German on Sunday morning ambles. Pick up a bottle of bitters, some Bavarian tunes, and a packet of Gummi bears at **Lehr's German Spe-**

Great San Francisco Views

- *Baker Beach. The bridge looms above to your right, the ocean extends endlessly to your left, and the craggy, green Marin Headlands lie in front of you. It's one of the most beautiful views in the city.*

- *Treasure Island. A slightly different angle reinvigorates the familiar San Francisco skyline. The Bay Bridge, dramatically draped in lights, frames the panorama. By car, take the Treasure Island exit from the Bay Bridge and park at the water's edge.*

- *Upper Market Street. Where Portola Street ends and Market Street begins, near Twin Peaks, you'll find a gorgeous view of the city and the East Bay.*

- *Tank Hill. Take Stanyan Street south and go left on Belgrave Avenue until it dead-ends. Follow the footpath to the high, craggy outlook and gaze to your heart's content. This is one of the finest views of San Francisco.*

- *Top of the Mark. The lookout point at the top of the Mark Hopkins Hotel, on Nob Hill at the corner of California and Mason streets, is accessible only to those in proper attire who are willing to pay dearly for a drink.*

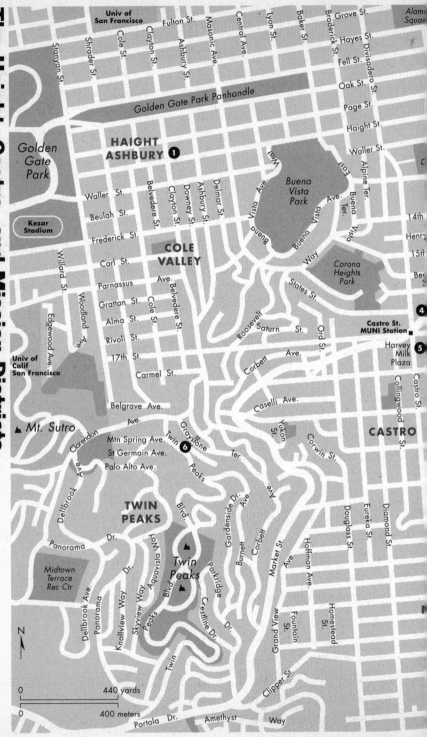

The Haight, Castro, and Mission Districts

Univ of San Francisco

Fulton St.

Golden Gate Park Panhandle

HAIGHT ASHBURY ❶

Golden Gate Park

Kezar Stadium

COLE VALLEY

Buena Vista Park

Corona Heights Park

14th

Henr

15t

Bec

Castro St. MUNI Station ❹

Harvey Milk Plaza ❺

Univ of Calif San Francisco

▲ Mt. Sutro

Mtn Spring Ave. ❻
St Germain Ave.
Palo Alto Ave.

CASTRO

TWIN PEAKS

Twin Peaks ▲

▲

Midtown Terrace Rec Ctr

N

0   440 yards

0   400 meters

Portola Dr.   Amethyst   Way

48

Café Flore, **3**
Castro Theatre, **5**
Collision Gallery, **9**
Four Walls, **10**
Gold Fire Hydrant, **14**
Haight-Ashbury Free Medical Clinic, **1**
The Lab, **12**
Levi Strauss Factory, **8**
Mission Cultural Center, **15**
Mission Dolores, **7**
NAMES Project, **4**
Painted Ladies, **2**
Pemberton Place Stairway, **6**
Precita Eyes Mural Arts Center, **16**
Roxie Cinema, **11**
Women's Building, **13**

cialties (1581 Church St. at Duncan St., tel. 415/282–6803). What goes best with Gummi bears? How about a sit-in-your-gut wurst and yummy goulash soup across the street at **Speckmann's** (1550 Church St., tel. 415/282–6850), which also has a deli stocked with your favorite German specialties (nothin' like bloodwurst for breakfast).

Noe Valley's main drag, **24th Street** beginning at Church Street and heading several blocks west, has plenty of solid, old-timey restaurants, pubs, and clothing stores, as well as a few trendy upstarts. **Global Exchange** (*see* Charitable Causes, in Chapter 3) satisfies the neighborhood's social conscience: It's an international organization that promotes exchange between the United States and developing countries. Gift shops that smell nice and invariably carry some combination of ethnic crafts, wind chimes, crystals, stationery, candles, lotions, oils, and fancy cookie cutters pop up at least once a block in this neighborhood. Doesn't sound tempting? Grab a cup of espresso at **Spinelli** (3966 24th St., near Noe St., tel. 415/550–7416), kick it on one of the benches outside, and contemplate which brie you're going to bring home from the **24th St. Cheese Co.** (3893 24th St., tel. 415/821–6658).

MISSION DISTRICT

Unplagued by fog, the sunny Mission District—named after the Mission Dolores (*see below*) and stretching from the South of Market area to César Chavez (Army) Street—was once San Francisco's prime real estate, first for Ohlone Native Americans and then for Spanish missionaries. Over the years, various populations, primarily European, have given way to immigrants from Central and South America, though the neighborhood also includes a significant contingent of artists and radicals of all ethnicities. The Mission is colorful, friendly, and a great place to hang out, but it can also be dangerous. Be particularly careful on Mission Street, 24th Street near Treat Avenue, and South Van Ness Avenue. Most women won't feel comfortable walking alone here at night, and while you can actually find a parking space, you might think twice about leaving your car. Luckily, public transportation is a snap: Two BART stations (one at Mission and 16th streets, the other at Mission and 24th streets) put you right in the heart of things.

The Mission provides a bounty of cheap food, especially in the form of huge burritos and succulent tacos made up fresh in the numerous storefront taquerías. The area also abounds with specialty bookstores, inexpensive alternative theater companies, and an increasing variety of bars, some of which offer live music, poetry readings, and dance spaces. The architecture is also well worth mentioning, since many of the Mission's large Victorians survived the '06 quake, such as the **Inn San Francisco** (*see box* Romantic Rendezvous, in Chapter 7). For a listing of cultural hubs in the Mission, pick up a free copy of *A Booklover's Guide to the Mission,* a foldout map that is available at most bookstores in the area.

Much of the artsy scene is concentrated in the northern half of the Mission, while the southern half is densely Mexican and Latin American, especially on **24th Street,** between Mission and Potrero. A lively, sometimes hectic area, the strip is filled with people shopping at the many cheap produce stands, markets, and *panaderías* (bakeries). In case you need to chase down your burrito with something sweet, head down to 24th and York streets, where you can have homemade ice cream at the **St. Francis Soda Fountain and Candy Store** (*see box* Sweet Treats, in Chapter 4)—in business since 1918. Or grab a pair of tongs and pick out a pastry or three at **La Mexicana Bakery** (2804 24th St., tel. 415/648–2633)—it'll still cost less than a scone from your favorite North Beach café.

A busy and dense offshoot of Valencia Street, **16th Street,** between Mission and Guerrero streets, has a notable collection of cafés, bars, cheap restaurants, unusual shops, and an independent movie theater, **The Roxie Cinema** (*see* Movie Houses, in Chapter 6). North of here, **Red Dora's Bearded Lady** (*see* Chapter 5), a lesbian-owned café, is the only full-time dyke space around.

VALENCIA STREET A good place to discover the offbeat side of the Mission is on Valencia Street (a block west of Mission St.) between 16th and 24th streets. A one-time low-key strip, Valencia Street is now lined with cafés, secondhand furniture and clothing stores, galleries, garages, **Epicenter** (*see box* Revolution at 33⅓, in Chapter 3), and a variety of bars to meet the needs of the urban hipsters who frequent the area. Around the corner is the **Women's Building** (3543 18th St., tel. 415/431–1180), a meeting place for progressive and radical political groups. Note the recently completed mural *Women's Wisdom Through Time.* Completed in 1995, more than 500 artists helped work on this mural honoring women from every culture. Look for Audre Lorde, Georgia O'Keefe, and Rigoberta Menchú, among many other women's names woven into the fabric of the mural (*also see box* Murals with a Mission, *below*).

Back on Valencia, **Yahoo Herb'an Ecology** (*see* Specialty Items, in Chapter 3) specializes in worm boxes for composting. They also sell herbal teas, organic seeds, and products made of hemp fiber. At **Botanica Yoruba** (998 Valencia St., at 21st St., tel. 415/826–4967), you can pick up incense, candles, herbs, and oils—or make an appointment for a *limpieza* (spiritual cleansing), one of the rituals of the Santeria religion. Valencia Street is also the site of several good bookstores, like the leftist **Modern Times** (*see* Books, in Chapter 3). Also check out **Good Vibrations** (*see* Specialty Items, in Chapter 3), a user-friendly vibrator and sex-toy store that's so respectful of the sacred act you could bring your mom here. If you have a craving for denim history and have never seen the insides of a sweatshop, stop by the 1906 **Levi Strauss** factory (250 Valencia St., tel. 415/565–9159)—Levi's oldest. Free museum tours happen Tuesdays and Wednesdays at 10:30 AM and Wednesdays again at 1 PM. Call ahead to reserve.

DOLORES STREET AND MISSION DOLORES West of the busy, sometimes dangerous, thoroughfares of Mission and Valencia streets, the scene becomes green, hilly, and residential. Dolores Street, bisected by a row of palm trees, marks the edge of the district. While the Castro, just west of here, is where many gay men call home, Dolores Street and the surrounding residential area is quietly, though not exclusively, lesbian. San Franciscans converge upon the expansive **Mission Dolores Park** (*see* Parks, *below*) to stretch their limbs, while tour buses make the obligatory stop at the old mission, 2 blocks away. Interestingly enough, the gold fire hydrant on the corner of 20th and Church streets kept pumping water when others went dry during the firestorm that followed the 1906 earthquake.

Though it's made of humble adobe, **Mission Dolores,** the oldest building in San Francisco, has survived some powerful earthquakes and fires. It was commissioned by Junípero Serra to honor San Francisco de Asis (St. Francis of Assisi) and completed in 1791. The Spanish nicknamed it Dolores after a nearby stream, *Arroyo de Nuestra Señora de los Dolores* (Stream of Our Lady of the Sorrows), and the name stuck (though the river is gone). Mission Dolores is both the simplest architecturally and the least restored of all the California missions, with a bright ceiling in a traditional Native American design painted by local Costanoan Indians. The mission bells still ring on holy days and the cemetery next door is the permanent home of a few early *rancheros,* including San Francisco's first mayor, Don Francisco de Haro. For the $2 admission

Murals with a Mission

For a little more than 20 years, artists in San Francisco have actively explored the tradition of mural painting originated by Mexican muralists like Diego Rivera by creating huge, vibrant works on walls all over the city. Approximately 60 murals are within an area of about 8 blocks in the southeast part of the Mission District. The Precita Eyes Mural Arts Center (348 Precita Ave., near Folsom St., tel. 415/285–2287) offers an excellent two-hour tour of said murals, led by one of its muralists-in-residence, along with an introductory slide show. Tours cost $4 and leave from the center every Saturday at 1:30 PM. Otherwise, stop by any weekday between 1 PM and 4 PM and pick up a copy of their handy "Mission Mural Walk" map for a $1.50 donation. To get to the center, take Bus 27 from 5th and Market streets downtown and get off at 27th and Harrison streets; the center is across the park.

fee, you get access to a small museum with old artifacts, plus as much time as you'd like in the fascinating old cemetery and the mission itself. *16th and Dolores Sts., tel. 415/621–8203. Admission: $2. Open daily 9–4.*

PORTRERO HILL Located just east of the Mission and South of SoMa, Potrero Hill is a sunny, quiet and relatively undiscovered community where you can feast your eyes on spectacular views of the Financial District skyline and the East Bay, as well as stimulate your olfactory senses with waffs of roasting grains and fresh hops from the **Anchor Brewing Company** (*see* Cheap Thrills, *below*). If the sun's down and the brewery is closed, head over to **Bottom of the Hill** (*see* Live Music, in Chapter 6) where you can enjoy a great selection of local bands and occasional surprise visits by big-timers. The main strip of "Goat Hill" is along 18th Street, between Arkansas and Connecticut streets, where you'll find an assortment of mellow restaurants, cafés, a bookstore, and **The Daily Scoop** (1401 18th

Sundays at 4 PM, head to the Bottom of the Hill for a true feast-o-rama. Three bucks buys you a bounty of barbecued goods (tater salad, pasta, chicken, patties—all you can stomach) AND three bands. What a deal!

St., tel. 415/824–3975)—an old-fashioned ice cream parlor. If you come on a Monday, your trek will be rewarded with the pizza extravaganza at **Goat Hill Pizza** (300 Connecticut St., at 18th St., tel. 415/641–1440). The wait staff circles around the restaurant with different slices, and $7.95 buys you all you can stuff in—plus a salad. Other nights, you can enjoy their fine slabs of dough and cheese with live tunes—piano Thursdays and Fridays, and jazz on Saturdays. Don't tell Lombard Street enthusiasts (*see* Nob Hill and Russian Hill, *above*), but **Vermont Street** (at 20th St.) is actually even *more* crooked, and without a tourist in sight. While you're there, picnic at McKinley Square. To get to Potrero Hill, take Bus 9 south from Civic Center to 16th Street and Potrero Avenue, and transfer to Bus 22 line heading east.

SOUTH OF MARKET

Until recently, South of Market (SoMa)—the area bordered by Mission Street, Townsend Street, the Embarcadero, and 12th Street—was merely a nondescript stretch of abandoned factories. Now, thanks to two factors—a resurgent art and theater scene and a happening nightlife—the region is coming alive. The SoMa nightlife scene centers around **Folsom Street,** where the city's predilection for loud music combines nicely with cheap warehouse space and a lack of neighbors to disturb, creating a heathen's haven of dance clubs (*see* Chapter 6).

Folsom Street is the center of the hypermacho leather-oriented gay circuit. At no time is this more obvious than during September's Folsom Street Fair (tel. 415/861–3247), when a multitude of studded bikers, cowboys, and construction workers choke the strip.

The brand-new Yerba Buena Gardens and the San Francisco Museum of Modern Art (*see below*) are the stars of the SoMa arts scene. Smaller, hipper galleries are relocating to the neighborhood as fast as they can, using light from the big names to draw attention to themselves. To test this theory, wander *behind* SFMOMA and try to count the warehouse-cum-gallery spaces within a 3-block radius. In particular, check out the **Capp Street Project** (525 2nd St., tel. 415/495–7059) and the two controversial murals they sponsor South of Market: The first, at 6th and Brannan streets, focuses on low-income housing; the second, at 10th and Brannan streets, points to the dearth of natural features in the city.

SoMa is home to the city's outlet stores and bargain warehouses (*see* Chapter 3). At **660 Center** (660 3rd St., btw Brannan and Townsend Sts., tel. 415/227–0464), you'll find the ultimate bargain basement—a conglomeration of 22 outlet stores under one roof. Toward the water, the downtown suits-and-heels crowd has infiltrated the SoMa area, but you'll still find several sorta-hip, sorta-yuppie cafés and restaurants around surprisingly green **South Park** (*see* Parks, *below*).

YERBA BUENA GARDENS This 8½-acre arts and performance space finally opened in October 1993, after more than 30 years of planning and bureaucratic disputes. On the east side of the garden complex, the **Center for the Arts** houses galleries (*see* Museums, *below*) and a theater (*see* Multimedia Performance Spaces, in Chapter 6) meant to celebrate the multi-cultural nature of the Bay Area. Critics point out that the multicultural emphasis may be to the exclusion of mainstream arts. Others smirk at the money spent building the center: a whopping $41 million. *701 Mission St., tel. 415/978–2787.*

Aside from the performing and visual arts, Yerba Buena Gardens offers a welcome respite from the frenzy of downtown—yet it's just a couple of blocks southeast of the Montgomery Street BART station. Take a walk along the paths of the grassy, spacious esplanade to the Martin Luther King, Jr. Memorial: 12 glass panels, all behind a shimmering waterfall, engraved with quotes from Dr. King in English and in the languages of each of San Francisco's sister cities.

Across the street from the Center for the Arts, 1995 also saw the opening of the new location of the **San Francisco Museum of Modern Art** (*see* Museums, *below*), and the relocation of the **California Historical Society** (678 Mission St., at 3rd St., tel. 415/357–1848). A Children's Center should open in 1997, and the Mexican Museum, now in cramped quarters at Fort Mason, will make its new home here around 1998.

Parks

Along with Golden Gate Park (*see* Major Sights, *above*), the city has an abundance of smaller strips of greenery where you can cavort like a hyperactive kid when your energy overflows or rest when your feet have become a little too accustomed to the feel of pavement. In several of these, the sheer horticultural magnificence and diversity will amaze you as you laze beneath cypress or gaze at palms and wonder: "If this is California, why is it so damn cold?"

BUENA VISTA It ain't called Buena Vista (good view) for nothing. Set on a steep hill covered with cypress and eucalyptus that tumbles down toward Haight Street at about 100 miles per hour, Buena Vista offers potheads, dog walkers, skateboarders, and lovers some serious inspiration to do their thing. The park has a reputation for being dangerous at night, but in the daytime it's a largely undiscovered escape from the Haight's asphalt chaos. From the summit, the views of the Golden Gate, the ocean, the Bay Bridge, and downtown create a mystical backdrop for whatever activity you choose to indulge in. The park fronts Haight Street at the intersection of Haight and Lyon streets; from Market Street downtown, take Bus 6, 7, 66, or 71.

DUBOCE PARK Twenty-year-olds with assorted dogs, tattoos, drug habits, and musical instruments seem especially drawn to this tiny park, which is crammed in between Lower Haight and Castro and offers no view beyond that of streetcars trundling by. (It's on the N Judah line, which runs from Market Street out to Ocean Beach.) Before you flop down, note that it's been dubbed "dog shit park" by locals thanks to its popularity with our four-legged friends. Despite its utter mediocrity compared to such jewels as nearby Buena Vista or Alamo Square (*see* Lower Haight and Western Addition, *above*), it's a grassy enough place to enjoy the cup of coffee or slice of pizza you just bought on Haight Street; unlike the other two, it requires barely any energy to reach.

GLEN CANYON Hidden in a part of the city that isn't crawling with visitors, a visit to Glen Canyon Park might just revitalize you after an overdose of city life. Eucalyptus trees loom above you and scent the air, zillions of birds sing to you and only you, and grass-covered slopes lead down to a shady path, equal parts poison oak and soothing stream. There are even rocks to climb on. Take BART to Glen Park, walk uphill on Bosworth Street to the end, and go hiking.

MISSION DOLORES PARK In a sunny residential area between the Mission and Castro, beautiful Dolores Park attracts picnickers, families with children, dogs and their owners, and men in Speedos if the weather is right. Set on a gently sloping hill, the park contains tennis courts, a basketball court, a playground, local kids playing soccer, palm trees, and wide expanses of grass where you can catch some of the city's elusive rays. Head toward the west and southwest edges of the park known, with tongue in cheek, as Castro Beach (where the serious sun-worshipers head) for spectacular views of the city and the Bay Bridge. While the open areas feel quite friendly and safe, the thoroughfare down the middle of the park is where drug dealers and other sketchy-looking types transact business. Avoid this area at night. On July

Fourth and Labor Day, the San Francisco Mime Troupe (*see* Theater, in Chapter 6) performs for free in the park. *Btw Dolores, Church, 18th, and 20th Sts. From downtown, J Church streetcar to 18th or 19th St.*

SOUTH PARK Set in the middle of the warehouse-laden and utterly ungreen SoMa district is a welcome surprise: South Park, a tree-filled square that looks like it just dropped in from Paris to say hi. With a playground, several cafés and restaurants, inviting benches, and a bit of quiet, it's a perfect old-fashioned antidote for those postmodern moments when you feel like you've spent the whole day on the set of *Mad Max.* During the week, graphic artists, writers, architects, and attorneys pass through here sipping lattes, and its proximity to the new "mut-limedia gulch" has earned it the moniker "South Spark." Sundays, when the surrounding cafés, offices, and galleries are closed, are quietest. *South Park Ave., off 2nd and 3rd Sts., btw Bryant and Brannan Sts.*

SUTRO FOREST Sometimes you'll be walking around the city and off in the distance you'll see a big patch of trees. You know it's not Golden Gate Park, but it looks awfully tempting anyway. This wild, densely forested place is Sutro Forest, off Stanyan Street behind the UCSF Medical Center. Just when you think it might be possible to get lost along one of its deserted, overgrown trails, among the ferns and ivy-covered eucalyptus trees, you stumble upon UCSF residence halls. The least strenuous way to get here is to take the N Judah streetcar to Willard Street, head south on Willard, right on Belmont Avenue, and left on Edgewood Avenue until it dead-ends. There's your hiking trail.

WASHINGTON SQUARE This park between Filbert, Union, Powell, and Stockton streets embodies the blending of cultures that makes San Francisco unique. Old Italian men chew on long-dead cigars as the bells of a Romanesque church ring on the hour. In the early morning, Chinese women engage in the graceful movements of tai chi, surrounded by lingering wisps of fog. An Italian-style picnic grabbed from any of North Beach's numerous delicatessens, a bottle of Chianti hidden discreetly in a brown paper bag, and someone you feel like relaxing with will only heighten the good vibes. From Market Street downtown, Bus 15 or 30 will bring you to the square.

Beaches

Step off the bus at Ocean Beach in your bikini top and flip-flops, all sunscreened and ready to catch some rays, and you may be in for a shock. San Francisco's beaches, though numerous and lovely, rarely greet you with the kind of sun that'll make you crave a swim. Locals quickly learn to use the city's beaches (listed below) for things other than swimming—like meditating, kite flying, or exercising their dogs. **Fort Funston,** San Francisco's southernmost beach, is great for watching hang gliders soaring overhead, and for starting the 7-mile trek from Fort Funston to the Cliff House at Ocean Beach. From Balboa Park BART, take Bus 88 west.

BAKER BEACH One end of Baker Beach sees families, tourists, anglers, and wealthy homeowners walking their dogs, while the other end sees a lot of skin as one of the city's most popular nude beaches. Beautiful views of the Marin Headlands, the Golden Gate Bridge, and the bay make this a great place to sunbathe. Take Bus 1 from Clay and Drumm streets near the Embarcadero, and transfer to Bus 29 heading into the Presidio.

CHINA BEACH Named after a Chinese fisherman who camped here in the 1870s, China Beach is one of the city's safest swimming beaches *and* the most convenient, with its free changing rooms and showers. (Although you must still watch out for the occasional deadly rip currents.) Stroll through Seacliff, with its million-dollar homes—you may see Robin Williams jogging by—tucked between Lands End and the Presidio. To reach this small beach with views of the Golden Gate, take Bus 1 from Clay and Drumm streets near the Embarcadero.

LANDS END Starting in the main parking lot of Sutro Baths, the mile-long Lands End circular trail is popular with mountain bikers, hikers, and picnickers. It offers amazing views of the Golden Gate, the ocean, and Mission headlands. Off to the side of the main trail you'll find Lands End Beach. A nude beach that's no longer exclusively gay, Lands End Beach is rocky and unsafe for swimming, but you'll find some sand, as well as a respite from the wind in the small walled-off areas that people have built. To get here from downtown, go west on Geary Street and turn right on El Camino del Mar, or take Bus 38 west from Union Square. From the parking lot at the end of the road, take the steps down by the flag and head east on the trail. When it branches, head down to the beach.

OCEAN BEACH The surfers' beach, the tourists' beach, the family beach, the walkers' beach. It's all-purpose. Have a drink at the **Cliff House,** a restaurant and historic San Francisco landmark perched on the cliffs, or pick up information on the Golden Gate National Recreation Area at the National Park Service office underneath the restaurant. Across the plaza from the park service office is the offbeat Musée Méchanique (*see* Museums, *below*). Just west of the Cliff House lie the ruins of the Sutro Baths, a huge complex of fresh and saltwater pools modeled after ancient Roman baths. In their heyday, the baths featured five saltwater tanks and one freshwater tank, all at different temperatures, as well as restaurants, art exhibits, and an amphitheater. Alas, the baths became victim to budget problems and were torn down in 1966. People still climb around on the foundation of the baths, trying to get a look at some sea lions or crustaceans. You'll also get a nice view of Seal Rock, so named because of the seals that used to sun themselves here before relocating to cozier digs by Fisherman's Wharf. To reach Ocean Beach, take the N Judah streetcar from any downtown underground MUNI station.

Museums

Although San Francisco has been trying to build a name for itself as a city of big, impressive institutions of art—note the newly relocated Museum of Modern Art and the renovated California Palace of the Legion of Honor—the increasing attention is also a boon to the smaller, funky spaces that fit more naturally into the city's eclectic cultural landscape.

AFRICAN AMERICAN MUSEUM This African American cultural center offers a contemporary art gallery featuring works by African and African American artists, an intriguing gift shop that sells jewelry and artifacts, and a historical archive and research library. In addition, the museum has performing arts classes and lecture series. *Fort Mason Center, Bldg. C, tel. 415/441–0640. Donation requested. Open Tues.–Sun. 11–5. $3 adults, $2 children.*

ANSEL ADAMS CENTER If you're even remotely interested in serious photography, come here. The largest repository of art photography on the West Coast, the center has five rotating exhibits, one of which is devoted to Adams's work (despite the name, there aren't that many works by Adams); the other exhibits range from traditional portraiture to computer-altered images. Born of the Friends of Photography, a national group founded by Adams, the center serves photographers with publications, awards, an educational series taught by famous shutterbugs, and an incredible bookstore. The center's 1993 Annie Leibovitz retrospective put it on the pop-culture map. *250 4th St., btw Howard and Folsom Sts., tel. 415/495–7000. Admission: $4, $3 students. Open Tues.–Sun. 11–5 (until 8 first Thurs. of month).*

ASIAN ART MUSEUM Housed in the same building as the M. H. de Young (*see below*), this is the West Coast's largest Asian museum. The first floor is devoted to Chinese and Korean art; the second floor holds treasures from Southeast Asia, India and the Himalayas, Japan, and Persia. The collection of more than 12,000 pieces from major periods of Asian art is rotated periodically, so everything comes out of storage once in awhile. Highlights of the permanent collection include the oldest known Buddha image (AD 338) and superb collections of jade and ancient Chinese ceramics. *John F. Kennedy and Tea Garden Drs., Golden Gate Park, tel. 415/668–8921. Admission: $6, $4 students; free first Wed. of month, first Sat. of month until noon. Open Wed.–Sun. 10–4:45 (until 8:45 first Wed. of month).*

CALIFORNIA ACADEMY OF SCIENCES This huge natural history complex houses one of the country's best natural history museums, subdivided into blockbuster sights that include the **Steinhart Aquarium** and **Morrison Planetarium** (*see* Golden Gate Park, in Major Sights, *above*). One big draw is the aquarium's **Fish Roundabout,** which places you in an underwater world of 14,500 different creatures. The living coral reef, with its fish, giant clams, and tropical sharks, is super cool. Go mid-morning so you can watch the penguins and dolphins at feeding time. If earthquakes are inextricably linked with San Francisco in your imagination, try the trembling earthquake floor in the Space and Earth Hall. Also worth checking out are the Life through Time Hall, which chronicles evolution from the dinosaurs through early mammals, and the Birds of a Feather exhibit, which explores the languages, songs, physical features, and learning of birds. Temporary exhibits often examine environmental issues. *Btw John F. Kennedy and Martin Luther King, Jr. Drs., Golden Gate Park, tel. 415/750–7145; laser shows at planetarium, tel. 415/750–7138. Admission to museum and aquarium: $7, $4 students; free first Wed. of month. Show your MUNI Fastpass or transfer and get $1 off. Admission to planetarium $2.50, to laser shows $7. Open daily 10–5.*

CENTER FOR THE ARTS The visual arts building at the Center for the Arts at Yerba Buena Gardens houses three spacious galleries exhibiting contemporary works, usually of emerging local and regional artists; a media screening room for video and film; and a multiuse forum. The idea of the center is to reflect San Francisco's multicultural community in a space that is welcoming, unpretentious, and appealing to as large a community as possible. *701 Mission St., at 3rd St., tel. 415/978–2700 or 415/978–2787. Admission: $4, $2 students; free first Thurs. of month 6 PM–8 PM. Open Tues.–Sun. 11–6 (until 8 first Thurs. of month).*

CHINESE HISTORICAL SOCIETY OF AMERICA This nonprofit organization houses a modest museum in its basement headquarters. Historical photos and graphics, accompanied by moving explanations, trace the experiences of Chinese Americans from the 1850s to the present. Among other artifacts, the small museum contains opium pipes, a queue (the long braid men wore as a symbol of allegiance to the Manchu emperor of China before the 1911 Revolution), an altar built in the 1880s, and a parade dragon head from 1909, one of the first to use lights. *650 Commercial St., btw Kearny and Montgomery Sts., tel. 415/391–1188. Admission free, donations accepted. Open Tues. and Fri. noon–4. Closed major holidays.*

EXPLORATORIUM Come here for the ultimate fourth-grade field trip you never took—it's a great place for children and grown-ups to learn about science and technology in a big, drafty warehouse. In the more than 650 exhibits, many of them computer-assisted, a strong emphasis is placed on interaction with the senses, making it especially popular with people on hallucinogenic drugs. Advance reservations are required for the excellent crawl-through Tactile Dome ($12 separate fee), where you slither through several differently textured small rooms in complete darkness. *3601 Lyon St., btw Marina Blvd. and Lombard St., tel. 415/561–0360. Admission: $9, $7 students, $5 disabled; free first Wed. of month. Open Tues.–Sun. 10–5 (Wed. until 9:30); Memorial Day through Labor Day 10–6.*

JEWISH MUSEUM This handsome, small museum features revolving exhibits that trace important moments in Jewish history and the works of Jewish artists—contemporary, as well as old masters. *121 Steuart St., btw Mission and Howard Sts., tel. 415/543–2090 or 415/543–8880 for recorded info. Admission: $3, $1.50 students; free first Mon. of month. Open Sun. 11–6, Mon.–Wed. noon–6, Thurs. noon–8. Closed Jewish holidays.*

LEGION OF HONOR San Francisco's European fine arts are on display, once again, in the newly reopened, seismically sound California Palace of the Legion of Honor. What was once a basement has become an underground complex of extra gallery space; what was once a café is now a full-service restaurant overlooking the Pacific Ocean. The collection is not exactly stunning, but it does include some fine pieces from the late 19th century, among them one of Monet's *Water Lilies* and several Rodin sculptures, including a cast of *The Thinker. In Lincoln Park, enter at 34th Ave. and Clement St., tel. 415/750–3600. Admission: $7; free second Wed. of month. Open Tues.–Sun. 10–4:45 (until 8:45 first Sat. of month). Take Bus 38 Geary west from Union Square to 33rd St., then transfer to Bus 18 north.*

M. H. DE YOUNG MEMORIAL MUSEUM While home to art from Africa, Oceania, and the Americas, the de Young is best known for its substantial survey collection of U.S. art, from paintings and sculpture to decorative arts, textiles, and furniture. Some pieces date from as far back as 1670; the artists represented include Sargent, Whistler, Church, and Wood—among the highlights are George Caleb Bingham's *Boatmen on the Missouri* and Georgia O'Keeffe's *Petunias.* Docent-led tours are offered on the hour. Call the recorded message to find out about special lectures and events. If you're a student, you can get a $35 membership that includes free admission for two adults for an entire year. *Golden Gate Park, btw John F. Kennedy Dr. and 8th Ave., tel. 415/750–3600 or 415/863–3330. Admission: $6, free first Wed. of month. Open Wed.–Sun. 10–4:45 (Wed. until 8:45), additional open hours during special exhibitions.*

MEXICAN MUSEUM It is the bittersweet curse of the Mexican Museum to have an enormous permanent collection (including works by Rodolfo Morales and Diego Rivera), a strong reputation as a national center for Mexican and Chicano culture, and only a few tiny rooms to move around in. The museum is trying to break out into new quarters at the Center for the Arts in Yerba Buena Gardens—they even have the building designed—but it'll be a few years yet. Meanwhile, come and enjoy the few pieces they can exhibit, usually by 20th-century artists. *Fort Mason Center, Bldg. D, tel. 415/441–0404. Admission: $3, $2 students; free first Wed. of month. Open Wed.–Sun. noon–5 (until 8 first Wed. of month).*

MUSEE MECHANIQUE This quirky museum lurks near the Cliff House at the end of Geary Boulevard. As museums go, the Méchanique is tops, stuffed with antique carnival attractions that include player pianos, marionette shows, fortune tellers, and a truly frightening mechanical laughing lady. Admission is free, but you'll want to spend handfuls of quarters playing with all of the gadgets. Don't miss the miniature amusement park—complete with a Ferris wheel—built out of toothpicks by inmates at San Quentin. *1090 Point Lobos Ave., tel. 415/386–1170. Admission free. Open weekdays 11–7, weekends 10–8.*

MUSEO ITALOAMERICANO If this little collection of 20th-century Italian and Italian American art seems oddly out of place, consider that it actually was founded two decades ago in North Beach. Though throngs of Italian Americans do not seem to be pouring in, the museum has stuck to its mission to research, collect, and display new works by Italians and Italian Americans, in an effort to restore appreciation of contemporary Italian art and culture. The one important work of the rotating permanent collection is Arnaldo Pomodoro's bronze sculpture *Tavola della Memoria* (1961). *Fort Mason Center, Bldg. C, tel. 415/673–2200. Admission: $2, $1 students; free first Wed. of month. Open Wed.–Sun. noon–5 (until 7 first Wed. of month).*

PACIFIC HERITAGE MUSEUM Check out rare works from private collections representing China, Taiwan, Japan, Thailand, and many other nations of Asia. Past exhibitions have featured Chinese Classical furniture, paintings, vases, and ceramics. Call for the latest exhibition information. *608 Commercial St., tel. 415/399–1124. Admission free. Open weekdays 10–4.*

SAN FRANCISCO MUSEUM OF MODERN ART Designed by Swiss architect Mario Botta, the new brick and stone home of the SFMOMA is dominated by a huge, cylindrical skylight trimmed with black-and-white stripes of stone. The interior is just as impressive: The spacious, attractive hall and galleries provide a sleek setting for the museum's sprawling exhibits. The space doubles that of the museum's prior home at the War Memorial Veterans Building, where it opened in 1935 as the West Coast's first museum devoted to 20th-century art. The excellent permanent collection includes works by Jackson Pollock, Jasper Johns, Frida Kahlo, Henri Matisse, and Frank Stella, as well as a healthy representation of contemporary photography and Bay Area figurative movement works. *151 3rd St., tel. 415/357–4000. Admission: $7, $3.50 students; free first Tues. of month, half-price Thurs. 6–9. Open Tues.–Sun. 11–6 (Thurs. until 9). Closed major holidays.*

Galleries

For those in higher tax brackets, galleries are stores where one might actually purchase a "little something" for the living room wall. For the rest of us, art galleries are minimuseums where the "look, but don't touch" rule holds firm. Except for the postcards, of course. The best time to wade into the gallery world is the first Thursday evening of each month, when many host receptions with free drinks, sometimes snacks, and occasionally some interesting new art. It's a great, and fairly casual, scene. For current happenings, keep an eye on publications like the *San Francisco Arts Monthly* and *San Francisco Gallery Guide*, both available at galleries throughout town.

DOWNTOWN No fewer than 30 galleries, most relatively mainstream and high-end, are in this area, a stone's throw from ritzy Union Square. The thickest concentrations are along the first 3 blocks of Grant Street, the 100 block of Geary, the 100 and 200 blocks of Post, and the 200 block of Sutter. For the most gallery per hour, head to **49 Geary Street,** where each of the second through fifth floors claims a separate swank gallery. On the fifth floor, **Robert Koch** gallery (tel. 415/421–0122) explores traditional and experimental photography. Other floors focus on painting or multimedia art. All four galleries are open at least Tuesday–Saturday 11– 5. You'll find unusual multimedia exhibits and funky sculpture at **A Luggage Store** (1007 Market St., tel. 415/255–5971). Call for current shows.

MISSION DISTRICT This neighborhood is the undisputed center of the city's Latino arts scene. **Galeria de la Raza** (2857 24th St., tel. 415/826–8009), founded in 1970 by members of the Chicano Arts movement, was the first Mexican museum in the United States; it remains an influential cultural resource with its exhibits of local Latin American art and community arts programs. Many galleries in the Mission also host occasional exhibits of women artists, for which you can thank the **Women's Building** (3543 18th St., tel. 415/431–1180), which itself sometimes hosts visual arts installments. Check out local and traveling artists and performances at these up-and-coming Mission galleries: **Southern Exposure** (410 Alabama St., at 17th St., tel. 415/863–2141); **Collision Gallery** (417 14th St., at Valencia St., tel. 415/431–4074); **Four Walls** (3160-A 16th St., btw Valencia and Guerrero Sts., entrance on Albion St., tel. 415/626–8515; and **The Lab** (2948 16th St., at Mission St., tel. 415/864–8855).

Mission Cultural Center. This Mission District landmark has not only gallery space but also classrooms, dance spaces, painting studios, and a theater, all devoted to promoting the Latino arts community. Current budget woes are keeping performance arts to a minimum, but visual arts exhibits continue, and the center is a great place to find out what's going on in the neighborhood. Call or stop by for a complete rundown of events, including exhibits, performances, lectures, and classes. *2868 Mission St., btw 24th and 25th Sts., tel. 415/821–1155. Donation requested. Open Tues.–Fri. 10–4, Sat. 11–3.*

SOUTH OF MARKET This is downtown's younger, more intriguing counterpart. In SoMa, plain old paintings won't draw a crowd anymore; everyone who's anyone is jumping on the mixed-media and multimedia bandwagons. Two galleries that are old hands at the multimedia game are **SOMAR** (934 Brannan St., tel. 415/552–2131), which does theater better than visual arts, and **New Langton Arts** (1246 Folsom St., btw 8th and 9th Sts., tel. 415/626–5416), the granddaddy of the city's mixed-media centers.

Also check out the endearingly awkward **Gallery 111** (111 Minna St., btw Mission and Howard Sts., tel. 415/974–1719), where you can catch installations by contemporary California artists and get a $1.50 cappuccino or similarly cheap glass of wine until 2 AM or so. Evenings often include music or other performances. **ACME** (667 Howard St., near 3rd St., tel. 415/777–2263) is another good, tiny space to see a strange creation or two. **Theater Concrete** (550 Natoma St., tel. 415/621–4068) offers unusual performances, often involving music and robots. Call for performance times.

If photography is your thing, try **Vision Gallery** (1155 Mission St., tel. 415/621–2107), a slightly upscale spot with consistently good exhibits. **SF Camera Work** (70 12th St., tel. 415/764–1001) is another good photography gallery with strong alternative shows in an airy warehouse space.

Cheap Thrills

San Francisco is a paradox. It's an expensive city that is also proud of its healthy contingent of bohemians and starving artists. In addition to the thrills listed below, consider some of the cheap forms of entertainment discussed in other sections, such as author readings, open mic nights at bars and cafés, museum free days, gallery hopping, Sunday morning celebrations at Glide Church (*see box* Welcome All Ye Sinners, *above*), and the many annual festivals and street fairs, especially in summer (*see* Festivals, in Chapter 1). Not to be missed are the free, accomplished musical pieces set in the Sunset's **Stern Grove** (*see* Festivals, in Chapter 1). The *San Francisco Bay Guardian* and the *SF Weekly* are excellent bets for the most updated information on local events.

Golden Gate Ferries (*see* Getting In, Out, and Around, in Chapter 1), the commuter ferry between San Francisco, Sausalito, and Larkspur, offers the cheapest way to experience the bay in a boat ($3–$5). They have all the features you've come to associate with fine ferry travel: outdoor decks, food for sale, a complete wet bar, and no irritating commentary. Bring stale bread to throw to (or at) the seagulls.

The **Anchor Brewing Company,** on Potrero Hill east of the Mission District, offers free brewery tours; these include a history of the brewery, a step-by-step explanation of the brewing process, and, yep, free samples at the end. Tours run twice a day June–August, and once a day the rest of the year. You *must* make reservations three to four weeks in advance. While you're there, pick up a copy of *Celebrator,* a publication of and guide to Bay Area breweries. *1705 Mariposa St., at De Haro St., tel. 415/863–8350.*

After pounding porters and ales at Anchor, go hang out with fuzzy, huggable bears at the **Basic Brown Bear Factory and Store** across the street (kiddie corner, you might say). This is one of the few remaining small and independent factories of its kind—watch 'em stuff and seal the suckers before your eyes. Free tours happen everyday at 1 PM. *444 De Haro St., at Mariposa St., tel. 415/626–0781.*

You may already be a member of the **Cacophony Society**—"a randomly gathered network of free spirits united in the pursuit of experiences beyond the pale of mainstream society . . . the canaries that swallow whole the paper tigers of authority"—in other words, upsetting the mundane flow of life as often as you can. Join in inspired events like the Urban Iditarod, a re-creation of the Alaskan dog sled race that substitutes barking humans for dogs, shopping carts for sleds, and the streets of San Francisco for the Alaskan tundra. More laid-back free spirits may prefer Dorothy Parker's Perpetual Perambulating Pedagogic Paperback Pow Wow. Call 415/665–0351 for information on these and other events, usually free, that surface randomly and irrationally throughout the year.

If you are in need of entertainment with a spiritual twist, head to the **Neptune Society Columbarium,** a four-story beaux arts structure displaying urns that contain the cremated remains of San Francisco's dearly departed. The domed structure alone can make you kind of dizzy: a perfect circle with niches carved throughout and doors leading to rooms with elaborate display cases and 19th-century stained glass. Get the greenskeeper going and he'll tell you all sorts of interesting stories. *1 Lorraine Ct., tel. 415/221–1838. Off Anza St. btw Stanyan and Arguello Sts. Admission free. Open weekdays 9–5, weekends 10–1.*

Wise Fool Puppet Intervention is a theater-arts project that brings giant puppets and stilt characters to the city's streets and public parks. The puppets and masks are handmade with recycled materials. The processions and performances are moving, magical, and just might inspire you to sign up for a volunteer program in your own community. They also hold open workshops, where you can help build a puppet or make a mask and then join one of the processions (you pay only for materials). For more info call 415/905–5958.

East Bay

So you've had a burrito at every taquería in the Mission. You've worn a groove in your seat at your favorite San Francisco café, and you know where each book at City Lights is shelved. You've had more than your share of great times in the city by the bay, but at the moment you're asking yourself somewhat anxiously: What next? Luckily, the funk and soul of San Francisco extend beyond the city limits. Only a bridge away lie Berkeley and Oakland, each with its own character and some attractions the city can't match—from the hip-hop Oaktown beat to the hippie parade in Berkeley. Whether you're looking for a New Age healing session or a grungy blues band, odds are good that you'll find it somewhere in the East Bay.

Berkeley

Berkeley and University of California may not be synonymous, but they're so interdependent that it's difficult to tell where one stops and the other begins. You won't find many backpack-toting students in the upscale neighborhoods that buffer the north and east sides of campus, but for the most part Berkeley is a student town, dominated by the massive U.C. campus and its 30,000 enrollees. Because of its offbeat, countercultural reputation, the university attracts every sort of person imaginable—from artists, anarchists, and hypergenius intellectuals to superjocks, sorority girls, and fashion slaves, not to mention the stubbornly apathetic and the piously ideological. Recent campus celebrities have included former math professor Theodore Kaczynski (the alleged Unabomber) and former student The Naked Guy (expelled for attending classes in the nude). But anyone who has watched the documentary *Berkeley in the Sixties* might be surprised to find out that the city isn't what it used to be. Berkeley *is* still a breeding ground for alternative social trends both important and inane, for posters and protesters that urge onlookers to "Resist Proposition 187" (the anti–illegal immigration initiative), "Fuck the Police," or "Legalize Marijuana." But with the 1994 election of a more conservative mayor, Shirley Dean, there seems to be a reaction by some Berkeley residents against the city's free-for-all reputation.

Perhaps the most poignant symbol of the conflict between '60s and '90s Berkeley is the continuing struggle over People's Park (*see* Major Sights, *below*). Activists consider the place a symbol of the people-power spirit of the 1960s, and want to keep the park pure open space. The university, however, has seen fit to install basketball and volleyball courts in the 2.8-acre park, and the Berkeley City Council has stated its commitment to curbing drug dealing and crime to make it more popular with students and other city residents. Those who continue their love affair with the '60s still influence the city, but others seem to want to drag them, kicking and screaming, into the '90s.

Berkeley's University of California **campus** is surprisingly beautiful, with walking paths, a creek, and eucalyptus and redwood groves. Southside, or the area south of campus, is dominated by chaotic **Telegraph Avenue,** and just east, **College Avenue,** heart of the Elmwood District, and lined with boutiques and cafés with a bohemian flair. North Berkeley, a more sedate and residential area, is where you'll find the **Gourmet Ghetto,** home of the famed restaurant Chez Panisse (*see* Chapter 4) and a number of excellent organic food markets. The Berkeley Hills, rising north and east of campus, offer the huge **Tilden Regional Park** and acres of densely forested slopes. Farther west, around **University** and **San Pablo avenues,** you'll find working-class Berkeley, a gritty neighborhood that is also among the city's most ethnically diverse. No matter what part of town you're in, you're never far from movie houses and bookstores geared toward the young and ideological, and restaurants and cafés that cater to student budgets.

MAJOR SIGHTS

TELEGRAPH AVENUE When most people think of Berkeley, they think of Telegraph Avenue, which begins at the campus and runs south into Oakland. Whether you love it or hate it, the first 5 blocks of this congested and colorful avenue form the spiritual heart of Berkeley—a jumble of cafés, bookstores, used-clothing stores, cheap restaurants, harried students, long-haired hippies, homeless buskers, metaphysical warriors, and wide-eyed tourists. Every day—rain or shine—street vendors line the avenue's sidewalks, selling everything from handmade jewelry and crafts to crystals, incense, and tie-dyed T-shirts. New Age prophets offer tarot and numerology readings to passersby while baggy-jeaned hip-hop fans skateboard down the sidewalks. Telegraph today is a unique fusion of '60s and '90s counterculture, and the two elements blend nicely. This is especially evident on Sundays between 11 and 3, when students, hippies, former hippies, and yuppies with a penchant for organic produce gather on Telegraph around Haste Street for the weekly farmers' market.

Shops along Telegraph (*see* Chapter 3) come and go, but neighborhood landmarks include **Amoeba** and **Rasputin's,** both of which feature a huge selection of vinyl, tapes, and CDs that could be music to your ears. Book lovers should check out **Cody's Books** (*see* Books, in Chap-

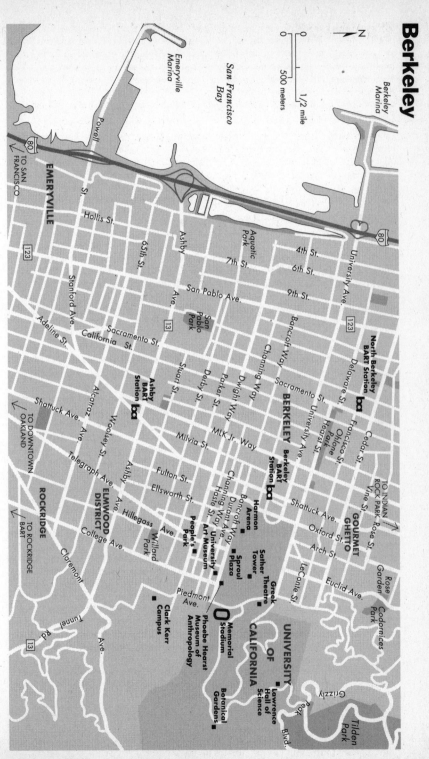

Berkeley

San Francisco Bay

Emeryville Marina

Berkeley Marina

TO SAN FRANCISCO

80

EMERYVILLE

123

Hollis St.

65th St.

Stanford Ave.

Adeline St.

Shattuck Ave.

TO DOWNTOWN OAKLAND

ROCKRIDGE

TO ROCKRIDGE BART

Claremont Ave.

Tunnel Rd.

13

Powell St.

Aquatic Park

Ashby Ave.

7th St.

San Pablo Ave.

Sacramento St.

California St.

13

San Pablo Park

Alcatraz Ave.

Woolsey St.

Telegraph Ave.

Ashby Ave.

Hillegass Ave.

College Ave.

Willard Park

ELMWOOD DISTRICT

Clark Kerr Campus

Piedmont Ave.

500 meters

1/2 mile

N

4th St.

6th St.

9th St.

Bancroft Way

Channing Way

Dwight Way

Parker St.

Derby St.

Stuart St.

MLK Jr. Way

Milvia St.

Fulton St.

Ellsworth St.

Ashby BART Station ba

People's Park

University Ave.

BERKELEY

Sacramento St.

Berkeley BART Station ba

Channing Way

Durant Ave.

Bancroft Way

Haste St.

University Ave.

Harmon Arena

University Art Museum

Phoebe Hearst Museum of Anthropology

Sather Tower

Sproul Plaza

Greek Theatre

Memorial Stadium

UNIVERSITY OF CALIFORNIA

Lawrence Hall of Science

Botanical Gardens

Delaware St.

Francisco St.

Ohlone Park

Hearst St.

Cedar St.

Vine St.

123

North Berkeley BART Station ba

GOURMET GHETTO

TO INDIAN ROCK PARK

Rose St.

Garden Codornices Park

Rose

Shattuck Ave.

Oxford St.

Arch St.

LeConte St.

Euclid Ave.

Grizzly Peak Blvd.

Tilden Park

80

61

ter 3) and **Moe's** (see Books, in Chapter 3). Cody's hosts regular readings and has probably the largest selection of new books, mags, and 'zines in the area, while Moe's specializes in used and rare books. For candles, incense, black-light posters, and other *recreational* needs, stop by Southside's head shop, **Annapurna** (see Specialty Items, in Chapter 3). One block south, **Caffè Mediterraneum** (see Chapter 5), opened in 1957, is more popular with long-time Berkeleyans than with students, who prefer to study in the cafés along Bancroft Way. The alleged workplace of Beat poet Allen Ginsberg, the Med was immortalized by an anxious Dustin Hoffman in the film *The Graduate*.

Telegraph Avenue is also a haven for **street musicians.** Most Fridays, a Peruvian band sets up on the corner of Telegraph and Bancroft avenues, while other afternoons bring folks hammering on dulcimers, drumming on buckets, and strumming on acoustic guitars. The first or second Sunday in October, Telegraph hosts a **jazz festival,** and authors, bookmakers, and musicians fill the street during the avenue's annual **book festival** in late July or early August. Call the Telegraph Avenue Association (tel. 510/649–9500) for news of upcoming fêtes.

PEOPLE'S PARK In 1969 the *Berkeley Barb* (a former local newspaper) urged people to "bring shovels, hoses, flowers, soil, colorful smiles, laughter, and lots of sweat" to convert a vacant lot, owned by the university, into a park for the people. Thousands of people showed up to work on and enjoy the new green space, and People's Park was born. The conflict began when the university erected a chain-link fence around the park in an attempt to assert their property rights and their plan to build a dormitory. Huge protests ensued, ending in nasty battles with police, a death, a 17-day occupation of Berkeley by the National Guard (sent for by then-governor Ronald Reagan), thousands of arrests, and the dropping of tear gas on Sproul Plaza. Over the years, the park has decayed into more of a community eyesore than a green haven as activists and university and city officials continue to struggle over the its future. In 1991, the university tried to beautify the park by installing volleyball courts, but many people saw the courts as a scheme to dislocate the homeless and hippies who call the park home, no doubt attracted by the now-controversial Free Box (filled with clothing, shoes, books, and other items there for the taking) and the free lunches (yes there is such a thing) served by Food Not Bombs. You'll still find flowers, smiles, and sweat at the park—along with activists, homeless families, drug dealers, and occasional acts upon its plywood stage. There isn't much to *do* here except contemplate why this little plot of land creates such passionate emotions, play basketball or volleyball on the much-disputed courts, and check out the elaborately graffitied bathrooms covered with murals, poetry, and antigovernment statements. Every year on the last Sunday in April, the anniversary of the creation of People's Park is celebrated with music, arts and crafts, and food. The sentiment of the park has been extended to **People's Park Annex** (Telegraph Ave., at Dwight Way), another vacant, fenced-in lot that regularly hosts witty graffiti and art displays made out of recycled material (toilet bowls are a frequent medium). *Btw Haste St. and Dwight Way, just east of Telegraph Ave.*

UNIVERSITY OF CALIFORNIA CAMPUS Established in 1868 as the first branch of the statewide University of California system, the U.C. Berkeley campus retains some of the beauty and gentility of its early years (especially in the old brick and stone buildings scattered about campus), some of the fire of the revolutionary 1960s (check out Sproul Plaza at noon), and some of the apathy and complacency of the 1980s (also visible on Sproul Plaza at noon). On a walk through campus you'll find peaceful glades, imposing academic buildings in the architectural style known as brutalism, as well as battalions of musicians, random dogs, zealots, and students "on their way to class" (i.e., napping in the sun). Free student-led tours of campus leave from the **visitor center** (101 University Hall, cnr of University Ave. and Oxford St., tel. 510/642–5215), on the west side of campus, weekdays at 10 AM. Tours also leave on Saturday at 10 AM from a small visitor center (tel. 510/642–4636), open Saturdays only, on the second floor of the Student Union Building on the west side of Sproul Plaza (see below). You can pick up a map or self-guided walking brochure from either office.

➤ **SPROUL PLAZA** • Just north of the Telegraph and Bancroft intersection, Sproul Plaza is widely known as the spot where the Free Speech Movement began in 1964. Look inside **Sproul Hall** (the nearby white, imposing administration building) for a display of photographs from this first demonstration, in which 3,000 students surrounded a police car that was holding Jack Weinberg, a U.C. Berkeley student arrested for distributing political flyers on Sproul Plaza. (This activity will no longer get you arrested, as five minutes spent on the plaza will attest.) Both the man and car were released after 32 hours, but the students, led by Mario Savio, continued to battle university head Clark Kerr. Today, Sproul Plaza is a source of endless entertainment for locals and tourists alike, where some of Berkeley's most famous loonies get a chance to match wits. Here's your chance to see the Hate Man (look for the man in a bra, high heels, long skirt, and lipstick), who has professed hatred for everything, heckle an evangelist who's preaching damnation and hellfire to fornicators and sodomites, or engage in a debate on foreign policy, affirmative action, or the existence of God with street philosophers of all stripes. Judging by the endless stream of bad show tunes sung by the intensely annoying Rick Starr, he apparently believes his unplugged Mr. Microphone will bring him international acclaim. **Lower Sproul Plaza,** just west of Sproul Plaza, is the site of occasional free noon concerts during the school year on Wednesdays (usually rock bands of various talent) and Thursdays (usually the Cal jazz band). Nearby **Zellerbach Hall** (*see* Classical Music, in Chapter 6) hosts professional (as opposed to street) theater and concerts; check the box office for upcoming events.

If you're lucky you may cross paths with the Bubble Lady (poet and bubble maker Julia Vinograd), Rare (lunatic and sports-trivia fiend), Pink Man (hot-pink unitard wearing unicyclist), or any of the other wacked-out denizens who give Berkeley its odd appeal.

➤ **SATHER GATE AND DOE LIBRARY** • North of Sproul Plaza, pass through Sather Gate, the main entrance to campus until expansion in the 1960s. The second building on your right, Doe Library, is worth a look for its cavernous and beautiful reference room and the cozy **Morrison Reading Room** (open weekdays noon–5). Stop in the latter if you want to curl up somewhere and recuperate from the incessant clamor of people outside. The subdued brass lamps, oak paneling, and ornate tapestries inspire calm; anyone is welcome to peruse the international newspapers and magazines, listen to the collection of compact discs and records with headphones, or just plant themselves in a cushy leather easy chair.

The Doe Library building also contains the **Bancroft Library,** accessible from the east side of the building, which houses a vast collection of historical documents, rare books, and old photographs. Anyone with a photo ID can get access to the huge, noncirculating collection. On permanent display in the administrative office is a gold nugget purported to have started the California Gold Rush when it was discovered on January 24, 1848 at Sutter's Mill.

The "Berkeleyan," a campus newspaper published every Wednesday, has a long list of free events and lectures— everything from "Double- strand break repair and the specific cloning of human DNA in yeast" to "Spatialization of Violence."

➤ **CAMPANILE AND AROUND** • Directly east of Bancroft Library is **Sather Tower** (more commonly known as the Campanile), a 307-foot clock tower modeled after the one in Venice's Piazza San Marco. The carillon is played daily, weekdays at 7:50 AM, noon, and 6 PM; Saturdays at noon and 6; and Sundays at 2 for an extended 45 minutes. You can watch the noon performances from the approximately 200-foot observation deck, open Monday–Saturday 10–3:30, Sunday 10–1:45. You reach the deck via an elevator (50¢). Even if you miss the carillon show, the views from the observation deck are stunning. Take note that the bell concerts are suspended during the final exam period. Southwest of the Campanile, the red-brick South Hall is the only one of the original university buildings still standing. Or walk northeast from the clock tower to check out the **Hearst Mining Building,** a masterpiece of beaux arts architecture designed by John Galen Howard.

NEIGHBORHOODS

Sure Berkeley may seem like another college town—with a bit more panache than most—but there *are* other neighborhoods beyond the student-dominated Southside well worth exploring.

A trip to working-class **West Berkeley** (along University Ave.), tony **North Berkeley**, or College Avenue's neighborly upscale/bohemian **Elmwood District** will show you other sides of Berkeley.

UNIVERSITY AVENUE University Avenue stretches all the way from I–80 and the bay to the U.C. campus, providing easy access to (or a quick escape from) downtown Berkeley and the university. It's not as trendy as some of Berkeley's other neighborhoods, and you won't find as many people wandering around, but it teems with cheap ethnic restaurants, cafés, and foreign clothing stores, as well as car-repair shops, futon shops, some seedy motels, and gas stations. In case you missed the first run of *Brazil* or this year's Festival of Animation, the **U.C. Theater** (*see* Movie Houses, in Chapter 6) shows a diverse range of classics, along with Saturday midnight performances of *The Rocky Horror Picture Show.*

A few miles west of the university, **San Pablo Avenue** crosses University at a perpetually gridlocked intersection. San Pablo used to be a largely uninteresting thoroughfare full of thrift stores and fast-food joints, but recently it has been attracting a more youthful crowd with a smattering of funky shops and bars, including a recently opened branch of the San Francisco–based feminist sex shop **Good Vibrations** (*see* Specialty Items, in Chapter 3); the hip chick-owned restaurants **Brick Hut Café** (*see* Chapter 4) and **Anne Kong's World-Famous Bleach Bottle Pig Farm** (2072 San Pablo Ave., tel. 510/848–7376); the ultracasual pub **The Albatross**; folk music club **Freight and Salvage**; and world-music emporium **Ashkenaz** (for more on Berkeley nightlife, *see* Chapter 6). That said, the area can be seedy at night and these gems are too few and far between for San Pablo to be conducive to exploration on foot.

Yuppie types drive straight past San Pablo Avenue another ½ mile west on University to the upscale shops on **4th Street,** roughly between University Avenue and Virginia Street. Stores here tend to sell overpriced goodies to those who blindly follow the gospel of Martha Stewart— home accoutrements such as sleigh beds, hummingbird feeders, organic cotton bathrobes— you get the idea. The only real bargains you'll find are at the Crate and Barrel outlet (*see* Household Furnishings, in Chapter 3). The street is still a fine place to browse, have brunch, and laugh at how much people will pay for a garlic smashing stone, complete with instructions. For a shopping experience of an altogether different variety, head to the **Vivarium** (1827 5th St., tel. 510/841–1400), where you can stroll among pythons, giant tortoises, iguanas, and the bunnies and rats they feed to them. If it's love at first sight, any one of the critters can be yours for a small fee. Once you've reached 5th Street, it would be a shame not to continue down University to the **Berkeley Marina** (*see* Parks and Gardens, *below*).

COLLEGE AVENUE/ELMWOOD DISTRICT Running south from campus, College Avenue (especially around Ashby Avenue) is the heart of what's known as the Elmwood District. This hopping residential area has some great examples of California Craftsmen homes as well as a plethora of cafés, specialty stores, and restaurants. Neighborhood destinations include **Nabolom Bakery** (2708 Russel St., tel. 510/845–2253), a cooperate effort that produces great breads and pastries, stylin' **Espresso Roma** (*see* Chapter 5), where hotshot composer John Adams has been known to quaff caffeine, and **Slash** (*see* Used Clothing, in Chapter 3), a great spot to buy used jeans. After much fund-raising and work, the newly refurbished **Elmwood Theatre** (*see* Movie Houses, in Chapter 6) is up and running almost-first-run movies and some classic double features for as little as $3.50 on Tuesdays.

NORTH BERKELEY Grad students, professors, and folks with steady jobs frequent Northside, lending it a calmer atmosphere than you'll find on the frenzied Southside. The hilly neighborhoods here are architecturally diverse, with many homes dating from the 1920s. On a jaunt through the **Gourmet Ghetto,** the area around Shattuck Avenue and Vine Street, you'll find hordes of tantalizing restaurants as well as specialty stores, clothing boutiques, and bookstores. Cafés and restaurants also line a block-long section of **Euclid Street,** where it dead-ends at the campus. After fortifying yourself, continue north on Euclid to reach the Berkeley Rose Garden (*see below*). Look for that obscure treatise on Nietzsche at **Black Oak Books** (*see* Books, in Chapter 3) or just grab a cuppa joe at **Peet's Coffee & Tea** (2124 Vine St., 1 block east of Shattuck Ave., tel. 510/841–0564) and kick back with the local caffeine fiends.

You'll find more stores, cafés, and movie theaters on **Solano Avenue** (Shattuck turns into Solano about 2 miles north of University), including the always packed **Zachary's Pizza** (*see*

Chapter 4) with their delicious Chicago-style pies running about $13. **The Bone Room** offers live tarantulas, dinosaur bones, and any other living or fossilized paleontological necessities (1569 Solano Ave., at Peralta Ave., tel. 510/526–5252).

PARKS AND GARDENS

TILDEN REGIONAL PARK Tilden Park's more than 2,000 acres of forests and grasslands are a wonderful escape from the urban congestion of the lowlands. Follow the signs to **Inspiration Point** for an uncluttered view of two reservoirs and rolling hills where lazy cows graze. If you feel inclined to stay a while, Tilden offers picnic spots (call 510/636–1684 to reserve a group picnic area) and miles of hiking and biking trails (*see* Chapter 8).

Tilden Nature Area Environmental Education Center (EEC) (tel. 510/525–2233; open Tues.–Sun. 10–5), at the north end of the park, has recently been renovated and now has a new exhibit on the Wildcat Canyon Watershed. EEC sponsors a number of naturalist-led programs; pick up a copy of the *Regional in Nature* quarterly at the center for more info. Independent types can borrow or buy a self-guided trail booklet ($2) at the center. For a nice, easy walk (about a mile), take the **Jewel Lake Trail** loop from the EEC office and look out for the salamanders. To make friends with furry or feathered animals, bring green, leafy vegetables to the nearby **Little Farm.**

Want to escape the heat of the dry hillside? If you don't mind sharing a small lakeside beach with toddlers in Mickey Mouse swimsuits, Tilden's **Lake Anza** (tel. 510/848–3028) makes a good swimming hole with a strip of sandy beach, but you may have to compete with a Girl Scout troop or two for precious towel space on hot summer days. A changing facility is open when the lifeguards are on duty, mid-May to mid-October, daily 11–6. While the lifeguards are around, adults pay $2.50. At all other times you swim for free and at your own risk.

Rumor has it that Lake Anza is a popular spot for skinny-dipping under a full moon.

Other park activities include pony rides ($2.50), a vintage carousel ($1), a botanical garden of California plants (open daily 8:30–5, free), the 18-hole **Tilden Golf Course** (tel. 510/848–7373 for reservations), and a miniature steam train ($1.50) that takes passengers on a 12-minute ride around the south end of the park. Rides operate on weekends and holidays when school is in session and daily during spring and summer vacations; call 510/843–2137 for specific hours.

To reach the park on weekends, take Bus 67 from Berkeley BART station to the end of the line. On weekdays, Bus 65 takes you from BART to the edge of the park. If you're driving, take Uni-

In for the Long Haul

Want to raise some hell about the latest exploits of the Republican-dominated Congress but don't know where to begin? Looking for an environmental organization to join but haven't found the right one? If you haven't completely succumbed to cynicism and apathy, go to the Long Haul, whose motto is "Information, Organization, Liberation." Groups like Food Not Bombs, Free Radio Berkeley, Industrial Workers of the World, and the radical gardening group Spiral Garden use the meeting space, while volunteers staff the "info shop," stocked with local and national progressive 'zines and pamphlets. A great way to get involved (and well fed) is to attend their Sunday night potluck dinners ($3– $5), cooked by a different group each week. Call or stop by for a schedule of events (held about five nights a week), including lectures, musical events, and movies. 3124 Shattuck Ave., at Woolsey St., tel. 510/540–0751. Info shop open Mon. 4 PM–8 PM for "wimmin only," Tues. and Thurs. 3–9, Wed. 6–9, Sat. 3–6, Sun. 3–9.

versity Avenue east from I–80 to Oxford Street, go left on Oxford, right on Rose, and left on Spruce to the top of the hill, cross Grizzly Peak Boulevard, make an immediate left on Canon Drive, and follow the signs. The park is open 5 AM–10 PM.

BERKELEY MARINA Warm days were meant to be spent at the Berkeley Marina, at the end of University Avenue a ½-mile west of I–80. First-time visitors head straight to the ¾-mile-long pier jutting out into the bay to enjoy the unbeatable views of the Golden Gate Bridge and Alcatraz Island. Bundle up (or snag one of the high-backed concrete benches) for protection against the cold wind that invariably whips up at the end of the pier. Long-time residents, however, are more likely to be found at the recently renamed **César E. Chávez Park** (formerly North Waterfront Park), a 92-acre expanse of grassy hills overlooking San Francisco Bay. The park is the only Berkeley open space with no leash law for dogs and is also one of the most popular kite-flying areas in the Bay Area.

For a map of the area, stop by the marina's **Nature Center** (160 University Ave., tel. 510/644–8623), which runs all sorts of educational and environmental programs like marine biology and waterskiing for the kiddies (and occasionally for grown-ups, too). For information on renting boats or hooking up with one of the sailing clubs stationed at the marina, stop by the **Marina Office** (201 University Ave., tel. 510/644–6376). To get to the marina, drive west on University Avenue across I–80 or take Bus 51M west from Berkeley BART station.

BERKELEY ROSE GARDEN/CODORNICES PARK Built during the Depression, the rose garden is an attractive spot for a picnic or to watch the sunset. There's the multilevel rose garden, an amphitheater with roses, benches aplenty, more roses, and a panoramic view of the bay. It's north of campus on Euclid Avenue, between Bayview Place and Eunice Street. If you're looking for the more traditional park accoutrements, head across the street to Codornices Park, where you'll find basketball courts, a baseball diamond, swings, grass and sand, and picnic areas—the star attraction is the long concrete slide; bring a piece of cardboard and join the local kids. At the back of the park, hiking paths lead up the hill along Codornices Creek. To reach the rose garden and the park, walk north from campus on Euclid Street for 20 minutes, or take Bus 65 from Berkeley BART station.

U. C. BOTANICAL GARDEN Haul yourself up to this horticultural haven to learn more about a rare species of plant, take a tour around the world of flora, or to just stop and smell the roses. Nestled in the hills east of Strawberry Canyon, the garden is a valuable research and education center with a diverse collection of plants—over 10,000 neatly labeled species from around the world. The garden is divided into regional areas with habitats ranging from South African deserts to Himalayan forests. It also features specialized plots like the Chinese Medicinal Herb Garden and the Garden of Economic Plants, as well as three indoor exhibits, and a slew of paths to explore. Relax on a rock along Strawberry Creek in the shady Asian Garden, on a bench near the sunny Cactus Garden, or head uphill for a lovely green-framed view of the Bay. The garden is especially colorful in spring when the extensive rhododendron collection is in full bloom. Check the visitor center for bulletins on various plant seminars and public education programs, then take home some outdoor plants, for sale at bargain prices. *200 Centennial Dr., tel. 510/642–3343. From Berkeley BART, take Bus 52 to Stadium Rimway and walk uphill for 25 min; or take Hill Service Shuttle (50¢) from Hearst Mining Circle on campus. Admission free. Open daily 9–4:45. Tours weekends at 1:30.*

BERKELEY HILLS FIRE TRAIL One of Berkeley's best semiurban hiking trails begins at a small dirt parking area just uphill from the Strawberry Canyon Recreational Facility on Centennial Drive (and just downhill from the U. C. Botanical Garden). Peppy joggers, thoughtful ramblers, and dog walkers of all ilks come to enjoy this wide dirt path, which, though sometimes crowded, provides a wonderful and accessible escape for nature seekers. After the beginning uphill stretch (pant, wheeze), the path levels off and weaves along the hillside through looming trees and clearings, which provide beautiful views of Berkeley and the Bay. *Off Centennial Dr. Follow directions to U. C. Botanical Garden (see above).*

INDIAN ROCK PARK As you head north, Shattuck Avenue dead-ends at Indian Rock Avenue, where you'll see enormous volcanic rock jutting from the hillside. Luckily, as there was no way for developers to sandblast the stone, the city eventually set it aside as a park. The view of Solano Avenue far below, Albany Hill in the distance, and the Marin Headlands is humbling. Rock climbers awkward and nimble converge here to practice their sport on the north side of the boulder, making it a great place to find climbing buddies. Steps are available for those who would prefer to saunter up the rock. The park is open from dawn to dusk.

MUSEUMS

LAWRENCE HALL OF SCIENCE Perched on a cliff overlooking the East Bay, the museum is a memorial to Ernest O. Lawrence, the university's first Nobel laureate, who helped design the atomic bomb. The exhibits here are mostly hands-on and geared toward children, with an emphasis on the life sciences. On weekends, and daily during summer, you can catch films, lectures, laboratory demonstrations, and planetarium shows. On the hillside outside the museum's rear patio, look for the long, slender pipes sticking out of the ground. The 36 harmonized aluminum pipes are part of a wind organ. If you walk among them when the wind is blowing, you'll hear their music; you can play with the tones by turning one of the six moveable pipes. *Centennial Dr., near Grizzly Peak Blvd., tel. 510/642–5132. Drive east on Hearst St., which borders campus on the north, and follow signs; or Bus 8 or 65 from Berkeley BART to end (ask driver for a transfer [25¢], redeemable for $1 off museum admission); or Hill Service Shuttle (50¢) from Hearst Mining Circle on campus. Admission: $6, $4 students and seniors; planetarium shows $2 more. Open daily 10–5.*

PHOEBE HEARST MUSEUM OF ANTHROPOLOGY This is one of Berkeley's best museums, with rotating exhibits that cover everything from ancient America to Neolithic China. Also on display are artifacts used by Ishi, the lone survivor of California's Yahi tribe, who was brought to live on the U.C. campus in 1911 after gold miners slaughtered the rest of his tribe. Frequent talks by artists, anthropologists, and other scholars shed light on the artifacts on display—call or look in the *Daily Californian* (the free student newspaper) to find out what's on tap. Keep your eyes open for the modern sculpture and painting in student art displays lining the halls to the museum entrance. *Kroeber Hall, U.C. Berkeley campus, tel. 510/642–3681. Admission: $2, free for U.C. students. Open Wed.–Sun. 10–4:30 (Thurs. until 9 during school year).*

UNIVERSITY ART MUSEUM The low concrete building housing the University Art Museum may not look like much from the street, but from the interior or from the whimsical sculpture garden in the rear, you can appreciate the artful arrangement of jutting concrete balconies that render the building both solid and surprisingly airy. The UAM houses the largest university-owned collection in the country. The works displayed are confoundingly diverse and may include anything from a 16th-century altar panel to a passel of sugar candy pastel Bibles made by a Berkeley MFA candidate. One of the museum's most impressive collections is a room full of violently colorful paintings by the abstract expressionist Hans Hofmann. Tables in many of the rooms contain a smattering of books related to the gallery's exhibits, giving you a chance to rest your feet and figure out what you're looking at. The UAM is also home to the **Pacific Film Archive** (*see* Movie Houses, in Chapter 6), on the ground floor. Pick up a schedule of upcoming exhibits and movies at the museum entrance. *2626 Bancroft Way, tel. 510/642–0808. Admission: $6, $4 students and seniors, free Thurs. 11–noon and 5–9. Open Wed.–Sun. 11–5, Thurs. 11–9.*

CHEAP THRILLS

For bay views from sea level, hook up with the **Cal Sailing Club** (west end of University Ave., tel. 510/287–5905) on the first full weekend of each month from 1 to 4 PM, when the club offers free spins around the bay to all comers. Wear warm, waterproof clothing and be prepared to get wet.

The free **Berkeley History Center and Museum** (1931 Center St., tel. 510/848–0181), open Thursday–Saturday 1–5, features changing exhibits of community interest such as The Berkeley literary scene. Get your karma healed at the **Berkeley Psychic Institute** (2436 Haste St., tel. 510/548–8020), popular with all sorts of New Agers and alternative enthusiasts. For more info, pick up their free tabloid, *The Psychic Reader,* which has listings of events, workshops, and classes, as well as photos of paranormal sightings. They offer a free weekly healing clinic Monday evenings at 7:30 and 10; psychic readings, by appointment only, are $20.

Those with musical leanings can hang out with the ragtag group of **bongo drummers** that has congregated on Lower Sproul Plaza most weekends (and many a weeknight) for the past 30 years, usually thumping away from early afternoon until late in the evening. Since the Berkeley Guides office overlooks Lower Sproul, we hesitate to endorse this activity—you try editing when you can't hear yourself *think*—but you might as well bring your own drum or pot (kitchen variety, of course) and join in. Or, better yet, join the dreadlocked, barefooted, wispy-skirted, and purple velvet pantsuit wearin' folks dancing silently to the rhythm of the drums. If you prefer a more formal musical setting, attend one of the free noon concerts Wednesdays during the school year at **Hertz Hall** (*see box* Classics on the Cheap, in Chapter 6).

The Berkeley Hills may not be the best place for stargazing, what with all the lights of San Francisco gleaming across the bay, but the free **Saturday Night Stargazing** at the Lawrence Hall of Science Plaza (*see* Museums, *above*) is still a lot of fun. Employees and local amateur astronomers break out their telescopes every clear Saturday night, from about 8 PM to 11 PM, to show any and all comers the moon, planets, star clusters, galaxies, and whatever else the universe has on show that night. Call the info number (tel. 510/642–5132) for specifics.

Thought you had to head to Napa Valley to sample free wine? Not if you go to **Takara Sake** (708 Addison St., at 4th St., tel. 510/540–8250), one of only three makers of sake (Japanese rice wine) in the United States. Enthusiastic employees offer a slide show and free samples of their product daily noon–6 in a minimally decorated room that seems out of place in this warehouse near the freeway.

Oakland

Oakland doesn't have the same dazzling affect on visitors as San Francisco, so if you're looking for glitz or chic you might want to save the $2 BART fare for a mocha. Oakland is more like a comfortable old bathrobe—a little ratty around the edges, but warm and familiar. A predominantly working-class city, Oakland locals go about their business during the week, and let loose for one hell of a good time on weekends. Voted "All American City" in 1993, Oakland offers visitors a typical example of American cities built after 1850: a diverse cultural landscape, a struggling downtown, some great architecture, some crime-ridden areas, and high hopes for community renewal. Oakland also has its own special flair as home to the West Coast blues, the Oaktown school of rap (heard in the music of local artists MC Hammer, Digital Underground, Too Short, Tony! Toni! Toné!, Oaktown 3-5-7, and Tupac Shakur), and a vibrant art scene from the many artists who live in the city's plentiful cheap warehouse spaces.

Developed in the 1850s in the midst of long-gone oak groves by three unsuccessful gold miners, Oakland prospered thanks to a thriving port, profitable manufacturing industries, and the arrival of the railroad. By the early 1990s, the city was home to a large number of businesses, a bustling electric streetcar system, and an ever increasing population of people from throughout the country lured by job prospects and cheap housing. Wealthy families crossed the Bay to escape San Francisco's urban blight, and still others migrated after damage wrought by the 1906 earthquake. Encouraged by this rapid growth, a group of powerful citizens spearheaded a beautification plan in hopes of changing Oakland's image from a suburb of San Francisco into a thriving metropolis in its own right. These boom days saw the construction of a flurry of new buildings downtown (many of which are now empty); a bigger, better City Hall (once the tallest building west of Chicago); and the creation of Lake Merritt. Unfortunately, the plan to turn the lake into the crowning recreational glory to a growing downtown was shattered by the Depression, the flight of wealthy citizens to the hills, and an incoherent development plan. Another blow to the city's fabric was the freeway built in the 1960s, resulting in the fracturing of neighborhoods and conflict between the "haves" and "have nots." Even today there are controversies about redlining in the area below I-580.

But there's a lot to discover in Oakland. The neighborhoods around **Grand, College,** and **Piedmont** avenues are lined with cafés, reasonable and upscale restaurants, bookstores, and bou-

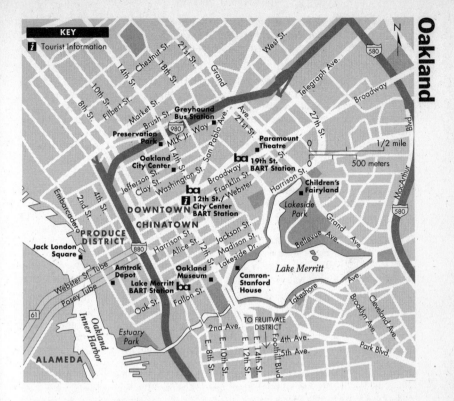

KEY

i Tourist Information

21st St.

Chestnut St.

14th St.

18th St.

West St.

Grand

10th St.

Filber St.

8th St.

2nd St.

4th St.

Market St.

Brush St.

MLK Jr. Way

San Pablo Ave.

21st St. Ave.

Telegraph Ave.

580

Broadway

27th St.

MacArthur Blvd.

Greyhound Bus Station

980

Preservation Park

Oakland City Center

Jefferson St.

Clay St.

14th St.

Washington St.

Broadway

Franklin St.

Webster

Paramount Theatre

ba 19th St. BART Station

Harrison St.

Children's Fairyland

ba

i 12th St./ City Center BART Station

DOWNTOWN

CHINATOWN

PRODUCE DISTRICT

880

Harrison St.

Jackson St.

Alice St.

12th St.

Madison St.

Lakeside Dr.

Lakeside Park

Grand Ave.

Bellevue Ave.

Lake Merritt

Jack London Square

Webster St. Tube

Posey Tube

Embarcadero

Amtrak Depot

Lake Merritt BART Station

Oakland Museum

ba

Oak St.

Fallon St.

Camron-Stanford House

Lakeshore

Lakeshore Ave.

Brooklyn Ave.

Cleveland Ave.

61

Estuary Park

Oakland Inner Harbor

2nd Ave.

E. 8th St.

E. 10th St.

E. 12th St.

E. 14th St.

TO FRUITVALE DISTRICT

Foothill Blvd.

4th Ave.

5th Ave.

Park Blvd.

ALAMEDA

0 ___ 1/2 mile

0 ___ 500 meters

N

580

tiques. Wander through **Chinatown** for lively restaurants and markets selling produce, pungent spices, and meats. Check out the downtown revitalization efforts around Jack London Square and City Center or, if the city is fraying your nerves, head for the parks in the hills to the east (*see* Chapter 8). Though some residential areas in these hills were devastated by a fire in October 1991, most of the multimillion dollar homes have been rebuilt in a variety of interesting architectural styles and the area manages to retain the look and feel of the 1930s, when much of Oakland was farms, ranches, and estates. You'll need a car or bike to explore the hills, but most everything else is within reach of a BART station.

WORTH SEEING

DOWNTOWN Downtown Oakland, spreading along Broadway roughly between 10th and 20th streets, is an odd conglomeration of shiny office complexes; art deco, beaux art, and Victorian buildings in various states of repair; and grimy concrete facades of abandoned businesses—the last remaining department store left in 1996, though a Sears is expected to take over the site by 1997. Though it's not a place you should visit alone at night, it's definitely worth a trip during the day to see some surprisingly impressive late 19th- and early 20th-century architecture. One of the most impressive art deco buildings in the Bay Area is the 1931 **Paramount Theater** (*see* Movies Houses, Chapter 6), decorated with an 80-foot mosaic outside and black marble and gilded plaster inside. Call the box office for information on dance, music, and film events held here, or come at 10 AM on the first or third Saturday of the month for a two-hour tour of the building ($1). Next to the

A timeless figure on downtown Oakland's skyline is the Tribune Tower (all of its clocks are wrong)—built in 1923 and the city's first landmark building—though its former tenant The Oakland Tribune has since moved to new digs in Jack London Square.

Paramount is the emerald green art deco I. Magnin Building; as if symbolizing downtown's problems, it now stands empty. Though many downtown businesses have moved, **De Laurer's Super Newsstand** (*see* Books, in Chapter 3) has been selling "your hometown newspaper" for years, as well magazines and paperbacks to all sorts of people all hours of the day.

Farther south, the new federal building at **Oakland City Center** (btw Clay, Jefferson, 12th, and 14th Sts.) is a study in contrast, with funky modern sculptures in the courtyard and a 70-foot-high glass rotunda that rises above a mosaic floor. During business hours, you can enter the building and go up to the two-tiered glass-enclosed walkway that connects the building's two towers. Security is pretty tight in the wake of the 1995 Oklahoma City bombing because the building houses the IRS and the Bureau of Alcohol, Tobacco, and Firearms (as well as other government agencies) and you may need to show a picture ID.

You'll find newly renovated buildings and red-brick sidewalks in **Old Oakland,** between 8th and 10th streets just west of Broadway. During the 1870s, this was a bustling Victorian business district—a boon the redevelopers of today must hope for as tenants slowly move in to the historic structures. A good sign are the many eateries opening in the area, including **Café 817** (817 Washington St., tel. 510/271–7965), the snazzy **Café Cheneville** (499 9th St., tel. 510/893–5439), and **Pacific Coast Brewing Company** (*see* Bars, in Chapter 6), which makes its own delicious brews. Another worthwhile stop is **Pro Arts Gallery** (461 9th St., tel. 510/763–4361), which displays local artists' work. Stop in for info about **East Bay Open Studios,** in which artists' work spaces are opened to the public for two weekends in June.

➢ **PRESERVATION PARK** • In the shadow of the brand-spankin' new City Center, Preservation Park (cnr Martin Luther King Jr. Way and 13th St.) is a recreation of an idyllic 19th-century Oakland neighborhood, complete with decorative wrought-iron fences and period streetlamps and benches. Forty years of architectural history can be seen in the 16 restored houses here (five are in their original location, the others were moved here after threats of demolition), including Queen Anne and Italianate cottages, colonial revival and Craftsman homes. Sitting near the fountain, you can almost believe that it's the turn of the century—except for the I–980 traffic noise from just over the hedges. The buildings are private office spaces and aren't open to visitors (unless you ask nicely or, oops, accidentally go into the wrong one). The adjacent **Pardee Home Museum** (672 11th St., tel. 510/444–2187) was the home of former Oakland mayor and California governor George C. Pardee. It now houses family and historical relics and is only open for guided tours ($4), offered Thursday–Saturday at 11, 1, and 2:30.

LAKE MERRITT Lake Merritt was built in the early 1900s as part of a city beautification program. A former swamp, this is now a 155-acre oasis in the middle of urban Oakland, surrounded by shady trees, meandering paths, and old men feeding the ducks. During the day sun seekers, joggers, power walkers on their lunch break, and stroller pushers circle the 3½-mile paved path around the lake and lounge on the lawns. Recently, those who live nearby have raised a ruckus about unruly teenagers who cruise around the lake after dark, resulting in a

Marching to a Different Beat

Like San Francisco and Berkeley, Oakland has a reputation for being a center of alternative culture and revolutionary politics. In the 1960s, the militant and still widely debated Black Panther Party began here. In the 1970s, the city was headquarters for the Symbionese Liberation Army, who kidnapped Patty Hearst and demanded as part of her ransom that food be distributed to Oakland's poor. Even the city's most famous literary figure, Jack London, was steeped in controversy—an ardent socialist and debauched troublemaker, he wanted California to form its own country (although that's hard to detect in those two novels about dogs).

controversial anticruising ordinance: Drive around the lake more than three times in four hours and you'll receive a citation—consider yourself warned. Near the southwest edge of the lake, you can tour the **Camron-Stanford House** (1418 Lakeside Dr., near 14th St., tel. 510/836–1976), the only remaining Victorian building in this formerly bourgeois neighborhood. Built in 1876, the house is meticulously decorated in the style of the 1880s. Tours ($4; free first Sun. of month) are offered Wednesday 11–4 and Sunday 1–5. **Lakeside Park** (tel. 510/238–3091), on the north shore, has picnic facilities, Japanese and herb gardens, the oldest urban bird sanctuary in the United States (1879), frequent music events, and boat rentals at the **Sailboat House** (568 Bellevue St., tel. 510/444–3807). For $6–$8 an hour (plus a $10 deposit) you can paddle a canoe on the lake; sailboats are $6–$12 an hour (plus $20 deposit). Also on the north side of the lake is **Children's Fairyland** (Grand and Bellevue Aves., tel. 510/238–6876), a storybook theme park for children with rides, puppet shows, trippy mushroom-, whale-, and shoe-shaped buildings, and other miniature delights. Walt Disney even visited Fairyland to gather ideas for his own theme parks. Unfortunately, you need a kid to enter the park—though it never hurts to ask—but you can see snippets of the fairytale buildings from outside the fence.

Grand Avenue, which runs into the north tip of the lake, is also a good place for a stroll, with a number of reasonably good ethnic restaurants and cafés, including **The Grand Bakery** (3264 Grand Ave., tel. 510/465–1110), which makes great breads, pastries, and kosher treats, and **The Coffee Mill** (3363 Grand Ave., tel. 510/465–4224), which claims to be Oakland's oldest coffeehouse and hosts readings and concerts. Across the street is **Walden Pond** (*see* Books, in Chapter 3), a nice little bookstore that also hosts poetry readings. On your way back to the lake, peek inside the **Grand Lake Theatre** (*see* Movie Houses, in Chapter 6), an art deco movie palace where an enormous chandelier and grand staircase remain from the 1920s. The theater now shows first-run movies on four screens. For information on the **Festival at the Lake** and the **Juneteenth Festival** that take place here every summer, *see* Festivals, in Chapter 1. To reach the south of the park, walk 3 blocks northeast from Lake Merritt BART station. To reach the north of the lake and Grand Avenue, take BART to 19th Street and walk east.

JACK LONDON SQUARE Although born in San Francisco, Jack London spent his early years in Oakland before shipping out on the adventures that inspired *The Call of the Wild, The Sea Wolf,* and *The Cruise of the Snark.* In an effort to make a buck and draw a Fisherman's Wharf–type crowd to the waterfront, Oakland created Jack London Square at the end of Broadway, west of downtown. Though several years ago the project resembled a ghost town with more FOR LEASE signs than tenants, the buildings have slowly been filled by the likes of specialty shops, boutiques, pricey eateries, cheap chain restaurants, a huge Barnes and Noble bookstore, and purveyor of reasonably priced liquids, Beverages & More. Weekends at the square can even be downright bustling these days with the Sunday Farmer's Market (10–2), a variety of performers on the small stage, and the recently open **Jack London Cinema** (100 Washington St., tel. 510/433–1320), which features first-run films. It is expected that the jazz club **Yoshi's** (*see* Live Music, in Chapter 6) will move here in early '97, and city planners hope that Jack London Square will become an "entertainment district" of sorts.

The public library's Oakland History Room (125 14th St., tel. 510/451–8218) has a collection of letters and photographs of Jack London, as well as wonderful photos of Oakland's early, more glamorous days.

Somewhat scant remnants of the square's namesake include **Heinhold's First and Last Chance Saloon** (56 Jack London Sq., tel. 510/839–6761), the former hangout of Jack London, as well as Robert Louis Stevenson and Joaquin Miller. The proprietors will proudly tell you about the memorabilia on the walls and the crazily sloping floor (a result of the 1906 earthquake)—but if they were shooting for authenticity, they would have nixed the neon JACK LONDON RENDEZVOUS sign outside. Next door, you can look through the window of a reassembled (and often litter strewn) cabin that Jack once spent a winter in—when it was in Alaska. Also near the saloon is the tiny **Jack London Museum** (Suite 104, tel. 510/451–8218), displaying a small collection of Jack-related artifacts ($1 donation requested).

MUSEUMS

Oakland has a number of excellent museums. In particular, stop by the **Ebony Museum of Art** (30 Jack London Sq., Suite 208–209, tel. 510/763–0745), which features work by African and African American artists. It's open Tuesday–Saturday 11–6, Sunday noon–5, and admission is free. Also free is the **Creative Growth Art Center** (355 24th St., tel. 510/836–2340), which displays arts and crafts by disabled artists. It's open weekdays 10–4, but closes one week out of every five for installation, so call ahead.

AFRICAN AMERICAN MUSEUM AND LIBRARY This branch of the Oakland public library focuses on the history of people of African descent in North America, with a special emphasis on Oakland and the Bay Area. The collection includes original manuscripts, photos, journals, audio tapes, and photographs of Bay Area residents, as well as special exhibits and a reference library for those interested in learning more about the history of black Americans. *5606 San Pablo Ave., at 56th St., tel. 510/597–5053. Open Tues. 11:30–7, Wed., Thurs., and Sat. 10–5:30, Fri. noon–5:30. From downtown, Bus 72 north on Broadway.*

OAKLAND MUSEUM This well-designed building, a few blocks from Lake Merritt, houses collections on the environment, history, and art of California. On the ground floor, the **Gallery of Natural Sciences** offers a simulated walk through the state's eight biotic zones and a view of the plants and animals in each; if the stuffed animals don't intrigue you, perhaps the quotes by eminent scientists and writers hanging overhead will. The **Cowell Hall of California History,** on the second floor, puts today's multicultural population in context. It documents the rise and fall of the Ohlone Native American people (the region's first inhabitants), the Spanish settlers, the suburban California dreamers, the 1967 "Summer of Love" (with hippy clothing, protest flyers, relics from the Beat scene, and Country Joe McDonald's guitar), and tackles present day issues of urban violence. The third floor **Gallery of California Art** showcases paintings, sculpture, crafts, and installations by international and local artists. Exhibits in 1997 will include "Hello Again" (Feb. 8–July 27), featuring all sorts of works created from recycled materials, the unusual furniture art of John Cederquist (Sept. 13–Dec. 14), and "Memory and Imagination" (Mar. 15–July 20), paintings and artifacts by the influential Konkow Maidu Indian artist Frank Day. Spend some time walking around the museum's terraced gardens and the nearby **Sculpture Court** (1111 Broadway) for a look at some surprisingly beautiful assemblages. *1000 Oak St., at 10th St., tel. 510/238–2200. 1 block east of Lake Merritt BART. Admission: $5, $3 students; free Sun. 4–7. Open Wed.–Sat. 10–5, Sun. noon–7. Wheelchair access.*

CHEAP THRILLS

No one ever said Oakland had the most picturesque downtown area, so if you need to get away from the bus exhaust fumes, stop by the **Oakland Rose Garden,** off Monte Vista Avenue about a mile northeast of Lake Merritt. The steeply terraced garden may not be as densely planted as the Berkeley Rose Garden (*see above*), but it's still a sublimely mellow place for a picnic.

Mountain View Cemetery (Piedmont Ave., tel. 510/658–2588) is another peaceful Oakland escape populated by the dearly departed, joggers, cyclists, and families feeding the ducks. Designed by Frederick Law Olmsted (of Central Park fame), it is open to strollers daily 8–5. Head uphill to see the ornate crypts of Oakland's powerful/wealthy citizens such as Anthony Chabot, former mayor Samuel Merritt, and Francis "Borax" Smith—this prime burial real estate commands excellent views. Free tours are offered at 10 AM on the second Saturday of each month. The adjacent **Chapel of the Chimes** (4499 Piedmont Ave.) seems part mausoleum, part greenhouse, and part library with its many fountains, glass roof, ornate detailing, and rows of urns displayed like books inside glass-enclosed cases.

Dying for a day at the beach but can't stand the thought of fighting the traffic to Marin County? Zip on over to **Robert Crown Memorial State Beach,** a long, thin slice of sand bordered by a swath of grassy picnic areas. The beach is in Alameda, a naval town that seems to be in a '50s timewarp. Located across the estuary from Oakland, Alameda is in shock due to the imminent closing of its naval base. The beach is in better shape than the local economy—though just barely. The sand is a bit mucky in spots and you get a view of South San Francisco instead of the pounding Pacific, but it's only a 10-minute drive from downtown Oakland and it's also one of the few places where you can safely swim in the bay. Parking is $3, but you can park for free anywhere along Shoreline Drive, which parallels the beach. To get here from downtown, drive south on Broadway, go through the Webster Street tube to Alameda, continue on Hwy. 61, turn right on 8th Street, and look for the sign. Or take Bus 51 south on Broadway from downtown to Webster and Santa Clara streets, then walk a ¼ mile west to the water.

Marin County

Just across the Golden Gate Bridge, Marin is the state's richest county, an upscale playground for children old enough to remember Woodstock. Everywhere you turn you'll see an odd combination of hippie ideals and yuppie wealth. Expensive estates are buffered by ragged log cabins and Porsches and BMWs park next to aging Volvo station wagons and VW vans.

The reason so many '60s-refugees-turned-'80s-success-stories want to live here—and the reason you'll want to visit despite the price tag—is Marin's incredible natural beauty. The stunning ocean views of western Marin give way to thick redwood forests along Mount Tamalpais. On the steep eastern side of the mountain are perched small, woodsy towns, including Mill Valley. You could spend a lifetime describing the pleasures of hiking in Muir Woods and the Point Reyes National Seashore, and it's hard to act blasé about the view from **Highway 1**, no matter how many times you've seen it.

Filmmaker George Lucas makes his home on Lucas Valley Road in Marin County. Believe it or not, that was the name of the road before George built Skywalker Ranch on it.

Marin's upscale, touristed bayside towns, like Tiburon and Sausalito, are tougher for the budget-conscious visitor to love. You'll have to pick your way through an ostentatious show of wealth to find a cheap organic grocery store where you can stock up on supplies for your hike; an isolated, sunny field hospitable to Frisbee; or an unpretentious restaurant that serves reasonably priced seafood. But these things do exist. Another aspect that keeps both locals and international tourists coming back is that even the most bucolic corners of Marin are little more than two hours from San Francisco (except during rush hour, when it can take nearly an hour just to cross the bridge).

Marin's jaw-dropping scenery will constantly make you want to pull over on the roadside to take in the view. You can make as many pit stops as you'd like if you leave the car behind and bike across the Golden Gate Bridge from San Francisco. After sweating up some steep hills, treat yourself to a ferry ride back to the city from Sausalito or Tiburon. If you opt for public transportation in this area, be forewarned of its complexity.

Marin Headlands

For a quick taste of what Marin County has to offer nature freaks, cross the Golden Gate Bridge, exit at Alexander Avenue, and drive up Conzelman Road to the Marin Headlands. Consisting of several small but steep bluffs overlooking San Francisco Bay and the Pacific Ocean, the undeveloped, 1,000-acre headlands are a great place to snap a few photos or while away an afternoon. Thick fog often whips across the headlands, obscuring everything but the top of the towers of the Golden Gate Bridge but, on a sunny day, the views of downtown San Francisco, the East Bay, and Point Reyes to the north are stunning. Hundreds of hiking and biking trails meander along the wind-beaten hills and cliffs (*see* Chapter 8).

The headlands were used as a military camp in the late 19th century, and during World War II emplacements were dug for huge naval guns to protect the approaches to the bay. The guns are long gone, but several overgrown concrete batteries still stand watch along the coast. One of the most impressive, Battery Wallace, is off Conzelman Road before you reach the Point Bonita Lighthouse. The two forbidding concrete structures you see today, once the site of 12-inch guns aimed 17 miles out to sea, are only part of the structure: They are connected by an inac-

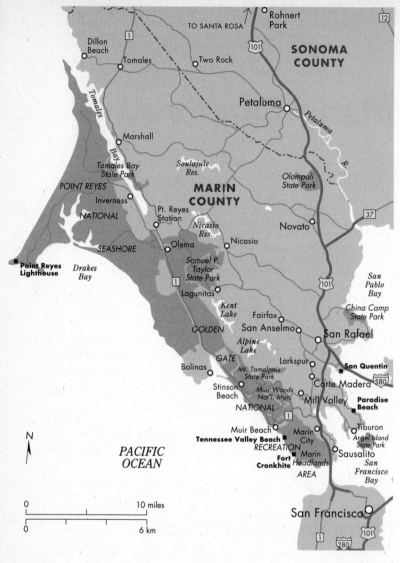

Marin County

cessible series of underground rooms used to hold troops and supplies. Call or stop by the Marin Headlands Visitor's Center (Field and Bunker Rds., tel. 415/331–1540) and pick up the free "Park Events" brochure or the almost indispensable map and guide to historic sites and wildlife ($1.60). Note that some trails (particularly the Miwok Trail) may be closed due to fires in fall 1995; call for details.

About a mile past the visitor's center (follow signs from Bunker Rd.) is the **Marine Mammal Center.** The center rehabilitates and rescues suffering marine mammals including sea lions, dolphins and whales. One of the more famous "rescuees" was Humphrey, an endangered humpback who was stuck in the mud for three days. Over 600 volunteers help operate the center alongside veterinary and medical staff. Docents will happily discuss this elephant seal's skin disease or that harbor seal's malnutrition while you watch the noisy critters flop around their pens. *Tel. 415/289–7325. Suggested donation: $1.*

Sausalito

Only a few miles north of San Francisco, Sausalito flourished during the 1880s and '90s as a small whaling town, infamous for its saloons, gambling dens, and bordellos. It had a reputation as the sort of place where sailors and riffraff could get drunk and cause trouble on the docks. Even after it became suburbanized in the 1940s, the town continued to attract an off-beat and raffish element, becoming a well-known artists' colony. Over the years, however, Sausalito's wharf rats have been replaced by a new sort of rat—lawyers and investment bankers—and this is now a bland, wealthy resort town, popular with yachters and San Francisco's upwardly mobile crowd. If you have unlimited time to explore the Bay Area, Sausalito is worth a gander, but don't go out of your way. Parking is next to impossible, shops and restaurants are shockingly expensive, and you have to dodge camera-toting tourists who fill the sidewalks and streets.

Still, Sausalito makes a reasonably good place to while away an afternoon (preferably a weekday) eating a picnic lunch while you watch the yachts drift by. **Stuffed Croissant** (43 Caledonia St., 1 block inland from Bridgeway, tel. 415/332–7103) sells an eclectic mix of mammoth scones ($1.95) and Indian food (curry chicken, $5.50), that you can eat in or take down to the waterfront. Health-conscious do-it-yourselfers should stop at the excellent **Real Food Store** (200 Caledonia St., tel. 415/332–9640).

Bridgeway is Sausalito's main thoroughfare, bordered on one side by waterfront restaurants and the bay, on the other by shops hawking pricey antiques or tacky pelican paperweights. At the south end of Bridgeway is the Sausalito Ferry Terminal, where the commuter ferry from San Francisco docks (*see* Getting In, Out, and Around, in Chapter 1). Farther south—near the end of Bridgeway at Richardson Street—is Sausalito's oldest restaurant, originally known as **Valhalla.** Built in 1893, it was used as a backdrop in the classic Orson Welles film *The Lady From Shanghai.* Today it's just a Chart House restaurant with fantastic views and expensive meals.

During the Great Depression, a local grocer graciously honored his customers' credit, preventing countless Sausalito residents from going hungry. Today, Yee Tock Chee Park stands as a monument to him, where Bridgeway meets the bay.

About a mile north on Bridgeway, look for the **Bay Model,** an enormous working model of San Francisco Bay and the Sacramento–San Joaquin Delta. Don't expect a cute replica of Coit Tower—this is strictly a scientific tool, used by the U.S. Army Corps of Engineers to study the tides and other forces affecting the bay. The detail of the model is amazing, right down to ebbing tides, actual South Bay mud flats, and rivers that flow at one-tenth of their actual velocity. *2100 Bridgeway, tel. 415/332–3871. Admission free. Open summer, Tues.–Fri. 9–4, weekends 10–6; fall–spring, Tues.–Sat. 9–4.*

Tiburon and Angel Island

Some folks come to Tiburon, a peninsula jutting into the bay just north of Sausalito, with picnic baskets in hand and set out their spread on the harbor-front lawns. Others dock their boats at the harbor and head to one of the many waterside restaurants. Do both these things and you'll have just about exhausted the possibilities here. The atmosphere is relaxed and the views of Angel Island and San Francisco are great, but the small cluster of gift shops and pricey boutiques housed in wooden shingle buildings along the waterfront will soon seem cloying. To rise above the strip of tourist shops on Main Street (both literally and figuratively), head up the hill to **Old St. Hilary's Historic Preserve,** which stands in a field of wildflowers on a lonely perch above town. The white, wooden carpenter Gothic church is run by the Landmarks Society as a historical and botanical museum. Come in May or June to see the rare black jewel wildflowers in bloom. *At top of Esperanza St., tel. 415/435–2567. Admission free. Open Apr.–Oct., Wed. and Sun. 1–4.*

Most of the restaurants and boutiques are on Main Street or on tree-lined Ark Row, which veers westish at the end of Main Street. For less expensive delis and grocery stores, look on Tiburon

Boulevard a few blocks from the waterfront. If you can't afford any wine to pack in your picnic basket, make a pre-picnic stop at **Windsor Vineyards** (72 Main St., tel. 415/435–3113), where you can sample up to six of their Russian River Valley wines for free. Some bottles sell for as little as $7.

If Tiburon is about to quaint you to death, take the 15-minute ferry ride to **Angel Island**—a 750-acre state park within spitting distance of the Golden Gate Bridge. The island used to be covered with eucalyptus groves, but in June of 1996 the park set in motion a controversial effort to eradicate all the nonnative flora. Park officials assure visitors that the island will soon return to native species, and eucalyptus or no, the surrounding view is stunning. **Ayala Cove,** the area around the ferry landing, is congested with picnickers taking advantage of tables and barbecue grills. The 5-mile perimeter road that rings the island offers access to plenty of scenic and historic sites (*see* Chapter 8), as well as plenty of tourists. Happily, it's easy to escape the crowds: For the ultimate isolated picnic, schlep your stuff about a mile from Ayala Cove to **Camp Reynolds,** which functioned as an army camp from the Civil War to World War II. Plenty of people linger at the Commanding Officer's House along the road, but about a ¼-mile past the old army barracks at the water's edge, you'll find some isolated picnic tables and an outstanding close-up view of the Golden Gate Bridge. Camping on the island is also an option (*see* Chapter 7).

On the other side of the island is **Immigration Station,** once known as "The Ellis Island of the West," where immigrants (mostly Asian) were detained when trying to enter the United States between 1910 and 1940. A few poems written by despairing detainees are still etched into the walls. A **visitor center** at Ayala Cove (tel. 415/435–1915) distributes a brochure with a history of the island and a map ($2).

COMING AND GOING To get to Tiburon, exit U.S. 101 at Tiburon Boulevard and drive 3 miles to the tip of the peninsula, where Main Street curves to the right. Ferries (tel. 415/435–2131) leave for Angel Island from Tiburon's Main Street Pier (21 Main St.) at 10 and 11 AM and 1 and 3 PM on spring and summer weekdays, and every hour from 10 to 5 on spring and summer weekends. Boats depart from Angel Island 20 minutes after they dock. Round-trip fares are $5, plus $1 for bicycles (no cars). Schedules are subject to change, so call ahead for the latest. Ferries also leave from Fisherman's Wharf in San Francisco in summer (*see* Getting In, Out, and Around, in Chapter 1). For information on bike rental on the island, *see* Chapter 8.

Mill Valley

Mill Valley, accessible via the East Blithedale exit from U.S. 101, is a community of millionaires and mountain bikers set amid the California redwoods on the eastern slope of Mt. Tamalpais. It's a mellow town where people have paid enormous sums of money for their solitude and want to keep it that way.

On weekends all the action is on the plaza at the corner of Miller Street and Throckmorton Avenue, where people play Hacky Sack and drink coffee bought at one of the three nearby coffeehouses. The best of the lot is the **Depot Bookstore & Café** (87 Throckmorton Ave., at Miller St., tel. 415/383–2665), a favorite of mountain bikers after a run down Mt. Tam. After you're properly wired, walk less than a block to **Village Music** (9 E. Blithedale Ave., at Throckmorton Ave., tel. 415/388–7400). John Goddard has run the record shop, which stocks almost exclusively vinyl, for more than 25 years. The store has become a landmark on the international music map, attracting many big-name customers. A local waiter boasts of having run into Mick Jagger outside Village Music one day. No guarantees of similar brushes with greatness, but the store's well worth a visit, if only to look at the memorabilia papering the walls. Consider sticking around Mill Valley after sunset to pay a visit to **Sweetwater** (153 Throckmorton Ave., at Madrona Ave., tel. 415/388–2820), a tiny club that attracts some of the finest jazz and R&B talents in the country. On any given night local resident Huey Lewis or bluesman Roy Rogers might show up to jam. Covers range from about $5 to $25 (plus a 2-drink minimum).

If you've come to enjoy more pastoral pursuits, take a "walk around the block," Mill Valley-style: The short **Three Wells** and **Cascade Falls** walks follow a gentle uphill route through the redwoods, along a creek, past more than one righteous and frigid swimming hole, to a small waterfall. To get here, walk or drive up Throckmorton and turn left on Cascade Drive until you see the THREE WELLS sign nailed to a tree. Follow the path starting at the sign for about ¼-mile, cross the street, and continue uphill at the CASCADES FALLS sign.

San Rafael

Unassuming San Rafael, set between the foot of Mt. Tamalpais and San Rafael Hill, would attract more day-trippers from foggy San Francisco if people realized it's almost always warmer here than elsewhere in the Bay Area. In fact, that's exactly why the town was founded in the first place. In 1817, when Native Americans at San Francisco's Mission Dolores started dying at an alarming rate, missionaries built a hospital here so the sick could receive care in a more hospitable climate. The original buildings of the Mission San Rafael Archangel were torn down in the 1870s, but a replica of the **chapel** (cnr 5th and A Sts.), built of stuccoed concrete instead of the original adobe, now sits next to a gift shop selling Catholic kitsch. A block away from the chapel, **4th Street** is the town's main drag, lined with used bookstores, a large contingent of department stores, and some good cafés. The best of the latter are **New George's** (842 4th St., at Cijos, tel. 415/457–1515) and **Cafe Kaldi** (835 4th St., at Cijos, tel. 415/457–6562): Both placed for "Best Nightlife in Marin." At New George's check out the live jazz, R&B, and acoustic entertainment, as well as New George's Cafe (tel. 415/454–1668), which serves an assortment of burgers and sandwiches. Airy Cafe Kaldi stays open late (midnight Sun.–Thurs., and 2 AM Fri.–Sat.) and serves up sandwiches ($5) and espresso to the local skater contingent. The best time to pay a visit to San Rafael is on summer Thursday evenings, when the **Farmers' Market** (tel. 415/457–2266) fills 4th Street around B Street. The market is more like a weekly block party than a simple produce sale; locals come in droves to buy handicrafts, listen to live music, and let the kids take pony rides.

Fourth Street is so quintessentially American that George Lucas used it as a backdrop for some scenes in his film "American Graffiti," based on his teenage years in Modesto.

North of downtown—take North San Pedro Road exit off U.S. 101—the enormous pink and blue **Marin Civic Center** (3501 Civic Center Dr., tel. 415/499–7407) offers guided tours (reserve ahead) of its impressive complex, designed by architect Frank Lloyd Wright. Concerned with preserving the natural contours of the site, Wright integrated the buildings into the surrounding landscape. The inside has been heralded as one of the most functional and offbeat office spaces ever conceived. There's a well-stocked information kiosk in the lobby (open weekdays 8–6) for walk-in visitors. For information on dance and drama performances in the adjoining theater, call 415/472–3500.

When concrete gets tiring, drive 4 miles east on North San Pedro Road to **China Camp State Park,** a beautiful 1,600-acre wilderness area on the fringe of civilization. Somehow this pristine slice of nature has remained undeveloped and unpublicized. Remnants of an old Chinese fishing village are still visible, and the oak knolls and saltwater marshes are great for hiking and camping (*see* Chapter 7). Parking at China Camp Point begins a 5-mile hike along the well-marked **Shoreline Trail.** The steeper **Bay View Trail** is an uncrowded favorite of park rangers. Pick up a trail map from the **ranger station** (tel. 415/456–0766) about a mile from the park entrance on North San Pedro Road. Parking is $3.

Muir Woods and Mt. Tamalpais

MUIR WOODS NATIONAL MONUMENT Judging from the crowded parking lot and tacky gift shop, the Muir Woods National Monument looks like just another overtouristed attraction to be avoided. This 550-acre park, however, contains one of the most impressive groves of coastal redwoods in the world, some more than 250 feet tall and over 800 years old. It's crowded, to be sure, but you can find rugged, unpopulated trails that meander along cool, fern-filled ridges high above the clogged canyon. The **Ocean View Trail,** one of the best for beating the crowds, ascends for 1¼ miles before connecting with the **Lost Trail,** which descends through forests of Douglas fir back into the redwoods. Lost Trail hooks up with **Fern Creek Trail,** taking you back to the parking lot. The moderate hike is 3 miles round-trip and passes some of the park's most impressive redwoods and many little streams. (For more trail tips, *see* Hiking, in Chapter 8).

Neither picnicking nor camping is allowed in the park, but snacks are available at the gift shop, along with every type of redwood souvenir imaginable. The **visitor center** (tel. 415/388–2595) organizes free nature walks through the woods; call for current schedules. From U.S. 101, take the Stinson Beach/Hwy. 1 exit and follow signs. The monument is open daily 8 AM–sunset, and parking is free, though on sunny weekends, Muir Woods is so crowded you may have to park a mile or more from the lot.

MUIR BEACH If you stick to Hwy. 1 instead of following the turnoff to Muir Woods, you come to **Muir Beach,** a quiet strip of sand cluttered with oddly shaped pieces of driftwood and hundreds of tidal pools. The strikingly scenic beach, the site of the first coastal settlement north of San Francisco, attracts folks looking to relax—not the Budweiser and volleyball crowd you'll find at Stinson Beach, 6 miles farther north.

If you really want to get a feel for Marin's landscape, park your car at Muir Beach and hike the **Coastal Trail** (*see* Hiking, in Chapter 8), which leads up a steep hill overlooking the ocean and crawls around a series of deserted coves and valleys. Return the same way and reward yourself with a pint of Guinness in front of the fire at the **Pelican Inn** (Hwy. 1 at Muir Beach, tel. 415/383–6000). You can eat lunch here for under $10—the cottage pie ($6.50) is excellent—but dinners run about $20. The dining room closes 3 PM–6 PM, but the adjoining pub, serving a healthy sampling of British ales and bitters, is open 11–11 every day but Monday, when both the pub and the restaurant are closed. There's a stone fireplace in the wood-paneled dining room and a dart board in the pub. Upstairs are seven Tudor-style rooms ($143–$165 a night) filled with antiques and canopied beds—about as atmospheric and romantic as they come. Ask the innkeeper about renting horses from the nearby stables: You can arrange moonlit gallops along the beach.

Less than a mile south of Stinson Beach, the **Green Gulch Farm Zen Center** (1601 Shoreline Hwy., tel. 415/383–3134) is worth a short visit, or, depending on your location on the path to

John Muir Demurs

It is somewhat ironic that Muir Woods—admittedly beautiful but annoyingly paved and crowded—should be named for John Muir (1838–1914). It's true enough that this naturalist and conservationist is largely responsible for the existence of his namesake national monument—he had a talent for gaining the favor of rich and powerful men who had the pull to preserve old-growth forests. But somehow you get the idea that Muir wouldn't be entirely happy about this slice of nature packaged neatly for your viewing pleasure. After all, Muir was a mountain man. He was so entranced with the awesome power of nature that, during the middle of a fierce storm in the Sierra Nevada, he climbed to the top of a wildly swaying Douglas Spruce to get his "ear close to the Æolian music of its topmost needles." What, then, would Muir, a tree hugger in the most literal sense of the word, think of the national monument's Cathedral Grove, where railings keep you from touching the trees and signs politely request that you not stray from the paths? Namesake or no, he would probably split for Mt. Tam.

spiritual enlightenment, a seven-week stay for intensive Zen training (*see* Chapter 7). The center offers classes in everything from walking meditation to Japanese tea ceremonies to gardening. (Green Gulch supplies organic produce to the famous vegetarian restaurant Greens, among other places.) One of the most popular activities here is the weekly Sunday program: instruction, meditation, a lecture, tea, a discussion period, and lunch ($5 donation). Even if you're not seeking instruction, you're welcome to wander the idyllic grounds and gardens. On Sundays between 8:45 AM and 10:30 AM, expect to pay a $5 parking fee unless you have three or more people in your car; another option is to carpool, as many people do, from the Manzanita Commuter Parking Lot underneath the Stinson Beach/Hwy. 1 exit off U.S. 101 (look for someone holding a GREEN GULCH CARPOOLING sign).

MT. TAMALPAIS STATE PARK There are several theories about the origin of the name Tamalpais, but the most commonly accepted one is that it is a combination of the Coastal Miwok words *tammal* (bay country) and *plis* (mountain). A good starting point for your exploration is the **Pantoll Ranger Station** (tel. 415/388–2070), where you can buy a $1 topo map of Mt. Tam with all the trails and roads clearly shown. Mountain biking is big here, and the map distinguishes the fire trails (where biking is allowed) from the walking trails (where biking nets you a fat $100-plus fine). One beautiful, strenuous, and popular hike, the 2-mile **Steep Ravine Trail** (*see* Hiking and Biking, in Chapter 8), starts from the Pantoll station and takes you down a series of ladders to the Steep Ravine cabins. Parking is $5 in the Pantoll parking lot, but you can park for free anywhere along the road. The place is packed on weekends, so you'll have trouble parking if you're not there before noon.

The **summit** of Mt. Tam can be reached by car (look for the turnoff opposite Pantoll station), and the gates are open dawn to dusk. Unfortunately, the military owned the summit until recently and left the kind of squat buildings and strange towers that only the military seems to build. According to one park aide, there are several full-size bowling alleys in one of the buildings (and no, you can't have a game). Also near the summit is the open-air **Mountain Theater** where, every summer for six consecutive Sundays, a play or musical is produced. Ask at the Pantoll station for performance and ticket information ($13–$18), or call 415/383–1100.

Stinson Beach

Six treacherous miles north of Muir Beach on Hwy. 1 lies Stinson Beach, one of the most popular coastal towns in Northern California. It's loaded with rickety wooden houses and friendly general stores, and its 3-mile-long beach—the longest in Marin County—has a beach-bum and barbecue appeal that's hard to find north of Santa Cruz. Despite Stinson's isolated location, the chilly water temperatures, and the threat of sharks lurking offshore, hordes of surfers and sun worshipers descend every weekend upon this town of 1,200. (For surfboard rental, *see* Surfing, in Chapter 8.) Even if you're not planning to surf or swim, the 20-minute (10-mile) drive from Muir Woods to Stinson, past towering cliffs and jagged granite peaks, is incredible. For groceries, stop by the **Beckers' by the Beach** (101 Calle del Mar, tel. 415/868–1923), next to the stop sign on Hwy. 1. Traffic can be a problem on summer weekends, but there are plenty of scenic overlooks along the way to cushion the blow of bumper-to-bumper traffic. To reach Stinson Beach by bus (weekends and holidays only), take Golden Gate Transit Bus 20 to Marin City from the Transbay Terminal in S.F. and transfer to Bus 63.

Along Bolinas Lagoon, just north of Stinson on Hwy. 1, you'll find the **Audubon Canyon Ranch** (tel. 415/868–9244). On weekends and holidays between mid-March and mid-July, this 1,000-acre bird sanctuary and ranch (and its 10 or so hiking trails) is open to the public from 10 to 4, offering bird lovers a chance to get up close and personal with blue herons and egrets. There's a small museum ($5 donation suggested) with geological and natural-history displays, a bookstore, gift shop, and a picnic area.

For a different slice of nature, walk down to **Red Rocks Beach** where, during extremely low tides, caves containing hot springs are revealed—as well as the bare buns of bathers. Even when the caves are concealed by water, the beach is peopled by nudists who one local claims are "the epitome of hipness." Leave your inhibitions in the car. To get here, drive ¾ mile south of Stinson Beach and park in the big gravel lot you'll see on the right (it's often full on sunny weekends). A path leads from there down to the beach.

Bolinas

A few miles north of the Audubon Canyon Ranch (*see above*), lies Bolinas, a town dedicated to discouraging tourism. Need proof? Locals are so tenacious about taking down the sign marking the Bolinas/Olema Road (it's the first left after you curve around the lagoon to your left), it's become a local legend. If you breeze into town to wander Main Street and do some shopping, you'll feel tolerated at best—locals loathe the idea of tacky Sausalito-style development. **Fourth of July** brings out the town's friendliest faces; past festivities have included outrageous parades and a tug-of-war with Stinson Beach (the loser ended up in the muddy mouth of the estuary between the two towns). One local described Bolinas as the "Zen-purity, earth-magnet, long-hair, free-to-do-what-you-want place to be, man," but a walk past the town's million-dollar homes makes you wonder how much residents really champion the ideals of the '60s.

Despite the wealth, you'll still find a few VW buses and bearded radicals strumming their guitars on street corners. The **Bolinas People's Store** (14 Wharf Rd., at Brighton Ave., tel. 415/868–1433) is famous for its fresh, high-quality local produce, grown by the same sweaty hippies who once gave Bolinas so much of its character. For a bite to eat, go next door to the **Bolinas Bay Bakery and Café** (20 Wharf Rd., tel. 415/868–0211), which offers fresh baked goods, pasta salads, and pizzas. Many items feature locally grown organic ingredients. The only nightlife in town is a few doors down at **Smiley's Schooner Saloon** (41 Wharf Rd., at Brighton Ave., tel. 415/868–1311), ostensibly the oldest continually operated saloon in California. Huddled around the pool table and jukebox are an odd combination of suit-and-tie professionals and tie-dyed fringies.

If the smell of patchouli is fraying your nerves, take Mesa Road 4½ miles north from the second stop sign on Bolinas/Olema Road to the **Point Reyes Bird Observatory** (tel. 415/868–0655), which harbors 225 species of birds. It's open year-round and admission is free. On your way, make the mile-long detour to **Duxberry Reef,** a peaceful breaker that's dotted with hundreds of tidal pools. To get there, go left on Overlook Drive from Mesa Road and right on Ocean Park Way. For hikes in this area, *see* Chapter 8.

Point Reyes National Seashore

Exploring the Point Reyes National Seashore—a 66,500-acre mosaic of marshes, ferocious cliffs, and undisturbed beaches—you'll feel a lot farther than 30 miles away from San Francisco, and for good reason. Point Reyes is on the Pacific tectonic plate, while most of the rest of California is on the North American Plate—as a result, its bedrock, plants, and the terrain are all very different from the rest of the Bay Area. Even though it's isolated, Point Reyes is a manageable day trip from San Francisco, a drive of about 90 minutes each way. There are hundreds of hiking trails on the peninsula (*see* Chapter 8) and, if you want to spend the night, four backpackers-only campgrounds and an excellent hostel (*see* Chapter 7).

With its lush grazing land and rambling farms, Point Reyes— a hammerhead-shaped peninsula that sticks 10 miles out into the ocean—could easily pass for western Ireland, minus the pubs.

Twelve miles north of Bolinas on Hwy. 1, past the block-long town of Olema, look for a sign marking the turnoff for Point Reyes at the end of the block of stores and head for the **Point Reyes Visitor Information Center** (tel. 415/663–1092) off Bear Valley Road. This is the best place to begin your exploration; you can sign up for ranger-led hikes or get trail maps and camping permits. A short walk away, look for the replica of a typical Coastal Miwok Native American village, built on the ruins of a 400-year-old Miwok farming settlement. Also nearby is the **Bear Valley Trail,** a lightly traveled 4-mile hike that wanders through the woods and down to a secluded beach offering a good overview of the peninsula.

Two miles farther down Bear Valley Road (which turns into Sir Francis Drake Boulevard), you'll pass through the quiet town of **Inverness.** Coming across this town's Czech restaurants and architecture—full of oddly colored, intricately carved wooden houses—can be disorienting after miles of uncluttered coast, but the town's Eastern European flavor is genuine. In 1935, after a freighter ran aground in San Francisco Bay, a number of its Czech deckhands jumped ship and settled here. Since then, dozens of Czech families have settled in Inverness, bringing both their culture and some of the best dumplings this side of Prague.

West of Inverness, at the end of Drake's Beach Road, which intersects Sir Francis Drake Boulevard, lies a massive stretch of white sand known as **Drake's Beach.** It's often windy here and too rough for swimming (plus great white sharks swim offshore), but the beach is great for relaxing in the sun. Supposedly, Sir Francis himself landed here on his world tour; hence the name. Check with the visitor center for current regulations; if they give the okay, there's plenty of driftwood on the beach for an early evening campfire.

A quarter mile north of Drake's Beach, a sign directs you to the **Point Reyes Lighthouse** (tel. 415/669–1534) 6 miles to the west. It's open Thursday–Monday 10–4:30, though closed during particularly windy weather, and admission is free. From the parking lot, a steep trail leads down to the lighthouse, and a dozen or so trails are etched into the surrounding cliffs. The ¾-mile hike to **Chimney Rock** is one of the most scenic; look for the trailhead in the parking lot. On clear days you can see San Francisco, but usually thick fog provides little visibility. From mid-December to April, and especially in January and March, this is a great place to look for the gray whales on their 12,000-mile round-trip migration along the Pacific coast.

To reach Point Reyes from San Francisco, cross the Golden Gate Bridge on U.S. 101. If speed is more important than scenery, exit at Sir Francis Drake Boulevard and follow it west for 21 miles to the coast. Eventually, you'll come to a "T" in the road and the town of Olema on Hwy. 1. Otherwise, take the Stinson Beach/Hwy. 1 exit and enjoy the curvy, 30-mile scenic drive along the coast. By bus (weekends only) take any Golden Gate Transit bus from the Transbay Terminal (1st and Mission Sts.) *except* Bus 10 to San Rafael (Bus 80 is the most direct) and transfer to Bus 65.

There aren't too many places to eat in Point Reyes, so stock up in San Francisco or at the **Bovine Bakery** (11315 Hwy. 1, 2 mi north of Olema, tel. 415/663–9420). They have excellent, reasonably priced sandwiches, pastries, and breads—the perfect fixings for a picnic. The most popular stop, however, is Inverness's **Perry's Delicatessen** (12301 Sir Francis Drake Blvd., near Vallejo Ave., tel. 415/663–1491). For under $6, you can brown-bag one of their shrimp or crab sandwiches and a pasta salad. Also in Inverness is the **Gray Whale Inn** (12781 Sir Francis Drake Blvd., tel. 415/669–1244), a good pit stop for home-style pizzas, pastries, sandwiches, coffee, and beer. It's more expensive than Perry's, but the sunny patio is a good place to watch day fade into night.

South Bay

Heading South on U.S. 101 brings both a change of scenery and pace. As the cosmopolitan frenzy of San Francisco fades away, you sense the bland surroundings of industrial parks, shopping malls, and tract housing. You've entered, not the Twilight Zone, but *suburbia*. But what do you expect from the diverse Bay Area? All of the aforementioned must exist somewhere. The South Bay has its own interesting, amusing, or just plain weird attractions that San Francisco snobs thoroughly underrate (or don't know about). The cities that stretch south from San Francisco to San Jose lie on what locals refer to as the **Peninsula,** a finger of land wedged between the San Francisco Bay on the east and the Pacific Ocean on the west; a number of cities, including Palo Alto—home to acclaimed Stanford University—make for easy day trips from San Francisco.

The best-kept secret of the South Bay is Hwy. 1 and the secluded **San Mateo County Coast**—more than 75 miles of winding shoreline and gently undulating hills that seem a world away from the overdeveloped inland communities. Along the highway are long, sandy beaches, frequently devoid of any life aside from the local sea lions, surfers, and gulls; small towns just beginning to awaken to their potential as tourist destinations; and redwood groves filled with great hiking trails. The only drag here is the weather: Though hilly inland areas like La Honda and Pescadero are nearly always cool to warm in spring and fall, and hot (but not oppressively so) in summer, the beaches more often than not are windswept and chilly—better suited for a brisk walk than an afternoon of sunbathing. The quickest way to reach the northern end of the San Mateo County Coast from San Francisco is to follow I–280 south to Hwy. 1; it'll only take 10–15 minutes to reach Pacifica from downtown. Public transportation is sketchy.

Palo Alto

Palo Alto, about 30 miles south of San Francisco, is mostly known as the location of Stanford University; it's certainly worth the drive just to check out the beautiful 8,200-acre campus. However, contrary to popular Bay Area opinion, the town of Palo Alto itself has some cultural attractions that are worth a look, as well as a cute, if overpriced, downtown area. Off U.S. 101, **University Avenue,** between Middlefield Road and High Street, is Palo Alto's main drag; west of El Camino Real it metamorphoses into **Palm Drive,** Stanford's entrance and main thorough-fare. University Avenue travels through Palo Alto's oldest and wealthiest neighborhood—keep your eyes peeled for mansions. In the downtown area, University Avenue and its side streets are loaded with restaurants, cafés, galleries, boutiques, and bookstores. All are disappointingly upscale for a student shopping district, but at least the streets are punctuated by pleasant lit-tle plazas with benches and plants.

As any Stanford student will lament, Palo Alto is seriously hurting in the nightlife department. To the rescue is the deliciously divey **Antonio's Nut House** (321 California Ave., at Birch St., tel. 415/321–2550), where you can get Guinness on tap ($3), free peanuts from the gorilla cage, and drinks until 2 AM nightly—a rarity around here. Most night crawlers head to San Francisco. When you're looking for that *other* buzz, head across the street to **Printer's Inc.** (310 California Ave., tel. 415/327–6500) and peruse the extensive 'zine selection (about 900 titles) while tossing back an espresso or three. On the other side of town, about a mile north of campus, **Café Borrone** (1010 El Camino Real, near Ravenswood Ave. in Menlo Park, tel. 415/327–0830), coupled with **Kepler's Books** (tel. 415/324–4321) next door, happily fuses caffeine and literature once again, attracting a yuppie college crowd that tends to sprawl out onto the brick patio. Dixieland jazz bands often play on weekend nights.

The huge, sprawling campus itself is best explored by bike, and the cycling is even better in the foothills west of the university. For rentals, try **Campus Bike Shop** (551 Salvatierra St., on campus, tel. 415/325–2945), which can get you rolling on a mountain bike for $15 or a three-speed for $8 per day. Either kind of bike requires a hefty cash, check, or credit card deposit.

STANFORD UNIVERSITY Sometimes called the Ivy League university of the West Coast, Stanford opened its doors to scholars in October 1891. Its cofounder, railroad mogul Leland Stanford, also served as governor and U.S. senator for California. Busy guy. Nicknamed "The Farm" because the land was once a stud farm (that's certainly no longer the case), Stanford consists of look-alike, mustard-colored buildings that combine Romanesque squatness with the ranchy feel of a Spanish mission, giving the campus an austere and refined flavor. Some of its more disenchanted students, however, refer to the university as an oversized Taco Bell.

From downtown, enter campus along the aptly named Palm Drive, which will take you to the **quad,** the heart of campus and a popular hangout. You can pick up free maps or take a guided walking tour from the **visitor center** (tel. 415/723–2560) in Memorial Hall. The hour-long tours leave from Memorial Hall at 11 and 3:15 daily. The quad is dominated by the sprightly, Romanesque **Memorial Church,** best known for its Venetian mosaics. Near the entrance to the quad, the grassy **Memorial Court** has a couple of Auguste Rodin statues—dedicated to Stanford men who died for their country—that depict 14th-century French martyrs, *The Burghers of Calais,* "at the moment of painful departure from their families and other citizens." A New Guinean **sculpture garden,** installed in 1995, can be found near the intersection of Lomita Drive and St. Theresa Street. Just to the south of the quad, the 280-foot **Hoover Tower** thrusts might-ily into the sky; home to the ultraconservative Hoover Institution for the Study of War, Revolution, and Peace. To get the classic view of campus and parts of Palo Alto, pay $2 to climb to the tower's observation deck, which offers an excellent 360° vista (open daily 9–4:30).

Rodin Sculpture Garden. For now, this is as close as you'll get to **Stanford's Museum of Art,** seriously damaged in the 1989 Loma Prieta earthquake. Expect the museum to reopen in the fall of 1998. The 20 or so works by French sculptor Auguste Rodin (1840–1917) are clustered in a small area to the left of the museum. Most pieces depict nudes in various stages of introspection, ecstasy, or anguish. Check out the particularly intense *Gates of Hell*; the giant iron doors are the scene of lots of wild action. The sculpture garden is open all hours, drawing late-night adventurers out to frolic with the lifelike figures. Descriptive tours are given at 2 PM Wednesday and on weekends; call for details. *Museum Way and Lomita Dr., tel. 415/723–3469. From Palm Dr., turn right on Museum Way, 1 block past Campus Dr.*

STANFORD LINEAR ACCELERATOR Even if you're only vaguely interested in science, make the trek up Sand Hill Road (west from campus toward I–280) to see this masterpiece of modern ingenuity. The 2-mile-long atom smasher is truly amazing—thousands of house-size machines, dials, diodes, and scientists who get excited when you mention n-orbits and electrons. Reserve space for the free two-hour tour, held twice a week, which includes a slide show and lecture (days and times vary); it's geared toward lay people and is extremely interesting. The accelerator is only open to the public during tour times. *2575 Sand Hill Rd., Menlo Park, tel. 415/926–2204. From I–280, exit east at Sand Hill Rd.*

BARBIE HALL OF FAME "Barbie mimics society; whatever we've done, she's done," says Evelyn Burkhalter, founder of the Barbie Hall of Fame. She's put together the largest collection of Barbie dolls on public display in the world, with 16,000 of the plastic bombshells in residence. Evelyn says that just about every fashion and lifestyle trend of the past few decades can be seen in these halls. Don't miss the infamous "talking-math Barbie," who says "math is *so hard*"—Mattel took a lot of heat from feminists for that one. *433 Waverly St., at University Ave. in Palo Alto, tel. 415/326–5841. Admission: $4. Open Tues.–Fri. 1:30–4:30, Sat. 10 AM–noon and 1:30–4:30.*

NEAR PALO ALTO

NASA AMES RESEARCH CENTER For a true technological trip, visit this 140-acre research center, devoted to the design of all types of flying machines, which is at Moffett Field in Mountain View (about 5 miles southeast of Palo Alto). The **NASA Visitor's Center Museum** (open weekdays 8–4:30) showcases aviation and space-flight paraphernalia, but the research facility itself is normally closed to the general public. The real score is to call two weeks ahead and sign up for one of the two or three escorted tours of the main plant they offer each week

Dying to Get to Colma

If you're driving south on I–280 to Palo Alto, you'll pass the small city of Colma, a modern-day necropolis filled with cemeteries and macabre graveyard art. In 1914, San Francisco's mayor ordered most city cemeteries to relocate their occupants to Colma, since the city needed the land for its more active residents. Since then, no new cemeteries have been created within San Francisco's city limits. The Colma Town Hall (1198 El Camino Real, at Serramonte Blvd., tel. 415/997–8300) offers a self-guided tour of the city's cemeteries ($2.50), from the prestigious Cypress Lawn to the eerie Pet's Rest, littered with flea collars and dog toys. Look for the graves of Dodge City's Wyatt Earp and a local baseball legend, former San Francisco Seals' manager Lefty O'Doul. Colma has more dead than living residents, the only such city in the US, although some might disparagingly claim this to be true of other South Bay towns.

(days and times vary). Depending on what's available that day, the two-hour free tour may take you around flight simulators, design centers, retired research crafts, or construction hangars. *Tel. 415/604–6274. From U.S. 101, exit at Moffett Field, left on Moffett Blvd. at main gate, and head toward space shuttle.*

San Jose

People are too hard on San Jose. True, Northern California's largest city is marked by the same minimall sprawl you'll find all over America. Emphatically middle-class, San Jose is the sort of charmless suburbia everyone loves to hate. Despite all this, San Jose has an oddly comfortable and cosmopolitan feel. Encircled by mountain ranges and buffered by city parks and gardens, San Jose is home to museums, symphonies, and wineries as well as industrial parks, computer companies, and corporate headquarters.

The new billion-dollar **downtown** is a good place to start exploring. Hop on the **Light Rail** (tel. 408/321–2300) that connects San Jose State University on one end with the Center for Performing Arts on the other (fare is $1.10); its numerous stops should give you a good overview of the city center, which is architecturally interesting in its—generally successful—attempt to meld existing Old West themes with modern styles and materials (note the traditional small-town clock tower built from marble and stainless steel). Cruising the heart of downtown, around the intersection of Market and San Carlos streets, there are a number of pedestrian plazas and a host of museums, including **The Tech** (145 W. San Carlos St., across from Convention Center, tel. 408/279–7150), a hands-on technology museum that definitely inspires admiration for the wizardry of the computer age; it's well worth the $6 admission. **Plaza de César Chavez** (S. Market St., in front of Fairmont Hotel) is a pleasant grassy strip that runs for 2 blocks, complete with benches and a fountain you can play in (the water shoots straight up out of grates in the ground).

The student population of San Jose State has gradually encouraged the growth of a trendier side of downtown that has become known as **SoFa** (South of First Street)—a small section of downtown roughly between East Carlos and West Reed streets. Make a beeline here if you find yourself in San Jose after dark; the rest of the city is infested with heavy metal discos and tedious sports bars. Join the hip, youngish crowd at **Café Matisse** (371 S. First St., at San Carlos St., tel. 408/298–7788), open daily until midnight, where you can sit back in one of the overstuffed chairs, nurse a latte ($2.50), and watch the people coming out of the tattoo parlor across the street.

San Jose's corporate image may overshadow its cultural diversity, but it does exist. The **San Jose America Festival** (tel. 408/534–4414) does its damnedest to convince you of this fact. Cultural groups from the area will be well-represented at this three-day July festival with live entertainment and crafts booths. On June 19th, the **Juneteenth Festival** (tel. 408/292–3157) showcases achievements of African Americans through lecture, cinema, art, and cultural foods. For a little hip action (literally) catch the **Tahiti Fête** (tel. 408/486–9177), a three-day dance competition in July that brings together Tahitian dance groups (*halaus*) from all over the Bay Area, and even draws dancers from as far as Hawaii. August nights heat up (as if it weren't already scorching) when the **San Jose Jazz Festival** (tel. 408/457–1141) rolls into town.

The **Rosicrucian Egyptian Museum and Planetarium** houses one of the most impressive collections of Egyptian, Assyrian, and Babylonian artifacts west of the Nile. Truly fascinating are the animal and human mummies, the underground tomb, and the decorative wall reliefs. The planetarium shows here also hold their own; call 408/947–3634 for show times and ticket prices. *1342 Naglee Ave., at Park Ave., tel. 408/947–3636. Get off I–880 at Alameda East exit, turn right at Naglee Ave. Admission: $6, $3.50 for ages 7–15, free for kids under 7. Open daily 9–5, last entry 4:35 PM.*

NEAR SAN JOSE

GARBAGE MUSEUM Californians generate more garbage per capita than any other group of people in the world, and this museum gives you some dramatic ways to feel guilty about it. The massive 100-foot "Wall of Garbage" exhibit represents merely one second's worth of what the country is continually throwing out. At least there's the Recycling Hall, where a huge magnet separates steel and iron from a mountain of tin cans. *1601 Dixon Landing Rd., Milpitas, tel. 408/432–1234. Take Dixon Landing exit off I-880, 5 mi north of San Jose; recyclery is visible from freeway. Admission free. Open weekdays 7:30–5.*

GREAT AMERICA If you've got the urge to spin around until you feel nauseous, eat gooey food, and buy tacky sunglasses, head to this Crayola-colored amusement park loaded with excellent roller coasters and hokey gift shops. It's owned by the Paramount/Viacom megacorporation, so you get movie-theme attractions like the **Days of Thunder** racing simulator and the **Top Gun Jet Coaster.** Popular favorites include the occasionally drenching water ride called **Logger's Run,** and the stand-up **Vortex** coaster, which cost a whopping $5 million to build. Newest is **The Drop Zone,** a 22 story free-fall drop guaranteed to bring your lunch up for an encore performance. To shave a few bucks off the price, call the number listed below and ask about any current discount schemes (usually by bringing a Coke can or a token from some fast-food restaurant). Another tip: They don't let people bring in food (so you'll be forced to buy their over-priced grease), but you *can* bring your own chow, leaving it in a locker near the front gate, and eat in the picnic area outside. *Great America Pkwy., Santa Clara, tel. 408/998–1776. Take Great America Pkwy. exit off U.S 101, about 10 mi north of San Jose. Admission: $28. Open spring and fall weekends; summer, daily 10–9 (Sat. until 11 PM).*

WINCHESTER MYSTERY HOUSE The continual construction of this 160-room Victorian mansion occupied Sarah Winchester's life for 38 years until her death. Apparently Mrs. Winchester was told by a fortuneteller to begin nonstop construction to placate the ghosts of those killed by Winchester guns. If she followed through with the project she would have eternal life. (Luckily her $20,000,000 inheritance was enough to fund her venture!) The end result was a floor plan so bizarre and complex that she and her servants got around using maps. On March 5, 1996, San Jose City Council designated the Winchester Mansion a city landmark. General building manager Keith Kittle was quoted in the *San Francisco Chronicle* as saying, "I think Sarah Winchester would be proud. We're going to have a seance and talk to her and see." *525 S. Winchester Blvd., tel. 408/247–2101. From I-280, take Stevens Creek exit to Winchester Blvd. Admission: $13. Open daily 9–5.*

The San Mateo County Coast

PACIFICA AND MONTARA

Pacifica and Montara—about 20 minutes south of San Francisco along Hwy. 1—mark the northern end of the spectacular, uncrowded San Mateo County Coast. Two sleepy seaside towns on a coastline known for its lethargy, Pacifica and Montara offer an easy escape from urban chaos. That's not to say, however, that they aren't without controversy. **Devil's Slide,** a spectacular stretch of Hwy. 1 between Pacifica and Montara, is determined to sink into the ocean while Bay Area environmentalists and coastal commuters battle hotly over a solution to this erosion problem—a bypass or tunnel has been proposed. Call 800/427–ROAD for the latest.

The "historic" section of Pacifica, located on the northernmost outskirts of town, is full of unpretentious, bungalow-style homes that once served as weekend retreats for wealthy San Franciscans but today house a majority of the town's locals. Pacifica's small commercial district, to the south, is an eclectic combination of old mom-and-pop stores and upscale specialty shops, the latter suggesting that the town is growing a little weary of its backwater authenticity and wants to start attracting some yuppie weekend tourists. Linking past and present are the recently renovated paved boardwalk and old fishing pier. Come here to smell the saltwater, feed the pigeons, and watch fishermen ply their trade; the pier also affords brilliant views of San Francisco and Marin County.

Pacifica's star attraction is its dark-sand beaches. About 2 miles south of old Pacifica is **Rockaway Beach,** consisting of two large dollops of sand on either end of a gorgeous cove—just large enough for half a dozen sunbathers and a handful of surfers and fishermen. The waves are pretty rough for swimming. Immediately south of Rockaway, you'll come to the more popular **Pacifica State Beach,** a longer stretch of sand favored by surfers and a fair number of local sun worshipers. Pacifica is also home to some fine hiking trails (*see* Chapter 8).

Just a few miles farther removed from San Francisco, Montara is pretty much all beach—its commercial district is virtually nonexistent. **Montara State Beach,** on the north end of town, 2 miles south of Devil's Slide, is a wide, picturesque stretch of sand, less crowded than Pacifica's beaches. It's a good place to catch some rays, play Frisbee, have a picnic, or walk along the beach. Half a mile farther north, **Gray Whale Cove State Beach** (tel. 415/728–5336) is an American anomaly: a government-supported clothing-optional beach. Entrance to the spectacular, secluded cove is $5 (or you can pay $175 for an annual pass). Keep your voyeuristic tendencies in check—cameras are strictly forbidden. Immediately south of the Montara city limits in Moss Beach, the rich tide pools of the **James V. Fitzgerald Marine Reserve** (tel. 415/728–3584) stretch along the coast for 4 miles. Go at low tide (call ahead to find out when) to check out abalone, barnacles, kelp, shells, and maybe an octopus or two; but remember, this is a reserve, so look, but don't touch. To reach the reserve from the Point Montara Lighthouse Hostel (*see* Chapter 7), where you can obtain a tidal timetable, take Hwy. 1 south to California Avenue and turn right. The beaches and reserve are open from dawn to dusk.

During Prohibition, the Moss Beach Distillery (Beach Way and Ocean Blvd., tel. 415/728–5595) served as a speakeasy roadhouse for politicians and silent film stars who came from San Francisco to drink bootlegged whiskey while enjoying the romantic ocean view over the cliffs.

For a meal in Pacifica, head straight to Francisco Boulevard, paralleling Hwy. 1 to the west. Here you'll find **Pacifica Thai Cuisine** (1966 Francisco Blvd., tel. 415/355–1678)—which features traditional specialties like chicken curry in coconut milk ($6)—and the oddly named **Pacifica Harry** (1780 Francisco Blvd., tel. 415/738–8300), an upscale Chinese restaurant with enticing entrées like cashew-nut shrimp ($8). Both restaurants have vegetarian options. In Montara, **A Coastal Affair** (Hwy. 1, at 8th St., tel. 415/728–5229), ⅓-mile north of the Point Montara Lighthouse Hostel (*see* Chapter 7), is a combination craft gallery and café with excellent espresso ($1.75–$2.75) and freshly made sandwiches (about $4). Half a mile south of the hostel in Moss Beach, **El Gran Amigo** (2448 Hwy. 1, at Virginia Ave., tel. 415/728–3815) serves up a wide variety of authentic Mexican specialties including enchiladas ($5) and nachos ($2.50). Across the street, **Coastside Market** (501 Virginia Ave., tel. 415/728–3142) is an amply stocked spot to buy picnic supplies.

Get to Pacifica and Montara via public transportation by taking BART to the Daly City or Colma station. From Daly City take SamTrans Bus 1L and from Colma take Bus 1C. Both bus lines will take you down Hwy. 1. Fares are $1.

HALF MOON BAY

Famous for growing Halloween pumpkins, Christmas trees, and flowers, Half Moon Bay—28 miles south of San Francisco—is the closest thing to a major town along the San Mateo County Coast. With its seaside/rural/small-town feel, immense surfing waves (*see box* Rebel Waves, in Chapter 8), natural beauty, and wealth of activities (well, compared to the other dinky villages around here), it's the most inviting of the coastal communities. The "revitalized" downtown area centers around **Main Street,** which parallels Hwy. 1; the cozy street is cluttered with craft stores, produce markets, gardens, cafés, and straightforward burger joints. If lolling on the beach is more your speed, follow Kelly Avenue west from Hwy. 1 to the popular **Half Moon Bay State Beach,** actually a series of beaches covering more than 2 miles. To avoid the $5 parking fee, walk from downtown. It will probably get chilly near the water before too long, a perfect excuse to trek 2 miles inland along Hwy. 92 and sample—for free—the local wines at **Obester Winery** (12341 San Mateo Rd., tel. 415/726–9463), open daily 10–5.

Half Moon Bay hosts literally dozens of annual festivals, any one of which you could plan a visit around. The largest and most popular one is the **Art and Pumpkin Festival,** held the weekend after Columbus Day. The high-spirited fall celebration includes live music, local foods, crafts, vendors, a children's parade, and outrageous pie-eating and pumpkin-carving contests. Also popular is the aptly named **Coastal Flower Market,** which takes place on the third Saturday of each month in May through September. Other yearly events include the riotous **Human Race** every May, in which entrants use every wacky scheme they can devise to carry other contestants along the course; the **Brew Ha-Ha** beer and sausage tasting festival each spring; and a daring **California Coast Air Show** that takes place at Half Moon Bay's tiny airport in the fall. For more information on any of these festivals, contact the **Half Moon Bay Chamber of Commerce** (520 Kelly Ave., at Hwy. 1, tel. 415/726–8380 or 415/726–5202). Traffic can be overwhelming during the festivals, so avoid gridlock headaches by visiting on a weekday when activity is more subdued. Better yet, leave your car behind and take SamTrans Bus 1L from the Daly City BART station (Bus 1C from Colma BART).

For a meal, Half Moon Bay offers everything from reasonably priced health food markets to way-outta-range seafood restaurants. The best of the former is **Healing Moon Natural Foods Market** (523 Main St., tel. 415/726–7881); if you're not looking for groceries, serve yourself a cup of soup and eat it on the peaceful outdoor patio. Across the street, colorful **McCoffee** (522 Main St., tel. 415/726–6241) serves sandwiches, salads, and milk shakes, each for less than $4. Despite its chain-restaurant exterior, **3 Amigos** (200 N. Cabrillo Hwy., on Hwy. 1 at Kelly Ave., tel. 415/726–6080) offers tasty, cheap Mexican food (veggie burritos $3) and every Mexican beer under the sun ($2.25) daily until midnight. You'll find reasonably priced seafood—a rarity in this area—at the **Flying Fish Grill** (99 Hwy. 92, at Main St., tel. 415/712–1125, open Tues.–Sun. 11–8). Chow down on clam chowder ($3) and a variety of deep-fried and grilled fresh fish ($7–$10).

SAN GREGORIO TO AÑO NUEVO

The desolate stretch of coastline south of Half Moon Bay is nearly deserted year-round, and for good reason. The beaches here are cold; the choice of affordable food and lodging is limited; and the number of worthwhile "sights," depending on your criteria, can be almost negligible. But the very fact that the area is so empty means that, with the exception of Año Nuevo State Reserve during the elephant seals' mating season, there's almost nothing you can do here that will require advance planning. Day-trippers seeking sand, sea, and forest in quiet simplicity are more likely to find it here than in the more touristed Half Moon Bay. The rich tide pools at Pescadero State Beach, the cliff-hugging Pigeon Point Lighthouse Hostel, and the sky-high trees lining Hwy. 84 through La Honda all make this chunk of coastline extremely worthwhile for people seeking serious solitude on short notice.

SAN GREGORIO Although not much of a destination in itself, San Gregorio is a worthwhile stop if you're traveling up or down the coast between Santa Cruz and Half Moon Bay. The drive in from the coast to this hitching-post of a town, at the junction of Hwys. 1 and 84, is half the fun, even if you don't come by the spectacular coast road. **Highway 84,** the east–west road running to San Gregorio from I–280 (also known as La Honda Road), is for the strong of stomach only; but if you can take it, the highway is so thick with redwoods you'll barely believe it's daytime. Best of all, the road spits you out at the isolated **San Gregorio State Beach,** where you can lie back and soak up some rays, or, more likely, throw on a sweater and battle the wind as the fog comes rolling in. If you get too cold, the bluff north of the parking lot is a good place for a brisk, blood-warming walk.

If you're in the area, don't miss the **San Gregorio General Store** (tel. 415/726–0565; open daily 9–6, Fri. until 7), a mile east of Hwy. 1 on Hwy. 84 at Stage Road. This eclectic, Old West–style store, which has served the ranching and farming community since 1889, sells everything from used books and stuffed animals to cast-iron pots and antiques—it also doubles as the town saloon and community center. Hell, you might even catch some Bulgarian bluegrass or Irish R&B if you show up on the right weekend night.

LA HONDA If you're getting tired of relentlessly magnificent coastal scenery, you should either seek psychiatric help or head inland to the densely forested community of La Honda, 11 miles east of Hwy. 1. About the size of a postage stamp, La Honda seems almost lost in the shadow of countless giant redwoods on Hwy. 84 (*see* San Gregorio, *above*). The town consists of **Pioneer Market** (La Honda Center, tel. 415/747–0551), where you can stock up on camping supplies and sandwiches ($3.50); the **Cool Water Café** (8725 La Honda Rd., tel. 415/747–9600), offering barbecued chicken sandwiches ($4.50) and espresso drinks (about $2), open daily until 8; a post office; and **Apple Jack's Tavern** (La Honda Rd., tel. 415/747–0331). The last is a scruffy bar that absolutely should not be missed, no matter what time of day you're passing through town. Open weekdays noon–2 AM and weekends 10 AM–2 AM, Apple Jack's is today's version of an Old West saloon: The men drink their whiskey straight-up, the women are loud and boisterous, and a brawl seems ready to erupt any minute. You'll feel equally comfortable pulling up on a Harley Davidson or on a horse.

Even more than Apple Jack's, though, it's the old-growth redwoods surrounding La Honda that will make your visit here a mind-blowing experience. If you don't have time to head north to California's redwood country, La Honda is a surprisingly good substitute. Four—that's right, four—state and county parks ring this tiny town, and their forested hills provide excellent terrain for hiking, biking, and being inspired by the ancient giants (for details, *see* Chapter 8).

Take Hwy. 84 about a mile west of La Honda, make a left on Alpine Road, and 4½ miles later you'll come to the parking lot of **Pescadero Creek County Park** (tel. 415/879–0212), a secluded expanse of fir- and pine-covered hills crisscrossed by a series of gentle streams. From the parking lot, follow the **Tarwater Trail Loop** in either direction for a moderate hike of about 2 miles, which will take you from a ridge with ocean views down through the scrub and into the redwoods. Don't blame Exxon for the crude oil bubbling in Tarwater Creek—it's natural. If you haven't had your fill of towering redwoods, Douglas fir, and pine trees, drive a bit farther along Alpine Road and you'll reach the turnoff for **Portola Redwood State Park** (Portola State Park Rd., tel. 415/948–9098), 2,400 acres of even more remote and scenic forest—the only drawback is the $5 parking fee. Just past the entrance to the park, the visitor center sells wood ($3) and trail maps ($1). For info on hikes here, *see* Chapter 8. And if night comes and you still can't tear yourself away, check it out: You can camp here (*see* South Bay, in Chapter 7).

Two more woodsy parks lie on Pescadero Road, which meets up with Alpine Road a mile south of Hwy. 84. The first is **Sam McDonald County Park** (for info call Memorial County Park, tel. 415/879–0238), a small, almost deserted redwood forest good for short hikes and complete solitude. Thankfully, there's no charge for day use of the park. A bit farther along Pescadero Road, you'll come to **Memorial County Park** (tel. 415/879–0238), the most developed of the four parks, whose attributes include a fresh-water swimming hole, picnic areas, fire roads popular with mountain bikers, and a number of short- and medium-length hiking trails through the redwoods (*see* Hiking and Biking, in Chapter 8). To avoid the $4 parking fee at Memorial, park on the side of the road just outside the entrance.

PESCADERO Over 100 years ago, all of the wooden buildings in the small fishing village of Pescadero were painted white with paint that washed up on shore when the clipper ship *Carrier Pigeon* crashed into the rocks off Pigeon Point, a few miles south of town. Today, the bakery, general store, bank, local post office, and other shops that populate Pescadero still retain

The Merry Pranksters

In the early 1960s La Honda was home to one of the hippie era's most renowned groups of psychedelic crazies, the Merry Pranksters. Led by the multitalented bohemian Ken Kesey, author of "One Flew Over the Cuckoo's Nest," the Merry Pranksters spent several years on a La Honda farm exploring "states of nonordinary reality," i.e., dropping acid, eating mushrooms, and smoking dope. When La Honda became too limiting, they outfitted an old school bus with psychedelic Day-Glo paintings and filming and recording equipment, and set off to travel across the country, a journey made famous by Tom Wolfe in his popular chronicle The Electric Kool-Aid Acid Test.

their whitewashed uniformity, giving this town, in the flatlands a mile inland from the coast on Pescadero Road, a calming, subdued ambience.

After you've rambled around the 3 blocks that make up Pescadero's commercial district, head to **Duarte's Tavern** (202 Stage Rd., at Pescadero Rd., tel. 415/879–0464), open 7 AM–9 PM daily, a combination bar and restaurant. Duarte's has been run by four generations of Duartes since 1894, and they're in no big hurry to serve you before the next generation takes over. The homey restaurant serves everything from peanut butter and jelly sandwiches ($3) to lamb chops ($14), but it's most famous for its cream of artichoke soup, made with local produce ($4), fresh seafood plates ($6–$20), and homemade pies ($3).

On the coast just west of town, you'll find **Pescadero State Beach,** a long, sandy expanse with vibrant tidal pools, perfect for checking out the Pacific's aquatic denizens. Just north of the beach, the **Pescadero Marsh Reserve** (tel. 415/879–2170) is a protected area favored by ornithologists. Free guided walks leave from the parking lot just south of Pescadero Creek on Saturdays (10:30 AM) and Sundays (1 PM) year-round, weather permitting. If you prefer to take to the hills, **Butano State Park** (tel. 415/879–0173), 5 miles south of Pescadero on Cloverdale Road, has 20 miles of trails on 2,700 acres (*see* Chapter 8). You can reach the park from Gazos Creek Road, off Hwy. 1 near Año Nuevo State Reserve (*see below*), or take Pescadero Road a couple miles east from town and head south on Cloverdale; there's a $5 parking fee.

ANO NUEVO STATE RESERVE Named by explorer Sebastian Viscaino on New Year's Day, 1603, the Punta del Año Nuevo is one of the few places in the world where you can safely view live elephant seals close up and personal. Not only that, if you're here between December and March, you get to watch them do the wild thing. During mating season, you'll need to make reservations up to eight weeks in advance through Destinet (tel. 800/444–PARK), and you can only visit the reserve on one of the 2½-hour guided walks ($4, plus a $4 parking fee). If you're lucky, you may catch sight of migrating gray whales at the same time. Sea lions, sea otters, and harbor seals have also been known to make appearances, mostly off the coast and on Año Nuevo Island, inhabited only by seals and birds.

Though not as thrilling as the fighting and preening of mating season, the elephant seals come ashore from April through September to shed their old, furry brown skin for a sleek, new one; the yearlings stick around until November, gaining strength for the upcoming months spent entirely in the water. At these times, you can gain access to the reserve by obtaining a free permit from the visitor center (tel. 415/879–2025; open Apr.–Sept. 8–6, Oct. and Nov. 8–4). To avoid the $4 parking fee, continue about ¼ mile south past the main reserve entrance and park on the west side of Hwy. 1 (where you'll also find an alternate trail to the reserve). The path to the elephant seals' beach from the main parking lot is 1½ miles long; and if you come in spring, you'll be treated to the sight of thousands of colorful wildflowers along the trail. The reserve, about 40 miles south of San Francisco, can be reached on SamTrans Bus 96C (*see* Getting In, Out, and Around, in Chapter 1). Wheelchair access to the viewing areas is available with one day's advance notice.

SHOPPING

By Stephan von Pohl

Even if you don't need a low-rider bicycle from the Mission, an extinct vinyl treasure from the Haight, or leather chaps from SoMa, San Francisco's stores merit some serious window shopping, and maybe a buck or two squeezed out of your billfold. Thankfully, Bay Area stores have a lot to offer those of limited means, as long as you avoid the overpriced, overperfumed emporia of downtown's Union Square. Trendy **Haight Street** is a good place to start, but prices include an "atmosphere and attitude" tax that makes the **Mission District**'s overflowing warehouses even more appealing. **Chinatown** has tons of cheap electronic goods and silk items; **North Beach** has unique (and often expensive) specialty stores that may still reek of pasta-chomping tourists; and the **South of Market** area has bargain warehouses that stock slightly flawed, brand-name threads at good prices.

Oakland's few viable shopping districts, like **Piedmont Avenue** and **Rockridge** (College Ave., btw Alcatraz Ave. and Broadway), are chock-full of boutiques and antique stores, but non-yuppies may also find something affordable. Meanwhile, Berkeley's incense- and patchouli-scented **Telegraph Avenue** (all student, all the time) offers books, vinyl, CDs, and new and used clothing to fit cheapskate student budgets. On weekends, even San Franciscans roam the Avenue to check out stands selling tie-dyes, cheap silver rings, and hair-weaving services. While most stores in San Francisco or Berkeley stay open until 8 or 9 PM, most Oakland stores close at 6 or 7 PM, and some are closed on Sunday.

Suburbia has one advantage over the cosmopolitan parts of the Bay Area: space. If outlet malls are your gig, the Peninsula is your paradise. Worth checking out are the **Metro 280 Center** (Colby Blvd., at I–280 in Colma) and **Marina Square** (Marina Blvd., at I–880 in San Leandro).

New Clothes

SAN FRANCISCO

You'll find everything from Armani suits to rubber dresses in the city. The huge department stores housed in the **San Francisco Shopping Centre** (865 Market St., btw 4th and 5th Sts.) may make you tired of shopping before you've even found the right floor, but deals can be found in some of the smaller stores, like **Cignal** (Third Floor, tel. 415/979–0209), where both men and women can find low-priced (compared to Union Square) suits and separates. The **Embarcadero Center** (Clay and Battery Sts., btw Drumm and Sacramento Sts.) is an eight-block complex of chichi shops customized for Financial District types rushing around on their lunch breaks. In general, the farther you venture from downtown, the better deal you'll find.

Behind the Post Office. Before X-Large came to the Haight, there was Behind the Post Office. Stocked with the latest and greatest hip-hop gear, including smart-ass T-shirts, skate-girl dresses, and baggy pants for when you're feeling phat, this tiny shop specializes in lesser-known local labels. On weekends local DJs spin tunes, and this is a great place to pick up info on underground jazz and hip-hop scenes. *1510 Haight St., at Ashbury St., tel. 415/861–2507.*

Betsey Johnson. Postmodern designer-goddess Betsey Johnson brings you her outrageous women's fashions in a campy art deco, neon-lit environment. The often silly clothes aren't cheap, but their limited appeal leads to regular half-off sales. *2031 Fillmore St., btw Pine and California Sts., tel. 415/567–2726. Other location: 160 Geary St., btw Stockton and Grant Sts., tel. 415/398–2516.*

Esprit Factory Outlet. You, too, can look like a fresh-scrubbed young American, and now at substantial savings! For best results, head for the back. *499 Illinois St., at 16th St., tel. 415/957–2550.*

Joshua Simon. This Noe Valley store stocks an eclectic selection of women's garments—from flowing pants and romantic-looking dresses to unusual woven vests and painted clothing. Some items are imported from Indonesia; others are fashioned by local designers. *3915 24th St., near Sanchez St., tel. 415/821–1068.*

Na Na. Part of a national chain that has stores in New York and Los Angeles, Na Na sells trendy shoes and clothes to ultra-hip Gen X-ers. The store carries a number of local labels, and the sales rack (up to 50% off) guarantees you won't go broke looking cool. *2276 Market St., near Noe St., tel. 415/861–NANA.*

Rolo. All four branches of this boutique, especially popular among gay and lesbian club-goers, carry groovy threads for those who like to see and be seen. The store on Market is heavy on flamboyant, expensive menswear; the Howard Street store features a flashy women's selection; Castro Street caters to style-conscious men; and the Mill Valley branch emphasizes casual clothes for women. *1301 Howard St., at 9th St., tel. 415/861–1999. Market Rolo: 2351 Market St., tel. 415/431–4545. Castro Rolo: 450 Castro St., tel. 415/626–7171. Mill Valley Rolo: 438 Miller Ave., tel. 415/383–4000.*

Shoe Biz. Satisfy the raver within with the latest European styles: platforms, hot pink, glitter, you name it. The last-size sale corner has tons of high-quality shoes at fantastic discounts. *1446 Haight St., at Masonic Ave., tel. 415/864–0990.*

EAST BAY

Although you can find almost anything in San Francisco, the East Bay, with its masses of students, holds its own. Come to Telegraph Avenue and environs to find street vendors, collegiate wear, and lower prices.

Deep Threads. Hip-hop fans, rejoice: Deep Threads has all the baggy jeans, baseball caps, beanies, and parkas you could possibly want. This is a good source of info on Oakland's hip-hop scene, so you can find out where to take your new duds for a test drive. *5243 College Ave., at Broadway, Oakland, tel. 510/653–4790.*

Futura. The eclectic blend of new and used clothes includes men's gas-station shirts, vintage jackets, and corduroy jeans. Women can find baby tees, pricey dresses, and baggy pants. For some of the cheapest prices this side of Goodwill, check out Futura's outlet store on the second floor next door above Bear Basics. *2360 Telegraph Ave., near Durant Ave., Berkeley, tel. 510/843–3037.*

New West. You're tired of flares and polyester, and your platforms give you too many sprained ankles. Guys and gals, head to New West to spruce up your wardrobe with big-name seconds and samples of a more practical (yet stylish) nature at markdown prices. *2967 College Ave., at Ashby Ave., Berkeley, tel. 510/849–0701. S.F. location: 426 Brannan St., btw 3rd and 4th Sts., tel. 415/882–4929.*

X-Large. X-Large brings cool clothes, phat hip-hop beats, and a comfortable couch to Telegraph Avenue. It's part of a chain fronted by Beastie Boy Mike D, and Sonic Youth bassist Kim Gordon has taken the time to design some of the threads for you Bettys—so you *know* they're cool. *2422 Telegraph Ave., Berkeley, tel. 510/849–9242. S.F. location: 1415 Haight St., tel. 415/626–9573.*

Secondhand Clothing

SAN FRANCISCO

Naturally, the **Mission** and the **Haight** abound with vintage clothing, secondhand duds, and thrift shops. The big name stores—Wasteland and Buffalo Exchange—are always dependable for flannel, a polyester shirt, or a basic black dress, but you'll find a better selection (at cheaper prices) at the city's smaller shops. For starters, try Mission and Valencia streets between 15th and 18th streets. If you want to shop Haight Street, start at Fillmore Street and work your way up to Stanyan Street; you'll find that you need to hold up a liquor store to afford looking like a '60s love child. Thrift-store sophisticates looking for a silk Chanel suit or a 1930s beaded satin gown will want to head off the beaten path to **Divisadero Street** (btw Pine and Bush Sts.) and **Fillmore Street** (btw Bush and Sacramento Sts.), where they'll find ritzy vintage shops and high-end secondhand stores that carry designer labels tossed aside by Pacific Heights society mavens. Up-and-coming in the boutique scene is the stretch of Hayes Street between Franklin and Buchanan streets, known as **Hayes Valley.**

560 Hayes Vintage Boutique. One of several Hayes Valley boutiques, Vintage stocks an odd assortment of used clothing, mostly women's. You'll find all sorts of pants, coats, and dresses, most of them reeking deliciously of the '70s. *560 Hayes St., btw Laguna and Octavia Sts., tel. 415/861–7993.*

AAardvark's Odd Ark. AAardvark's keeps the thrift crowd coming back with a wide selection of used clothing. It's your local source for men's basics, cotton dress shirts, hats, and vintage Levi's. *1501 Haight St., at Ashbury St., tel. 415/621–3141.*

American Rag. This store stocks old and new, and precious little is cheap; but the dregs have been filtered out, the clothes are in good shape, and everything is sanitized for your protection. They arguably have the best selection of black vintage dresses in San Francisco, plus racks of stylish suits and jackets classy enough for the day job. *1305 Van Ness Ave., btw Sutter and Bush Sts., tel. 415/474–5214.*

Buffalo Exchange. This thrift store doesn't try to be cutting-edge, but the selection is consistent and pretty cheap. The store mixes vintage with contemporary clothes—keep this in mind if you want to sell that Gap stuff you got for your birthday. *1555 Haight St., btw Ashbury and Clayton Sts., tel. 415/431–7733. Other locations: 1800 Polk St., near Washington St., tel. 415/346–5726; 2512 Telegraph Ave., Berkeley, tel. 510/644–9202; 3333 Lake Shore Ave., Oakland, tel. 510/452–4464.*

Clothes Contact. You really can't go wrong, as just about everything here—used, vintage, old jeans, jackets—is $6 per pound. Come here if you have a weakness for funky old dresses or are in dire need of a suit and a Hawaiian-print tie. *473 Valencia St., near 16th St., tel. 415/621–3212.*

Crossroads Trading Co. This secondhand clothing store has three locations in the Bay Area, each with a small, carefully selected, and relatively cheap stock. The Fillmore store tends to be rife with early '80s wear, while the other two stores are better for jeans (under $20), unusual dresses, and classic vintage wear. *2231 Market St., btw Sanchez and Noe Sts., tel. 415/626–8989. Other locations: 1901 Fillmore St., at Bush St., tel. 415/775–8885; 5636 College Ave., near Keith St., Oakland, tel. 510/420–1952.*

Departures From the Past. This immaculate vintage shop has formal attire and costumes plus casual wear from eras past. Though prices are slightly higher than you'll find elsewhere, you can rent some of the items on display—a tux goes for $40–$65 per night. Their other store,

Costumes on Haight (735 Haight St., tel. 415/621–1356), rents costumes and has some vintage for sale. *2028 Fillmore St., btw California and Pine Sts., tel. 415/885–3377.*

Thrift Town. Fashion victims will swoon at the racks upon racks of clothing basics. Where else can you get a pair of pants for $5 or shoes for $15? Upstairs you can skip among tennis rackets, kitchen doodads, lamps, and appliances (they even provide an outlet so you can test them out). *2101 Mission St., at 17th St., tel. 415/861–1132.*

Wasteland. One of the more popular (but pricier) secondhand stores in San Francisco, Wasteland brings you the trendy and outrageous—including a groovy selection of bell-bottoms and other fashion items you hoped never to see again. It's also a good source for vintage costume jewelry, gowns, and suits. *1660 Haight St., btw Belvedere and Clayton Sts., tel. 415/863–3150.*

Worn Out West. This Castro District store provides secondhand western wear and leather goods to budget-conscious cowboys. *582 Castro St., near 19th St., tel. 415/431–6020.*

EAST BAY

The East Bay has a great variety of thrift stores, especially along Telegraph Avenue near the U.C. campus in Berkeley and on College Avenue in Rockridge. The farther you stray from the stores with velvet in the windows, the more likely you are to find a real steal, like a $5 pair of Levi's that some collector would pay $50 for.

Madame Butterfly. Not the cheapest place, but you might find a good deal on '50s and '60s vintage clothing. The hats and gloves, summer dresses, pants, and a small selection of men's jackets go for $15–$40. Funkier dresses start at $70 and creep up from there. *5474 College Ave., at Taft St., Oakland, tel. 510/653–1525.*

Mars Mercantile. Mars is the most reliable used and vintage clothing store on Telegraph. The prices aren't rock-bottom, but they're reasonable. Peruse the racks of vintage dresses, acrylic

A Barter Society

When the stretch from paycheck to paycheck seems longer than usual, clean out your closets, bookshelves, and CD racks, and head to one of the Bay Area's secondhand stores, where you can get cash or trade for the stuff you don't want anymore. Clothing stores pay a percentage of what they can sell the item for, which is determined by the buyers—the dragons at the gate, so to speak—based on style, age, and condition. Wasteland, Buffalo Exchange, Futura, and Crossroads all give about 40% in cash or 60% in trade. Pay attention to the season when you sell: If it's summer, you're going to have a hard time unloading your fake fur.

Music stores subscribe to the chaos theory of buying and set no definite guidelines. Expect anywhere from $1 to $6 in trade or cash for a basic domestic CD, and anywhere from 5¢ to $5 for records and cassettes. Buyers include Reckless, Recycled Records, Streetlight, and Rough Trade. Book stores are even less forgiving. Prices vary based on a book's condition and reputation: If a book didn't sell well the first time around, chances are good you'll get a fat rejection at the counter. San Franciscans in the know head east to Berkeley to sell books—specifically to Moe's (see below), Shakespeare's (2499 Telegraph Ave., tel. 510/841–8916), and Half-Price Books (2525 Telegraph Ave., tel. 510/843–6412).

men's shirts, fake fur, and genuine leather, but you'd be out of your gourd to buy one of the '50s-era jeans—$300! *2398 Telegraph Ave., at Channing Way, Berkeley, tel. 510/843–6711.*

Rockridge Rags. Browse through the orderly racks of secondhand clothing (conveniently arranged by size) and you'll find lots of stuff to wear when you're doing temp work downtown, including the occasional Anne Klein suit or Polo chinos at bargain basement prices. *5711 College Ave., near Rockridge BART, Oakland, tel. 510/655–2289.*

Slash. With its piles (literally) of cheap Levi's ($15–$25), overalls ($20), and corduroys of all colors, Slash looks like someone's messy closet. Owners Carla Bell and Ocean Edgars are always happy to help you dig through the denim—which is half the fun anyway—to find the perfect pair of 5-O-whatevers. *2840 College Ave., at Russell St., Berkeley, tel. 510/841–7803.*

Books

SAN FRANCISCO

Looking for a good book to take to bed, to act as a prop when you're lounging in a café, or to read on that 12-hour flight? This city has more than 200 bookstores—new and used, tiny and huge, nonprofit and corporate—for every language, political bent, or cultural interest. Don't forget to support smaller, local bookstores: You'll find them peppered throughout the city, but concentrated in the Mission and the Haight. Every bookstore has its own personality and loyal following; it's up to you to sniff around and find one to suit your literary fantasies.

The Abandoned Planet Bookstore. Duck into this cool and quiet spot to have a chat with the friendly owner, pat the cats, and browse the used books. Music, theater, and art history are well-represented here, and they occasionally have new publishers' overstock books at rock-bottom prices. Someone usually strolls in to play the old piano in the corner. *518 Valencia St., near 16th St., tel. 415/861–4695.*

Acorn Books. Desperate customers in search of antiquarian, out-of-print, or used books know the friendly staff at Acorn would hunt down a book to the ends of the earth—although the well-stocked store probably already has it somewhere on its shelves. *740 Polk St., at Ellis St., tel. 415/563–1736.*

Adobe Books. Specializing in the used and rare, and possibly the cheapest bookstore of its kind in the city, Adobe is an excellent source for books on art and modern philosophy. The well-worn easy chair by the front desk attests to the amiability of the erudite staff. *3166 16th St., btw Valencia and Guerrero Sts., tel. 415/864–3936.*

Bound Together Bookstore Collective. Before the age of the Internet, budding anarchists had to come here for their bomb-making manuals. Bound Together recently celebrated its 20th anniversary, and it continues to be the city's best source for underground magazines, political tracts, and generally subversive materials. *1369 Haight St., near Masonic St., tel. 415/431–8355.*

City Lights. For some, a trip to San Francisco is not complete without an evening spent browsing the stacks at City Lights, surely the city's most famous bookstore. Owned by poet Lawrence Ferlinghetti, City Lights is *the* source for Beat literature, much of it published under the store's own imprint. Opened in 1955, this beautiful bookshop has a fantastic upstairs room filled with poetry, beat literature, and a few used books. There's also a "little press" alcove of local journals and 'zines; nonfiction is downstairs. *261 Columbus Ave., at Broadway, tel. 415/362–8193.*

City Lights, the legendary home of the Beat Generation, was once busted on obscenity charges for selling Allen Ginsberg's "Howl."

A Different Light. Come here for lesbian, transgender, and gay-oriented literature, as well as queerzines, T-shirts, and stickers. Regular book signings and readings attract the local gay community. *489 Castro St., near 18th St., tel. 415/431–0891.*

Dog Eared Books. There's something for everyone in this homey Mission District bookstore. Whether it's literature, queer fiction, gender issues, mysteries, or art, you'll find new and used books at rock-bottom prices. A lot of the new books are publishers' overstock, sold at 20%–50% off the cover price. *1173 Valencia St., at 23rd St., tel. 415/282–1901.*

Eastwind Books and Arts, Inc. Stocking new books on China, Asia, and Asian America, Eastwind has both Chinese- and English-language sections. *1435A Stockton St., at Vallejo St., tel. 415/772–5877.*

European Book Company. This is *the* spot for French, German, and Spanish-language books, magazines, and newspapers, as well as foreign-language dictionaries and travel guides. *925 Larkin St., near Geary St., tel. 415/474–0626.*

Green Apple Books. Not for those who demand order and neatness, this ramshackle Richmond District store jumbles together the new, the used, and the rare in a space reminiscent of Grandma's attic. Consistently voted the Bay Area's best bookstore by *San Francisco Bay Guardian* readers, Green Apple is also known for its knowledgeable and friendly staff. *506 Clement St., btw 6th and 7th Aves., tel. 415/387–2272.*

Modern Times. Leftists can choose from lots of new titles with a politically progressive, multicultural bent; oft-browsed sections include cultural theory, gay/lesbian issues, Spanish-language books, art, and current affairs. Modern Times is collectively run, carries underground papers and 'zines, and hosts regular readings and forums, often with a political focus. *888 Valencia St., btw 19th and 20th Sts., tel. 415/282–9246.*

San Francisco Mystery Bookstore. This Noe Valley shop stocks everything imaginable for the armchair gumshoe in your life. New and used books, both in and out of print, abound; they also stock a few gay and lesbian mysteries. *4175 24th St., btw Castro and Diamond Sts., tel. 415/282–7444. Closed Mon. and Tues.*

Sierra Club Bookstore. Along with a wide range of shiny-new titles on all aspects of environmentalism—including political tomes, nature poetry, and practical guides for hiking and camping—you'll find topo maps and kids' books. You can also find newsletters and postings listing upcoming hikes, meetings, and events. *730 Polk St., btw Eddy and Ellis Sts., tel. 415/923–5600. Oakland location: 6014 College Ave., tel. 510/658–7470.*

William Stout Architectural Books. This store stocks an international, professional collection of architecture and design books and periodicals. Even nonindustry types should admire the store's collection of out-of-print books. *804 Montgomery St., btw Jackson and Pacific Sts., tel. 415/391–6757.*

EAST BAY

The East Bay intelligentsia doesn't have to trek to San Francisco to look for quality new and used books. With a huge university in its midst and more pretentious intellectuals per square mile than anywhere outside the Académie Française, you'll find enough bookstores here to keep you occupied for a year. **Telegraph Avenue** has the highest concentration of tried-and-true general bookstores, though some fine shops lie further from campus.

Black Oak Books. Locals, professors, and local professors frequent this friendly, well-stocked, new and used bookstore in North Berkeley. Boasting an impressive collection of both rare books and cheap paperback fiction ($1 and up), Black Oak also sells a beautiful collection of broadsides (quotations from literary works, artfully printed on heavy decorative paper)—an excellent gift for the serious bookworm. There are weekly author readings and book signings (including occasional big-name writers). *1491 Shattuck Ave., at Vine St., Berkeley, tel. 510/486–0698.*

Cody's. Here's a Berkeley institution if there ever was one. Take a break from Telegraph Avenue and wander among the stacks upon stacks of shiny new volumes, covering every imaginable genre—from poetry and philosophy to self-defense and women's studies. Cody's also has an impressive newsstand, a cheery kids' substore, foreign-language books upstairs, and free gift wrapping. Regular readings by famous and almost-famous authors are crowded social events;

arrive early if you want a shot at a seat. *2454 Telegraph Ave., at Haste St., Berkeley, tel. 510/ 845–7852.*

De Lauer's Super Newsstand. De Lauer's isn't kidding. Open 24 hours daily, they carry maps, foreign language and domestic newspapers, and an overwhelming number of magazines—from the *Columbia Journalism Review* to *Beauty Pageant* magazine. *1310 Broadway Ave., at 14th St., Oakland, tel. 510/451–6157.*

Diesel. A Bookstore. Diesel stands out among Rockridge bookstores with its excellent collection of fiction, history, politics, and other genres, much of it with a social or California bent. Weekly readings and book signings, running the gamut from local history to poetry, attract creative types from the nearby College of Arts and Crafts. *5433 College Ave., near Hudson St., Oakland, tel. 510/653–9965.*

Gaia Books. The East Bay's home for books on spirituality, ecology, holistic health, sexuality, and anything else in the "well-being" category, Gaia occupies a bright, airy space that's perfect for its regular readings and lectures. *1400 Shattuck Ave., at Rose St., Berkeley, tel. 510/ 548–4172.*

Mama Bears. This friendly bookstore/café carries new and used books on feminist political theory and lesbian issues, plus fiction by women writers. The beautiful garden is the perfect place to peruse or discuss your purchases. The coffeehouse doubles as a space for readings and workshops. *6536 Telegraph Ave., at 66th St., Oakland, tel. 510/428–9684.*

Marcus Books. Specializing in books "by and about African-Americans," Marcus Books is a longtime community resource for new publications on history, religion, fiction, art, and more. There's a great selection of children's and young adult literature. Readings are held almost every week. *3900 Martin Luther King Jr. Way, tel. 510/652–2344. S.F. location: 1712 Fillmore St., near Post St., tel. 415/346–4222.*

Moe's. Moe's is one of Berkeley's most successful bookstores, thanks to the efforts of the gruff, cigar-chomping owner, Moe Moskowitz. Browse his five floors of new, used, and antique books, with a strong emphasis on the used and antique. Moe's is a good first stop when you're trying to sell. *2476 Telegraph Ave., btw Haste St. and Dwight Way, Berkeley, tel. 510/849–2087.*

Shambhala. Specializing in Eastern religions (and Western slants on Eastern religions), Shambhala also stocks new and used books on alternative medicine, the "new" sciences, mysticism, psychology, and theology. *2482 Telegraph Ave., btw Haste St. and Dwight Way, Berkeley, tel. 510/848–8443.*

University Press Books. Titles from over 100 university presses represent the absolute latest in intellectual thought. All disciplines are represented here. Buy a hot treatise on cultural theory and read it at the Musical Offering café next door—make sure everyone can see the title as you read. *2430 Bancroft Way, near Telegraph Ave., Berkeley, tel. 510/548–0585.*

On Friday and Saturday nights, Bay Area bookstores become somewhat of a pickup joint for earnest intellectuals.

Walden Pond. Everything a bookstore should be, with a great selection of new and used titles in all categories, and plenty of nooks where you can plop down on the wooden floor and sample a few pages. You can dive right into your new purchase at nearby Lake Merritt, or down the street at **The Coffee Mill** (3363 Grand Ave., tel. 510/465–4224). *3316 Grand Ave., near Grand Lake Theater, Oakland, tel. 510/832–4438.*

Records, Tapes, and CDs

When you're ready to blow a few hundred greenbacks on tunes, you can't do much better than the Bay Area. Berkeley's Telegraph Avenue boasts no fewer than four mammoth record stores within five blocks of the U.C. campus. Basically, if you can't find what you need there, it probably doesn't exist. Granted you can always find an overpriced new CD at the new **Virgin Megastore** (2 Stockton St., at Market St., tel. 415/397-4525), but wouldn't you rather support

The quality and quantity of vinyl available at Bay Area music stores will have you begging Dad for his old turntable.

your friendly neighborhood store (bound to be cheaper and better stocked with used goods and vinyl)? The **Upper Haight** is a good place to look for obscure titles and classic punk, while the **Mission District** is great for Latin music. Most places guarantee their records against scratches; check to make sure.

SAN FRANCISCO

Groove Merchant. Groove Merchant's owners run the highly recommended Luv 'n Haight and Ubiquity labels, both of which put the spotlight on the local acid jazz scene. The store has plenty of great finds for the collector, DJ, or serious amateur. *687 Haight St., btw Pierce and Steiner Sts., tel. 415/252–5766.*

Prince Neville's Reggae Run-Ins. Jah, mon, this is a reggae wonderland, with records, tapes, videos, T-shirts, jewelry, and other paraphernalia in red, gold, black, and green. *505 Divisadero St., btw Fell and Hayes Sts., tel. 415/922–2442.*

Reckless Records. A reliable source for used cassettes and CDs, Reckless also carries new music, T-shirts, posters, and used videos. They specialize in independent and mainstream rock, hip-hop, and soul. *1401 Haight St., at Masonic St., tel. 415/431–3434.*

Recycled Records. Vinyl junkies will find their fix among the great selection of new and used (mostly used) records. The collection focuses on rock, but other genres are well represented. *1377 Haight St., at Masonic St., tel. 415/626–4075.*

Ritmo Latino. This colorful, Carnaval-esque store in the heart of the Mission sells an enormous variety of Latin music: ranchero, mariachi, salsa, Tex-Mex, merengue, norteño, and more. Best of all, the store has listening stations where you can check out any of the store's CDs before laying down cold cash. *2401 Mission St., at 20th St., tel. 415/824–8556.*

For Middle Eastern music (come on, shake that belly), try Samiramis Imports (2990 Mission St., tel. 415/824–6555).

Star Classics. The Blockbuster Video of classical music, Star Classics stocks only new classical CDs and cassettes. The adjoining Star Classics Recital Hall hosts vocal and musical performances every Friday and Sunday. *425 Hayes St., at Gough St., tel. 415/552–9622.*

Streetlight Records. Because they buy and sell for great prices to a diverse clientele, the selection of records, tapes, and CDs is usually offbeat and always fresh. True to their quirky TV ads, Streetlight will buy back almost anything. The Noe Valley store is smaller, but has a better selection of vinyl. *3979 24th St., btw Noe and Sanchez Sts., tel. 415/282–3550. Other location: 2350 Market St., near Castro St., tel. 415/282–8000.*

EAST BAY

Amoeba. Employees claim their store has more used CDs than any other in the country, and they've certainly been expanding with amoebalike growth since they arrived on the scene. Offer-

Revolution at 33⅓

In San Francisco you can buy records and incite revolution at the same time. Epicenter (475 Valencia St., at 16th St., tel. 415/431–2725), an anarchist-oriented community center, has a huge selection of new and used punk rock albums, as well as pool tables, bulletin boards, and a library with tons of independent zines. It's an ideal resource for the new radical in town. Come by weekdays 3–8, Saturday noon–8, or Sunday noon–7.

ing the widest and choicest selection of used CDs and new and used 7" records in the Bay Area, their collection includes well-rounded jazz, international, indie, import, and rock sections. The experienced staff will show you the newest artists, dig out their rarest records, and cut you a fair deal for your used goods. *2455 Telegraph Ave., at Haste St., Berkeley, tel. 510/549–1125.*

Groove Yard. Used jazz and soul records and a fair number of Latin and Brazilian discs reward anyone who ventures to this Temescal neighborhood store halfway between downtown Oakland and Berkeley. They also carry a little acid jazz, a little funk, and a bit of blues. Groove Yard happily gives trade or cash for high quality LPs and CDs. *4770 Telegraph Ave., at 48th St., Oakland, tel. 510/655–8400.*

Mod Lang. A single from your favorite long-haired British band is released overseas. Four days later you'll find it at Mod Lang, where shipments of ambient, indie, and psychedelic '60s music come in every week and sell at lower prices than on Telegraph. *2136 University Ave., near Shattuck Ave., Berkeley, tel. 510/486–1880.*

Rasputin's. Rasputin's had the lock on Telegraph cool until Amoeba showed up in 1990. In a game of catch-up, the store has moved twice in as many years, each time into bigger digs, though with less and less vinyl. But the CDs, oh the CDs! The store regularly hosts live performances; otherwise, entertain yourself by further provoking the already rude staff. *2401 Telegraph Ave., at Channing Ave., Berkeley, tel. 510/848–9005.*

Reid's. Preacher putting you to sleep? A visit to Reid's will reaffirm your faith in gospel—they stock CDs, cassettes, robes, the works. *3101 Sacramento St., at Prince St., Berkeley, tel. 510/843–7282.*

Saturn Records. Who would have guessed that the yup-scale neighborhood of Rockridge would house some of the best hard-to-find vinyl? The wall-to-wall racks contain excellent and extensive selections of rock, jazz, blues, oldies, show tunes, and soundtracks as well as some used CDs. *5488 College Ave., at Lawton St., Oakland, tel. 510/654–0335.*

Household Furnishings

The Bay Area might be a nightmare when it comes to finding a place to live, but it's a dream when it comes to furnishing your pad. Garage, sidewalk, estate, and yard sales abound; check the *Bay Guardian, SF Weekly,* or *San Francisco Chronicle,* and watch for fliers on telephone poles, especially on summer weekends. **Thrift stores** abound: Try Goodwill or Salvation Army (*see box, below*) or Valencia Street, in the Mission. Stores like **Hocus Pocus** (900 Valencia St., at 20th St., tel. 415/824–2900) and **Jim's Used Furniture** (1499 Valencia St., at 26th St., tel. 415/285–2049) are piled high with furniture and knickknacks. **Thrift Town** (*see* Secondhand Clothing, *above*) has one of the largest selections at great prices. In the East Bay, Berkeley has nearly perfected the art of furnishing student apartments cheaply. You'll find moderately priced furniture basics on San Pablo Avenue near University Avenue; University itself is lined with futon shops; and north of University, Fourth Street is slowly accumulating upscale furniture outlet stores (a good place to window shop for decorating ideas). Nearby, venerable **Whole Earth Access** (2907 7th St., at Ashby Ave., tel. 510/845–3000) is a convenient one-stop shop with moderate prices.

SAN FRANCISCO

Community Thrift. Come here to rummage around the selection of furniture (including sofas, desks, and easy chairs) starting around $30. They also stock clothing, books, some kitchenware, and a few bikes. *623 Valencia St., btw 17th and 18th Sts., tel. 415/861–4910.*

Cookin': Recycled Gourmet Appurtenances. Here are used fondue makers, espresso machines, cookie cutters, Jell-O molds, pots, pans, and everything else you can't afford new. *339 Divisadero St., btw Oak and Page Sts., tel. 415/861–1854.*

Super Thrift. Though not as "thrifty" as Community Thrift, their furniture is in better condition and still cheaper than antique stores: Kitschy lamps start at around $20. All said, the real reason to seek out Super Thrift is their aisles of kitchen supplies. *560 Valencia St., near 17th St., tel. 415/255–4877.*

EAST BAY

Crate and Barrel Outlet. This is the only outlet store in California for Crate and Barrel's popular wooden furniture, kitchenware, and decorative items. Most of the stock consists of irregular or discontinued items (only a few pieces of furniture), but everything is functional and priced about 30%–50% lower than at their regular stores. *1785 4th St., near Hearst St., Berkeley, tel. 510/528–5500.*

Urban Ore. Eureka! It's the mother lode of all garage sales. You could outfit your entire house with the choice of sofas, chairs, tables, and dressers from this giant warehouse/junkyard. Couches start around $15, as do bicycles (as long as you don't mind doing some repair work). If you don't find anything you like, check back a week or two later. *7th St., at Gilman St., Berkeley, tel. 510/559–4450.*

Flea Markets

Flea markets are overwhelming anywhere, and in the Bay Area they can approach the size of small towns. Entire fairgrounds, parking lots, and football fields are all full of good deals on antique furniture, clothes, toys, books, bikes . . . anything remotely old, quirky, or dusty. For more complete listings, pick up a copy of the free *Classified Flea Market,* available at most newsstands and convenience stores. If you're a real hound, either set the alarm clock and get there before the professionals move in, or go late in the day when sellers would rather lower prices than reload the damn truck. Noe Valley, particularly Church Street between 19th and 27th streets, is garage-sale paradise. So, too, are Dolores and Guerrero streets between 16th and 24th and 18th Street between Church and Castro streets.

Ashby BART Flea Market. The mix of goods here is decidedly "Berkeley." Vendors of used furniture and clothing always have some funky desks or a good vintage coat they're willing to lower the price on, as well as manly man tools, blenders, African-American jewelry, used

One Person's Garbage. . .

The cheapest furniture of all comes from the street. Scavenging is best on the first and last days of every month, when people move out of their apartments and leave their sofas and other furniture to the winds of fate. Even better, however, are the legendary Neighborhood Cleanups, when residents of a particular neighborhood are allowed to leave furniture, appliances, and any other hefty pieces of so-called junk on the street; in the morning, the city hauls it away for free. Most folks will put their stuff out around 8 or 9 PM; get at it early, before the secondhand-furniture salespeople sweep everything into their big trucks. Russian Hill, Pacific Heights, and the Marina generally have the toniest goods. For specific San Francisco Neighborhood Cleanup dates, call Sunset Scavenger (tel. 415/330–1355). In Berkeley, where Neighborhood Cleanup happens only once a year in each neighborhood, call Berkeley Refuse (tel. 510/644–8856). A better deal in the East Bay, though, comes every May when year-round residents "dumpster dive" for the stuff departing U.C. students can't fit in the U-Haul. Before you start your search, remember that free don't always mean tasteful; the lower your standards and the better your sense of humor, the more luck you'll have.

bikes, and secondhand (or thirdhand) books. To top it off, you'll find fresh produce from local farmers. *Ashby BART station, cnr Ashby Ave. and MLK Jr. Way, Berkeley, tel. 510/644–0744. Open weekends 8–7.*

Coliseum Swap Meet. This vast flea market sprawls across the drive-in movie theater parking lot next to the Oakland Coliseum. You'll find furniture, clothing, electronic goods—everything but the kitchen sink (well, maybe that too). *5401 Coliseum Way, tel. 510/534-0325. Hwy. 880 and Coliseum Way, near Coliseum BART station. Open weekends 8-4.*

NorCal Swap Meet. Larger than Ashby but smaller than the Coliseum, this market at Laney College in Oakland is especially good for wacky, off-the-wall items and lots of fresh produce. Although there are plenty of organized stands, the best finds require digging through the vendors' piles. *7th and Fallon Sts., near Lake Merritt BART station, tel. 510/769-7266. Open weekends 7:30–4.*

San Jose Flea Market. One of the world's largest, this market to end all markets houses some 2,600 vendors over a 120-acre area. Selling everything from furniture to car parts to clothes to farm-fresh produce, this site may be bigger than your hometown. *12000 Berryessa Rd., tel. 408/453–1110. 13th St. exit from U.S. 101, or Bus 36 (direction: East San Jose) from College Park CalTrain station. Open Wed.–Sun. dawn–dusk.*

Specialty Items

The Bay Area attracts weird specialty goods the way a black hole attracts . . . well, you get the idea. Maybe it's because San Francisco and Berkeley harbor such an abundance of special-interest groups and bizarre individuals; maybe it's because people come here to create a niche for themselves and need the proper accessories. In the city, the **Castro** abounds with places that complement almost any kind of queer lifestyle; the **Haight** offers lots of head shops and tie-dye boutiques for the neo-hippie crowd; and both the **Mission** and the Haight provide *botanicas* and other "magic" shops for those who want to flirt with the occult. If you prefer mass-produced style, try Macy's downtown. Head to **Berkeley** if you're looking for political consumerism, "herbal" goods, or the street-fair atmosphere of Telegraph Avenue.

ART AND PHOTOGRAPHY **Adolph Gasser.** Your best source for photography and video equipment, Gasser has the largest inventory of such items in Northern California. *181 2nd St., btw Howard and Mission Sts., tel. 415/495–3852. Other location: 5733 Geary Blvd., at 22nd Ave., tel. 415/751–0145.*

Amsterdam Art. A favorite of local artists for years, Amsterdam Art stocks supplies for painting, printmaking, ceramics, and more. If you need canvas, frames, or merely a good set of pens,

It's Musty, It's Dusty, but It's Mine

Can't stand to pay $20 for a beach-glass ashtray at Z Gallerie, or $30 for a candlestick at Urban Outfitters? Join the too-cool-to-be-suckered club and head to your neighborhood Salvation Army, Goodwill, or St. Vincent de Paul—where you can flick around a fiver and get more than attitude back. Goodwill (2279 Mission St., tel. 415/826–5759 or 1700 Haight St., tel. 415/387–1192) is best for clothing and tries hard to look like a department store, not a thrift shop. The Salvation Army's Oakland store (601 Webster St., tel. 510/451–4514) has lots of good furniture and household items, and St. Vincent de Paul (1529 Haight St., tel. 415/621–7375 ;1745 Folsom St., tel. 415/626–1515; 2009 San Pablo, Berkeley, tel. 510/841–1504) has a great selection of virtually everything. Now you know. And knowing is half the battle.

this is the place. *1013 University Ave., near San Pablo Ave., Berkeley, tel. 510/649–4800. SF location: 5424 Geary Blvd., tel. 415/751–6248.*

Art Rock Gallery. Put Hole or the Grateful Dead on your wall for $10 and up. Handmade silkscreened posters—many in an artsy-vintage style—run $15–$20. *1153 Mission St., btw 7th and 8th Sts., tel. 415/255–7390.*

Looking Glass. This small store sells tripods, paper, film, books, and other photographic supplies. They also offer classes and darkroom space ($6 per hour). *2848 Telegraph Ave., at Oregon St., Berkeley, tel. 510/548–6888.*

CHARITABLE CAUSES **Global Exchange.** Specializing in handmade crafts (from African jewelry to Guatemalan backpacks), Global Exchange hosts occasional lectures and has info on Third World tours and seminars. *2840 College Ave., at Russell St., Berkeley, tel. 510/548–0370. S.F. location: 3900 24th St., at Sanchez St., tel. 415/648–8088; Mill Valley location: 167B Throckmorton Ave., tel. 415/389–6950.*

Planet Weavers Treasure Store. Indulge your socially conscious side with an international hand-crafted gift or toy from this UNICEF-run store. Also on hand is a good selection of world music, bongos, and Australian didgeridoos. A portion of the proceeds goes to the U.N. children's fund. *1573 Haight St., btw Ashbury and Clayton Sts., tel. 415/864–4415.*

Under One Roof. They share a roof with the NAMES project and sell goods gathered from 62 AIDS organizations. You'll find all kinds of gifts, including radical queer T-shirts, household goods, and cards. *2362B Market St., btw Noe and Castro Sts., tel. 415/252–9430.*

BODY DECORATIONS **Blue Buddha Tattoo.** The location of this basic, anything-but-flashy tattoo parlor across from Ashby BART is prime. Tattoos run the gamut from basic flesh art to elaborate designs, their needles are always sterile, and prices are lower than those at most other parlors. *1959 Ashby Ave., Berkeley, tel. 510/549–9860.*

Gauntlet. The only reminders of its hard-core S&M past are a few intimidating black leather and metal displays in the lobby. Gauntlet's well-informed staff has great bedside manners and has been piercing safely since 1975. This is the place to get your tongue pierced, your questions answered, and to learn how to care for your new hole. *2377 Market St., at 17th St., tel. 415/431–3133.*

Nomad. The employees are versed in tribal mythologies, and piercings lean toward wood and ivory, though they're educated in the ways of the implant-grade, surgical-steel spike as well. Piercings take place among lush plants and soothing African rhythms. *1881 Hayes St., btw Ashbury St. and Masonic Ave., tel. 415/563-7771.*

Primal Urge. If you feel the need to tattoo an ancient Sumerian hieroglyph from the post-Mesolithic period on your bum, Primal Urge will accommodate, provided you have an ID proving you're over 18. Appointments are necessary if your interests are much more complicated than a heart or "Mom." *2703 Geary Blvd., at Masonic, tel. 415/474–3442. Closed Mon.–Tues.*

GAMES AND TOYS **FAO Schwarz Fifth Avenue.** The dancing bears, singing dolls, and non-stop incantations of "Welcome to Our World of Toys" are guaranteed to further stimulate already sugar-crazed youngsters. Here you'll find the home of some of the most lavish, elaborate toys you never knew you needed, including that giant keyboard that Tom Hanks played on in the movie *Big. 48 Stockton St., at O'Farrell St., tel. 415/394–8700.*

Games of Berkeley. This store is for the immature geek in all of us: Dungeons and Dragons, board games, puzzles, modeling kits, or small plastic thingies that hang off pencils. *2010 Shattuck Ave., near University Ave., Berkeley, tel. 510/540–7822.*

Gamescape. They've got sci-fi and war board games, playing cards, gambling paraphernalia (for recreational use only, of course), tarot cards, and lots more for those long, boring winter nights. *333 Divisadero St., btw Page and Oak Sts., tel. 415/621–4263.*

HATS AND JEWELRY **African Outlet.** Reasonably priced African textiles, shell jewelry, hats, and other accessories line the walls here. *524 Octavia St., btw Hayes and Grove Sts., tel. 415/ 864–3576.*

Gallery of Jewels. Gallery of Jewels stocks rhinestone, glass, silver, and metal jewelry crafted by local artisans. The styles are eclectic, the prices high—it's not Tiffany & Co., nor is it cheap-o-rama junk. *1400 Haight St., at Masonic Ave., tel. 415/255–1180.*

Zeitgeist. Remember when watches were built to last? So do the fully apprenticed owners of Zeitgeist, who repair and restore clocks, jewelry, and any watch worth salvaging. They also sell beautiful vintage wristwatches and pocket watches from the likes of Grüen and Bulova. *437B Hayes St., at Gough St., tel. 415/864–0185.*

PAPER, CARDS, AND STATIONERY **Does Your Mother Know . . .** This queer card shop features coming-out cards, same-sex love cards, and *fabulous* gay humor cards. *4079 18th St., near Castro St., tel. 415/ 864–3160.*

Kozo Bookbinding. Beautiful Japanese stationery, blank books, and other frivolities cost a pretty penny here. The poster-sized silk-screened wall-hangings range from $4 for a basic print to $40 for elaborate designs on handmade paper. *531 Castro St., btw 18th and 19th Sts., tel. 415/621–0869.*

Tilt. Looking for anything *other* than a postcard with a fog-shrouded bridge? Head straight to the colorful walls of this wacky shop. The selection includes old pictures of SF, weird snapshots of Americana, and postcards from the fifties. They're also the exclusive distributor of posters by Frank Kozik, whose psychedelic art has advertised bands like the Butthole Surfers, Melvins, and Green Day. *1441 Grant St., btw Green and Union Sts., tel. 415/986–8866. Other locations: 507 Columbus Ave., near Stockton St., tel. 415/788–1112; 1427 Haight St., near Masonic St., tel. 415/255–1199.*

SEX ACCESSORIES **Good Vibrations.** This cooperatively owned, feminist sex shop for people of all persuasions stocks a dazzling selection of vibrators (there's even an antique vibrator museum), other sex toys, videos, and literature on all topics sexual. If you think all sex shops are sleazy, you haven't been here. *1210 Valencia St., at 23rd St., tel. 415/974–8980, http://www.goodvibes.com. Berkeley location: 2504 San Pablo Ave., at Dwight Way, tel. 510/841–8987.*

Image Leather. Accommodate all your intimate leather needs with a wide variety of nipple rings, harnesses, whips, collars, and boots. Looking for something a bit more . . . physical? Descend to the "Dungeon Room" for things to go "bump" with in the night. *2199 Market St., at Sanchez St., tel. 415/621–7551.*

SKATEBOARDS AND MOTORCYCLES **Deluxe.** Kick back with a regular posse of skaters and watch skate videos in a relatively upscale environment. Street wear and decks ($40–$45) abound, and the store features work (including display mannequins) by local skater/artist Kevin Ancell. *1831 Market St., btw Guerrero and Octavia Sts., tel. 415/626–5588.*

Dudley Perkins Harley-Davidson. This is the oldest Harley-Davidson dealership in the world. Check out the vintage Harleys for sale and on exhibit, and start saving up. *66 Page St., btw Franklin and Gough Sts., tel. 415/703–9494.*

Skates on Haight. S.O.H. is a long-time favorite of Bay Area skaters and their entourage. They sell decks (starting around $25) and snowboards, and rent in-line skates ($7 an hour or $28 a day) and snowboards (starting at $20 a day). Rentals include pads and boots, respectively. *1818 Haight St., btw Shrader and Stanyan Sts., tel. 415/752–8375.*

Wanna skate? Cruise over to Harrison Street between 16th and 20th streets, where the warehouses function as makeshift skate playgrounds.

VIDEO **Movie Image.** Film buffs will appreciate the great selection of film noir and other American classics, as well as the foreign and independent sections. If you're looking for a certain director, check the racks in the center of the store, where several famous moviemakers are showcased. *64 Shattuck Sq., near University Ave., Berkeley, tel. 510/649–0296.*

Naked Eye News and Video. This is definitely not Blockbuster. Come here for offbeat and hard-to-find titles (to rent or buy), and to peruse the racks of obscure, foreign, and alternative comics and 'zines. *533 Haight St., btw Fillmore and Steiner Sts., tel. 415/864–2985.*

Leather Tongue. This Mission institution rents the whole nine yards—cult, film noir, sci-fi, porn—plus they sell a lot of their titles outside on the sidewalk on weekends. Leather Tongue's greatest claim to fame, however, is their extensive collection of films by local and independent filmmakers. *714 Valencia St., tel. 415/552–2900.*

MISCELLANEOUS **Annapurna.** A "trip" to Berkeley is incomplete without a visit to the city's infamous head shop to pick up some incense, specialty cigarettes, hookahs, or a decorative pipe (for tobacco, of course). *2416 Telegraph Ave., near Haste St., Berkeley, tel. 510/841–6187.*

Capezio. When Bob Mandell's costume shop went out of business, Capezio bought some of his gear, and continues to keep the ball rolling. Fake hands, clown ruffles, vampire teeth, ball gowns, capes, and other miscellany await you—for the holidays or for every day. *126 Post St., btw Grant Ave., and Kearny St., tel. 415/421–5657.*

Guitar Solo. You probably can't afford a 1968 Ramirez or one of the upper-end steel-string guitars sold here, but it's still fun to dream. Their stock is expansive, but if they don't have that obscure piece of music you're searching for, they'll order it. *1411 Clement St., btw 15th and 16th Aves., tel. 415/386–0395.*

Lady Luck Candle Shop. The proprietor of this tiny shop is so convincing that even the most bitter cynic will feel compelled to buy a hope candle. The devotional candles, love potions, and wide selection of incense will thrill your favorite mystic. *311 Valencia St., btw 14th and 15th Sts., tel. 415/621–0358.*

Lhasa Karnak. An excellent source for herbs and herbal information, Lhasa Karnak's staff is knowledgeable and friendly. Take advantage now—before the FDA regulates or outlaws herbs. *2513 Telegraph Ave., at Dwight Way, Berkeley, tel. 510/548–0380. Other location: 1938 Shattuck Ave., Berkeley, tel. 510/548–0372.*

Yahoo Herb'an Ecology. Yahoo promotes urban ecology through the sale of compost materials (like worm boxes and organic seeds), and their fund-raising benefits include hip-hop shows and poetry readings. Call before stopping by as the staff takes occasional siestas. *968 Valencia St., btw 20th and 21st Sts., tel. 415/282–WORM. Open Fri.–Mon. noon–6.*

FOOD

4

Tara Duggan and Maureen Klier, with Charlene Pinzon

The Bay Area is blessed with enough restaurants to satisfy a staggering variety of tastes—from shellfish to tofu to the exotic beyond. Waves of Asian and Mexican immigrants have made San Francisco a flavorful and festive hotbed of cheap taquerías, backstreet Chinese holes-in-the wall, gracious Thai and Vietnamese establishments, reasonably priced sushi houses, and Korean barbecue joints. Oakland is known for southern-style eats and its less-touristy version of Chinatown. Berkeley has an entire Gourmet Ghetto, and even Marin County and the suburban South Bay host dining spots to boast of—if only for their waterfront views.

Besides restaurants with a regional, national, or ethnic theme, you'll also encounter a strange breed of establishments offering Southeast Asian and Mediterranean food, with a little traditional American thrown in, and always with a new twist. Though these nouvelle menus may offend your sense of authenticity (and indulgence), don't be afraid to take a jump into the eclectic abyss of California cuisine. This regional food-as-art has won world renown for its commitment to the idea that fresh, home-cultivated ingredients (no matter how expensive) are vital to the success of a dish. Of course, presentation is key, too, which you can experience most fully at the **Flying Saucer** (*see below*), a fashionable restaurant in San Francisco's Mission District where food is architecture. Who knows, if it weren't for Berkeley chef Alice Waters, who in 1971 supposedly started the whole California dining scene by opening the now legendary **Chez Panisse** (*see below*), you might—horror of horrors—never have heard of polenta, goat cheese, or arugula.

Not all of us have $65 to drop on a prix-fixe dinner, and you certainly don't have to. A huge, messy burrito or a bounteous bowl of fresh Chinese noodles can be yours for less than $5. If you want more ambience with your chow, there are hundreds of excellent sit-down restaurants throughout the Bay Area in the $10–$15 range. Or spend a few bucks more and get your quota of food and entertainment all in the same place at one of San Francisco's flashy supper clubs (*see box* Music to the Mouth, in Chapter 6).

While searching out the perfect place to feed your head, you may notice that a surprising (if not suspicious) number of the Bay Area's more than 4,000 restaurants have received favorable reviews, which they display in their windows, usually conspicuously close to their menus. Always check the dates of reviews, because restaurants regularly change hands, and chefs sometimes bask too much in enthusiastic press coverage. *Examiner* food critic Jim Wood is pretty reliable, except that his audience tends to have fat wallets. The *Bay Guardian*'s main reviewers are Stephanie Rosenbaum, who hits the more upscale restaurants, and Dan Leone, who covers dives; both can be trusted for their wit and taste. As a matter of fact, both the *Guardian* and the *S.F. Weekly* have extensive, wisely chosen Bay Area restaurant listings.

San Francisco

CASTRO/NOE VALLEY

The Castro District teems with lively restaurants, many with outdoor patios to optimize your people-watching pleasure. Brunch seems to be the district's most popular meal. Mimosas and espressos flow freely on weekend mornings, and the crowd is always jovial and loud. Follow the sunglass-wearing masses to the two hottest brunch spots, **Café Flore** (*see* Chapter 5) and the **Patio Café** (*see below*), and brace yourself for a long afternoon of Bloody Marys. The after-hours eating scene around **Castro Street** is just as vibrant—you don't have to look too far for a casual dinner spot, even late into the night (*see box* Late-Night Grubbing, *below*). But if you really want to impress someone, the new, super-trendy **2223 Market** (2223 Market, at Noe St., tel. 415/431–0692) is considered the best restaurant in the neighborhood. The cuisine is all Californian, and entrées cost about $15 each.

Just over the hill from the Castro around 24th Street, **Noe Valley** is a placid oasis awash in young liberal professionals, including a sizable lesbian contingent. It's a popular destination on sunny weekend mornings for a lazy brunch and a bit of window-shopping with the dog and/or the stroller. At night, Noe gets fairly quiet, as it's mostly residential.

➤ **UNDER $5** • **Hot 'n Hunky.** This pink, perky little restaurant with a preponderance of Marilyn Monroe posters on the walls is a Castro institution for thick, juicy burgers. With names like the Macho Man (three patties; $4), I Wanna Hold Your Ham (burger with ham and Swiss; $4),

Waiters on Wheels (tel. 415/252–1470) and Dine-One-One (tel. 415/771–DINE) will deliver anything from burgers to Italian to Cajun to Japanese from San Francisco restaurants for a $6-per-stop fee. Pick up one of their free delivery guides at a newspaper stand.

and Ms. Piggy (burger with cheddar and bacon; $3.50), ordering your food is half the fun. (Their garden burgers, at $4, are also dee-lish.) *4039 18th St., near Castro St., tel. 415/621–6365. Open Sun.–Thurs. 11 AM–midnight, Fri.–Sat. 11 AM–1 AM. No credit cards.*

Marcello's. These guys conjure up some of the best pizza in San Francisco, and it's right across the street from the Castro Theatre (*see* Movie Houses, in Chapter 6)—very convenient when it's almost show time. They sell by the slice ($1.75–$2.50) or the pie ($9.20–$18.50), and you can always find interesting combo slices like ham and pineapple or spinach with black olives and feta. They're open late on weekends, and they deliver for free. *420 Castro St., near Market St., tel. 415/863–3900. Open Sun.–Thurs. 11 AM–1 AM, Fri.–Sat. 11 AM–2 AM. Wheelchair access. No credit cards.*

Tom Peasant Pies. Tom serves only one thing—pies. Not big, meaty pies, but butter-and-cholesterol-free, fresh-outta-the-oven pies, at $2.50 a pop. One fits neatly into the palm of your hand, and two will easily satisfy your hunger. Start with ratatouille or potato-rosemary and finish with cherry anjou pear. This Noe Valley snack stand consists of a few bar stools lined against the front window, so plan to get your pies to go. *4108 24th St., at Castro St., tel. 415/642–1316. Open daily 8:30–7. Castro location: 4117 18th St., at Castro St., tel. 415/621–3632. Wheelchair access. No credit cards.*

➤ **UNDER $10** • **Eric's Hunan and Mandarin.** Looks can be deceiving at this popular Noe Valley restaurant. The airy space, hardwood floors, and scattered orchids that would normally adorn a more upscale eatery shelter a casual, neighborhoody crowd. If the reasonable prices don't shock you, the authentic and first-rate Chinese food will. An order of tangy sesame beef ($6.50) with the Hoisin string beans ($5.25) will stuff a party of two. Weekday lunch specials ($4) include an entrée and a soup. After you've eaten yourself silly, browse the sidewalk flower stand just outside. *1500 Church St., at 27th St., tel. 415/282–0919. Open weekdays 10:30–9:15, Sat. 10:30–10, Sun. 12:30–9:15.*

Josie's Cabaret and Juice Joint. By night it's a well-known performance venue featuring gay comedy acts like the Kinsey Sicks—a hilarious drag, a cappella, beauty-shop quartet. By day it's an easygoing neighborhood hangout with a 100% vegetarian menu of fresh organic juices, salads, sandwiches, and breakfast items. Pastas are $6.50; and you can get a small salad, or soup, or a fruit smoothie for less than $3. Come on a sunny day and eat outside on the pretty back patio. *3583 16th St., at Market St., tel. 415/861–7933. Restaurant open daily 9–8. Cabaret performances Wed.–Sun. 8 PM; cover $5–$12. No credit cards.*

La Méditerranée. This small, personable restaurant on the edge of the Castro District serves great—you guessed it—Mediterranean food, including dolmas, salads, hummus, baba-ghanoush, and levant sandwiches (appetizers: $4–$7; entrées: $6–$10). If you can't decide, get the Middle Eastern combination plate (vegetarian or not): two phyllo pastries, a levant sandwich, luleh kabob, and salad for $7.50. Dessert lovers shouldn't miss the decadent *datil* ($3.50), a dense roll made of dates, phyllo dough, nuts, and cream. *288 Noe St., at Market St., tel. 415/431–7210. Open Sun. and Tues.–Thurs. 11–10, Fri.–Sat. 11–11. Other locations: 2210 Fillmore St., at Sacramento St., tel. 415/921–2956; 2936 College Ave., at Ashby Ave., Berkeley, tel. 510/540–7773.*

Miss Millie's. This cute-as-a-button breakfast spot opened up recently in Noe Valley looking like Grandma's (freshly painted) kitchen. The carved wood booths, frilly curtains, and antique fixtures will get you in the mood for homemade jams, scones, and cinnamon rolls. The menu isn't as extensive or cheap as in breakfast joints in the Mission or Haight, but what Miss Millie's crew does whip up is excellent. Try the lemon ricotta pancakes in blueberry syrup ($7), or a fluffy omelet ($7.75) filled with oven-roasted tomatoes, basil, and feta cheese and served with a scone and roasted root vegetables. *4123 24th St., at Castro St., tel. 415/285–5598. Open Tues.–Fri. 7:30–2:30 (breakfast until 11:15), weekends 9–2. Wheelchair access. $15 minimum on credit cards.*

No-Name (Nippon) Sushi. Everybody calls it No-Name Sushi, even though the proprietors did eventually put up a tiny sign in the window officially dubbing it "Nippon." This small wood-paneled restaurant on Church Street almost always has a line out the door because it serves huge sushi combos at prices that are hard to believe—try $6–$10 on for size. (If you're a sushi snob, you'll know that such low prices do come at the price of freshness.) No alcohol is served, but most people bring theirs in a bag. *314 Church St., at 15th St., no phone. Open Mon.–Sat. noon–10. No credit cards.*

Pasta Pomodoro. At this bustling Castro hangout, you can eat a super-cheap plate of pasta and do a bit of cruising on the side. It's always full of people, but the wait list moves fast. Try the polenta with fontina cheese and tomato sauce ($3.75), or the penne *puttanesca* (with black olives, capers, anchovies, and tomato; $5). The scrumdeleeicious caprese sandwich ($5), with fresh mozzarella, tomatoes, basil, and olive purée, comes with a side salad. *2304 Market St., at 16th St., tel. 415/558–8123. Open Mon.–Thurs. 11 AM–midnight, Fri. and Sat. 11 AM–1 AM, Sun. noon–midnight. Other locations: 2027 Chestnut St., at Fillmore St., tel. 415/474–3400; 655 Union St., near Columbus St., tel. 415/399–0300. Wheelchair access.*

Patio Café. The Castro's premiere brunch spot operates out of an enormous converted greenhouse complete with fake parrots perched among the foliage. Enough Bloody Marys ($3) are consumed here to conk out a small army. Eggs or omelets with home fries go for $4–$7, and sinful cheese blintzes with cherry sauce are $7. Later in the day, you can chow down on sandwiches, burgers, and pastas ($5–$8), or come for a more formal dinner, like a grilled New York steak ($11). *531 Castro St., btw 18th and 19th Sts., tel. 415/621–4640. Open Mon.–Thurs. 8 AM–10:30 PM, Fri. and Sat. 8 AM–11 PM, Sun. 8:30 AM–10 PM.*

If you get stuck waiting for a table at Thai House on Noe, meander around the coveted Duboce Triangle neighborhood: Both Henry and Noe streets are thickly lined with trees, well-tended flower gardens, and some of the most beloved Victorians in the city.

> **UNDER $15 • Thai House on Noe.** The rich, spicy curries and elegant dining room, graced with white tablecloths and intricately carved wood panels, make this Duboce Triangle restaurant a popular choice for an intimate dinner. Try the duck on a bed of spinach with hot chili sauce ($9) or the mixed seafood in red curry with vegetables and basil ($10). There's often a wait, so reserve ahead. **Thai House II,** right around the corner on Market Street, is not quite as good but has

more room and an outdoor patio. *151 Noe St., at Henry St., tel. 415/863–0374. Open daily 5 PM–10 PM. Thai House II: 2200 Market St., at Sanchez St., tel. 415/864–5006.*

➤ **SPLURGE** • **Firefly.** Firefly's artsy, homey atmosphere captures Noe Valley's small-town charm. The menu changes weekly and revolves around the world in typical California fashion— you could choose between Mediterranean or Southeast Asian or American home cooking (or a variation on the above) on any given night. Budget room in your stomach to sample a few of their innovative appetizers ($5–$7), like golden beet soup or shrimp and scallop pot stickers. There are usually at least a couple of veggie and seafood entrées ($12–$17), such as halibut on polenta with asparagus and tarragon butter. *4288 24th St., at Douglass St., tel. 415/821– 7652. Open daily 5:30–9:30. Reservations advised. Wheelchair access.*

Late-Night Grubbing

Sadly, San Francisco is not a 24-hour city in the Berlin or NYC sense. In fact, most of the city's restaurants close by 11 PM, even on weekends. But if you just danced up an appetite at the DNA Lounge or ingested something likely to keep you up until tomorrow afternoon, you indeed can find a few places serving omelets and burgers, or even pot stickers, into the wee hours.

- *Bagdad Café. This 24-hour restaurant in the Castro—where people-watching is a high art—is as famous for its expansive street-level windows as its home-style breakfasts. 2295 Market St., at 16th St., tel. 415/621–4434.*

- *El Farolito. Stagger in here for a burrito as late as 2:45 AM (3:45 AM on Fri. and Sat.). If you've had a few, you probably won't even notice the grimy, cafeteria-style atmosphere. 2777 Mission St., btw 23rd and 24th Sts., tel. 415/824–7877.*

- *Grubstake. Housed in a converted railroad car, this diner fits right in to the grungy late-night Polk Gulch scene. 1525 Pine St., btw Polk St. and Van Ness Ave., tel. 415/673–8268. Open weekdays 5 PM–4 AM, weekends 10 AM–4 AM.*

- *Orphan Andy's. This all-hours Castro hangout is adorned with red vinyl booths, a lunch counter, and a jukebox—bring a date and stare dreamily into his eyes over a burger and a shake. 3991A 17th St., at Market and Castro Sts., tel. 415/864–9795.*

- *Pinecrest. A real-live retro diner—complete with a long formica counter and a bunch of old vinyl booths—Pinecrest has been serving juicy charbroiled half-pounders to late-night downtowners for decades. 401 Geary St., at Mason St., tel. 415/885– 6407. Open daily 24 hours.*

- *Silver. Reputedly popular with Chinatown gangsters, Silver offers all-hours Chinese cuisine (including dim sum) in a glaring fluorescent setting. 737 Washington St., at Grant Ave., tel. 415/433–8888. Open daily 24 hours.*

- *Sparky's. The menu might remind you of Denny's but—for what it's worth—they serve a much trendier post-club clientele on the edge of the Castro. They even deliver. 242 Church St., near Market St., tel. 415/626-8666. Open daily 24 hrs.*

Finding something to eat in Chinatown is a cinch. Finding something *good* to eat—well, that's a little trickier. Steer clear of the glaringly tourist-oriented places (where you have to ask for chopsticks and the patrons are all carrying shopping bags of souvenirs) and instead wander through the heart of Chinatown—**Washington, Clay,** and **Sacramento streets** between Mason and Kearny streets—until you find a restaurant that has the four elements that spell success: small, spare, cheap, and packed with locals. **Stockton Street** is the main market street, where you can load up on chow fun, ginger roots, and live turtles. If you're looking for dim sum, *see box, below.*

➤ **UNDER $5 • Kowloon.** This is one of the few places in the city where you can get all-vegetarian dim sum, which makes it popular with tree huggers and Buddhists alike. A cabbage-stuffed pot sticker or a crispy mushroom-potato cake sells for only about 60¢. If you'd rather go for a rice dish (brown rice optional; $3–$6), choose from a huge list that includes such exotica as vegetarian duck gizzards or vegetarian eel. *909 Grant Ave., near Washington St., tel. 415/362–9888. Open daily 9–9. Wheelchair access.*

Lucky Creation. This small restaurant in the heart of Chinatown serves fantastic meatless fare. From the green sign to the green menus, this place declares loud and clear its aim to please the vegetarian palate—and it's cheap. Spicy bean cake over rice goes for $4, and braised egg-plant in a clay pot will run you $4.25. *854 Washington St., btw Grant Ave. and Stockton St., tel. 415/989–0818. Open Thurs.–Tues. 11–9:30. Wheelchair access. No credit cards.*

➤ **UNDER $10 • Chef Jia's.** A few doors down from the ever-popular House of Nanking (*see below*), Chef Jia's manages to survive, indeed thrive, thanks to its top-notch Hunan and Mandarin cuisine. It's noisy and crowded, and the decor leaves a lot to be desired, but the onion cakes ($2) and the spicy string beans with yam ($5) are both to die for. Best of all, you'll be halfway through your mouthwatering honey-chili chicken ($5) before the Nanking diehards even reach the front door. *925 Kearny St., btw Jackson and Columbus Sts., tel. 415/398–1626. Open weekdays 11–10, weekends noon–10. No credit cards.*

House of Nanking. This Chinatown hole-in-the-wall recently added a new room to accommo-date the hordes in the know about Nanking's excellent Shanghai home cooking and righteously low prices. You'll be crammed into tiny tables with total strangers and the no-nonsense waiters will keep you on your toes, but all that only adds to the Nanking experience. Ask for the deli-

Dim Sum, a Cantonese Breakfast

Dim sum, or Chinese finger food, is to Chinatown as bagels are to New York. The meal is traditionally served early in the day in large banquet halls, where servers push around carts full of food—not your typical stir-fry, but savory pastries and dumplings you dip in a little soy sauce and pay for by the plate (the cart pushers stamp your bill every time you select a plate). Typical offerings include flaky potato cakes, sticky rice (steamed in bamboo leaves with meat and spices), shrimp and pork dumplings, steamed buns filled with barbecued pork or ginger-chicken, and large rice noodles rolled around shrimp.

Traditional dim sum specialties are greasy and pork-based, so you may not want to ask what's inside your pot stickers, and vegetarians should definitely stick to Kowloon (see above). Bustling Meriwa (see below) is good, cheap, and makes you feel like you've been beamed to Hong Kong; while Yank Sing (see Downtown restaurants, below) is more elegant and expensive. If your wallet's feeling light, a number of bakery/cafés around Chinatown and the Richmond district sell dim sum to go at about $1 for three items.

cious shrimp cakes in peanut sauce ($4)—they're not on the menu—or try the Nanking chicken ($5), a version of General Tso's chicken. *919 Kearny St., btw Jackson and Columbus Sts., tel. 415/421–1429. Open weekdays 11–10, Sat. noon–10, Sun. 4–10. No credit cards.*

Meriwa. This wood-paneled, red-bannered banquet hall is the place for a real Chinatown dim sum experience, chicken feet and all. It may be hard to hear yourself think amidst all the chatting Chinese-American families and gossiping old men sharing rounds of schnapps; but that's okay, you'll be too busy stuffing yourself with tasty dumplings and sticky rice. A reasonably hungry person can fill up for around $6 or less. *728 Pacific Ave., at Stockton St., 2nd Floor, tel. 415/989–8868. Open daily 7 AM–2:30 PM.*

Yuet Lee. This ambience-free joint on the congested corner of Broadway and Stockton feeds both tourists and locals authentic Cantonese cuisine, which means milder sauces and lots of exotic seafood. Share a huge platter of New Zealand mussels with black bean sauce ($8.50), or try a nonfishy dish, like the home-style beef stew clay pot ($5.50). They're open until 3 AM, if you're ever jonesin' sautéed fresh frogs ($16) late at night. *1300 Stockton St., at Broadway, tel. 415/982–6020. Open Wed.–Mon. 11 AM–3 AM. Wheelchair access. No credit cards.*

➤ **UNDER $15** • **R&G Lounge.** No one is going to accuse this upscale, somewhat sterile restaurant of being too festive, but it's worth the minisplurge for super-fresh Cantonese and seafood dishes, such as clams with spicy black bean sauce ($9.50) or mushrooms with tender greens ($8.50). Lunch prices—around $5 a rice plate—are easier to swallow. *631B Kearny St., btw Sacramento and Clay Sts., tel. 415/982–7877. Open daily 11–9:30.*

THE CIVIC CENTER AREA

This dining category comprises a few low-lying neighborhoods that aren't exactly what you'd call classy, except, of course, for the area immediately surrounding the Opera House and the Symphony Hall (*see* Chapter 6). **Hayes Valley,** to the west of **Civic Center** along Hayes and Grove streets between Franklin and Laguna streets, is a good example of gentrification in progress, with wine bars and chichi restaurants sprouting up beside fledgling art galleries (meanwhile, condemned public housing buildings loom a few blocks away). Running north of Civic Center on Polk Street, **Polk Gulch** gets some of the runoff from the drug and male prostitution trade in the nearby Tenderloin. But a bunch of movie theaters (*see* Chapter 6), laid-back cafés (*see* Chapter 5), and terrific international and ethnic dives might convince you of the Gulch's seedy charm. Stretching northeast of the Civic Center toward Downtown, the **Tenderloin** is definitely *not* where you want to take Grandma to dinner. Very few dining experiences are worth a stroll through the area surrounding Larkin, Market, O'Farrell and Mason streets after dark if you don't know your way around—except maybe an evening at Miss Pearl's Jam House (*see below*)—so try to stick to lunch or take a cab.

➤ **UNDER $5** • **Aladdin.** This recently opened Mediterranean restaurant in Polk Gulch, offers amazing deals on *shawerma* (rotisserie-roasted meat; $4.75) and falafels ($3.75). This is how it works: They hand you the pita full of meat or falafel, and you fill it up as much as you can at their generous buffet of scrumptious Mediterranean salads, sauces, and grilled veggies. The friendly guys behind the counter are always trying to force-feed you bonus falafel balls, but sadly, the place is often empty. They also deliver. *1300 Polk St., at Bush St., tel. 415/441–2212. Open Sun.–Thurs. 11–11, Fri. and Sat. 11–midnight.*

Main Squeeze. If you are overcome by the despair on display around the Civic Center, duck over to this space-age juice bar on Polk Street, innovatively designed with industrial materials molded into postmodern pieces of fruit. They specialize in juices and smoothies ($2.75–$4) and have mostly vegetarian and vegan lunch and breakfast items. Focaccia and pita sandwiches ($3–$4.50) and frozen yogurt ($2) cater to the health-conscious crowd. *1515 Polk St., at California St., tel. 415/567–1515. Open daily 8:30–8. Wheelchair access. No credit cards.*

Moishe's Pippic. This Hayes Valley Jewish deli will satisfy the corned-beef pangs of relocated, alienated East Coasters. They've got it all: kosher salami, hot dogs, corned beef, chopped liver, tongue, bagels and lox, matzo ball soup, Polish sausage, knishes . . . a big wet Bronx cheer to obsessively healthy California cuisine. Hot dogs are $2.50, sandwiches start at $4.25. *425A Hayes St., at Gough St., tel. 415/431–2440. Open weekdays 8–4, Sat. 9–4. No credit cards.*

Soups. In the middle of the Tenderloin, this place reaches out to the community with filling, homemade soups and a friendly, small-town atmosphere. For $2.75–$3.75, you get a huge bowl of soup (and half a bowl refill if you can hack it), limitless crackers, and a cup of either milk, coffee, or hot tea. A sign on the window welcomes anyone to use the bathroom, which goes to show how much the owner cares about the local homeless population. *784 O'Farrell St., at Larkin St., tel. 415/775–6406. Open Mon.–Sat. 10–6:30. Wheelchair access. No credit cards.*

➤ **UNDER $10** • **Ananda Fuara.** Escape from grimy Market Street into this soothing vegan/vegetarian restaurant with sky-blue walls and draped ivy plants. Servers sway by the tables in flowing saris, bringing sandwiches ($5) and entrées like curry with rice and chutney ($8). The massive Brahma burrito ($5.25) will fill you up for the rest of the day. *1298 Market St., at 9th St., tel. 415/621–1994. Open Mon.–Sat. 8–8 (Wed. until 3); free delivery weekdays 11–6, Sat. 11–3. Wheelchair access. No credit cards.*

Cordon Bleu. If you're on your way to the Lumiere Theater (in Polk Gulch), stop right next door at this tiny Vietnamese counter for a satisfying meal prepared right before your eyes. The two women who own the place only make a few things—kabobs, rice with a rich meat sauce, crispy imperial rolls, and Five-Spice Roast Chicken—but they're all dangerously addictive. Special # 5 ($6.25) includes all of the above, and can satisfy two carnivores. Lunch specials go for $3.50. *1574 California St., btw Polk and Larkin Sts., tel. 415/673–5637. Open Tues.–Sat. 11:30–2:30 and 5–10, Sun. 4–10. No credit cards.*

Racha Café. This industrial-meets-tropical (note the silver support pole/palm tree) Thai restaurant is right on the edge of the Tenderloin; it's best to come here via Polk Street at night. They offer a wide range of vegetarian, seafood, and meat entrées ($4.50–$10), and the coconut milk–based soups (with chicken, seafood, or vegetables; $6.50) are out of this world, flavored with lime, cilantro, and Thai spices. *771 Ellis St., btw Polk and Larkin Sts., tel. 415/885–0725. Open daily 11–9:30. Wheelchair access.*

Tu Lan. This greasy little dive in a really seedy section near Civic Center is famous for its fantastic Vietnamese grub—Herb Caen even documented Julia Child chowing down here at one point. The imperial rolls with rice noodles ($4.25) and lemon beef salad ($4.25) are among the favorite dishes on the expansive menu, which includes quite a few vegetarian choices. Bottles of imported beer are only $2 if you can ever get someone to bring you one. *8 6th St., at Market St., tel. 415/626–0927. Open Mon.–Sat. 11–9. No credit cards.*

Swan Oyster Depot. Politicians from the nearby City Hall can open their mouths wider than this fish market, which consists of nothing more than one long counter and some of the best damn seafood in town. The genial staff welcomes you with open arms and will promptly set you up with a bowl of clam chowder, thick sourdough bread, and an Anchor Steam beer for a fiver. Who knows, you might even see Mayor Willie Brown downing a crab cocktail or a salad ($5.50–$7.50) on the bar stool next to you. *1517 Polk St., btw California and Sacramento Sts., tel. 415/673–1101. Open Mon.–Sat. 8–5:30. No credit cards.*

➤ **UNDER $15** • **Nori Sushi.** Tucked on a small annex of Market Street in the no man's land between Civic Center and the Castro, this joint consists of an L-shaped bar, two booths, and one sushi master, Nori himself. Nori's only been in business for a year or so, but his place is always packed with people who know about his super-fresh AND incredibly inexpensive fish. Most *nigiri* (finger-size pieces of fish on a roll of rice) and six-piece rolls are only $3, so two people can have a sushi fest for less than $25 (not including sake). *1815 Market St. No. 5, btw Guerrero and Valencia Sts., tel. 415/621–1114. Open Tues.–Thurs. 11:30–2 and 5–10, Fri. 11:30–2 and 5–11, Sat. 5–11, Sun. 4–9. Wheelchair access. No credit cards.*

➤ **SPLURGE** • **Miss Pearl's Jam House.** Miss Pearl's frequent live reggae and calypso performances and DJ/dance bar (*see box* Music to the Mouth, in Chapter 6) attracts a young, lively crowd. You'll feel like you're in the tropics whether you drink a few aquarium-size fruit cocktails by the pool (weekends only; the pool belongs to the attached Phoenix Hotel) or dine on scrumptious Caribbean food in the Jamaican-style dining room. Try a round of unique appetizers like vegetarian white corn tamales with smoked tomatoes and a cilantro sauce ($6). As far as main courses ($11–$16) go, the Jamaican-style jerk chicken ($11) is famous in these parts, and they always have a vegetarian blue-plate special ($12). *601 Eddy St., at Larkin St., tel. 415/775–5267. Open Wed.–Thurs. 6 PM–10 PM, Fri.–Sat. 6 PM–11 PM, Sun. 11–2 and 5:30–9:30.*

Suppenküche. In the Asian- and Mediterranean-oriented Bay Area dining scene, it's hard to find a place serving German food that isn't dark, dingy, and full of crusty men with beer bellies. Yet this Hayes Valley restaurant has a lively yet elegant atmosphere and authentic but dignified German cuisine. Share a bowl of their creamy, delicious soup ($3.50), and then brace yourself for a main course, like venison sautéed in red wine sauce with red cabbage and noodles ($14.50) or farmer's sausage with sauerkraut and mashed potatoes ($9.50). It's not the best place for healthy eaters, but there's usually one vegetarian entrée and a fish of the day. *601 Hayes St., at Laguna St., tel. 415/252–9289. Open weekdays 5 PM–10 PM, weekends 10–3 (brunch) and 5–10. Reservations advised.*

At Suppenküche, simple long pine tables and whitewashed walls are set off with Bavarian Catholic touches, like candles and crucifixes. If you find yourself waiting for a table, head to the cozy bar, which is equipped with as many German beers on tap as Munich itself (well, almost).

Zuni Café. Zuni offers a slick atmosphere and extravagant food for those times when you're in a what-the-hell frame of mind. Lots of people just grab a ringside seat near the perennially packed bar and order appetizers and drinks. Sample from their wide selection of oysters ($1.50 each) or try the Caesar salad ($8)—regulars swear it's the best they've ever had. If you're ready for a full meal, go for the wonderfully crisp and tender roasted chicken with Tuscan stuffing ($28 for two). But be prepared to get a few sneers from the wait staff if you look any younger than 30. *1658 Market St., btw Franklin and Gough Sts., tel. 415/552–2522. Open Tues.–Sat. 7:30 AM–midnight, Sun. 7:30 AM–11 PM.*

DOWNTOWN/EMBARCADERO

Downtown abounds with both old, classic restaurants that evoke San Francisco's golden years and trendy, new, let's-do-lunch-and-expense-it bistros; both take advantage of the high-rolling Financial District's need to dispose of income. Except for a few options below, it's difficult to find a decent *and* inexpensive sit-down restaurant in this area—but it's usually worth it when you decide to blow a few bucks, especially in the "French Quarter," which offers the almost identical cafés **Claude** and **Bastille** (*see below*). On the other end of the fiscal spectrum, it's not so hard to find healthy soup-and-salad buffets trying to keep all those working stiffs from succumbing to heart disease at a young age. As Downtown flows into the **Embarcadero,** stop by the bakery at **Il Fornaio** (1265 Battery St., at Greenwich St., tel. 415/986–0100) for a slice of pizza or panino picnic on the pier.

➤ **UNDER $5 • Specialty's.** These four tiny take-out stands bake 14 kinds of bread, including potato-cheese and carrot-curry, with which they will make any of 40—count 'em, 40—fresh sandwiches (most $3–$5). They also sell coffee and pastries (around $1.50), like zucchini bran muffins, and insanely rich sweets. If you don't feel like eating on the sidewalk, take your lunch over to the rooftop garden at Crocker Galleria (cnr Kearny and Post Sts.) and relax. *312 Kearny St., btw Bush and Pine Sts.; 22 Battery St., btw Market and Bush Sts.; 150 Spear St., btw Mission and Howard Sts.; 1 Post St., at Market St. Tel. 415/896–BAKE for daily specials, 415/512–9550 for phone orders. Open weekdays 6–6. No credit cards.*

➤ **UNDER $10 • 101 Restaurant.** Just steps from the Powell Street station towards the Tenderloin, this weary-looking but very reasonable restaurant serves up Vietnamese favorites like barbecue beef with rice noodles, lettuce, mint, peanuts, and bean sprouts ($4.50) or chicken in coconut-milk curry with lemongrass ($5.25). The lunch special ($4.75) includes soup, an imperial roll, and your choice of barbecued beef, chicken, or pork. *101 Eddy St., at Mason St., tel. 415/928–4490. Open Mon.–Sat. 11–9. Wheelchair access.*

➤ **UNDER $15** • **Café Bastille.** Stop by for neat little French appetizers, like onion soup, pâté, or baked goat cheese on eggplant ($4–$6), in a happening, Frenchy atmosphere. For a more substantial meal, try a sandwich ($7–$8), crêpe dinner ($7.25), or real meat-and-potatoes fare ($7–$12). Filled with quasi-hip Financial District workers and bohemians with a few bucks to blow, the café gets pretty fun and friendly, especially Wednesday through Saturday when there's live jazz. *22 Belden Pl., btw Pine and Bush Sts. and Kearny and Montgomery Sts., tel. 415/986–5673. Open Mon.–Thurs. 11–10, Fri. 11–11, Sat. 11 AM–2 AM.*

Café Claude. Live jazz accompanies your meal most nights at this youthful but bourgeois French bistro in an alley right near Chinatown's gates. With a more relaxed atmosphere than Café Bastille (*see above*), this is a great place to while away a lazy afternoon or a late evening with a few glasses of wine—there's no doubt you'll feel like you've been magically transported to Paris. As far as food goes, stick to the appetizers and specials menus, like the rich pâté plate ($5.50) or decadently rich *coq au vin* (chicken in wine sauce) with creamy au gratin potatoes ($12). *7 Claude Ln., off Bush St. btw Grant and Kearny Sts., tel. 415/392–3515. Open Mon.–Wed. 8 AM–9:30 PM, Thurs. and Fri. 8 AM–11 PM, Sat. 10 AM–11 PM (closing times vary depending on the crowd).*

There's a running debate in the city as to whether the waiters' accents at Café Claude are French or faux. Either way, their winning smiles and Gaulish good looks may persuade you to order up a storm.

Caffe Macaroni. They're not kidding when they say caffe—this place is tiny and usually packed elbow to elbow (though there's an additional room upstairs). But it's worth the wait for some of the city's most affordable, authentic Southern Italian food, served with a Neopolitan flair. No plate (even grilled swordfish) is ever over $14, and the crowd includes anyone from students to suits from the Transamerica Pyramid looming a few blocks away. A "small" antipasti plate ($6) will warm up at least three people's appetites, and the pasta dishes ($8.50–$9.25) are generous and delicious. Look for specials like squid-ink fettucine heaped with fresh mussels, clams, calamari, and crab legs. *59 Columbus Ave., at Jackson St., tel. 415/956–9737. Open weekdays 11:30–2:30 and 5:30–10:30, Sat. 5:30–10:30. No credit cards.*

Yank Sing. With a location in the Financial District and one South of Market, Yank Sing is a great place to feast on dim sum in a tasteful, modern setting. A meal should cost about $10–$15, but watch out: Let your appetite run away with you, and next thing you know, your pants are unbuttoned, your head is nodding, stacks of plates are sliding off the table, and the waiter is handing you a bill the size of Beijing. *427 Battery St., at Clay St., tel. 415/362–1640. Open weekdays 11–3, weekends 10–4. Other location: 49 Stevenson Pl., btw 1st and 2nd Sts., tel. 415/541–4949.*

FISHERMAN'S WHARF

Steer clear of the mediocre, high-priced seafood restaurants that compete for tourist bucks all along the wharf. The best dining experience you could have here would involve a loaf of sourdough, some cracked crab, a bottle of wine, a seat on the pier, and a tantalizing dining partner. The corner of **Jefferson** and **Taylor streets** is jam-packed with street stands that hawk all sorts of seafood goodies, including shrimp, prawn, or crab cups ($2.50–$4) and thick clam chowder in a bread bowl ($4). The only authentically rustic place to sit down and eat around here is **Eagle Café** (Upper level, Pier 39, tel. 415/433–3689), where windows and patio tables offer a view of the waterfront and Alcatraz. It's a good place to eat a bowl of clam chowder ($4.50) or a burger ($6) and plan your escape from Fisherman's Wharf. If the crowds are getting to you, soothe your nerves with an Irish coffee at the old-fashioned **Buena Vista Café** (2765 Hyde St., tel. 415/474–5044), who purportedly introduced the drink to America. The B.V.—as it's often called—manages to retain its dignity with its brass-and-wood interior, black-tie clad bartenders, and view of the Bay and Mt. Tamalpais, despite the hordes of tourists clamoring for a seat at the bar. Otherwise, nothing satisfies more than a scoop of **Ben and Jerry's** (near the Red and White Fleet's ticket booth) ice-cream.

THE HAIGHT

The Haight (both Lower and Upper) is renowned for its breakfast spots, including the **Pork Store Café**, the **Crescent City Café**, and **Kate's Kitchen** (*see below*). These places are full of the youth of today—in case you can't tell, they're the ones smoking, looking ragged, and sucking up coffee like it's the primal life force. For dinner, the Haight offers a few trendy hot spots and a preponderance of pizza, falafel, and burrito joints, which cheaply provide the necessary carbohydrates to propel you to the next bar.

➤ **UNDER $5** • **Balazo.** This isn't the Mission, but that's precisely Balazo's appeal—its new-agey Cal-Mex food. Choose from three kinds of veggie burritos ($3.85), stuffed with saffron rice, beans, Mexican goat cheese, and/or vegetables sautéed on a vegetarian grill. The burrito vallarta ($5), with sautéed rock prawns, tender nopales cactus, red peppers, and black beans, is so good you'll want to come back tomorrow and eat it again. They also have huge dinner platters ($5) that are meant to be shared. Eat in the back room and listen to live flamenco guitar. *1654 Haight St., btw Belvedere and Clayton Sts., tel. 415/864–8608. Open Sun.–Thurs. 10 AM–11 PM, Fri.–Sat. 10 AM–1 AM. No credit cards.*

Studio Café. This tiny café-eatery features whitewashed walls, old farmhouse furniture, a friendly atmosphere, and a great lookout on Lower Haight's crazy-colored Victorians. The Morning Special, available daily until 11 AM, includes three steamed eggs (like scrambled but without the butter or oil), a bagel or pastry, and a cup of coffee for $3.50; Studio Spuds are an extra 50¢. The baked tofu scrambled with mushrooms, tomato, onion, and cheese ($5) is also a wonderful way to brunch. Sandwiches or scrumptious quiches run about $5 and include a side salad. *248 Fillmore St., btw Haight and Waller Sts., tel. 415/863–8982. Open weekdays 7 AM–9 PM (Fri. until 10 PM), Sat. 8 AM–10 PM, Sun. 9 AM–9 PM. No credit cards.*

➤ **UNDER $10** • **Crescent City Café.** This New Orleans-style café has just six small tables and maybe a dozen counter seats—you might annoy loyal customers if you come for brunch on weekends, when it gets packed to the gills. Then again, the call of Andouille hash ($5.75) or eggs Creole ($6.75; like eggs Benedict except with avocado and Creole sauce), can be pretty irresistible. The same goes for the Thursday night barbecued-rib special ($9). *1418 Haight St., at Masonic St., tel. 415/863–1374. Open daily 8–4 and 5–10.*

Kan Zaman. Patrons pack into this trendy Mediterranean restaurant to listen to hypnotic Middle Eastern music and indulge in hummus ($3), babaghanoush ($3), and spinach pies ($3.25). If you need that final push to reach a dreamlike state, fork over $7 for a huge hookah (a traditional water pipe) with your choice of flavored tobacco—the apple is excellent. (Because of San Francisco's new anti-smoking laws, you can only smoke hookahs at the bar or in the dining area after the kitchen closes.) On Friday, Saturday, and Sunday nights the Fat Chance Belly Dancers do their seductive thing. *1793 Haight St., at Shrader St., tel. 415/751–9656. Kitchen open Mon. 5 PM–11 PM, Tues.–Thurs. and Sun. noon–11, Fri. and Sat. noon–midnight; bar open weekends until 2 AM. No credit cards.*

Kate's Kitchen. Get to this popular breakfast spot early, especially on weekends, unless you want to wait forever for a table. The wholesome food, though, is worth the wait. Chummy servers bring you specials like buttermilk-cornmeal pancakes ($4 short, $6 tall) or hush puppies with honey butter ($2.25 for six). The fruit orgy ($5)—comprised of fresh fruit, yogurt, honey, and granola—is aptly named. *471 Haight St., btw Fillmore and Webster Sts., tel. 415/626–3984. Open Mon. 9 AM–2:45 PM, Tues.–Fri. 8 AM–2:45 PM, weekends 9–3:45.*

Massawa. If you've never had Ethiopian food before, and you (1) like to eat with your hands and (2) relish unusual spices, then you must come here. You get a dinner platter filled with tender lamb or beef ($8–$10), usually with side portions of lentils, greens, or yellow split-pea paste. (Vegetarian dishes run $6–$9.) All plates come with *injera*, a flat, spongy bread used instead of silverware to scoop up food. *1538 Haight St., btw Ashbury and Clayton Sts., tel. 415/621–4129. Open Tues.–Sun. 11:30–10.*

Pork Store Café. This Haight Street joint is a great place to eat away your hangover. Mounds of grits ($1 for a side order), big fluffy omelets ($4.25–$6), and plate-size pancakes (a chocolate short stack is $4) are all slapped together on the same griddle. The café serves lunch, too—try the pork chops and applesauce ($6.75) when you need a little comfort food. While you're waiting in line (with a cup of complimentary coffee), check out the collection of posters from Haight-Ashbury street fairs past—they're almost as entertaining as the stream of locals strutting by. *1451 Haight St., btw Ashbury St. and Masonic Ave., tel. 415/864–6981. Open weekdays 7 AM–3:30 PM, weekends 8 AM–4 PM. Other location: 372 5th St., btw Harrison and Folsom Sts., tel. 415/495–3669.*

Spaghetti Western. The pierced-and-tattooed set eats breakfast and then hangs around all day at this chaotic Lower Haight spot. Gorge yourself on the Spuds O'Rama ($4.75), a huge, quivering mound of home-fried potatoes topped with cheese and sour cream, or the thick sourdough French toast ($5). *576 Haight St., near Steiner St., tel. 415/864–8461. Open weekdays 7 AM–3 PM, weekends 8 AM–4 PM.*

Squat and Gobble Café. This sprawling café-turned-breakfast-spot serves up home-style breakfasts to Lower Haight types who come armed with the Sunday paper, a pack of Marlboro reds, and nothing to do all day. Try the massive Lower Haight omelet, with fresh veggies, pesto, and cheese ($5.35), or any number of inventive crêpes, including the Zorba the Greek, with feta, olives, artichokes, spinach, and cheddar ($6). They also have a decent selection of salads and sandwiches. If you're the type who needs a pot of coffee before you can focus, be aware that refills are not free. *237 Fillmore St., btw Haight and Waller Sts., tel. 415/487–0551. Open daily 8 AM–10 PM. Other location: 1428 Haight St., btw Ashbury and Masonic Sts., tel. 415/ 864–8484.*

Ya Halla. This Lower Haight Middle Eastern restaurant is on a particularly grimy stretch of Haight Street, but inside you'll find a peaceful little enclave, replete with soothing Middle Eastern music. Chef Nadia attracts loyal customers with extremely fresh, delicious falafel and homestyle main dishes ($5.25–$8). All meals come with a plate of feta and olives, but the *meze* (appetizers; $3.25) are worth getting stuffed for. Beware, this place is extremely addictive: Both the eggplant *musakaa'h* (with roasted tomato, garlic, pine nuts and rice pilaf; $6) and the super falafel (with hummus, *mulabal*, and tabouleh in a burrito-style *lavash* wrap; $4) are incredible. *494 Haight St., near Fillmore St., tel. 415/522–1509. Open daily 11–11. Wheelchair access.*

➤ **UNDER $15** • **Cha Cha Cha.** You'll enjoy the skillfully prepared tapas and the pseudo-Catholic icons on the walls, but you'll wait all night for a table. Entrées range from $10 to $13, but it's de rigueur to stick to tapas like fried plantains with black beans and sour cream ($5.25) or shrimp sautéed in Cajun spices ($6.75). Wash it all down with plenty of sangria (which can help you pass your possibly two-hour wait in a painless haze). To avoid the crowds, come for a late lunch. *1801 Haight St., at Shrader St., tel. 415/386–7670. Open Mon.–Thurs. 11:30–3 and 5–11, Fri. 11:30–3 and 5–11:30, Sat. 11:30–4 and 5–11:30, Sun. 11:30–4 and 5–11.*

JAPANTOWN

In the **Japan Center** (1737 Post St., btw Geary and Fillmore Sts.), the veritable essence of Japantown, a bunch of decent restaurants—spanning a wide range of price categories—display their edibles via shiny photos or shellacked plastic miniatures. If nothing piques your interest, explore the surrounding streets, especially **Buchanan** and **Webster streets** to the north of the center, for older, more divey places that occasionally turn out to be gems. The cheapest option of all is to visit the Japanese market **Maruwa** (open Mon.–Sat. 10–7, Sun. 10–6), on the corner of Post and Webster streets. Along with fruits and vegetables and all manner of Japanese products, the delicatessen offers sushi, rice and noodle dishes, and individual cuts of meat. When you're done eating, go blow the rest of your money on a cheesy action movie at the multiscreen Kabuki 8 (*see* Movie Houses, in Chapter 6), in the same complex as the center.

➤ **UNDER $10** • **Isobune.** Patrons at this touristy but fun sushi restaurant pack in around a large table, elbow to elbow, and fish their sushi off little boats that bob about in the water in front of them. Kimono-clad chefs deftly mold the sushi and replenish the boats' cargoes as fast as they are emptied. Prices range from $1.20 for two pieces of mackerel or fried bean cake to $3 for two pieces of salmon roe or red clam. It may not be the best sushi you'll ever eat, but it's good enough for the price. *Japan Center, 1737 Post St., tel. 415/563–1030. Open daily 11:30–10. Oakland location: 5897 College Ave., at Chabot St., tel. 510/601–1424. Wheelchair access.*

Mifune. A steady stream of Asian and American patrons slurp up cheap, tasty *udon* (thick white noodles), *soba* (thin buckwheat noodles), and *donburi* (rice) dishes in the simple Mifune dining room. The noodles, which come with various meats and vegetables, cost anywhere from $3.50 for a plain broth to $8.50 for one with jumbo shrimp. *Japan Center, 1737 Post St., tel. 415/922–0337. Open daily 11–9:30. Wheelchair access.*

➢ **UNDER $15** • **Izumiya.** Ignore the requisite plastic sushi prototypes in the window and the cheesy decor—this place is almost always packed with a young crowd, giving it a kind of Japanese Mel's Diner atmosphere. The house special, orange roughy steamed in foil with lemon and noodles ($10.50; including salad, soup, and rice), is special for a reason, and the appetizers, such as the clams steamed in sake ($5.25), are equally fantastic. The menu is full of teriyaki and tempura combos ($9–$12), as well as sushi, though raw fish is not the main draw here. *Japan Center, 1737 Post St., tel. 415/441–6867. Open Tues.–Thurs. 11:30–3 and 5:30–10:30, Fri. 11:30–3 and 5:30–11, Sat. 11:30–11, Sun. 11:30–10. Wheelchair access.*

Now and Zen. This "enlightened vegan restaurant" about a block from the Japan Center began as a wholesale vegan bakery. So, of course, the highlights here are cakes and pastries that contain no eggs, milk, or sugar. Also offered at this friendly little café is a full range of delicious vegan meals made from organic ingredients with a Japanese twist. For lunch try the *vermicelli japonais* (pasta with oyster, shiitake, and enoki mushrooms in a soy, sake, Japanese basil, and seaweed sauce; $7); for dinner, the *macro sukiyaki* (vegetable medley with tofu and Japanese mountain yam noodles in a savory soy broth with brown rice; $12). *1826B Buchanan St., tel. 415/922–9696. Open Mon. 10–4:30, Tues.–Thurs. 10–4:30 and 5:30–9, Fri. 10–4:30 and 5:30–10, Sat. 10–3 and 5:30–10, Sun. 10–3 and 5:30–9. Wheelchair access.*

MARINA DISTRICT/COW HOLLOW

Although not exactly a budget locale, the Marina has recently been flooded with scores of new culinary hot spots. A 10-minute walk west of Fisherman's Wharf, lots of upscale restaurants—from grills to sushi spots to California-cuisine eateries—line **Chestnut** and **Union streets.** It's a nice place to take your honey for dinner when she passes the bar exam.

➢ **UNDER $10** • **Hahn's Hibachi.** This tiny restaurant, little more than a takeout counter, dishes up healthy portions of Korean-barbecued chicken, beef, or pork with rice and kimchi for about $6. Vegetarians will pay even less ($4) for a bowl of vegetable *udon* (noodle soup), and can shudder at menu items like "pile o' pork" and "meat mountain." So many people order takeout that there's rarely a wait for the five or so tables. *3318 Steiner St., btw Chestnut and Lombard Sts., tel. 415/931–6284. Open Mon.–Sat. 11:30–10. Other locations: 1710 Polk St., at Clay St., tel. 415/776–1095; 1305 Castro St. at 24th St., tel. 415/642–8151. No credit cards.*

Pluto's. The modern decor at this casual place includes an entire wall covered with countless adjectives describing food—an almost subliminal attempt at making you hungry. But chances are, you'll already be ravenous after waiting in line with the young Marina folks who come here in droves. The biggest line forms for the salad bar, where you can create a custom-made salad ($3.25–$4.50). The herb-roasted Sonoma turkey ($3.25) with the smashed spuds of the day ($1.45) will make you feel like you're having a top-notch Thanksgiving dinner. *3258 Scott St., at Chestnut St., tel. 415/7-PLUTOS. Open Mon.–Thurs. 11:30–10:00, Fri. 11:30–11, Sat. 9:30 AM–11:00 PM, Sun. 9:30 AM–10 PM.*

➢ **SPLURGE** • **Greens.** Head here for a treat after a long day of museums and cultural enrichment—or any time for that matter. This place will make you entirely reevaluate your notion of vegetarian dining. Greens serves state-of-the-art meals in a beautifully spacious, gallerylike setting with a romantic view of the Golden Gate Bridge. The menu is always fresh, and you might see such things as Moroccan carrot soup with spiced yogurt and cilantro, or soft polenta with chipotle butter and smoked cheese. "Café Dinners" (weekdays 5:30–9:30) feature entrées in the $10–$13 range, while the Saturday evening (mandatory) prix-fixe menu costs $38. *Fort Mason, Bldg. A, tel. 415/771–6222. Open Mon. 5:30 PM–9:30 PM, Tues.–Fri. 11:30–2 and 5:30–9:30, Sat. 11:30–2:30 and 6–9:30, Sun. 10 AM–2 PM. Wheelchair access.*

MISSION DISTRICT

Here you can wander from taquería to café to bookstore to taquería again in a salsa-and-cerveza-induced state of bliss. To add to the zillions of Mexican and Central American spots that already crowd the neighborhood, a smattering of trendy restaurants has sprouted up in recent years around the intersection of **16th** and **Valencia streets**—this is without a doubt the favorite area in town for young hipsters to wine and dine. The Mission's restaurants are accessible from either the 16th St./Mission or the 24th St./Mission BART stations.

If you're looking to celebrate, grab your friends and head to one of the Mission's many Mediterranean or Spanish tapas restaurants, where live music keeps things lively, red wine flows freely, and plates are meant to be shared and lingered over.

➤ **UNDER $5 • Casa Sanchez.** With a colorful outdoor patio, home-style cooking, and a friendly atmosphere, Casa Sanchez might just become your favorite taquería. Hefty combo platters ($4–$5.50) and limitless chips y salsa (both of which are homemade, as are the tortillas) will fill you to the bursting point. *2778 24th St., btw York and Hampshire Sts., tel. 415/282–2400. Open weekdays 10–6, weekends 10–5. Wheelchair access. No credit cards.*

El Toro. This lively, gringo-frequented taquería provides a wealth of choice: Spanish or vegetarian rice, four kinds of salsa, four colors of tortillas (white, wheat, red chile, or green chile), and no less than 10 types of protein to chose from, including *lengua* (beef tongue) and tofu ranchero. You'll have plenty of time to make up your mind, since the line often snakes out the door. Tacos run $1–$3, burritos $2.25–$6.25. *598 Valencia St., at 17th St., tel. 415/431–3351. Open daily 10–10. No credit cards.*

El Trébol. What El Trébol lacks in decor it quickly makes up for with incredibly cheap Central American fare and an animated, Spanish-speaking clientele. Specialties include *salpicón* (chopped beef), *chancho con yuca* (fried pork with cassava), and *pollo encebollado* (chicken with onions). Most entrées come with beans, rice, and tortillas, and all cost under $4. *3324 24th St., at Mission St., tel. 415/285–6298. Open weekdays noon–9, Sat. noon–8. Wheelchair access.*

La Cumbre. Large, colorful Mexican paintings line the walls, and the requisite Virgin Mary statue guards the front door of this bustling taquería. The tacos and burritos with *carne asada* (marinated beef; $2–$5.50) are so good you'll forget all about your high cholesterol. Meat ($7) and veggie ($5) dinner platters, which include beans and rice, will fuel you through the night and most of the next day. *515 Valencia St., btw 16th and 17th Sts., tel. 415/863–8205. Open Mon.–Sat. 11–10, Sun. noon–9. Wheelchair access.*

New Dawn. You'll find the most bizarre collection of kitsch you've ever seen in this slacker hangout, including a life-size Jesus wearing sunglasses. The decor is the main reason to come here—this is *not* haute cuisine—but the breakfasts, loaded with cholesterol, fat, starch, and everything else you need to remain immobilized for the rest of the day, effectively serve the role of hangover-helper. Share an enormous plate of veggie home fries (vegetables topped with a load of potatoes; $7), or go the familiar route with a three-egg breakfast ($4). *3174 16th St., btw Valencia and Guerrero Sts., no phone. Open Mon. and Tues. 8:30–2:30, Wed.–Fri. 8:30–8:30, weekends 8:30 AM–9:30 PM. No credit cards.*

Pancho Villa. This always-packed taquería is a step above the myriad others, with a full range of dinner plates that feature seafood, like garlic prawns ($7). Of course, you can always get a basic burrito ($4). The eclectic, ever-changing artwork is always fun to peruse, and mariachi bands often come in to perform on weekends. *3071 16th St., btw Mission and Valencia Sts., tel. 415/864–8840. Open daily 10 AM–midnight. Wheelchair access.*

Taquería Cancun. Surrounded by countless empty restaurants in the midst of Mission Street's mayhem, this *típico* taquería is always packed with locals. They serve one of the best veggie burritos ($3) around, chock-full of beans, rice, and thick avocado slices, which goes great with their spicy salsa verde. *2288 Mission St., btw 18th and 19th Sts., tel. 415/252–9560. Open Sun.–Thurs. 10 AM–12:30 AM, Fri.–Sat. 10 AM–1:30 AM. No credit cards.*

Truly Mediterranean. This tiny takeout counter serves up all your basic Mediterranean salads and pita sandwiches; but their falafel deluxe (with eggplant and potatoes; $3.50) and shawerma ($5) compete with neighboring taqerías when it comes to a cheap, filling, and tasty meal to go. *3109 16th St., btw Valencia and Guerrero Sts., tel. 415/252-PITA. Open Mon.–Sat. 11 AM–midnight, Sun. 11–10. No credit cards.*

➤ **UNDER $10 • Boogaloos.** Under the same ownership as the Spaghetti Western (*see* The Haight, *above*), Boogaloos has quickly become a popular breakfast spot for carefully disheveled young locals. Choose a sidewalk table for people watching, or sit indoors and enjoy the colorful walls decorated with shards of pottery and abstract art. One of the better breakfast dishes is the polenta and eggs with salsa, black beans, and sour cream ($5.50). Wash it down with a mimosa ($2.75) if you're feeling frisky. *3296 Valencia St., at 22nd St., 415/824-3211. Open Mon. and Tues. 8 AM–3 PM, Wed.–Fri. 8–3 and 5–10 (Fri. until 11), weekends 8–4 and 5–10 (Sat. until 11 PM). Wheelchair access. No credit cards.*

La Rondalla. A strolling mariachi band follows iron-haired waitresses in a room decorated with Christmas ornaments year-round (and probably has been doing so since La Rondalla opened in 1951). The Mexican food, though decent and reasonably priced, isn't the main draw here—it's the margaritas ($10.50 a pitcher), the crazy atmosphere, and the fact that it's open until 3:30 AM. An enchilada, taco, and chili relleno combination dinner goes for $8.50. *901 Valencia St., at 20th St., tel. 415/647–7474. Open Tues.–Sun. 11:30 AM–3:30 AM. Wheelchair access. No credit cards.*

Nicaragua. The fried plantain and cheese dinners ($4–$8.75) are, in the words of one Nicaraguan, an "explosion of flavors." The restaurant is a classic dive, with plastic tablecloths and cheesy pictures of Nicaragua on the walls. The area is seedy, so be careful at night. *3015 Mission St., btw 26th and César Chavez (Army) Sts., tel. 415/826–3672. Open daily 11–9:30. No credit cards.*

Panchita's. You could walk down 16th Street a hundred times without noticing this basic but fantastic El Salvadoran/Mexican restaurant. If your idea of charming includes home cooking, mismatched silverware, and a jukebox loaded with mariachi tunes, plan on eating many meals here. For breakfast there's *huevos rancheros* (eggs with tortillas, cheese, and salsa; $4.25), for dinner *carne desilachada* (shredded beef with egg, tomatoes, peppers, beans and rice; $5.50). Be sure to order some *plantanos con crema* (fried plantains with refried beans and cream; $4.25) on the side. *3091 16th St., at Valencia St., tel. 415/431–4232. Open Sun.–Thurs. 9 AM–11 PM, Fri.–Sat. 9 AM–2 AM.*

Ti Couz. An impatient crowd hangs around the bar sipping cider out of *bols,* waiting (they don't accept reservations) to get a taste of the succulent, piping-hot crêpes whipped up after the style of Breton crêperies in western France. You'll want one of the light pancakes for dinner *and* dessert, no doubt. A main course, with savory fillings like ratatouille or mushrooms, will run you $3–$5, while a sweet crêpe, like one filled with Nutella and banana, will set you back $2–$5. Warm and friendly, Ti Couz is perfect for dessert on a long summer evening or lunch on a rainy afternoon. *3108 16th St., at Valencia St., tel. 415/25–CREPE. Open weekdays 11–11, Sat. 10 AM–11 PM, Sun. 10–10. Wheelchair access.*

➤ **UNDER $15 • Amira.** This is the place to lie back on low couches, order a bunch of *maza* (appetizers) and bottles of wine, and ogle belly dancers. The designer took the sheik's tent look over the top, and you're likely to get a little indulgent yourself amid all the velveteen cushions and the purple drapery. Start off with the chef's mind-altering walnut-garlic dip ($3.75), and then try a "Pan-Arabic" entrée (ranging from Libyan chicken to Moroccan couscous, $8–$11). Belly dancers perform nightly, with live Near Eastern music on Wednesdays, Fridays and Saturdays, when reservations are essential and there's a $1 cover. *590 Valencia St., btw. 16th and 17th Sts., tel. 415/621–6213. Open Tues., Thurs., and Sun. 5 PM–10 PM, Wed. 5 PM–11 PM, Fri. and Sat. 5 PM–midnight. Wheelchair access.*

Esperpento. When this tapas joint opened in the Mission in 1992, it skyrocketed to instant popularity, as lines out the door on weekends will attest. Decorated with colorful Miró-esque touches, Esperpento serves delicacies like clams with white beans ($6), *calamares en su tinta* (squid in its own ink; $4), and *tortilla de patatas* (potato and onion pancake; $4.75), as well as huge *paella* (saffron rice cooked with chicken, sausage, and shellfish) dinners ($26 for two). The sangria is tastier and cheaper than at most tapas joints, so come with a bunch of people to celebrate something—like the end of the day. *3295 22nd St., btw Valencia and Mission Sts., tel. 415/282–8867. Open Mon.–Thurs. 11 AM–3 PM and 5 PM–10 PM, Fri. and Sat. 11 AM–3 PM and 5 PM–10:30 PM, Sun. noon–10 PM . Partial wheelchair access. No credit cards.*

Scenic India. This small restaurant serves up tasty *shaag bhajee* (spinach with tomato and onion; $5), chicken tandoori (half chicken baked in a clay oven; $10), and other traditional Indian specialties. Delicious breads ($2 each) help keep the curries and other spicy sauces from a-wastin' in the bottom of your bowl. Think of the slow service as a bonus, not a drawback—just that much more time to knock back your fill of Taj Mahal beer. If the portions were a little bigger, and the prices a little lower, Scenic India would be perfect. *532 Valencia St., btw 16th and 17th Sts., tel. 415/621–7226. Open Mon. 5–10, Tues.–Sun. 11–3 and 5–10. Wheelchair access.*

Slanted Door. A decidedly subdued atmosphere pervades this upscale Vietnamese restaurant— especially when compared with all of the party-oriented restaurants surrounding it. The elegant decor makes it a good place to take your main (or latest) squeeze. The vegetarian-friendly menu includes subtle dishes like vegetable curry ($7.50), with shitake mushrooms, yams, and cauliflower; or "spicy squid stir fried" ($8.50), delicately infused with red pepper, garlic, and other spices. Wash it down with a pot of exotic tea ($3.50–$5) or a microbrew ($3). This place is new and trendy, so reserve ahead. *584 Valencia St., at 17th St., tel. 415/861–8032. Open Tues.–Sun. 11:30–3:30 and 5:30–10. Partial wheelchair access.*

Timo's. The menu at this dimly lit, cozy restaurant features a huge selection of South American-, Spanish-, and Mediterranean-style tapas ($3.75–$11.75), including delicate salads, roasted potatoes with garlic mayonnaise, grilled prawns, quail, and salt-cod potato cake with mint salsa. Gather together a huge group so that you can try as many different tapas as is humanly possible to go with your Sangre de Toro wine. *842 Valencia St., btw 19th and 20th Sts., tel. 415/647–0558. Open Sun.–Wed. 5–10:30, Thurs.–Sat. 5–11:30.*

➤ **SPLURGE • Flying Saucer.** This is a place to experience California cuisine at its most outrageous, but in a not-so-stuffy Mission District setting. The chefs take the spaceship theme and apply it to incredible three-dimensional dishes, adding flounces to each plate like "pineapples" constructed out of potatoes or crazy, caramelized antenna to desserts. The menu changes four times a year, but always includes fanciful appetizers ($6–$10.50), like Pacific oysters on the half shell dressed with a cranberry-anis ice. Entrées get pretty pricey ($14–$24), but each is a work of art. Don't miss the exquisite homemade desserts ($6), such as nectarine tart with green pistachio ice cream. *1000 Guerrero St., at 22nd St., tel. 415/641–9955. Open Tues.–Sat. 5:30 PM–9:30 PM. Reservations advised. Wheelchair access.*

NORTH BEACH/ RUSSIAN HILL

The old-time Italian neighborhood of North Beach is about strong espresso, lotsa pasta, fresh tomatoes, and the highest concentration of restaurants (and lowest concentration of parking) in the city. **Columbus** and **Grant avenues** north of Columbus are lined with reasonably priced restaurants featuring everything from old-fashioned "American-style" Italian food to trendy neo-Italian cuisine. But watch out for traps— this has been a restaurant district for decades, and many establishments come and go with each tourist season.

A preponderance of intimate restaurants, sidewalk cafés, and dimly lit bars makes North Beach a prime destination for a romantic tête-à-tête. If dinner and drinks don't do the trick, head up to Coit Tower for a view (and hike) that will have your date swooning in no time.

➤ **UNDER $5 • Golden Boy Pizza.** Young North Beach residents and anybody trying to prevent a hangover crowd the bar stools at this tiny dive for fat, greasy slices. Check out what's available in the window—pesto vegetarian or clam garlic (both $2.75) are good bets. The pur-ple-coiffed people behind the bar might even smile at you as they warm up your square. If you're not already too loaded, wash it down with one of the cheap microbrews on tap ($2.75). *542 Green St., btw Grant and Stockton, tel. 415/982–9738. Open Sun.–Thurs. 11:30–11:30, Fri. and Sat. 11:30–1:30. Wheelchair access. No credit cards.*

San Francisco Art Institute Café. Usually the only way you can eat with a view like this is by dressing up, subjecting yourself to a rude wait staff, and dishing out lot of cash at the top-floor restaurant of a downtown skyscraper. But at this café inside an art school a couple of steep blocks up Russian Hill from North Beach, nose rings and tattoos are de rigueur, and a sign promises PSEDUO BOHEMIANS WELCOME. On top of that, you get great food cheap: Superlative gar-den burgers, regular burgers, and sandwiches all run about $4. *800 Chestnut St., btw Leav-enworth and Jones Sts., tel. 415/749–4567. Open winter, Mon.–Thurs. 8 AM–9 AM, Fri. 8–4, Sat. 9–2; summer, weekdays 9 AM–2 PM. No credit cards.*

➤ **UNDER $10** • **Bocce Café.** The choose-your-own-adventure menu might not blow you away, but Bocce continues to pack 'em in with its reasonable prices, jovial atmosphere, and cozy decor. Sit back on cushions and admire the high ceilings graced with baskets and ornate mirrors while you slurp up your custom-made pasta dish ($6–$8)—there are five pastas and about 15 sauces (including clams, pesto, or sautéed eggplant) to choose from. On warm Fri-day and Saturday evenings you can eat in the garden to the strains of live jazz. *478 Green St., at Grant Ave., tel. 415/981–2044. Open Mon.–Thurs. 11:30–11, Fri.–Sat. 11:30–12:30.*

Il Pollaio. This small Italian kitchen serves up tasty grilled chicken, and lots of it, in a homey atmosphere. It's kind of greasy around the edges, but the Italian old-timers who have been coming here for years don't seem to mind. Fill up on a fantastic half chicken with salad, crusty bread, and wine for less than $10; without the wine it's only $6.25. *555 Columbus Ave., btw Union and Green Sts., tel. 415/362–7727. Open Mon.–Sat. 11:30–9. Wheelchair access.*

L'Osteria del Forno. Two Italian women have created an affordable menu and a chic-but-casual atmosphere for their tiny Italian restaurant. Antipasti and focaccia sandwiches ($3–$6.50) or thin-crust pizza ($2–$4 by the slice; $10–$13 by the small pie) are deliciously authentic. There are usually only one or two pastas available daily, but they're homemade and filled with nummy stuff like spinach or pumpkin ($8). The only drawback is the small portions. *519 Columbus Ave., at Green St., tel. 415/982–1124. Open Mon., Wed., and Thurs. 11:30–10, Fri.–Sat. 11:30–10:30, Sun. 1–10. Wheelchair access. No credit cards.*

North Beach Pizza. On weekends you'll have to stand on the street like a dog and be tortured by the smell of garlic while you wait for a table. Once inside, you can sink your teeth into these thick-crusted babies—they're absolutely heaped with toppings, like spinach, pesto, onions, and feta cheese on the Verdi's special (medium: $15). They don't sell by the slice, but they do offer free delivery from the location nearest you. *1499 Grant Ave., at Union St., tel. 415/433–2444. Open Sun.–Thurs. 11 AM–1 AM, Fri.–Sat. 11 AM–3 AM. Wheelchair access. Other loca-tions: 1310 Grant Ave., at Vallejo St., tel. 415/433–2444; 800 Stanyan St., at Beulah St., tel. 415/751–2300; 4787 Mission St., at Ocean Ave., tel. 415/586–1400; 1598 University Ave., at California St., Berkeley, tel. 510/849–9800.*

➤ **UNDER $15** • **Ristorante Ideale.** This is like a true Roman restaurant—the waiters are distracted but warm-hearted, the antipasti are top-notch, and the atmosphere is refined but relaxed. You can stick to the antipasti menu and sample delectable *cozze con fagioli* (steamed mussels with garlic and fava beans; $7) or the *antipasto vegetariano* (grilled and marinated vegetables; $9), which includes radicchio, eggplant, and artichokes. Or go for a perfectly *al dente* pasta dish, like *papardelle all'agnello* (homemade wide noodles with lamb-tomato sauce; $10). The most wonderful and Roman thing about it is you don't have to hurry, because this place is big enough to handle the crowds. *1309 Grant St., btw Green and Vallejo Sts., tel. 415/391–4129. Open Tues.–Thurs. 5:30–10:30, Fri. and Sat. 5:30–11, Sun. 5–10. Wheel-chair access.*

Zarzuela. This Spanish restaurant suits its Russian Hill setting—though it's always bustling, it doesn't have the "PAR-dee!" feel of tapas joints in the Mission (despite the efforts of the jolly waiters, who force you to clink glasses when they serve the wine). You might see real-live Spaniards under the timbered ceilings of this warm and rustic place, passing around small but satisfying plates of mushrooms in garlic sauce ($3.50), tortilla española ($3.25), or steamed mussels ($4.50). The paella is saffron-rich and abundant with shellfish, but extravagant at $13 per serving (a minimum of two servings is required). *2000 Hyde St., at Union St., tel. 415/346–0800. Open Mon.–Sat. noon–10:30.*

➤ **SPLURGE** • **Rose Pistola.** The hottest new North Beach joint was opened by the makers of Lulu (*see below*) as an all-Italian counterpart. It's the kind of place you would see in a Visa commercial—lots of nouveau light fixtures and wait people rushing in and out of every aisle. The casually dressed crowd is an odd mix of young trendsetters with happenin' hairdos to older folks with a few cosmetic surgery nips and tucks. And the food is pretty incredible. Antipasti ($3.50–$10.50), like *crostini* (oven-fired toasts) topped with prosciutto and asparagus, are a good way to start. Then move on to a bowl of pasta, like the amazing gnocchi with calamari bolognese (potato dumplings in a rich tomato-squid sauce; $8.50). Second courses ($11–$17) like grilled Japanese snapper with potatoes, green garlic, and lemon are meant to be passed around. *532 Columbus Ave., btw Union and Green Sts., tel. 415/399–0499. Open Sun.–Thurs. 11:30 AM–midnight, Fri. and Sat. 11:30 AM–1 AM. Reservations advised. Wheelchair access.*

RICHMOND AND SUNSET DISTRICTS

From the way San Franciscans talk, you'd think the Richmond and Sunset districts were in another county. Fact is, these districts (flanking Golden Gate Park) are only a few minutes away from the Haight and Japantown by car or just three to four more stops on the MUNI. For a little extra effort you get good, cheap food and the opportunity to brag about exploring the city to your friends. In the Richmond District, Vietnamese, Chinese, Burmese, and Japanese places line **Clement** and **Geary streets** between Arguello Boulevard and 9th Avenue and between 20th and 25th avenues, where you'll also find produce markets brimming with items strange to a Western eye. On the other side of the park, in the Sunset, **Irving Street** between 5th and 25th avenues yields numerous Chinese and Thai restaurants.

➤ **UNDER $10** • **Empress Garden.** Although the Sunset teems with Chinese restaurants, this tastefully decorated establishment has muscled its way to the top. Every night of the week, Asian locals pack in around the party-size tables. Chicken dishes run about $5, but the house specialty, minced or deep-fried squab ($8–$10), is worth the splurge. An inlaid fish tank filled with live, kicking crabs (poor fellas) attests to the food's freshness. *1386 9th Ave., btw Irving and Judah Sts., tel. 415/731–2388. Open daily 11:30–9:30.*

Shangri-La. This all-vegetarian Chinese restaurant in the Sunset offers a delicious array of dishes ($4–$6), including bean-curd balls with garlic sauce, vegetarian chicken with black-bean sauce, and golden-brown gluten with sweet-and-sour sauce. Although the faux-wood walls and inadequate lighting may be a turnoff, the food definitely makes up for the blah decor. *2026 Irving St., btw 21st and 22nd Aves., tel. 415/731–2548. Open daily 11:30–9:30.*

➤ **UNDER $15** • **Brother's Restaurant.** Come to this minimalist Richmond joint for authentic Korean barbecue—and much more of it than you think you could, or at least should, ever eat. Each table comes equipped with its very own piping-hot wood-charcoal grill. Once you order your servings of marinated short ribs, chicken, or shrimp ($10–$14), servers start bringing out never-ending bowls of kimchi, assorted pickled veggies, sushi seaweed wraps, and rice. Then comes the raw meat, and you're ready to grill. Three plates and a big bowl of soup ($7) will stuff four hungry people. There are two locations only a block apart from each other; the one between 5th and 6th is more lively. *4128 Geary Blvd., btw 5th and 6th Aves., tel. 415/387–7991. Open daily 11 AM–3 AM. Other location: 4014 Geary Blvd., near 4th Ave., tel. 415/668–2028. Wheelchair access.*

Ebisu. This Inner Sunset sushi bar is one of the city's most popular—there's always a line out the door. The sushi specials ($9.50–$14), which include miso soup and tea, are a good way to sample some rolls and traditional nigiri. Or sidle up to the bar and ask the sushi masters what exotica is on special. Nigiri run about $3.50 for two à la carte; some of Ebisu's best are the delicate *hirame* (halibut) or the slippery, pearly white *kaibashira* (scallops). If you're not into raw fish, there's also plenty of teriyaki ($11–$12.50) and tempura ($8–$10). *1283 Ninth Ave., at Irving, tel. 415/566–1770. Open Mon.–Wed. 5 PM–10 PM, Thurs.–Sat. 5 PM–midnight. Wheelchair access.*

Khan Toke Thai House. In this dimly lit Richmond District restaurant, you sit on the floor with your shoes off surrounded by delicately carved wood panels and a wild garden. They always seem to be winning some prize in a "Best of the Bay Area" contest, despite the fact that most dishes cost only $5–$10. If you're feeling especially erudite, choose from a special section of the menu called "Thai curries mentioned in Thai literature." Don't forget to tip the shoe guy. *5937 Geary Blvd., at 24th Ave., tel. 415/668–6654. Open daily 5–10:30. Wheelchair access.*

If P.J.'s Oyster Bed is all booked up, put your name on the list and tell them you're going across the street to Yancy's, a cavernous dive bar that's connected to the restaurant via an intercom.

P.J.'s Oyster Bed. As you're walking down Irving Street towards this happening Cajun restaurant, inhale deeply if you're a fish lover. Prices are a bit steep, but you'll be sorry if you don't share—with an appetizer thrown in, most entrées will successfully employ two big eaters. The best stuff here is the super-fresh oysters ($1.50 each), gigantic bowls of gumbo ($7), and the enormous shellfish roast ($19), which features spicy crawdaddies and lots of bivalves. If you get caught up in P.J.'s Mardi Gras atmosphere, go for the alligator steak ($19). *737 Irving, at Ninth Ave., tel. 415/566–7775. Open Mon.–Thurs. 11:30–2:30 and 5–10, Fri. 11:30–2:30 and 5–11, Sat. 11–3 and 5–11, Sun. 11–3 and 5–10. Wheelchair access.*

SOUTH OF MARKET

The SoMa warehouse wasteland yields surprisingly attractive and friendly restaurants on the unlikeliest, grimiest corners. Wander along **Folsom Street** between 7th and 12th streets, or along **11th** and **9th streets** between Howard and Harrison streets, and you'll have the SoMa eating scene in the palm of your hand. Oddly, there are few late-night eating spots to satiate clubbers' cravings. Besides **Hamburger Mary's** and **Club Za Pizza** (*see below*), you can try **20 Tank Brewery** (*see* Bars, in Chapter 6), which serves sandwiches, nachos, and other munchies ($4–$7) most nights until 1 AM and beer until 1:30.

➤ **UNDER $5** • **Club Za Pizza.** Right next to the DNA Lounge (*see* Chapter 6), Club Za is a convenient spot for a $3 slice (or "zlice" as they say) when you're clubbin' late at night. Fancifully named pies range from "vegan friendly" (with cilantro pesto and lots of veggies) to "vegan nightmare" (with extra cheese and lots of meats); but the "potesto" (with pesto, cheese, and potatoes) is king. Za is also popular with the lunchtime SoMa multimedia crowd, when you can get zalads ($1.50–$6) and zoups ($2.50). *371 11th St., btw Folsom and Harrison Sts., tel. 415/552–5599. Open Sun.–Thurs. 11:30 AM–midnight, Fri. and Sat. 11:30 AM–3 AM. Wheelchair access.*

➤ **UNDER $10** • **Hamburger Mary's.** The messy hamburgers ($6–$11) and the cluttered decor go together wonderfully. Come by at 1 AM to hang out with SoMa clubbers in various states of drunkenness and undress. Vegetarians can feast on the tofu burger ($6) or the Meatless Meaty, a hot sandwich of mushrooms, cream cheese, and olives ($7). *1582 Folsom St., at 12th St., tel. 415/626–5767. Open Mon.–Thurs. 11:30 AM–1 AM, Fri. 11:30–2 AM, Sat. 10 AM–2 AM, Sun. 10 AM–1 AM. Wheelchair access.*

Manora's Thai Cuisine. The location on Folsom is trendier than most Thai restaurants in the city, and big crowds wait at the bar before being seated—but the fresh, attractive dishes here are worth the wait. Garlic quail is $8, and spicy Japanese eggplant with prawns, chicken, and pork goes for $7. *1600 Folsom St., at 12th St., tel. 415/861–6224. Open weekdays 11:30–2:30 and 5:30–10:30, Sat. 5:30–10:30, Sun. 5–10. Wheelchair access.*

➤ **UNDER $15** • **South Park Café.** Pretend you're Hemingway, Gertrude Stein, or Henry Miller in glorious Parisian exile while you gnaw on *boudin noir* (blood sausage; $7.50 lunch $11) and *frites* (french fries; $2) and watch the world go by. This French bistro opens at 7:30

AM with fresh croissants and coffee and stays open for country-cooked lunches ($7.50–$10) and dinners ($10–$15.50). *108 South Park Ave., btw 2nd and 3rd and Bryant and Brannan Sts., tel. 415/495–7275. Open for coffee weekdays 7:30 AM–10 PM, for meals weekdays 11:30–2:30 and 6–10, Sat. 6 PM–10 PM.*

➤ **SPLURGE • Lulu.** A nouvelle French/Italian/Californian meal at Lulu's is worth the money. Besides, dishes are served family style, which lends an informal side to things and means that you can try a little of everything and not spend too much. Roasted meat entrées ($11–$16.50)— as well as grilled vegetables—are the specialty: Watch the designated roasters at the wood-fired oven with their official-looking walkie-talkies. Pastas ($8.25–$10.50), such as butternut squash gnocchi in sage and olive oil, are fantastically rustic, and thin-crust pizzas ($9–$10.25) taste as amazing as they look. Or, sample oysters ($1.35 each) at the bar or adjacent café, where you can order from the regular menu if the main dining room is full. *816 Folsom St. at 4th St. tel. 415/495–5775. Open Sun.–Thurs. 11:30–2:30 and 5:30–10:30, Fri. and Sat. 11:30–2:30 and 5:30–11:30; café open for breakfast 7 AM–11 AM. Wheelchair access.*

East Bay

Sure San Francisco has enough restaurants to keep a gourmand feasting for years, but the East Bay outdoes San Francisco in some types of cuisine. Not only is it the home of "California Cui-

Sweet Treats

• *Lovejoy's Antiques and Tea Room. This Noe Valley shop serves up English high tea, with scones, finger sandwiches, and crumpets galore. 1195 Church St., at 24th St., tel. 415/648–5895.*

• *Just Desserts. This bakery has captured the hearts and stomachs of the Bay Area since 1974. Just think lemon tarts, cheesecakes, scones, muffins, cookies . . . ($1.25–$3.50 a pop). Look for 10 branches throughout the Bay Area; the main location on Church Street in San Francisco has a secluded outdoor courtyard. 248 Church St., at Market St., tel. 415/626–5774.*

• *Mitchell's Ice Cream. This popular, family-owned shop in the Mission features a variety of weird and delicious homemade ice creams, in addition to traditional flavors for the vanilla-ice-cream types. If you're a daredevil there's always avocado and yam flavors. 688 San Jose Ave., at 29th St., tel. 415/648–2300.*

• *St. Francis Soda Fountain and Candy Store. This soda shop has been in the Mission since 1918, and they still make their own ice cream, syrups, and candy. Order a phosphate, an egg cream, or a chocolate malt and wax nostalgic. 2801 24th St., at York St., tel. 415/826–4200.*

• *Swensen's. Climb to the top of Russian Hill, and you'll find the original Swensen's ice cream parlor. You might need a chocolate double dip (if not a respirator) to get going again. 1999 Hyde St., at Union St., tel. 415/775–6818.*

• *Toy Boat. Come here for a scoop and marvel for hours at the hundreds of old and new toys lining the walls. 401 Clement St., at 5th Ave., tel. 415/751–7505.*

sine," but it's also the best place to find an Ethiopian meal, or to pick up a barbecued-rib dinner. Oakland's Chinatown rivals San Francisco's in authenticity, and Berkeley offers a classier breakfast scene than the Haight for about the same price.

BERKELEY

California cuisine, that designer fuel for the yuppie generation, got its start in Berkeley, and locals take their food very seriously. The area around Shattuck Avenue at Vine Street has become known as the **Gourmet Ghetto** and is home to a number of high quality restaurants, including the famed **Chez Panisse** (*see below*). On **Telegraph Avenue** between Dwight Way and the U.C. campus, you'll find the city's cheapest restaurants serving fast-food with a Berkeley twist (heaping green salads and gourmet sandwiches are far more common than burgers). West of campus, along **University Avenue,** there's a string of mostly Asian and Indian restaurants. Both **College Avenue** (running south from campus into Oakland) and **Solano Avenue** (just north of Berkeley in Albany) are lined with cafés, sandwich shops, and upscale restaurants that cater to the neighborhood's students, professors, and granolafied yuppies.

➤ **UNDER $5** • Telegraph Avenue near the Berkeley campus is full of places that cater to students' thin pocketbooks. At Telegraph Avenue and Bancroft Way, you'll find a cluster of food carts selling everything from burritos and smoothies to Japanese food, falafel sandwiches, and wonderfully stuffed potatoes—try the "Berkeley's Best" spud ($2.75) with pesto and mozzarella. The ever-popular **Noah's Bagels** (2344 Telegraph Ave., tel. 510/849–9951; 3170 College Ave., Oakland, tel. 510/654–0941; 1883 Solano Ave., tel. 510/525–4447) spreads flavored cream-cheese shmears ($1.75), lox shmear ($2.25), tuna and hummus ($3.75) around the holes of its chewy New York-style bagels. Though service is occasionally less than intelligent, **Smart Alec's** (2355 Telegraph Ave., tel. 510/704–4000) is a new, vegan fast-food spot, where you can get a veggie burger, air-baked fries, and soda for $3.29. For pizza with an "eat-it-or-screw-you" attitude, stop by Blondie's (2340 Telegraph Ave., near Durant Ave., tel.

If you have ID to prove it, Blondie's will hand you a free slice of pizza on your birthday.

510/548–1129), popular with street freaks and bleary-eyed students in need of a pepperoni fix at 1 AM (2 AM Fridays and Saturdays). The jaded, underpaid employees provide constant entertainment, the stand-up counter is always packed, and your basic, greasy, filling slice costs $2. **Bongo Burger** (2505 Dwight Way, at Telegraph Ave., tel. 510/540–9147; 1839 Euclid Ave., tel. 510/540–9573; 2154 Center St., tel. 510/540–9014) serves some of the cheapest meals in town—two eggs, home fries, and toast; a Polish dog; or a falafel sandwich cost about $2 each. A few blocks south of campus at Dwight Way, **Ann's Soup Kitchen and Restaurant** (2498 Telegraph Ave., tel. 510/548–8885) dishes out exceptionally cheap breakfasts, homemade soups, and sandwiches ($1.75–$4).

Café Intermezzo. This Berkeley institution, with a harried, occasionally rude staff, indisputably serves the biggest and best salads around. The veggie delight ($4.75) is a family-size mound of greens topped with kidney and garbanzo beans, hard-boiled egg, sprouts, avocado, and croutons. Salads are served with your choice of homemade dressings—try the poppyseed—and include a bookend-size slab of fresh-from-the-oven, honey-wheat bread. Or try one of the humongous sandwiches on inch-thick slices of the same delicious bread ($4.15). *2442 Telegraph Ave., at Haste St., tel. 510/849–4592. Open daily 7:30 AM–11 PM. Wheelchair access.*

Crêpes-a-Go-Go. Slimane Djili, the owner of this small café, used to sell crêpes on the streets of Paris. Now, bless him, he's settled on busy University Avenue, offering sweet and savory crêpes like Nutella and banana ($3.25) or spinach, green onions, and cheeses ($3.75). One is filling, two will leave you staggering out the door. *2125 University Ave., at Shattuck Ave., tel. 510/841–7722. 2 blocks north of Berkeley BART. Open daily 9 AM–10 PM. No credit cards.*

Juice Bar Collective. Smack in the middle of the Gourmet Ghetto, the Juice Bar offers fresh and organic sandwiches as well as hot dishes ($3–$4) like spinach lasagna. But their focus, as the name suggests, is conjuring up smoothies like the Sunset ($3.25), made with bananas, orange juice, and yogurt. *2114 Vine St., tel. 510/548–8473. Open Mon.–Sat. Wheelchair access. No credit cards.*

> **UNDER $10** • **Berkeley Thai House.** Locals and students in the know come to this restaurant near the Berkeley campus to wolf down pad Thai ($4.85) and other reasonably priced lunch specials ($5–$6). For dinner, try the *mus-s-mun* (beef with red curry, peanuts, potatoes, carrots, and coconut milk; $6.25), or basil tofu ($5.75). On a sunny day, dine on the peaceful patio, sheltered from the street by tall bushes. *2511 Channing Way, at Telegraph Ave., tel. 510/843–7352. Open Mon.–Thurs. 11–9:30, Fri.–Sat. 11–10, Sun. 2–9:30.*

Bette's Oceanview Diner. On the recently yuppified stretch of 4th Street near I–80, this bright, crowded, '50s-style diner offers yummy breakfasts and lunches from the grill ($5–$8). But, Bette's takes a more upscale approach than the usual diner. Grilled American cheese and white bread? Try jack and cheddar on sourdough ($4.75). If you're not up for a half-hour wait on weekends, grab a cup of strong coffee and a heavenly scone, or takeout salads ($2–$4 for ½ pint) and sandwiches ($3.50–$4.50) from **Bette's To Go**, next door, and head for the marina. *1807A 4th St., near University Ave., tel. 510/644–3230. Open Mon.–Thurs. 6:30 AM–2:30 PM, Fri.–Sun. 6:30 AM–4 PM. Wheelchair access.*

Blue Nile. This is one of Berkeley's best Ethiopian eateries, serving everything from thick split-pea stew and pepper-cooked beef to *tej* (honey wine) and freshly blended fruit shakes. The food is served family style, and you use *injera* bread instead of silverware to scoop it up. As with most restaurants along Telegraph Avenue, the Blue Nile attracts lots of U.C. students and faculty for lunch ($5) and dinner ($6–$8). *2525 Telegraph Ave., btw Dwight Way and Parker St., tel. 510/540–6777. Open Mon.–Sat. 11:30–10, Sun. 5–10. Wheelchair access.*

Brick Hut Café. This mom-and-mom café, a collective owned and operated by women, is one of the best breakfast joints around. It's also a hot lesbian pickup spot on an increasingly womanish stretch of San Pablo Avenue. The pesto eggs ($5.50) are a house favorite, or try the well-prepared salads, burgers, and sandwiches. The high ceilings, exposed-brick walls, polished wooden floors, and friendly wait staff create an atmosphere conducive to postmeal lingering. *2512 San Pablo Ave., at Dwight Way, tel. 510/486–1124. Open Sun.–Tues. 8–3, Wed.–Sat. 8–3 and 5:30–10. Wheelchair access.*

Cha Am. This airy restaurant—one of Berkeley's best Thai spots—feels removed from Shattuck Avenue, even though its greenhouselike window seats overlook the street. Try the magical *Tom ka gai* (chicken and coconut soup; $7.25) or the mixed seafood plate with chili, garlic, and vegetables ($9). *1543 Shattuck Ave., at Cedar St., tel. 510/848–9664. 7 blocks north of Berkeley BART. Open Mon.–Thurs. 11:30–4 and 5:30–9:30, Fri.–Sat. 11:30–4 and 5:30–10, Sun. 5:30–9:30.*

Little Bit of Buddha in Every Bite

Sundays between 10 and 2 (or later, depending on the crowd), families set up food stands in the courtyard behind the Thai Buddhist Temple and Cultural Center in Berkeley and serve up homemade specialties. In fair or foul weather, exchange your money for tokens and choose among a heaping plate of pad Thai; a spicy soup of noodles, meatballs, and beef; or various seafood curries ($3 each). The freshly sliced mango over sticky rice with coconut cream ($3) is heavenly. Side dishes, including neat packages of glutinous rice filled with taro root, banana, or coconut and wrapped in banana leaves, are $1. Be brave and taste one of the artistic but hard-to-identify desserts ($1.50) stacked next to Thai iced tea, iced coffee, and logan drink ($1 each). This brunch is popular among Thai families and anthropologist types; proceeds benefit the temple. 1911 Russell St., btw Martin Luther King Jr. Way and Otis St., tel. 510/540–9734. 1 block west of Ashby BART.

Chester's Café. Looking out over the bay from Chester's sunny upstairs deck is one of the best ways to start a lazy weekend morning. The friendly staff will do you up with mug after mug of hot coffee and a brunch with all the fixings. Weekend specials include eggs Juneau (poached eggs and smoked salmon on an English muffin topped with Hollandaise sauce; $7.50). If you wake up on the lunch side of brunch, console yourself with warm chicken salad with sautéed red, yellow, and green bell peppers ($6.75). *1508B Walnut Ave., at Vine St., tel. 510/849–9995. Open weekdays 8–4, weekends 8–5.*

Homemade Café. You'll have a hard time deciding what to order from the extensive menu, and you'll probably have to wait for a table (at least on weekends), so grab a cup of coffee and a menu, park yourself on the sidewalk, and start deliberating. The whole-wheat buttermilk waffle made with cinnamon and nutmeg ($3) seems like one of the less indulgent items until you start adding pecans (75¢) and homemade blueberry sauce ($1.50). Also popular are the *matzoh brei* (matzo with scrambled eggs and cheese; $5.50) and the famous Home-Fry Heaven (home fries with cheese, salsa, sour cream, and guacamole or pesto; $4.75). *2454 Sacramento St., at Dwight Way, tel. 510/845–1940. Open weekdays 7 AM–2 PM, weekends 8–3.*

Juan's Place. This traditional Mexican restaurant has the feel of an old cantina, complete with piñatas, mirrored beer ads, and cheesy portraits of matadors. Juan's dishes out large portions of standard fare, including tacos, burritos, and tamales. The crab enchilada with red sauce and cheese ($7 for two) overflows with tender crabmeat. Try a wine margarita ($2.50 a glass, $10 a pitcher) from the adjoining bar. Juan's is stuck on the fringes of Berkeley, surrounded by steel factories and warehouses. *941 Carleton St., at 9th St., tel. 510/845–6904. 2 blocks west of San Pablo Ave. Open weekdays 11–10, weekends 2–10.*

Kabana. Okay, so it's not much to look at, but don't be deterred by the piecemeal decor, or you'll miss out on the deliciously spicy Pakistani food served by a friendly, helpful staff. Choose from vegetarian dishes ($5)—made with eggplant, potatoes, chic peas, or greens—or try a hefty portion of *biryani* (rice dish) or curry made with lamb ($7) or chicken ($6), both tender as could be from baking in the clay oven. The fresh veggies with mint sauce, roti ($1), and a wonderful mango *lassi* (sweetened yogurt shake; $2.50) are lovely accompaniments. *1106 University Ave., at San Pablo Ave., tel. 845–3355. Open daily 11–10. Wheelchair access.*

Long Life Vegi House. Just west of campus, sits this long-time favorite of locals who appreciate big portions of healthy Chinese food for very reasonable prices. They have daily specials in addition to a long menu of vegetarian (including vegi-chicken, vegi-beef, and vegi-pork options, made with wheat gluten and soy protein for the organ shy) and seafood dishes. Feast on cold tan tan noodles with peanut sauce ($4) or the prawns and string beans in black bean sauce ($8.75). Lunch specials ($3.65–$4.39), served daily 11:30–3, include soup, a spring roll, and entreé over surprisingly tasty rice. *2129 University Ave., near Shattuck Ave., tel. 510/845–6072. Open daily 11:30–9:30 (in summer until 10:30). Wheelchair access.*

Rick and Ann's. Join East Bay yuppies in bicycle shorts (babies and dogs in tow) as you wait for the best breakfast in town—and in Berkeley, that's really saying something. Try the Down South ($7.45), a combo of two cornmeal pancakes, two spicy turkey sausages, and two fluffy scrambled eggs with cheese. The special omelets and scrambles are also delicious, as is the French toast, made with challah (egg bread). *2922 Domingo St., near Ashby St., tel. 510/649–8538. Across from Claremont Resort. Open daily 8–2:30 and 5:30–9:30.*

Saul's. This Gourmet Ghetto nosherie is the closest thing to a New York deli in the East Bay. Shelves of Manischewitz products line the entryway, and a glass deli counter displays bowls of chopped liver, sauerkraut, and whole smoked fish. Sandwiches ($5–$8) are stuffed with pastrami, corned beef, brisket, or tongue. Jewish specialties include knishes ($3), potato latkes with sour cream and applesauce ($6.25 for three), and matzo-ball soup ($3.50). Saul's gets noisy and crowded during peak hours; avoid the lunch-hour wait by getting your food to go. *1475 Shattuck Ave., at Vine St., tel. 510/848–3354. 8 blocks north of Berkeley BART. Open daily 8–9.*

➤ **UNDER $15** • **Pasand Madras Cuisine.** If you feel like going for the gusto at this southern Indian restaurant, get a complete *thali* dinner, including lentil curry, lentil vegetable soup, spicy tamarind soup, yogurt with vegetables, a selection of Indian flat breads, rice pilaf, sweet

mango chutney, and a dessert surprise. The boneless ginger chicken Masala curry ($8.50 à la carte, $11 thali) is a winner, as are the vegetable curries ($6–$9.50)—though even the ones labeled "spicy" are pretty tame. A raised seating area offers views of cross-legged sitar and tabla players who whip *Stuff yourself silly for $6.50 at Pasand's all-you-can-eat lunch buffet (noon–2:30 PM).*
up a musical frenzy during dinner. A downstairs lounge features live jazz nightly and salsa dancing Thursdays. *2286 Shattuck Ave., at Bancroft Way, tel. 510/549–2559. 2 blocks south of Berkeley BART. Open Sun.–Thurs. 11–10:30, Fri. and Sat. 11–11. Wheelchair access.*

➤ **UNDER $20** • **Kirala.** Voted best East Bay Japanese restaurant in 1996, Kirala is the place for those in the mood for a fine meal. Locals crowd in for delicious dishes such as vegetable tempura ($5), umpteen varieties of *robata* (grilled skewered meats or vegetables; $2–$5), and soba noodles ($7.50), followed by a fresh and delicious array of sushi ($2.20–$5), or a full dinner ($8.75–$14.75) served with good-for-the-soul miso soup, Japanese salad, and rice. Some nights the line for a table spills around the corner, but there's probably a spot at the sushi bar. *2100 Ward St., at Shattuck Ave., tel. 510/549–3486. Open Tues.–Fri. 11:30–1:45 and 5:30–9:30, Sat. and Mon. 5:30–9:30, Sun 5–9.*

Venezia. This restaurant goes to great lengths to evoke the atmosphere of a Venetian piazza. The walls are painted to look like Italian shops and houses and have protruding wrought-iron balconies and flower boxes. There's even a clothesline strung overhead, complete with drying boxers. Luckily, the food measures up to the decor. Start with the insalata di pollo (salad with smoked chicken, pistachios, grapefruit, and scallions; $6) and check the board for daily pasta and fresh fish specials, like grilled salmon with olive-fennel relish ($13). *1799 University Ave., at Grant St., tel. 510/849–4681. Reservations advised. Open Mon.–Thurs. 11:30–2:30 and 5:30–10, Fri. 11:30–2:30 and 5–10, Sat. 5–10, Sun. 5–9:30. Wheelchair access.*

➤ **SPLURGE** • **Chez Panisse.** Chef Alice Waters started this world-famous restaurant 25 years ago with a commitment to serve "produce and meat from local farms and ranches producing ecologically sound agriculture." Her thorough attention to detail produced a revolution in dining called California cuisine, and though that may translate to a plate with an oh-so-elegantly arranged tangerine surrounded by three dates, it just may be the best darn tangerine you ever tasted—as one diner said, "I remember every meal I ever ate here." The four-course dinner menu ($35–$65), served in the downstairs restaurant, changes nightly, but you can be assured of innovative, seasonal, combinations. If you would rather not spend your weekly grocery budget on one meal, the upstairs **Chez Panisse Café** serves many of the same dishes for half the price. Carefully prepared entrées range from $14–$16. You can make same-day reservations for lunch, but for dinner go early and expect to wait an hour or more for a table. Though it may be a dubious distinction, President Clinton made a special trip across the bay to eat here. *1517 Shattuck Ave., at Cedar St., tel. 510/548–5049. 7 blocks north of Berkeley BART. Open Mon.–Thurs. 11:30–3 and 5–10, Fri.–Sat. 11:30–4 and 5–11:30.*

OAKLAND

From southern-style barbecue shacks to El Salvadoran holes-in-the-wall, Oakland is loaded with cheap and colorful eateries. Because the city's population is so diverse, you can find just about every type of cuisine imaginable—explore with eager taste buds and an open mind. Oakland's **Chinatown** is a less touristy version of its counterpart across the bay. Bounded by 7th, 10th, Broadway, and Alice streets downtown, Chinatown offers increasing numbers of Southeast Asian restaurants and markets, as well as the older and more established Chinese ones. The **Fruitvale** district, encompassing the neighborhoods around the Fruitvale BART station, has dozens of cheap Mexican and Central American restaurants. It is safest, however, to restrict your visits here to main streets and daylight hours. Join the young professionals on **College Avenue** or **Piedmont Avenue,** and you'll find a wide selection of familiar delis, burger joints, gringo burrito shops, and upscale bistros: From downtown Oakland, take Bus 59 or 59A to Piedmont Avenue; for College Avenue, take BART to Rockridge.

➤ **UNDER $5** • **Taquería Morelia.** Come to this Oakland joint for one of the best quesadillas ($2) around, a fried flour or corn tortilla oozing cheese and sprinkled with chopped tomatoes and cilantro. Locals of all ages flow between the restaurant and adjacent dive bar, Talk of the Town, carrying cheap beer and plastic baskets of tacos and burritos ($2.50–$4 each). *4491 E. 14th St., near High St., tel. 510/535–6030. About 7 blocks southeast of Fruitvale BART. Open Sun.–Wed. 10–10, Thurs. 10–11, Fri.–Sat. 10–midnight.*

➤ **UNDER $10** • **Asmara Restaurant.** Colorful baskets and rugs suspended from the ceiling cheer up the interior of this East African restaurant in North Oakland. Sample three of the excellent entrées in the meat ($5.50 lunch, $8 dinner) or vegetarian ($5.50 lunch, $7.95 dinner) combination platter. The red lentil stew is the most flavorful of the vegetarian dishes. Those who like lamb should try *ye-beg alicha*, made with curry and spices ($4.75 lunch, $7.50 dinner). In keeping with Ethiopian tradition, food is served family style with *injera* (bread) and a notable lack of utensils—use your fingers. *5020 Telegraph Ave., near 51st St., tel. 510/547–5100. Open Mon., Wed.–Fri. 11:30–11, Tues. 5–11, weekends noon–11. Wheelchair access.*

Barney's Gourmet Hamburger. Welcome to the international house of hamburgers: Barney's serves over 20 different kinds of burgers—including the Greek, Canadian, Russian, Western, Popeye(?!)—for $5–$7. For those who like their burger experience without the red meat, tofu and garden burgers ($4.25–$6) are bunned in a variety of styles. Would you like fries ($1.75) with that? How about a chocolate shake ($3)? *5819 College Ave., near Chabot Ave., tel. 510/601–0444. Open Sun.–Thurs. 11–10, Fri.–Sat. 11–10:30. Other Locations. 4162 Piedmont Ave., Oakland, tel. 510/655–7180; 1591 Solano Ave., Albany, tel. 510/526–8185; 24th St., at Castro St., San Francisco, tel. 415/282–7770; 3344 Steiner St., at Lombard St., tel. 415/563–0307.*

Cactus Taquería. This festive cafeteria-style Mexican restaurant in Rockridge offers a dizzying array of fillings for your burrito ($3.55–$6), taco ($2.55–$4.50), torta ($4.25–$5.75), or quesadilla ($4–$5.45). Try to choose from excellently spiced vegetables, shrimp, *carne asada* (marinated beef), red or green chicken mole, etc., served with delicious chips and addictive salsa. Or try the heaping plates of tamales ($4.50), or enchiladas ($5.50) and *nopales* (cactus; $5.70) served with rice and brown or black beans. *5525 College Ave., tel. 510/547–1305. One block south of Rockridge BART. Open Mon.–Sat. 11–10, Sun. 11–9. Other location: 1881 Solano Ave., Berkeley, tel. 510/528–1881. Open daily 11–9.*

Flint's. Regarded by some as the best barbecue shack in the world, Flint's caters to large appetites during the wee hours. Choose from pork or beef ribs, links, or chicken ($8–$9) piled high on a sturdy paper plate, crowned with a couple slices of all-American white bread (to soak up the grease) and potato salad. Sandwiches are around $6.50. You'll be getting your food to go, as there are no seats here. Keep your wits about you at both locations after dark. *3114 San Pablo Ave., at 31st St., tel. 510/658–9912. Open daily 11 AM–midnight. Other location: 6609 Shattuck Ave., at Alcatraz Ave., tel. 510/653–0593. Open Mon.–Sat. 11–2, Sun. 11–7.*

Lois the Pie Queen. Despite the name, most people come to this Oakland eatery for breakfast, not dessert. A family-run diner (vinyl swivel chairs, checkered tablecloths, and root-beer floats) that's gone California chic (pink walls, salmon croquettes, and espresso drinks), Lois's offers all the breakfast favorites as well as excellent burgers and fries. Two eggs with homemade biscuits and grits is $3.75, the "Reggie Jackson Special" (pork chops, eggs, hash browns or grits, and coffee or tea) is $7. Don't forget the pies that made Lois a monarch; a slice of sweet potato or lemon ice-box goes for $2.50–$3. *851 60th St., at Adeline St., tel. 510/658–5616. Open weekdays 8 AM–2 PM, Sat. 7–3, Sun. 7–4.*

Los Cocos. Fruitvale's best (and only) El Salvadoran restaurant is famous for its fried bananas ($4.50) and *pupusas* (stuffed tortillas; $3 for two). It may not look like much from the outside (or the inside), but the food is excellent and cheap. The friendly family of cooks chatting in the small open kitchen brings life to the sparse yellow room. *1449 Fruitvale Ave., at 14th St., tel. 510/536–3079. Open Tues.–Thurs. 10–9:30, Fri.–Sun. 10–10. Wheelchair access.*

Lucy's Creole Kitchen. This sunny, friendly diner, trapped on a traffic island in downtown Oakland, has some of the best southern seafood west of the Mississippi River Delta. Daily hot lunch specials like jambalaya ($6) or smothered short ribs ($7.95) attract crowds from the neighborhood, as does straight-up southern fare like black-eyed peas, yams, and greens

($1.25 each) cooked with smoked turkey. Lucy also serves a veggie burger ($3.25) in addition to the more southerly spicy crab burger ($5) and catfish with fries, coleslaw, or potato salad ($6.25). *1601 San Pablo Ave., at 16th St., tel. 510/763–6706. 7 blocks SW of 19th St. BART. Open Mon.–Thurs. 11–4, Fri.–Sat. 10:30–7 (Closed third weekend of each month). Wheelchair access. No credit cards.*

Mama's Royal Café. Although you can get lunch here after 11:30, the restaurant's real *raison d'être* is breakfast (served until closing). Huge omelets ($6–$9), which come with home-style potatoes, fruit, and a muffin, are available in no fewer than 31 varieties. The seasonal fresh-fruit crêpes ($6.50) and the popular eggs Benedict ($8.25) could send you into a coma. Weekend mornings, bring the Sunday paper and be prepared to wait outside with all the other twentysomethings with the same idea. *4012 Broadway, at 40th St., tel. 510/547–7600. Open weekdays 7 AM–3 PM, weekends 8–3. No credit cards.*

Mexicali Rose. Come to this bright pink building with a bunch of friends late at night when you need to make lots of noise and gorge yourselves on Mexican food. The massive portions are served on sizzling hot platters (not plates, *platters*). The bilingual menu is heavy on the meat dishes, though there are some vegetarian items. The *nopales* (cactus) with eggs, rice, beans, and tortillas ($8) is a delicious—though acquired—taste. Two people could easily split the Mexicali Rose combo ($9.75): taco, stuffed chile, green enchilada, guacamole salad, rice, beans, and a drink (phew!). Right across from the Oakland jail, Mexicali's regular clientele sometimes includes both recently released jailbirds and their arresting officers. *701 Clay St., at 7th St., tel. 510/451–2450. 6 blocks SW of 12th St. BART. Open daily 10 AM–3:30 AM.*

Nan Yang. Step into this airy Rockridge restaurant for delicious Burmese food. Especially tasty dishes are the ginger salad ($6.50), garlic noodles with cold mixed vegetables ($7.50), and curried tofu with shrimp ($7.50). Service is friendly, and there is an extensive vegetarian menu. *6048 College Ave., at Claremont Ave., tel. 655–3298. Open Tues.–Sat. 11:30–10, Sun. noon–9. Wheelchair access.*

Phó' Lâm Viên. This Vietnamese restaurant in Oakland's Chinatown is worth a trip for those with a sense of culinary adventure. Ignore the piped-in Muzak and focus on pork with fish sauce, spicy lemongrass gluten, and all sorts of Phó (noodle soups), bún (thin rice noodles) and rice dishes ($4–$6). The beverages are no less exotic—you can quench your thirst with a tall glass of pennywort juice ($1) or a concoction made from seaweed, barley, dried logan, lotus seed, and apples ($1.50). *930 Webster St., btw 10th and 11th Sts., tel. 510/763–1484. Open Sun.–Mon., Wed.–Thurs. 11–11, Fri.–Sat. 11 AM–midnight.*

Spettro. A fine time should be had by all at this funky world-food restaurant near Lake Merritt. The friendly staff creates interesting specials nightly, in addition to main menu treats such as mussels ($7), pastas ($7–$9), and pizzas ($10–$16), with aberrant toppings like peanut butter. On weekend nights, sign your name on the list near the door and join the small crowds waiting happily (thanks to the complimentary house wine or beer) for a table. *3355 Lake Shore Ave., at Mandana Blvd., tel. 465–8320. Open daily 5–10. Wheelchair access.*

Zachary's Chicago Pizza Inc. Even if you've never been to Chicago, come to Zachary's for a slice (or two) of their unforgettable stuffed pizza. People rave about the spinach and mushroom special (medium, $16.40), but whatever toppings you choose, they'll come surrounded by a wall of chewy crust and topped with a layer of oozing mozzarella and stewed tomatoes. Voted #1 East Bay pizzeria for 10 years running, Zachary's typically has a line snaking around the corner, so be prepared to wait: Utilize this time by placing your order, so the pizza will be ready when your table is. At lunch, get a thin slice ($1.75–$2) to go. *5801 College Ave., near Rockridge BART, tel. 510/655–6385. Open Sun.–Thurs. 11–10, Fri.–Sat. 11–10:30. Other location: 1853 Solano Ave., Berkeley, tel. 510/525–5950. Open Sun.–Thurs. 11–9:30, Fri.–Sat. 11–10:30. Both locations wheelchair accessible.*

➤ **UNDER $15** • **Le Cheval I.** Customers of all sorts come to this gleaming restaurant in downtown Oakland for delicious Vietnamese food with a French twist. Firepot soup (medium $6), with prawns, calamari, clams, fish balls, and vegetables, Singapore noodles ($7), marinated beef ($8.75), and a variety of fish dishes are generously proportioned and uniquely spiced. An appetizer not to be missed is the shrimp or tofu imperial rolls ($3.75) served with an addictive peanut sauce. **Le Cheval II** (Kaiser Center, 344 20th St., tel. 510/763–8953) serves lunch weekdays 11–3. *1007 Clay St., at 10th St., tel. 510/763–8957. Open Mon.–Thurs. 11–9:30, Fri.–Sat. 11–10, Sun. 5–9:30. Wheelchair access.*

➤ **SPLURGE** • **Bay Wolf.** As you enter this elegant restaurant, you might think you are visiting someone's beautiful home. Inside you're treated to friendly service and excellent food that mixes Provençal, northern Italian, and California influences. The menu, with entrées in the $13–$17 range, changes every two weeks and includes such tasty creations as grilled duck with ginger-peach chutney and smoked trout salad with arugula, pickled beets, and dill crème fraîche. When it's warm enough, you can dine on the outdoor patio. *3853 Piedmont Ave., btw 40th St. and MacArthur Blvd., tel. 510/655–6004. Open weekdays 11:30–2 and 6–9, weekends 5:30–10.*

Kincaid's Bayhouse. On the waterfront at Jack London Square, this spiffy restaurant spit-roasts, sear-grills, and hardwood-broils steaks and seafood. Savor the renowned crab cakes ($17, $8 as an appetizer) or the coconut-beer prawns ($15, $7 as an appetizer). Even if you can't afford a meal here, you can hang out at the bar during happy hour (weekdays 4:30–6:30) and watch sailboats breeze into the harbor. *1 Franklin St., in Jack London Sq., tel. 510/835–8600. Open Mon.–Thurs. 11:15–10, Fri. 11:15–10:30, Sat. 11:30–10:30, Sun. 10:30–9. Wheelchair access.*

Marin County

In this land of the rich and established, it's hardly surprising that most restaurants cater to older folks with plenty of cash to spare. You'll have to look hard for budget eats, and don't expect anything too exciting—Marin is no hotbed of ethnic diversity. Your best bet is to pack a picnic and dine in the open, far from the din of well-heeled civilization. For Marin County picnic supplies, and for restaurants on the Marin County Coast, including Stinson Beach, Bolinas, and Point Reyes, *see* Marin County, in Chapter 2.

SAUSALITO

Restaurants and cafés line **Bridgeway,** Sausalito's main street, but they're generally overpriced and touristy. Expect to pay at least $15–$20 for seafood on the waterfront. If you head one block inland to **Caledonia Street,** you'll find much better bargains without the tourist brouhaha. Your cheapest bet is to picnic at one of the grassy areas between Bridgeway and the bay.

After dark, a rowdy over-thirty crowd congregates at Sausalito's No Name Bar (757 Bridgeway, tel. 415/332-1392) to enjoy free live jazz, blues, or Dixieland music Wednesday–Sunday.

➤ **UNDER $10** • **Hamburgers.** If you're lucky enough to see a few locals in Sausalito, it'll be in the line outside this hole-in-the-wall. As the name suggests, all they do here are a few variations on the hamburger ($4–$5) and fries ($1.50) theme. Most people take their food to one of the benches in the park rather than eat in the steamy restaurant. If neither option appeals, head to Paterson's Bar next door, where they'll serve you the same burger for about a buck more. *737 Bridgeway, tel. 415/332–9471. Open daily 11–5.*

Lighthouse Coffee Shop. Open daily at the crack of dawn, hungry folks trek all the way from Berkeley and S.F. for the Lighthouse's huge fruit pancakes ($5). Hearty Danish food is the owner's specialty: Try the meatballs with potato salad ($7) or the Copenhagen burger ($8) with horseradish, pickles, capers, onion, and egg yolk at this popular, no-frills sort of place. *1311 Bridgeway, tel. 415/331–3034. Open weekdays 6:30 AM–3 PM, weekends 7–3.*

➤ **UNDER $15** • **Arawan.** It ain't much to look at, but once you eat at unpretentious Arawan, you'll see why loyal Thai-food devotees patronize the place regularly. Though the lunch specials are standard (pad Thai is $6), they pull out all the stops at dinner serving up savory entrées ($8.50–$11) like *Pla Muk Kra Tiem* (sautéed calamari with garlic, pepper, and fresh mushrooms in oyster sauce). *47 Caledonia St., 1 block inland from Bridgeway, tel. 415/332–0882. Open weekdays 11:30–3 and 4:30–10, weekends 4:30–10.*

TIBURON

In general, Tiburon's restaurants—found mostly on **Main Street**—are more notable for their views than for their food. Most offer decks hanging out over the bay, but you'll pay for the privilege of gazing at the San Francisco skyline or Angel Island. If you're really short on money, pack a picnic, take a ferry over from San Francisco (*see* Getting In, Out, and Around, in Chapter 1), and eat on the grass at the tip of the peninsula.

➢ **UNDER $10 • Sweden House Café.** The Swedish chef at this Tiburon café serves up fresh and unusual breakfast and lunch on a peaceful wooden deck jutting out over the water. Regulars order the Swedish pancakes with lingonberries and sour cream ($6.75). Also check out the granola with yogurt ($5.50). For lunch, your options are mainly salads ($6–$8.25) and open-faced sandwiches ($6–$8.25). Ordering one of the decadent pastries ($3) for dessert is practically a moral imperative. *35 Main St., tel. 415/435–9767. Open for coffee weekdays 7:30–6, weekends 8–7; kitchen open weekdays 8–3, weekends 8–4, shorter hrs off-season.*

➢ **UNDER $15 • Sam's Anchor Café.** One of the cheaper waterfront restaurants, Sam's attracts a lot of locals, who cram onto the deck and sip Famous Ramos gin fizzes ($4.50) and Bloody Marys. Even on wet and windy days, diehards take brunch (served on weekends until 2 PM) or dinner on the deck. Hearty breakfast dishes are $7–$9; if you're feeling adventurous, try the Hangtown Fry omelet ($7.50) with oysters, bacon, scallions, and cheese. Fresh seafood dishes are $8–$16, burgers $7–$9, sandwiches $7 and up. *27 Main St., tel. 415/435–4527. Open Mon.–Thurs. 11–10:00, Fri. 11–10:30, Sat. 10 AM–10:30 PM, Sun. 9:30 AM–10:00 PM. Wheelchair access.*

➢ **SPLURGE • Guaymas.** It's not cheap, but this restaurant next to the Tiburon ferry landing serves some of the best, most innovative Mexican food in the Bay Area. If you're on a tight budget, fill up on the fresh corn tortillas and three salsas brought to your table before you order, and stick to the appetizers ($4–$9). Look for *chalupas* (tortilla pockets with chicken breast, cheese, and jalapeños; $4.95) and *cazuelitas* (potato and corn tortillas with baked zucchini and cheese; $4). If you want to go all out, tack on a main course ($9–$18)—there are heaps of seafood options. The outside deck is heated, but in this case the colorful interior is as attractive as the view. *5 Main St., tel. 415/435–6300. Open Mon.–Thurs. 11:30–10:30, Fri.–Sat. 11:30–11:30, Sun. 10:30–10:30, shorter hrs off season. Wheelchair access.*

Order a Guaymas margarita ($4.50) to find out what the drink is supposed to taste like.

MILL VALLEY

You'll pass through Mill Valley on your way to Muir Woods, Mt. Tamalpais, Stinson Beach, or Point Reyes. If you're eager to push on through to the coast, grab a quick slice of thin pizza ($2–$3)—served by a guy who actually speaks Italian—at **Stefano's Pizza** (8 E. Blithedale Ave., at Throckmorton Ave., tel. 415/383–9666).

➢ **UNDER $10 • Joe's Taco Lounge.** The colorful walls lined with hot-sauce bottles and religious memorabilia from Mexico make for a festive dining atmosphere at Joe's. Hunker down with the locals to enjoy excellent meat and vegi-burritos ($4.50–$5). *382 Miller Ave., at La Goma Ave., tel. 415/383–8164. Open Mon.–Thurs. 11:30–10, Fri. 11:30–11, Sat. 11–11, Sun. 11–10. Wheelchair access.*

Mama's Royal Café. If you're anxious to get an early start on the day, this funky café serves unbeatable *huevos rancheros* ($6) and omelets ($5–$7.50). It's full of thrift-store artifacts and psychedelic murals and has outdoor seating. For lunch and dinner, Mama's features the Caspar Whineburger ($6), a jack

Mama's Royal Café victoriously battled a local ordinance banning live music in Mill Valley, and they have reinstated acoustic rock and jazz Tuesday through Saturday from 6–10 PM.

cheeseburger with green chilies. Mama's also has an assortment of board games, so you can play a round of Battleship while waiting for your cappuccino to cool down. *393 Miller Ave., at La Goma Ave., tel. 415/388–3261. Open Mon. 7:30–2:30, Tues.–Sat. 7:30–2:30, 6–10, Sun. 8:30–3.*

SAN RAFAEL

Compared to most of Marin County, San Rafael has a down-to-earth restaurant scene with lots of cafés, Mexican joints, and other ethnic eateries lining **4th Street** downtown.

➢ **UNDER $10** • **Royal Thai.** You'd hardly expect to find great Thai food in a leafy court-yard called the French Quarter in San Rafael, but Bay Area folks rave about this restaurant, started by a couple who defected from the kitchen at San Francisco's popular Khan Toke Thai House (*see* Richmond and Sunset Districts, San Francisco, *above*). The friendly staff serves up no-frills seafood and curry dishes for less than $10 in a restored Victorian house. *610 3rd St., btw Hetherton and Irwin Sts., tel. 415/485–1074. Open weekdays 11–2:30 and 5–10, week-ends 5–10. Wheelchair access. S.F. location: 951 Clement St., tel. 415/386–1795.*

San Rafael Station Café. This breakfast and lunch spot has a real neighborhood feel—pictures of people's pooches line the mirror behind the counter, and locals hang out on weekends read-ing the paper and ingesting phenomenal amounts of cholesterol. Omelets of every persuasion run $5–$8. Sandwiches are $3.50–$7.50. *1013 B St., btw 4th and 5th Sts., tel. 415/456–0191. Open weekdays 6:30–3, weekends 8–3. Wheelchair access.*

➢ **UNDER $15** • **Mayflower Pub and Grill.** Few people would mistake the British pub grub here for haute cuisine. Still, their fish 'n' chips ($7.50) and hearty sandwiches ($6) are some of the best deals in town. If you're sick of skimpy California cuisine, you'll appreciate dinners ($10–$11) like the huge ploughman's platter or *bangers 'n' mash* (juicy pork sausages with mashed potatoes, vegetables and gravy). Chummy locals congregate around the bar all day long, breaking out into badly sung folk tunes on Friday and Saturday nights. Next door, you'll find a British food items specialty store. *1533 4th St., tel. 415/456–1011. From U.S. 101 north, take Central San Rafael exit to 4th St. and turn left. Kitchen open weekdays 11:30–3 and 4–9, weekends 5–9. Wheelchair access.*

South Bay

Most restaurants on the suburbanized peninsula south of San Francisco are predictably bland. You'll find a cluster of semi-intriguing restaurants around Palo Alto and the Stanford campus, but they're not as cheap as the eats in most student areas. You might do better to head out to the coast—the food's certainly no more exciting, but it's bound to taste better when you're gaz-ing out at the roaring Pacific (*see* South Bay, in Chapter 2).

PALO ALTO

University Avenue, which runs west from U.S. 101 into the Stanford University campus, is one long food court with cutesy, yuppified restaurants everywhere you look. You'll pay just enough more than usual for your burrito, your burger, or your beer to make it annoying. If you really want to eat cheaply, head to **El Camino Real,** home to both fast-food chains and a number of local takeouts. At **Mr. Chau** (3781 El Camino Real, at Curtner Ave., tel. 415/856–8938), open daily until 9, $3 goes a long way for buffet-style Chinese food. Another alternative is casual California Avenue, east of Stanford, where you'll find café/bookstore **Printer's Inc.** (310 Cali-fornia Ave., at Birch St., tel. 415/327–6500) serving sandwiches and salads for less than $8.

➢ **UNDER $10** • **Jing Jing.** This popular Chinese restaurant near the Stanford campus is the place to come for spicy food. Though it's now slightly overshadowed by the new south-western-style bar next door, you're sure to run into students and professors, as the large tables host many a departmental lunch. Most dishes are in the $5–$10 range, with $4–$5 lunch specials (11:30–2). Expect a wait. *443 Emerson St., off University Ave., tel. 415/328–6885. Open daily. 11:30–2 and 4:30–9:30 (Fri. and Sat. until 10).*

Mango Café. The Mango just settled into a new, splashier location, but the food remains the same: authentic Caribbean dishes like hot curried goat with vegetables ($9) and jerked joints ($5.50), a spicy chicken dish. Fruit-juice smoothies ($3), served in glasses the size of fish-bowls, come in a wide range of exotic flavors. They also cater to vegetarians. *435 Hamilton Ave., at Fulton Ave., tel. 415/325–3229. From U.S. 101, take University Ave. exit west (toward Stanford), left on Fulton Ave. Open weekdays 11–2:30, weekends 6–9:30. Wheelchair access. No credit cards.*

Miyake. Despite the din of sake-drinking college students and waiters yelling greetings to customers across the restaurant, you get surprisingly good sushi at a truly reasonable price—about $1–$2 per piece. For just a bit more you can order specialties like the Tazana roll (yellowtail, wild carrots, sprouts, and flying fish roe; $4). They also have a small menu of filling teriyaki and tempura dinners ($7–$12). There's almost always a wait, so consider squeezing in at the sushi bar. *140 University Ave., tel. 415/323–9449. Open daily 11:30–10. Wheelchair access.*

Oasis Beer Garden. This grubby but immensely popular college hangout near the Palo Alto–Menlo Park border serves tasty burgers and sandwiches ($4–$7). Vegetarians will have to stick to the pizza. You can play pinball, watch sports on TV, or soak up sun at one of the outdoor tables. *241 El Camino Real, Menlo Park, tel. 415/326–8896. Just north of Stanford campus, at Cambridge St. Kitchen open daily 11 AM–1:30 AM.*

➤ **UNDER $15** • **Sushi Ya.** The regular clientele, a mix of students and office workers, will more than vouch for the sushi and sashimi here. This inconspicuous restaurant near Stanford's campus does a good business in all the staples, from yellowtail and tuna rolls ($3.50 each) to *kaiso* (seaweed) salad ($6.15). The soft-shell crab ($6.50) is especially good. There are a few tables, but most patrons prefer to sit at the bar and chat with the owner while he skillfully prepares the food. *380 University Ave., btw Waverly and Florence Sts., tel. 415/322–0330. From U.S. 101, take University Ave. exit west. Open weekdays 11:30–2 and 5:30–9:30, Sat. 5–9:30. Wheelchair access.*

SAN JOSE

The Bay Area's biggest city has it's fair share of good eats, but it's too far from San Francisco to make a special trip. If you find yourself in San Jose—perhaps at the Garbage Museum (*see* Chapter 2)—and need a good, cheap meal, try **Taco Al Pastor** (400 Bascom Ave., at San Carlos St., tel. 408/275–1619), which has been serving excellent Mexican food for more than 15 years. You'll find the best grub in the downtown area between Santa Clara and San Salvador streets (which run east-west) and Almaden and 3rd streets (running north-south). The **Flying Pig Pub** (78. S. First St., btw San Carlons and San Fernando Sts., tel. 408/298–6710) is recommendable for its variety of finger foods (crab cakes and pig skins) and salads for under $7.

San Jose is home to some of the best Vietnamese food in the Bay Area. Locals recommend the South Vietnamese cuisine found near Kelley Park at **Phuong Nam** (2168 Story Rd., tel. 408/254–4823), where entrées fall under $10. From downtown go south on First Street, then turn left on Keyes Street which turns into Story Road.

Chez Sovan. Every weekend, carloads of Bay Area residents make the 45-minute trek to San Jose for Chez Sovan's incredible Cambodian cuisine. The owners have just opened a second Chez Sovan just south of San Jose in Campbell (2425 S. Bascom Ave., Campbell, tel. 408/371–7711), and now the original location serves lunch only. The food—including a selection of ginger-cooked meats and vegetables, coconut and leek soups, and other traditional Cambodian specials—at both locations is well worth the journey; most dishes start at $5. *923 Oakland Rd., I block north of Hedding, where 13th St. becomes Oakland Rd., tel. 408/287–7619. Open weekdays 11–3.*

Markets and Specialty Stores

SAN FRANCISCO

Grocery shopping in San Francisco need not be a mundane chore. Not only is there an outlet for every imaginable cuisine, ethnicity, and dietary restriction, but time spent searching for the ideal ingredients can yield greater rewards: a date, perhaps. In one easy step you can check out a potential love interest *and* make sure they're not committing any food faux pas'. Stores whose windows can be counted on to steam up on occasion include the **Marina Safeway,** where young financial consultants size up each other's sportswear and fret about the onset of love handles; the **Harvest Ranch Market** (*see below*), for the health- and fashion-conscious rainbow coalition; the **Safeway** on Market and Church streets, for queers and Lower Haight fashion victims; and the **Rainbow Grocery** (*see below*), for politically radical types of all persuasions. You may leave the house with a list reading "lettuce, toilet paper, marshmallow cream" and come home with a whole lot more.

If all you want is cheap and unusual food items, head to San Francisco's neighborhood markets. In the Mission you'll find bodegas stacked with piñatas, fresh tortillas, and myriad varieties of dried chilies. The Asian markets on Clement Street in the Richmond District will cheaply accommodate your every produce need; and the delis in North Beach will load you down with extra-virgin olive oil and fresh mozzarella. Once you see all the city has to offer, you'll never go back to Safeway again—unless you're lonely.

Harvest Ranch Market. This always-busy Castro market is packed with organic produce, organic bulk foods (including 10 varieties of cereal), and tons of canned goods—most sans fat and preservatives. They also offer an organic salad bar and the ever-popular Tassajara bread. The outside benches are popular munching (and flirting) spots on the weekends. *2285 Market St., near 16th St., tel. 415/626–0805. Open daily 9 AM–11 PM. Wheelchair access.*

House of Bagels. Besides serving 15 kinds of fresh, chewy bagels with four different flavors of cream cheeses, this friendly neighborhood deli in the Inner Richmond District also has an entire *wall* of fresh-baked breads, both baguettes and loaves. You can get a basic garlic bagel with veggie cream cheese for $2.15; bags of a dozen day-olds cost only $2.50. *5030 Geary Blvd., btw 14th and 15th Aves., tel. 415/752–6000. Open daily 6–5:45.*

Molinari Delicatessen and **Lucca Ravioli Delicatessen.** Although these two establishments lie worlds apart from each other (Molinari is in the heart of North Beach, Lucca in the Mission District), they have similar selections, prices, and jovial Italian service. At both you can get reasonably priced homemade pastas, cheeses, vino, bread, and a wide variety of specialty items. Enormous sandwiches (around $5), dripping with fresh mozzarella and a trillion slices of salami, make both places popular lunchtime spots. *Molinari: 373 Columbus Ave., at Vallejo St., tel. 415/421–2337. Open weekdays 8–5:30, Sat. 7:30–5:30. Lucca: 1100 Valencia St., at 22nd St., tel. 415/647–5581. Open Mon.–Sat. 9–6.*

Rainbow Grocery. This co-operatively owned-and-run grocery store recently moved from the Mission to a bigger, slicker location in SoMa. They've got just about every food item a vegetarian or vegan could dream of, including organic produce, oils, honey, syrup, grains, pastas, herbs, spices, and other stuff in bulk, and the prices are reasonable for organic foods. You can also choose from a large variety of vitamins, herbal supplements, health books, and natural soaps. Check out their bulletin board if you're looking for a room, a ride, a dog, or a cause. *1745 Folsom St., at 13th St., tel. 415/863–0620. Open Mon.–Sat. 9–9, Sun. 10–9.*

Real Foods. This delicatessen on the upscale stretch of Polk Street sells all sorts of prepared gourmet food items (salads, casseroles, noodle dishes, desserts) to folks who have sauntered down from Russian Hill to see what the peasants are up to. If you've got a little extra cash to blow on a gourmet picnic, you're in the right place; if not, you can always enjoy a coffee and a cookie while those around you spend the big bucks. Look for their grocery store next door; Real Foods has a number of these healthy markets around the city and the Bay Area. *2164 Polk St., at Vallejo St., tel. 415/775–2805. Open daily 8–8. S.F. grocery locations: 1023 Stanyan St.,* *btw Parnassus and Carl Sts., tel. 415/564–2800; 3939 24th St., btw Sanchez and Noe Sts., tel. 415/282–9500.*

EAST BAY

In addition to the farmers' markets (*see box below*), Berkeley is home to one of the best stores for produce in the Bay area, **Berkeley Bowl Marketplace** (2777 Shattuck Ave., at Stuart St., tel. 510/843-6929). Housed in a former bowling alley, Berkeley Bowl represents alternative and co-operative grocery shopping at its finest: The vegetable and fruit selection (including organic) is endless, the bulk grains come cheap, most local bakeries stock their loaves here, and the attached seafood department features the freshest of fish for excellent prices. Another great place to shop is **Trader Joe's** (5796 Christie Ave., at Powell St., tel. 510/658–8091), which sells inexpensive, international gourmet food, and most reasonably priced wine and beer. **Seabreeze Market** (598 University Ave., tel. 486–8119) offers fresh shellfish, fruits, and vegetables. They also serve sandwiches, but get yours to go because the market is right next to an 1-80 on ramp; fortunately, the Berkeley Marina is close by. **Whole Foods** (3000 Telegraph Ave., at Ashby Ave., tel. 510/649–1333) is a health food supermarket, with a good variety of food at "a little higher than they should be" prices. The store has a deli, bakery, organic salad bar, and a massage chair, making it quite the gathering place.

Berkeley has a bounty of European-style markets, but even these come with a Berkeley twist (i.e., heavy on organic produce and vegan pastries, light on butcher shops). The renowned **Cheese Board** (1504 Shattuck Ave., btw Cedar and Vine Sts., tel. 510/549–3183) features an incredible selection of cheeses and freshly baked breads. Stop by in the morning for a scone

Farmers' Markets

One of the best ways to get seasonal and organic produce cheaply is to go to local farmers' markets, which usually take place once or twice a week. The farmers' market at San Francisco's United Nations Plaza happens Wednesdays and Sundays 8 AM–5 PM and is chock-full of fruits, vegetables, greens, flowers, and nuts. A decidedly more upscale market bustles at the Ferry Building, at the downtown end of Market Street, Tuesdays 11 AM–3 PM and Saturdays 8 AM–1:30 PM. This market is a gourmet paradise: Try free samples of home-grown and homemade yogurts, cheeses, tortillas, salsas, fresh juices, breads, and even items from Lulu's restaurant (the latter at a small price). It's also one of the best places in the city to get shellfish straight out of Tamales Bay. At 100 Alemany Boulevard, near Crescent Avenue (tel. 415/647–9423) in Bernal Heights, residents do some serious produce shopping Saturdays from dawn to dusk and Thursdays in summer from 3 to 8.

Every Friday from 8 to 2 you can buy from East Bay farmers and bakers at the Old Oakland Certified Farmers' Market (Broadway and 9th St., tel. 510/452–FARM). Oakland's other farmers' market takes place at Jack London Square (Broadway and Embarcadero, Sundays 10–2). You can also stock up on farm-fresh products at one of Berkeley's farmers' markets, sponsored by the Ecology Center (tel. 510/548–3333). They happen every Saturday 10–2 on Center Street at Martin Luther King Jr. Way; Sunday 11–3 on Haste Street at Telegraph Avenue (May through November); and Tuesday from 2 until 7 on Derby Street at Martin Luther King Jr. Way.

($1) or a sourdough cheese roll ($1). The store is collectively owned, and the staff will explain the subtle variations in cheeses to you and give you samples to help you choose. A few doors down, their offshoot **Cheese Board Pizza Collective** (1512 Shattuck Ave., tel. 510/549–3055) has ridiculously short open hours (Tues.–Thurs. 11:30–2, Mon. and Fri. 4:30–6:30, and Sat. noon–3), but pizza that would wow the most finicky of connoisseurs. They make just one kind of vegetarian pizza each day, with toppings like eggplant, red peppers, pesto, and feta cheese (slices $1.75, whole pies $14).

For fresh baked loaves—such as seeded baguettes or potato-rosemary bread—stop by the retail outlets of **Semifreddi's** (372 Colusa Ave., Kensington, tel. 510/596–9935) and **Acme** (1601 San Pablo Ave., Berkeley, tel. 510/524–1327; 2730 9th St., Berkeley, tel. 510/843–2978). They both supply many Bay Area markets with fresh bread daily. Or visit **Il Fornaio** (2059 Mountain Blvd., Oakland, tel. 510/339–3108), a slick European-café chain with branches in Oakland, San Francisco, and Marin. If you can deal with the atmosphere, you'll be rewarded with interesting (albeit expensive) breads. Specializing in "good-for-you" baked goods, **Your Black Muslim Bakery** (5832 San Pablo Ave., btw Stanford Ave. and 59th St., Oakland, tel. 510/658–7080), with six outlets in the East Bay and one in San Francisco, is a haven for vegans and the health conscious: Most items contain no sugar, salt, milk, or eggs. On the cultural side, the bakeries carry books on black history and promote African American community events.

In Oakland's Rockridge district, **Market Hall** (5565 College Ave., at Shafer St.) is a one-stop gourmet haven for yuppies. Sip a nonfat decaf mocha from **Peaberry's Coffee and Tea** between bites of delicious pastry from **Grace Bakery.** Drool at the fresh pastas and salads at **The Pasta Shop,** ponder why anyone would pay $1.65 for a box of macaroni and cheese, and then partake in some free samples of olives, cheese, or sun-dried tomato dip. Pick up meat, poultry, fish, and fine wine from **Enzo's** and produce from **Market Hall Produce,** to make your own feast, or join the upscale crowd dining on Italian delicacies at **Oliveto** (tel. 510/547–5356).

In downtown Oakland you'll find a huge variety of ethnic markets, especially in Chinatown, which is full of Chinese and Southeast Asian groceries. On the other side of Broadway, **Mi Rancho Tortilla Factory** (464 7th St., at Broadway, tel. 510/451–2393) sells the fixings for making your own burritos and tacos. **Housewives Marketplace** (9th and Clay Sts., tel. 510/444–4396) is a warehouse full of specialty stands with a southern flair. You'll find a small grocery store, a deli, a butcher, a fish and seafood counter, a sausage shop, and dry goods such as beans, roasted peanuts, and mix for Cajun jambalaya. Locals come here for fresh produce and smoked meats, such as ham hocks. A few stands offer fast-food items like Louisiana burgers with jalapeño cheese ($3.50). **G.B. Ratto & Company** (821 Washington St., btw 8th and 9th Sts., tel. 510/832–6503) is your source for delicacies like buffalo-milk mozzarella and many varieties of olive oil. They also prepare sandwiches (about $4) and have everything you need for a gourmet picnic.

Reference Listings

BY CUISINE

AMERICAN

UNDER $5
Café Intermezzo (Berkeley)
Moishe's Pippic (Civic Center)
New Dawn (Mission)
San Francisco Art Institute Café (North Beach/ Russian Hill)
Soups (Civic Center)
Specialty's (Downtown)

Studio Café (The Haight)
Tom Peasant Pies (Castro/ Noe Valley)

UNDER $10
Bagdad Café (Castro/ Noe Valley)
Bette's Oceanview Diner (Berkeley)
Boogaloos (Mission)
Brick Hut Café (Berkeley)

Buena Vista Café (Fisherman's Wharf)
Chester's Café (Berkeley)
Crescent City Café (The Haight)
Flint's (Oakland)
Homemade Café (Berkeley)
Kate's Kitchen (The Haight)
Lois the Pie Queen (Oakland)

Lucy's Creole Kitchen
(Oakland)
Mama's Royal Café (Oakland,
Mill Valley)
Miss Millie's (Castro/
Noe Valley)
Orphan Andy's (Castro/
Noe Valley)
Patio Café (Castro/Noe Valley)
Pork Store Café (The Haight)
Rick and Ann's (Berkeley)
San Rafael Station Café
(San Rafael)
Saul's (Berkeley)
Spaghetti Western (The
Haight)
Sparky's (Castro/Noe Valley)
Squat and Gobble Café
(The Haight)

UNDER $15
Sam's Anchor Café (Tiburon)

BURGERS

UNDER $5
Bongo Burger (Berkeley)
Hot 'n' Hunky (Castro/
Noe Valley)

UNDER $10
Barney's Gourmet Hamburger
(Oakland)
Grubstake (Civic Center)
Hamburger Mary's (SoMa)
Hamburgers (Sausalito)
Oasis Beer Garden (Palo Alto)
Pinecrest (Downtown)

CALIFORNIAN

UNDER $5
Juice Bar Collective (Berkeley)
Main Squeeze (Civic Center)

UNDER $10
Josie's Cabaret and Juice
Joint (Castro/Noe Valley)
Pluto's (Marina)

SPLURGE
Bay Wolf (Oakland)
Chez Panisse (Berkeley)
Firefly (Castro/Noe Valley)
Flying Saucer (Mission)

Greens (Marina)
Lulu (SoMa)
Zuni Café (Civic Center)

CHINESE

UNDER $5
Kowloon (Chinatown)
Lucky Creation (Chinatown)

UNDER $10
Chef Jia's (Chinatown)
Eric's Hunan and Mandarin
(Castro/Noe Valley)
Empress Garden
(Richmond/Sunset)
Jing Jing (Palo Alto)
House of Nanking (Chinatown)
Long Life Vegi House
(Berkeley)
Meriwa (Chinatown)
Shangri-La (Richmond/
Sunset)
Silver (Chinatown)
Yuet Lee (Chinatown)

UNDER $15
R&G Lounge (Chinatown)
Yank Sing (Downtown)

ETHIOPIAN

UNDER $10
Asmara (Oakland)
Blue Nile (Berkeley)
Massawa (The Haight)

FRENCH

UNDER $5
Crêpes-a-Go-Go (Berkeley)

UNDER $10
Ti Couz (Mission)

UNDER $15
Café Bastille (Downtown)
Café Claude (Downtown)
South Park Café (SoMa)

SPLURGE
Bay Wolf (Oakland)
Lulu (SoMa)

INDIAN

UNDER $10
Ananda Fuara (Civic Center)

UNDER $15
Pasand Madras Cuisine
(Berkeley)
Scenic India (Mission)

ITALIAN

UNDER $10
Bocce Café (North Beach/
Russian Hill)
Il Pollaio (North Beach/
Russian Hill)
L'Osteria del Forno (North
Beach/Russian Hill)
Pasta Pomodoro (Castro/
Noe Valley)
Spettro (Oakland)

UNDER $15
Caffe Macaroni (Downtown)
Ristorante Ideale (North
Beach/Russian Hill)

UNDER $20
Venezia (Berkeley)

SPLURGE
Bay Wolf (Oakland)
Lulu (SoMa)
Rose Pistola (North
Beach/Russian Hill)

JAPANESE

UNDER $10
Isobune (Japantown)
Mifune (Japantown)
Miyake Sushi (Palo Alto)
No-Name (a.k.a. Nippon)
Sushi (Castro/Noe Valley)

UNDER $15
Ebisu (Richmond/Sunset)
Izumiya (Japantown)
Nori Sushi (Civic Center)
Now and Zen (Japantown)
Sushi Ya (Palo Alto)

UNDER $20
Kirala (Berkeley)

MEDITERRANEAN AND MIDDLE EASTERN

UNDER $5
Aladdin (Civic Center)
Truly Mediterranean (Mission)

UNDER $10
Kan Zaman (The Haight)
La Méditerranée (Castro/ Noe Valley)
Ya Halla (The Haight)

UNDER $15
Amira (Mission)

MEXICAN AND CENTRAL AMERICAN

UNDER $5
Balazo (The Haight)
Casa Sanchez (Mission)
El Farolito (Mission)
Joe's Taco Lounge (Mill Valley)
El Toro (Mission)
El Trébol (Mission)
La Cumbre (Mission)
Pancho Villa (Mission)
Taquería Cancun (Mission)
Taquería Morelia (Oakland)

UNDER $10
Cactus Taquería (Oakland)
Juan's Place (Berkeley)
La Rondalla (Mission)
Los Cocos (Oakland)
Mexicali Rose (Oakland)
Nicaragua (Mission)
Panchita's (Mission)

SPLURGE
Guaymas (Tiburon)

PIZZA

UNDER $5
Club Za Pizza (SoMa)
Golden Boy Pizza (North Beach/Russian Hill)
Marcello's (Castro/ Noe Valley)

UNDER $10
North Beach Pizza (North Beach/Russian Hill)
Spettro (Oakland)
Zachary's Chicago Pizza Inc. (Berkeley)

SEAFOOD

UNDER $10
Lucy's Creole Kitchen (Oakland)
Swan Oyster Depot (Civic Center)

UNDER $15
P.J.'s Oyster Bed (Richmond/Sunset)
R&G Lounge (Chinatown)
Sam's Anchor Café (Tiburon)

UNDER $25
Kincaid's Bayhouse (Oakland)

SPANISH AND CARIBBEAN

UNDER $10
Mango Café (Palo Alto)

UNDER $15
Cha Cha Cha (The Haight)
Esperpento (Mission)
Timo's (Mission)
Zarzuela (North Beach/ Russian Hill)

SPLURGE
Miss Pearl's Jam House (Civic Center)

THAI

UNDER $5
Thai Buddhist Temple (Berkeley)

UNDER $10
Berkeley Thai House (Berkeley)

Cha Am (Berkeley)
Manora's Thai Cuisine (SoMa)
Racha Café (Civic Center)
Royal Thai (San Rafael)

UNDER $15
Arawan (Sausalito)
Khan Toke Thai House (Richmond/Sunset)
Thai House on Noe (Castro/Noe Valley)

VIETNAMESE AND CAMBODIAN

UNDER $10
101 Restaurant (Downtown)
Chez Sovan (San Jose)
Cordon Bleu (Civic Center)
Phó' Lâm Viên (Oakland)
Tu Lan (Downtown)

UNDER $15
Le Cheval I (Oakland)
Slanted Door (Mission)

OTHER

UNDER $10
Hahn's Hibachi (Korean; Marina)
Kabana (Pakistani; Berkeley)
Lighthouse Coffee Shop (Danish; Sausalito)
Nan Yang (Burmese; Oakland)
Sweden House Café (Swedish; Tiburon)

UNDER $15
Brother's Restaurant (Korean; Richmond/Sunset)
Mayflower Pub and Grill (British; San Rafael)

SPLURGE
Suppenküche (German; Civic Center)

SPECIAL FEATURES

BREAKFAST/BRUNCH

UNDER $5
New Dawn (Mission)
Studio Café (The Haight)
Thai Buddhist Temple
  (Berkeley)

UNDER $10
Bette's Oceanview Diner
  (Berkeley)
Boogaloos (Mission)
Brick Hut Café (Berkeley)
Chester's Café (Berkeley)
Crescent City Café (The
  Haight)
Homemade Café (Berkeley)
Kate's Kitchen (The Haight)
Lighthouse Coffee Shop
  (Sausalito)
Lois the Pie Queen (Oakland)
Mama's Royal Café (Oakland,
  Mill Valley)
Miss Millie's (Castro/Noe
  Valley)
Patio Café (Castro/Noe Valley)
Pork Store Café (The Haight)
Rick and Ann's (Berkeley)
San Rafael Station Café (San
  Rafael)
Spaghetti Western (The
  Haight)
Squat and Gobble Café (The
  Haight)
Sweden House Café (Tiburon)

UNDER $15
Sam's Anchor Café (Tiburon)

DINNER AND ENTERTAINMENT

UNDER $10
Balazo (The Haight)
Bocce Café (North Beach/
  Russian Hill)
Josie's Cabaret and Juice Bar
  (Castro/Noe Valley)
Kan Zaman (The Haight)
Mama's Royal Café (Mill
  Valley)
La Rondalla (Mission)

UNDER $15
Amira (Mission)
Café Bastille (Downtown)
Café Claude (Downtown)
Pasand Madras Cuisine
  (Berkeley)

SPLURGE
Miss Pearl's Jam House
  (Civic Center)

LATE-NIGHT EATS (AFTER 1 AM)

UNDER $5
Club Za Pizza (SoMa)
El Farolito (Mission)
Hot 'n' Hunky (Castro/
  Noe Valley)
Marcello's (Castro/Noe Valley)
Taquería Cancun (Mission)

UNDER $10
Bagdad Café (Castro/
  Noe Valley)
Grubstake (Civic Center)
Hamburger Mary's (SoMa)
Kan Zaman (The Haight)
La Rondalla (Mission)
Mexicali Rose (Oakland)
North Beach Pizza (North
  Beach/Russian Hill)
Oasis Beer Garden (Palo Alto)
Orphan Andy's (Castro/
  Noe Valley)
Panchita's (Mission)
Pinecrest (Downtown)
Silver (Chinatown)
Sparky's (Castro/Noe Valley)

UNDER $15
Café Bastille (Downtown)

OUTDOOR EATING

UNDER $5
Casa Sanchez (Mission)
Juice Bar Collective (Berkeley)
Thai Buddhist Temple
  (Berkeley)

UNDER $10
Berkeley Thai House
  (Berkeley)
Bocce Café (North Beach/
  Russian Hill)
Boogaloos (Mission)
Chester's Café (Berkeley)
Josie's Cabaret and Juice
  Joint (Castro/Noe Valley)
Oasis Beer Garden (Palo Alto)
Sweden House Café (Tiburon)

UNDER $15
Café Bastille (Downtown)
Café Claude (Downtown)
Sam's Anchor Café (Tiburon)

SPLURGE
Bay Wolf (Oakland)
Guaymas (Tiburon)
Miss Pearl's Jam House (Civic
  Center)

VEGETARIAN

UNDER $5
Juice Bar Collective (Berkeley)
Kowloon (Chinatown)
Lucky Creation (Chinatown)
Main Squeeze (Civic Center)

UNDER $10
Ananda Fuara (Civic Center)
Josie's Cabaret and Juice
  Joint (Castro/Noe Valley)
Long Life Vegi House
  (Berkeley)
Shangri-La (Richmond/
  Sunset)

UNDER $15
Now and Zen (Japantown)

SPLURGE
Greens (Marina)

CAFÉ CULTURE   5

By Stephan von Pohl

For many people living in the Bay Area, coffee is the fuel that drives them to do . . . whatever it is they do. Indeed, after spending some time in the Bay Area's many cafés, you may wonder if they do anything at all. No mere filling stations, cafés are where locals come to meet and yak with friends, spend hours poring over books and homework, or just drink themselves into a caffeine-induced stupor. In Berkeley and San Francisco in particular, cafés can be as crowded on Friday nights as local bars, and a few establishments can boast of having the same java-obsessed customers for more than 30 years. Though you'll find a few mega-chains like Starbucks, most coffeehouses are family-run or local chains with no more than three or four outlets. In San Francisco, meeting for coffee isn't just something to do when you're bored; it's a cherished way of life. San Franciscans are well aware that four shots of espresso is the best legal high around.

Bay Area cafés come in every style imaginable. You can drink your morning espresso in a small establishment with sofas and classical music, take your noon latte in a postmodern warehouse space where Armani suits rub elbows with bloodied bike messengers, and sip your evening cappuccino in a place where English is a rarity and the jukebox plays opera. If you like to hang out with students, politicos, or New Age prophets, head to Berkeley. Otherwise, your scene—be it a stylish, older crowd (North Beach), black leather and body piercings (either the Haight or the Castro, depending on sexual orientation), or something else entirely—can be found somewhere in San Francisco. In an effort to be true to the "culture" part of café culture, many Bay Area cafés do a lot more than crank out coffee. Local artists are invited to display their works, Bay Area bands ply their trade, and open-mic poetry readings (where anyone can read their work, no matter how silly, crazy, or both) can be found every night of the week.

Proper café etiquette includes busing your own table and tipping the counterperson.

SAN FRANCISCO

San Francisco is a city of people who believe strongly in the connection between coffee and the arts. Early converts to the café-as-muse philosophy include renegades Jack Kerouac and Allen Ginsberg, who held all manner of performances at the still-hopping Caffè Trieste in North Beach. With its European-style park and tiny streets, North Beach is still a popular place to grab a demitasse on a rainy day, especially if you have someone to hold hands with under the table. Postmodern hipsters, however, would be more comfortable South of Market, in the Haight, and especially in the Mission. The new hotbed for experimental art in San Francisco, the Mission has recently sprouted all manner of java dens for bohemians new and old, who write poems, novels, letters, and laundry lists as they soak up the atmosphere.

141

CASTRO DISTRICT **Café Flore.** A bit heavy in the black turtleneck department, Flore is nevertheless one of the Castro's premier gathering spots, drawing pseudo-artists, political activists, and trendy boys. If you can't find a place at one of the outside tables, strike a pose and loiter until someone makes room—sharing tables is de rigueur. Expect noise, commotion, and, in the midst of it all, an incredibly attractive someone sipping chamomile tea and looking furtively your way. Preferred reading material: Jean Genet (just pretend to read). *2298 Market St., at Noe St., tel. 415/621–8579. Open daily 7:30 AM–11:30 PM (Fri.–Sat. until midnight).*

Cup a Joe. This funky place with maroon walls has all the ingredients of a successful café: a mean cuppa joe ($1.10 for an espresso), tasty pastries (75¢ after 5:30 PM), and an art-student clientele. They occasionally hold spoken word performances; call for details. Preferred reading material: the *Bay Times,* Armistead Maupin's *Tales of the City. 3801 17th St., at Sanchez St., tel. 415/252–0536. Open weekdays 7 AM–10 PM, weekends 8 AM–10 PM.*

Jumpin' Java. The quiet, tree-lined neighborhood of Duboce Triangle is a relaxing contrast to its chaotic Market Street and Lower Haight neighbors. Although the *Bay Guardian* deems this café "the best place to cruise nerdy gay guys," you'll also find a mix of students and couples. Make a night of it here and sit down with a good read, a powerful cup of coffee ($1.25 for a large), and a spinach-and-cheddar quiche ($3.25). Hell, come here every night. Preferred reading material: *A Tree Grows in Brooklyn. 139 Noe St., btw Henry and 14th Sts., tel. 415/431–5282. Open weekdays 6 AM–10 PM, weekends 7 AM–10 PM.*

Morning Due. Not as grungy as most cafés in the Mission, nor as trendy as those in the Castro, this place smack on the border of these two neighborhoods is a refreshingly airy, well-lit café with a good selection of oat cakes, light meals, pastries and cookies. It's rarely crowded (half the people grab an iced coffee to go), and the studious crowds and mellow world-beat music on the stereo means it's a good place to read that novel. And, if you forgot to bring your book, they'll be happy to sell you one from their shelves. Aspiring poets and folk musicians show up for the open mic on Saturday nights. Preferred reading material: Charlotte Brontë's works. *3698 17th St. at Church St., tel 415/621–7156. Open daily 7 AM–10 PM. Wheelchair access.*

Pasqua Coffee. Normally, Pasqua is the most standardized and impersonal of local chains, but here, the friendly Castro crowd adds more than enough personality. Pasqua stays packed with toned, tanned locals who come for the excellent scones and coffee and stay for the stylish social scene. Preferred reading material: *GQ* magazine. *4094 18th St., at Castro St., tel. 415/626–6263. Open Mon.–Tues. 6:30 AM–10 PM, Weds.–Thurs. 6:30 AM–11 PM, Fri. 6:30 AM–midnight, Sat. 7 AM–midnight, Sun. 8 AM–10 PM.*

CIVIC CENTER/HAYES VALLEY **Mad Magda's Russian Tea Room and Café.** More like the Mad Hatter's Café. The deep-blue ceiling, red walls, and eerily peaceful "magic" garden in back give Magda's an otherworldly feel. Have your palm read ($13, Wed. 1:30–5) or attend one of their daily workshops ($25, 11 AM and 3 PM) on topics ranging from Wiccan rituals to Tarot reading. Those who wish destiny to remain unknown can simply kick back with an herbal tea and a sandwich. Preferred reading material: Tea leaves. *579 Hayes St., near Octavia St., tel. 415/864–7654. Open Mon.–Tues. 9–9, Wed.–Sat. 9 AM–midnight, Sun. 10–7.*

In January 1995, San Francisco banned smoking in all cafés, though a liquor license provides a convenient loophole for those who want to light up with a beer or booze.

Momi Toby's Revolution Café. A Sunday-morning hangout for Hayes Valley locals, Momi Toby's encourages artistic expression by providing a piano, sketchbook, crayons, and markers. Prefer to read quietly? You'll find a small shelf of quality literature next to the counter. Momi Toby's also serves appealing snacks like tuna bagels ($3) and veggie or chicken burritos ($3), as well as beer and wine. Occasional live music happens on weekends. Preferred reading material: *Mother Jones* magazine. *528 Laguna St., at Fell St., tel. 415/626–1508. Open weekdays 7:30 AM–9:30 PM, weekends 8 AM–9:30 PM.*

DOWNTOWN **Cafe de la Presse.** This café near the German and French cultural centers doubles as a European newsstand, so you won't hear much English spoken here. You can enjoy your espresso outdoors under sidewalk umbrellas, but the Parisian café fantasy ends there:

One look across busy Bush Street at the Chinatown Gate will remind you this is a West Coast metropolis. While you're here, take a peek inside the Hotel Triton's funky Alice in Wonderland lobby. Preferred reading material: *Der Spiegel, Le Monde. 352 Grant St., at Bush St., tel. 415/398–2680. Open daily 7 AM–11 PM.*

Yakety Yak. The bright facade of this mellow coffeehouse contrasts rebelliously with the gray surroundings. Hopeful artists from the nearby Academy of Arts find their caffeine fixes, a huge selection of fresh pastries, and a respite from the bustling downtown traffic here. Yakety Yak has an S.F. Net hookup (*see box* Plug In, Tune In, Drink Up, *below*) and open-mic poetry readings Fridays 7–9. Preferred reading material: *Cups: A Café Journal, What Color is your Parachute? 679 Sutter St., at Taylor St., tel. 415/885–6908. Open Mon.-Sat. 7 AM–10 PM, Sun. 8 AM–10 PM.*

HAIGHT-ASHBURY AND WESTERN ADDITION **Bean There.** Once you set foot inside this airy, high-ceilinged space, it's hard to believe you're a mere block from grimy Lower Haight. This is a great place to kick back Parisian-style with a game of chess and indulge in specialties like the Caffè Duboce (a potent latte with a twist of almond, caramel, or vanilla, $2–$3) or a spinach and tomato scone ($1.35). Weekends, neighborhood residents laze over sidewalk tables with the Sunday crossword and the family dog. Weekday mornings, locals line up for a java jump-start of their excellent organic coffees (sold by the pound). Preferred reading material: the e-mail off your laptop. *201 Steiner St., at Waller St., tel. 415/255–8855. 1 block south of Haight St. Open weekdays 7 AM–10 PM, weekends 8 AM–10 PM.*

Café International. The sofas, homey furniture, and mural-covered backyard patio give this Lower Haight café a friendly touch. Besides caffeine, International serves up fruit juices ($2.75) and snacks. Fridays at 9 PM, poets and their angst-ridden wanna-bes ply their verse at the open mic. Preferred reading material: *The Anarchist's Cookbook. 508 Haight St., at Fillmore St., tel. 415/552–7370. Open daily 7 AM–11 PM (Fri.–Sat. until midnight).*

The Horseshoe. Here you'll find more disaffected youths with tattoos, piercings, and time on their hands than perhaps anywhere else in the city. Regulars come for chess, shouted conversation over the blasting music, or to post flyers seeking band members or advertising artistic events. You might even leave toying with the idea of just a small tattoo. Preferred reading material: *Trainspotting, Guitar magazine. 566 Haight St., near Steiner St., tel. 415/626–8852. Open daily 7:30 AM–1 AM.*

Jammin' Java. This sunny, neighborhood café one block south of frantic Haight Street serves great, strong coffee ($1.25–$2), light food (quiche is $3.50), and lackluster desserts. The indoor and outdoor tables are populated day and night, and an interesting variety of music plays in the background. Preferred reading material: *The Electric Kool-Aid Acid Test. 701 Cole St., tel. 415/668–JAVA. Open daily 7 AM–11 PM. Other location: 398 Judah St., at 9th Ave., tel. 415/566–JAVA.*

Would You Like Coffee With That?

Pretension and cafés go hand-in-hand: Witness the way in which coffeehouses attempt to give self-important names to what is, after all, flavored water. Beyond the basic espresso, cappuccino, latte, or mocha, some cafés list a half-dozen or more caffeine concoctions. Figuring out how to order becomes a struggle in and of itself. Gone are the days of small, medium, and large. Instead you must decide between a single or double (bonus pretense points for ordering a "doppio"); short, tall, or grande; and wet or dry foam. Occasionally, cafés adopt an absurdist mix-and-match attitude. If you are asked, "Would you like the doppio in a grande cup with dry foam?" you have our permission to strangle the counterperson.

MISSION DISTRICT **Café Istanbul.** The Syrian owner of this unique café serves authentic and delicious Middle Eastern food ($2–$5) and beverages ($1–$3) in an exotic, tapestried setting. Definitely a contrast to your average café, Istanbul boasts a pillowed platform area and intricately scrolled, gold-colored trays that function as tabletops. Take off your shoes and hunker down with a pot of mint tea and delicately flavored dolmas (grape leaves), or baklava and cardamom-spiked Turkish coffee. A wide variety of Middle Eastern music completes the ambience, along with belly dancing on Wednesday and Saturday nights. There's a $1 cover charge for the dancing. Preferred reading material: anything by Rumi. *525 Valencia St., btw 16th and 17th Sts., tel. 415/863–8854. Open daily 11–11.*

Café Macondo. It's encouraging that, even in the trendiest part of the Mission, a down-to-earth neighborhood coffeehouse lives on. The walls are plastered with revolutionary posters from all over Latin America, and a mix of students, intellectuals, and revolutionaries sits at the heavy wooden tables to read, study, or talk politics over steamy cups of *café*. Preferred reading material: *Pasajes de la guerra revolucionaria. 3159 16th St., btw Valencia and Guerrero Sts., tel. 415/863–6517. Open daily 11 AM–10 PM (Fri.–Sat. until 11 PM).*

La Bohème. Though it recently changed owners, this Mission District institution continues to draw a multiracial, all-ages clientele that feasts on the deli's variety of American, Greek, and Middle Eastern sandwiches. Word has it the new owners hope to expand the occasional live guitar music. Preferred reading material: anything by Pablo Neruda (*en español, por supuesto*). *3318 24th St., at Mission St., tel. 415/643–0481. Open weekdays 6 AM–11 PM, weekends 7:30 AM–11 PM.*

Mission Grounds. Most of the friendly locals who hang out here do so during the day or on weekends. Found near the popular Kilowatt club (*see* Live Music, in Chapter 6), this is a good place to caffeinate yourself before hitting the Mission's nightlife, but this isn't really an evening café; come nightfall, it's just you and the dustbunnies. They serve crêpes ($2–$6) and omelets ($4) all day. Preferred reading material: anything by Bukowski. *3170 16th St., at Guerrero St., tel. 415/621–1539. Open daily 7 AM–10 PM.*

Radio Valencia. In June of 1995, two fire trucks collided into each other and went careening into the storefront of Radio Valencia, but you'd never know it from the beautifully rebuilt glass windows, and cheery, brightly painted café tables. This friendly place is all about music, from the vinyl and vintage instruments on the walls, to the carefully selected tunes playing over the speakers. Owner Don Allen used to work in radio in Wisconsin, and now he (and other staff members) create a daily "menu" of hand-picked songs that they display on each table—many from local jazz and indie groups—and play all day long. Fridays through Sundays, live music sets up in the corner to the sounds of jazz, blues, bluegrass, and swing. Tap your foot while nursing a cappuccino or hum along while downing a pint of one of the 12 microbrews they have on tap. Preferred reading material: CD liner notes. *1199 Valencia St., at 23rd St., tel. 415/826–1199. Open Mon.–Tues. 5 PM–midnight, Wed.–Sun. noon–midnight.*

Red Dora's Bearded Lady. A self-proclaimed "dyke café (everybody welcome)," this small coffeehouse is an expression of San Francisco's young, energetic queer culture. Especially in the afternoon and on weekends, the pierced-but-unpretentious come to chill among the mismatched furniture or in the lovely garden in back. Dora's serves the usual café eats, plus a tasty breakfast burrito ($4) and a tofu burger ($4.50). Spoken-word and musical performances take place on some Fridays and Saturdays at 8 PM after the café closes, but call ahead to confirm. Preferred reading material: *On Our Backs* (for arousal), *Off Our Backs* (for edification). *485 14th St., at Guerrero St., tel. 415/626–2805. Open weekdays 7–7, weekends 9–7.*

NORTH BEACH **Caffè Greco.** An international crowd fills this attractive café, whose windows overlook Columbus Avenue. Rich Italian espresso ($1.40 a cup) accompanies a variety of music (from Edith Piaf to Italian pop) in a bustling atmosphere. You'll find a colorful selection of desserts—regulars worship the decadent tiramisù ($4). Preferred reading material: *The New Yorker. 423 Columbus Ave., btw Vallejo and Stockton Sts., tel. 415/397–6261. Open daily 7 AM–midnight (weekends until 1 AM).*

Caffè Trieste. This is the legendary home of the Beat generation; it was here that Kerouac and his gang oozed cool from every pore. The café doesn't seem to have changed a bit—heck, the '50s jukebox still spouts opera. Saturday afternoons at 2 PM, local Italian performers serenade guests with old Italian tunes—many times accompanied by a live mini orchestra. Coffee drinks cost $1–$3. Preferred reading material: Ginsberg's *Howl*. *601 Vallejo St., at Grant Ave., tel. 415/392–6739. Open daily 6:30 AM–11:30 PM (Fri.–Sat. until 12:30 AM).*

Gathering Caffè. Jazz aficionados should not miss this spot, where there's no cover charge for the nightly live music—you'll just pay an extra 50¢ for your coffee drink. The small marble tables and black-and-white checkered floor evoke a tiny jazz bar in Paris, not a San Francisco café three blocks from the "Girls! Girls! Girls!" of Broadway. Sunny weekends, you can take your cappuccino outside while listening to the strains of a stand-up bass. Preferred reading material: Nat Shapiro's *The Jazz Makers*. *1326 Grant Ave., btw, Green and Vallejo Sts., tel. 415/433–4247. Open weekdays 7 PM–2 AM, weekends 11 AM–2 AM.*

Mario's Bohemian Cigar Store and Café. With about eight tables and a big polished-wood bar, this old-time Italian café has been feeding 'em strong espresso, a glass of Chianti, or a beer for the last 50 years. You can also get a fine grilled sandwich (meatball or roasted eggplant among others; around $6) on homemade focaccia or a Neopolitan pizza ($9). The windows overlook Washington Square Park and the Church of Saints Peter and Paul, in case you didn't already feel like you were in Italy. Preferred reading material: *How to Speak Italian in 30 Days or Less*. *566 Columbus Ave., at Union St., tel. 415/362–0536. Open Mon.–Sat. 10 AM–midnight, Sun. 10 AM–11 PM. Wheelchair access.*

North End Café. The young and the restless congregate at this cozy café over massive bowl-sized cups of coffee. While you can easily sit and read a book undisturbed, the urge to gaze at the beautiful people may overpower you. The coffee is strong—one cup should render you giddy, two will leave you babbling incessantly. Preferred reading material: *Details* magazine. *1402 Grant Ave., at Green St., tel. 415/956–3350. Open weekdays 7:30 AM–10 PM, weekends 8:30 AM–10 PM.*

The Steps of Rome. Well-dressed—correction, make that *very* well-dressed—young urbanites crowd this large, bright, café. The music is loud, the conversation (ranging from intellectual banter to cheezy come-ons) louder, and the waiters might hit on your girlfriend or break into spontaneous song. Preferred reading material: Read?! You came here to look good! *348 Columbus Ave., near Grant Ave., tel. 415/397–0435. Open weekdays 7:30 AM–10 PM, weekends 8:30 AM–10 PM.*

SOUTH OF MARKET **Brain Wash.** Much more than a laundromat, more than a café . . . Brain Wash is a way of life. Where else can you drink a beer, listen to live music, play pinball, and eat a veggie burger ($5.25) while you wash your clothes? The music is hip and the decor Jetsons-like, so even if you don't have your load with you, it's fun to come here for a cuppa joe,

Plug In, Tune In, Drink Up

If you're yearning to jump on the Internet bandwagon, try SF NET, a computer network found in more than a dozen cafés in the Bay Area. As you drink your latte, you can dive into cyberspace and exchange messages with people at other cafés hooked up to the system. Here's how it works: You put in your quarter (yes, it costs money), log on with a nickname of your liking, and chat away, feeding the computer more money every so often. Your quarter also lets you connect with the Bay Guardian's on-line service, Gay Net, Greenpeace, and the San Francisco Library's on-line catalog. You can also log on at home if you have a modem. The remote access number is 415/824–8747. You'll find S.F. Net in more than 13 cafés, including Jammin' Java and Yakety Yak (see above).

a two-egg breakfast ($4), or just to stare through the big windows out at lonely, warehouse-lined Folsom Street. There's live music (from acoustic to punk) every weekend at 10 PM, and occasionally during the week at 8 PM. Preferred reading material: clothing tags. *1122 Folsom St., btw 7th and 8th Sts., tel. 415/861–FOOD. Open for coffee and pastries weekdays at 7 AM; kitchen open Sun.–Thurs. 8–9, Fri. and Sat. 9–11. $10 minimum on credit cards.*

Café Natoma. This lunch-hour café in the shadow of the impressive 1925 Pacific Telephone and Telegraph company's office tower names its sandwiches after SoMa streets and alleys, such as the Natoma Street Original (smoked ham; $4) and the Yerba Buena (veggie; $4). A shot of espresso is 95¢. Because the café is directly behind the Museum of Modern Art, office workers and museum-goers vie for tables. Preferred reading material: *Forbes* and *Interview* magazines. *145 Natoma St., btw. 3rd and New Montgomery Sts., tel. 415/495–3289. Open weekdays 7 AM–4:30 PM.*

Caffè Centro. Workers from the new "multimedia gulch" snag the sidewalk tables of this café overlooking South Park—a beautiful patch of green surrounded by beautiful old (and modern) homes. Grab a light lunch or coffee and bask barefoot in the park with young graphic artists, programmers, and designers. Preferred reading material: *Wired* magazine. *102 South Park Ave., btw 2nd and 3rd and Bryant and Brannan Sts., tel. 415/882–1500. Open weekdays 8 AM–7:30 PM, Sat. 9 AM-5 PM.*

Mr. Ralph's. Stroll down Natoma, off Second Street, and you'll find a tiny, bright-green tile building that houses this funky little coffeehouse with exposed brick walls and imaginatively painted furniture. Unwind with the mellow, artsy-professional crowd after a few hours of cultural overload at the MOMA. During happy hour (4:30–6:30), pints are $2, and Friday evenings there's free live jazz. Preferred reading material: *Candide. 90 Natoma St., near 2nd St., tel. 415/243–9330. Open Mon.–Wed. 7–7, Thurs.–Fri. 7 AM–9 PM, Sat. 8:30–2:30.*

OUTLYING NEIGHBORHOODS So you've ventured beyond the parts of the city where espresso bars run two to a block. Shame on you. Luckily, whether you're out and about visiting your aunt, expanding your horizons, getting a part for your car, or going to the dentist, there are places in almost every neighborhood to get your caffeine fix.

Blue Danube. Bring your purchases from nearby Green Apple Books (*see* Chapter 3), and soak in the homey Richmond District atmosphere with college students, resident youth, and thirtysomethings who still remember how to laze away the weekend. On sunny days, the windows are wide open and provide a ledge for putting your feet up and people watching. Preferred reading material: *The Tao of Pooh. 306 Clement St., btw 4th and 5th Aves., tel. 415/221–9041. Open Mon.–Thurs. 7 AM–11:30 PM, Fri.–Sat. 7 AM–12:30 AM, Sun. 7 AM–10:30 PM.*

Cool Beans. If you're looking for the equivalent of a west coast "Cheers" set (minus Carla's scathing sarcasm), make the trip out to this brighty painted Inner Richmond café. Owners Sam and Henry—one of whom is usually behind the bar—will learn your name by your second visit, and it's easy to make the acquaintance of the locals who spend many of their daylight hours here. Besides the usual café breakfast amenities, they also serve great sandwiches and homemade soups. Preferred reading material: *The New York Times Crossword Puzzle. California St., at 6th Ave, tel. 415/750–1955. From downtown, take Bus 1 west to cnr of California St. and 6th Ave. Open daily 7 AM–8 PM. Wheelchair access.*

Farley's. Besides the classic features of a good café—strong coffee, local art displays, lots of sidewalk tables—this Potrero Hill coffeehouse has a magazine rack with more than 20 titles, a stack of games, and loads of journals. Farley's holds occasional music and poetry nights, and storytelling events for big and small kids. Preferred reading material: *The Phantom Tollbooth. 1315 18th St., btw Texas and Missouri Sts., tel. 415/648–1545. Open weekdays 7 AM–10 PM, weekends 8 AM–10 PM.*

Java Beach. What do surfers at Ocean Beach do when the waves are blown out? They go to Java Beach, the only decent café in the Outer Sunset, to lounge on the couches and swap tales of conquered swells. Nonsurfers come to read, chat, study, or catch some of the occasional live music. Preferred reading material: Bill Morris's *Stoked. 1396 La Playa St., at Judah St., tel. 415/665–JAVA. Open weekdays 6 AM–11 PM, weekends 7 AM–11 PM.*

Royal Ground Coffee. If you're on Fillmore Street or in Japantown, come here to take a load off. Even if the outside tables are taken, the large windows let in plenty of sunshine. The upwardly mobile patrons (local families and twentysomethings) insist on calling this neighborhood "lower" Pacific Heights to distinguish it from the seedy stretch of Fillmore south of Geary. Preferred reading material: *Sunset* magazine. *2060 Fillmore St., at California St., tel. 415/567–8823. Open daily 6:30 AM–11 PM (Fri.–Sat. until midnight).*

Tart to Tart. Another friendly neighborhood café, Tart to Tart whips up a mean cup of coffee and plenty of excellent desserts ($2–$4), salads ($4), and entrées for Inner Sunset locals and UCSF medical students. Preferred reading material: *Gray's Anatomy. 641 Irving St., btw 7th and 8th Aves., tel. 415/753–0643. Open weekdays 7:30 AM–11 PM, Sat. 8:30 AM–midnight, Sun. 8:30 AM–11 PM.*

EAST BAY

Without its many cafés, the People's Republic of Berkeley would collapse. Students would have nowhere to be seen while "studying"; skate punks would have nowhere to hang while cutting class; artists and poets would have no place to share their angst. Around **Telegraph Avenue** south of campus and **Euclid Avenue** north of campus you'll find cafés crowded day and night with students; while the crowds downtown and on **College Avenue** are more mixed. Oakland isn't exactly a latte town, but locals do gather at the cafés in the **Rockridge, Piedmont Avenue,** and **Grand Lake** areas, especially on sunny weekends. Smokers, however, should take note: In 1994, Berkeley banned smoking in all indoor *and* outdoor cafés.

Started in the '60s, Peets Coffee (2124 Vine St., at Walnut St., tel. 510/841–0564) began at this unassuming café. It now distributes its roasts worldwide and has over a dozen cafés in the Bay Area providing super-strong blends to experienced coffee swillers.

BERKELEY **Au Cocquelet.** There *is* life in Berkeley after midnight, and you'll find it here, a couple of doors down from the U.C. Theatre. Au Cocquelet is always packed with moviegoers, students, and people reading into the night. Brunch is served weekends until 3 PM. Preferred reading material: Film reviews. *2000 University Ave., at Milvia St., tel. 510/845–0433. Open weekdays 6 AM–1:30 AM (Fri. until 2 AM), Sat. 8 AM–2 AM, Sun. 8 AM–1:30 AM.*

Café Fanny. Opened by Chez Panisse maven Alice Waters and named for her daughter Fanny, this west Berkeley café draws weekend crowds of young mothers and aging yuppies to its trellised patio. The food is not exactly cheap, and the portions are small: If you're on a tight budget, get a bowl-sized latte ($2) and homemade granola ($4), or try the buckwheat crêpes ($4.75), available with a variety of fillings. On your way home, stop next door at Acme Bread for a fresh-baked baguette. Preferred reading material: *A Year in Provence. 1603 San Pablo Ave., at Cedar St., tel. 510/524–5447. Open weekdays 7–3, Sat. 8–4, Sun. 9–3.*

Caffè Mediterraneum. Featured in the film *The Graduate*, the Med has nurtured countless bursts of inspiration and the occasional failed revolution. These days, it's one of the few places where lifelong Berkeleyans and open-minded students converge for conversation over a shot of caffeine (most students stick closer to campus). Besides espresso drinks and desserts, the Med's small kitchen (open daily 7–3) serves omelets, sandwiches, burgers, and pasta at reasonable prices. The café—but not the second-floor rest room—is wheelchair accessible. Preferred reading material: Berkeley celebrity Julia Vinograd's poetry, which if you don't already have, she'll come by and sell you at the café. *2475 Telegraph Ave., btw Haste St. and Dwight Way, tel. 510/549–1128. Open daily 7 AM–midnight.*

Caffè Strada. There's little indoor seating, but the sprawling outdoor patio attracts a good mix of architecture students, frat and sorority types, and visiting foreigners. It's a social spot, so don't expect to get much work done. Instead, bring a newspaper, relax in the sun, and eavesdrop while you sip your latte ($1.50) and munch on your pastry ($1–$2). Preferred reading material: *The East Bay Express* and *The Daily Cal*, available for free at a stand across the street. *2300 College Ave., at Bancroft Way, tel. 510/843–5282. Open daily 7 AM–11:30 PM.*

Espresso Roma. It may be in the sleepy Elmwood neighborhood, but Roma is one of Berkeley's favorite late-night hangouts—the large café is always packed on weekends with locals from all walks of life. They also serve a variety of beers ($2.50), some overpriced salads and sandwiches ($4–$6) and have a S.F. Net terminal. Preferred reading material: Jane Austen's *Persuasion*. *2960 College Ave., at Ashby Ave., tel. 510/644–3773. Open Mon.–Thurs. 6:30 AM–11 PM, Fri. 6:30 AM–midnight, Sat. 7:30 AM–midnight, Sun. 7:30 AM–11 PM.*

Nefeli Caffè. This Greek north side coffeehouse is popular with students and professors for its innovative, reasonably priced menu. The impressive selection of Italian-style panini includes an unusually delectable sandwich with eggplant, roasted peppers, feta, and Kalamata olive spread ($4.25). Nefeli also has a variety of wine and beer, as well as sangria ($2.75), and you shouldn't leave without sampling the house specialty, caffè freddo (espresso, sugar, and Sambuca, $2.50). Poetry readings take place Monday nights, followed by open-mic performances. Preferred reading material: anything by Nikos Kazantzakis. *1854 Euclid Ave., at Hearst St., tel. 510/841–6374. Open Mon.–Thurs. 7 AM–10 PM, Fri. 7 AM–midnight, Sat. 8 AM–midnight, Sun. 8 AM–10 PM.*

Red Café. This gem of a café-bar, one of a few as yet undiscovered by students, fills with an older, artsy, postgrad crowd. The red-brick walls, exposed beam ceiling, and massive skylight (that actually opens) create a warm, welcoming ambience. The full kitchen serves carefully prepared, mostly vegetarian sandwiches, salads, and pastas ($3–$6), and the café has a fine selection of beers. The coffee is smooth, the service is super-friendly, and you'll find frequent live jazz. Preferred reading material: the want ads. *1941A University Ave., at Bonita St., tel. 510/843–8607. Open weekdays 7–7, Sat. 9–5. Wheelchair access.*

OAKLAND **Carraras Café and Gallery.** Emeryville—a former industrial enclave of a few thousand inhabitants wedged between Oakland and Berkeley—has seen many of its warehouses turned into artists' lofts and communal live/work spaces. Carraras, housed in a one-story brick warehouse, is an excellent place to experience this neo-urban mélange while sucking on an Anchor Steam beer ($2.50). Local artists (no shortage of those) display their work on the walls. Preferred reading material: *The Spirit of Community and the Reinvention of American Society*. *1290 Powell St., at Hollis St., tel. 510/547–6763. From I–80, take Powell St. exit north 3 blocks. Open weekdays 7 AM–midnight (Mon. until 11 PM), Sat. 9 AM–midnight. Wheelchair access.*

Edible Complex. Oaklanders (primarily students from nearby California College of Arts and Crafts) stay late into the night—late by Oakland standards, anyway—at this large Rockridge café. Sandwiches and salads are $3–$6, and artwork by different local artists graces the walls. Preferred reading material: *Jansen's History of Art*. *5600 College Ave., Oakland, one block south of Rockridge BART, tel. 510/658–2172. Open weekdays 7:30 AM–midnight (Fri. until 1 AM), Sat. 8:30 AM–1 AM, Sun. 8:30 AM–midnight.*

AFTER DARK   6

By Mylah de la Rosa, with Simon Dang

The sun has edged its way into the ocean, leaving you to face that all-consuming question: What am I going to do tonight? Well, the Bay Area's got a lot of answers. If you don't find your scene in one of the area's 10,000 bars, you can go see a movie classic in a funky theater, check out a live show at a local club, head to a performance space to watch some unbridled genius, or dance all night long at an underground party. In this chapter, nightlife has been broken down into bars, live music, and clubs, but these distinctions are *not* hard and fast. More often than not, your favorite café will also serve beer, host a local band, cram the chairs in back for disco, and cater to folks of various persuasions depending on the night.

San Francisco has traditionally been a place to invent and reinvent oneself, dating back to when the first criminals and gold-diggers came to the bay in search of fortune and a little bit of anonymity. Although saloons and brothels have since been supplanted by thousands of bars and clubs, the live-and-let-live attitude still thrives in the city's nightlife. Check *SF Weekly* or the *Bay Guardian* (both available free at newsstands and cafés citywide), or the *SF Chronicle*'s Sunday "Datebook" section for listings of current happenings after dark. The free weeklies, *Bay Times, Bay Area Reporter,* and the magazine *Q San Francisco* ($2.95) are good sources for gay and lesbian listings.

If your interests involve hard-core clubbing, tattooed rockers, or the gay scene and all of its subscenes, you're best off in San Francisco. Otherwise, the East Bay boasts plenty of bars and a handful of live music venues: Come to Oakland to sample world-class blues and jazz, and a burgeoning improv scene, or to Berkeley to drink with a predominately collegiate crowd. Pore through the free weekly *East Bay Express* for a complete events calendar, including films, lectures, readings, and music. For live music, consult *The List* (found at most independent record stores), which details dates, times, and locations for punk, ska, and rock shows in the East Bay.

While both Marin County and the South Bay can be entertaining during daylight hours, when the sun sets, these areas become very, very quiet. Still, you should be able to ferret out a local bar and maybe some live music in Marin; even the South Bay offers a few diversions near the Stanford campus. For nightlife in Marin and the South Bay, *see* Chapter 2.

Bars

SAN FRANCISCO

In San Francisco, choosing a place to drink is no easy matter. Anarchist punks with piercings, highbrow cocktail-lounge swingers, black-leather-and-chaps bikers, fresh-faced college students in sweatshirts and baseball caps, cowboys in pickup trucks—you name it, San Francisco's got it. The city caters to tastes both subtle and flamboyant, and you shouldn't have any trouble finding a new favorite bar. Keep in mind that hills, fog, and one-way streets prove particularly treacherous for those who drink and drive; instead, take the bus or call a cab.

CASTRO DISTRICT This safe, very gay quarter of San Francisco plays host to some of the wildest festivals in the city. You're far more likely to kindle a romance here if you're enamored of the same sex, but open-minded straight folks frequent a few of the less intense pickup bars after an evening at the grand old Castro Theatre (see Movie Houses, below) or one of the area's fine restaurants.

The Café. Formerly known as Café San Marco, this large, lively bar with mirrored walls and neon lights used to cater mainly to lesbians, although it's mostly men now. If there's no room on the dance floor, you can hang out on the balcony and watch the Castro strut by. 2367 Market St., near Castro St., tel. 415/861–3846.

The Detour. Minimally decorated with a chain-link fence and pool table, this bar caters to a youngish leather-queen-wanna-be crowd sporting goatees. Even with no dance floor, the urgent

Happy hour at the Detour means draft beer is 75¢ from 2 PM to 8 PM, Monday–Friday.

techno-house music causes the level of sexual frustration in the room to skyrocket. If you forget the address, listen for the music, since the black-on-black sign is impossible to see at night. 2348 Market St., btw Castro and Noe Sts., tel. 415/861–6053.

Midnight Sun. Two large video screens help alleviate the need for conversation in this crowded, colorful bar that shows a mix of weird TV shows and current music videos. 4067 18th St., near Castro St., tel. 415/861–4186. Wheelchair access.

The Orbit Room. Besides having a groovy name, the Orbit has a smart-looking, high-ceilinged drinking area where you can enjoy a cocktail or espresso with a mostly straight crowd that doesn't mind the artsy, slightly uncomfortable bar stools. The subdued lighting, stucco walls, and innovative design scheme make you feel like you're on display at some swank art gallery. 1900 Market St., at Laguna St., tel. 415/252–9525. Wheelchair access.

The Phoenix. This is a good place for shy types to pick up a sexy new lover boy. Admission is only $1 on Fridays and Saturdays, and it features Castro Street's oldest gay dance floor. 482 Castro St., btw 17th and 18th Sts., tel. 415/552–6827.

Twin Peaks. David Lynch has nothing to do with this casual, loungelike gay bar; in fact, the Peaks has been around for more than 15 years, and proudly claims to have been the first gay bar in the city with clear—as in, not tinted—floor-to-ceiling windows. Twin Peaks enjoys its high visibility on the corner of Market and Castro; on weekends expect big crowds of both newcomers and an older, established clientele. 401 Castro St., at Market St., tel. 415/864–9470.

CHINATOWN By day a maelstrom of gaudy souvenir shops, pungent markets, and overcrowded sidewalks, Chinatown transforms into a quiet, genuine neighborhood at night. Step into one of the local bars for a reminder of whose part of town this is.

Li Po's. The dark, cavernous setting and incense-burning altar lend an oddly mystical feel to Li Po's. By 1 AM the coveted back booths are filled with boisterous escapees from the North Beach scene, who are almost daring—and drunk—enough to join in the occasional karaoke. After last call, stop into Sam Wo's around the corner for some downright cheap chow mein. 916 Grant St., btw Jackson and Washington Sts., tel. 415/982–0072.

Mr. Bing's. This horseshoe-shape spot on the edge of Chinatown draws a heterogeneous mix of drinkers who line the narrow bar and, when given the chance, gladly share their latest misadventures. There's also the ubiquitous video-poker machines and a jukebox that plays scratchy Sinatra tunes. 201 Columbus Ave., at Pacific St., tel. 415/362–1545.

DOWNTOWN AND CIVIC CENTER AREA The downtown area isn't the greatest place to be after sundown, unless you enjoy getting heckled by streetwalkers in microminis or witnessing shady business transactions. Nevertheless, there are a few bars worth braving if you have door-to-door transportation. Be especially careful in the Tenderloin, which is loosely bordered by Larkin, O'Farrell, Mason, and Market streets.

Edinburgh Castle. This diamond in the rough was established before the Tenderloin earned its reputation for squalor. A British pub with a beautiful bar, it's a great place to play darts, eat *real* fish 'n' chips, down pints of Guinness or Bass, and make friends with thick-accented U.K. types. Other benign reasons to visit include occasional local bands, Scottish bagpipe troupes, and plays hosted in the upstairs theater space. *950 Geary St., btw Polk and Larkin Sts., tel. 415/885–4074.*

Jacks. Posters of blues legends still hang on the wall, and John Lee Hooker has been known to stop by on occasion, but Jacks has stopped having live music for the time being. Jacks does, however, still serve a wide selection of draft beer (as well as 70 different bottled kinds), and maintains a casual, down-home atmosphere. This lower Fillmore club is not in the best of San Francisco's neighborhoods. *1601 Fillmore St., at Geary Blvd., tel. 415/567–3227.*

Motherlode. This Tenderloin landmark is the city's most popular transvestite haven, although there's no "dress" code posted at the door. The area is often dangerous and the crowd occasionally seedy, but the flamboyant patrons provide an energetic, entertaining night of thrills. Come for the free drag shows on Friday and Saturday nights—but please refrain from gawking. *1002 Post St., at Larkin St., tel. 415/928–6006.*

Place Pigalle. The vibes are hip and European (but definitely not pretentious) at this sleek, low-key, French-owned, Hayes Valley wine bar and gallery space. Stop in for a glass of wine after work and stay for the evening; there's live jazz Thursday through Saturday nights, and occasional spoken-word performances during the week. *520 Hayes St., btw Octavia and Laguna Sts., tel. 415/552–2671. Cover: up to $3. Wheelchair access.*

HAIGHT AND THE WESTERN ADDITION Ah, Haight-Ashbury—more than 25 years of hipness. This neighborhood might overdo it at times, and the crowd is always hot on the heels of the latest trend, but there are a variety of low-key spots where you can toss down a few. Upper Haight is still host to vacant-looking hippies mourning Jerry and their dogs, as well as lots of cocktail-quaffing tourists who've just spent the day buying pricey "flower child" togs. When you want a watering hole that's slightly rougher around the edges, head downhill to Lower Haight.

Club Deluxe. Come on the weekend to this slick, retro bar in Upper Haight, order a martini, and take a look around: You'll get the uncanny feeling that the year is 1945. Patrons enjoy donning their finest '40s duds (hairdos and shoes included) and acting *very* cool. There will usually be a crooner, with backup swing band, or at least owner Jay Johnson doing Sinatra his way. Denim-wearers are welcome. *1511 Haight St., btw Ashbury and Clayton Sts., tel. 415/552–6949. Cover: $3–$5 weekends.*

Mad Dog in the Fog. This British-style pub in the heart of Lower Haight is frequented by neighborhood folk jonesin' for cold, frothy beer and a rugby match. The Dog offers diversions galore: darts inside, a beer garden outside, and lively trivia competitions for beer and cash prizes on Mondays and Thursdays. Mornings, they serve up greasy breakfasts like the Greedy Bastard (bacon, sausage, baked beans, scrambled eggs, and tomato; $6)—and all dishes over $6 include a free pint until 2:30 PM. *530 Haight St., btw Fillmore and Steiner Sts., tel. 415/626–7279.*

Midtown. Watch lower Haight Street have a beer. The clientele is young, tattooed, perpetually smoking, and good at pool. Arrive early on weekends to snag the lone table, as the crowd can be fierce in the standing room. *582 Haight St., btw Fillmore and Steiner Sts., tel. 415/558–8019.*

Murio's Trophy Room. Murio's, in Upper Haight, is often overcrowded with bikers and Haight Street slackers, but it can be fun and low-key on weekdays. When the conversation lags, there's a pool table, jukebox, and TV. *1811 Haight St., btw Shrader and Stanyan Sts., tel. 415/752–2971.*

Noc Noc. Step inside this Lower Haight institution and you'll find yourself in a postmodern cave complete with chunky Flintstones-style furniture and a very eclectic music repertoire.

Expect a healthy variety of beers, a couple kinds of wine, and sake—but no hard liquor. *557 Haight St., btw Fillmore and Steiner Sts., tel. 415/861–5811.*

The Toronado. A narrow, dark dive in Lower Haight with lots of folks in leather, the Toronado features one of the widest selections of microbrews in the city. The jukebox blares a refreshing mix of kitschy country and western in addition to the standard grunge anthems. *547 Haight St., btw Fillmore and Steiner Sts., tel. 415/863–2276.*

MARINA DISTRICT The nightlife in this affluent, homogenous section of Lower Pacific Heights is typified by the bevy of bars in the "Triangle," the intersection of Fillmore and Greenwich streets, which attract hordes of sporty professionals (i.e., postcollege frat boys). You'll find this one of the safest areas to knock back a few (at least in terms of stumbling to MUNI, BART, or a cab without getting mugged).

Pierce Street Annex Drinking Establishment. Packed with the young and beautiful, this festive bar has a dance floor, pool tables, and nightly drink specials. Tuesdays are karaoke nights and Wednesdays feature live reggae. *3138 Fillmore St., near Greenwich St., tel. 415/567–1400.*

MISSION DISTRICT Lately, the Mission has been sprouting hip bars, cafés, restaurants, and clubs faster than a Chia Pet sprouts alfalfa, attracting a young bohemian crowd with a predilection for thrift stores. The neighborhood, however, has long had a shady reputation. The poorly lit side streets are the diciest, but even on more heavily trafficked streets like Valencia and Mission, late-night bar-hoppers should take care.

The city's best margaritas are mixed at Puerto Alegre (546 Valencia St., near 16th St., tel. 415/626–2922), about a block from the Elbo Room. Order a strawberry and munch on some tortilla chips to get fueled up for the evening ahead.

The 500 Club. Here's a little slice of Americana—complete with a huge neon sign, two cramped pool tables, and three comfy vinyl booths. Check your attitude at the door, and join the locals at this friendly neighborhood dive. *500 Guerrero St., at 17th St., tel. 415/861–2500.*

The Albion. Elbow your way into this cramped bar and fight for a seat under the glow of pink neon lights. If you're left standing, you can always shoot some stick or edge your way closer to the occasional loud, live music. *3139 16th St., btw Valencia and Guerrero Sts., tel. 415/552–8558.*

The Lone Palm. Push open the huge black door and you will enter an oasis of class. Dimly lit tables, a '40s retro atmosphere, and skilled cocktail shakers behind the bar combine to make

Rack 'Em

Intimidated shooting stick in front of an unsympathetic bar crowd? Tired of waiting half an hour for a table, only to scratch the eight ball on your first shot? Pay a visit to one of San Francisco's pool halls, where, for an hourly fee, you can practice that bank shot or hustle your friends without interruption. Serious players should head to one of the 37 tables at Hollywood Billiards (61 Golden Gate Ave., near Market St., tel. 415/252–9643). Mondays, students play for up to five hours for $5; Tuesdays and Thursdays it jumps to $10. Hollywood is open 24 hours and has a full bar, but the downside is that it's not in the best neighborhood. At South Beach Billiards (270 Brannan St., near 2nd St., tel. 415/495–5939)—a sleek SoMa pool hall open until 2 AM nightly—tables are $10 an hour after 6 PM, and there are weekly beer specials. With only five tables, the pool room at Park Bowl (1851 Haight St., btw Shrader and Stanyan Sts., tel. 415/752–2366) occasionally fills up, but the dirt-cheap tables ($5.50 an hour for two people) are worth the wait, and it's a casual place to hang with some friends and a cue ball.

this an intimate setting to sip martinis with that certain someone. *3394 22nd St., near Guerrero St., tel. 415/648–0109.*

The Make Out Room. The dark, quiet street and beckoning marquee may have you convinced that this is some shady strip joint. Once inside, however, you'll discover a popular hot spot on the Mission bar scene. You may not see a whole lot of making out, but you *will* see plenty of room in this spacious bar—enough for a pool table and a stage that hosts live bands. *3225 22nd Ave., btw Mission and Valencia Sts., tel. 415/647–2888. Cover: $3–$6 (when there's a band).*

The Rite Spot. The piano in the corner, candlelit tables, and understated decor all lend a sense of timelessness to this outer Mission bar that's a favorite among locals. They also serve light meals, so you won't have to leave if you get the munchies. *2099 Folsom St., at 17th St., tel. 415/552–6066.*

The Uptown. Sit at the long oak bar and get rowdy with friendly barflies, grab a game of pool with neighborhood hipsters, or stand outside watching hookers and drug dealers do their thing. Several well-worn couches in back make you feel right at home. *200 Capp St., at 17th St., tel. 415/861–8231.*

Zeitgeist. This is the original no-frills biker bar—albeit a bit trendier and friendlier—for every kind of biker. In the afternoons, it fills with bike messengers relating the day's near encounters with the Big Grille in the Sky; by night the BMW motorbike crowd clogs the outdoor deck, waiting its turn at the lone pool table. *199 Valencia St., at Duboce Ave., tel. 415/255–7505.*

NOB HILL AND RUSSIAN HILL This area caters to an upscale, often touristy crowd—it's very safe at night. There are a few bars that the city's more conservative youth swear by, but Nob and Russian hills are dominated by four- and five-star hotels, and don't offer much to dive-bar aficionados.

Johnny Love's. Young urban professionals let their hair down and dance on the tables at this Russian Hill lounge, much touted by the press as *the* singles bar for postcollege types who have managed to find a steady job. In other words, it's the most upscale meat market in town. *1500 Broadway, at Polk St., tel. 415/931–8021.*

Red Room. Owned by a Manhattan socialite, this lounge-y cocktail bar attracts the trendy, clubbing crowd. Its impressive entrance opens to a curved wall of red bottles stacked to the ceiling and a thoroughly red interior—quite entrancing. Wear black to be better seen, and prepare to match wits against the top 10% of the social food chain. *827 Sutter St., at Jones St., tel. 415/346–7666.*

The Tonga Room. This Tiki kitsch-o-rama bar is custom-made for tourists who wish it was still 1955, but you'll secretly love the bamboo-and-palm-leaf decor as much as they do. The waiters wear muumuus; a simulated rainstorm regularly occurs in the artificial lagoon; and, best of all, your potent drink comes with fruit, umbrellas, and all sorts of paraphernalia. Of course, you'll pay handsomely for all this—even during happy hour (5 PM–7 PM), drinks will set you back $2.50–

Every 30 minutes or so, a small hurricane blows through the Tonga Room, and at 8 PM most nights a soft-rock band performs from a thatched hut in the middle of a lagoon.

$4.50. In addition, you'll fork over $5 for the all-you-can-eat, greasy happy hour Dim sum buffet. *Fairmont Hotel, California and Mason Sts., tel. 415/772–5278. Enter on California St., btw Mason and Powell Sts.; turn down the first hall on the right. Wheelchair access.*

NORTH BEACH North Beach is famous for its Italian restaurants, cafés, and tiny cobblestone alleys. While it does have a small red-light district on Broadway, the generally civil crowd, which usually includes a number of out-of-towners, is more attracted to the bars and cafés that line Columbus and Grant avenues.

Highball Lounge. Found near the Wall-to-Wall Sex Parlor, this swank new bar features some of its own red-light district furnishings—leopard-skin drapery and red velvet booths—but none of the sleazy clientele. Highball caters to the swing scene crowd, but is happily devoid of much of the attitude found in other such bars. Before the Highball days, this spot used to be a hangout for jazz greats such as John Coltrane and Miles Davis, and the bar tries to maintain its legendary atmosphere with nightly live bands. Slip into your favorite cocktail attire, and swill smooth martinis. *473 Broadway St., near Columbus Ave., tel. 415/39-SWING. Cover: $5 Thurs. and Sun., $7 Fri. and Sat., free Tues.–Wed.*

Savoy-Tivoli. This North Beach institution caters to an amorous set recuperating from a hard day in the Financial District. The large, covered front patio opens when the weather's nice, making the Savoy prime territory to drink wine, watch the world go by, and generally feel like you're in Italy. If it's raining, shoot pool in the back. *1434 Grant Ave., btw Union and Green Sts., tel. 415/362–7023.*

Specs'. Its given name is Specs' Twelve Adler Museum Café, but this classic North Beach hangout for the perennially half-sloshed is popularly known as Specs'. It's a jovial, divey, no-attitude sort of place where, if the conversation sucks, you can gaze for hours at the quirky memorabilia papering the walls. *12 Saroyan Pl., tel. 415/421–4112. Off Columbus Ave., next to Tosca (see below), btw Broadway and Pacific Sts.*

Tosca. This classic vintage establishment in North Beach is renowned for its liqueur-laced coffee drinks, its beautiful old espresso machine, its mostly opera jukebox, and its celebrity patrons (Francis Ford Coppola and Mikhail Baryshnikov occasionally pop in). *242 Columbus Ave., near Broadway, tel. 415/391–1244. Wheelchair access.*

Vesuvio. A bohemian hangout during the Beat era, Vesuvio has somehow managed to avoid having the life stamped out of it by tourist boots. Have a glass of red and peruse the copy of *Howl* you just bought next door at City Lights, or listen for words of wisdom from the crowd of wizened regulars. Check out the "Booth for Lady Psychiatrists" upstairs. *255 Columbus Ave., near Broadway, tel. 415/362–3370.*

If you prefer cocktails with your sunrise, head to Vesuvio (see above), the Motherlode (see above), or Twin Peaks (1316 Castro St., near 24th St., tel. 415/826–0100), all of which open at 6 AM for your drinking pleasure.

SOUTH OF MARKET A roughshod area of warehouses, outlet stores, and a few upscale spots, South of Market has few bars but lots of dance clubs. However, there are several gems you should go out of your way to check out—come early and toss back a few before the sweaty crowds invade.

20 Tank Brewery. Catch a few pints (brewed on the premises) before heading across the street to DNA (*see Clubs, below*) or Slim's (*see Live Music, below*), or skip the clubs and just catch the pints. Located in a beautiful old warehouse, 20 Tank is a great place to enjoy a large selection of microbrews, although on weekends it can feel like a frat party. They also serve hearty appetizers and sandwiches. *316 11th St., near Folsom St., tel. 415/255–9455. Wheelchair access.*

Hotel Utah. All manner of local rock, jazz, and acoustic sounds reverberate in the woody interior of this casual SoMa bar. If you don't want to hang in the tiny music room, take a seat at the long mahogany bar (shipped from Belgium during the Civil War) and avail yourself of the

Moe's Tavern

Now that The Simpsons airs on Sunday nights, you may not feel so lame when you stay home to watch it. But you'll have a lot more fun getting your Homer fix at the Rat and Raven (4054 24th St., near Church St., tel. 415/550–9145), where every Sunday you can enjoy a loud and clear episode of The Simpsons, plenty of beer (though no Flaming Moes), and a crowd of folks who know what you mean when you say, "It's funny, because it's true." Arrive by 7 PM to get a seat. If you can't make it all the way to Noe Valley, watch Marge and Homer at the Zeitgeist (see above), the Toronado (see above), or Club Chameleon (see Live Music, below).

fine assortment of beer and liquor. The friendly crowd ranges from lawyers to bikers to dogs (yes, dogs); the wood floor occasionally creaks; and a fine view of a U.S. 101 off-ramp is yours through the front windows. *500 4th St., at Bryant St., tel. 415/421–8308. Wheelchair access.*

Julie's Supper Club. Past music greats (captured in black-and-white photos) gaze down at professionals and preprofessionals nibbling interesting appetizers and sipping cocktails. As the name implies, Julie's is a place to dine, but the art-deco interior and innovative munchies, including calamari and quesadillas ($4–$6), make this a good place for an after-work or pre-club cocktail as well. Julie's features live music on Fridays and Saturdays ($5 cover, free if you're eating dinner). *1123 Folsom St., near 7th St., tel. 415/861–0707.*

Mars Café. Although it's situated in a somewhat removed area of SoMa, Mars is a happening bar and frequently fills to the gills. On Wednesdays the bar becomes the "cosmic lounge" as DJs spin the latest jungle tunes and spacey jazz. Other nights, shoot pool in the back, and enjoy Martian Martinis, made with Finlandia cranberry vodka with a dried cranberry twist ($4.75), and delicious tapas from the kitchen. *798 Brannan St., near 7th St., tel 415/621–6277.*

EAST BAY

BERKELEY Berkeley doesn't offer high-concept bars, but you'll find plenty of casual places to have a beer. The bars along Telegraph Avenue can't help but appeal to student tastes and budgets. To peer more deeply into Berkeley's psyche, head to one of the watering holes scattered along San Pablo Avenue, which tend to be seedier, but more genuine. Even here, though, it's hard to escape the collegiate contingent completely.

The Albatross. This no-nonsense watering hole attracts both students and working folk. The cheap draft beer (starting at $1.25) tastes even better with the free popcorn, and there's a cozy fireplace and a whole row of dart boards occupying a good-size portion of the bar. *1822 San Pablo Ave., btw Hearst Ave. and Delaware St., tel. 510/849–4714. From Berkeley BART, Bus 51 west to San Pablo Ave., walk 1½ blocks north.*

Le Bateau Ivre. Beautifully decorated in French château style, this elegant establishment nevertheless felt it necessary to install a new neon sign translating its name (from an Arthur Rimbaud poem) into English. Once inside, however, "The Drunken Boat" still retains a romantic and subdued quality, complete with fireplace, and candlelit tables, and still serves one of the creamiest pints of Guinness ($3) this side of Dublin. On summer evenings, the outdoor patio feels like a Parisian sidewalk, that is if Telegraph Avenue were in Paris. *2629 Telegraph Ave., at Carleton St., tel. 510/849–1100. 6 blocks south of U.C. campus.*

Bison Brewing Company. Homemade stout, cider, ale, and snakebites ($3 a pint) bring in Berkeley's most raucous crowd. Happy hour (weekdays 4–6, 3–8 during "daylight savings") features $2.25 pints and attracts masses of tattooed humanity. Live bands, ranging from blues to Irish folk, entertain Thursday through Saturday (occasional $1–$2 cover). Shout over the

Cruisin' for a Boozin'

One Sunday every month, a boat cruises up and down the bay hauling a cargo of fashionable, intoxicated partiers. These "Bulletproof Boat Parties" (hosted by Bulletproof clothing) feature two floors of progressive house and acid jazz, each with a DJ spinning his own unrelenting mix. The boat is equipped with an excellent sound system, as well as a full bar, so you can drink in the sounds of deep bass as the boat sways to the rhythm of the sea. Guests assemble at the Ferry Building before 7 PM, and the excursion lasts until midnight. For tickets ($25) and directions, contact Bulletproof (629 Haight St., at Steiner St., tel. 415/255–7168).

music, or steal away to the upstairs patio or one of the new sidewalk tables if you're in need of a quiet moment. Free live jazz on Sunday afternoons. *2598 Telegraph Ave., at Parker St., tel. 510/841–7734. 5 blocks south of U.C. campus. Wheelchair access.*

The Ivy Room. This self-styled dive-bar, where Bud is $2 a bottle, attracts a congenial mix of students, working-class folks, and retired bikers. The welcoming bar staff and colorful cast of regulars make for excellent company when you're out to pull a few pints, even on a weeknight. *860 San Pablo Ave., at Solano Ave., tel. 510/524–9220. From Berkeley BART, Bus 43 west to Solano Ave. Wheelchair access.*

Jupiter. This spacious wine-and-beer bar across from Berkeley BART is popular for its outdoor beer garden, 20 microbrews on tap, and live jazz on Wednesday, Friday, and Saturday (no cover). All of this makes for a great place to relax with friends. Weekends draw large down-to-earth crowds, but it's almost always mellow enough to allow for conversation. Beers run $2.75–$3.50. *2181 Shattuck Ave., near Center St., tel. 510/843–8277. Wheelchair access.*

The Pub. Officially titled Schmidt's Tobacco & Trading Co., The Pub is a cozy gathering spot for cheap pints and thick coffee. The overstuffed sofas, oak tables, and pipe-tobacco aroma complement a game of chess or a good novel. If you forget your book, borrow one of theirs. The Pub teems with students downing $3.25 pints on weekend nights, but during the week things are generally quiet. *1492 Solano Ave., tel. 510/525–1900. From Berkeley BART, Bus 43 north to Santa Fe Ave.*

Spats. The inventive drink selection rivals anyone's anywhere: Choose from concoctions like the Borneo Fogcutter (rum, brandy, fruit juices, and liqueurs, heaving on a bed of dry ice; $5) or the Nutty Buddy (Frangelico, cream, and crème de cacao; $4.25). Then settle into a cushy, old Victorian sofa in the parlorlike bar. *1974 Shattuck Ave., tel. 510/841–7225. 2 blocks north of Berkeley BART. Wheelchair access.*

Triple Rock Brewery. At this popular microbrewery, the 1950s reign supreme, with vintage posters and nostalgic knickknacks lining the walls. The crowd is noisy in a collegiate sort of way, but folks are friendly. The outdoor patio area is the best place to enjoy one of their homebrews ($2.75–$3.25) and excellent munchies (nachos and the like). *1920 Shattuck Ave., at Hearst Ave., tel. 510/843–2739. 3 blocks north of Berkeley BART. Wheelchair access.*

OAKLAND Oakland's bars tend to be cheaper, more sincere, and generally rougher around the edges. Rockridge bars, however, often fill with students—from U.C. Berkeley and the nearby art school—and are barely distinguishable from those in Berkeley. Downtown bars, near Jack London Square, appeal mostly to the gainfully employed and get hopelessly crowded on payday Fridays. The farther you venture from central Oakland, the seedier the bars become; exercise caution when walking around at night.

The Alley. This is the only bar in Oakland where you can sit at a piano and sing along with your drunken compadres. It's been in business since the late 1940s and has the clientele and bar staff to prove it. It's dark, musty, and unassuming—a great place to hang out with low-key locals. Live piano music usually begins at 9 PM; drinks are $2.50–$5. *3325 Grand Ave., 3 blocks east of Lake Merritt, tel. 510/444–8505. From 19th St. BART, Bus 12 east to Santa Clara Ave. Wheelchair access.*

At the Alley, sit next to the piano and don't be shy about singing your favorite Barry Manilow or Sinatra song. It's like karaoke, but without the cheesy video.

E-line Ale House. Recently founded by former Triple Rock staff and the previous head brewer of 20 Tank Brewery (*see above*) this casual, down-to-earth pub is fast becoming a favorite among locals and students for its 16 microbrews (around $3) and hearty pub grub. Grab a seat at the long, wooden bar, or snag a table with a couple of friends. The Ale House is popular but never cramped. *5612 College Ave., 1 block south of Rockridge BART., tel. 510/547–8786.*

George and Walt's. G&W's celebrated its 50th anniversary in 1996, and its regular clientele remains loyal (though whether it's to the bar or the big-screen TV remains a mystery). The dim, smoky, but comfortable setting attracts students and sports fans alike to its full bar and beers on tap ($2.25–$3.25). *5445 College Ave., tel. 510/653–7441. 1 block north of McNally's (see below).*

McNally's Irish Pub. This place has the smell, feel, and whiskeys of a real Dublin pub. Grab a pint of Guinness, Bass, or Harp ($3.25) and warm yourself by the stone fireplace, or groove to the jukebox while playing bumper-pool in back. *5352 College Ave., tel. 510/654–9463. 4 blocks south of Rockridge BART.*

Pacific Coast Brewing Company. In historic Oakland, this brew pub serves four homebrews and has 15 other beers on tap. Its polished appearance attracts a thirstysomething, slightly yuppie crowd, but the beers are top drawer. Drinks are around $3. *906 Washington St., near 10th St., tel. 510/836–2739. From 12th St. BART, 3 blocks SW on Broadway, 1 block west to Washington St.*

Stork Club. With patrons present for this dive bar's 6 AM opening, it would seem that only hardcore boozers would be drawn to the country-western decor and store-bought Christmas lighting. Lately, however, the Stork has been booking some decent local bands, and has started to attract a hipper crowd. Drinks are about $3; live-music cover runs $4–$5. *380 12th St., tel. 510/444–6174. 1½ blocks east of Broadway.*

Live Music

SAN FRANCISCO

Because of its propensity to draw people willing to be outlandish for art's sake, San Francisco—while not at the forefront of any new musical revolution—has an eclectic and extensive music scene. Bars and clubs feature live music on any given night of the week, usually for a modest cover. Sometimes you can see hugely talented bands for free in parks, music stores, bars, cultural centers, and the occasional alley; in such venues, your money will go a long way (Bud in a brown paper bag is cheap). For a price, you can also see lots of national and international acts, as befits a world-class metropolis. Your best bets for up-to-the-minute music listings are the *SF Weekly* and the *Bay Guardian.*

The **Great American Music Hall** (859 O'Farrell St., btw Polk and Larkin Sts., tel. 415/885–0750), a gorgeous old theater that serves as a midsize concert venue, books an innovative blend of rock and world music. Tickets cost around $9–$15. Boz Scagg's club, **Slim's** (333 11th St., tel. 415/522–0333), specializes in bluesy rock icons and the occasional indie band; tickets are $10–$20. MTV-friendly bands often play at the **Warfield** (982 Market St., btw 5th and 6th Sts., tel. 415/775–7722) or at the historic **Fillmore** (1805 Geary Blvd., at Fillmore St., tel. 415/346–6000), where tickets run $15–$25. **Bimbo's 365 Club** (1025 Columbus, at Chestnut St., tel. 415/474–0365), a stylish concert venue swathed in red draperies, books a lot of big names in jazz, alterna-pop, and world music; tickets are $10–$20, with a two-drink minimum at most shows (drinks are $4–$5).

ROCK **Bottom of the Hill.** Squeeze into this tiny neighborhood space at the bottom of Potrero Hill to acquire a comprehensive sense of the local music scene. You'll be mere feet from promising local talent and touring bands in this eclectic venue, and to make it even better, they recently improved their sound system. On Sunday afternoons, $3 will not only gain you admission to the live music, but also to the all-you-can-eat barbecue (4 PM). *1233 17th St., at Texas St., tel. 415/626–4455. Cover: $5–$15.*

Club Chameleon. This cheap, cramped bar in the Mission is a haven for indie bands and local, experimental music. When your eardrums start to hurt, head downstairs for Ping-Pong and video games. On Sundays at 8 PM, the Chameleon hosts wacky viewings of the Simpsons—during commercials, they turn the sound off and give you the opportunity to win prizes for guessing the names of obscure '70s hits. *853 Valencia St., btw 19th and 20th Sts., tel. 415/821–1891. Cover: up to $5.*

Kilowatt. Saturdays and Sundays, this Mission bar hosts local, alternative rock bands reaching maximum noise levels. Fridays, *The X-Files* fanatics congregate around the boob tube at 9 PM. *3160 16th St., btw Guerrero and Valencia Sts., tel. 415/861–2595. Cover: $5–$7.*

Paradise Lounge. The Paradise is like a carnival fun house with something different around every corner: three different musical stages to choose from, Sunday night poetry slams, pool tables, free-flowing booze, and a constant flow of people. Although the quality of music varies widely (to put it kindly), its almost always a reliable weekend destination. *1501 Folsom St., at 11th St., tel. 415/861–6906. Cover: about $5.*

The Purple Onion. Indulge in pints of Pabst Blue Ribbon, kick back in one of the oversize red vinyl booths, and enjoy garage-style punk and surf music at this underground North Beach lounge, a popular hangout for what's left of the overdressed mod scene. The Onion is open Fridays and Saturdays only. *140 Columbus Ave., btw Pacific Ave. and Jackson St., tel. 415/398–8415. Cover: $5.*

JAZZ San Francisco has been spearheading a rash of local bands who have taken it upon themselves to fuse the edges of funk, hip-hop, and jazz to create a distinctive new sound. Venues like the Elbo Room (*see below*), Café du Nord (*see below*), and Eleven (*see box Music to the Mouth, below*) devote much space to these new acts: Look for the **Broun Fellinis** (freestyle jazz with a funky bass line), **Alphabet Soup** (upbeat, reggae-influenced jazz with a pair of rappers), **Slide-Five** (a jazz trio that blends classic sounds with a modern sassiness), the **Supernaturals** (a lounge-y new direction taken by former members of the band The Loved Ones), and the **Charlie Hunter Trio** (more straight-ahead jazz).

The message is in the music at St. John Coltrane's African Orthodox Church (351 Divisadero St., near Oak St., tel. 415/621–4054), where services consist of a rousing two hours of the jazz great's sounds of salvation. All are welcome at both the Sunday (11:45 AM) and Wednesday (6 PM) services.

Bruno's. Bruno's is three acts in one: a full-scale restaurant, a lounge-y bar/supper club and—the latest addition—the extremely popular **Cork Club.** Every night of the week, the intimate club showcases local jazz and swing acts, many of them up-and-coming new stars of the San Francisco scene. Relax in the red vinyl booths with a martini, or squeeze up closer (if that's possible) to the band. *2389 Mission St., at 20th St., tel. 415/550–7455. Cover: $3–$5.*

Café du Nord. The specialty at this often overcrowded Castro club is jazz you can afford. Saturday nights usually feature local faves LaVay Smith & the Red Hot Skillet Lickers whose sultry crooning rivals that of Billie Holiday or Dinah Washington. Wednesdays bring the Downhear Experimental Series, showcasing some of the finest local talent, and other nights feature lounge, salsa, swing, and big band. While hot with urban hipsters, Café du Nord retains a friendly aura. *2170 Market St., at Sanchez St., tel. 415/861–5016. Cover: $3–$5.*

CoCo Club. A variety of acts come through this small woman-owned restaurant and performance space South of Market—everything from acoustic rock to avant-garde jazz and blues. The tiny, comfortable interior also plays home to a few lesbian events each week. *139 8th St., btw Mission and Howard Sts., tel. 415/626–7668. Cover: $3–$5. Entrance to bar on Minna St.*

The Elbo Room. This stylish Mission watering hole becomes unmanageably popular as the night progresses. Head upstairs for some of the best local live jazz and hip-hop acts, as well as occasional DJs. Forgot your dancing shoes? Join the locals packed around the pool table—the drinks are cheap enough ($2–$3) to keep you around until closing. *647 Valencia St., near 17th St., tel. 415/552–7788. Upstairs cover: about $5.*

Jazz at Pearl's. This all-ages North Beach joint generally showcases mainstream, traditional jazz in a dimly-lit, comfy setting. However, if you stick around late (after the tourists have left) you might catch some smoking improvisational jams. *256 Columbus Ave., at Broadway, tel. 415/291–8255. No cover; 2-drink minimum (drinks $3–$5).*

Noe Valley Ministry. An adventurous booking policy draws some serious talent—from experimental jazz and blues artists to world music acts—into this nonsmoking/occasional-drinking church in Noe Valley that moonlights as a performance space. *1021 Sanchez St., btw 23rd and Elizabeth Sts., tel. 415/282–2317. Cover: $10–$15.*

Up and Down Club. Sleek deco digs and live jazz give this multilevel SoMa supper club the feel of a New York lounge. Upstairs you'll find a DJ laying down tracks, but little room to dance. *1151 Folsom St., btw 7th and 8th Sts., tel. 415/626–2388. Cover: $5, free Wed. Closed Sun.*

BLUES While Oakland's blues scene is more renowned, San Francisco's devoted blues followers are pros at supporting local acts and making the most out of what their city has to offer. Several venues, most notably **Slim's** (*see above*) and the **Great American Music Hall** (*see above*), are often stops for traveling blues legends.

The Blue Lamp. This friendly, downtown bar books a variety of blues, jazz, folk, and rock bands nightly, and attracts an equally diverse mix of patrons. Arrive early to stake your spot near the fireplace. *561 Geary St., btw Taylor and Jones Sts., tel. 415/885–1464. Cover: $2–$5.*

Grant and Green Blues Club. This dark, smoky bar hosts some raucous blues shows, a welcome change in North Beach, where too many folks sit stiffly in coffeehouses discussing obscure lit-crits over bottles of wine. *1731 Grant Ave., at Green St., tel. 415/693–9565. Cover: $3–$5.*

EAST BAY

The quality of the East Bay's music scene is sporadic: Some nights you won't be able to choose from the number of events taking place in the area, others will leave you hunting for something to do. Berkeley is better known for its student bars and cafés than for its music venues. Though rock, folk, jazz, and world music are prevalent in the East Bay, it's the soulful blues that lure people into the depths of Oakland, home of West Coast blues.

ROCK **924 Gilman Street.** This all-ages, alcohol-free co-operative features local hard-core garage and punk bands. Green Day first got its start here (and has brought the place a fair amount of fame), but now that they have gone major label they couldn't even *pay* to play here. Most shows cost $5, but you have to buy a $2 membership (valid for one year) to get in the

Music to the Mouth

Want more than a mariachi band with your meal? Supper clubs, an old concept combining live music, classy duds, and fancy food, are making a grand reappearance in San Francisco's nightlife. In the classic vein, the plush Eleven (374 11th St., at Harrison St., tel. 415/431–3337) serves a moderately priced Italian menu ($10–$15) while sultry jazz ensembles play from atop a 15-foot loft. 330 Ritch Street (330 Ritch St., off Townsend St., btw 3rd and 4th Sts., tel. 415/522–9558) attracts a classy crowd with jazz and salsa, tapas ($8), and dinner served until 3:30 AM Fridays and Saturdays. At the apex of sophistication, Julie Ring's Heart and Soul (1695 Polk St., tel. 415/673–7100) attracts polished urban professionals and features jazz, jump, jive, and swing. Dress is casually formal, the crowd unpretentious. Fridays and Saturdays Miss Pearl's Jam House (601 Eddy St., tel. 415/775–5267) offers dining and dancing in an unabashedly Caribbean setting.

Other supper clubs worth checking out include: Julie's Supper Club (see Bars, above), with California cuisine and the feel of an exclusive 1950s coterie, Bruno's (see Live Music, above) and Coconut Grove (1415 Van Ness Ave., tel. 415/776–1616), the most upscale joint in town—Tom Jones was featured on opening night.

first time. To attend a show for free, arrive at 7 PM and get on the work list. *924 Gilman St., at 8th St., Berkeley, tel. 510/525–9926. From Berkeley BART, Bus 9 north to 8th St.*

The Berkeley Square. Once the finest venue in Berkeley for live alternative music, this 18-and-over club still occasionally attracts big names. However, the current booking policy—which caters primarily to teenage skate punks—can't ensure success for this live music venue. Losing their liquor license didn't help either. Call for current schedule. *1333 University Ave., Berkeley, tel. 510/841–6555. From Berkeley BART, Bus 51 west. Cover: $5–$6.*

Formula. The brainchild of everyone's favorite former bartender from Berkeley's Bison Brewery (*see* Bars, *above*), this Emeryville venue—housed in what was once a cottage-style restaurant called The Bavarian Village—is already one of the coolest scenes in the East Bay. The music ranges from alternative to progressive blues-rock most nights. *1411 Powell St., at Hollis St., Emeryville, tel. 510/595–8008. Cover: $3–$6.*

JAZZ Jazz greats come through Oakland on a regular basis, making appearances at established venues and putting on special shows. **Koncepts Cultural Gallery** (tel. 510/763–0682), in collaboration with the nonprofit Pro Arts organization, hosts their monthly poetry-with-music series, "Word Songs," a forum that combines live jazz instruments with rhythmic—often spontaneous—poetry.

Kimball's East. In Emeryville, a small community tucked between Berkeley and Oakland, look for this excellent jazz and supper club, which books well-known jazz musicians Wednesday through Sunday. Downstairs, **Kimball's Carnival** draws big names in Latin jazz and Caribbean music, with an audience of mostly older professionals. *5800 Shellmound St., Emeryville, tel. 510/658–2555. From MacArthur BART, Bus 6 or 57 west on 40th St. to Pacific Park Plaza. Cover: $10–$25.*

Yoshi's. Yoshi's is an historic club and restaurant, serving up sushi and jazz in sophisticated style. The clientele knows its music, and past acts have included Cecil Taylor, Anthony Braxton, and Ornette Coleman. Yoshi's will be relocating to Jack London Square in early 1997. Check listings or call information for its current whereabouts. *6030 Claremont Ave., Oakland, tel. 510/652–9200. Cover: $5–$35.*

BLUES In the years following World War II, Oakland gave birth to the gritty, hurts-so-bad-I'm-gonna-die music known as West Coast blues. Even after 50 years, it still flourishes in clubs and bars all over town. Dedicated to the preservation of blues, jazz, and gospel, the **Bay Area Blues Society** (tel. 510/836–2227) sponsors shows and festivals year-round, and is a wellspring of information about West Coast blues. These folks are also the ones to call about the famed **Oakland Blues and Heritage Festival** happening every September.

Blake's. This restaurant and jazz joint opened in the late 1940s, and since then it's become a Berkeley institution. The ground-floor dining room serves decent food, and the upstairs bar (Leona's) provides brews and booze to a polished, student crowd, but the cramped basement downstairs—a no-frills bar with a sawdust-covered floor—hosts some of the best blues acts in the area, plus the occasional alternative rock band. If you venture downstairs to use the bathroom, you'll get an earful of the band, and you can decide if they're worth the cover charge. *2367 Telegraph Ave., near Durant Ave., Berkeley, tel. 510/848–0886. 1 block from U.C. campus. Cover: $5 and up.*

Eli's Mile High Club. The reputed birthplace of West Coast blues remains a consistently good bet, continuing to highlight promising local acts plus more renowned performers. It's a small club with a pool table, soul food, and music Thursday–Sunday. The kitchen opens around 6:30 PM and music starts by 9. *3629 Martin Luther King Jr. Way, Oakland, tel. 510/655–6661. From Berkeley, Bus 15 south on Martin Luther King Jr. Way. Cover: $4–$8. Wheelchair access.*

The Fifth Amendment. High-quality blues and jazz acts play to a largely African-American crowd of professionals, students, and local old-timers. Dress up a bit for some absolutely searing music. *3255 Lakeshore Ave., Oakland, tel. 510/832–3242. From MacArthur BART, Bus 57 to cnr of Lakeshore Ave. and Lake Park Way. No cover. Wheelchair access.*

FOLK **The Freight and Salvage.** At this low-key coffeehouse you'll find Berkeley's thriving (and aging) folk-music community enjoying a wide variety of entertainment—everything from world-class accordionists to spoken-word performers to lefty singer/songwriters. *1111 Addison St., near San Pablo Ave., Berkeley, tel. 510/548–1761. From Berkeley BART, Bus 51 west to San Pablo Ave.; 1 block south to Addison St. Cover: $10–$14 ($2.50 open-mike night some Tuesdays). Wheelchair access.*

The Starry Plough. This popular Irish pub near the Berkeley–Oakland border offers an eclectic mix of folk music and not-too-extreme rock bands. Join the older, politically left crowd for a pint or two of Guinness, Bass, or Anchor Steam and a game of darts. *3101 Shattuck Ave., at Prince St., Berkeley, tel. 510/ 841–2082. From Ashby BART, walk 1 block east on Prince St. Cover: up to $6. Wheelchair access.*

Join both the pros and the amateurs at the Starry Plough on Monday nights at 7 PM for free Irish dance lessons.

WORLD MUSIC **Ashkenaz.** There's a different live beat here every night, from African to Cajun to Bulgarian folk. You can take dance lessons first or just come and wing it. You won't find any brain-dead ravers here, only a devoted group of older locals and students out to broaden their cultural horizons. Light vegetarian fare (around $3) is served starting at 8 PM. *1317 San Pablo Ave., Berkeley, tel. 510/525–5054. From Berkeley BART, Bus 9 west to San Pablo Ave. Cover: $5–$10. Wheelchair access.*

La Peña. This Latin American cultural center offers a wide selection of live music, political lectures, performance pieces, and films on Central and South American issues. Many shows are benefits, so covers often masquerade as "donations," ranging from $5 to $15. *3105 Shattuck Ave., Berkeley, tel. 510/849–2568. Next to Starry Plough (see above). Wheelchair access.*

Clubs

Hard-core club-hoppers take their nightlife more seriously than their jobs. As a result, it can be hard for the uninitiated to break the ice with the club-going crowd and plug into the underground scene. Your best bet is to check smaller, more alternative retail and record shops for flyers. Many spaces host different clubs on different nights of the week; check the *Guardian* or the *SF Weekly* for complete listings of the Bay Area's rotating club nights, and always call ahead—the hot spots change as quickly as the clothing of the fashion victims who frequent them.

SAN FRANCISCO

Spaces large and small play music for every age, style, and level of rhythmic ability. There's a huge variety of quite cheap and casual dance venues, as well as some that ooze pretension. Dance purists can even find spaces that allow no alcohol or smoking. On the other end of the spectrum are raves and gothic dance parties—still going strong in warehouses and fields—where substance abuse is by no means limited to alcohol and smoking. For current listings of gay and lesbian clubs (as well as the latest gossip), flip through the free monthly *Odyssey*, available in cafés and bookstores around the Castro District.

STRAIGHT **Bahia Cabana.** A multigenerational, international crowd comes to samba at this tropical downtown supper club with mural-covered walls. Thursday is salsa night; other nights feature Afro-Brazilian music and shows by local dance troupes. *1600 Market St., at Franklin St., tel. 415/282–4020 or 415/861–4202. Cover: $5–$10.*

Barefoot Boogie. Neither a drop of alcohol nor a puff of smoke invades this groove venue, but the moves people execute in various states of undress belie your expectation of a nice, straight dance party. The event now takes place at a newer, more spacious location, at the back of **Café Mardi Gras,** every Sunday and Wednesday 7:30–10:30, and the music ranges from classical to deep house to samba to hip-hop. People often bring their own drums and other rhythm machines. Women should exercise precaution in the neighborhood surrounding the alley where the club is located. *50 Brady St., near Market and 12th Sts., tel. 415/864–6788. Cover: $7.*

Cat's Grill and Alley Club. The small back room of this mostly after-hours club in SoMa features everything from jazz to jungle to ambient house. Thursday night is "Popscene," a weekly tribute to BritPop; Saturdays, the club hosts "So What," featuring hard-core industrial music and the occasional mosh pit. *1190 Folsom St., near 8th St., tel. 415/431–3332. Cover: about $5.*

Cesar's Latin Palace. Cesar's Latin All-Stars play fiery salsa most nights, with occasional guest artists from all over Latin America. Early on you'll find older folks and even families here; things heat up later in the evening when it's mostly young, well-dressed Latinos. Open Fridays and Saturdays only, the club keeps going until 5 AM. *3140 Mission St., near César Chavez (Army) St., tel. 415/648–6611. Cover: about $10.*

Deco. If it weren't for the strains of funk, hip-hop, and dance-hall rhythms spilling out the front entrance of this low-rent downtown club, it might be mistaken for a neighborhood bar with an impressive selection of beer. Three floors, each with its own spin jockey and ambience, will amuse you till the wee hours of the morning. *510 Larkin St., btw Turk and Eddy Sts., tel. 415/441–4007. Cover: up to $5; women usually enter free before 11 PM.*

DNA Lounge. This dependable choice for after-hours dancing (weekends until 4 AM) has eclectic acts that range from rockabilly nights to tattoo and piercing shows. The crowd isn't afraid to break a sweat on the dance floor, but many come just to kick back in dimly lit corners downstairs. On Fridays, dance to the '70s retro-band, Grooveline, performing covers of songs that tweaked a generation. DJs usually come on after the live music. *375 11th St., at Harrison St., tel. 415/626–1409. Cover: $5–$10.*

Nickie's BBQ. Red-vinyl booths and Christmas lights decorate this urban, Lower Haight hole-in-the-wall that's entirely lacking in pretension. Everything from '70s funk, soul, and hip-hop to reggae, Latin, and world beat booms through the speakers every night of the week. This is the cool venue pictured on the album cover of the sizzling modern dance floor jazz compilation, "Home Cookin'" (Ubiquity Records). *460 Haight St., btw Webster and Fillmore Sts., tel. 415/621–6508. Cover: $3–$5.*

MIXED **The Box.** This Thursdays-only SoMa club plays hard-core hip-hop, funk, soul, and house, and you'll find little attitude here because everybody's out on the dance floor. For an extra treat, go-go platforms mounted on the walls showcase dancers who gyrate at full throttle. The city's most accomplished DJs—including Page Hodel, S.F.'s most famous queer DJ—and club dance troupes appear here. While the club is lesbian-run, the multicultural crowd includes straights, too. *715 Harrison St., btw 3rd and 4th Sts., tel. 415/972–8087. Cover: $6; $5 for members. Wheelchair access.*

Club 1015. This SoMa spot hosts various clubs on a nightly basis. Three separate "dance scenes"—disco, techno, and house—and themed parties like "Eurotrash" should satisfy any taste in dance music. Saturdays, the ever-popular "Release" (tel. 415/337–7457) keeps you

"Tripping" the Light Fantastic

If you find yourself stumbling over two left feet instead of cutting a rug, don't be dismayed. Inexpensive lessons are available at a number of Bay Area locations. At Café du Nord (see Live Music, above), samba, mambo, and cha-cha lessons can be had for the $3 cover Tuesdays at 9 PM, and Sundays mean free swing lessons at 8 PM, $3 after 9 PM. Head to 330 Ritch Street (330 Ritch St., off Townsend St., btw 3rd and 4th Sts., tel. 415/522–9558) for free swing lessons on Wednesdays at 8:30 PM, and steamy Latin dance steps Saturdays at 8:30 PM for $5. Ten dollars buys you salsa lessons and dancing every Friday and Saturday at 9 PM at Kimballs East (see Live Music, above). Barring the above, a coy glance and a polite inquiry might enlist the company of a willing, and hopefully, capable partner.

up all night with '70s funk and disco, deep house, and acid jazz. Though the club suffers from an ostentatious dress-code policy on weekends, the club's more casual weeknight after-hours events consistently showcase quality turntable talent, and there's a cozy fireplace upstairs. Call for a complete listing of club nights. *1015 Folsom St., at 6th St., tel. 415/431–1200. Cover: $10 weekends; $5 weeknights.*

DV8. With four levels and seven dance floors, this enormous SoMa club often has more than one event happening at a time. "Lift" on Thursdays, midnight to 5 AM (tel. 415/267–5984), has become a San Francisco institution for pulsating house. Celebrity doorman Robnoxious will be sure to greet you at the 55 Natoma Street back entrance. On weekends, don't be daunted by the long line wrapping around the block—that's the line for the guest list; paying customers get in more quickly than the promoter's friends. Call for up-to-date listings. *540 Howard St., btw 1st and 2nd Sts; tel. 415/957–1730. Cover: $5–$10.*

El Río. This casual neighborhood hangout in the Mission attracts a healthy mix of men and women, straight and gay, and all those in between. Different dance parties are held here every night of the week. Sunny afternoons, nothing is more relaxing than a cold brew under the palm tree on El Río's back patio, and if you come on a Sunday, you can work off the beer with some fiery salsa dancing. Friday nights, locals turn out for the free oyster fest. The neighborhood isn't the best; women especially should avoid walking alone on Mission Street at night. *3158 Mission St., near César Chavez (Army) St., tel. 415/282–3325. Cover: up to $7.*

All aboard for some serious salsa. Friday and Saturday nights the "Mexican Bus" winds its way through the city depositing dancers at various Latin clubs. Join the fun for $25 (cover charges included). Call 415/546–3747 for details.

The Sound Factory. This club is tame and mainstream by city standards, but Friday night's "Twirl," a mixed, deep house dance extravaganza has been embraced by all-nighters as a favorite after-hours hangout. Modeled after New York and L.A. clubs, this large SoMa space hosts a literal maze of pulsating rooms. Call for upcoming clubs and events. *525 Harrison St., at 1st St., tel. 415/543–1300. Cover: about $10.*

Trocadero Transfer. Wednesdays only, Trocadero hosts the oldest fetish dance club in California: "Bondage A Go-Go." It's a light intro to the real S&M subculture, where you may engage in acts of light bondage, get whipped by a professional dominatrix, or just stand to the side and gawk. Other nights, this SoMa club features industrial dancing and live hard-core music. The Trocadero is all-ages when the music is live, and 18-and-over for "Bondage A Go-Go." *520 4th St., btw Bryant and Brannan Sts., tel. 415/995–4600. Cover: $5.*

GAY AND LESBIAN **Club Townsend.** This vast SoMa disco hosts the high-energy Sunday "Pleasuredome," with local DJs churning out sounds for a largely male crowd, followed by a where-do-they-get-the-energy "Sunday Tea Dance" until 6 AM. DJs spin, sounds weave, but Monday's looming right around the corner. "Club Universe," on Saturdays, is less gender-specific, and the artsy decor changes to create a stunning new illusion each week. *177 Townsend St., btw 2nd and 3rd Sts., tel. 415/974–1156. Cover: $10.*

Covered Wagon. Black light illuminates the Western decor on the walls, as well as the lint on your shirt, at this dark SoMa bar. Afternoons, the CW sees a lot of bike messengers taking a breather, but at night it caters primarily to women-loving women, with live funk and soul some nights, DJs and dancing on others. Wednesdays at 9 PM, "Faster, Pussycat!" starts off with a DJ, and continues with one or two bands of the riot-grrl persuasion. The bar serves as a pre-club watering hole to a mixed crowd early on weekend nights, and grows increasingly female by the end of the night. *917 Folsom St., at 5th St., tel. 415/974–1585. Cover: $3–$6.*

The EndUp. Home of the "misplaced weekend," this primarily gay bar has an outdoor patio (threatened by closure due to neighborhood complaints), a pool table, and a waterfall, all surrealistically situated almost underneath U.S. 101. The elevated dance floor couldn't possibly accommodate everyone, so the sweaty crowd gets down wherever it suits them. Come at 9 AM for the "Sunday Tea Dance"—happening here for nearly a quarter of a century. Three dollars buys you all the dancing you can handle until 2 AM Monday—nice way to start the work week.

Call The EndUp's info line for event listings. *401 6th St., at Harrison St., tel. 415/487–6277. Cover: $5–$10.*

Esta Noche. Tucked away in the Mission, Esta Noche plays a good mix of hard-pumping Latin, house music, and '70s disco. The crowd consists mostly of young Latino men, and European-American patrons are respectfully requested to refrain from doing the cha-cha. *3079 16th St., at Valencia St., tel. 415/861–5757. Cover: $3–$4.*

The Stud. This SoMa club is a San Francisco legend and a good watering hole any night of the week. Dress up or come as you are, and have fun flirting with innocent out-of-towners. Thursday nights are often set aside for lesbian events; Wednesdays, the club draws in a postcollegiate crowd for dancing to '70s and early '80s classics. *399 9th St., at Harrison St., tel. 415/863–6623. Cover: $3–$6.*

EAST BAY

With San Francisco just across the bay, there was never a need for the East Bay to come into a dance club scene of its own. You can check the *East Bay Express* under "Dance Clubs" for a thorough listing, but you're likely to discover that East Bay clubbers make the trek to the city when they want serious after-hours dancing. **Blake's** (*see* Live Music, *above*) provides a sweaty basement ruled by funk, soul, hip-hop, and rare grooves. Blake's might not be the pinnacle of cool, but it should serve your dance needs just fine.

The Caribee Dance Center. Occasional live music is supplemented six nights a week (closed Thursday) with dancing to reggae, salsa, and African music. Drinks cost $2–$5. *1408 Webster St., Oakland, tel. 510/835–4006. From 12th St. BART, 2 blocks east on 14th St. Cover: $5–$10.*

White Horse Inn. Get down under a gleaming disco ball at this easygoing place on the Oakland–Berkeley border. Most patrons are gay or lesbian, but other fun-seekers are welcome as long as they behave themselves. A DJ is in the house Thursday–Saturday after 9 PM, and the bar's open daily 3 PM–2 AM. *6551 Telegraph Ave., at 66th St., Oakland, tel. 510/652–3820. From MacArthur BART, Bus 40 south on Telegraph to 66th St. No cover.*

Movie Houses

The Bay Area is fortunate to have more than a handful of independent theaters, where fervent buffs insist on viewing "films" and not "movies." While billion-dollar formula blockbusters get made in Hollywood, a little-known fact is that San Francisco is one of the nation's most prolific cities for independent filmmaking—in particular, documentary, short, experimental, and avant-garde. Many natives have gone on to nationwide fame for their small-budget ventures, such as the docudramatist, Marlon Riggs, who died recently of AIDS. Francis Ford Coppola's production company, Zoetrope, dedicated to small independent filmmakers, still makes its home in San Francisco. The city houses almost as many quirky, interesting theaters, as it does filmmakers.

SAN FRANCISCO

If all this inspires you to make your own movies, a great resource is **Artists' Television Access** (992 Valencia St., at 21st St., tel. 415/824–3890), a nonprofit media-arts center in the Mission founded in 1986 to perpetuate knowledge about television, video, and film. You can rent editing facilities at reasonable rates—or take workshops on production and editing—then show your homemade video to other artists and get feedback. Their screenings of offbeat films provide a night of entertainment for $5.

During spring and summer, five big film festivals roll through town, starting in March with the 15-year-old **San Francisco Asian-American Film Festival** (tel. 415/863–0814). In mid-April look for the **San Francisco International Film Festival** (tel. 415/931–3456), which features quality films from all over the world. During the last two weeks in June, the much-loved **International Lesbian and Gay Film Festival** (tel. 415/703–8650) coincides with Gay Pride Week and is the largest such event in the world. The **Jewish Film Festival** (tel. 510/548–0556) breezes into town—one week at the Castro Theatre in San Francisco and one week at the U.C. Theatre in Berkeley—at the end of July and beginning of August. Finally, September brings the increasingly popular **Festival Cine Latino** (tel. 415/553–8135).

For new and, sometimes, obscure releases, everyone goes to the **Kabuki 8** (1881 Post St., at Fillmore St., tel. 415/931–9800), even though some of the octoplex's screens are pretty tiny and seating is limited. Tickets run $8, but you get a discount with student ID. Take advantage of the validated parking in Japan Center since this isn't the safest place to leave your car. **Landmark Theaters** recently consolidated a number of houses in the city, such as the Embarcadero Center Cinema (One Embarcadero Center), Clay Theatre (2261 Fillmore St., at Clay St.), Opera Plaza (601 Van Ness Ave., at Golden Gate Ave.), and Bridge Theatre (3010 Geary Blvd., at Blake St.); all host artsy and foreign films, and show-time information may now be obtained using one telephone number (tel. 415/352–0810). The Landmark Theater card, for use at any of their numerous locations throughout the Bay Area, gets you five admissions for $25. The *Bay Guardian* and *SF Weekly* have complete listings and reviews for both first-run theaters and rep houses.

The Casting Couch Micro Theatre. Come to this deluxe 46-person screening room for an intimate and unique viewing experience. Sink into one of the sofas and let the wait staff bring you cookies while you check out not-so-recent releases and older, hidden gems. *950 Battery St., btw Green and Vallejo Sts., tel. 415/986–7001. Admission: $8.50. Arrive 15 minutes prior to show time to secure a seat.*

Castro Theatre. The most beautiful place to see a film in San Francisco, the Castro shows a wide selection of rare, foreign, and unusual films that play for anywhere from a night to a week or two. However, the specialties here are camp, classics of all genres, and new releases of interest to lesbian and gay viewers. And the man who rises out of the floor playing the Wurlitzer organ is guaranteed to make you giggle for the sheer kitschiness of it all. *429 Castro St., btw Market and 18th Sts., tel. 415/621–6120. Admission: $6.50.*

The Red Vic. Films at this co-op range from the artsy to the cultish to the rare, and you can have your herbal tea in a real mug to accompany your popcorn with yeast. If you get there early, snag one of the couches before love birds beat you to it. *1727 Haight St., btw Cole and Shrader Sts., tel. 415/668–3994. Admission: $6.*

The Roxie. This Mission theater shows political, cult, and otherwise bent films. The audience can get raucous; insightful critiques are shouted at the screen as you're watching the film. *3117 16th St., at Valencia St., tel. 415/863–1087. Admission: $6.*

During the Film Arts Festival, in late October and early November, the Roxie Cinema features films, shorts, and documentaries from independent Bay Area filmmakers. Call 415/552–FILM for more info.

San Francisco Cinemateque. This S.F. Art Institute's non-profit theater celebrated its 35th anniversary in 1996. Dedicated to the perpetuation of experimental filmmaking, it screens rare avant-garde films, documentaries, and independent films. Screenings take place at either the Yerba Buena Center for the Arts (*see* Multimedia Performance Spaces, *below*), or at the Institute every Sunday and Thursday night. *S.F. Art Institute., 800 Chestnut St., btw Jones and Leavenworth Sts., tel. 415/558–8129. Admission: $6.*

EAST BAY

Of the several big cinema complexes that show first-run releases in the East Bay, the **Grand Lake Theatre** (3200 Grand Ave., tel. 510/452–3556) is by far the most stylish. Built in 1926, this ornate movie house just east of Oakland's Lake Merritt has been (regrettably) divided into four midsize theaters—slightly diminishing its grandeur. In Berkeley, Landmark's **U.C. Theatre**

(2036 University Ave., tel. 510/843–6267), in operation since 1917, shows foreign films and classics; double features are juxtaposed with great creativity, and billings change daily. The theater is cavernous, the seats lumpy, and you get to see John Waters ask you not to light up. Admission is $6. If you've never seen *The Rocky Horror Picture Show*, it plays here at midnight Saturdays: Come armed with toilet paper and a garter belt, if you dare. The **Elmwood Theatre** (2966 College Ave., at Ashby Ave., tel. 510/869–3999) shows both mainstream and revival films for only $3.50 on Tuesdays, all day.

For $25 ($10 for Cal students) the P.F.A. will set you up in a private screening room with a film of your choice: Choose from their vast library— particularly strong in Soviet and Japanese films—of 16mm films. Call their reference line (tel. 510/642–1437) for details.

Pacific Film Archive. Housed in the U.C. Berkeley Art Museum, the P.F.A. caters to hard-core film enthusiasts with its impressive collection of rare and foreign titles. Films change nightly and often center around a certain theme—past offerings have included "Space, Time, and Memory" and an evening with Ingmar Bergman. Filmmakers often show up to discuss their work before the show. *2621 Durant Ave., tel. 510/642–1124. Admission: $6–$7.*

Paramount Theatre. An art-deco landmark in downtown Oakland, the Paramount Theatre is a beautifully restored motion picture palace that now houses both the Oakland Symphony and the Oakland Ballet (*see* Dance, *below*). Classic and silent films are featured intermittently on Friday or Saturday evenings, complete with pre-show organ music and old newsreel clips. Live rock or jazz performances are also held at this stately venue. Tours of the theater are available the first and third Saturday of the month at 10 AM for $1. *2025 Broadway, near 19th St., tel. 510/465–6400. Wheelchair access.*

Theater

Mainstream Bay Area theater tends to rely more on the cult of personality of big name *artistes* than on quality of production or acting. It's the smaller multicultural and experimental theater ensembles, those willing to take risks, that are the ones to look out for. Local troupes worth pursuing include the **Sick and Twisted Players** (tel. 415/861–8972), a mostly gay group that specializes in campy, staged interpretations of films (like *The Rocky Horror Picture Show*). Also keep an eye on **A Traveling Jewish Theater** (2860 Mariposa St., tel. 415/399–1809); they received a large NEA grant in 1995 and are growing nicely into their new Project Artaud space. If your tastes are less experimental, **ACT** (American Contemporary Theater; tel. 415/749–2228) and the Berkeley Repertory Theater (*see below*) are both large operations that generally present quality productions. The truly mainstream, Broadway-type shows usually appear at the downtown **Curran Theater** (445 Geary St., at Mason St., tel. 415/474–3800).

The San Francisco Fringe Festival is a must-see if you're interested in modern theater. This festival brings local, national, and international experimental theater to venues throughout the city just after Labor Day (Sept. 4–14 in 1997). Call 415/931–1094 for more info.

Sometimes a night of theater involves more conflict, climax, and denouement than you're prepared to commit to, when you just feel like a little no-brainer entertainment. The productions ($10–$12) at **Josie's Cabaret & Juice Joint** (*see* Castro District, in Chapter 4), an established gay cultural center, lean toward campy cabaret and riotous stand-up, though you'll see the occasional serious piece as well. At **Climate Theater** (252 9th St., at Tehama St., tel. 415/978–2345), you can catch small ensembles and solo performers doing original work. Tickets are $7–$10.

SAN FRANCISCO

Asian-American Theater Company. At press time, this company was in the process of moving, so call ahead for the latest. Tickets for in-house productions of the works of Asian playwrights (both American and foreign) go for $8–$21 (some student discounts offered). *Administrative office: 1840 Sutter St., at Webster St., Suite 207, tel. 415/440–5545.*

Beach Blanket Babylon. This treasure trove of San Francisco lore has been selling out most nights for the past three decades. The revue still entertains with talented musicians, polished performers, impeccable timing, extra-large headgear, and a zesty, zany script that changes to incorporate topical references and characters (not to mention an on-going love affair with the British Royal Family). A significant chunk of your $18–$45 ticket goes to local charities. Those under 21 may attend Sunday matinee performances only. *Club Fugazi, 678 Green St., at Powell St., tel. 415/421–4222.*

Brava! Theater Center. Brava! For Women in the Arts is the official name of this resident theater company, a stronghold of women's stage work. The mostly experimental programming includes works by local playwrights and performance artists, and frequently showcases the work of the Latina community. Tickets cost up to $16. *2789 24th St., at York, tel. 415/487–5401.*

Exit Theater. One of the best venues downtown is this café/theater, where small but imaginative productions sometimes draw on video, music, or other media. Absurdism is a favored topic of many productions, and no one is safe from their far-reaching comedic jabs. Tickets range $5–$10. *156 Eddy St., at Mason St., tel. 415/673–3847.*

Lorraine Hansberry Theatre. A consistently high-quality locus of African-American theater, the Lorraine Hansberry performs experimental, musical, and classical works by African Americans and other writers of color. The work of talented young playwrights is often premiered at the theater. Tickets cost $15–$22. Student discounts include $3-off regular tickets and a shot at same-day, half-price seats. *620 Sutter St., at Mason St., tel. 415/474–8800.*

Magic Theater. The Magic is San Francisco's standby for the modern and mildly experimental. Sam Shepherd wrote a lot of his plays for this venue in the late '70s and early '80s; the theater continues to premiere innovative American works, and Sam himself returns from time to time. Tickets for performances run $18–$24, with discounts for students with ID. *Fort Mason Center, Bldg. D, tel. 415/441–8822.*

The Marsh. This "breeding ground for new performances" (get it?) hosts primarily new works by local artists, and has been a springboard to greater fame. Though the shows are not consistently excellent, they are almost always intriguing. The 99 house seats include a cozy corner of sofas. Tickets cost $8–$12 weekdays, $15 weekends. New material is tested during their late-night performances, Friday and Saturday at 10:15 PM, where admission is on a pay-what-you-can-basis. *1062 Valencia St., near 22nd St., tel. 415/826–5750.*

San Francisco Mime Troupe. This provocative ensemble puts on free, scathing political comedies and musicals in Golden Gate Park and other Bay Area parks on weekends at 2 PM, July 4 through Labor Day, and has been doing so since 1961. Recent cuts from the NEA, however, have put the program in jeopardy; if you'd like to support their anticorporate, anticlassist agenda, send contributions to 855 Treat Avenue, San Francisco 94110. Call for their current whereabouts. *Tel. 415/285–1717.*

Sassy Mouth. John Fisher's youthful ensemble of Berkeley grads has finally taken to the San Francisco stage, with much critical acclaim. A commitment to exploring issues like homosexuality and feminism, sophisticated gender-bending, well-placed sight gags, and thespian self-parody have helped make a name for this troupe. You can catch Sassy Mouth's latest (usually campy) act at **The Stage Door Theater** (520 Mason St.; tickets $22–$26) or call for more information. *Tel. 510/832–4636.*

Theatre Rhinoceros. The only strictly gay and lesbian theater company in San Francisco stages consistently reliable dramas and comedies in its tiny Mission District hall. Ticket prices are $12–$18, with $2 off for students; student previews are half off the general admission price. Stagings for 1997 include *Stand-In* by Keith Curran, a comic drama about a closeted actor consistently cast in gay screen roles. *2926 16th St., tel. 415/861–5079.*

Theater of Yugen/Noh Space. The mission of this theater is to bring the Japanese aesthetic to Western audiences. Of the four East–West fusion works staged each year, three are

The "Noh Space" is more than a meaningless bad pun: It's a bad pun based on "noh," the 600-year-old tradition of Japanese tragedy.

primarily in English and deal with Japanese stories or themes, while the fourth is *kyogen*, traditional Japanese comedy, performed in Japanese on a simple, black-draped stage. Tickets cost $10–$15, with reduced rates for previews, as well as for students with ID. *2840 Mariposa St., at Alabama St., tel. 415/621–7978.*

EAST BAY

Berkeley Repertory Theater. Berkeley is currently cultivating an arts movement downtown, with the Berkeley Repertory Theater as its keystone. The company stages performances every night except Mondays; they also have some matinees in the smaller theater. The works are rarely experimental, but they are meticulously produced and well worth the $22–$35 ticket price—and only half of that if you can score student-rush tickets a half hour before the show. *2025 Addison St., tel. 510/845–4700.*

Black Repertory Group. Founded in 1965, this Oakland company continues to be committed to the production of works by black authors and the celebration of black culture in the United States. The likes of Langston Hughes and James Weldon Johnson are most frequently represented, in amateur but heartfelt musical and dramatic productions. Admission is $10 ($8 students) and Saturday matinees are $5. Sometimes the most interesting works are the one-act plays shown for $3 on Sundays. *3201 Adeline St., tel. 510/652–2120.*

Multimedia Performance Spaces

As technology increasingly affects theater, video, dance, and music, it also becomes a link for different types of creative expression. At the same time, technology, as the point of fusion, can become a powerful medium itself. The following venues are most committed to exploring the evolving relationship among performance media.

Audium. This theater explores the relationship between music and space. Audiences sit in pitch darkness, surrounded by 169 speakers, which saturate them with sounds that seem to move around them as they remain still in their chairs. The effect is both intense and unsettling, with Stan Shaff's "sound-sculpted" performances lasting 72 minutes in the tiny 49-seat theater. *1616 Bush St., at Franklin St., tel. 415/771–1616. Admission: $10. Open Fri. and Sat. only. Be there promptly at 8:30 PM.*

Cramped Quarters

San Francisco artists have a wonderful habit of gathering together groups of friends and devising tiny performance venues of their own. We can't guarantee the longevity of any of the following, but we can promise intimate, intriguing shows, often for less than $10. These spaces can also provide an entry into other facets of San Francisco's alternative arts culture. Luna Sea (2926 16th St., tel. 415/863–2989) is a women's group upstairs from Theatre Rhinoceros in the Mission; they sponsor readings, music, and other events, often as benefits, and offer three work-exchange positions a night in lieu of the $8–$10 admission fee. In the Western Addition, 848 Community Space (848 Divisadero St., tel. 415/387–9410) specializes in screwy productions in a variety of media—sometimes all at once. Z Space (940 Howard St., tel. 415/543–9505), formed by Zuni Café's wait staff (see Civic Center, in Chapter 4), often hosts spoken-word performances and readings of new plays by local writers in its SoMa locale.

Center for the Arts at Yerba Buena Gardens. The bright yellow and red of this modern theater's lobby give way to the more metallic luster of the interior space. Though budget problems have threatened the center's ambitious mission, it still draws top dancers, musicians, and dramatists and sometimes combines them in large-scale ways. The theater itself has superb acoustics and is absolutely souped-up technologically. Despite the 750 seats, it feels like an intimate space. Tickets start at $9. *700 Howard St., at 3rd St., tel. 415/978–2787.*

George Coates Performance Works. Fresh from a tour in South America, technological wizard George Coates brings his prowess to the theater, where he mixes the latest computer technology with the stage. Performances, held under the soaring vaulted ceiling of a former church, involve music, video, and motion and use only a scrim to create "virtual" sets. The program for 1997 includes digitized images of poet William Blake's engravings, which incorporate both text and image, making him a multimedia pioneer by Coates' definition. There are a few seats that go for $14, but most cost $25–$34. *110 McAllister St., at Leavenworth St., tel. 415/863–8520.*

Intersection for the Arts. This stark, stone-walled space in the Mission seats 65 for viewing performance art, performative readings, competitive "Poetry Slam Finals," workshops, and lectures. The gallery space upstairs features intriguing sound and/or visual installations. The 30-year-old Intersection is San Francisco's oldest alternative art space; shows here are not only experimental but also consistently good. Ticket prices vary widely but are usually around $10–$20, less for students. *446 Valencia St., btw 15th and 16th Sts., tel. 415/626–2787. Free evening parking at 670 Valencia St.*

New Langton Arts. This far-reaching organization has been around for a couple decades, providing local performance and installation artists with both grants to complete their work and an audience to appreciate it. New Langton's work is similar to that of Theater Artaud (*see below*), but on a smaller scale. Upstairs is a bright, continually changing gallery; downstairs is a 75-seat, well-equipped multimedia theater. Admission is $6–$8, with discounts for students with ID. *1246 Folsom St., at 8th St., tel. 415/626–5416.*

Theater Artaud. Artaud boasts one of the most interesting performance halls in town: a cavernous converted cannery that you enter from behind the scaffolding of 300 seats. Sound echoes eerily through the space, generally adding to the effect. The local and traveling shows—often dance, drama, and music all at once—are excellent and provide insight into the experimental scene both in San Francisco and internationally. Tickets run $10–$25 and are cheaper weeknights. The neighborhood is seedy, but the experience is worth it. *450 Florida St., btw 17th and Mariposa Sts., tel. 415/621–7797 (for tickets).*

Classical Music

SAN FRANCISCO

Herbst Theater. World-class soloists and occasional groups play at the elegant Herbst, in the Veterans Building downtown, usually drawing $20 and up per seat. Though the theater is plush, the acoustics are mediocre. *401 Van Ness Ave., tel. 415/392–4400.*

San Francisco Conservatory. The city's major music school has something going on almost nightly, whether it's performed by students, faculty, or the Conservatory Orchestra. Quality is unpredictable, but with the school's fine reputation, odds are you'll see something worthwhile. General admission is $10, $6 students; most student recitals are free. *1201 Ortega St., at 19th Ave., tel. 415/759–3477.*

San Francisco Contemporary Music Players. The biggest-name contemporary company in the area sadly hosts only six performances a year at Center for the Arts (*see* Multimedia Performance Spaces, *above*) in both the main theater and the intimate 300-seat Forum Theater. Concerts generally feature brand-new works by contemporary composers, and some by "oldies" like Steve Reich. Tickets are $14 for general admission, $6 for students with ID. *700 Howard St., at 3rd St., tel. 415/978–ARTS or 415/252–6235 for programming info.*

San Francisco Opera. In the tradition of expensive wigs, lavish costumes, and lusty sopranos, the local opera company puts on grand-scale quality performances each season. The well-benefacted company usually puts on one exorbitantly costly production each year, 1997's program includes a 4½ hour program of Wagner's *Lohengrin*. Ticket prices range from uneconomical ($20–$30) to outrageous (more than $50 for decent seats). Student-rush tickets go on sale two hours before curtain and cost $15–$20, and there's almost always something left. The War Memorial Opera House (301 Van Ness Ave.), closed for earthquake retrofitting, is anticipated to reopen in September of 1997; until then the company will stage its operas at the Bill Graham Memorial Civic Auditorium (cnr of Grove and Polk Sts.) and at the Orpheum Theater (1192 Market St., near 8th St.). *Box office: 199 Grove St., at Van Ness Ave., tel. 415/864–3330.*

San Francisco Symphony. The big news here is Michael Tilson Thomas, the vibrant new conductor who's already shaken things up after 10 years of Herbert Blomstedt's steady but less than daring leadership. Tilson Thomas made a name for himself with the London Symphony Orchestra and is bringing new and needed energy to San Francisco's biggest symphony. Promising 1997 season programs include Shostakovich's *Battleship Potemkin*, with the orchestra accompanying Sergei Eisenstein's silent film of the same title. The Lego-inspired interior of Davies Symphony Hall is surreal at first glance, but the odd interior architecture creates good acoustics for even the cheapest balcony seats ($25). The best deals, though, are the $10–$12 center terrace seats: A limited number are available in advance but sell out quickly; 40 more go on sale two hours before the show. The seats hover directly over the orchestra, yielding an off-balance sound but a fantastic, face-on view of the conductor and an intimate look at the musicians' work. *Louise M. Davies Symphony Hall, 201 Van Ness Ave., at Grove St., tel. 415/864–6000.*

EAST BAY

While the East Bay puts on fewer major productions, you can easily find an inexpensive venue for a concert. For chamber music, jazz, or world music in a beautiful, intimate setting, try the **Maybeck Recital Hall** (1537 Euclid Ave., Berkeley, tel. 510/848–3228), designed by revered Berkeley architect Bernard Maybeck. U.C. Berkeley's **Zellerbach Hall** (Lower Sproul Plaza, on

Classics on the Cheap

On summer Sundays, the Stern Grove Midsummer Music Festival (tel. 415/252–6252) brings the symphony and ballet to Stern Grove in San Francisco for 2 PM performances. During spring, summer, and the Christmas season, the Brown Bag Opera series (tel. 415/565–6434) pitches divas against traffic noise for your listening pleasure: Performances are held at 12:15 at 1 Bush Street, among other Bay Area locations. You can also find free, or nearly free, concerts at local universities: Berkeley's free Wednesday Noon Concerts (tel. 510/642–4864 or 510/642–2678) showcase talented professors and students at Hertz Hall on campus; Oakland's Mills College (see below) is well known for its sometimes-free contemporary music program; and the San Francisco Conservatory (see above) hosts free performances, which feature amateur and upcoming musical talent.

If you're willing to spend a little, try TIX Bay Area (251 Stockton St., btw Post and Geary Sts., tel. 415/433–7827), a same-day, half-price ticket booth on Union Square. Otherwise, most venues provide discounts for students with ID, and larger venues often offer student-rush tickets.

campus, tel. 510/642–9988) presents solo recitals, as well as chamber, orchestra, and contemporary classical performances from some of the finest names in the world.

Berkeley Opera. For a company that began only 17 years ago by a former professor who just wanted to *sing,* the Berkeley Opera is coming into its own. The company stages four operas each season in small 200-seat venues, like the Maybeck-designed Hillside Club (2286 Cedar St.) in North Berkeley, or the intimate Julia Morgan Theater (2640 College Ave.) on the south side of campus. Most productions are fully staged with orchestra, and the smaller venues are wonderful for catching every little nuance of a performance. The leads often come from the San Francisco Opera Chorus—younger singers looking for a break—and a few have reportedly gone on to the Met. Tickets sound pricey at up to $25 (student discounts available; student-rush tickets available 20 minutes prior to show time for $8 with ID), but for opera-lovers who have experienced only large houses, this is a pleasant change. Tickets can be purchased by phone or at the opera venue. *Tel. 510/841–1903.*

Berkeley Symphony Orchestra. By an unbelievable stroke of luck, the Berkeley Symphony Orchestra has managed to hang onto Kent Nagano, a world-famous conductor who spends part of the year with Berkeley, part with the renowned Lyon Opera in France. His inspired performances—at venues throughout town—are well worth the $25–$30 ticket. *Tel. 510/841–2800.*

Mills College. One of the hottest places around for contemporary composition and performance, Mills College hosts an extensive season of classical and experimental concerts during the academic year. Fred Frith and Alvin Curran will be 1997's composers in residence, and the season will also include a tribute to Lou Harrison. Their whimsical and outlandish hall is in the Oakland hills; if you're coming by car, call ahead for directions. Many shows are free; some run $5–$10. *5000 MacArthur Blvd., Oakland, tel. 510/430–2296. From Coliseum BART, Bus 56 west. Wheelchair access.*

Dance

The world's very best dance troupes pass through the Bay Area, many of them stopping at **Zellerbach Hall** (*see* Classical Music introduction, *above*) or at the neoclassical **Palace of Fine Arts** (3301 Lyon St., S.F., tel. 415/563–6504). Modern dance has been embraced locally, with a fervor, and the Bay Area is fortunate to have more than a handful of progressive and experimental companies. One Oakland-based troupe to watch for is the **Dance Brigade** (tel. 510/652–0752), a casually feminist, very cool troupe that subverts the classics. Also in Oakland, look for **Dimensions Dance Theater** (1428 Alice St., tel. 510/465–3363), a young, vibrant company that produces "choreo-dramas," teeming with African influences. Check the *Bay Guardian* for schedules and dependable recommendations from dance critic Rita Felciano.

Cal Performances (tel. 510/642–9988), a first-class series of dance, theater, and music performances, takes place in Zellerbach Hall, on the Berkeley campus.

SAN FRANCISCO

Asian-American Dance Performances. This studio and its fantastically energetic resident dance company, Unbound Spirit, meld modern and traditional Asian movements into unique dance forms. They perform the fascinating results both in-house and at theaters throughout town (mostly $15, with nearly half off for students). At least one show each year features the work of an independent Asian-American choreographer. At press time, the company was moving; call for their current location. *Tel. 415/441–8831.*

Dancer's Group/Footwork. This small, informal space is packed to capacity most Friday and Saturday nights with avid audiences enjoying the vibrant creativity of local choreographers. Many performances incorporate text with music and movement to examine a variety of personal and political themes. The first Thursday of each run is free for students; otherwise, students get a couple dollars off the usual $5–$15 admission. Beginning and intermediate dance lessons are also offered at $9 a session. *3221 22nd St., at Mission St., tel. 415/824–5044.*

San Francisco Ballet. This company, which has built a reputation as one of the premier ballets in the country, has never been considered progressive by any leap (or pirouette) of the imagination. The productions are mainstream, and the performances are competent but uninspired. While the War Memorial Opera House is closed for renovations, performances will rotate between the Center for the Arts (700 Howard St.), the Palace of Fine Arts (3301 Lyon St.) and Zellerbach Hall (U.C. Berkeley campus). Ticket prices can be steep, ranging anywhere from $12 to $60. *Box office: 455 Franklin St., at Fulton St., tel. 415/703–9400.*

Third Wave Dance House. The spirit of Third Wave is African-driven. Performances, which cost $10–$15, are often experimental and almost always feature live percussionists. Dance classes for all abilities, at $10 a pop, delve into Cuban, Haitian, hip-hop, and West African dance traditions, among others. *3316 24th St., at Mission St., tel. 415/282–4020.*

EAST BAY

Oakland Ballet. Thirty years in the business hasn't corrupted this company. By staying flexible, it's avoided the trap of mediocrity that constantly threatens San Francisco's ballet, symphony, and opera. This a classical troupe, but company productions often bear heavy thematic weight, exploring the outer boundaries of classicism. Seasons often feature revivals of early 1900s classics as well as new works set to contemporary music. Performances are held in the grand old Paramount Theater downtown (*see* Movie Houses, *above*); tickets run $12–$34. *Oakland Ballet box office: 2025 Broadway, tel. 510/452–9288.*

WHERE TO SLEEP   7

By Simon Dang, with Maureen Klier and Charlene Pinzon

San Francisco offers the best selection of lodging in the Bay Area. You'll find some truly unusual bed-and-breakfasts here; even the cheap hotels have a little bit of character. For those who are looking for gorgeous open space surprisingly close to the city, Marin County offers a night at a woodsy hostel or beach campsite for less than $12. But the best-kept secret in the Bay Area is the San Mateo County Coast—its hostels and campgrounds are as beautifully situated as those in Marin, but are much less populated. Other options are less attractive—grimy motels in the East Bay, astronomically priced bed-and-breakfasts in Marin County, or chain hotels in the South Bay that cater to business travelers.

San Francisco

San Francisco's neighborhoods are each quite distinctive—the sanitized hipness of North Beach and Russian Hill; the pierced and tattooed youth scene in the Haight; the gay culture of the Castro; and the city's Latino and bohemian hangout, the Mission District. Only in San Francisco will you find a leather-and-Levi's gay B&B, an artist's B&B complete with easels and plenty of light, or an inn whose nightly accommodations include "The Summer of Love Room" and "The Japanese Tea Garden Room."

For an expensive city, San Francisco has a surprisingly large assortment of reasonably priced accommodations. For a great no-frills deal, stay in one of the city's nine hostels, where a bed will set you back only about $12, or in one of the residential hotels that populate Downtown and North Beach. For a little bit more ($30–$50 a night), many small downtown hotels offer charming "European-style" rooms (i.e., the toilet's down the hall). These prices might be worthwhile since Downtown is also the public transportation hub. And while there are no campgrounds within the city limits, free—and beautiful—sites are available just north of the Golden Gate Bridge in the Marin Headlands (*see* Sausalito, *below*).

If you don't reserve one to two weeks in advance in summer, you may be exiled to the strip of generic motels along Lombard Street in the Marina District. These motels are about a 20-minute bus ride from Downtown (on Bus 76) but are quite close to Fisherman's Wharf, the Marina Green, and the Golden Gate Bridge. On Lombard, you'll pay $60–$80 for a double—stay here only if you're desperate. The area South of Market has its share of similar "last resort" places on 6th Street, but the neighborhood can be unsafe; if you do want to stay in SoMa, try a hostel. The places listed below will put you up for a night, a week, or (in some cases) a month. If you can't bear to leave, we've included some tips on how to find a long-term home.

HOTELS AND MOTELS

Directions below are given from the Downtown BART/MUNI stations along Market Street. To reach the stations from San Francisco International Airport, take SamTrans (see Getting In, Out, and Around, in Chapter 1): The 7F is an express bus that has luggage limits, and the 7B is a local bus that allows heavy bags. Either one will drop you off on Mission Street, one block south of Market Street; just ask the driver for the stop nearest your station.

THE CASTRO Not surprisingly, the most prominent gay neighborhood in the United States offers a wide variety of accommodations tailored to gay and lesbian travelers, though breeders are welcome as well. The hotels nearest Castro Street are pricey, but those on upper Market Street are more affordable; the neighborhood, in general, is a safe area at night. In June, reserve way in advance as thousands of visitors arrive in the area for the San Francisco Lesbian, Gay, Bisexual, Transgender Pride Celebration—San Francisco Pride, for short (formerly known as the Gay and Lesbian Freedom Day Parade). For a map of Castro lodging, see Haight, Castro, and Mission Lodging map, *below*.

➤ **UNDER $55** • **Twin Peaks.** Despite being redone in pastels, the generic motel decor is still nondescript, though firm beds and clean bathrooms more than compensate. Doubles range $35–$41 ($45–$51 with bath); weekly rates are $135–$170, depending on room size. You should be able to get a room anytime, though they recommend calling first. *2160 Market St., btw Church and Sanchez Sts., tel. 415/621–9467, fax 415/863–1545. From Montgomery St. BART/MUNI, MUNI F, K, L, or M Streetcar to Church St.; walk 1 block SW on Market St. 60 rooms, 3 with bath.*

➤ **UNDER $85** • **24 Henry.** This charming B&B has six doubles (two with bath) and caters to a mostly gay and lesbian clientele. The rooms are colorful and cozy, the showers are big enough for two, and a complimentary breakfast is served in the Victorian-style parlor. Rian and Walter, the proprietors, are very informative and happy to answer any questions about the neighborhood. Singles are $55–$80 per night, doubles $75–$90, suites for 3 people with kitchens ($95–120). *24 Henry St., btw 14th and 15th Sts., tel. 415/864–5686 or 800/900–5686, fax 415/864–0406. From Montgomery St. BART/MUNI, MUNI N Judah Streetcar to Noe St.; walk 4 blocks south to Henry St. Reservations advised.*

➤ **UNDER $120** • **The Black Stallion.** The city's only leather-and-Levi's B&B provides gay men—as well as a few lesbians and adventurous straight couples—with an immaculate, comfortable home base three blocks south of Harvey Milk Plaza. The Black Stallion boasts gorgeous woodwork and a working fireplace, as well as eight rooms, each with a variety of original artwork and sculptures. All rooms share baths and rates (singles from $80, doubles $90–$110) include breakfast and use of the full kitchen and sun deck. *635 Castro St., at 19th St., tel. 415/863–0131. From Montgomery St. BART/MUNI, MUNI F, K, L, or M Streetcar to Castro St.; walk 2 blocks south on Castro St. Reservations a must in summer.*

Inn on Castro. This immaculate B&B in a restored Edwardian affords a cheery stay with its colorful contemporary/pop art designs and collection of orchids. Relax, lounge around the fireplace, and sip your complimentary brandy. The prices range from $85 for a double with shared bath to $120 for a suite with private bath and sun deck—all include a full breakfast. *321 Castro St., near Market St., tel. 415/861–0321. From Montgomery St. BART/MUNI, MUNI F, K, L, or M Streetcar to Castro St.; walk 1 block north. 8 rooms, 7 with bath. Reserve ahead.*

CHINATOWN Chinatown—its narrow sidewalks lined with storefront meat and produce markets catering to crowds of recent immigrants—is, in a word, noisy. It also serves as a convenient location as it's bounded by North Beach, the Financial District, and Union Square, and it's chock-full of inexpensive restaurants. Surprisingly, the neighborhood is almost as quiet at night as it is busy during the day, and can provide a peaceful and safe place to rest your head after a night out on the town. If you'd rather hang with those of the same sex, Chinatown's **YMCA** (855 Sacramento St., near Grant St., tel. 415/982–4412) has 33 beds for men only with free access to a swimming pool, gym, and basketball court. Room rates range from $28 for a single with shared bath to $40 for a double with private bath. Women can seek out the **Gum Moon Women's Residence** (940 Washington St., at Stockton St., tel. 415/421–6937). Doubles in this clean and quiet establishment are available for $20 per night or $85 per week. There are also full kitchen and laundry facilities and two spacious common rooms with TV. For a map of Chinatown hotels, *see* Downtown San Francisco Lodging map, *below.*

➤ **UNDER $45** • **Hotel Astoria.** Steps from the Chinatown Gate, this hotel can be a real bargain—provided you're willing to share a bathroom. Singles with TV cost $36 a night, doubles with two twin beds are $40. Expect to pay about $15 extra for a private bath. Although the rooms are decent and clean, the best thing about this place is its location in a relatively safe neighborhood a few blocks from Union Square and North Beach and inches from Chinatown. *510 Bush St., at Grant Ave., tel. 415/434–8889 or 800/666–6696, fax 415/434–8919. From Montgomery St. BART/MUNI, walk 2 blocks west on Post St., 2 blocks north on Grant Ave. 70 rooms, 50 with bath. Credit card required for reservations.*

➤ **UNDER $60** • **Grant Plaza.** If you've got a group, this large, characterless hotel offers a bargain comparable to hostel rates—two double beds for $79. You also get some luxuries that AYH doesn't provide: private baths, color TVs, phones, free toothbrushes, and use of irons, sewing kits, and hot pots at the front desk. If you're not traveling in a posse, expect to pay $47 for one person, $59 for two. The small, clean rooms are popular with families and older travelers. *465 Grant Ave., btw Bush and Pine Sts., tel. 415/434–3883 or 800/472–6899, fax 415/434–3886. From Montgomery St. BART/MUNI, walk 2 blocks west on Post St., 2½ blocks north on Grant Ave. 72 rooms, all with bath. 1 wheelchair accessible room.*

CIVIC CENTER The area around the Civic Center *should* be a great place to stay: Davies Symphony Hall, the Opera House, and a host of theaters are all within easy walking distance, and many of the city's public transport lines converge here. Sadly, the Civic Center can be quite dangerous, especially at night, due to an active drug scene in the Tenderloin. After dark, solo travelers—particularly women—should avoid the triangle formed by Market, Polk, and Geary streets. For a map of Civic Center hotels, *see* Downtown San Francisco Lodging map, *below.*

➤ **UNDER $40** • **YMCA.** Although it's in possibly the shadiest part of the Tenderloin, the Y's amenities might make you forget about its sketchy surroundings: free access to a full-size swimming pool, sauna, fully equipped weight room, aerobics classes, and morning muffins and coffee. Tired-looking singles with shared bath and clean sheets start at $28. Singles with private bath go for $40, but the cheapest sleeps of all are the six hostel beds that set you back only $17. Ask for special weekly and winter rates. *220 Golden Gate Ave., at Leavenworth St., tel. 415/885–0460, fax 415/885–5439. From Civic Center BART/MUNI, walk 1 block east on Market St., 1 block north on Leavenworth St. 106 rooms, 6 with bath. 28-day max. stay, laundry. 6 wheelchair accessible rooms.*

➤ **UNDER $55** • **Aida Hotel.** Tourists from all over the world sleep at this centrally located hotel one block from Civic Center BART. Doubles with TV and phone cost $45; rooms with private bath cost $10 more. Show this book to the desk staff, and you'll get a $5–$10 discount. The generic motel decor wouldn't satisfy a true diva, but at least the rooms are new and clean. Since there are 174 rooms, you can probably get something at the last minute, even during high season. *1087 Market St., at 7th St., tel. 415/863–4141 or 800/863–AIDA, fax 415/863–5151. From Civic Center BART/MUNI, walk 1 block NE on Market St. 174 rooms, 100 with bath. Breakfast, luggage storage.*

Albergo Verona. In a central but dicey neighborhood, this beautifully renovated turn-of-the-century hotel is a safe haven attracting all sorts of international tourists. Lounge in the cozy lobby and slide a dime into the art deco jukebox for hits by the likes of Glen Miller and Louis Armstrong—all on vinyl. Rooms are a good deal at $40–$55 per double. The 14 dorm spaces in two-, four-, and six-person rooms rent for $18–$20 per person. All rates include morning coffee and doughnuts; ask about weekly rates. *317 Leavenworth St., at Eddy St., tel. 415/771–4242 or 800/422–3646, fax 415/863–5151. From Powell St. BART/MUNI, walk 4 blocks west on Eddy St. 65 rooms, 50 with bath. Free parking.*

➤ **UNDER $100** • **Phoenix Hotel.** Nestled among the strip bars and streetwalkers of the Tenderloin, this lively hotel has a strong reputation among young hipsters. A whole host of bands has stayed here, including the Red Hot Chili Peppers, NRBQ, Simple Minds, and Living

A special legal exemption was obtained for the Phoenix's swirling black-tile swimming pool floor, since an obscure state law requires pool bottoms to be a certain shade of blue.

Colour; original work by Bay Area artists spices up the alternately tropical and Southwestern design scheme. The Phoenix is joined at the hip, as it were, to the lively Miss Pearl's Jam House (*see* Chapter 4). If you seek a quiet night, request a room away from Miss Pearl's, or ask at the front desk for earplugs (where you'll also find complimentary condoms and dental floss). In high season, you'll pay $90 for a single or double, but rates go down as much as $20 in winter. *601 Larkin St., at Eddy St., tel. 415/776–1380 or 800/CITY INN, fax 415/885-3109. From Powell St. BART/MUNI, Bus 31 west on Eddy St. 44 rooms, all with bath. Continental breakfast, free parking.*

DOWNTOWN This fog-shrouded neighborhood is home to San Francisco's Theater District, a host of shady local bars, and a handful of snazzy restaurants. Its many turn-of-the-century and Victorian buildings lend the area an old-world charm, and its central location affords easy access to North Beach, the Financial District, and Chinatown. Downtown, however, also adjoins the Tenderloin: Be cautious of the assortment of suspect characters that emerges at night. The safest area is west of Mason Street and north of Sutter Street.

➢ **UNDER $40** • **Alexander Inn.** This marginally decent hotel two blocks west of Union Square has dingy but clean rooms with TVs, and free coffee and tea. If you're willing to share a bath, you'll pay a rock-bottom $35; rooms with private bath are $64–$72. Pick up a coupon (for $20 off rooms with baths) at the Powell Street Visitor Information Center (in Hallidie Plaza) or the Transbay Terminal. *415 O'Farrell St., at Taylor St., tel. 415/928–6800 or 800/843–8709, fax 415/928–3354. 62 rooms, 4 with bath. Breakfast, laundry, luggage storage.*

Nob Hill Pensione. This European-style inn offers basic furnishings in newly remodeled, spacious, sunny rooms, most with shared baths. Doubles go for $36 ($60 with private bath). The hotel's friendly staff and perks (i.e., e-mail, fax, and voice-mail services) attract a few live-in residents. *835 Hyde St., near Sutter St., tel. 415/885–2987, fax 415/921–1648. From Powell St. BART/MUNI, walk 5 blocks north to Sutter St., then 10 blocks west or take Bus 2, 3, or 4 to Hyde St. 50 rooms, 8 with bath. Cable TV, laundry, luggage storage.*

➢ **UNDER $55** • **Adelaide Inn.** The comfortable Adelaide, on a short, dead-end street just minutes from Union Square, is popular with Europeans. The decor will remind you of a kitschy Swiss chalet—the kind of place where, if they had a mantelpiece, you'd expect to see a cuckoo clock on it. Rates include a continental breakfast; some kitchen facilities are also available. Singles from $42, doubles from $52, depending on room size and availability. All share baths. *5 Isadora Duncan Ln., near Taylor St., tel. 415/441–2261, fax 415/441-0161. From Montgomery St. BART/MUNI, Bus 38 NW to Geary and Taylor Sts.; walk ¾ block north on Taylor St. and turn left. 18 rooms. Reservations advised in summer.*

Zen and the Art of Sleeping

If you have an honest interest in enlightenment and aren't just looking for a cheap place to crash, the San Francisco Zen Center, between the Civic Center and Lower Haight, has a few rooms for visitors. For $35–$40 (single) or $50–$55 (double with shared bath) you get a spotless, nicely furnished room overlooking a courtyard, plus a hearty breakfast. This working temple also offers a guest-student program ($10 a night), during which monks-in-training adhere to the center's meditation, work, and meal schedule for one to six weeks. Reserve in advance, especially during summer. 300 Page St., at Laguna St., tel. 415/863–3136. From Market St. downtown, take Bus 7 or 71 west to Page and Laguna Sts.

Herbert Hotel. If you're the "get up and go" type, then this just might be the place for you. Located one block from Union Square on Powell Street—a main artery on tourists' agendas—this hotel lies right along a cable-car route. Surprisingly, it's also very affordable: clean singles from $25 ($35 with private bath), doubles from $40 ($50 with private bath), weekly rates for singles with shared bath from $125. These low prices woo many live-in residents and travelers year-round, so book ahead. *161 Powell St., at O'Farrell St., tel. 415/362–1600, fax 415/398–3688. From Powell St. BART/MUNI, walk 2 blocks north on Powell St. 101 rooms, 50 with bath. Laundry, luggage storage.*

➤ **UNDER $65 • San Francisco Residence Club.** An excellent deal at an excellent location atop Nob Hill. Built in 1907 and recently renovated, this friendly, family-owned pension offers full breakfast *and* dinner with a night's stay. Clean, spacious rooms have Victorian furnishings and some boast spectacular views of Angel Island. Even if your room doesn't come with a view, you can still enjoy the sunny garden or dabble on the lobby's Steinway. Singles are $38–$95 nightly, $235–$600 weekly; doubles are $58–$95 nightly, $330–$600 weekly. Rates depend on room size and availability of private bath. *851 California St., at Powell St., tel. 415/421–2220, fax 415/421–2335. From Powell St. BART/MUNI, walk 8 blocks north or take cable car to California St. 84 rooms, 6 with bath. Laundry. Reservations advised.*

➤ **UNDER $85 • Amsterdam.** A very comfortable and clean Victorian B&B two blocks from Nob Hill. Singles with queen beds are $70–$80, doubles start at $80 (deluxe doubles with private Jacuzzi and outdoor patio go for $130). The sunny, cloistered deck garden is a great spot to enjoy the complimentary breakfast. *749 Taylor St., btw Sutter and Bush Sts., tel. 415/673–3277 or 800/637–3444. From Montgomery St. BART/MUNI, Bus 2, 3, or 4 west to Sutter St. 34 rooms, all with bath.*

Biltmore Hotel. Run by the same folks who run the Amsterdam next door, the Biltmore offers newly remodeled, sunny rooms at attractively low prices. The clean rooms, some with great downtown views, go for $55 (singles), $65 (doubles), or $75 (deluxe suites with wet bar, microwave, and refrigerator). *735 Taylor St., tel. 415/775–0630, fax 415/673–0458. 61 rooms, all with bath.*

Brady Acres. Come to this small, comfortable hotel near the Theater District if you're sick of being on the road and miss the comforts of home. Each room comes with a microwave, toaster, coffee maker, and a minifridge filled with chocolates and jam; the bathrooms feature apricot and papaya shampoos; and the beds are laden with colorful quilts. Your room also comes with an answering machine, TV, and a radio/cassette player. Singles are $55–$65, doubles $60–$85; ask about weekly specials. *649 Jones St., btw Post and Geary Sts., tel. 415/929–8033 or 800/627–2396. From Montgomery St. BART/MUNI, Bus 38 west to Geary and Jones Sts. 25 rooms, all with bath. Laundry. Reservations advised in summer.*

➤ **UNDER $100 • Cornell.** This small, French country–style hotel on Nob Hill offers beautifully decorated (though slightly heavy on the flowers and lace) singles for $75–$90 and doubles for $85–$100. The French owners also operate a small restaurant in the cellar with a $19 prix-fixe menu, stained glass, and groovy medieval accoutrements on the walls. *715 Bush St., btw Powell and Mason Sts., tel. 415/421–3154 or 800/232–9698, fax 415/399–1442. From Powell St. BART/MUNI, walk 5½ blocks north on Powell St., left on Bush St. 58 rooms, 48 with bath, all no-smoking. Laundry.*

David's Hotel. David's deli, the main act at this joint hotel/restaurant, has been serving up kishkes on Theater Row for more than 40 years, and everything else on the menu is fantastic, too. Stay at the hotel, and you get a free breakfast and a 15% discount on lunch and dinner at the deli. As the ultimate compliment, this hotel is popular among visitors from New York. The sterile singles are $70–$80, doubles $90–$100. David's also provides free pickup from San Francisco International Airport and free parking for guests who stay two nights or more. Two floors of the hotel are reserved for nonsmokers. *480 Geary St., at Taylor St., tel. 415/771–1600 or 800/524–1888, fax 415/931–5442. From Powell St. BART/MUNI, walk 2½ blocks north on Powell St., 2 blocks west on Geary St. 54 rooms, all with bath. Cable TV. Wheelchair access.*

MARINA

Chestnut St.

Lombard St.

101

Octavia St.

Gough St.

Franklin St.

Van Ness Ave.

Polk St.

Larkin St.

Hyde St.

Leavenworth St.

Greenw

Filbert

Union S

RUSSIAN HILL

Green St.

Vallejo St.

Broadway

Broadway Tunnel

PACIFIC HEIGHTS

Pacific St.

Jackson St.

Alta Plaza

Washington St.

101

Lafayette Park

Clay St.

Sacramento St.

Pierce St.

Steiner St.

Fillmore St.

California St.

Leavenworth St.

Jones St.

NH

Pine St.

Bush St.

Webster St.

Buchanan St.

Laguna St.

Sutter St.

Hyde St.

JAPANTOWN

Gough St.

Franklin St.

Van Ness Ave.

POLK GULCH

Larkin St.

Post St.

Geary St.

Geary Expressway

O'Farrell St.

Ellis St.

Eddy St.

Turk St.

Golden Gate Ave.

McAllister St.

Fulton St.

CIVIC CENTER

Market St.

Alamo Square

Grove St.

Civic Center BART Station

Hayes St.

7th St.

8th St.

Adelaide Inn, **26**
Aida Hotel, **21**
Albergo Verona, **23**
Alexander Inn, **24**
Amsterdam, **13**
Art Center Bed and Breakfast, **2**
Auberge des Artistes, **7**
AYH Hostel at Union Square, **33**
Biltmore Hotel, **14**
Brady Acres, **15**
Cornell, **27**

David's Hotel, **25**
European Guest House, **18**
Ft. Mason International Hostel, **3**
Globetrotter's Inn, **35**
Grand Central Hostel, **17**
Grant Plaza, **31**
Green Tortoise Guest House, **11**
Gum Moon Women's Residence, **12**

Herbert Hotel, **34**
Hotel Astoria, **32**
Hotel Bohème, **10**
Interclub Globe Hostel, **19**
Lombard Plaza, **1**
The Mansions Hotel, **5**
Nob Hill Pensione, **9**
Pacific Tradewinds, **30**
Phoenix Hotel, **16**

San Francisco International Student Center, **20**
San Francisco Residence Club, **28**
San Francisco Zen Center, **8**
San Remo Hotel, **6**
Travelodge, **4**
YMCA Chinatown, **29**
YMCA Downtown, **22**

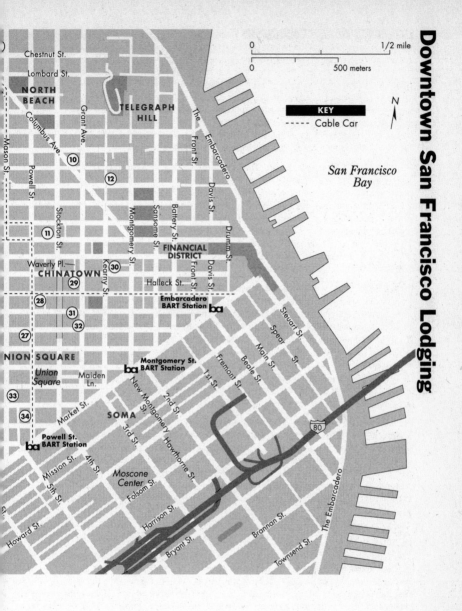

Chestnut St.

Lombard St.

NORTH BEACH

TELEGRAPH HILL

Columbus Ave.

Grant Ave.

Mason St.

Powell St.

Stockton St.

(10)

(12)

(11)

Montgomery St.

Sansome St.

Battery St.

Davis St.

Front St.

The Embarcadero

Drumm St.

FINANCIAL DISTRICT

Waverly Pl.

CHINATOWN

Kearny St.

(30)

(29)

Halleck St.

Davis St.

(28)

(31)

(32)

(27)

NION SQUARE

Union Square

Maiden Ln.

(33)

(34)

Market St.

SOMA

New Montgomery St.

2nd St.

3rd St.

1st St.

Hawthorne St.

Fremont St.

Beale St.

Main St.

Spear St.

Steuart St.

Powell St. BART Station

Mission St.

4th St.

5th St.

Moscone Center

Folsom St.

Harrison St.

Howard St.

Bryant St.

Brannan St.

Townsend St.

The Embarcadero

Embarcadero BART Station

Montgomery St. BART Station

San Francisco Bay

80

N

0   1/2 mile

0   500 meters

KEY

- - - - Cable Car

HAIGHT AND WESTERN ADDITION Rock stars (the Dead, Janis Joplin), poets (Allen Ginsberg), psycho cults (the Manson family), and runaway hippie children have settled in the Haight at various times; it remains a fun, eclectic neighborhood. Staying here will give you a great introduction into how the postcollege set lives in San Francisco; it also puts you close to other fine neighborhoods like the Castro and Mission districts. Lower **Haight Street** (especially between Laguna and Pierce streets) can be dicey at night, but the Upper Haight only seems seedier than it actually is. The Western Addition, on the other hand, was genuinely seedy a few years ago, but is now undergoing something of a revival as artists and musicians discover its (relatively) cheap rents. Nevertheless, caution is advised at night, as it can get hairy in the Western Addition near the subsidized housing west of Webster Street.

➤ **UNDER $55** • **Metro Hotel.** The first thing you'll notice about the Metro is its neon sign, which lights up Divisadero Street, a major thoroughfare in the Western Addition. This is a good middle-range option; the whole place was recently redone and the high-ceilinged rooms are large, clean, and comfortable. Ask for a room in the back, away from the street noise. Singles and doubles go for $50 (add $10 for a third person). If you're lucky, you might run into a rock band scheduled to play at a nearby club. *319 Divisadero St., btw Oak and Page Sts., tel. 415/861–5364, fax 415/863–1970. From Market St. downtown, Bus 7 or 71 west to Divisadero and Haight Sts.; walk 1½ blocks north on Divisadero. 24 rooms, all with bath. Cable TV. Reservations advised in summer.*

➤ **UNDER $70** • **Auberge des Artistes.** If your lowbrow friends are dragging down your lofty ideals, then this très hip B&B on the outskirts of Alamo Square Park is the place for you. The stunning Victorian (circa 1901) has an extensive collection of art books, a sunny garden, and rich art nouveau decor; a free gourmet breakfast is served in the dining room, painted with a full-scale replica of a Gustav Klimt mural. If you're feeling the urge to create, ask about accessing the darkroom or arranging live-model drawing sessions. Luxurious doubles (some with fireplace) with shared bath start at $65, larger suites range $85–$100. *829 Fillmore St., at Grove St., tel. 415/776–2530, fax 415/441–8242. From Montgomery St. BART/MUNI, MUNI F, K, L, or M Streetcar to Church St., then Bus 22 Fillmore north to Grove St. 5 rooms, 2 with bath. Parking. Reservations highly advised.*

➤ **UNDER $90** • **The Red Victorian.** At the Red Vic, an immensely popular Haight Street landmark, each room is decorated according to a particular theme. Come here if you want to spend the night in The Japanese Tea Garden Room (single $77, double $96); The Summer of Love Room (single $69, double $86), complete with a tie-dyed canopy and authentic '60s concert posters; or The Skylight Room (single $69, double $86), painted in deep jewel tones and featuring a skylighted ceiling. Some rooms are more gimmicky than others, but it's clear from the moment you walk in that the Red Vic's proprietors and employees have taken great care with every aspect of the place. *1665 Haight St., btw Belvedere and Cole Sts., tel. 415/864–1978, fax 415/863–3293. From Market St. downtown, Bus 7 or 71 west to Haight and Cole Sts. 18 rooms, 4 with bath. Reservations advised in summer.*

Stanyan Park Hotel. So your bell-bottoms reek of stale incense, you've been humming Grateful Dead tunes for days, and you can't bear to look at anything tie-dyed ever again. This hotel on the eastern edge of Golden Gate Park offers a respite from the Haight's hectic pace—Victorian furniture, brass fixtures, and intelligent conversation. The immaculate but unspectacular rooms cost $85 per day, and the staff is friendly. Breakfast is included. *750 Stanyan St., btw Waller and Beulah Sts., tel. 415/751–1000, fax 415/668–5454. From Market St. downtown, Bus 71 west to Haight and Stanyan Sts.; walk 2 blocks south on Stanyan St. 36 rooms, all with bath. Reservations advised. 2 wheelchair accessible rooms.*

THE MARINA AND PACIFIC HEIGHTS The **Marina District** is a quiet, safe residential neighborhood popular with young folks climbing the corporate ladder. It's a long walk from North Beach, Chinatown, and Downtown, but the views of the bay and the Golden Gate Bridge from the nearby waterfront are tremendous. The posh **Pacific Heights** sits above the Marina and shares its spectacular views; this neighborhood, too, is safe, quiet, and very dull at night, though a star-studded cast slumbers within its confines (Meg Ryan, Danielle Steele, and Nicolas Cage, to name a few). Union and Fillmore streets offer a good selection of yuppified restaurants and singles bars. Unfortunately, most of the cheap lodging in this area lies along busy

Haight, Castro, and Mission Lodging

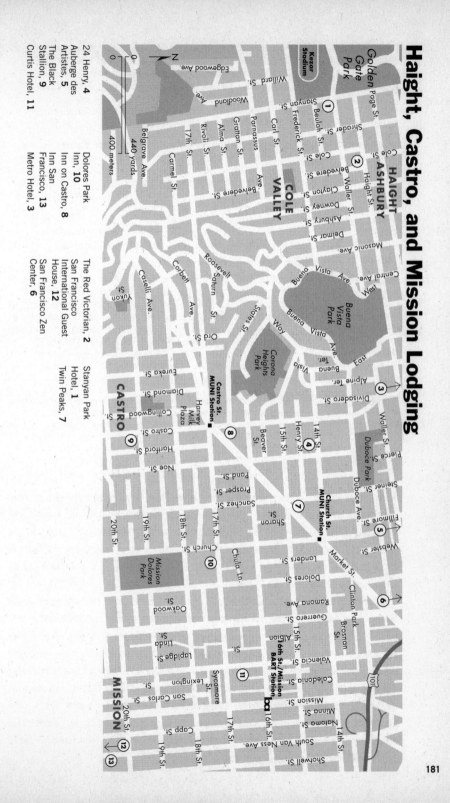

24 Henry, **4**
Auberge des
Artistes, **5**
The Black
Stallion, **9**
Curtis Hotel, **11**

Dolores Park
Inn, **10**
Inn on Castro, **8**
Inn San
Francisco, **13**
Metro Hotel, **3**

The Red Victorian, **2**
San Francisco
International Guest
House, **12**
Twin Peaks, **7**

Stanyan Park
Hotel, **1**
San Francisco Zen
Center, **6**

Golden Gate Park

Kezar Stadium

Page St.

Edgewood Ave.

Willard St.

Stanyan St.

Beulah St.

Shrader St.

Cole St.

HAIGHT ASHBURY

Cole St.

Woodland Ave.

Frederick St.

Belvedere St.

Waller St.

Haight St.

Clayton St.

COLE VALLEY

Downey St.

Ashbury St.

Parnassus Ave.

Grattan St.

Carl St.

Alma St.

Rivoli St.

17th St.

Belgrave Ave.

Carmel St.

Delmar St.

Masonic Ave.

Central Ave.

Belvedere St.

Roosevelt

Saturn St.

Corbett Ave.

Caselli Ave.

Ord St.

Yukon St.

Buena Vista Ave.

West

Buena Vista Park

Buena Vista

East

Buena Vista

Vista

Buena Ter.

Alpine Ter.

Way

Corona Heights Park

Divisadero St.

Waller St.

Duboce Park

Pierce St.

Duboce Ave.

Steiner St.

Eureka St.

Diamond St.

Collingwood St.

Castro St. MUNI Station

Harvey Milk Plaza

Beaver St.

14th St.

Henry St.

15th St.

CASTRO

Castro St.

Hartford St.

Noe St.

Pond St.

Prosper St.

Sanchez St.

Sharon St.

Church St. MUNI Station

Fillmore St.

Webster St.

Market St.

Clinton Park

Brosnan St.

18th St.

19th St.

20th St.

Church St.

Chula Ln.

Landers St.

Dolores St.

Ramona Ave.

Guerrero St.

Mission Dolores Park

Oakwood St.

15th St.

Albion St.

Caledonia St.

Valencia St.

Linda St.

Lapidge St.

16th St./Mission BART Station

Mission St.

Lexington St.

San Carlos St.

Sycamore St.

MISSION

20th St.

Capp St.

Shotwell St.

19th St.

18th St.

17th St.

South Van Ness Ave.

Minna St.

Natoma St.

14th St.

101

① ② ③ ④ ⑤ ⑥ ⑦ ⑧ ⑨ ⑩ ⑪ ⑫ ⑬

N

0   440 yards
0   400 meters

Lombard Street (not on the world's crookedest part), a major thoroughfare leading to the Golden Gate Bridge. The **Travelodge** (1450 Lombard St., at Van Ness Ave., tel. 415/673–0691) isn't too bad—in a last-resort kind of way—with clean singles ($45) and doubles ($55); expect $30 rate increases May–November. Another decent bet is the **Lombard Plaza** (2026 Lombard St., at Fillmore St., tel. 415/921–2444, fax 415/921–5275), where doubles start at $40–$60 depending on the season. For a map of Marina and Pacific Heights hotels, *see* Downtown San Francisco Lodging map, *above*.

➢ **UNDER $100 • Art Center Bed and Breakfast.** The owners like to call this place a country inn with a city built around it; when you see it, you'll understand why. The inn, near the Presidio and the yuppie bars of Union Street, is cluttered with paintings and art-related knickknacks. If you want to take brush to canvas, the proprietors will be glad to set up an easel for you, and you can go to the garden in back for inspiration. Three studios and a pair of two-room suites ($95 per day) have double beds, TV and radio, microwave ovens, hot plates, and refrigerators. A three-room apartment with the same amenities runs $125 for two people. *1902 Filbert St., at Laguna St., tel. 415/567–1526 or 800/927–8236. From Embarcadero BART/MUNI, Bus 41 NW to Laguna St.; walk 1 block north and turn left. 5 rooms, all with bath. Reserve 2 weeks in advance in summer.*

The Mansions Hotel. This historic 1887 landmark in Pacific Heights boasts a host of ghastly residents and a list of celebrity visitors, including Barbra Streisand, Paul Simon, and Joe Montana. The hotel has all the refinement of a schlocky Pier 39 tourist attraction (check out the international pig museum), but it's cheesy fun, and the cost of a comfortable room includes breakfast and entrance to the nightly show featuring the hauntress Claudia. The tiny Tom Thumb double with detached bath costs $89; otherwise guest suites range $129 to $350 for the insanely extravagant presidential suite. Expect a $20 rate increase on weekends. *220 Sacramento St., at Laguna St., tel. 415/929–9444 or 800/826–9398, fax 415/567–9391. From Embarcadero BART/MUNI, Bus 1 west to Laguna St. 21 rooms, all with bath.*

MISSION DISTRICT This lively, colorful neighborhood is home not only to the city's sizable Mexican and Central American communities, but also to lesbians, riot grrrls, and young, politically radical types. Sadly, your housing options here are limited to either expensive or cheap

Romantic Rendezvous

After an evening at the symphony (or a show at the Fillmore), and after the last bottle of wine (or whiskey) is empty, the nearest cookie-cutter motel just won't do. Luckily, the San Remo Hotel (see below) has a penthouse room for $85 that will help put both of you in the mood. Up on the roof, you're removed from the prying eyes of the world—all the better to enjoy the views of the bay and Marina. Others may prefer soaking in a private hot tub at the sumptuous Inn San Francisco (943 S. Van Ness Ave., near 21st St., tel. 415/641–0188), in the Mission District. This luxury's $195 price tag may deter all but the most infatuated, but the inn also has smaller rooms with shared bath ($75), furnished with antiques, crystal, stained glass, and Oriental rugs. Other perks include breakfast, a peaceful garden with gazebo and hot tub, and complimentary sherry. Larger rooms come with extras such as a sun deck, fireplace, or claw-foot bathtub. A third amorous option is the women-only House O' Chicks (tel. 415/861–9849), near the Castro, with an atmosphere that is artsy, homey, and very sex- and gay-positive. Each of the two rooms ($75) has a custom-made mattress, TV, and stereo with CDs; all guests share a bath and the video library, which includes lesbian erotica. The proprietors prefer to speak with potential guests before accepting reservations.

and grimy. The Mission is not the safest area, so if you're traveling solo, stick to Valencia, Dolores, and Guerrero streets and avoid taking a room east of Valencia Street. If you don't mind walking, try the San Francisco International Guest House Hotel (*see* Hostels, *below*). For a map of Mission District hotels, *see* Haight, Castro, and Mission Lodging map, *above*.

➤ **UNDER $40** • **Curtis Hotel.** The Mission has its share of shady characters, but the owner of this residential hotel works hard to keep the riffraff out—sometimes successfully. The rules include a ban on loud noises after 9 PM, no alcohol, and no parties. If you get too wild, you'll get thrown out. A sweet deal awaits those who can hold their reveling tendencies in check: Clean singles with shared bath are just $75–$90 per week (no doubles). Talk to the manager about shorter stays. Guests must pay in advance (cash only) and flash a picture ID. *559 Valencia St., near 16th St., tel. 415/621–9337. From Mission/16th St. BART/MUNI, walk 1 block west on 16th St., turn left on Valencia St. 60 rooms, none with bath. Key deposit ($2).*

➤ **UNDER $100** • **Dolores Park Inn.** This lovely B&B—actually a Victorian home built in 1874—is quiet, restful, and almost entirely furnished with antiques. It's on a sedate street between the Mission and the Castro, one block south of Mission Dolores Park. Singles are $60, doubles $90–$165; both include breakfast and access to the garden and parlor. Check out the private suite in the garden—perfect if you've got wealthy friends who enjoy partying like rock stars. For $250 you get creature comforts galore *and* a super-large eight-foot Jacuzzi with '70s lava-rock decor. *3641 17th St., near Dolores St., tel. 415/621–0482. From any downtown BART/MUNI station, MUNI J Streetcar to 16th and Church Sts.; walk 1 block south on Church St. to 17th St. 5 rooms, 1 with bath, all nonsmoking. Two-night min. stay.*

NORTH BEACH North Beach—where Italian immigrants and Beat poets have converged on narrow sidewalks—is a uniquely San Francisco experience and a great place to stay. Near Downtown, Chinatown, and Fisherman's Wharf, this is also where most tourists congregate— hotel rates are accordingly high. While North Beach is close to many of the city's best restaurants, bars and cafés; another "attraction" to be aware of is the row of tacky strip joints along Broadway. An appealing, low-cost option is the **Green Tortoise Guest House** (*see* Hostels, *below*). For a map of North Beach hotels, *see* Downtown San Francisco Lodging, *above.*

➤ **UNDER $75** • **San Remo Hotel.** A short walk from both Fisherman's Wharf and North Beach, the friendly San Remo is an incredible bargain in a pricey area. Doubles with shared bath cost $55–$75; the more you spend, the better your view. The hotel boasts beautiful redwood furnishings, stained-glass windows, and quiet, spotless rooms. *2237 Mason St., btw Francisco and Chestnut Sts., tel. 415/776–8688 or 800/352–REMO, fax 415/776–2811. From Montgomery St. BART/MUNI Bus 15 north to Chestnut St.; walk 1 block west to Mason St. 64 rooms, 1 with bath. Laundry. Reservations advised in summer.*

➤ **UNDER $125** • **Hotel Bohème.** Near the outdoor cafés that sidle up to Columbus Avenue, Bohème offers 15 newly remodeled rooms; plush, striped carpeting; and black-and-white snapshots on the hallway walls. Enter, and you'll feel like you've just stepped into a smoky, suspenseful scene from an old private-eye show—well, minus the smoke (all rooms are nonsmoking). Indeed, this was once a hangout for beatnik poets like Allen Ginsberg. Enlist three friends to burden the cost of a double with two beds ($120); there's also one suite that goes for $125 (for three) or $130 (for four). *444 Columbus Ave., at Vallejo St., tel. 415/433–9111, fax 415/362–6292. From Montgomery St. BART/MUNI, Bus 41 north to Vallejo St. 15 rooms, all with bath.*

HOSTELS

Hostels affiliated with American Youth Hostels (AYH), the American branch of Hostelling International (HI), offer a certain welcomed predictability, but private hostels are often cheaper and filled with a more diverse crowd. Due perhaps to the dearth of budget lodging in the area, hostels are extremely popular; make reservations before you arrive. In a pinch, you can also try **Albergo Verona** (*see* Civic Center, *above*), which charges $18 for one of 14 dorm spaces. For more info, hit the hostel website (http://www.hostels.com).

AYH Hostel at Union Square. This huge hostel one block from Union Square sleeps 230 people in rooms with one to four beds ($14 for members, $17 for nonmembers). The interior is bright and pleasant, filled mostly with an international student crowd; amenities include a TV room, smoking room, library, and kitchen (with microwaves, toasters, and refrigerators). Bulletin boards offer info on San Francisco nightlife and other attractions. About 40% of the rooms are set aside for reservations, which must be made at least 48 hours in advance ($14 deposit). You can stay a maximum of six days (14 days off-season). *312 Mason St., btw O'Farrell and Geary Sts., tel. 415/788–5604 or 800/444–6111. From Powell St. BART/MUNI, walk 1½ blocks north on Powell St., 1 block west on O'Farrell St., turn right. No curfew, no lockout. Reception open daily 24 hrs. Wheelchair access.*

European Guest House. A good choice for those who want to take advantage of the nightlife south of Market, this mid-size hostel offers decent, if unspectacular, lodging in one 15-bed room ($12 per person), four-person dorms ($12 per person), and doubles ($14 per person). It's got a sun deck, common room, and cozy kitchen. True to its name, it hosts European guests. *761 Minna St., near Mission St. btw 8th and 9th Sts., tel. 415/861–6634, fax 415/621–4428. From Civic Center BART/MUNI, walk 2 blocks south on 8th St., turn right on Minna St. 24 beds. No curfew, no lockout. Reception open 24 hrs. 3-week max. stay, deposit ($5), laundry. Reservations advised in summer.*

Ft. Mason International Hostel. This AYH hostel, perched high above the waterfront, will dazzle you with its views of the bay and the Golden Gate Bridge. The rules are tedious and complex, however, so listen up. It's almost impossible to stay here unless you reserve in advance. Reservations (by phone or in person) must be made at least 24 hours ahead with a credit card, or by sending the cost of your first night's stay at least two weeks prior to your arrival, with the names and genders of the people in your party and the dates you intend to stay. Get here *really* early if you don't have a reservation. Beds are $13–$15 a night. During the summer, you can stay a maximum of 14 nights. You're required to perform a chore each day. No smoking or alcohol allowed. Whew. *Mailing address: Ft. Mason, Bldg. 240, Box A, San Francisco, CA 94123, tel. 415/771–7277 or 800/444–6111, fax 415/788–3023. From Transbay Terminal, Bus 42 to Van Ness Ave. and Bay St.; turn right on Bay St. and follow signs. 160 beds. No curfew, lockout 11 AM–3 PM. Reception open daily 7–2 and 3–midnight. Bike and luggage storage, common room, kitchen, laundry, free linens.*

Globetrotter's Inn. The lack of restrictions and small size (it sleeps only 39 people) are among the strengths of this independent hostel on the edge of the down-and-out Tenderloin District. It's not as new or as sunny as some of the others, but the staff has done its best, putting artwork on the walls and creating a comfortable common space with a TV, plants, and a 24-hour kitchen. A space in a double or in a four- or six-person dorm costs $12; singles are $24 ($75 per week). Many young Europeans stay here while looking for a more permanent situation, and the bulletin board lists job openings on a regular basis. *225 Ellis St., btw Mason and Taylor Sts., tel. 415/346–5786. From Powell St. BART/MUNI, walk ½ block north on Powell St., 1½ blocks west on Ellis St. No curfew, no lockout. Reception open daily 8–1 and 5–9. Key deposit ($5), laundry.*

Grand Central Hostel. This former flophouse, in a central but seedy location, has been transformed into a decent hostel. Dorm space costs $12 per night ($75 per week); singles are $20 per night, doubles $30. Other perks include an exercise room, free coffee, breakfast, social events, free linens, a pool table, a jukebox, table tennis, and TV rooms. All visitors, even Americans traveling within the United States, must show travel documents to stay here. *1412 Market St., at 10th and Fell Sts., tel. 415/703–9988, fax 415/703–9986. From Van Ness Ave. MUNI, walk 1 block NE on Market St. 250 beds. No curfew or lockout. Reception open 24 hrs. 21-day max. stay.*

Green Tortoise Guest House. From the popular people who have brought you budget bus travel for the past 20 years comes one of the best hostels in San Francisco. Green Tortoise is found in the cheesy red-light district, minutes from North Beach, and just blocks from Downtown and Chinatown. Cool Euro-backpackers fill most of the rooms, which are clean, spacious, and rarely vacant—call ahead. There's no curfew or lockout, and the managers are friendly and mellow. Single bunks cost $15 per night, private singles $20, private doubles $35. *494 Broadway, btw Montgomery and Kearny Sts., tel. 415/834–1000, fax 415/956–4900. From Montgomery St.*

BART/MUNI, Bus 15 or 9X north. 40 rooms (110 beds). Reception open 24 hrs. Breakfast (free), kitchen, laundry, sauna. No credit cards.

Interclub Globe Hostel. Intended for international travelers (but passport-carrying Americans are not turned away), this SoMa hostel has few rules and a warm, relaxed atmosphere—not to mention a pool table and a sun deck that has a grand view of the city. With more than 100 beds, guests sleep four to a room, and each room has a bathroom; two floors are reserved for nonsmokers. A bed is $15 per night in summer ($10 for your first night off-season) and $80 a week. At the lively adjoining canteen, you can get dinner for less than $5. *10 Hallam Pl., near Folsom St. btw 7th and 8th Sts., tel. 415/ 431–0540, fax 415/431–3286. From Civic Center BART/MUNI, walk 3 blocks south on 8th St., turn left on Folsom St. No curfew. Reception open 24 hrs. Laundry.*

The bar next door to the Interclub Globe Hostel hosts weekly $1 beer nights for guests of the hostel.

Pacific Tradewinds. The antithesis of an institutional hostel, this homey place in Chinatown has only four rooms (with a total of 28 beds), plus a friendly common space and kitchen. There's no official lockout (although they like people to be gone during the afternoon), and if you want to come in after midnight, the proprietors will give you a key ($10 deposit). They'll also let you know about cheap restaurants and other attractions in the area. Beds are usually $16 per night, but the price fluctuates, so call ahead. If you stay seven nights, you pay for only six; in summer, they ask that you pay for the week in advance. *680 Sacramento St., near Kearny St., tel. 415/433–7970, fax 415/291–8801. From Montgomery St. BART/MUNI, walk 1 block west on Post St., then Bus 15 north on Kearny St. Reception open daily 8 AM–midnight. 40-day max. stay.*

San Francisco International Guest House. Tucked away on the outskirts of the Mission District, this clean, remodeled, 100-year-old hostel is friendly and cozy. With its five-day minimum stay requirement, this hostel is also known for breeding "intimacy." You need to flash travel documents to stay here, and it's filled mostly with European student travelers. There are two full kitchens, a TV room, and a funky, orange-colored reading room. Rooms of two to four people go for $12 ($11 if you stay more than 28 days); couples can ask for private rooms. *2976 23rd St., at Harrison St., tel. 415/641-1411. From 24th St. BART/MUNI, walk 1 block north on Mission St. to 23rd St., then 6½ blocks east. 28 beds. No curfew.*

San Francisco International Student Center. Small, homey, and right in the middle of hip SoMa, this student center has 16 rooms with three to five beds in each, a small kitchen, a common room, and an owner who doesn't believe in television. Beds cost $13 a night, $84 a week. *1188 Folsom St., near 8th St., tel. 415/255–8800, fax 510/938–0113. From Civic Center BART/MUNI, walk 3 blocks south on 8th St. to Folsom St. No curfew, no lockout. Reception open 9 AM–11 PM. 28-day max. stay.*

LONGER STAYS

So you think you want to stay awhile? Monthly rents in San Francisco range from $250 for a closet in an eight-bedroom house to $350–$450 for an average room to $500–$850 for studios and one-bedroom apartments. Still want to stay? If so, there are several ways to find a semiaffordable place to live in the city. If you need a whole apartment or house, investigate the classified ads in the **San Francisco Chronicle** or the **San Francisco Examiner**. Buy the Sunday papers on Saturday night to get a jump start on your search. Another option is to visit a rental agency with private listings. For example, **Community Rentals** (470 Castro St., tel. 415/552–8868) provides listings of vacant apartments, flats, and houses all over San Francisco. You tell them what you're looking for (price range, neighborhood, type of housing) and they give you listings, each with about a quarter-page of info. They also feature the largest selection of gay roommate resources in San Francisco ($30 for 2 months). Their fee is $75 for two months, $50 of which is refund-

To find their soul (room)mate, folks with a room for rent will often put flyers in cafés or laundromats with 10 to 15 adjectives strung together: "Bass-playing, cat-owning vegetarian household seeks gay, guitar-playing, nonsmoking, spiritual roommate for jam sessions and hearty soup . . . ."

able if you don't find a place through them. **Metro Rents** (2021 Fillmore St., tel. 415/563-7368) charges $65 for 40 days, refunds $40 if you don't find a place, and has good info for neighborhoods between Fillmore Street and the Marina. Look in the Yellow Pages for other agencies and keep in mind that a service's most comprehensive listings are likely to be for the neighborhoods adjacent to it. Summer means cheaper sublet prices as students leave for vacation; try to get housing before August (when returning students nab the best places and don't plan to leave anytime soon). Bring your checkbook and references when apartment hunting, so you can give them a security deposit on the spot—fierce doesn't even begin to describe the competition.

One of the cheapest ways to find an apartment is simply by walking around. Look up, and you'll see countless FOR RENT signs in windows, with a few details about the apartment and a phone number to call.

If you're looking for a sublet, or a room in someone else's apartment, you have all kinds of options. Struggling artists and other poor folks often take their chances with the bulletin boards that appear in just about every café in the city. Another free way to find roommates is at **Rainbow Grocery** (*see* Markets and Specialty Stores, in Chapter 4). A set of file boxes at the store contains listings, both short- and long-term, for your dream San Francisco roommate—a cynical leftist with a futon and two standoffish cats. Those who can spend a little bit of money to find a home often have good luck with roommate referral agencies. For a fee of $25–$50, these agencies will give you access to computer databases of places with vacant rooms. The listings are tailored to your price range, personality, room requirements, tastes in music, food preferences, neuroses, and whatever else you and your potential housemates want to divulge about your inner selves. Most agencies let you view the listings for as long as it takes to find a good living situation. **Community Rentals** (*see above*) has information on shares in the Castro, Noe Valley, and the Haight. Other agencies include **The Original S.F. Roommate Referral Service** (610A Cole St., at Haight St., tel. 415/558–9191), which charges $34 for four months of service, and the **Roommate Network** (3129 Fillmore St., near Filbert St., tel. 415/441–6334), which charges "working professionals" $55–$90 (depending on whether you want a shared or private rental) for an indefinite period of time. Many people also find roommates through the classified ads under "Shared Housing" in the *Bay Guardian* and *S.F. Weekly,* San Francisco's largest free weeklies.

East Bay

BERKELEY

Lodging in Berkeley is often either shabby or downright expensive—sometimes both. If that isn't enough, it's also hard to come by: In mid-May, when thousands of graduating Berkeley students don caps and gowns, reservations become *absolutely* essential, since most of the nicer hotels sell out four to five months in advance. To add insult to injury, all Berkeley lodgings add 12% tax to the prices listed below.

Most of the city's motels are on **University Avenue,** west of campus, and most of these motels are not recommended. Your life isn't necessarily in danger here, but expect a general air of seediness (i.e., velvet curtains, the reek of cheap perfume). It's best to stick to the campus end of University Avenue; the farther west you go, the shoddier the surroundings become. To reach all of the motels in the vicinity from Berkeley BART, walk two blocks north to University Avenue and head west, or take Bus 51.

Berkeley has no youth hostels, but the **YMCA** (2185 Milvia St., tel. 510/848–6800, fax 510/848–6835)—open to both men and women—is cheap and within easy reach of Berkeley's sights. Clean, dorm-style singles with shared bath cost $25; there are also a few doubles ($33) and triples ($40) available. After 14 days, you're eligible to stay longer, for around $100 per week. And, if the price isn't reason enough to stay here, guests have access to a kitchen and the recently remodeled fitness center next door.

➤ **UNDER $55** • **Campus Motel.** This place is right on noisy University Avenue, but it *is* close to campus (six blocks west) and the rooms are neat and clean. Some rooms allow smoking, and all have cable TV and coffee makers. Singles are $45, doubles $50. *1619 University Ave., btw McGee Ave. and California St., tel. 510/841–3844, fax 510/841–8134. 23 rooms, all with bath. Wheelchair access.*

Golden Bear Motel. One of the nicer budget lodgings in town, the Golden Bear has clean doubles for $49. The surrounding neighborhood isn't that great, so be careful walking around at night. Bus 52 across the street will whisk you to the Berkeley campus. *1620 San Pablo Ave., tel. 510/525–6770, fax 510/525–6999. From North Berkeley BART, walk 3 blocks west to San Pablo Ave. and turn right. 42 rooms, all with bath. Wheelchair access.*

Travel Inn. This pink motel is cheap, clean, far enough away from the street to escape traffic noise, and has plenty of parking. The rooms are decorated with an eclectic array of furnishings, and the management is friendly. Singles cost $40, doubles $50. *1461 University Ave., btw Sacramento and Acton Sts., tel. 510/848–3840, fax 510/848–3846. 3 blocks south of North Berkeley BART. 42 rooms, all with bath.*

➤ **UNDER $80** • **Travelodge.** If you're not concerned about price or atmosphere, you can always settle for the generic blue-and-white Travelodge, three blocks from campus, where basic, very clean doubles start at $78. *1820 University Ave., near Grant St., tel. 510/843–4262, fax 510/848–1480. 30 rooms, all with bath. Wheelchair access.*

➤ **UNDER $100** • **Berkeley City Club.** This beautiful building with gorgeous high ceilings and Moorish-Gothic architecture was designed in 1927 by famed northern California architect Julia Morgan. It is now simultaneously an historic landmark, private social club, and hotel with rather spartan singles for $80, and doubles for $90 (continental breakfast included). Many of the rooms have bay views, and guests have access to the club's fitness center and pool. *2315 Durant Ave., tel 510/848–7800, fax 510/848–5900. From Berkeley BART, walk 3 blocks south on Shattuck Ave., turn left on Durant Ave. 42 rooms, all with bath. Wheelchair access.*

French Hotel. This little Euro hotel in North Berkeley's "Gourmet Ghetto" is close to excellent restaurants and bookstores. Doubles with a minuscule patio cost $85–$95 (there's one room available for $68) and most include a complimentary breakfast. You can join yuppies sipping espresso in the popular café downstairs. *1538 Shattuck Ave., btw Cedar and Vine Sts., tel. and fax 510/548–9930. From Berkeley BART, walk 6 blocks north on Shattuck Ave. 18 rooms, all with bath. Wheelchair access.*

Gramma's Rose Garden Inn. The froufrou set will be delighted with this compound of quaintness on grimy Telegraph Avenue. As you open the little gates, you enter a wonderland of flower beds, cute stone paths, and chintz. Doubles in the main house are $89–$99; the surrounding cottages offer more spacious, higher-priced rooms ($110–$145). Many rooms have fireplaces, balconies, and bay views, and all include a tasty breakfast. *2740 Telegraph Ave., at Stuart St., tel. 510/549–2145, fax 510/549–1085. From Ashby BART, walk 5 blocks east on Ashby Ave., turn left on Telegraph Ave. 40 rooms, all with bath. Wheelchair access.*

➤ **UNDER $110** • **Hotel Durant.** An elegant lobby, friendly staff, and convenient location one block from campus make this hotel a popular choice with visiting parents and Cal Bears fans (book ahead for graduation and big football games). The spacious, earth-toned rooms all have big, comfy beds and include a continental breakfast. Singles cost $91, doubles $101 (rooms with 2 double beds are $111). *2600 Durant Ave., tel. 510/845–8981 or 800/238–7268, fax 510/486–8336. From Berkeley BART, walk 3 blocks south on Shattuck Ave., turn left on Durant Ave. 103 rooms, all with bath. Wheelchair access.*

UNIVERSITY HOUSING University Summer Visitor Housing (2601 Warring St., tel. 510/642–4444) offers summer dorm accommodations at 2424 Channing Way for $38–$50 per night. Rooms are nothing to write home about (bed, desk, chair, phone). For an additional $3 per day, you'll get linens, soap (maybe write home about the university's generosity), and parking. There are lots of young people around, and the dorms are a very safe place to stay.

LONGER STAYS Finding long-term housing is most difficult in the fall, when thousands of Berkeley students scramble for a place to live. Those who hit the jackpot with a cheap room or apartment close to campus are too wise to give it up come summer vacation: Their solution is to sublet the space (at about two-thirds the normal rent). Still, you should expect to pay around $300 per month for a room in shared housing, and at least $400 for a studio apartment. Good resources for rental listings include the campus newspaper *The Daily Californian*, *East Bay Express*, and *East Bay Guardian*, all of which are available for free in most cafés around Bancroft Way and Telegraph Avenue. A number of cafés have large bulletin boards that boast a glorious mess of flyers and scraps of paper advertising apartments for rent. **Sproul Plaza,** on the Berkeley campus, is another bulletin-board hot spot.

Those who have access to a valid Berkeley student ID can browse the rental listings at the **Community Living Office** (2405 Bowditch St., tel. 510/642–3642). During summer, the office provides nonstudents with 10 days of customized sublet listings for $20. You can also look in the Yellow Pages for a rental agency. Popular ones include **Berkeley Connection** (2840 College Ave., tel. 510/845–7821), which charges $50 for one month (if you don't find anything, you get a $25 refund or a second month free), and **Homefinders** (2158 University Ave., tel. 510/549–6450), which charges $55 for 30 days (if nothing comes up, you get a $30 refund or a second month free). These companies will give you a long list of properties for rent in the area; for short-term housing, however, you're better off looking on your own.

Another option is staying in the student-owned and -operated co-ops. Inquire and make all reservations at the **University Students' Cooperative Association** (2424 Ridge Rd., tel. 510/848–1936). The co-ops are open to students from any college; for $729–$1,227 you can stay all summer (mid-May–mid-August) in a shared apartment or studio. Ask about the vegetarian-only **Lothlorien** (2415 and 2405 Prospect St.) southeast of campus, where you can frolic in the Jacuzzi, or the women-only **Sherman Hall** (2250 Prospect St.), one of the cleanest and best-maintained co-ops. Also worth looking into are **Rochdale Village** (2424 Haste St.) and the **Northside Co-op** (2526 and 2540 Le Conte Ave.), both of which are part co-op and part apartment complex. If you're not a student, you might get them to bend the rules at one of the larger co-ops, such as grimy **Cloyne Court** (2600 Ridge Rd., tel. 510/549–6300). Show desperation, share whatever you have on you, and you may be offered someone's floor space.

Berkeley's fraternities offer cheap summer lodging, if you can stand dirt, loud music, a plain room (just a bed and a desk), and the constant company of frat boys.

Berkeley's **fraternities** also rent rooms in the summer—and during the school year depending on space—as do some of the sororities (women can comfortably stay in the frats, too). Rents vary, but you can usually stay the whole summer for about $500. The group of frats and sororities that rent rooms changes, so stop by **102 Sproul Hall** (Sproul Plaza, at Bancroft Way and Telegraph Ave., tel. 510/642–5171) for an updated list of addresses and phone numbers. Most fraternities are southeast of campus, on and around Piedmont Avenue, Warring Street, and Channing Way. You can try calling them, but generally no one answers the house phone; you're better off just scouting the neighborhood on foot. Head east up Bancroft Way, turn right at Piedmont Avenue, and start your hunting. Fraternities often advertise by hanging a big sign on their house. When something catches your eye, knock on the door and ask for the house manager. Scope out the bathrooms and kitchens—one glance should tell you if the place is livable.

OAKLAND

Travelers concerned about price and safety should consider staying in San Francisco since Oakland's budget lodging scene is pretty bleak. Hotels are either geared toward executives with expense accounts, or they're in the middle of grimy, scary neighborhoods. And, sad to say, Oakland has no youth hostel. If you're desperate, there are faceless chain motels in downtown Oakland and near the airport with rooms for $50–$75 per night. If you're *really* desperate, there are a number of motels used for illicit, after-hours business transactions along **West MacArthur Boulevard,** near MacArthur BART in North Oakland. Those east of Telegraph Avenue are marginally safer, though women should not stay here alone. Among them, the **Regency Inn**

(3720 Telegraph Ave., at W. MacArthur Blvd., tel. and fax 510/652–9800) has mediocre singles for $35, doubles for $45.

➤ **UNDER $55 • Civic Center Lodge.** One of the few centrally located and cheap hotels in Oakland, this basic, no-frills hotel is right next to a highway and a boarded-up gas station but within easy reach of the waterfront, Lake Merritt, and downtown bars and restaurants. Singles cost $38 per night, doubles $48. *50 6th St., tel. 510/444–4139. From Lake Merritt BART, walk 3 blocks down Oak St. to 6th St., turn left. 32 rooms, all with bath.*

SPLURGE **Claremont Resort, Spa, and Tennis Club.** If you really want luxury, head into the Oakland-Berkeley hills for this striking, all-white palace that has been a favorite of the wealthy since the 1920s. The prices will stun you as much as the building does. Bay-view doubles go for $220, hill-side doubles for a mere $190. They sometimes offer weekend packages starting at $160 per night. *Ashby and Domingo Aves., tel. 510/843–3000, fax 5110/843–6239. 239 rooms, all with bath. Wheelchair access.*

CAMPING **Lake Chabot Regional Park.** Three campgrounds are perched above Lake Chabot in this park southeast of downtown Oakland. Tent sites in a pleasant wooded area are $13 per night, RV hookups are $19; you also have to pay a $5 reservation charge. The campground has showers and is close to hiking and biking trails (*see* Hiking and Biking, in Chapter 8). The lake is a popular spot for fishing, so try to reserve ahead in summer. Unfortunately, the nearest bus stop is 1½ miles from the park entrance. *Tel. 510/562–CAMP. From I-80, I-580 east to Redwood Road exit, turn left, follow Redwood Road 4½ mi to park gate (it's another 2½–3 mi to campgrounds).*

Marin County

Across the Golden Gate Bridge from San Francisco, Marin County is the home of scenic views, quaint B&Bs, and hot-tubbing former hippies who no longer believe that owning property is a form of theft. Unfortunately, hotel accommodations here aren't cheap. Your least expensive option is one of the area's many campgrounds. If you've got cash to spare, though, the **Bed and Breakfast Exchange of Marin** (tel. 415/485–1971) books brief or extended stays in private homes and B&Bs; expect to pay $55–$150 per night. They can also set four to six people up in a houseboat for about $225 per night. More enlightened accommodations can be found less than a mile from Stinson Beach, at the **Green Gulch Farm Zen Center** (1601 Shoreline Hwy., tel. 415/383–3134). Green Gulch offers meditation sessions and overnight stays that run $12–$15; this isn't for gawkers, but for those serious about beginning or continuing Zen practice. If you're interested in applying as a guest student, contact Katie Whitehead (*also see* Muir Beach, in Chapter 2).

ALONG U.S. 101

SAUSALITO Though tourists crowd Sausalito's streets during the day, all but the richest have to find somewhere else to spend the night. Luckily, an excellent hostel and free camping are only a 10-minute drive away.

➤ **UNDER $85 • Alta Mira Continental Hotel.** This Spanish-style hotel in the Sausalito hills offers amazing views of the bay, but you'll pay dearly for them. Doubles start at $80; rooms with a view are $115–$170. Even if you stay in one of the cheaper rooms, you can still take in the view from the hotel terrace. The stately rooms are tastefully decorated with antiques, and all come with a TV and telephone. *125 Bulkley Ave., tel. 415/332–1350, fax 415/331–3862. From U.S. 101, Sausalito exit, follow signs to Bridgeway, turn right at Princess Ave. (the 9th stoplight), continue 3 blocks. 29 rooms, all with bath. Reservations advised.*

➤ **HOSTEL • Golden Gate AYH-Hostel.** Built in 1907, this beautiful, friendly hostel is housed in the Marin Headlands in historic Ft. Barry. There's a communal kitchen, laundry room, tennis court, Ping-Pong table, pool table, and a common room with a fireplace. Dorm beds cost $12 per night, but a recently opened second building has "family rooms" that sleep up to four; couples may get their own room on slow nights. Membership is not required. Getting to the hostel by public transit is tricky, but well worth the effort. From San Francisco, catch Golden Gate Transit Bus 10 or 50 from the Transbay Terminal and ask to be let off at the bottom of the Alexander Avenue off-ramp. From here, it's a stiff 4-mile hike to the hostel. On Sundays only, Bus 76 goes from the Transbay Terminal all the way to the Marin Headlands Visitor Center, one block from the hostel. *Ft. Barry, Bldg. 941, tel. 415/331–2777. From U.S. 101, Alexander Ave. exit, cross under freeway, make first right after MARIN HEADLANDS sign, continue 1 mi, turn right on McCullough Rd., left on Bunker Rd., follow signs to visitor center (hostel is just up hill). 103 beds. No curfew, lockout 9:30–3:30. Reception open daily 7:30 AM–9:30 PM. Key deposit ($10).*

➤ **CAMPING** • **Marin Headlands.** Four free tent-camping areas are available in the headlands, which are part of the Golden Gate National Recreational Area and only a few miles north of San Francisco. **Hawkcamp** is the most primitive; entering entails a 3½-mile hike. Fires are not allowed here. Campers can drive right up to **Bicentennial,** the only campground with piped-in water. Backcountry permits are required; to reserve a site, call between 9:30 and noon no more than 90 days in advance. *Tel. 415/331–1540. Picnic tables, pit toilets.*

TIBURON AND ANGEL ISLAND Not surprisingly, chichi Tiburon has no cheap lodging. If you don't want to head to the Golden Gate Hostel a few miles south (*see above*), consider a ferry trip to Angel Island for a night of camping.

➤ **CAMPING** • **Angel Island State Park.** Get away from it all without losing sight of good old San Francisco. Nine showerless, primitive, sites ($10) are scattered around the island. Sites 3 and 4, with views of the Golden Gate Bridge, are the most popular; Sites 1 and 2, surrounded by pine trees and with a view of the East Bay, offer more privacy and shelter from the wind. Wherever you camp, prepare for a 2-mile hike. Reserve a few weeks ahead for a weekend stay; on weekdays, you can almost always get a site on the same day. For directions, *see* Tiburon and Angel Island, in Chapter 2. *Tel. 415/435–1915 (info) or 800/444–PARK (reservations). Barbecue grills, food lockers, picnic tables, pit toilets, running water.*

SAN RAFAEL San Rafael is Marin's most down-to-earth town and boasts the county's best nightlife, shops, and cafés. While the hotels here could hardly be called budget, they're more affordable than the options in the surrounding area.

➤ **UNDER $55** • **Panama Hotel.** The owner is terrific, the setting is perfect, the location is convenient, and—most amazing—the prices are reasonable. Rooms without bath start at $45 ($70–$110 with bath). Each room is individually decorated, some with canopy queen beds and some with claw-foot tubs. All but one comes with TV, and some of the higher-priced rooms offer kitchenettes and patios. The hotel's restaurant has a mouth-watering menu (lunch costs around $10, dinner $15–$20) and a beautiful outdoor area draped with wisteria. *4 Bayview St., tel. 415/457–3993 or 800/899–3993, fax 415/457–6240. From U.S. 101, Central San Rafael exit, left on 3rd St., left on B St., continue 4 blocks to where B St. becomes Bayview St. 15 rooms, 9 with bath. Reservations advised.*

➤ **UNDER $100** • **425 Mission.** An easy walk from Old San Rafael, this wood-shingled cottage offers homey rooms furnished with antiques, rosewood and wicker furniture, and the occasional claw-foot tub. You can hang out on the deck when the weather is nice, or lounge in the comfortable downstairs living room. Rooms cost $85 on weekdays and $95 on weekends, and include a gourmet breakfast and use of a hot tub in the backyard. If you stay awhile, the innkeeper will do your laundry for free, just like Mom. *425 Mission Ave., tel. 415/453–1365. From U.S. 101, Central San Rafael exit, continue 5 blocks to Mission Ave., turn right. 4 rooms, 2 with bath. Reservations advised.*

➤ **CAMPING** • **China Camp State Park.** The trappings of civilization fade away as you enter the 1,600-acre China Camp State Park, 4 miles northeast of San Rafael. Here you can pitch your tent at one of 30 walk-in campsites near San Pablo Bay. The sites aren't far from the parking lot, or from each other, but they're well sheltered by oak trees. And you get hot water to boot. Sites are $15 per night ($12 off-season), and parking costs an additional $3. Call Destinet (tel. 800/444–PARK) to reserve. *Tel. 415/456–0766. From U.S. 101, N. San Pedro Rd. exit, follow signs. Fire pits, flush toilets, showers. Closed Nov.–Mar.*

COASTAL HIGHWAY 1

MARIN COUNTY

MT. TAMALPAIS The Pantoll campsites (*see below*), near the Mt. Tamalpais Ranger Station and many trailheads, are perfect for hard-core hikers who want to make tracks up and down the mountain. The Steep Ravine cabins, perched along the rocky coast, are perfect for solitude seekers who want to get away from it all (including roads and flush toilets).

➤ **CAMPING** • **Pantoll.** Fifteen campsites, relatively close together but well sheltered by trees, are about a 100-yard walk from the parking lot of the Pantoll Ranger Station in Mt. Tamalpais State Park and cost only $15 per night. A 16th site ($3 per person) is reserved for those without a car. All sites are available on a first-come, first-served basis. *Tel. 415/388–2070. From Hwy. 1, follow signs to Mt. Tamalpais State Park, then Panoramic Hwy. to Pantoll Ranger Station. Drinking water, flush toilets.*

Steep Ravine Campground and Cabins. Off Highway 1 in Mt. Tamalpais State Park, Steep Ravine has six walk-in campsites for $9 per night, $7 off-season. Cabins with two double beds and two small bunk beds, as well as an indoor wood stove and outdoor barbecue, cost $30 per night. If you can deal with a pit toilet, this place is absolutely unbeatable—just you and a few other guests with an endless view of the dramatic coastline. Unfortunately, Steep Ravine is not an unknown gem, so cabins are booked well in advance, except in winter. *Tel. 800/444–PARK for reservations. From U.S. 101, Stinson Beach/Hwy. 1 exit, follow Hwy. 1 until you see signs.*

STINSON BEACH Stinson Beach is full of B&Bs that are quaint in every detail except price. Expect to pay upwards of $90 a night. The only semicheap option is the **Stinson Beach Motel** (3416 Hwy. 1, tel. 415/868–1712), which has inviting doubles with private bath ($60–$80) set around a shady garden.

POINT REYES In addition to its excellent hostel, **Point Reyes National Seashore** has four free campgrounds, open to backpackers only, in isolated wilderness areas. You may have to hike in as far as 6 miles to reach one, but if you could drive there, it wouldn't be nature anymore, would it?

➤ **HOSTEL** • **Point Reyes AYH-Hostel.** Eight miles west of the Point Reyes Visitor Center, this hostel is popular with both foreign travelers and local college kids. It makes a great base camp as there are hundreds of hiking trails nearby. The two common rooms have wood-burning stoves and plentiful reading material. Dorm beds cost $10 per night for members, $12 for nonmembers. Reservations are advised; if you want them to hold a bed, call and use your Visa or MasterCard or mail them a check. *Mailing address: Box 247, Point Reyes Station, CA 94956, tel. 415/663–8811. From Hwy. 1, head left (west) on Bear Valley Rd. (1 block beyond stop sign in Olema), continue 1½ mi, turn left at LIGHTHOUSE/BEACHES/HOSTEL sign, left after 6 mi onto Crossroads Rd. 44 beds. Curfew 10 PM, lockout 9:30–4:30. Reception open daily 7:30–9:30 and 4:30–9:30. Kitchen, linen rental, parking.*

➤ **CAMPING** • To reserve a campsite up to two months in advance in Point Reyes, call the **Point Reyes Visitor Information Center** (tel. 415/663–1092) weekdays between 9 and noon. Trails to the campgrounds leave from the visitor center, which is on the entrance road (turn left off Hwy. 1 just past Olema on Bear Valley Road). All sites have picnic tables, pit toilets, food storage lockers, a charcoal grill, and running water.

Coast Camp is a 2-mile hike from the youth hostel parking lot (*see above*) or an 8-mile trek from the visitor center, but you'll sleep within a stone's throw (100 yards) of the ocean at any of the 14 sites. People tend to avoid **Glenn Camp** because it's 5 miles from the nearest road, but it's in a quiet valley surrounded by trees, perfect for those who want to get away from civilization. The two group and 12 individual sites at **Sky Camp** are the most popular; they're a 2½-mile walk from the visitor center and 2 miles from the nearest parking area. The campground is perched on a small mountain ridge with an outstanding view. For the true misanthrope, **Wildcat Camp,** a stiff 6½ miles from the nearest road, has seven sites on a bluff, just a short walk from the beach. Privacy is never a problem.

Samuel P. Taylor State Park. Six miles east of Point Reyes on Sir Francis Drake Boulevard, 60 campsites are available for $12–$16 per night (hike/bike sites cost $3 per person). They feature—blessing of all blessings—hot showers, at 50¢ for five minutes. Reservations can be made through Destinet (tel. 800/444–PARK); during summer, even weeknights are booked up. Think about hiking up to Barnaby Peak (4–5 hours round-trip)—it's a beautiful campground and redwood grove, not as overrun as Muir Woods. Golden Gate Transit Bus 65 stops at the park on weekends and holidays (see Getting In, Out, and Around, in Chapter 1). *Tel. 415/488–9897. From U.S. 101, take Sir Francis Drake Blvd. about 15 mi west.*

South Bay

The area along U.S. 101 resembles many other parts of the United States; strip malls, fast food, and chain motels abound. You'll find the latter at just about every freeway off-ramp, and double rooms invariably cost $50–$70 per night. For a cheap weekend getaway, the San Mateo County Coast has two excellent hostels and several secluded campgrounds. For longer stays, consult Santa Clara County's free weekly newspaper *Metro*. It's available in cafés, bookstores, and sidewalk vending machines and lists summer sublets and long-term rentals. College bulletin boards, such as the one in Tressider Student Union at Stanford University in Palo Alto, are also promising places to look for apartments.

PALO ALTO

Although Palo Alto isn't exactly a mecca of budget accommodations, it's probably the most happening place to stay in the South Bay—a healthy number of pricey restaurants, bars, and cafés cater to Stanford University students. Most of Palo Alto's budget motels are along **El Camino Real.**

➤ **UNDER $55 • Coronet Motel.** Traffic on El Camino Real makes it noisy, but the Coronet wins points for location and value (there's even a tiny pool). It's only a few blocks from Stanford University, and Stanford Shopping Center is a short drive away. Doubles are $50, and the rooms—some with kitchenettes—are comfortable, if not exactly modern. *2455 El Camino Real, btw California Ave. and Page Mill Rd., tel. 415/326–1081. From U.S. 101, Embarcadero Rd. exit west, turn left on El Camino Real. 21 rooms, all with bath.*

➤ **UNDER $100 • Cowper Inn.** This Victorian B&B is the perfect place for your folks to stay. The spacious, airy rooms are filled with antiques, and all have phones and cable TV. Doubles start at $60 with shared bath, $105 with private bath (breakfast included). Mom and Dad can sip sherry and munch on almonds in the parlor before taking you out for an expensive dinner. *705 Cowper St., at Forest Ave., tel. 415/327–4475, fax 415/329–1703. From U.S. 101, University Ave. west 2–3 mi, turn left on Cowper St., continue 2 blocks. 14 rooms, 12 with bath. Reservations advised.*

HOSTELS **Hidden Villa Hostel.** This is an actual working farm—complete with animals and organic gardens. Set in a 1,500-acre canyon in the Los Altos Hills between Palo Alto and San Jose, the hostel offers easy access to hiking trails and peaceful dirt roads. Large, rustic dorm-style cabins dot the canyon, and each cabin has communal bathroom facilities. HI members pay $10 per night, nonmembers $13. There's no curfew, but lockout occurs 9:30–4:30. *26870 Moody Rd., Los Altos, tel. 415/949–8648. From San Francisco, I-280 south past Palo Alto to El Monte/Moody Rd. exit, turn right on El Monte Ave., left on Moody Rd. (at stop sign), continue 1.7 mi. Or, from San Francisco, SamTrans Bus 7F from Transbay Terminal (see Getting In, Out and Around, in Chapter 1) to Palo Alto, then SamTrans Bus 35 to Foothill College; walk 2 mi to hostel. 35 beds. Reception open daily 8–9:30 and 4:30–9:30. Closed June–Aug.*

Sanborn Park Hostel. This is one of the most attractive hostels in California, perfectly situated for avid hikers and easily reached by public transit. The main cottage, a log cabin that dates from 1908, is surrounded by the dense 300-acre redwood forest of Sanborn Park—also home to a nearby nature museum. Hostelers stay in a large hall and have access to a rec room, volleyball court, grill, laundry facilities, and the standard HI kitchen—all for $9 per night for members or $11 for nonmembers. It's a busy place, but they try to find room for anyone who shows up. You need to bring your own food; the only restaurants and grocery stores are 4 miles away in downtown Saratoga. *15808 Sanborn Rd., Saratoga, tel. 408/741–0166. From San Francisco, I–280 south to Saratoga/Sunnyvale exit, turn right, go 5½ mi to Hwy. 9, turn right (toward Big Basin), go 2½ mi, turn left at SANBORN SKYLINE COUNTY PARK sign, go 1 mi, and turn right. Or, from Sunnyvale CalTrain station, Santa Clara County Transit Bus 54 or 27 to Saratoga post office; call hostel for ride. 39 beds. Curfew 11 PM, lockout 9–5. Reception open daily 5 PM–11 PM. Sheet rental (50¢). Wheelchair access.*

SAN MATEO COUNTY COAST

The desolate coastline south of San Francisco has some of the area's most striking scenery. **Half Moon Bay,** the largest and most centrally located town, is not the best choice for accommodations, since all of its offerings are quite expensive. Instead, head for one of two gorgeous hostels—either of which could be the best lodging deal in the Bay Area.

PACIFICA AND MONTARA This area features a number of generic budget motels that are virtually indistinguishable from each other. The hostels are far more memorable.

➢ **UNDER $60** • **Marine View Motel.** With roomy doubles ($55) that include enough carpeted floor space for at least six, this run-down but acceptably clean motel is the best bet in Pacifica. It's an easy walk to the beach and the old town, but the noise from Highway 1 is slightly annoying. *2040 Francisco Blvd., Pacifica, tel. 415/355–2543. 12 rooms, all with bath. Wheelchair access.*

➢ **HOSTEL** • **Point Montara Lighthouse AYH-Hostel.** This functioning lighthouse and its adjoining hostel are perched on a cliff a half-mile south of Montara State Beach. As if that weren't enough, it has incredible views of the coastline and access to a beach and tide pools. Inside, there's a fireplace in the comfortable living room, a communal kitchen, dining area, and an outdoor redwood hot tub ($5 per person per hour, two-person minimum). Beds go for $12 per night ($14 for nonmembers), and everyone must perform a small chore. The range of guests is greater than at most hostels; expect to see anyone from locals on a weekend holiday to German travelers on a cross-country trek. Reservations can be made up to six months in advance with a night's deposit and are advised for summer weekends. *Hwy. 1, at 16th St., Montara, tel. 415/728–7177. From Daly City BART, SamTrans Bus 1L or 1C southbound; ask driver to let you off at 14th St. 45 beds. Curfew 11 PM, lockout 9:30–4:30. Reception open daily 7:30–9:30 and 4:30–9:30. Laundry.*

HALF MOON BAY If you can afford it, the **Old Thyme Inn** (779 Main St., tel. 415/726–1616), dating from 1899, is the nicest B&B in town. Each of its seven rooms is named for and decorated with a different herb, and each has an old-fashioned claw-foot bathtub. Some rooms also have a whirlpool or a fireplace. Rates range from $85–$165 per night on weekdays to $105–$220 on the weekends and include a hearty breakfast. The **San Benito House** (356 Main St., tel. 415/726–3425), built at the turn of the century, has 12 rooms, a beautiful backyard garden, and a pricey restaurant overlooking Main Street. Nightly rates are $60–$120 (depending on availability of bath) with a 20% weekday discount. If all else fails, a 20-room **Ramada Inn** (3020 Hwy. 1, tel. 415/726–9700 or 800/2–RAMADA) at the north end of town has doubles starting at $85 weekdays, $95 weekends, including breakfast.

➢ **UNDER $70** • **Cameron's Inn.** This tiny hotel on the southern outskirts of town has three clean, simple doubles that feel distinctly European. Big beds and fine-art prints lend some style to the rooms, all of which share a common bath. You'll hear big-rigs downshifting on the highway as you drift off, but at $60 on weekdays and $70 on weekends, it's about as cheap as you'll find anywhere in the area. *1410 S. Cabrillo Hwy. (Hwy. 1), tel. 415/726–5705.*

➢ **CAMPING** • **Half Moon Bay State Beach.** Because of its proximity to downtown, this place attracts teenage partiers and weekend-warrior types, especially during summer. You'll fall asleep to the sound of waves and arise to the smell of the sea, but it's hardly the great outdoors. Located at the base of a small sand dune, the 55 characterless sites cost $14 per night ($12 off-season); all sites are doled out on a first-come, first-served basis. *95 Kelly Ave., Half Moon*

Bay, tel. 415/726–8820. From Hwy. 1, Kelly Ave. west. Cold showers, fire pits, flush toilets, food lockers, picnic tables.

LA HONDA Outdoorsy types have four excellent choices of lodging in La Honda. There's a hostel that caters to backpackers, and three of the area's parks have campgrounds.

➢ **HOSTEL • Hiker's Hut.** This hostel in Sam McDonald County Park ($10 per night per person, $8 for Sierra Club members) has sleeping space for 14 (bring a sleeping bag). The Scandinavian A-frame cabin sits atop a ridge—a fairly steep 1½-mile hike from the parking lot. From the deck, you can see the ocean on a clear day. Reservations (which require a 50% check deposit) must be made well in advance, especially during summer weekends. Reserve through the Loma Prieta chapter of the Sierra Club (3921 E. Bayshore Rd., Palo Alto, CA 94303, tel. 415/390–8411). *For more info and directions to Sam McDonald County Park, see South Bay, in Chapter 2. Kitchen facilities, pit toilets.*

➢ **CAMPING • Memorial County Park** offers 135 quiet sites ($14) with picnic tables, fire pits, and hot showers in a thick old-growth forest. Although popular with car campers on summer weekends, the campground is sparsely visited at other times. Sites are allotted on a first-come, first-served basis. In **Portola Redwood State Park,** the 53 "family" and seven hike-in sites ($15–$16) see little light in their cool berth beneath the redwoods. The family sites have running water, showers, fire pits, and picnic tables. Reserve through Destinet (tel. 800/444–PARK). **Pescadero Creek County Park** has 15 hike-in sites ($7), located in dense second-growth forest along the river. Contact the rangers at Portola Redwood State Park (tel. 415/948–9098) to secure a spot. For directions to these parks and info on exploring them, *see* San Mateo County Coast, South Bay, in Chapter 2.

PESCADERO This pristine town overlooks miles of unblemished coastline; an enchanting hostel and peaceful campgrounds are situated among the redwoods.

➢ **HOSTEL • Pigeon Point Lighthouse Youth Hostel.** Perched on a small bluff 5 miles south of Pescadero State Beach are four bungalow-style dorms, including an outdoor, bluff-side hot tub ($3 per person per half hour). Free tours of the historic lighthouse on the grounds are also available. One night in any of the 54 comfortable beds costs $11 ($14 for nonmembers); another $10 secures a private room for two. Bring your own food to cook in their kitchen. All guests must do a chore each day of their stay. The maximum stay is three nights. Bummer. *Pigeon Point Rd. and Hwy. 1, tel. 415/879–0633. From Daly City BART, take SamTrans Bus 1L to Half Moon Bay then SamTrans bus 96C. Curfew 11 PM, lockout 9:30–4:30. Reception open daily 7:30–9:30 and 4:30–9:30. Reservations advised. Wheelchair access.*

➢ **CAMPING •** Surprisingly few visitors venture to the 27 campsites ($17) and 18 hike-in sites ($7) in quiet **Butano State Park** (tel. 415/879–2040). The drive-in sites have fire rings, picnic tables, and food lockers. Reservations can be made through Destinet (tel. 800/444–PARK) up to eight weeks in advance, but are usually not necessary. None of the sites has showers, but, hey, welcome to the great outdoors. For directions to Butano and more info on the park, *see* San Mateo County Coast, South Bay, in Chapter 8.

THE GREAT OUTDOORS

8

By Mylah de la Rosa

Denizens of the Bay Area have cultivated a discriminating palate for the outdoors.
It's no surprise—many people choose to live in the Bay Area precisely because it's so easy to drive 15 minutes from the city and enjoy some of the most spectacular natural attractions this country has to offer. Those weary of battling traffic on their way to work may easily trade the quacking of car horns for the joyful honks of waterfowl at a nearby shoreline preserve, and the cool, moist woodlands of Marin Country are prime territory for hikers, bikers, horseback riders, and bird-watchers. On weekends this means you may have to fight for a view in Marin and Point Reyes. The afternoon breezes make San Francisco Bay ideal for windsurfing. And when the summer winds die down, you can put away your sail and dust off the surfboard for the winter waves. Rock climbers, in-line skaters, mountain bikers, and sea kayakers will have no trouble finding new challenges in the Bay Area. This is California, after all, where even Silicon Valley professionals surf more than the Internet.

Within the city, the numerous neighborhood parks and rec centers have a full range of pickup sports; from the same grassy knoll, you can observe a homeless person wrestle $5 from an unwitting chess opponent, and a hostile takeover by a corporate hoopster. Armchair athletes will want to nuke another bag of popcorn, as the Bay Area is fertile ground for spectator sports. Grab a beer and join the thousands of loyal fans following American and National League baseball, NFL football, NBA basketball, ice hockey, Major League soccer, and enthusiastic college sports rivalries. With so many sporting options and such a moderate climate, it's hard for Bay Area residents to think of excuses to stay inside.

A great place to get the inside scoop on the outdoors is **Outdoors Unlimited** (OU), a co-op fueled by funds from U.C. San Francisco and the community. OU volunteers teach everything from fly fishing to CPR, organize backpacking and cycling outings, lead moonlight kayak trips, and rent out top-notch equipment. While UCSF students have priority in signing up for some of the activities (which are thankfully inexpensive, and sometimes even free), the general public is welcome and well represented. The bulletin board and staff at OU are a great resource for all your recreation needs—even for hiking buddies. To receive their quarterly newsletter, send one stamped (55¢), self-addressed envelope to Outdoors Unlimited, Box 0234A, University of California, San Francisco 94143. *Office: 550 Parnassus Ave., at 3rd Ave., tel. 415/476–2078. Open Tues.–Thurs. 5 PM –8 PM, Mon. and Fri. 11 AM–1:30 PM.*

Berkeley's **Cal Adventures**—similar in scope to OU—reserves the best deals for U.C. students, but it's also a great resource for the East Bay community, with a wide variety of affordable outings and lessons in such sports as sailing, kayaking, wind surfing, backpacking, and rock climbing. Located on the U.C. campus, Cal Adventures rents equipment at low prices. Call for a brochure. *Recreational Sports Facility, 2301 Bancroft Way, tel. 510/642–4000 or 510/643–8029. Open Mon.–Thurs. 10–6, Fri. 10–7.*

Another East Bay resource for competition as well as recreation is the **Cal Sport Club Program.** Individual clubs include boxing, fencing, ultimate Frisbee, and cycling. Membership eligibility varies from club to club—call ahead and check it out. *Recreational Sports Facility, 2301 Bancroft Way, Suite 4420, on the U.C. Berkeley campus, tel. 510/643–8024.*

Environmental Traveling Companions (ETC) is a nonprofit organization that leads sea-kayaking, river-rafting, and cross-country skiing expeditions in and around the Bay Area for people with special needs—physical and developmental disabilities, financial hardship—as well as the population at large (*see* Resources for People With Disabilities, in Chapter 1). *Fort Mason Center, Bldg. C, tel. 415/474–7662.*

The best places to stock up on pamphlets, books, and maps are **Rand McNally** (595 Market St., at 2nd. St., S.F., tel. 415/777–3131), the Oakland **Sierra Club Bookstore** (6014 College Ave., tel. 510/658–7470), and the Berkeley **REI** (1338 San Pablo Ave., tel. 510/527–4140), which also offers free wilderness lectures, book signings, and slide presentations. An invaluable resource for folks sans car is **Transit Outdoors,** a free guide to accessing Bay Area parks and trailheads via public transportation. The map, put out by the Bay Area Open Space Council, is available at public libraries and park districts as well as on the Web (http://server.berkeley.edu/Transit/Outdoors/).

League Sports and Pickup Games

For city folk, pickup games and organized sports leagues represent the most convenient and civilized way to relieve the stress of urban living. You can join pickup games on virtually every court and field in the Bay Area, though skill levels and rules vary by location. Weekends draw the largest crowds, but warm weekdays and long evenings generally guarantee activity. Contact a local community center, park department, or YMCA to get involved with activities in your neighborhood.

For women's sports info try "The Women's Sports Page," published in Berkeley (Box 5187, Berkeley 94705, tel. 510/655–6750), or call the Women's Sports Connection in San Francisco (tel. 415/241–8879).

The **San Francisco Urban Professionals Athletic League** offers two indoor basketball leagues and four indoor volleyball leagues, including one coed and one gay/lesbian league. The end of each season is marked with barbecues and a competitive all-star game. For more information, call 415/431–6339. The **Bay Area Outreach and Recreation Program** (830 Bancroft Way, Berkeley, tel. 510/849–4663) sponsors athletics for people with physical disabilities, including motorized- and manual-chair basketball and soccer.

BASKETBALL Pickup games are almost universally male, and competition levels vary dramatically. In other words, peruse neighborhood courts before lacing up your high-tops. For information on city leagues, contact the **San Francisco Recreation and Park Department** (tel. 415/753–7027). Nancy Dito at the **Eureka Valley Recreation Center** (100 Collingwood St., 1 block from 18th St., tel. 415/554–9528) is an excellent source of information on women's league activity in the city.

In the East Bay, the **City of Berkeley Recreation Department** (2180 Milvia St., at Center St. in City Hall, tel. 510/644–6530) offers men's and women's leagues January–March. The **Oakland Recreation Department** (1520 Lakeside Dr., at 14th St., tel. 510/238–3494) also offers winter and spring leagues for men, and spring leagues for women.

➤ **WHERE TO PLAY** • The following San Francisco courts usually get going weekday afternoons and weekend mornings between 8 and 11. **Grattan Playground** (Alma and Stanyan Sts.), near Golden Gate Park, sees casual play weekday afternoons around 3:30; weekends draw larger crowds and more ferocious competition. In the Marina, the popular **Moscone Recreation Center** (Chestnut and Laguna Sts.) has courts with night lighting and unforgiving double rims. Weekends tend to be a zoo. The skill level varies at the **Chinese Playground** (Broadway and Larkin St.), but it's among the city's few lit courts, and people are almost always here in the evenings. Games at the **Potrero Hill Recreation Center** (Arkansas and 22nd Sts.) get highly competitive, especially Monday and Thursday nights. Four-on-four games begin early on weekends at the small courts of Noe Valley's **James Lick Middle School** (Clipper and Castro Sts.). The small courts in the Panhandle of Golden Gate Park, between Oak and Fell streets, have competitive games going all the time. The Eureka Valley Recreation Center (*see above*) hosts half-court play for women on Monday nights, and Wednesdays the full gym is off-limits to the y-chromosome for "Women's Night."

In North Berkeley, the short court at **Live Oak Park** (Shattuck Ave. and Berryman St.) hosts weekend three-on-three games, but the wait can be unbearable. A more intimidating game goes on at **Ohlone Park** (Hearst St., near California St.). In South Berkeley, the court at **People's Park** (Haste St., btw Telegraph Ave. and Bowditch St.) is always hopping, though the skill level swings wildly. If you *really* want to get serious, you'll find competitive players on the courts at the **Recreational Sports Facility** on the U.C. Berkeley campus (2301 Bancroft Way, tel. 510/643–8038), but you'll have to shell out $8 a day to play.

SOCCER The **Golden Gate Women's Soccer League** has four divisions in the East Bay, Marin County, and San Francisco. To join either the fall or spring season, contact Ashley Young (tel. 510/658–8337). In the highly competitive men's **San Francisco Football Soccer League,** the players are a truly international crew. The season runs September–May, with six divisions playing citywide on Sundays. **Sunset Soccer Supply** (3214 Irving St., near 33rd Ave., S.F., tel. 415/753–2666) has a list of coaches' phone numbers and game locations; tryouts are required. The high-caliber **Latin American Soccer League** (tel. 510/732–6804), with half as many divisions, fills in the summer gap for men's soccer. Contact the **San Francisco Coed Recreational Soccer League** (tel. 415/330–8900) for coed league information.

➤ **WHERE TO PLAY** • Sunday mornings, year-round, a crowd gathers at Golden Gate Park's **Polo Field** (Middle Dr. W, near Martin Luther King Jr. Dr.) for impromptu soccer games, where the almost exclusively male players represent a wide range of skill levels. League teams square off at **Beach Chalet,** also at the western edge of the park. You'll find women's teams there on Saturdays and men's on Sundays. Wednesdays after work, postcollege footsters play at the **Marina Green** (Marina Blvd. and Fillmore St.), where lack of night lighting means less play on shorter winter days.

While San Francisco's got it going on with league teams, Berkeley's the winner when it comes to pickup games. The field, a.k.a. Dwight/Derby (off Dwight Way, east of Warring St.), at the top of Berkeley's **Clark Kerr Campus,** has coed pickup games weekday evenings, women's (usually)

Don't Call It Hacky Sack

San Francisco is home to the Bay Area Footbag League (BAFL)—the world's largest— and is one of the best places to acquire or improve your footbag proficiency. There are two kinds of play: "Freestyle" involves circle kicking where you pass the bag around with varying levels of success, while "net" is a competitive game involving getting the bag over a net (duh) with scoring similar to that of volleyball. Call the BAFL Footbag Hotline (tel. 415/308–KICK) for info on upcoming kicks, events, tournaments, and the yearly benefit for cystic fibrosis, or contact Steve Goldberg (tel. 408/974–8478).

Don't know where to play? All ability levels are welcome (and represented) at the pickup games held Sundays 1–5 in Golden Gate Park on JFK Drive just east of the Conservatory of Flowers. You'll also find footbaggers Tuesdays 3–5 at Stanford University on the White Plaza in front of the post office.

Tuesday or Thursday evenings, and mostly men's on weekend mornings. A good place to come if you're looking for fun rather than competition, the scene here quiets down when the university is not in session. Down the hill, **Willard Park** (Derby St., btw Hillegass Ave. and Regent St.) usually has Friday afternoon pickup games from 2 or 3 until 6. Look for a friendly coed game (i.e., varied ages and skill levels) Tuesday, Thursday, and Friday noon to 1 at **San Pablo Field** (btw Mabel, Russell, Park, and Ward Sts.). Serious, testosterone-charged pickup games take place weekdays at 5 and weekends at 4 on **Kleeberger Field's** AstroTurf (Piedmont Ave., at Stadium Rim Way).

ULTIMATE FRISBEE The rules of ultimate combine those of football and soccer, except that ultimate is a noncontact sport with no referees, and players call their own fouls—truly the most democratic game in all of the United States. The best way to get the scoop on leagues, club teams, and tournaments is to go to the pickup games at the parks listed below, or call the **Cal Sport Club Program** (*see* chapter introduction, *above*). For East Bay resources, your best bets are Ken Frauwirth (tel. 510/643–9196), who organizes informal games, and the **Ultimate Frisbee Hotline** (tel. 510/464–4494), a recording of pickup game times and locations.

➤ **WHERE TO PLAY** • **Sharon Meadow,** off Kezar Drive in Golden Gate Park, sometimes sees coed pickup games of up to 40 people. Frisbee fanatics gather here every Tuesday and Thursday evening while it's still light out and on late mornings every weekend. **Julius Kahn Playground** (W. Pacific Ave., btw Spruce and Locust Sts.), near the southeast corner of the Presidio, hosts pickup games Wednesday evenings and Saturday mornings. In Berkeley, pickup ultimate follows soccer at 6 on Fridays in **Willard Park** (*see* Soccer, *above*). Other popular places to play in the East Bay are **Cedar Rose Park** (btw Cedar and Rose Sts.), which hosts games Sunday mornings at 11 and summer Thursdays at 6 PM, and **Oakland Tech High School** (4351 Broadway, at 43rd St.).

VOLLEYBALL The **Central YMCA** (220 Golden Gate Ave., at Leavenworth St., tel. 415/885–0460) and the Richmond district's **S.F. Volleyball Association** (tel. 415/931–6385) have coed leagues nearly year-round. Roger Underhill (tel. 415/931–6385) is the man to contact about these leagues and others. He can also send you an informational newsletter ($10) that lists all the leagues and spaces for open play. To join a women's volleyball league in San Francisco, contact the **San Francisco Recreation and Park Department** (*see* Basketball, *above*), which sponsors several leagues for different skill levels; the season runs from October to mid-December.

The **City of Berkeley Recreation Department** (*see* Basketball, *above*) organizes a coed league for advanced and recreational players. **City Beach Sports and Recreation Center** (4701 Doyle St., at 47th St., tel. 510/428–1221) in Emeryville offers some serious choices: Five levels of play in men, and "reverse" coed leagues (three men, three women, playing on a women's net), made up of teams of two, four, five, or six people. They have three hard courts and two sand, all indoors.

➤ **WHERE TO PLAY** • On weekends in San Francisco, people set up their own nets at the **Marina Green** (*see* Soccer, *above*) and nearby at the **Moscone Recreation Center** (*see* Basketball, *above*). At both locations you'll usually find high-skill two-on-two games. Also intimidating are the six-on-six weekend games at several spots along JFK Drive in **Golden Gate Park.** You can rent nets for $13 for the weekend at **Outdoors Unlimited** (*see* chapter introduction, *above*).

The S.F. Recreation and Park Department hosts friendly open play 8 PM Tuesday and Thursday nights (Monday during summer) at **Kezar Pavilion** (Stanyan and Waller Sts.), and Tuesday and Wednesday nights at **Potrero Hill Recreation Center** (*see* Basketball, *above*). Kezar Pavilion also hosts Saturday women's games at noon, 2, and 4.

In the East Bay, **People's Park** (*see* Basketball, *above*) has two outdoor sand courts, but you may have to fight for your right to play. Pickup games take place Tuesday night at the asphalt court in **Live Oak Park** (*see* Basketball, *above*). Players also set up on the grass in **Ohlone Park** (Hearst Ave., btw. Sacramento Ave. and Milvia St.) and goof around Saturday morning. For $5, summers only, you can take part in open play in Emeryville at **City Beach** (*see above*). Games take place weekdays 11–2, Fridays 5–11, and Sundays 5–9. Tournaments take place most Saturdays 10–6.

Hiking and Biking

The Bay Area is punctuated by an impressive array of hiking and biking spots, where one can easily escape, if just for an afternoon. The notoriously hilly Bay Area provides some of the nation's best testing ground for climbing machines, both human and mechanical. Unfortunately, there's intense competition for this prime real estate: Many hikers see bikers as a threat to their safety and to the land. The controversy has grown into a fight for control of state parkland, and bikers seem to be losing the battle. Bikes have been banned from most single-track trails in the Bay Area, leaving only fire roads for pedaling.

If you want to hit the trail with just your feet, contact the **Golden Gate Hikers,** sponsored by Hostelling International. You don't have to be an HI member to hike—just bring a buck for each event, a bag lunch, and a $3–$5 carpool fee. For free information on upcoming hikes, write to 1717 Cabrillo St., San Francisco 94121, or call the **Hikers' Hotline** (tel. 415/550–6321). At **Outdoors Unlimited** (*see* chapter introduction, *above*), in true co-op spirit, all of the hiking trips are free—save the cost of transportation. Anyone may sign up on the trip sheet posted at the OU office (550 Parnassus Ave., tel. 415/476–2078) up to 11 days prior to a scheduled jaunt. The **Sierra Club** also sponsors hikes all over the Bay Area. They're free, though a donation may be requested, and carpoolers are expected to share gas, parking, and bridge tolls. Pick up a schedule at the Sierra Club Bookstore (*see* chapter introduction, *above*) or send a check for $4.50 (payable to the Sierra Club) to Chapter Schedule, 5237 College Avenue, Oakland 94618.

Northern Californians have the dubious distinction of having reinvented the wheel with the creation of the mountain bike. If you want to rub spokes with other cyclists on a planned recreational ride, check out the calendar of events in the free monthly *Northern California Bicyclist,* available at bike shops. The **Sierra Club** (*see above*) organizes group rides on terrains that range from farmland to challenging hills. You need at least a 10-speed bike for all but the most level routes, and you must show up with a helmet. Pick up their activities schedule for a list of planned rides. The **Bicycling Group** co-op organizes rides about once a month with an emphasis on social as well as physical activity; check out the bulletin board at **Outdoors Unlimited** (*see above*) for specifics.

EQUIPMENT RENTAL **Pedal Revolution** (3085 21st St., at So. Van Ness Ave., tel. 415/641-1264) in the Mission sells used bikes and parts at low prices, *and* they donate all their proceeds to Youth Industry, which provides vocational training for the disadvantaged. In San Francisco, **Park Cyclery** (1865 Haight St., at Stanyan St., tel. 415/751–RENT) rents mountain bikes for $5 an hour or $25 a day. If you're renting in the East Bay, you can hook up with the friendly, knowledgeable folks at **Missing Link Bicycle Co-op** (1988 Shattuck Ave., Berkeley, tel. 510/843–7471), who will rent you a mountain bike for $25 a day and then load you down with biking info. Across the bay in Marin, **Wheel Escapes** (30 Liberty Ship Way, No. 210, Sausalito, tel. 415/332–0218) rents mountain bikes for $6 an hour or $23 a day.

SAN FRANCISCO

HIKING The **Coastal Trail** follows 9 miles of San Francisco's shoreline, from the cliffs near Golden Gate Bridge over dirt roads, onto residential sidewalks, around craggy headlands, and along the beach all the way down to Fort Funston.

Begin at the **Golden Gate Bridge** toll plaza parking lot. Walk west underneath the toll plaza, turn left onto Merchant Road, and continue west to find the trailhead. After about 10 minutes you get your first hint of why this hike is not to be missed: The view takes in 200-foot cliffs, the Golden Gate Bridge, and the Marin Headlands all at once. The trail then heads inland; when the path ends on Lincoln Boulevard, take the dirt road to the right that leads to **Baker Beach.** Enjoy the sandy dunes and salty air as you forge ahead in a westerly direction; cross the parking lot and head into the forest (keep to the right every time the trail forks). About five minutes later, the trail spits you out onto **El Camino Del Mar,** which travels through the extravagant **Seacliff** neighborhood. The dirt trail begins again on the right just where the houses end. The next 1.7 miles of the trail, passing through **Lands End,** takes you past San Francisco's wildest little corner, full of rocky cliffs, grassy fields, crashing surf, and magnificent views. Wise hikers will heed the warning signs and stay off the unstable cliffs, though a quick peek over the edge won't hurt (look for seal lions diving among the rocks). The dirt trail ends in a parking lot overlooking the **Sutro Baths**; head downhill past the aptly named **Cliff House** to **Ocean Beach**. From here to **Fort Funston** (4.7 mi south) you'll pass **Golden Gate Park** and the **San Francisco Zoo** on your left. If you make it all the way to Fort Funston, you'll find picnicking areas with great views of the ocean and local hang gliders practicing their craft. Once you hit Ocean Beach, you can catch a bus back to downtown at almost any cross street. For a map, call or visit the **Golden Gate National Recreation Area Visitor Center.** *West end of Point Lobos Ave., at the Great Highway, under the Cliff House, tel. 415/556–8642. From Montgomery BART, Bus M38 to Cliff House. Open daily 10–5.*

For a less strenuous and time-consuming urban stroll, try the **Golden Gate Promenade.** Starting from the same parking lot as the Coastal Trail, head east down the stairs that lead to **Fort Point National Historic Site** (*also see* Beaches, in Chapter 2). From here follow the 3.5-mile, mostly asphalt path, which traces the bay from Fort Point to the **Hyde Street Pier.** The popular jogging route takes you by the windsurfers at Crissy Field, around the yacht harbor, past Marina Green, and over the hill of Fort Mason to Aquatic Park near Fisherman's Wharf.

➤ **THE PRESIDIO** • For another intimate encounter with the native flora and fauna of San Francisco, try the Presidio (*see* Neighborhoods, in Chapter 2). Check out the 2-mile **Ecology Trail** that starts at the southeasternmost corner (Presidio Blvd. and Pacific Ave.) of the Presidio. The trail travels through cool, springy forest beds and provides an intimate introduction to some of San Francisco's most distinctive plant life, including the endangered, pink-flowered *Presidio clarkia* and the small, white-flowered *Marin duarte* flax. You can get more information on the Ecology Trail or the guided tours offered by the National Park Service at the **Presidio Visitor Information Center.** *Montgomery St., Bldg. 102, tel. 415/556–0865. Open daily 10–5.*

BIKING San Francisco can be a tough city to ride in; you've got cars, jaywalkers, cable-car tracks, one-way streets, and thigh-straining hills. But you also have an incredible variety of scenery within a relatively small area and less smog than most big cities. If you plan on doing a lot of riding in the city, take a look at the *San Francisco Biking/Walking Guide* ($3) that shows street grades and bike-friendly routes (*see* Getting In, Out, and Around, By Bike, in Chapter 1). For those who take a more political interest in bike riding, a group called **Critical Mass** sweeps through the city once a month in a show of grass-roots support for alternative means of transportation. Everyone is welcome and encouraged to join them in their effort to get people out of cars and onto bikes. For more specific information on the location and time, *see* Getting In, Out, and Around, By Bike, in Chapter 1.

The following 21-mile ride takes you through Golden Gate Park, into the Presidio, across the Golden Gate Bridge, and along the coast. Start at the west end of Golden Gate Park, where **John F. Kennedy Drive** hits the Great Highway. Follow JFK Drive along a slight incline to the east end of the park, turn left on **Conservatory Road,** left again on **Arguello Boulevard,** exit the park, and head through residential neighborhoods and onto the curvy, downhill roads of the **Presidio.** Hang a right on Moraga Avenue, then take another right onto **Presidio Boulevard** for a quick tour of the historic former military base. Make a hard left onto **Lincoln Boulevard** almost immediately; it leads to the windy view area/toll plaza of the Golden Gate Bridge, where signs tell you how to cross according to the time and day of the week. When you return, follow Lincoln Boulevard west; it turns into **El Camino del Mar** and runs through the beautiful, grand **Seacliff** neighborhood. At the Palace of Legion of Honor, the road veers right and becomes **Legion of Honor Drive** before dumping you back onto **Clement Street.** Turn right on Clement, and when it dead-ends, take **Point Lobos Avenue** past the **Cliff House** back to the Great Highway, where you can either collapse on the beach for some well-earned rest, continue down the coast, or head back into Golden Gate Park.

EAST BAY

The extensive **East Bay Regional Park District** (tel. 510/562–PARK) spans two counties, includes more than 75,000 acres of parkland, and provides a varied terrain of dark redwood forests, blustery hills with ocean views, lakes, and grassy fields. At any one of six visitor centers you can get free maps, and for one well-spent dollar, you can own the "Regional Parks" brochure; it includes information on all the parks and attractions, including the 31-mile **Skyline Trail**, which connects the six East Bay regional parks running through the Berkeley–Oakland hills. From the northern trailhead in **Wildcat Canyon Park,** the trail snakes south through **Tilden Regional Park** (*see below*); **Sibley Volcanic National Reserve,** with its volcanic dikes and new-age pagan stone circles; **Huckleberry Botanic Regional Reserve,** known for its endangered and rare plant life, such as the pallid manzanita, which only grows two places in the world; and **Redwood Regional Park** (*see below*). It finally reaches the southern trail terminus at **Anthony Chabot Regional Park.** Parking and admission to all East Bay parks is free unless otherwise noted.

TILDEN Named after Major Charles Lee Tilden, first president of the park district board, Tilden Park contains 2,078 acres of eucalyptus trees and rolling hills, filled with hikers, cyclists, picnickers, and poison oak. As in most Bay Area parks, mountain bikes are limited to the fire trails.

To reach Tilden Park, take University Avenue east from I–80 to Oxford Street; go left on Oxford, right on Rose, and left on Spruce to the top of the hill. Cross Grizzly Peak Boulevard, make an immediate left on Canon Drive, and follow the signs. From Berkeley BART, AC Bus 67 gets you as far as Spruce and Grizzly Peak on weekdays, and directly to **Lake Anza** on weekends. Summers, AC Bus 65 will transport both you and your bike from Berkeley BART to the top of Spruce Street at Grizzly Peak. To reach **Inspiration Point** by car from University Avenue, turn left on Oxford Street, right on Rose Street, and left on Spruce Street. Follow Spruce to the top of the hill, then turn right on Wildcat Canyon Road; the Inspiration Point parking lot is on your left after about 15 minutes. Stop by the **Environmental Education Center** (tel. 510/525–2233) at the north end of the park for maps and info, or call 510/562–7275 to speak with a ranger.

➤ **HIKING** • Tilden contains two of the highest points in the East Bay: **Volmer Peak** (1,913 feet) to the south and **Wildcat Peak** (1,250 feet) to the north. The hike to Wildcat Peak from **Inspiration Point** is just a moderate sweat-breaker. In fact, the trail, called **Nimitz Way,** is 4½ miles of wheelchair-accessible road. The hike takes a good two hours, during which you'll have plenty of time to absorb views of the bay and of the San Pablo and Briones reservoirs. Nimitz Way is a better bet than most of Tilden's poorly maintained dirt trails, where poison oak and brambles run rampant.

You can disentangle yourself from the overgrown trails by heading to the central part of Tilden Park where it's more open and grassy. Starting at the Lake Anza parking lot, head northeast on the **Lake Anza Trail,** which encircles the lake. When you reach the far northeast corner of the lake, look for the **Wildcat Gorge Trail** on your left. The initial steep descent past a century-old springhouse is no indication of things to come: The trail tunnels through a wide, rocky gorge but eventually rises to 80 feet above the creek that carved it. Continue for a half-mile until the trail forks. To the right, the **Curran Trail** rises sharply for .7 mile to Inspiration Point. Otherwise, the Wildcat Gorge Trail, one of the nicest in Tilden, continues on through groves of California bay laurels. About .3 mile up the trail on your right, you'll pass a hill with a practically vertical path upward (this isn't on the official Tilden map). At the top of the hill you'll have a 360° view of the park. Return to the Wildcat Gorge Trail and backtrack to Lake Anza for an easy to moderate 1½-hour hike.

The moderate 1½-hour, 800-foot climb through woods and fields to the top of Wildcat Peak begins at the Environmental Education Center: Head east on **Laurel Canyon Trail,** cross the fire road, continue uphill, and turn left onto the **Wildcat Peak Trail.** A turnoff to the right leads all the way to the top, where you can look out over Oakland, San Francisco, and Marin. Head back down the way you came, turn right onto Wildcat Peak Trail, and go left on the **Sylvan Trail,** which leads back to the nature center.

➤ **BIKING** • To escape the asphalt obstacle course of Berkeley's streets, take this strenuous 7-mile loop along the ridge of the Berkeley Hills and into Tilden Park. From the intersection of **Grizzly Peak Boulevard** and **Spruce Street** in North Berkeley, head south up Grizzly Peak Boulevard. This is the hardest part of the ride; the winding, steep street at times has only a narrow shoulder and can be hairy. Not far beyond the two lookouts, make a left on **South Park**

Drive, which takes you down through Tilden Park and past several picnic grounds. The street dead-ends at **Wildcat Canyon Road**; go left and ride over rolling hills past Lake Anza, back to the intersection with Grizzly Peak Boulevard. Taking this loop in the opposite direction involves potentially dangerous sharp curves and limited visibility. Spruce Street is the main access road to Grizzly Peak Boulevard north of town; **Tunnel Road,** which goes up into the hills past the Caldecott Tunnel, is the main access road to the south.

A beautiful, moderately strenuous 13½-mile loop through both Tilden and Wildcat Canyon Park begins just west of the Inspiration Point parking lot (*see above*). Head down the rocky **Meadows Canyon Trail,** which starts to the left of the paved Nimitz Trail; when you come to **Loop Road** hang a left, which will lead you to the **Environmental Education Center.** On the west side of the EEC, pick up **Wildcat Creek Trail,** and 6 miles farther head right on the **Belgum Trail** for a steep and often muddy ascent of just less than a mile. Make another right onto the **San Pablo Ridge Trail,** a steep uphill grade that affords spectacular views of the bay. From here, you can pick up the paved **Nimitz Way Trail,** which leads back to Inspiration Point. For a shorter ride that avoids the most challenging stretch of the Belgum Trail, turn right off Wildcat Creek Trail onto **Conlon Trail.**

WILDCAT CANYON REGIONAL PARK During summer and fall, Wildcat Canyon is the dried-up fire hazard adjoining Tilden to the north; it's often hard to tell where one park ends and the next begins. Nowhere near as developed or crowded as Tilden, the overall ambience of the park is that of a forgotten country back road, and you'll share the grassy hills and stunning views of San Pablo Bay with grazing cattle. The main entrance to Wildcat Canyon is on **Park Avenue** at the north end of the canyon; parking is readily available, and you'll also find a **park office** (tel. 510/236–1262). Residents of the surrounding neighborhood near the park entrance caution that the park can be unsafe for solo women in the evening. To get here, take I–80 to the Solano/Amador exit. Turn left on Amador, and at the second stop sign, turn right on McBryde Street, and follow signs to the park office from the first stop sign. From El Cerrito del Norte BART, take AC Bus 68, which stops a few hundred feet from the park entrance.

➢ **HIKING** • The best trail loop is a moderate 4-mile hike: From the **Wildcat Creek Trail**—which starts at the EEC in Tilden Park and is different from Wildcat *Peak* Trail—head up 1½ miles through the tall grass on the **Mezue Trail** for an excellent view; then turn right and continue for ¾ mile along the paved **Nimitz Way.** Turning right onto the **Havey Canyon Trail** will return you to the Wildcat Creek Trail on a winding 1½-mile path; note: when the trail's wet, you'll spend more time on your bum than your feet.

REDWOOD REGIONAL PARK More than a hundred years ago, sailors entering San Francisco Bay used the giant redwood trees growing on the hills east of Oakland as a landmark from the water. Unfortunately, most of those trees were mowed down at the start of the California gold rush. Only a few virgin redwoods remain in Redwood Regional Park, but the second-growth forest is still impressive.

To get to the **Skyline Gate Entrance** (tel. 510/635–0135, ext. 2578), where you'll find free trail maps, take I–580 to Hwy. 24; head east to Hwy. 13 south. Exit north on Joaquin Miller Road and turn left on Skyline Boulevard; the Skyline Gate entrance is about 4 miles farther on the right. From Coliseum BART, AC Bus 46 takes you to Skyline Boulevard, head uphill ⅓ mile to the park. To get to **Redwood Gate,** take I–580 east toward Hayward and exit at 35th Avenue/MacArthur Boulevard. Take 35th Avenue, which becomes Redwood Road, east past Skyline Boulevard. The park entrance is about 2 miles farther down the road. Parking inside costs $3 on weekends, but you can park along the road for free. There is no public transit to Redwood Gate.

➢ **HIKING** • The key to enjoying hikes in this park is to avoid the dusty perimeter trails by staying at the bottom of the canyon under the moist redwood canopy. Connecting the northern and southern entrances are two main trails, the **East Ridge Trail** and the **West Ridge Trail.** Both, along with the **Stream Trail,** start at the Skyline Gate parking lot. The West Ridge Trail is the main thoroughfare through the park, and too much time on its broad path may get you flattened by a charging mountain biker, but most of the other trails are limited to just hikers. From the Skyline Gate entrance, take the 3-mile (one-way) **Stream Trail,** which, after a steep (and often hot and dry) descent to the valley floor, meanders through the redwoods. If you'd rather have shade and the company of redwood groves on your way down, follow the West Ridge Trail a little farther to the strenuous **French Trail.** To return to the Skyline Gate entrance from the valley floor, simply pick any trail heading up and to the right; you'll soon connect with the West Ridge Trail, which will lead you back to the park entrance.

➢ **BIKING** • The 9-mile bike loop through the redwood forest is moderately difficult, with some strenuous areas. From **Redwood Gate** follow the road past the picnic areas to the trailhead. **Canyon Trail** begins with a steep climb (which gets nice and muddy in the rainy season). After ½ mile, bear left on the **East Ridge Trail** for a gentle 3½-mile ascent up to the **West Ridge Trail.** The road levels out for a bit, but the downhill stretch has plenty of danger zones, so watch your speed. After about 5 miles, the West Ridge Trail becomes the **Bridle Trail,** which runs into the Fern Dell picnic area. From here, turn right and take the **Stream Trail** all the way back.

Hike the nature trail at Huckleberry Botanical Preserve in early spring, and you might spy the first blossoms of the season. Since the park is outside the fog belt, the plants bloom one to two months ahead of others in the vicinity. To reach Huckleberry, follow the directions for Redwood Regional Park.

ANTHONY CHABOT REGIONAL PARK South of Redwood Regional Park, Chabot covers almost 5,000 acres. This is one of the few East Bay parks with a campground (*see* Chapter 7), and the blue waters of Lake Chabot are a refreshing sight after a long haul. Not refreshing, however, is the "No Swimming Allowed" rule. On weekends and holidays, the grassy expanse near the **Marina Entrance** is overcrowded with noisy picnickers. Best to stay away and enjoy the more remote areas of the lake shore; you can rent a rowboat, canoe, or pedal boat ($10 per hr, $25 per day) to escape the masses. For hiking, biking, and camping info, dial 510/635–0135, ext. 2570; for lake info, dial 510/582–2198. To get to the park from I–580 east, exit at 150th Avenue/Fairmont Drive east, which merges with Lake Chabot Road; then follow signs. Parking is $3; park along road for free.

➢ **HIKING** • The walk around the lake's perimeter, about 9 miles, is mostly flat, so if you're looking for a workout you should head elsewhere. The real reason to take this walk is for a close-up view of the wildflowers and waterfowl that abound in this habitat.

➢ **BIKING** • Bikers enjoy making the hilly 14-mile loop around Chabot Park because it affords all sorts of terrain. From the parking area at the marina, take the **East Shore Trail.** Cross the bridge, turn right on **Live Oak Trail** for a steep, rutted ascent of just under a mile that will deter any 10-speeder and even a few mountain bikers. Then turn right on **Towhee Trail** to the **Red Tail Trail.** Follow Red Tail—where you will be serenaded by the sounds of gunshots from the local rifle range—until you meet the **Grass Valley Trail,** which may inspire you to stop and talk with the nearby cows just for a chance to rest. Follow the **Brandon Trail**—a u-turn after the gate at the end of Grass Valley Trail—to the **Goldenrod Trail**; if you make it this far, your reward is a drinking fountain for cows and humans to share. Nope, you're not *even* done. Next is the **Bass Cove Trail,** another rain-rutted trail that ends up on the **West Shore Trail,** which takes you back to the lake.

MARIN COUNTY

A short drive north from San Francisco over the Golden Gate Bridge deposits you in Marin County, chock full of the kind of hiking most people will travel hours for—virgin redwoods, grassy mountain fields, the roaring sound of the Pacific as it dashes against cliffs. Many of Marin's best hiking and biking spots—Muir Woods, Mt. Tamalpais, and Point Reyes National Seashore—lie along Hwy. 1, which winds up the coast.

Ironically, the birthplace of the mountain bike is now a battleground where bikers are squaring off with hikers who want to keep the two-wheelers off the trails. Marin County has been particularly zealous about curtailing the use of mountain bikes. Trails that haven't been closed to bikers have a 15-mph speed limit (5 mph around turns), and rangers aren't shy about giving out hefty tickets ($180–$200) for violations. Some cyclists deliberately don't carry identification and give false names when rangers stop them. Other bikers have formed organizations to encourage better relations among everyone who wants to enjoy the wilderness. The **Bicycle Trails Council of Marin** (tel. 415/456–7512) maintains contact with park administrators and performs acts of community service, like leading bike trips for underprivileged urban kids and working on trail maintenance.

MARIN HEADLANDS Part of the **Golden Gate National Recreation Area,** the headlands are so close to San Francisco that most people leave the car at home and just bike across the Golden Gate Bridge. The Marin Headlands are home to rolling hills covered with coyote bush, low-lying grasses, precipitous bluffs, hardy wildflowers, and sandy beaches—dress in layers, as wind and fog are always present. The trails, which start almost immediately on the north side of the bridge, are sure to be crowded on rare sunny weekends.

If you're driving from the city, cross the Golden Gate Bridge and take the first exit (Alexander Ave.). Pass under the freeway, turn right before the entrance to U.S. 101 south, and follow the signs to the **visitor center** (tel. 415/331–1540; open daily 9:30–4:30), where you can pick up a map ($1.50) and get trail suggestions from the staff. Most trails start here, and parking is free. By bus, use the often overcrowded M76 from the Transbay Terminal or the Golden Gate Bridge toll plaza.

➤ **HIKING** • For a leisurely stroll, take a spin around the perimeter of the **Rodeo Lagoon.** With all the opportunities to stop and look at the waterfowl, the 1½-mile tour may take longer than you think. For a better view and a more strenuous hike, charge north up the **Coastal Trail.** From the visitor center parking lot, head up the closed-off road (*not* the left stairway). Persevere for about 2 miles, turn right onto the **Wolf Ridge Trail,** and head up the grassy hill (alias Wolf Ridge) for 1.6 miles to the top. When you're ready to stop gazing at the Tennessee Valley, continue for .7 mile down the verdant leeward side of the hill until it hooks up with the **Miwok Trail,** which you follow south. The trail wanders above the edge of the grassy Gerbode Valley, where you may spot a black-tailed deer or bobcat basking in the chaparral. Two miles later, you'll be back at the visitor center.

The **Tennessee Valley Trail,** at the end of Tennessee Valley Road (from U.S. 101 north, take the Hwy. 1 exit west and make the first left), is a broad path that meanders next to a small creek and through grassy fields for an easy 2 miles. In no time you'll be on black, sandy **Tennessee Beach,** in the company of many families. Here you can see the namesake of the valley—the shipwreck of the S.S. *Tennessee* (only at *very* low tide, however). If you're in the mood for a more strenuous hike, follow the Tennessee Valley Trail 1.3 miles from the parking lot and veer right onto the **Coastal Trail.** You may start to regret your decision when the going gets tough after ¾ mile; the trail wildly snakes above the secluded **Pirates Cove** for 2.2 miles, with stunning views of the jagged coast, and eventually leads you down to **Muir Beach** in the next .8 mile. Before you head back, relax a while at the pub of the **Pelican Inn** (*see* Muir Beach, in Chapter 2). On your return, see the less dramatic side of the Tennessee Valley by turning left off the Coastal Trail at **Coyote Ridge Trail** after .8 mile. Here, keep your eyes peeled for deer, bobcats, hawks, and great horned owls. Continue for 1½ miles and take the **Fox Trail** back to the Tennessee Valley Trail. You complete the 8-mile round trip with a short walk north back to the parking lot.

➤ **BIKING** • A popular series of fire trails offers a great panorama of the Golden Gate and the Pacific. The 11½-mile loop described below is moderate, with some pretty steep sections. Take the **Miwok Trail** (from the parking area near the visitor center) to the **Bobcat Trail,** and continue 3½ miles uphill to the **Marincello Trail.** This gravelly downhill run drops you on **Tennessee Valley Road,** which leads to the beach. To return, go back up Tennessee Valley Road and pick up **Old Springs Trail,** which picks up on the road leading into Miwok Stables. Once you get back to the Miwok Trail, hang a right and head back down to the trailhead. Rangers sometimes lead mountain-biking tours; call for details.

ANGEL ISLAND Almost all 750 acres of this island in San Francisco Bay, accessible by ferry, are covered with forest or sweeping grasses. In June of 1996, Angel Island began a controversial campaign to eradicate all the non-native flora—eucalyptus trees were hit the hardest—but you can still gaze in awe at sweeping ocean views. **Perimeter Road,** which encircles the island, is wheelchair accessible, though very steep and gravelly in some places. For information on how to reach the island, *see* Tiburon and Angel Island, in Chapter 2. For recorded information, call 415/435–1915; dial 415/435–5390 to speak to a ranger.

➢ **HIKING** • All trails lead in from Perimeter Road. On the **Sunset Trail,** immediately southeast of park headquarters (behind the picnic area, west of the ferry landing), 2 miles of ascending switchbacks afford stunning views of San Francisco to the west. As you circle the 781-foot summit, **Mt. Caroline Livermore,** you'll reach a crossroads; take a left up the paved road to the top for a 360° view of the Bay Area. After you backtrack to the crossroads, return to the ferry via the **North Ridge Trail** to view the eastern side of the island. The entire loop, Angel Island's most difficult hike, takes 2½–3 hours. On a sunny day, however, the hardest part is tearing yourself away from the secluded beaches on the western side of the island.

➢ **BIKING** • Angel Island offers relatively easy spinning, and not hard-core, grit-your-teeth rides; this is mainly because much of the island is off-limits to cyclists. However, two-wheeling is still very popular, and you'll find many people bringing their bikes over on the ferry. Otherwise, you can rent mountain bikes by the ferry landing for $9 an hour, or $25 per day (including helmet). There are two accessible trails: The **Perimeter Road** is a 5½-mile twirl around the island, while the **Fire Road** is a 3½-mile, more elevated loop. Pick up a free trail map at the bike rental shack.

MUIR WOODS You'll share the awe-inspiring sight of ancient, towering redwoods (the oldest has been around more than 1,200 years) with droves of tourists who clog the paved paths on the valley floor. An estimated two million sightseers shuffle past the redwoods annually, but happily, less than 10% venture forth onto the network of hiking trails that start here. You can make a quick escape by following any of the trails that head up from the valley floor. The trail guide for sale at the park entrance ($1) provides great explanations of flora and fauna. Don't plan on penetrating much of Muir Woods with your bike; cyclists are prohibited on everything but fire roads. You'll find free bike maps at the Muir Woods Visitor Center/Kiosk detailing where you can and cannot go. For recorded info call 415/388–2595.

One way to avoid the crowds at Muir Woods is to come on a rainy day. The forest's canopy is so dense that it keeps out much of the rain, and the dripping ferns and moss give the illusion that you've ventured into a rain forest.

For a spectacular view and workout, head up the **Ben Johnson Trail,** after crossing the fourth bridge from the park entrance. You'll climb up through the forest for 2 miles (the last half-mile is quite steep despite the switchbacks) until you reach the top of a hill with postcard views of several canyons and the Pacific. You can either head east on the **Dipsea Trail** to complete a 4½-mile hike, or if you're still full of energy, follow it 2 miles west down a steep gulch to **Stinson Beach.** The round-trip hike is one of the best around, and it's more than 9 miles, so you'll be damn pleased with yourself when you're done. Weekends and holidays only, you can cut down on the hike back by hopping on the hourly Golden Gate Transit Bus 63 (*see* Stinson Beach, in Chapter 2) at the Stinson Beach park entrance. For $1.25 it'll transport you to Mountain Home Inn, where you can pick up the **Panoramic/Ocean View Trail,** which leads 2 miles downhill to the parking lot. *Tel. 415/388–2596. From U.S. 101, follow signs from Stinson Beach/Hwy. 1 exit.*

MT. TAMALPAIS Home to the Coastal Miwok Native Americans for thousand of years before the first European explorers arrived, Mt. Tamalpais ("Mt. Tam") is now home to explorers of a different sort, hiking and biking around the forested canyons and up to the 2,571-foot summit (on a clear day you can spot the Sierra Nevada from the top). More than 50 miles of trails crisscross the park, which contains more than 750 species of plant life, from the hardy coastal redwood to the persnickety Calypso orchid.

➢ **HIKING** • Of all Mt. Tam's well-worn trails, the trip to the top is the most popular. If you want to sweat a lot and hike more than 3 miles to the summit, park at the Bootjack Day-Use Area (5 miles from Panoramic Hwy.; *see below*) and head north on the **Bootjack Trail** (which also connects Mt. Tam to Muir Woods). At the Mountain Theater, turn right onto Ridgecrest Boulevard, following the well-marked paths to the summit. Or conserve your energy and drive

In the annual 7-mile Dipsea Race, usually held the second Sunday in June, runners take off from Mill Valley and sprint over Mt. Tamalpais before collapsing on Stinson Beach at the finish line. The race originated in 1905 and is now limited to 1,500 manic runners.

up most of the way. If you park at the free East Peak parking lot, an easy .7 mile on a paved road gets you to the top for a humbling view. Those traveling by bus may take Golden Gate Transit Bus 10, 20, or 50 from the Golden Gate toll plaza and transfer to Golden Gate Transit 63 to the Pantoll park headquarters.

The 2-mile **Steep Ravine Trail** follows a redwood-lined creek down to the ocean. The trail begins at the west end of the parking lot at **Pantoll Ranger Station** (tel. 415/388–2070); the trail map for sale here ($1) is an excellent investment. Look for waterfalls along the trail, especially in springtime. It's all downhill to **Stinson Beach**; take the brutal but scenic, 1½-mile **Dipsea Trail** or stick to the trail that leads to **Rocky Point** and the **Steep Ravine Environmental Camp** (1 mi south of Stinson Beach on Hwy. 1), where you can get a close look at marine life such as seals, sea lions, star fish, and beach crabs. To get to the Pantoll Ranger Station from U.S. 101, take the Stinson Beach/Hwy. 1 exit, turn left at the first traffic light onto Hwy. 1, and right again onto Panoramic Hwy. Parking at the station is $5, but you can park for free at roadside pullouts.

➤ **BIKING** • Mt. Tam's rangers take trail restrictions seriously—some spend their whole day hunting for mountain bikers who are speeding or riding illegal trails. You should definitely get a map ($1) from the **Pantoll Ranger Station** (tel. 415/388–2070) to see which trails are legal.

The following bike ride takes you up to Mt. Tam's **East Peak,** for an exhilarating view from the top. Though you're climbing a mountain, the gradual gain in elevation makes this a relatively easy ride. If you continue past the East Peak, you're in for an all-day journey. From the ranger station, take the **Old Stage Road** uphill ½ mile to the West Point Inn, where you can grab a glass of lemonade. From the inn, go left on **Old Railroad Grade,** which runs for 2 miles almost to the top of Mt. Tam. It's one of the most popular rides on the mountain and gets quite crowded on weekends.

From the top, you can either head back the way you came or turn your ride into a 20-mile loop (total) that takes you back down Mt. Tam and halfway up again. If you've got the stamina, go down **East Ridgecrest Drive** and pick up the **Lagunitas–Rock Springs Trail,** which begins on the other side of the dirt parking lot. After a short climb, the trail descends to Lake Lagunitas, where you should turn right and go around the lake. Turn right again on **Lakeview,** and eventually you'll meet **Eldridge Grade,** where you start another ascent. Go left at **Indian** and enjoy a steep and bumpy downhill ride. Turn right on **Blithedale Ridge** (past the Hoo Koo E Koo Trail), and take either of two spurs that drop down to the right toward the **Old Railroad Grade.** When you hit West Point Inn—now are you ready for that lemonade?—go left on **Old Stage Road** and head back to the ranger station.

BOLINAS Serious hikers should consider the 45-mile **Coast Trail,** which stretches from the Palo Marin trailhead in Bolinas (*see* Marin County, in Chapter 2) into the middle of the Point Reyes National Seashore. The trailhead is at the end of Mesa Road, just past the bird observatory. For a healthy day hike, follow the trail to **Bass Lake** (5½ mi round-trip) or **Pelican Lake** (7 mi round-trip). Either way, you'll walk through eucalyptus groves and untamed wetlands and along the edge of the cliffs that overlook the Pacific Ocean. Camping along the trail is allowed only within the boundaries of the national seashore and in designated campgrounds; permits are required.

POINT REYES Even though it's close to the city, Point Reyes seems a world away. Gazing out at the rest of Marin County from this national seashore, you might get the feeling that you're on a separate island, which is almost true, except that the Tomales Valley joins the little peninsula to the mainland. In August of 1995, Point Reyes was ravaged by flames after some teenagers purportedly left an illegal campfire burning. Luckily the park has recovered well, and the fire was actually good for most of the wildflowers and native trees, which need the undergrowth to be burned out once in a while. The San Andreas fault runs right through the valley, putting Point Reyes on a different tectonic plate than the rest of the continent. Within the peninsula, the geography varies greatly; in just a few miles you can see meadows, forests, peaks with panoramic vistas, craggy cliffs overlooking the ocean, and isolated coves. The area erupts with wildflowers from mid-February through July, and though winter sees a lot of rain, that's when the rivers and ponds teem with life and the whales migrate south. Point Reyes feels so far removed that you may not want to go home; fortunately, there are plenty of places to camp here (see Marin County, in Chapter 7).

The best place to gear up is the **Bear Valley Visitor Center** (tel. 415/663–1092), where you can get a trail map and talk to the rangers. To get here, take Bear Valley Road off Route 1 just west of the village of Olema. Golden Gate Transit Bus 50, 70, and 80 from the Transbay Terminal connect with Bus 65, which takes you as far as the visitor center. Be sure to call ahead for bus schedules—Bus 65 runs only once a day in each direction.

➤ **HIKING** • For a hike along a narrow peninsula, with the Pacific crashing on one side of you and Tomales Bay gently lapping the other side, head out to **Tomales Point,** the northern-most spot in the park. From the visitor center, take Bear Valley Road, go left at the stop sign on Sir Francis Drake Boulevard, and bear right at Pierce Point Road, which ends at the Historic Pierce Point Ranch. The **Tomales Point Trail** picks up here and heads right through the Tule Elk Range; keep your eyes peeled for the graceful animals. Three miles down the road, the official trail ends, and the sandy footpaths to the cliffs (1½ mi) begin.

For a steep, strenuous hike, head to the highest point in the park, Mt. Wittenberg (1,407 feet). The **Mt. Wittenberg Trail** begins .2 mile from the Bear Valley Trailhead, at the south end of the park. The trail rises 1,250 feet in elevation; the final push follows an unmaintained offshoot up to the peak, where you'll be rewarded with a panorama of land and sea. To get down, head back to the Mt. Wittenberg Trail, hang a right, then take the **Horse Trail** to the Bear Valley Trail, where another right completes your 6-mile loop.

➤ **BIKING** • Most of the pristine trails in Point Reyes National Seashore are closed to bik-ers, but a few open paths and the park's paved roads make for scenic riding. For an easy, beau-tiful ride, take the **Bear Valley Trail** from the south end of the parking lot. About 3 miles into the ride, you'll reach a rack where you can lock your bike while you hike .8 mile out to the coast.

If you're up for something more serious, a strenuous 13-mile ride leaves from Five Brooks, a well-marked parking area off Hwy. 1 about 3 miles south of Olema. Pick up the **Olema Valley Trail,** which leads to the **Randall Trail** (on the left); cross Hwy. 1, ascend to Bolinas Ridge, and go right on the **Bolinas Ridge Trail.** About 1½ miles down the road, pick up the **McCurdy Trail,** cross Hwy. 1 again, and take the Olema Valley Trail all the way back.

SOUTH BAY

The gently rolling hills that shelter the San Mateo County Coast provide excellent opportunities for hiking and biking. You'll actually feel like you're heading into the country as you pass the small towns and farms south of San Francisco. Less popular than those in Marin County, the South Bay's parks offer solitude—although, unfortunately, most of them are inaccessible by public transit. The inland town of **La Honda** on Hwy. 84 (see San Mateo County Coast, in Chap-ter 2) is a good place to stop for picnic supplies before you head into one of the nearby state or county parks.

Most parks in the South Bay are completely closed to mountain bikers—fire trails and paved roads are pretty much it—but the relative lack of crowds can still make the South Bay an appealing biking destination.

PACIFICA The hiking along **Sweeney Ridge** is mediocre, but its proximity to the city and amazing view of the coastline make it a worthwhile getaway. To reach the peak, hike 2 miles up a moderate grade through coastal scrub and grasslands that bloom with wildflowers in spring; the trailhead is at the end of Sneath Lane. A monument to the Spanish captain, Gas-par de Portola, who supposedly discovered San Francisco Bay from this point in 1769, stands atop the peak. Most people are content to contemplate the view from here, but if you want to keep going, you can hike the **Baquiano Trail** about 2 more miles down to Pacifica. Since the ridge is so close to the coast, you'll definitely encounter some wind, and you may have to combat zero visibility on foggy summer afternoons. To get here, take I–280 or Skyline Boulevard (Hwy. 35) to the Sneath Lane exit in San Bruno. Follow Sneath Lane west for 10 minutes all the way to the Sweeney Ridge Gate. For information on ranger-led hikes, call 415/556–8371.

San Pedro Valley County Park has several mellow hiking trails that take you through shady woods and meadows exploding with wildflowers. In winter and spring, the ½-mile **Brooks Falls Overlook Trail** offers great views of a three-tiered, 275-foot waterfall. The even-shorter **Plaskon Nature Trail,** which gives you the opportunity to get up close and personal with a variety of plant species and wildlife, is wheelchair accessible. For more trail tips or a detailed guide to the nature trail, stop by the **visitor center** (600 Oddstad Blvd., tel. 415/355–8289). To reach the park, take Hwy. 1 into Pacifica and turn east on Linda Mar Boulevard. When it dead-ends, make a right onto Oddstad Boulevard; the entrance is 50 yards up on the left.

LA HONDA Eleven miles east of Hwy. 1 along Hwy. 84 lies the beautiful and secluded **Portola Redwood State Park.** Stop by the **visitor center** (tel. 415/948–9098) at the entrance where you must pay a $5 day-use fee (walk-ins are free). Here, you can also purchase a trail map for 75¢ or get info on guided nature walks and other activities.

➤ **HIKING** • For a moderately difficult 4½-mile hike through towering redwood groves, catch the steep **Coyote Ridge Trail** just north of the visitor center and follow it to Upper Escape Road, where you'll turn left; hang a left again onto the **Slate Creek Trail,** shoot downhill on the steep **Summit Trail,** and follow the service road back to the visitor center. All told, the hike lasts two to three hours. To reach Portola, take I–280 to Hwy. 84 west to Skyline Boulevard (Hwy. 35). Go south 7 miles, then turn west on Alpine Road.

➤ **BIKING** • Some of the best mountain biking in the area is to be found in **Pescadero Creek County Park,** near La Honda. You can access the trails from nearby San Mateo County Memorial Park (9500 Pescadero Rd., Loma Mar, tel. 415/879–0212): From Memorial's visitor center, take Pescadero Road back toward La Honda, turn right on Wurr Road, cross the bridge, and you'll come to the well-maintained, dirt-and-gravel **Old Haul Road,** where you can ride to your heart's content.

BUTANO STATE PARK This little-known state park in the Santa Cruz Mountains occupies a small canyon with diverse flora and fauna. Even when its campsites are full, you can still find solitude in Butano. Definitely invest in the 50¢ map available at the entrance station. In addition to marking the trails, it has information on the park's wildlife communities.

Saddle Sores? . . . Bums the Word

Seeing the sights saddleside means less work for you and more ground covered. Golden Gate Park Stables (JFK Dr., at 36th Ave., in Golden Gate Park, tel. 415/668–7360) has daily guided walks for $20 a ride, and one-hour rides that end with a BBQ the last Friday of each month ($35). In the East Bay, Chabot Riding Stables (14600 Skyline Blvd., tel. 510/638–0610) will guide you trotting and walking along a large, two-hour loop through the hills and valleys surrounding Anthony Chabot Regional Park. South of San Francisco on Hwy. 1 lies the Half Moon Bay coastal gem known as Sea Horse Ranch (tel. 415/726–9903). Rent a horse and ride, unguided, through 10 miles of verdant trails, ending in a breathtaking stretch of sandy beach that simply invites your horse to break into a canter. One hour will set you back $22, two hours go for $40; tack on $15 if you want an expert guide.

➢ **HIKING** • A great hike, one that will introduce you to the park's beautiful terrain, starts at the **Año Nuevo Trail** to the right of the entrance station. This trail is so dense with lush growth that the narrow path is constantly under the threat of being overgrown: Watch out here for stinging nettles and poison oak. The first half-mile, a steep ascent, is punctuated with benches; at the second bench you'll find the **Año Overlook**—on a clear day, you can see south to Año Nuevo Island. Continuing on, you'll run into **Olmo Fire Road.** Turn left, and left again on **Goat Hill Trail** for a 2-mile walk through the quiet forests. When the trail hits the main road, follow it to the right for the highlight of the hike: **Little Butano Creek Trail,** where the trail meanders along Little Butano Creek, crisscrossed by fallen redwoods. You will also see banana slugs and California newts with their bright orange stomachs. At the end of the trail you can turn right onto the main road, right onto **Mill Ox Trail,** then left onto **Jackson Flat Trail,** which takes you through forests and fields of wildflowers, while the creek rushes along far below. Jackson Flat will deposit you back at the entrance station for a total hike of about 7 miles.

For a gentler introduction to Butano, check out one of the ranger-led, 1½-hour nature walks, which happen every Saturday and Sunday at 2 and leave from the park entrance. To get to Butano, take Hwy. 1 about 15 miles south of Half Moon Bay to Pescadero; turn left on Pescadero Road, right on Cloverdale Road, and go about 5 miles to the park entrance. It costs $5 to park within the grounds, but you can usually ditch your car for free at the turnoff just south of the Cloverdale Road entrance.

➢ **BIKING** • You can ride on any of the fire roads, though mountain bikes are forbidden on trails. Your best bet is to park at the entrance gate near the corner of Cloverdale and Canyon roads, about a mile north of the main park entrance, and ride the **Butano Fire Road.** If you're in good shape, you can take it all the way to the **Olmo Fire Road,** which leads back to the park's main road, and pedal back to your car.

In-Line Skating

The beauty of in-line skating rests in the fact that you can do it just about anywhere—although you'd better learn to stop before daring San Francisco's hills. On Sundays, **Golden Gate Park** closes to motor vehicles to make way for the confluence of skaters and cyclists that glide through the park. This is a great place to learn on the flat pavement or to practice your '70s disco moves on '90s blades. San Francisco's **Marina District** is another hotbed for bladed youths on weekday afternoons and weekends. The numerous parks around the Bay Area are agreeable for sportblading (skating on unpaved surfaces), and devotees highly recommend **Angel Island**—but it's bumpy going for novices.

Skates on Haight (1818 Haight St., tel. 415/752–8375) rents in-line skates ($7 per hour, $28 per day) right near the entrance to Golden Gate Park, so you can just strap them on and go. Also near the park, **Skate Pro Sports** (2549 Irving St., at 27th Ave., in the Sunset District, tel. 415/752–8776) rents them for a couple of bucks cheaper. **Marina Skate and Snowboards** (2271 Chestnut St., near Scott St., tel. 415/567–8400) is the place to go if you want to skate along the Marina Green boardwalk. They rent skates and pads for $6 an hour, $19 a day. All

For a Wheel Good Time . . .

Every Friday night in San Francisco you can catch the sight of (literally) hundreds of in-line skaters flying through the city on a 13-mile figure eight. If you'd like to join in the fun, the Midnight Rollers meet at the Ferry Building at 8 PM—okay, so the name's off by a couple hours—to promote alternative, nonmotorized transportation (but mostly just to have one hell of a good time). Contact organizer David Miles (tel. 415/752–1967, CAblader@ix.netcom.com).

stores give free (!) lessons (Marina Skate and Snowboards and Skate Pro Sports even throw in a free rental for the duration of the lesson). Call for details.

Rock Climbing

It takes a certain psyche to scale rock faces knowing a nylon rope is all that separates you from a grisly plunge, and the Bay Area is a breeding ground for just this kind of insanity. Actually, a climb with the right equipment and instruction can be safer than crossing Market Street during rush hour, and far more exhilarating.

INSTRUCTION AND EQUIPMENT

Although the proper rigging can be expensive, it's a death wish to buy used gear, and nobody rents ropes in the Bay Area for liability reasons. **REI** (*see* chapter introduction, *above*) is a good place to go for the essentials; they also rent climbing shoes for $8 the first day, $3 for each subsequent day. **Marmot Mountain Works** in Berkeley (3049 Adeline St., tel. 510/849–0735) also has a knowledgeable staff that can outfit you with the climbing basics.

The reason to start rock climbing is so you can go outdoors and climb rocks—not indoor walls. That said, it's often easiest to learn the basics on a rock wall, and indoor climbing gyms have become popular places for newcomers to learn the sport and meet climbing buddies. **Cal Adventures** (*see* chapter introduction, *above*) offers all sorts of classes, from one day rock-wall introductions ($40) to weekend climbing classes that include camping at Pinnacles National Monument ($175) to women-only seminars. Cal Adventures also has an outdoor climbing wall available to all those who can pass a belay proficiency test. You can rent equipment (shoes, harness, belay device, and a helmet) for $3 and a day's access to the wall for $2; a three-month pass is $60 (including rentals). Housed in a 6,000-square-foot warehouse, **CityRock Gym** in Emeryville (1250 45th St., tel. 510/654–2510) is considered one of nation's best climbing facilities, with sculpted walls up to 40 feet high and a separate area for bouldering (free climbing). A day spent climbing the walls will cost you $20, including shoe and harness rental. They also offer a full-service climbing school, where introductory and intermediate lessons taught by some of the nation's top climbers cost $35. **Class 5 Fitness** in San Rafael (25B Bodie St., tel. 415/485–6931) has 35-foot walls ($12 day fee) and rents shoes and harness ($5) for in-house use. All of the above facilities offer private instruction on request.

WHERE TO CLIMB

One of the best places for new climbers to practice and meet seasoned veterans in the East Bay is **Indian Rock Park** in North Berkeley where Shattuck Avenue dead-ends (*see* East Bay, in Chapter 2). Arid **Mt. Diablo State Park** offers excellent top-roping and lead routes up to 120 feet high in some areas. The sandstone rock varies in hardness, with new routes simply waiting to be discovered. The two main climbing areas are the more charted Boy Scout Rocks in the southeastern corner of the park, and Pine Canyon just past the North Gate fee station, which is closed from early February to late June for the raptor nesting season. Head east on Hwy. 24 toward Walnut Creek, then south on I–680. Exit at Diablo Road, follow it to the park entrance ($5 day-use fee), and look for the Rock City parking lot to the right.

Castle Rock State Park in the Santa Cruz Mountains is in a beautiful wooded area with some routes recommended for novices. The sandstone rock is appropriate for bouldering as well as top-roping. To get here, take I–280 south past Palo Alto, continue south on Rte. 85, west on Big Basin Road, and then left on Skyline Boulevard. Look for the parking lot to the right after 2 miles. Directly south of Stinson Beach along Hwy. 1 lies **Mickey's Beach**—popular with nude bathers as well as serious rock climbers. The greenstone rock edges its way toward the ocean, making for 30–65 feet of spectacular climbing on well-established routes with names like "Eggfart" and the "Endless Bummer." The rocky outcropping to the north is suitable for bouldering. Look for the dirt pullout about a mile south of Stinson. For more information on other locations, including route maps and difficulty levels, look for the superlative guidebook, "Bay Area Rock," by local expert, Jim Thornburg, available at CityRock and other stores ($9.95).

Sailing

No view of San Francisco is greater than from sea level, but it isn't postcard scenery that draws sailors to the bay—it's the remarkably consistent west wind. The San Francisco Bay is one of the most challenging places in the country to sail. Even if you don't have the means to buy a yacht, a little charm—and a tolerance for grunt work—can earn you a job working crew on a boat. **Crewing** is the cheapest way to learn about sailing, and the water makes the best classroom. Post an ad at your local marina and talk to boaters, and your eagerness will likely win you a sailing invitation. The California sailing magazine *Latitude 38* (look for it in boating stores) is an excellent resource for finding used boats or placing an ad for a crew. They also print a schedule of races every March, just in time for the beginning of the season.

INSTRUCTION AND EQUIPMENT

The Berkeley Marina (west end of University Ave.) is one of the greatest places to learn to sail. **Cal Sailing Club** (tel. 510/287–5905), across from the marina, offers three months of unlimited lessons and equipment use for a membership cost of $45, $40 for U.C. students. You can sail to your heart's content on their 8- to 15-foot (not necessarily well-maintained) boats. To check out the club, take a free sail the first full weekend of each month from 1 PM to 4 PM—don't forget to wear something warm and waterproof. Just next door to the Cal Sailing Club, **Cal Adventures** (*see* chapter introduction, *above*), offers equipment rental if you have the appropriate qualifications, and reasonably priced classes ($80 for three weeks) if you don't. Also consider **Olympic Circle Sailing Club** (1 Spinnaker Way, near the Berkeley Marina, tel. 800/223–2984), which has expensive but highly recommended courses. If you can't afford a class, show up on a summer Wednesday for the 5:30 sunset sail. The two-hour ride (reservations required) costs $35 per person. AC Transit Bus 51M heads to the marina from downtown Berkeley. **Spinnaker Sailing/Rendezvous Charter** (Pier 40, South Beach Harbor, San Francisco, tel. 415/543–7333) charters boats and teaches sailing in the city. They also offer a two-hour sunset sail ($23) on Wednesday, Friday, and Saturday.

Sea Kayaking

The Bay Area's many lagoons, estuaries, inlets, and of course, ocean waters allow both novices and experts to roll their kayaks gleefully year-round. Sea kayaking provides the prime opportunity to take in stunning scenery, paddle by the light of the moon, make friends with affable seals, and bird-watch—all without getting your feet wet (hopefully).

INSTRUCTION AND EQUIPMENT

To get in touch with the Bay Area kayak scene, contact Penny Welles of the 400-member **Bay Area Sea Kayakers Co-op** (tel. 415/457–6094). For $25 a year, you'll receive a newsletter and info about their frequent trips throughout the Bay Area. Also check the quarterly bulletin published by **Outdoors Unlimited** (*see* chapter introduction, *above*) for listings of free kayak and canoe workshops and volunteer-led trips. OU's day trips and moonlight paddles are some of the cheapest around—some are free, and others cost $60. Berkeley's **Cal Adventures** (*see above*) also offers sea-kayaking day trips, instruction, and rentals at cut-rate prices.

California Canoe and Kayak (409 Water St., Jack London Sq., Oakland, tel. 510/893–7833 or 800/366–9804) offers the widest range of classes and trips, including lessons and outings for women only. Two-day introductory classes run about $80, and outings cost $80–$600, depending on destination and length of the trip. **Sea Trek** (Schoonmaker Point Marina, Sausalito, tel. 415/488–1000 or 415/332–4465) also has classes and rentals, and they offer special kayak trips with naturalist guides. Sea Trek rents equipment for about $7–$8 an hour, and a seven-hour introductory class costs $90. Other outings include a $45 sunset or full-moon paddle and a $110 full-day trip to Angel Island. If you're looking to buy equipment, take a free spin during Sea Trek's "Demo Days." Like California Canoe and Kayak, they offer free testing of canoes and kayaks on a designated day each month from early spring through early fall.

WHERE TO KAYAK

Beginners will get acquainted early on with **Richardson Bay,** between Tiburon and Sausalito in Marin County. With its calm waters, gorgeous locale, and bird-watching opportunities, Richardson is a hot spot for novices, and it makes a good launching point for an intermediate-level trip to Angel Island or an advanced trip through the rough and dangerous currents under the Golden Gate Bridge. For even calmer waters, head farther north to **Bolinas Lagoon,** a protected estuary where you'll paddle past egret nesting sites and see more birds than you ever imagined. **Drake's Estuary,** another bird-infested spot, is a beautiful bay on the Point Reyes peninsula with calm waters for beginners. The placid waters of **Tomales Bay,** also off the coast of Point Reyes National Seashore, claim a resident flock of white pelicans as well as jellyfish and starfish. Beginners and intermediates will feel comfortable in the western part of the bay, which offers stunning views of coves and beaches on shore.

Surfing

The closest surf is brutal, paddling out can be exasperating, and the water is cold enough to remind men that they, too, have nipples. Surfers looking for more merciful conditions head south toward Santa Cruz. Anywhere you go in the Bay Area, though, swells are best during fall and winter, when storms far out at sea send ripples across the Pacific. Call **Wise Surfboards** (tel. 415/665–WISE) for a recorded message on conditions in the city. For conditions at Stinson Beach call **Livewater** surf shop (*see below*); for Santa Cruz conditions call the **O'Neil Surf Shop** hot line (tel. 408/475–2275); and for Pacifica conditions call **Nor-Cal** surf shop (*see below*).

Local surfers are territorial about their waves and less forgiving than the ocean when you violate surf etiquette, particularly the unwritten law that the first person riding the wave has ownership. Novices should avoid practicing at popular spots like Rockaway Beach (*see below*), where there's stiff competition for waves. In addition, the current around San Francisco claims lives every year; beginners are best off heading north to Stinson Beach or south to Santa Cruz.

INSTRUCTION AND EQUIPMENT

If you can't find a friend to teach you, two world-class surfing instructors offer lessons near Santa Cruz. **Richard Schmidt** (tel. 408/423–0928) is a champion whose graceful style inspires his peers to sit back and take notes. The cheapest way to get any of the man's time is to take a surf class through the **Santa Cruz Parks and Recreation Department** (tel. 408/429–3663). A two-day group lesson, two hours each day, costs $60 for residents of Santa Cruz, $68 for anyone else. You must reserve months in advance. Schmidt also offers private instruction; he guarantees to have first-time surfers riding their boards. A one-hour private lesson costs $60; equipment is included. **CLUB ED Surf and Windsurf School** (tel. 800/287–7873), run by Ed Guzman, also offers classes in Santa Cruz. Ed owns a concession stand on Cowell Beach between the Dream Inn and the wharf. He's got boogie boards, windsurfers, kayaks, skim boards, surfboards, and an instructor for every skill level. His one-hour ($50) and two-hour ($75) group lessons start you off on an oversize board, perfect for beginners who don't yet have their balance. If you don't get the hang of it the first time, you can come back for another two-hour lesson for only $45.

In terms of equipment, locals wear artificial blubber (boots, gloves, and full wet suits, 3/2–4/3 mm thick) year-round. A common mistake of neophytes is buying a board that's too small; a slightly longer, thicker board will help inexperienced surfers catch more waves. Check out the bulletin boards in surf shops to find something secondhand; you should be able to find something for about $200–$350. **Wise Surfboards** (3149 Vicente St., tel. 415/665–7745) helps customers resell boards without taking a commission.

To rent wet suits in the city, go to **Outdoors Unlimited** (*see* chapter introduction, *above*), where weekend rentals run $15–$19. **Livewater** (3450 Hwy. 1, Stinson Beach, tel. 415/868–0333) rents buoyant foam boards ($25 a day) for beginners. To the south, local surfers staff **Nor-Cal Surfshop** (5460 Cabrillo Hwy., Pacifica, tel. 415/738–9283), where you can rent a soft board for $10 a day. **O'Neil Surf Shop** (1149 41st Ave., tel. 408/475–4151) in Santa Cruz rents boards for $10 a day and wet suits for $8 a day.

WHERE TO SURF

A frightening number of great white sharks make their home off the coastline stretching from Davenport (near Santa Cruz) to Stinson Beach. Unfortunately, sharks have bad eyesight and mistake slick wet suits for shiny seal fur. Sharks attack a few people annually, but that doesn't keep anyone out of the water. Surfers who have been bitten suggest hitting the shark on the nose to break its grip, then swimming like hell for shore.

Surf's up at **Ocean Beach,** west of Golden Gate Park, but you may wish it would go back down. Winter waves here get as big as anywhere in the world (20–25 feet), but only the insane tackle the biggest ones since their shape is often poor. Even when the swells are manageable, the current is strong. You don't have to be an expert to surf Ocean Beach, but it's not a place to learn unless you're into self-abuse. Waves are cleaner at **Fort Point,** beneath the Golden Gate Bridge on the southeast side. This oft-overlooked haven is convenient for city surfers, but the current and rocks may deter beginners.

If you're just starting out, drive north along Hwy. 1 to **Stinson Beach.** The shallow beach break is not demanding, and the waves are neither fast nor big. Stinson is a popular beach for sunbathing, but the water is rarely crowded. **Pacifica State Beach,** also known as **Linda Mar Beach,** is about 45 minutes south of San Francisco along Hwy. 1. Pacifica breaks best at high tide, with smaller waves for beginners at the southern end of the beach. Just north of the rocky promontory, **Rockaway Beach** offers bigger waves, but it's more crowded and competitive. If you're adventurous, check out the isolated state beaches between Pacifica and Santa Cruz.

Windsurfing

The San Francisco Bay ranks the third-best spot for windsurfing in the United States, after Oregon's Royal Gorge and Maui. Take advantage. Summer is the season to tack across the bay: From April to August, westerly winds provide optimal conditions for windsurfing almost anywhere in the Bay Area. Winds are sporadic during the rest of the year, blowing either north or

Rebel Wave

Some of the biggest waves in the world can be found at Mavericks in Half Moon Bay. Surfers tackle the 35- to 40-foot behemoths armed with nothing but tiny fiberglass boards: A testament to both the awesome power of the Pacific and the equally awesome audacity of humans. Do not surf here unless you know what you are doing; even then, this reef break can be lethal. In December 1994, Mavericks (named after the dog of a local surfer) claimed the life of Mark Foo, a native Hawaiian and the most famous big-wave surfer in the world. His death—a shocking blow to the surfing world—was caught on video, but it remains a mystery as to why he went under. This is one wave you might want to sit out.

south. During winter, the air can be as cold as the water, and you'll need a wet suit 3/2- or 4/3-mm thick. Some summer days are hot enough to go bottomless (in regard to wet suits, that is).

INSTRUCTION AND EQUIPMENT

Cal Adventures (*see* chapter introduction, *above*) offers cheap windsurfing lessons; six hours of instruction on the bay with an added hour of recreational windsurfing, board included, cost $60, $55 for students. After you've completed the course, you can buy a two-month pass for $100 that allows you to use windsurfing equipment during business hours (Mon. morning and all day Wed.–Sun.; closed Thurs. Nov.–May).

The conditions on the bay are harsh for a beginning windsurfer; consider learning on a lake. **Spinnaker Sailing** (3160 N. Shoreline Blvd., Mountain View, tel. 415/965–7474) offers beginning and advanced classes on an artificial lake. The two-day beginners' course costs $135. **Windsurf Del Valle** (Lake Del Valle, Livermore, tel. 510/455–4008) has the largest windsurfing school in the country and is excellent for beginners. The site, on a lake about a half hour's drive east of Oakland, is the perfect windsurfing location: The water and air temperatures hover in the 80s from April through October. The water is flat, with few waves, and the wind is light. The $95 beginners' course usually lasts two days and earns you the certification necessary for renting equipment at most shops. They guarantee that you will learn the sport and will give you additional days of instruction for free if you need more help.

The **San Francisco School of Windsurfing** (3Com Park or Lake Merced, tel. 415/753–3235) specializes in increasing your skill level quickly. Beginners start at Lake Merced, but you soon learn to tackle the more popular bay. The school is renowned for dramatically improving intermediate students' abilities. The owner recommends that you not buy equipment until you've finished the entire course, since your beginning or intermediate board will become obsolete once you've improved. The two-day beginning course costs $95 (equipment included). Rentals cost $15 an hour, including wet suit, booties, and harness; a 10-hour pass is $100.

New windsurfing equipment is expensive—a grand, easy—so you may be forced to nickel and dime yourself with rentals. In addition to their main store, **Berkeley Boardsports** (843 Gilman St., Berkeley, tel. 510/527–7873) has set up shop next to the water at Alameda's Crown Beach and at Larkspur Landing in San Rafael. One hour on a board costs $10, but you can use the board all day for $40, including a wet suit. If you're going to buy, it's best to look for secondhand equipment. Most windsurfing shops have a bulletin board and free magazines with ads for used gear.

WHERE TO WINDSURF

BEGINNING Alameda's **Crown Beach,** with easy access to shallow waters, offers the best conditions in the East Bay for learning the sport. Forces of nature work to the novice's advantage—the wind is usually light and blows towards the shore, so if you zig when you should have zagged, you won't be lost at sea. For directions to the beach, *see* Oakland, Cheap Thrills, in Chapter 2.

Larkspur Landing, in Marin County, is good for mixed windsurfing abilities. The light wind close to shore accommodates beginners, while the more advanced windsurfer will be challenged farther out in the bay. Mornings are calmest and best for beginners; the wind picks up in the afternoon. The area is not without its weaknesses—parking your car, for example, is a major hassle. And when the wind is light, it's no fun to access the water: From a rocky shore, you have to paddle out into the bay while keeping a wary eye out for ferries. From U.S. 101, take the San Rafael/Richmond exit east, and continue ¼ mile past the Larkspur Ferry Terminal.

INTERMEDIATE/ADVANCED The **Berkeley Marina,** at the west end of University Avenue, requires intermediate to advanced skills. Access to the water is problematic, since you must launch off either the dock or the rocks. The windy and choppy conditions are tough on a beginner but provide lots of wave-jumping opportunities for experienced windsurfers who like to spend time in the air. From I–80, take the University Avenue exit west to the end.

Crissy Field, in San Francisco's Presidio, should challenge advanced windsurfers. Beach access makes getting into the water easy, but with the strong tides and currents, getting out is a task. The current could easily sweep an unprepared windsurfer under the Golden Gate into the Pacific or across the bay to Treasure Island. In addition, boat and ship traffic make the water about as easy to navigate as the freeway at rush hour. If you're up to the challenge, you'll find Crissy Field just southeast of the Golden Gate Bridge.

At **3Com Park** (formerly known as Candlestick) on the Peninsula, not everyone is going to the ball game. Flat water, strong winds, and easy bay access make Candlestick a favorite with windsurfers who want speed. Winds average 19–25 mph, but they can get as high as 55 mph. You have to be an expert to handle the offshore winds, which carry you right out into the bay— if the wind dies, you'll be stranded out there. Think twice before windsurfing here on game days: Parking costs $8 during baseball season and $20 during football.

The onshore wind and big chops make **Coyote Point,** south of the San Francisco International Airport, an advanced area. On the inside (close to shore), the wind is moderate, but on the out-side, it increases, and the waves become choppy. The entrance fee for **Coyote Point Park** (tel. 415/573–2592) is $4, well worth it for the use of the hot showers. Follow U.S. 101 south past the airport to the Poplar Avenue exit, take Humboldt Street, turn right on Peninsula Avenue, go right across the overpass, and bear left onto Coyote Point Drive.

Spectator Sports

BASEBALL The baseball rivalry between San Francisco and the East Bay came to a dramatic head in the 1989 "Bay Bridge Series," when the American League's **Oakland A's** and the National League's **San Francisco Giants** duked it out for the championship, and fate intervened to sever the bridge between east and west with a major earthquake during the game. The Giants (tel. 415/467–8000) expect to have a new downtown ballpark completed by 2000. In the meantime, they continue to play at **3Com Park** in the far southeastern corner of the city. Tickets are $5.50 for bleachers, $7–$20 for plaza level. Bus 9x ($5 round-trip) heads for 3Com Park from Montgomery BART on game days, or take U.S. 101 south to the 3Com Park exit. The A's (tel. 510/638–0500) play at the newly renovated **Oakland Coliseum.** Bleachers cost $4.50, plaza level $11–$13. The stadium is connected via an elevated walkway with the Coliseum BART station.

FOOTBALL Because of their consistent success, the **San Francisco '49ers** have built up a huge fan base from all over Northern California, and tickets for home games at 3Com Park (the season runs Sept.–Jan.) are nearly impossible to get. Season-ticket holders have a lock on most seats, and when the rest go on sale in July, they usually sell out within the hour, despite the $40 price tag. Call the ticket office (tel. 415/468–2249) to find out what day tickets go on sale (usually in mid-July). Then all you can do is call BASS (tel. 415/776–1999 or 510/762–BASS) at 9 AM that day and hope you get through before someone else snatches the last ticket.

The big news is the return of the **Oakland Raiders** from Los Angeles, a move that is bringing Raiders fans out of closets all over the Bay Area. The city of Oakland is also thrilled, no doubt by the revenue and publicity that the popular team, who left Oakland for L.A. in 1982 ("L.A. Traitors"), will rake in. The Raiders play at the Oakland Coliseum.

BASKETBALL Having secured first pick in the 1995 NBA draft, many people feel that the **Golden State Warriors** are now a team worth watching. Tickets ($17.50–$28; no student dis-counts) go on sale in late September or early October and are available through BASS. They sell out fast. The Warriors play at the Oakland Coliseum Arena.

HOCKEY The **San Jose Sharks** (tel. 408/287–4275) repeated their miraculous '94 playoffs performance in '95, beating the Calgary Flames in a seventh game double-overtime victory to win the first round of the Stanley Cup Games. They eventually lost in the second round to New Jersey. Sharks aficionados continue to be one of hockey's most enthused group of fans, and tickets to games in the new San Jose Arena ($15–$71) sell quickly. The season runs Octo-ber–April. From San Francisco, CalTrain will get you to the San Jose Arena. There's also a shuttle to and from parking lots in downtown San Jose. The **San Francisco Spiders** of the International Hockey League are gaining a cult following as well. They play at the Cow Palace; take Bus 9X from Balboa Park BART.

SOCCER On April 6, 1996, the **San Jose Clash** (tel. 408/985–GOAL) kicked off Major League Soccer at **Spartan Stadium** with an exciting win over D.C. United. Whether San Jose embraces the Clash as it did the Sharks remains to be seen, but all signs point to "yes." The season runs April–September; tickets are $12–$19. Take CalTrain to the San Jose Station, then take Bus 25 (direction: East San Jose).

COLLEGE SPORTS The Bay Area's two big universities—U.C. Berkeley ("Cal") and Stanford University in Palo Alto—have been arch rivals for close to a century. Each year, the **Big Game** pits Berkeley's and Stanford's football teams against each other. Both schools are supported by huge alumni bases that love to recapture their youth by getting sloshed and cheering like banshees at school events. The **Cal Bears** football team, which plays in Memorial Stadium on the east side of campus, has improved a bit in recent years, and you'll find that even the most blasé Berkeley bohemian may work up a sweat over the cutthroat Big Game. The Cal men's and women's **basketball** teams aren't exactly championship teams, but they have a loyal fan base, and tickets go fast. Some games are played at the Oakland Coliseum, most at Harmon Gym on the Berkeley campus.

To buy tickets for Cal sports, call 800/GO–BEARS. Football tickets cost $12 for general admission, $20 for reserved seating. Basketball tickets for games at the Coliseum cost about $16. Baseball, played at Evans Diamond on the corner of Bancroft Way and Oxford Street, costs $5 for adults, $3 for Cal students and minors. Women's basketball tickets are $5, or $3 for Cal students and youth.

Stanford's spectator sports revolve mainly around the university's football team, the **Cardinal** (named for the color, not the bird), which plays at Stanford Stadium. The other strong team on campus is women's basketball, a consistent NCAA championship contender that made the Final Four in '95. Palo Alto may seem a little out of the way to some people, but Stanford fans are gung-ho. The school is also notorious for its wacky band. For information on tickets for all Stanford sports, call 800/BEAT–CAL weekdays 9–4. Football tickets cost $9 general admission ($7 for youth), $22 reserved, and $35 for the "Big Game," and they go on sale at the beginning of June. Tickets to **basketball** games, played at Maples Pavilion, go on sale in September and cost $5 general admission ($3 for youth), $11 reserved.

DAY AND WEEKEND TRIPS

By Michelle Kaye, Irene J. Nexica, Charlene Pinzon, and Jeff Stark

Whether you're looking for a day at the beach or a weekend in the mountains, a New Age healing session or an isolated cross-country ski trail, odds are good that you'll find what you want somewhere in the diverse and gorgeous country surrounding San Francisco. Perhaps more than any other major American city, San Francisco is distinguished by its proximity to dramatic natural terrain and interesting small towns. North of the city lies California's world-famous **Wine Country**; and to the south, **Santa Cruz** is a gathering point for surfers, New Agers, and neo-hippies. Continuing south, **Monterey** brims with tourists, harbor seals, and an incredible aquarium, while **Big Sur** rewards hardy campers and hikers with its rugged beauty. An afternoon's drive east at the right time of year will bring you to that most un-Californian phenomenon, snow, in the mountains surrounding **Lake Tahoe** or in **Yosemite**, California's favorite national park. Tahoe is home to some of the country's best skiing, while Yosemite provides Northern Californians with a place to rock climb, hike, and hang out with the bears and other wildlife of the Sierra Nevada. You can escape to any one of these world-class spots in no more than four hours if you've got access to a car; or with patience and a little pre-trip planning, public transit will get you into the great wide open as well.

The Wine Country

Sipping wine amidst the rustic beauty and relaxed surroundings of the Wine Country makes the 50-mile trek northeast from San Francisco a worthwhile venture. Wine novices shouldn't feel intimidated—just drink away and ask questions later. Many of the wineries will pour you glass after glass of free samples. Choose carefully, though: A number of Napa Valley wineries charge a $2 or $3 tasting fee, which can add up if you're making the rounds. In some places you may have to take a tour or watch a film before you can get to the tasting, but luckily the tours are usually interesting (especially at the smaller wineries).

Most vineyards are concentrated in the Napa and Sonoma valleys, but the Wine Country actually stretches north through Santa Rosa and all the way into Lake and Mendocino counties. Vintners have been making wine here for well over 100 years, but it was only in 1976, when a cabernet sauvignon from Stag's Leap won a blind taste test in Paris, that Californians began boasting and people all over the world began buying. Since then, production has skyrocketed. Twenty-five years ago there were only about 25 wineries; now there are more than 200.

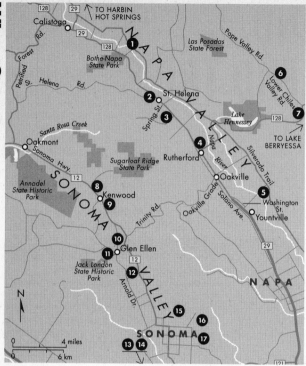

Beaulieu
Vineyards, **4**
Benziger, **11**
Beringer Winery, **2**
Buena Vista, **16**
Château St. Jean, **8**
Cline Cellars, **14**
Gundlach-
Bundschu, **17**
Kunde, **9**
Nichelini, **7**
Prager Port Works, **3**
Ravenswood, **15**
Rustridge, **6**
S. Anderson, **5**
Schug, **13**
Valley of
the Moon, **12**
Wellington, **10**
Wermuth, **1**

Napa Valley has the greatest number of wineries, but many are expensive and pretentious. Once upon a time, visitors were greeted with open arms—and flowing bottles—by jolly vintners thankful for even a trickle of business. These days you'll have to search out the Napa Valley's tiniest wineries to get this kind of reception. A better option is to make a beeline for the Sonoma Valley. While Sonoma has some big, impersonal wineries, it draws fewer tourists and is home to a greater share of rustic, unassuming vineyards. In both counties, the farther you stray from the main drag, the better off you'll be. Remember that it doesn't always work to just drop in at a winery, especially if you want to take a tour—you may need an appointment.

Before stocking up on vino at a winery, check the local supermarket—they often have lower prices.

If you need a break from the wineries, you can luxuriate in the hot springs, mud baths, and mineral baths of Calistoga, loiter in the lovely Spanish mission and old adobes of Sonoma, or browse through the small museums devoted to former residents Jack London and Robert Louis Stevenson, both of whom wrote about the area. Be forewarned, though: An overnight stay in the Wine Country can take a monster-size bite out of your budget. Lodging tends to be even more expensive than in San Francisco, and food is pricey as well. You can survive cheaply by eating at roadside produce stands, drinking free wine, and sleeping in a state park. Otherwise, expect to pay through the nose.

BASICS

VISITOR INFORMATION Before you go (or once you arrive), you may want to call the **Napa Chamber of Commerce** (1556 1st St., Napa, tel. 707/226-7455), open weekdays 9–5, which can help you organize your trip and provide you with more maps than you'll ever need. The **Sonoma Valley Visitors' Bureau** (453 1st St. E, Sonoma, tel. 707/996-1090), open weekdays 9–5 and weekends until 6, gives friendly advice on what to see and do in the "other" valley.

Additionally, most wineries carry the *California Visitor's Review*, a free weekly that has maps and winery info.

WHEN TO GO The best time to visit is during the autumn harvest season, when you'll see some real action in the wine cellars. In both spring and fall, wildflowers bloom amid the endless rows of manicured vines. Try to avoid the Wine Country in summer, though. The dry, dusty valleys become even drier and dustier, and the crowds can be suffocating—it sometimes feels as if each and every one of the 2.5 million annual visitors is backed up along Hwy. 29, impatient for another glass of zinfandel.

COMING AND GOING

BY CAR Though traffic can be heavy, especially on weekends and during rush hours (7–9 AM and 4–6 PM), the easiest way to reach the Wine Country is by car. From San Francisco, the best option is to take **U.S. 101** north over the Golden Gate Bridge and connect with **Highway 37** east near Ignacio. From here take **Highway 121** north to **Highway 12** north for Sonoma, or follow Hwy. 121 as it curves east toward **Highway 29** for Napa. If you're only visiting the Napa Valley or are coming from the East Bay, it's quicker to take **I-80** north and exit to Hwy. 37 west in Vallejo. Hwy. 37 joins up with Hwy. 29 north to Napa. Even when traffic is heavy it shouldn't take more than two hours; on good days you'll be there in an hour.

BY BUS **Golden Gate Transit** (tel. 415/455–2000 or 707/541–2000) provides bus service from San Francisco and Marin County to towns throughout Sonoma County. Bus 90 makes the trek from San Francisco to Sonoma (2 hrs, $4.50) twice daily. **Greyhound** has service from San Francisco's Transbay Terminal (*see* Getting In, Out, and Around, in Chapter 1) once daily to Napa (2½ hrs, $15 one-way) and Middletown (4¼ hrs, $17 one-way), twice daily to Sonoma (3–4 hrs, change in Vallejo or Santa Rosa, $15 one-way). Tickets are cheaper midweek.

GETTING AROUND

Unless you've hit one winery too many, orienting yourself in the Wine Country shouldn't be too difficult: Both the Napa and Sonoma valleys have main north–south arteries (Hwys. 29 and 12, respectively) that connect towns and vineyards alike. **Highway 29** begins in the medium-size town of Napa and stretches north through Yountville, Oakville, Rutherford, St. Helena, and Calistoga, continuing north to Middletown and Clear Lake. A parallel route, **Silverado Trail,** avoids most of Hwy. 29's traffic lights (and jams), making for a more scenic and speedy ride. In the Sonoma Valley, **Highway 12** runs north from Sonoma's main plaza, zigzagging east and then north through the towns of Glen Ellen and Kenwood before reaching Santa Rosa. East–west crossroads between the two valleys include **Highway 121** from Napa, the scenic **Oakville Grade/Trinity Road** from Oakville, and the **Petrified Forest Trail** from Calistoga.

Quaint and tempting as the **Napa Valley Wine Train** (1275 McKinstry St., Napa, tel. 707/253–2111) may sound, the train is more of a moving restaurant than a means of transportation—no stopping for a taste of the grape. In addition, it's resented by the locals for polluting the valley and bringing too many tourists. If you're *still* interested, $24 buys you a joyride to St. Helena and back. For that kind of money, rent a car—you can't get drunk, but at least you have the liberty to stop when and where you want.

BY CAR When you tour the Wine Country by car, please do everyone a favor and choose a designated driver. In summer, much of the traffic can be avoided by staying off Hwy. 29 and exploring the less crowded and more scenic Silverado Trail, which runs parallel to Hwy. 29 a mile to the east. Exit Hwy. 29 at any point between Napa and Calistoga and follow the Silverado Trail signs.

BY BUS It requires creativity to see the Wine Country on public transit, but hey—that's half the fun. In particular, **Sonoma County Transit** (tel. 707/576–7433) connects all cities in Sonoma County, with buses running weekdays 6 AM–6:30 PM (some until 10 PM), weekends 8–6. Fares are less than $2 to most places (ask for student and disabled discounts), and buses can get you within walking distance of a few wineries: Kunde, Château St. Jean, and Valley of the Moon. **Napa Valley Transit** (1151 Pearl St., at Main St., tel. 707/255–7631) offers frequent service between Napa and Yountville ($1), St. Helena ($2), and Calistoga ($2) Monday–Saturday. In between, you can be dropped off at Beaulieu, Beringer, Prager Port Works, and Sutter Home wineries.

BY BIKE Biking is perhaps the best way to see the Wine Country, and both Napa and Sonoma are relatively flat and easy on the legs. In Napa, wineries are closer together, making bicycling ideal if wine tasting is your thing. As for scenery, the valleys are comparable, although Sonoma offers less congestion. The 50-mile haul from Sonoma to St. Helena may not be too appealing, but within each region the wineries tend to be clumped close together, making them easy to see on two wheels. Cyclists on Hwy. 29 risk being run over by tipsy drivers, especially on summer weekends—stick to Silverado Trail or Solano Avenue (an access road that parallels Hwy. 29 from Napa to Yountville). In the town of Sonoma, cyclists can avoid most of the traffic and drunk drivers by traveling along Arnold Drive; it splits off from Highway 12 about 4 miles south of town and rejoins the highway just south of Glen Ellen. **Napa Valley Cyclery** (4080 Byway E, at Salvador Ave., tel. 707/255–3380 or 800/707–BIKE), at the northern end of Napa, rents bikes for $6 per hour or $20 per day. Farther north, **St. Helena Cyclery** (1156 Main St., at Spring St., tel. 707/963–7736) charges $7 per hour, $25 per day, or $140 per week. **Sonoma Valley Cyclery** (1061 Broadway, Sonoma, tel. 707/935–3377), on Hwy. 12, can set you up with a mountain bike for $6 per hour or $20 per day. All these shops offer biking maps and tour suggestions, so squeeze as much info out of them as possible.

One of the best winery routes takes cyclists on an easy ride through Sonoma's fields and vineyards. From Sonoma's downtown plaza, take East Napa Street east, turn left at Sebastiani Winery (4th St. E), then right on Lovall Valley Road. From here follow signs to any of several wineries in the foothills, including **Bartholomew Park** (1000 Vineyard Ln., off Castle Rd., tel. 707/935–9511), **Ravenswood,** and **Buena Vista** (*see* Wineries, *below*). For a longer ride, continue on Lovall Valley Road and turn right on Thornsberry Road, which leads to **Gundlach-Bundschu** winery (*see* Wineries, *below*). After a pit stop at the tasting room, take Denmark Street back toward town. The whole trip is about 7 miles.

Sonoma Valley

Although Napa Valley receives most of the hype, Sonoma Valley is the birthplace of California's wine industry, and it's a better bet for budget travelers. For one thing, almost all of Sonoma's wineries offer free tastings, meaning you can imbibe to your heart's content without spending a dime. In addition, most of the wineries are small, family-owned concerns, more relaxed and less crowded than those in Napa.

The town of **Sonoma** may have recently grown into an upscale bedroom community for San Francisco commuters, but behind the trendy restaurants and chic clothing boutiques lie a small-town sense of humor and a rich California history. It was here that Father José Altimira built the last and northernmost of the California missions, **Mission San Francisco Solano** (1st and Spain Sts., tel. 707/938–1519). The missionaries planted the region's first vines here in 1823 to make sacramental wine. For a $2 fee (also good for entrance to Lachryma Montis and

The Bear Flag Republic

For a short period in 1846, Sonoma belonged not to Mexico, Spain, or the United States, but to the lesser-known Bear Flag Republic—the brainchild of Captain John C. Frémont and a ragtag group of Yankee trappers who decided to resolve tensions between the Mexican government and non-Mexican immigrants by throwing the Mexican commander in prison and creating their own country. The republic was broken up a month later when the U.S. Navy arrived, but the bear remains on the California state flag.

the army barracks) you can see the reconstructed priests' quarters and a collection of 19th-century watercolors by Chris Jorgenson. Kitty-corner to the mission lies grassy **Sonoma Plaza,** the largest such plaza in California and the epicenter of Sonoma life. Around the plaza, many adobe buildings remain from the days of Spanish and Mexican rule, including old army barracks and the restored **Toscana Hotel** (20 E. Spain St., tel. 707/938–5889). Friday–Sunday between 1 and 4, kindly gray-haired docents will recount the hotel's colorful past as a general store, library, and home to Italian stone masons. Behind the hotel is Depot Park and the free **Sonoma Depot Museum** (270 1st St. W, tel. 707/938–1762), which chronicles Sonoma Valley history on and off the rails. It's worth a quick peek inside to see a pair of grizzly bear feet worn by Ulysses S. Grant to a San Francisco masquerade ball in the 1860s. Three blocks west of the plaza lies **Lachryma Montis** (3rd St. W, off W. Spain St., tel. 707/938–1519), the ornate home of the last Mexican governor, General Vallejo. Admission to the grounds is $2.

WHERE TO SLEEP Beds don't come cheap in the Sonoma Valley. If you have a tent, your best bet is to camp. Otherwise you'll probably want to make the half-hour drive north on Hwy. 12 to Santa Rosa for an affordable room. Even at Sonoma's least expensive motel, **El Pueblo Motel** (896 W. Napa St., on Hwy. 12, tel. 707/996–3651 or 800/900–8844), a clean and generic double will run you a whopping $77 on weekdays, $88 on weekends ($66 daily in winter). At least the motel has a great swimming pool and is close to the central square and several wineries.

Since prices are comparable, consider staying at one of Sonoma's bed-and-breakfasts. **Hollyhock House** (1541 Denmark St., off 8th St. E, tel. 707/938–1809) attracts adventurous, bohemian types to its old two-story farmhouse on a quiet country road, with geese, a friendly gray cat, and a comfy back porch. The two doubles cost $80–$90 on summer weekends ($55 in winter), but you can lower the price of the cheaper room to $55–$65 by staying more than one weekend night or coming on a weekday. In Glen Ellen, the **Jack London Lodge** (13740 Arnold Dr., at London Ranch Rd., tel. 707/938–8510) offers comfortable doubles with antique decor for $75; off-season specials can lower rates to $55–$60. The lodge has a pool, a saloon, and a decent restaurant. Reservations are strongly advised, especially in summer.

➢ **CAMPING** • **Sugarloaf Ridge State Park.** Only 8 miles north of Sonoma on Hwy. 12, Sugarloaf has 49 campsites scattered around a large meadow (dry and uninviting in summer). There are 25 miles of trails for hiking, biking, and horseback riding (*see* Outdoor Activities, *below*). If you hike up the trail to your left as you enter the park, you're likely to see deer, especially around sunset when they come out for early evening grazing. Campsites cost $15 ($12 in winter). In summer and on weekends, it's a good idea to reserve ahead through Destinet (tel. 800/444–PARK). *2605 Adobe Canyon Rd., Kenwood, tel. 707/833–5712. From Sonoma, Hwy. 12 north, right on Adobe Canyon Rd., which dead-ends at park. Day use fee ($5), barbecues, drinking water, flush toilets.*

FOOD Sonoma is *the* place to get your fill of gourmet-pesto this and roasted-goat-cheese that. Fortunately, there are some options for those unable to lay out huge sums of cash: Put together a picnic at the **Sonoma Farmer's Market** Friday 9–noon in Depot Park. An additional market is held in the plaza Tuesday evenings from 4:30 until dusk. Both markets take place during the summer months. Sonoma's best breakfast deal is at the **Feed Store Café and Bakery** (529 1st St. W, off central plaza, tel. 707/938–2122). From 7 AM–2:30 PM you can get a two-egg breakfast, fruity granola, or orange-brandy French toast for under $5.

Come dinner time, dive into delicious pasta dishes ($7–$11) on the patio at **Pasta Nostra** (139 E. Napa St., tel. 707/938–4166). Or head down the alley east of the plaza to lively **Murphy's Irish Pub** (464 1st St. E, tel. 707/935–0660) for homemade lamb stew and vegetables ($6.50), a pint of stout ($3.50), and live Irish tunes (summer weekends). For a Mexican-food fix, the roadside **Cocina Cha Cha** (897 W. Napa St., tel. 707/996–1735) is open daily until 9 PM and serves crisp tacos with ground beef for only 99¢. Two people can easily split the enormous burrito grande ($6.75), filled with the works and topped with a spicy homemade sauce.

For an excellent sit-down meal, trek out to the one-street town of Glen Ellen, where you'll find the **Sonoma Mountain Grill** (13690 Arnold Dr., tel. 707/938–2370), open Monday and Wednesday–Friday 11–9, weekends 9–9. The fresh fish special—with a heaping salad, vegetables, and rice—is the most expensive thing on the menu ($12–$14), but it's well worth it; with an appetizer, it could feed two.

WINERIES Sonoma Valley is home to some 30 wineries and 6,000 acres of vineyards. It was here that California began its upstart drive to compete with old-world wineries, when Count Agoston Haraszthy, the "father of California wine," brought thousands of European grapevine cuttings to the United States in 1857 and started the **Buena Vista** winery (18000 Old Winery Rd., Sonoma, tel. 800/926–1266). You can easily spend a leisurely day driving up Hwy. 12 through the 17-mile-long valley, stopping to sip a little wine, learn a little history, have a picnic, and nap in the sun.

Benziger. You're encouraged to roam the beautiful grounds, enjoy the fragrant rose gardens, picnic in any spot you choose, and indulge in many a free taster. Benziger is currently in the process of tearing out some of their merlot vines to make room for hops (yes, beer hops!). They are jumping on the microbrewery bandwagon with the opening of the Sonoma Mountain Brewing Company. Vino lovers can breathe easy—they plan on continuing their line of wines. *1883 London Ranch Rd., Glen Ellen, tel. 707/935–3000. From Hwy. 12, take Glen Ellen (Arnold Dr.) turnoff and follow signs for Jack London State Park. Open daily 10–5. Wheelchair access.*

Château St. Jean. The palatial grounds include a fish pond, a fountain, and an observation tower from which you get a spectacular view of the vineyard and surrounding area. Though tasting is free, the room is crowded, and the staff may be too busy to be very helpful. For a more relaxed time, kick back on the lawn with a picnic and a bottle of their excellent gewürztraminer ($8). *8555 Hwy. 12, Kenwood, tel. 707/833–4134, or 800/543–7572. From Sonoma, Hwy. 12 north past Glen Ellen and look for sign on right. Open daily 10–4:30. Wheelchair access.*

Cline Cellars. You'll pass through grapevines and roses on the way to the tasting room, in an old farmhouse dating from the mid-1800s. At the tasting bar, you can try four of the six wines, as well as homemade mustards, for free. If you've brought your Brie and baguettes, you can picnic on the porch beside one of six ponds fed by neighboring hot springs. *24737 Arnold Dr. (Hwy. 121), Sonoma, tel. 707/935–4310. Btw Hwys. 12 and 37. Open daily 10–6. Wheelchair access.*

Gundlach-Bundschu. Someone at this 137-year-old, family-owned winery has a sense of humor. In the main building (surrounded by trellised wisteria), old photographs of the family and winery sit alongside a picture of Bacchus in shades. Then there are the corks, inscribed: "Leave the kids the land and money—drink the wine yourself." Free tasters of up to five different wines get you in the proper hedonistic mood. *2000 Denmark St., Sonoma, tel. 707/938–5277. From plaza, take E. Napa St. east, turn right on E. 8th St., left on Denmark St., and look for sign on left. Open daily 11–4:30. Wheelchair access.*

Kunde. The folks at Kunde claim it's the friendliest winery in the valley, and they mean it—step into the large tasting room and you'll be greeted by a glass and a smile. Enjoy free tastings in their airy tasting room or take the half-hour tour through the vast cave cellars. If things are slow, you may even get a tour of the property, including the owner's duck sanctuary and the ruined stone winery where Geena Davis was married. *10155 Hwy. 12, Kenwood, tel. 707/833–5501. From Sonoma, Hwy. 12 north 7 mi; winery is on right, just past Glen Ellen. Open daily 11–5. Wheelchair access.*

Ravenswood. This small, stone winery in the Sonoma foothills has a relaxed, intimate feel. Their motto is *Nulla Vinum Flaccidum* (No Wimpy Wines), and their merlots and zinfandels are definitely worth writing home about. If you didn't bring a picnic to savor on the terrace, try their barbecued chicken or ribs with bread, coleslaw, and potato salad ($6–$7.25), available on summer weekends only. *18701 Gehricke Rd., Sonoma, tel. 707/938–1960. From plaza, take Spain St. east, turn left on 4th St. E, right onto Lovall Valley Rd., left on Gehricke Rd. Open daily 10–4:30. Wheelchair access.*

Schug. Walter Schug will pour you free tastes of his European-style wines at this mellow, family-run winery. Not many tourists come here, so the family members (who are viticultural experts) have plenty of time to answer questions. They'll give you a tour if you're interested, and you can explore the rooms where the wines are aged and bottled. *602 Bonneau Rd.,*

Sonoma, tel. 707/939–9363, or 800/966–9365. From plaza, Hwy. 12 south, then Hwy. 121 west until it hits Hwy. 116 at stop sign; Bonneau Rd. is straight ahead. Open daily 10–5. Wheelchair access.

Valley of the Moon. This intimate winery off the main drag is a breath of fresh air compared to the more crowded vineyards in the upper valley. The staff is friendly and helpful, and in that fine Sonoma Valley tradition, tasting is free. Be sure to sample their port, a brandy-fortified wine that packs a punch. *777 Madrone Rd., Glen Ellen, tel. 707/996–6941. From Sonoma, Hwy. 12 north 6 mi to Madrone Rd. Open Apr.–Oct., daily 10–5; Nov.–Mar., daily 10–4:30. Wheelchair access.*

Wellington. Run by a father-son team, this tiny winery just opened its doors in 1994, and it's still obscure enough to escape the tourist hordes. The tasting room is a down-to-earth affair with a small terrace and a view of the Sonoma Mountains. Tastings of their delicious wines are unlimited—be sure to try the Estate Chardonnay, a combination of fruit and clove flavors that tastes like liquid Christmas. *11600 Dunbar Rd., Glen Ellen, tel. 707/939–0708. From Sonoma, Hwy. 12 north 7 mi, exit left at Dunbar Rd. Open daily 11–5. Wheelchair access.*

CHEAP THRILLS Wine isn't the only thing that's free in the Sonoma Valley. If you're pinching pennies, don't miss the free samples at the **Sonoma Cheese Factory** (2 Spain St., Sonoma, tel. 707/996–1931), where the popular Sonoma Jack cheese is made. At the mellower, family-owned **Vella Cheese Company** (315 2nd St. E, Sonoma, tel. 707/938–3232), watch cheese being rolled by hand Monday–Wednesday from noon to 2 PM. Hard-core freeloaders will have a field day at **Viansa** (25200 Arnold Dr., on Hwy. 121, tel. 707/935–4700), a slick, commercial winery equipped with an Italian-style marketplace. Be prepared to fight tooth-and-nail with hungry tourists for free tastes of chocolate sauces, preserves, mustards, oils, and, of course, wine. At Sonoma's central **plaza,** you can throw a Frisbee around, feed the resident ducks, or regress to childhood on the swings and the slide. In summer the **Sonoma Valley Jazz Society** offers free concerts around town. Call 707/996–7423 for schedule info.

OUTDOOR ACTIVITIES Towns like Sonoma and Glen Ellen may be overrun by a wine-sipping, Volvo-driving crowd, but in the rest of this largely rural valley you'll find gentle hills covered with live oak and wildflowers. Spring and autumn, when the weather is cool, are the best times for hiking and mountain biking in area parks. One of the more popular routes, either on foot or two wheels, is the Bald Mountain Trail in **Sugarloaf Ridge State Park** (*also see* Where to Sleep, *above*); you face a steep 3½-mile trek to the summit, but you'll be rewarded by a view that, on a clear day, stretches all the way to the Sierra Nevada. When the summer heat makes the backs of your legs stick to the car seat, head to **Morton's Warm Springs** (1651 Warm Springs Rd., off Hwy. 12 in Kenwood, tel. 707/833–5511), a low-key resort full of picnicking families and splashing kids. An entrance fee ($4.25, $5.75 weekends) gets you access to two spring-water pools, a small creek, a grassy picnic area, snack bar, and game room. Morton's is open daily from mid-May through August (weekends only in early May and September).

Napa Valley

While Sonoma is cheaper and more welcoming, it's Napa Valley, about a 20-minute drive east of Sonoma on Hwy. 121, that lures most visitors to the Wine Country. When the traffic backs up for miles on Hwy. 29, it's clear that Napa Valley has become one of the Bay Area's biggest tourist attractions north of Fisherman's Wharf. The scenery is still beautiful, the wine (in some cases) still free, the town of **Napa** still lined with attractive Victorian houses and California bungalows, but the Napa Valley is losing some of its old-time charm with each trampling tourist.

Stock up on groceries in the quiet, but touristy town of St. Helena, 16 miles north of Napa on Hwy. 29. You might even bump into Francis Ford Coppola (who makes his home here) while bagging picnic supplies.

Wine may take center stage in the Napa Valley, but a fair share of hedonists come here solely for a peaceful soak in the valley's hot springs and mud baths, most in or near Calistoga. Though you'd perhaps hesitate to throw yourself in a roadside ditch and roll around in the muck, folks in the Wine Country believe that mud baths and sulfur springs heal all manner of ills. Poverty is not one of them: You'll pay a pretty penny for a day of pampering. On the bright side, you can spend the night at any of several resorts for a decent price, and get free access to mineral pools and Jacuzzis.

WHERE TO SLEEP Although some of the most expensive lodging in the Wine Country is here in the posh Napa Valley, budget travelers can survive by camping or checking into one of Napa's lower-end motels. In summer, reserve at least three weeks ahead.

➤ **NAPA** • One of Napa's cheapest options is the **Silverado Motel** (500 Silverado Trail, tel. 707/253–0892), where a tacky but cleanish room is $38 weekdays, $55 weekends ($38 daily in winter). The rooms at the **Napa Motel** (314 Soscol Ave., tel. 707/226–1878) are equally homely and equally cheap ($42 weekdays, $52 weekends). The **Napa Valley Budget Inn** (3380 Solano Ave., off Hwy. 29, tel. 707/257–6111) has clean but spartan doubles starting at $60 ($76 on Friday or Saturday). The swimming pool is perfect after a long day at the wineries, many of which are within biking distance. At the **Wine Valley Lodge** (200 S. Coombs St., tel. 707/224–7911), comfy rooms cost $60 on weekdays, $90 on weekends—unless you want to stay in the room where Elvis slept, in which case you must shell out $150. Amenities include a pool and a barbecue in the courtyard, and one room is wheelchair accessible.

➤ **CALISTOGA** • Pleasure-seekers planning to hit both the wineries and the hot springs should consider staying in Calistoga. If you want to stay on the main drag, the **Calistoga Inn** (1250 Lincoln Ave., tel. 707/942–4101) has clean, simple bed-and-breakfast rooms with shared baths and full-size beds for $49 ($60 Fri.–Sat.). For $54 (second night $5 off), you can get a cabin for two at the **Triple S Ranch** (4600 Mt. Home Ranch Rd., tel. 707/942–6730). There's no phone or TV, but the complex does include a swimming pool and a pricey steak house. The ranch is north of Calistoga off Hwy. 128; take Petrified Forest Road west for 2½ miles until you reach Mt. Home Ranch Road. If you can't spend the night without a color TV, try the **Holiday House** (3514 Hwy. 128, tel. 707/942–6174), 3 miles north of Calistoga; watch for the white picket fence. From the outside it looks like you're pulling into a friend's house, but the three rooms ($60) are strictly Motel 6.

➤ **CAMPING** • Camping is your best budget option in Napa (and the Wine Country in general). Unfortunately, there isn't any public transportation to the campgrounds; unless you have a car, you'll have to hitchhike, walk, or bike back to civilization. If you're getting desperate, head 20 miles east from Rutherford on Hwy. 128 to Lake Berryessa. The lake is divided into seven campgrounds, including **Pleasure Cove** (tel. 707/966–2172) and **Spanish Flat** (tel. 707/966–7700), for a total of 225 campsites (about $16) near the water. While you get direct access to swimming, fishing, picnicking, and waterskiing facilities, the area around the lake is barren, dusty, and very hot during summer. Summer weekends, reserve ahead.

Bothe-Napa State Park. This is the Wine Country's most attractive campground, situated in the Napa foothills amid redwoods, madrone, and tan oaks, only 5 miles north of St. Helena and its wineries. The sites are reasonably private, and the park is one of the few with a swimming pool ($3 separate fee), much used on hot summer days. The fee is $15–$16 April–October or $12 off-season (half-price disabled camping pass available through Destinet), and reservations are suggested in summer, especially on weekends. For reservations call Destinet (tel. 800/444–PARK). *3801 St. Helena Hwy. N, Calistoga, tel. 707/942–4575. From St. Helena, north on Hwy. 29. 48 sites. No cooking facilities, day use fee ($5), drinking water, flush toilets, hot showers. Wheelchair access.*

FOOD If wine tasting is Napa Valley's main attraction, gourmet cuisine runs a close second. The best way to eat well without breaking the bank is to stock up at one of the area's makeshift farmers' markets (*see below*), with bushels of fresh produce at reasonable prices. If you're spending the day in Calistoga, cruise down to the **Calistoga Roastery** (1631 Lincoln Ave., tel. 707/942–5757), open daily 7–6. The bottomless cup of coffee ($1) is a good deal, and the ice cream latte ($2.50) makes a great dessert. For cheap Mexican food, head to the west end of Lincoln Avenue, where it dead-ends at the wheelchair accessible **Calistoga Drive-In Taquería** (1207 Foothill Blvd., tel. 707/942–0543). A veggie burrito here runs $3.50, and the tortillas and chips are great.

Calistoga Inn. The California cuisine at this casual restaurant is excellent, and—for once—the portions are fair for the price. Try the grilled lemon-chicken sausage with sauerkraut, roasted potatoes, and coleslaw ($7.75), or cool off in the shady garden with one of their award-winning home-brew ales or lagers—only $2 during happy hour (weekdays 4–6 PM). *1250 Lincoln Ave., tel. 707/942–4101. Open daily 11:30–3 and 5:30–9:30 (weekends until 10); shorter hrs off-season.*

The Diner. Several good restaurants line Washington Street in Yountville, but this is the best for the price. You can get huge plates of American or Mexican food for lunch and dinner, or specialty eggs and pancakes for breakfast. Most meals are $7–$10, but portions are generous (consider splitting an appetizer and a main course with a friend). *6476 Washington St., Yountville, tel. 707/944–2626. Open Tues.–Sun. 8–3 and 5:30–9.*

The Red Hen Cantina. Pull into the Red Hen for their popular fajitas ($22 for two people) and margaritas ($5), or one of the hefty side dishes (tamales, burritos, chili rellenos) starting at about $3. Then take a seat on the large outdoor patio and watch people race to the wineries. You, on the other hand, can search for the perfect souvenir at the attached antique store (open 10–5). *5091 St. Helena Hwy. (Hwy. 29), tel. 707/255–8125. 5 mi north of Napa off Oak Knoll Rd. Open weekdays 11–9, weekends 11–10.*

➤ **MARKETS AND DELICATESSENS • Napa Valley Farmers' Market.** This market is held on Tuesdays in Napa and Fridays in St. Helena, with fruits and veggies, cheese, eggs, honey, dressings, cut flowers, baked goods, and countless other edibles. *Napa: West St., btw 1st and Pearl Sts., tel. 707/252–2105. Just west of Cinedome Theater, which has free parking. Open May–Oct., Tues. 7:30–noon. St. Helena: Old Railroad Depot, tel. 707/252–2105. East on Adams St. off Hwy. 29, left at stop sign, and 1 block up on right. Open May–Oct., Fri. 7:30–11:30 AM.*

Pometta's Deli. This place is famous for its barbecued chicken platters ($7), but you can also get box lunches to go ($9.50–$12.50). Especially good is the vegetarian sandwich (about $4), stuffed with avocado, provolone, zucchini, and jalapeños. The restaurant has indoor and outdoor seating and—wonder of wonders—tournament horseshoe pits (free). *Hwy. 29, at Oakville Grade in Oakville, tel. 707/944–2365. Open weekdays 9–5, Sat. 10–5, Sun. 10–4.*

If you let enough wine go to your head, starve yourself for a week, and reserve two months ahead, you can dine at Yountville's French Laundry (6640 Washington St., at Creek St., tel. 707/944–2380)— reputed to be California's BEST restaurant. The nine-course, prix-fixe menu will set you back $75, so it damn well better be good.

WINERIES With literally hundreds of wineries crammed into the 35-mile-long Napa Valley, it's difficult to decide which to visit. Some, like **Sutter Home Winery** (277 Hwy. 29, St. Helena, tel. 707/963–3104), right on the main drag, are packed with drunken revelers, while others, like **Trefethen Vineyards** (1160 Oak Knoll Ave., Napa, tel. 707/255–7700), draw a sedate crowd able to hold forth about a wine's bouquet and tannins. If you're irked by the idea of paying a $3 tasting fee, you'll have to choose wineries carefully. Seek out the freebies at some of the smaller wineries, where the extra attention paid to the product often means better wine. As one vintner explained, "I know every barrel like it was my own child."

Beaulieu Vineyards. Affectionately known as "BV," Beaulieu has supplied wine to President Eisenhower and Queen Elizabeth, among other notables. Unbelievably, BV is far from snooty. The staff greets you with a glass of wine at the door of the octagonal tasting room and encourages you to indulge in free samples. If you like dessert wine, be sure to taste their lovely muscat. Free, informative, half-hour tours cover the wine-making process and BV's 100-year history. *1960 Hwy. 29, Rutherford, tel. 707/963–2411. Open daily 10–5. Wheelchair access.*

Nichelini. Napa's oldest family-owned winery (since 1890) lies 11 miles east of Rutherford and is worth every minute of the beautiful drive. Outside, under the shade of walnut trees and next to an old Roman grape press (which looks like a giant garlic press), you can sample several wines for free. Picnic to the strains of traditional Italian music on a hill overlooking the countryside. *Hwy. 128, St. Helena, tel. 707/963–0717 or 800/WE–TASTE. Open May–Oct., weekends 10–6; Nov.–Apr., weekends 10–5.*

Beringer Winery (2000 Hwy. 29, St. Helena, tel. 707/963–7115) is one of the few wineries to remain in continuous operation since 1876. A government license to make sacramental wine kept Beringer in business during Prohibition. Now, Beringer is owned by the Nestlé corporation and has its own winery clothing line!

Prager Port Works. Owner Jim Prager and the family dog Eno (short for "Enology") know the meaning of hospitality. This rustic winery doesn't even produce enough cases a year to be classified as "small." ("That makes us 'tiny,'" quips Jim.) Tastings run $3, but the fee can be applied toward a bottle of Prager's special port ($35), available only at the winery. The homey garden provides a quiet break from the Highway 29 crowds. *1281 Lewelling Ln., St. Helena, tel. 707/963–PORT or 800/969–PORT. On Hwy. 29, next to Sutter Home. Open daily 10:30–4:30, or whenever the last person leaves. Wheelchair access.*

Rustridge. While you're traipsing through Napa's backwoods, check out this winery, ranch, and B&B ($100–$155). You'll probably be the only visitor indulging in the free tasters, served in a converted barn. Someone might even have to run in from the fields to open the tasting room. You can picnic on the serene grounds of Catacula (Valley of the Oaks), as the native people once called this land. *2910 Lower Chiles Valley Rd., St. Helena, tel. 707/965–9353 or 800/788–0263. From Hwy. 29 north, Hwy. 128 east. Cross Silverado Trail, left at*

How to Taste Like a Master

If you want to pass yourself off as a wine aficionado (as opposed to a freeloading swiller), you'll need to know some rules of tasting. First of all, move from light wines to dark, so as not to "clutter your palate," as a vintner might say. Begin by vigorously swirling an ounce of wine in your glass. Put your hand over the glass to hold in the aromas (as well as the wine, if you're new to the swirling business). Raise the glass to your nose and inhale deeply. In young wines, you smell only the grapes (for example, the smell of the pinot noir grape might remind you of black cherries); with aging, the wine becomes more complex, emitting a whole "bouquet" of aromas (in pinot, that can include violets, vanilla, spicy pepper, or even leather). Next, take a sip—you're encouraged to slurp, because air helps you taste the wine. Swish the wine around in your mouth to pick up the more subtle flavors. Before downing the rest of your glass, notice the aftertaste (or "finish"), and then decide what you think. ("It's a cheeky little wine, reminiscent of running naked through verdant pastures.")

If you're seriously interested in viticulture—and not just trying to impress your date—take a course through City College of San Francisco's Extension Program (Fort Mason Art Campus, tel. 415/561–1860). They have Saturday afternoon seminars ($24, wine included) or six-week evening classes for under $100. In the East Bay, U.C. Berkeley Extension's Wine Studies department offers classes on Wines of California and Europe, Country Wines of France, and others. The fees are steep ($125–$150 for a six-week course, plus $65 for the wine), but the courses are fun and incredibly informative. Contact U.C. Berkeley Extension (2223 Fulton St., Berkeley 94720, tel. 510/642–4111) for more info.

fork (look for Pope Valley sign), first right on Lower Chiles Valley Rd. Open daily 10–5 (winter until 4).

S. Anderson. Tours are given twice daily, frequently by John Anderson, son of the late Stan (as in "S.") Anderson. He does a wonderful job guiding you through his vineyards and candlelit, stone wine caves, modeled after those in the Champagne region of France. The caves hold over 400,000 bottles of sparkling wine, awaiting their "turn" (champagne bottles are turned by hand in a labor-intensive process that removes the yeast). The tour, with tasting, costs $3, but it's more than worth it. Plan for over an hour—John doesn't need much prompting to extend the visit. *1473 Yountville Crossroad, Yountville, tel. 800/4–BUBBLY. From Hwy. 29 in Yountville, take Madison exit and follow signs for Yountville Crossroad. Open daily 10–5; tours at 10:30 and 2:30.*

Wermuth. Vintner Ralph Wermuth presides over the tiny tasting room and is more entertaining than a barrel of monkeys: He's one part philosopher, one part mad scientist, and one part stand-up comedian. For $1 you get tastings of Gamay accompanied by chocolate chips to "bring out the flavor," and colombard paired with that gourmet standby, Cheez-Its. Wife and partner Smitty Wermuth designs the winery logos, which depict the old Italian basket presses still used here in the crush. *3942 Silverado Trail, Calistoga, tel. 707/942–5924. From Hwy. 29 north, Hwy. 128 east to Silverado Trail; continue north past Bale Ln. and look for sign on right. Open Tues.–Sun. 11–5.*

HOT SPRINGS The majority of the Napa Valley's mud and mineral baths are in the curious little town of Calistoga, at the northern end of the valley. The town's bubbling mineral spring became a spa in 1859, when entrepreneur Sam Brannan slurred together the word California with the name of New York's Saratoga Springs resort; Calistoga has been attracting health seekers ever since. Unfortunately, most visitors are loaded and willing to pay up the wazoo to get their wazoo steam-wrapped. Prices at the Calistoga spas are uniformly steep, varying by only a couple of dollars. Be sure to pick up 10%-off coupons at the **Calistoga Chamber of Commerce** (1458 Lincoln Ave., tel. 707/942–6333), open weekdays 10–5, Sat. 10–4.

A cheaper option is open-air bathing at rustic retreats like Harbin Hot Springs or White Sulphur Springs (*see below*). You won't get to play human mud pie at the outdoor spas, but you can bathe in natural springs and hike through rolling grounds far from the buzz of urbanity. Not only do these resorts offer many of the same amenities as the Calistoga spas, but you get an affordable room for the night to boot. If you opt for one of the indoor spas, call ahead for a reservation. Most accept walk-ins, but nothing is more stressful than being turned away from the massage you've been aching for.

Golden Haven Hot Springs. A favorite with hetero couples, Golden Haven is the only Calistoga spa to offer private co-ed mud baths (sorry lovebirds, there's still an attendant). The full treatment (mud bath, mineral Jacuzzi, blanket wrap, and 30-minute massage) will run you $64 per person. If you're too relaxed to make it past the front door, you can crash in one of their rooms for $59 ($49 Sept.–June), which includes use of the swimming pool and hot mineral pool. *1713 Lake St., Calistoga, tel. 707/942–6793. From Lincoln Ave. east, left on Stevenson St., right on Lake St. Open daily 9–9.*

Harbin Hot Springs. Forty minutes north of Calistoga, this 1,200-acre, laid-back community is run by the Heart Consciousness Church, a group that advocates holistic health and spiritual renewal. The retreat, popular with gay men, has three natural mineral pools, varying in temperature from tepid to *very* hot, and a cold, spring-fed "plunge" pool, all open 24 hours. To use the pools you must pay $5 for a one-month membership or $15 for a year (only one member per group required), plus an additional day-use fee ($13 Mon.–Thurs., $18 Fri.–Sun. and holidays). There's also an acclaimed massage school, whose graduates would be happy to show you their stuff ($46 per hour, $60 for 90 minutes). You're welcome to use the vegetarian-only communal kitchen or eat their veggie-only meals ($8–$12). Rustic dorm beds start at $23 ($35 on weekends and holidays), and you have to provide your own sheets or sleeping bag. Private rooms

They say "clothing optional" but you're going to feel pretty out of place if you wear anything but a smile into the pools at Harbin Hot Springs.

with shared bath are $60 ($90 on weekends). There are campsites along the creek and in nearby meadows, but at $14 per person ($23 Fri.–Sat., $17 Sun.), it's a lot to pay for a night in a tent, especially when the grounds are unkempt and the bathrooms few and far between. Despite the cost, expect a crowd on weekends. *Tel. 707/987–2477 or 800/622–2477 (Northern California only). Hwy. 29 north to Middletown, turn left at junction for Hwy. 175, right on Barnes St.; go 1½ mi to Harbin Springs Rd. and turn left. Rides can be arranged for those taking Greyhound.*

Lincoln Avenue Spa. With pleasant stone-and-wood massage rooms and a central location, this spa is posh for the price. Their Body Mud Treatment ($38) is the ideal alternative for those squeamish about wallowing in mud someone else has already wallowed in: You get your choice of mud (herbal, sea, or mint) slathered over your body, a relaxing nap on the steam table, and a soothing facial mask. *1339 Lincoln Ave., Calistoga, tel. 707/942–5296. Open daily 9–9.*

Nance's Spa. Of the Calistoga spas, Nance's is one of the cheapest, offering "the works" for $62. You begin by sliding into a tub of hot volcanic mud, then you shower and simmer in a bubbling mineral bath. Next you're swaddled in soft sheets and left to "set" like a human dumpling in preparation for a half-hour massage. The process is supposed to relieve tension and extract toxins from your skin and muscles. Nance's facilities are sex segregated and none too private: The amorous and the modest may opt to go elsewhere. *1614 Lincoln Ave., Calistoga, tel. 707/942–6211. Open weekdays 9–5, weekends 9–7.*

White Sulphur Springs. If you're planning to stay the night in Napa Valley, this St. Helena resort is a bargain. For $75 you get access to 300 acres of land, plenty of hiking and biking trails, a Jacuzzi, a natural mineral bath, even a stand of redwoods; *and* you get a decent room for the night, either in the rustic, dormitory-style carriage house or in the inn, where each room has a half-bath. It's a day and night of decadence for the price of an hour or two at some of Calistoga's spas. Reserve two weeks ahead of time. *3100 White Sulphur Springs Rd., St. Helena, tel. 707/963–8588. From Hwy. 29 north, turn left on Spring St. in St. Helena and go 2.8 mi. Note: Do NOT take Sulphur Springs Rd. from Hwy. 29.*

CHEAP THRILLS If you blow your last buck on a bottle of wine or a mud wrap, you'll still find fun in Napa Valley. In summer, the chamber of commerce sponsors free concerts in downtown Napa's **Veterans Memorial Park** (cnr 3rd and Main Sts.). One of the most popular is the **Napa Valley Jazz Festival,** held annually in mid-July. Sundays from 6–5, junk lovers can rummage among the used furniture, silver jewelry, and Harley-Davidson T-shirts at the **Napa Valley Flea Market** (303 S. Kelly Rd., tel. 707/226–8862), located south of Napa on Hwy. 29.

For a lesson in maximizing the potential of junk, trek out to **Litto's Hubcap Ranch** in Pope Valley. The Litto legacy began when Emanuelle "Litto" Damonte discovered that several hubcaps had been lost on a turn of the road near his property. Being a kindly fellow, he placed them on the fence for the owners to retrieve. Thirty years and over 2,000 hubcaps later, the metallic splendor of his house and property are a tribute to American folk art. Litto's grandson and family now live in the house and are surprisingly cordial to gawkers. To reach the ranch from Hwy. 29, take Hwy. 128 east, cross Silverado Trail, and bear left at the fork. When you reach Pope Valley, turn left on Pope Valley Road—it's a couple miles farther on the right.

OUTDOOR ACTIVITIES If you're determined to beat the heat, it's a half-hour drive from Napa or Rutherford to **Lake Berryessa** (*see* Camping, *above*), where you can rent almost any kind of water vessel—from a Jet Ski to a ski boat—from one of the lake's many resorts. If you're spending the day in Calistoga, pay a visit to **Robert Louis Stevenson State Park** off Hwy. 29, 9 miles northeast of Calistoga. Here you can hike to the bunkhouse of the Silverado Mine, where the impoverished author honeymooned with his wife, Fanny Osbourne, in the summer of 1880. The stay inspired Stevenson's *The Silverado Squatters.* The park is perched at the top of Mt. St. Helena, which is said to be the model for Spyglass Hill in *Treasure Island.* Its 3,000 acres are largely undeveloped; picnicking is permitted but overnight camping is not.

Skyline Wilderness Park. Perhaps the best way to experience the beauty of the Napa Valley is to get out and hike, preferably on Skyline's 2½-mile Lake Marie Trail, which runs along a shady creek and past overgrown orchards and ruined stone dairies. Swimming in Lake Marie isn't allowed, but you can try your luck fishing for bluegill and bass. *2201 Imola Ave, tel. 707/252–0481. Open Mon.–Thurs. 9–8, Fri.–Sun. 8–8; shorter hrs in winter.*

Lake Tahoe

Straddling the border of California and Nevada on the northern flank of the Sierra Nevada range, Lake Tahoe is one of the West Coast's most popular outdoor playgrounds. During spring and summer, when temperatures hover in the 70s, the lake (about a 3½-hour drive east of San Francisco on I–80) offers boating, fishing, waterskiing, and jet skiing; and the mountains surrounding Tahoe Basin satiate the desires of even the most demanding rock climbers, hikers, bikers, equestrians, and anglers. During the winter season (usually December–April, sometimes extending into May), attention shifts to downhill and cross-country skiing and snowboarding. Tahoe has earned a worldwide reputation for its "extreme" conditions, thanks to the sheer cliffs and steep faces of the Sierra Nevada, while the Donner Summit is famed for its challenging rock climbing faces.

Given the array of pleasures, it's no wonder Lake Tahoe draws up to 100,000 tourists at peak periods. On weekends, the traffic on I–80 between the Bay Area and Lake Tahoe has to be seen to be believed. The lake itself is 6,225 feet above sea level, for its size the highest in the U.S. The water is so clear you can see 75 feet below the surface, and it holds enough water to cover the state of California to a depth of 14 inches. Those who come to the lake and spend all their time in the hermetically sealed casinos are missing out on one of the most varied and incredible natural areas in the country.

Besides being deep and blue, Lake Tahoe is also damn cold (40°-70° throughout the year). You can swim in it, but most visitors just dip their feet in and scamper back to shore. On the other hand, a quick dip is said by locals to be the best way to cure a hangover.

Although it's a somewhat subjective division, the lake's locales are usually designated as belonging to either the north shore or the south shore. Thanks largely to the popularity of fifteen or so ski areas (compared with two in the south), the north shore is the domain of Tahoe's athletic set. The south shore, on the other hand, is largely overrun with family vacationers and casino-bound gamblers. Places like **Desolation Wilderness** have, as one local ranger put it, "been loved to death," and have quotas regulating just how many people can enter.

The north shore's largest town is **Truckee,** about a 30-minute drive (12 miles) north of the lake, with a modern downtown area to the west and an Old Town (complete with a boardwalk, wood-frame storefronts, and an ancient railroad) to the east. Donner Pass Road connects the two sides of town and serves as the main commercial boulevard. To the west, **Tahoe City** has a small-town warmth largely lacking in Truckee. On the south shore, the city center of **South Lake Tahoe** is packed to the gills with restaurants, motels, and rental shops. The pace never flags in summer, and in winter popular ski areas like Heavenly keep the town jumping. Butting up against the east side of South Lake Tahoe is the imaginatively named town of **Stateline,** Nevada, a jumble of brightly lit casinos, hotels, and tacky gift shops.

BASICS

The **North Lake Tahoe Chamber of Commerce** (245 Hwy. 89, Tahoe City, tel. 916/581–6900) lies north of the Bank of America across from the Tahoe City "Y" (the intersection of Hwys. 89 and 28 that is impossible to miss). This site has free guides and maps, lots of community and historical facts, info on kids activities, resources for travelers with disabilities, and details on camping. The **Tahoe North Visitors and Convention Bureau** in Tahoe City (950 North Lake Blvd., near the Safeway, tel. 916/583–3494 or 800/824–6348) has deals on activity and accommodation packages year-round. The **Lake Tahoe Forest Service Visitor Center** (Hwy. 89, btw Emerald Bay and South Lake Tahoe, tel. 916/573–2674) has beach access and nature trails, many of which are wheelchair accessible. The staff will tell you all you want to know about the lake's natural and human history. This is also the place to pick up campfire and wilderness permits for the Desolation and Mokelumne wilderness areas. Permits are free, but

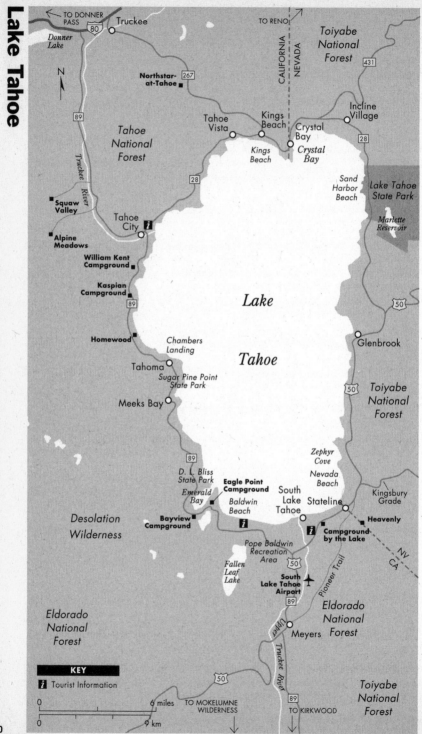

Lake Tahoe

TO DONNER PASS
80
Truckee
TO RENO
Donner Lake
Truckee River
N
89
Tahoe National Forest
Northstar-at-Tahoe
267

CALIFORNIA
NEVADA

Toiyabe National Forest
431

Tahoe Vista
Kings Beach
Crystal Bay
Incline Village
28
Kings Beach
Crystal Bay

Sand Harbor Beach
Lake Tahoe State Park

Squaw Valley
Alpine Meadows
Tahoe City
Marlette Reservoir

William Kent Campground
Kaspian Campground
89

Lake Tahoe

50
Homewood
Chambers Landing
Tahoma
Glenbrook
Sugar Pine Point State Park
50
Meeks Bay

Toiyabe National Forest

89
D.L. Bliss State Park
Eagle Point Campground
Zephyr Cove
Nevada Beach

Emerald Bay
Baldwin Beach
South Lake Tahoe
Stateline
Kingsbury Grade

Desolation Wilderness
Bayview Campground
Heavenly
Campground by the Lake
NV CA

Pope Baldwin Recreation Area
50
Fallen Leaf Lake
South Lake Tahoe Airport
89
Pioneer Trail
Eldorado National Forest

Eldorado National Forest
Upper Truckee River
Meyers

KEY
Tourist Information
0   6 miles
0   9 km

50
TO MOKELUMNE WILDERNESS
89
TO KIRKWOOD

Toiyabe National Forest

230

only a limited number are available. Depending on funding, the visitor center may be closed on certain days of the week—call ahead.

The **South Lake Tahoe Women's Center** (3140 Lake Tahoe Blvd., tel. 916/544–2118) has Spanish and English services and also operates a crisis line (tel. 916/544–4444) we hope you'll never have to use. Gay-friendly info on recreational activities, support groups, businesses, and accommodations is found through the **Tahoe Gay Hotline** (tel. 916/541–GAYS). **Disabled Sports USA of Northern California** (6060 Sunrise Vista Dr., Suite 3030, Citrus Heights, CA 95610, tel. 916/722–6447) has information on skiing, waterskiing, rafting, and other outdoor activities.

COMING AND GOING

BY CAR Both routes to Lake Tahoe take 3–3½ hours from the Bay Area when road and traffic conditions are at their best. To reach the north shore, follow I-80 east all the way to Truckee. For the south shore, take U.S. 50 east from Sacramento, which leads directly to South Lake Tahoe. You won't be allowed into the mountains without chains if it snows; bring your own or you'll have to pay inflated prices for a set near the CalTrans checkpoint. Even if you bring your own, consider paying (about $10) to let someone else put them on for you. You will see swarms of jumpsuit-clad people with numbers on their backs at every checkpoint waiting to perform this service.

For recorded info on road conditions, call CalTrans at 800/427–ROAD.

If snow doesn't slow you down, traffic might, especially on Friday and Sunday afternoons, and during summer and holiday weekends. If you must drive to Tahoe on Friday, wait until 7 or 8 PM. Traffic is usually worst on I-80, so consider taking U.S. 50, even if you're headed for the north shore.

BY BUS Greyhound (tel. 800/231–2222) runs five buses a day between San Francisco and Truckee (5–6 hrs, $32 one-way) and four between Truckee and Reno (1 hr, $9 one-way). If you're headed to the south shore, Greyhound makes the trip between Sacramento and **Harrah's Hotel and Casino** in Stateline, NV (3 hrs, $18 one-way) three times a day, with a $5 cash bonus on arrival. Both Amtrak and Greyhound use the **Transit Depot** (Donner Pass Rd., in Old Town Truckee, tel. 916/587–3822), a safe place to wait for connections or pick up info at the tourist office. There are a few coin-operated lockers here.

BY TRAIN Amtrak (tel. 800/USA–RAIL) runs three train/bus routes a day between Emeryville and Truckee (transfer in Sacramento, 5 hrs, $54 round-trip). If you're coming from San Francisco, take the free bus from the CalTrain Station at 4th and Townsend streets to the Emeryville Amtrak Station (5885 Landregan St., at Powell St., tel. 510/450–1081). Amtrak also has four trains a week traveling the hour-long route between Truckee and Reno ($13 one-way). All trains arrive at the Truckee Transit Depot (*see* By Bus, *above*). Another train/bus

Keep Tahoe Blue

Lake Tahoe is a magnificent sight, and with all the visitors, attention has to be paid so that it can stay that way. It's a tricky business to provide locals with jobs without bulldozing the unique surroundings, but the League to Save Lake Tahoe (around since 1957) has been trying to work with local businesses in its conservation efforts. The league is responsible for halting casino development on the north shore, buying up land for public use, monitoring industries to ensure that environmental regulations are being followed, and all those "Keep Tahoe Blue" bumper stickers. They also encourage appreciation of the natural setting by hosting free hiking, biking, and ski tours. Contact them at 916/541–5388 or 916/546–5410.

combination serves South Lake Tahoe from Emeryville (transfer in Sacramento, 5 hrs, $33 round-trip).

BY PLANE At press time, no commercial flights were flying into the Tahoe area, but Boone Air (tel. 209/982–1600) promises to be up and running by January 1997 with flights to the tiny **South Lake Tahoe Airport** (off Hwy. 89, about 2 miles south of the "Y" in South Lake Tahoe, tel. 916/541–4080) from San Francisco. Otherwise, your best bet is to get a flight to the **Reno Cannon International Airport** (2001 E. Plumb Ln., tel. 702/328–6499).

GETTING AROUND

Three intersecting highways form a loop around the lake: **Highway 89** (a.k.a. Emerald Bay Road) skirts the western shore of the lake between Tahoe City and South Lake Tahoe; **U.S. 50** (a.k.a. Lake Tahoe Boulevard) intersects Hwy. 89 in South Lake Tahoe and follows the lake's eastern shore; and **Highway 28** (a.k.a. North Lake Boulevard or Lake Shore Boulevard) runs along the north part of the shore back into Tahoe City. The intersections of Hwys. 28 and 89 in Tahoe City and Hwy. 89 and U.S. 50 in South Lake Tahoe are commonly referred to as the **Tahoe City "Y"** and the **South Lake Tahoe "Y,"** respectively.

Tahoe Area Regional Transit (TART) (tel. 916/581–6365 or 800/736–6365) has wheelchair accessible buses, most equipped with ski and bike racks, that serve the north and west shores of Lake Tahoe, traveling from Meeks Bay on the southwest shore to Incline Village in the north, and up Hwy. 89 to Truckee. The fare is $1.25, and buses run until 1 AM in summer. Between **BUS PLUS** (tel. 916/542–6077) and the **South Tahoe Area Ground Express (STAGE)**, service runs 24 hours from the South Lake Tahoe "Y" to Stateline, Nevada; the fare is $1.25 for STAGE, $2–$3 for BUS PLUS. BUS PLUS is for people who are too far from bus stops; if you call the number (*see above*) they will pick you up and drop you at the nearest STAGE stop. Schedules and maps are available from the tourist info centers. Pending continued funding, the new **Lake Lapper** (tel. 916/542–5900) is a great deal—$5 for an all day pass on coaches that circle the lake, stopping at scenic points of interest, connecting with STAGE and TART, and running 8 AM to 1:45 AM.

WHERE TO SLEEP

You face a mind-boggling number of options in choosing a place to stay in Tahoe. Hostels, motels, condos, cabins, and campgrounds abound. If you're just passing through for a night or two in summer, a motel or campground is the cheapest and most convenient alternative. But if you're coming for a week in winter to ski with a group of friends, consider a condo or cabin on the north shore: It's more affordable than you might think (*see below*).

The quickest way to find a cheap (and perhaps fleabaggy) place to crash is to head to U.S. 50 between South Lake Tahoe and Stateline—cruise the strip and keep your eyes open for the neon. For a safer, quieter stay, opt for the area west of the South Tahoe "Y," and travel up to either the north shore or Stateline from there. As a last resort, look for cheap deals at the casinos on the Nevada side of both the south and north shores. No matter where you stay, reserve as far ahead as possible. On holidays and summer weekends everything is completely packed, despite the fact that most places raise their prices indiscriminately at these times.

➤ **SOUTH SHORE • Emerald Motel.** The well-maintained building is 35 years old, making for a homey setting with exceptionally friendly proprietors. Pope Beach and the woods are less than 2 miles away. Standard doubles start at $40 on weekdays and $50 on weekends, with rates $10 lower in winter; groups get the best deal—two beds, sleeping four, for $40 on summer weekdays. Rates are negotiable for stays of four nights or more. *515 Emerald Bay Rd. (Hwy. 89), tel. 916/544–5515. 1 mi north of South Lake Tahoe "Y." 9 rooms, all with bath. Wheelchair access.*

El Nido Motel. If you're seeking comfort at a reasonable price, the El Nido should end your search. Its excellent amenities include a hot tub and small, modern rooms with TV, VCR, and telephone. Flawlessly clean doubles start at $40 on weekdays, $50 on summer weekends; in the winter prices are about $10 lower. Call for details on discount lift ticket deals. *2215 Lake*

Tahoe Blvd. (U.S. 50), tel. and fax 916/541–2711. About ½ mile NE of South Lake Tahoe "Y." 21 rooms, all with bath.

Ridgewood Inn. Set on a 2-acre wooded lot you can explore, and boasting a Jacuzzi, these clean, well-kept rooms, some with kitchenettes, are a swell deal. Doubles in summer are $45, and a self-contained suite that sleeps five goes for $110. Some rooms even have tubs for a private post-hike soak. *1341 Emerald Bay Rd., tel. 916/541–8589 or 800/800–4640, fax 916/541–8712. 1 mi south of "Y." 12 rooms, all with bath. Wheelchair access.*

➤ **NORTH SHORE** • It's hard to find a budget motel on the north shore, especially in Truckee. For better prices and better location, check out the smaller communities around the lakeshore, like Tahoe Vista or Kings Beach. One of the cheapest hotels on the North Shore is in Kings Beach: **The Big 7** (8171 North Lake Blvd., tel. 916/546–2541 or 800/354–6970), with weekday doubles at $40, $65 weekends.

Family Tree Motel. In the middle of the commercial area, this motel has rooms that are plain and very '70s, but also large and clean. The attached restaurant serves up decent diner fare. Off-season double rates are $33 weekdays, $43 weekends. *551 North Lake Blvd., Tahoe City, tel. 916/583–0287, fax 916/583–0405. 9 rooms, all with bath. Wheelchair access.*

North Shore Lodge. Across from Kings Beach, $55 gets you a double room in the lodge with a kitchen and the smell of stale smoke. The cabins are the best deal: One sleeps six ($115), one sleeps eight ($125). Negotiate in winter, as they've been known to take what they can get— sometimes as low as $25. In summer, you have use of a heated pool. *8755 North Lake Blvd. (Hwy. 28) at Chipmunk St., tel. 916/546–4833, fax 916/546–0265. In Kings Beach, 1 mi west of California–Nevada border. 11 rooms, all with bath.*

River Ranch Lodge. For a great splurge, head to the classy River Ranch Lodge, beside the Truckee River between Truckee and Tahoe City. The rustic rooms (all no-smoking) come complete with tasteful wallpaper and antique furniture, and half have small decks overlooking the river. Doubles start at $40 on spring and fall weekdays ($50 on weekends), $55 on winter and summer weekdays ($70 on weekends). Several of the noisier rooms above the bar go for $10 less, and there's a cheaper double facing the parking lot. *Hwy. 89 and Alpine Meadows Rd., tel. 916/583–4264 or 800/535–9900. 21 rooms, all with bath. Continental breakfast.*

Tamarack Lodge Motel. This is the best budget lodging on the North Shore! The air smells great (it's the pines), the beach is a short walk away, and friendly managers lay on the charm. Knotty pine paneling and bike trail access bring people back here year after year. The TART bus stops across the street. Doubles start at $35 weekdays, kitchenettes are $10 more, and rates go up by $10 in high season. Stay over four non-holiday days and it's $10 off per day. *2311 North Lake Blvd. (Hwy. 28), 1 mi north of Tahoe City, tel. 916/583–3350, fax 916/583–3531. 21 rooms, all with bath.*

HOSTELS **Clair Tappaan Lodge.** Managed by the Sierra Club, this co-ed hostel is about 45 minutes away from Tahoe City. There are cross-country trails on site, and they rent snowshoes and nordic skis in winter. In the summer they lead bird-watching, wildflower, and hiking workshops. Summer rates are $37 for nonmembers ($33 members) and include three meals per day. Rates in winter are about $5 higher. *19940 Donner Pass Rd., Norden, tel. 916/426–3632, fax 916/426–0742. From Tahoe City, take Hwy. 89 E., exit at Soda Springs/Norden. 140 beds. No curfew.*

Doug's Mellow Mountain Retreat. Billed as "The Perfect Place to Chill Out," this laid-back private hostel rents bikes for $5 per day, offers laundry services for $3, and has a Rastafarian theme. Doug's a friendly guy, and he'll let you sit in front of the fireplace and watch movies (he has over 200), use his kitchen, and have barbecues on the deck. He'll even pick you up from the Greyhound station at Harrah's if you call ahead. Doug's house, in a quiet residential neighborhood, is about a mile from Heavenly and from the casinos. Beds in co-ed rooms go for $13. Reserve ahead; if you're a party of three, ask for the studio ($35) with its own kitchen, TV, and bath. *3787 Forest St., just west of CA–NV border, tel. 916/544–8065. From South Lake Tahoe, U.S. 50 east, right on Wildwood Rd., left on Forest St. 15 beds in 3 rooms. No curfew, no lockout. Reception hours flexible. Luggage storage.*

Squaw Valley Hostel. This privately run hostel, within walking distance of the Squaw Valley ski area, opens only during winter, usually from November 15 to April 15. During the week a dorm bed runs $20, $25 weekends. On weekends, when the hostel hosts groups, it's next to impossible to get a room unless you call well in advance and are blessed with good luck. *1900 Squaw Valley Rd., tel. and fax 916/581–3246. From Truckee, Hwy. 89 south, right on Squaw Valley Rd. 100 beds in 9 rooms.*

WEEKEND AND WEEKLY RENTALS As a rule of thumb, the more people in your group and the longer the stay, the more affordable rentals become. Contact the **Lake Tahoe Visitors' Authority** (1156 Ski Run Blvd., South Lake Tahoe, tel. 916/544–5050 or 800/AT–TAHOE) or the **Tahoe North Visitors' and Convention Bureau** (tel. 916/583–3494 or 800/TAHOE–4U) to find out about weekend or weekly rentals. You should be able to find a basic two- to four-person condo for about $75 a night or $425 a week in the off-season, with prices rising roughly 10% in summer. **R. RENT** (tel. 916/546–2549) specializes in north-shore budget rentals. If you have the time, you can save a few bucks by arranging a rental directly through a property owner. To find out what's available, check the classified ads in the *Tahoe Daily Tribune* for south-shore listings, or the *Tahoe World,* a north-shore paper that comes out each Thursday.

CAMPING You can hardly drive a half mile in Lake Tahoe without bumping into a public or private campground, and almost all of them lie in beautiful pine forests. For obvious reasons, all campgrounds close in winter until about Memorial Day. Temperatures can fluctuate widely in the region (from 60° to less than zero in a day), and many of the areas have snow until May. It's a good idea to call the Forest Service (*see* Basics, *above*) for advice and weather conditions before setting out. Free camping in the Tahoe area is restricted, but still available at some lesser-known primitive campgrounds scattered around the lake. The Forest Service has maps, tips, and directions to free spots as well as a complete listing of campgrounds.

➤ **SOUTH SHORE** • Two inviting campgrounds are just south of Emerald Bay on Hwy. 89. **Bayview** (tel. 916/544–5994), on the inland side of Hwy. 89, has 10 primitive sites amid the pines, with picnic tables and fire pits but no drinking water. A stopping-off point for journeys into Desolation Wilderness, it imposes a two-night limit on stays; but for those two nights you'll sleep for free. If all the sites in Bayview are full, head just up the road to beautiful **Eagle Point** (Hwy. 89, 1 mi south of Emerald Bay, tel. 916/525–7277 or 800/444–PARK for reservations). Here you'll find 100 well-spaced sites ($14)—all with fire pits, barbecues, drinking water, picnic tables, food lockers, and access to bathrooms and showers—on a hillside covered with brush and pines. Some sites offer incredible views of Emerald Bay.

The most conveniently located, though certainly not the most picturesque, spot on the south shore is the **Campground by the Lake** (1150 Rufus Allen Blvd., at U.S. 50, tel. 916/542–6096), a spacious campground with 170 sites shaded by young pines. Sites go for $11–$17 and are surprisingly isolated, considering how close you are to downtown South Lake Tahoe (the campground lies between Stateline and the South Lake Tahoe "Y," where U.S. 50 meets the lake). There are toilets, showers, and drinking water. Reservations are necessary only on holiday weekends, and a shuttle to the casinos is provided.

➤ **NORTH SHORE** • On the north shore, dispersed camping is available near Homewood ski resort in **Blackwood Canyon.** From Hwy. 89 south of Tahoe City, look for a sign to BLACKWOOD CANYON on the right. After 2½ miles, veer to the right on an unmarked dirt road, and camp anywhere you please.

William Kent Campground (off Hwy. 89, tel. 916/544–5994 or 800/444–PARK for reservations) is a 95-site National Forest campground set well off the highway, 2 miles south of Tahoe City. William Kent lies in a moderately dense pine forest and is within walking distance of the lake. Sites are $12. Just down the road to the south, the **Kaspian Campground** (tel. 916/544–5994) is specially equipped for wheelchair travelers.

FOOD

On the south shore, eateries are concentrated along U.S. 50 between South Lake Tahoe and Stateline, Nevada. In Stateline itself, you can get cheap (if generic) food at all-you-can-eat casino buffets. On the north shore, there's a heap of restaurants in downtown Truckee (especially on Donner Pass Road) and on Hwy. 28 in Tahoe City. For fresh organic produce and bulk foods, head to **Grass Roots** (2040 Dunlap Dr., at South Lake Tahoe "Y," tel. 916/541–7788) on the south shore. **The Mustard Seed** (7411 North Lake Blvd., Tahoe Vista, tel. 916/546-3525), a small health food shop and deli on the north shore, is another good bet.

SOUTH SHORE **Ernie's Coffee Shop.** An unpretentious greasy spoon serving breakfast and lunch only, Ernie's has a host of regulars that keep their personalized coffee mugs hanging on the wall. Breakfast is served all day in retro green vinyl booths. Meals range from the standard two-egg-and-toast breakfast ($4) to more adventurous creations like the tostada omelet ($6.50). *1146 Emerald Bay Rd. (Hwy. 89), at C St., South Lake Tahoe, tel. 916/541–2161. ¼ mi south of South Lake Tahoe "Y." Open daily 6 AM–2 PM.*

Hunan Garden. The friendly, sometimes wisecracking staff makes this a good place to refuel at the end of the day. Special vegetarian dishes, no MSG, and a willingness to alter any order are also pluses. If you need another reason to enter the flower-festooned joint, they have a lunch buffet (11:30–2:30) for $5.50, and another for dinner (5–9) for $7.95. *900 Emerald Bay Rd. (Hwy. 89), just NW of South Lake Tahoe "Y", tel. 916/544–5868 or 916/544–7268. Open daily 11:30–9:30. Wheelchair access.*

Sprouts. At South Lake Tahoe's vegetarian paradise, you can feast on great sandwiches ($4–$6), rice and vegetable plates ($4.25–$4.75), tempeh burgers ($4.50), and incredible fruit smoothies ($2.50–$3) and beer. The produce is largely organic. The restaurant itself is small and cheery, with a few wooden tables and a small outdoor patio. *3123 Harrison Ave., at U.S. 50, South Lake Tahoe, tel. 916/541–6969. Intersection of U.S. 50 and Alameda Ave. Open daily 8 AM–10 PM. Wheelchair access.*

Taquería Jalisco. With a rockin' jukebox and great food, this spot attracts Tahoe's sizable Latino population. Hidden behind Rojo's eatery and next to the Sierra Veterinary, Taquería Jalisco sells burritos, nachos, and tacos (some vegetarian) for under $2.50. *3097 Harrison Ave. at San Francisco Ave., South Lake Tahoe, tel. 916/541–6516. Open daily 11 AM–8 PM. Wheelchair access.*

NORTH SHORE **Bridgetender Tavern and Grill.** Housed in an old wooden cabin with high-beam ceilings and tree trunks poking through the roof, the Bridgetender is a worthy burgers-and-beer spot. Huge beef patties ($4) and tasty veggie burgers ($6) are both served with hefty french fries. Sit on a patio overlooking the Truckee River, or drink beer and shoot pool inside. *30 Emerald Bay Rd. (Hwy. 89), Tahoe City, tel. 916/583–3342. Next to bridge at Tahoe City "Y." Open daily 11–11.*

China Garden. One of Truckee's best restaurants serves up veggie dishes ($6–$6.50), seafood ($7–$9), and other Mandarin standards (no MSG) in a family-style dining room. Lunch specials (which come with soup, egg roll, fried rice, and your choice of entrée) run just $4.25–$5.25; dinner specials for two or more start at $8.50; The Mongolian BBQ buffet goes for $6.75–$8.75. *11361 Deerfield Dr., tel. 916/587–7625. In Crossroads Center, off Hwy. 89 just south of I-80. Open Mon.–Sat. 11–3 and 5–9, Sun. 5–9. Wheelchair access.*

Coyote's Mexican Grill. Whether you sit on the sun-drenched patio or in the tranquil southwestern dining room, you're bound to like the tasty grub at this woman-owned and -operated Mexican eatery. Aside from the regular old burritos, tacos, and quesadillas—most under $5— Coyote's also features specialties like tequila-and-lime fajitas ($7.25) and mesquite chicken ($5). If you're still not satisfied, head to the adjoining Café Luna for a cappuccino. *521 North Lake Blvd. (Hwy. 28), Tahoe City, tel. 916/583–6653. ½ mi east of Tahoe City "Y." Open daily 10–10 in summer, 11–9 in winter.*

Seedling Café and Coffeehouse. This vegetarian and very vegan-friendly spot offers a hubbub of activity throughout the week. On any given night you'll find poetry readings or live music. Their microbrews pass German purity tests, the coffee is organic, and all food is cooked on site. Try the plain focaccia ($5.95) or add in toppings. Throw in a salad ($2.25–$7.50). Seasoned polenta is $8.50, or look out for the specials, which change regularly. *7081 North Lake Blvd., Tahoe Vista, tel. 916/546–3936. Across from Agatam State Beach. Open daily 7 AM–10 PM. Wheelchair access.*

Truckee River Coffee Company. For coffee and dessert in Truckee, head to this homey café furnished with couches, a few tables, and a piano. You can get a calzone for $3, but the real reason to come is for dessert. Try the old-fashioned hot chocolate ($1.75), or the Coffee Nut ($4); made of hazelnut espresso, hazelnut syrup, and vanilla yogurt. *11373 Deerfield Dr., Truckee, tel. 916/587–2583. In Crossroads Center just south of I–80/Hwy. 89 junction. Open Sun.–Thurs. 7–6, Fri. 7–7, Sat. 7–9.*

AFTER DARK

Events on the south shore are covered in *Lake Tahoe Action,* a free weekly entertainment magazine put out by the *Tahoe Daily Tribune,* available at most motels, as is the *Tahoe–Truckee Review,* which covers the north shore.

SOUTH SHORE The south shore is surprisingly quiet by night. On the Nevada side of the border in Stateline, you'll find a number of casinos and the usual array of shows and "revues." Just north of the stateline, **Faces** (270 Kingsbury Grade, just west of Hwy. 50, tel. 702/588–2333) offers a relaxed, friendly, queer atmosphere with dancing three nights a week until 4 AM (no cover). **The Brewery at Lake Tahoe** (3542 U.S. 50, tel. 916/544–BREW), 1½ miles west of the California–Nevada border, is a microbrewery popular with the après-ski crowd. **Ellis Island Café** (4093 Lake Tahoe Blvd., tel. 916/542–1142) is a new arrival on the scene: a queer-friendly spot with 10 microbrews on tap, live music every night, and fresh food.

NORTH SHORE Tahoe City is without a doubt the center of the lake's nightlife. Loud, crowded, and filled with hard-drinking youth, **Humpty's** (877 North Lake Blvd., 1 mi NE of Tahoe City "Y," tel. 916/583–4867) features the best live indie music in the area most nights (cover $2–$7). When Humpty's closes on Tuesdays, the crowd heads a few doors down to **Rosie's Cafe** (571 North Lake Blvd., Tahoe City, tel. 916/583–8504), a large restaurant and bar housed in an old cabin full of Tahoe City memorabilia. Across the street at the **Blue Water Brewery** (850 North Lake Blvd., behind Safeway in Tahoe City, tel. 916/581–2583) you can suck down microbrews, munch on some veggie chili ($7) or fish and chips in beer batter ($7.50), and shoot a game of pool; live bands play Thursday–Saturday nights, more often in summer.

Catering to a mellower clientele, the **Naughty Dawg** (255 North Lake Blvd., ¼ mi NE of Tahoe City "Y," tel. 916/581–DAWG) has a good selection of high-quality beers, as well as surprisingly good salads, burgers, and pizza ($3–$7). With a large deck next to the Truckee River and a stylish indoor bar, the **River Ranch Lodge** (Hwy. 89, at Alpine Meadows Rd., tel. 916/583–4264) is an excellent place for a quiet drink. During the summer this place hosts an outdoor concert series with eclectic bookings ranging from jazz to hard rock (cover $5–$25).

SKIING

Whether you prefer downhill or cross-country, you've come to the right place. Unbelievably sheer faces, narrow chutes, and huge cliffs have attracted a new breed of downhill skier and snowboarder bent on pushing the sport to extremes. But novices shouldn't be intimidated: With more than 24 ski resorts, Lake Tahoe offers ample opportunity for beginners and experts alike on downhill and cross-country slopes. In addition to the millions of discount rental and lift ticket flyers you'll find all over the area, the tourist centers can give you the *Skier's Planning Guide,* the *Winter Travel Planner,* and the *Winter Visitor's Guide.* All have info on the various lift operators and advice about skiing in the area. Call the **North Lake Tahoe Chamber of Commerce** (*see* Basics, *above*) for info on skiing specials—they change throughout the season.

EQUIPMENT RENTAL As a rule of thumb, the closer you get to the ski resorts, the higher the cost of renting equipment. On the other hand, if you choose to rent from the shops run by the resorts, it'll be easier to get an adjustment, repair, or replacement midday. You'll save money by renting from any one of the hundreds of rental stores crowding the lake's major roads. The best deal anywhere is the south shore's **Don Cheepo's** (3349 U.S. 50, about ¾ mi west of Heavenly, tel. 916/544–0356), which offers full downhill and cross-country rental packages (skis, boots, and poles) for $10, or the unbelievably low price of $7.60 if you produce a coupon (scattered around local motels and tourist info centers). Snowboards rent for $25, including boots—a very competitive price.

Of north-shore rental outfits, **Porter's** has low rates (full ski packages $10–$14, snowboards $15–$22) and three locations, including one in Tahoe City (501 North Lake Blvd., just east of Tahoe City "Y," tel. 916/583–2314) and one in Truckee (in Crossroads Center on Hwy. 89, south of I-80, tel. 916/587–1500).

DOWNHILL The "Big Five" ski resorts (*see below*) all charge in the neighborhood of $45 a day, but if you're careful you can avoid paying these prices. Buying multiple-day or weekday tickets will save you $3–$7 per day; also scour local papers, motels, gas stations, and supermarkets (try Safeway) for discounts and deals. Beginners and intermediate skiers can save money and still get their money's worth at one of the smaller, less expensive resorts, some of which even offer midweek discounts. If you're coming from the Bay Area, you can save 30–45 minutes driving time by skiing at any of the Donner Pass ski resorts—Soda Springs, Sugar Bowl, Donner Ranch, Boreal, or Tahoe Donner. Of these five, **Sugar Bowl** (tel. 916/426–3847 for snow report), off the Soda Springs/Norden exit of I-80, is the largest and most beautiful. Sugar Bowl is especially attractive for experienced skiers, with 50% of its runs designated advanced, including some of the best tree skiing in Tahoe. A few miles farther down the road, **Donner Ranch** (Soda Springs/Norden exit off I-80, tel. 916/426–3635 for snow report) is Tahoe's cheapest ski resort, with lift tickets starting at just $10 on weekdays and $20 on weekends. If you have more than a day for skiing, consider the underrated, 1,260-acre **Homewood** (Hwy. 89, btw Tahoe City and South Lake Tahoe, tel. 916/525–2900 for snow report). Homewood offers outstanding views of the lake and a wide variety of terrain. Lift tickets go for $25 weekdays and $29 on weekends and holidays. Better still, Wednesday is two-for-one day, when you and a friend can ski for $12.50 each.

➤ **THE BIG FIVE** • **Squaw Valley** (on Hwy. 89, 8 mi south of Truckee, tel. 916/583–6955 for snow report) is a vast resort with over 8,000 acres of open bowls, 2,850 vertical feet, and more than 25 chairlifts. Squaw Valley is unofficially known as the home of "extreme" skiing, but the beauty of Squaw is that it's truly an all-around ski area—70% of the mountain is suited to beginning and novice skiers. **Alpine Meadows** (off Hwy. 89, 6 mi NW of Tahoe City, tel. 916/581–8374 for snow report) has a high base elevation of 7,000 feet (allowing for a longer season) and 12 lifts servicing over 100 runs. Alpine has built its reputation on the abundant snow and sunshine that grace its two mountains—most locals agree that Alpine Meadows is the best place for spring skiing. Alpine Meadows is also home to the **Tahoe Handicapped Ski School** (tel. 916/581–4161), the first school in the area to offer ski programs for the mentally and physically challenged. **Northstar-at-Tahoe** (Hwy. 267, 7 mi south of Truckee, tel. 916/562–1330 for snow report) certainly tries to be all things to all people, with a split of 25% beginner runs, 50% intermediate runs, and 25% advanced runs. It's definitely worth coming here for a day, if only for the incredible views of the basin from the top of the 8,610-foot **Mt. Pluto**. **Heavenly** (west entrance off Lake Tahoe Boulevard, in South Lake Tahoe, tel. 916/541–SKII for snow report) is officially the largest ski area in the United States. That means you'll find over 4,300 acres of skiable terrain, an incredible 3,500-foot vertical drop, and 25 lifts scattered over no less than nine peaks—a ski resort of Vegas-size proportions. **Kirkwood** (Hwy. 88 east, off Hwy. 89 south from South Lake Tahoe, tel. 209/258–3000 for snow report) boasts the driest snow, which experienced skiers know means the best powder—all told, 85% of Kirkwood's runs are designated intermediate or advanced.

Alpine Meadows is one of the few resorts that does not allow snowboarders.

CROSS-COUNTRY SKIING You'll have no problem finding a trail to suit your abilities at Tahoe's 13 cross-country ski areas, the most famous of which is the north shore's **Royal Gorge** (Soda Springs/Norden exit south from I-80, tel. 916/426–3871 or 800/500–3871), the largest cross-country ski resort in the United States. You can choose from 200 miles of trails running along a ridge above the north fork of the American River; fees are $16.50 midweek.

Strictly for skiers with at least some experience, **Eagle Mountain** (tel. 916/389–2254), dubbed "one of the area's best-kept secrets" by locals, offers incredible vistas along 45 miles of trails (fee $11). About an hour west of Truckee, Eagle is Tahoe's closest nordic resort. Exit I–80 at Yuba Gap and follow signs. Two other cross-country resorts on the north shore, **North-star-at-Tahoe** (tel. 916/562–1330; fee $14), and **Squaw Creek** (tel. 916/583–6300; fee $10) are right next to downhill ski areas (*see above*), making them great choices for vacation groups with divided loyalties. Of the two, Northstar, with 40 miles of trails, is the more exciting destination.

On the south shore, only **Kirkwood** (*see above,* tel. 209/258–7248) offers both alpine and nordic ski trails, with over 50 miles of cross-country for skiers of all levels ($12). The best deal on the south shore is **Hope Valley** (Hwy. 88 east, off Hwy. 89, tel. 916/694–2266), located in a beautiful valley of the Toiyabe (say it: TOY-ah-bee) National Forest, on the grounds of Soren-son's Resort. It offers 60 miles of trails for all levels—free! (Donation requested.) The Tahoe North Visitors & Convention Bureau (*see Basics, above*) can also hook you up with packages, such as a $33 three-day ticket that can be used at any of seven resorts.

SUMMER ACTIVITIES

Lake Tahoe offers opportunities for just about every fair-weather sport imaginable. An abbreviated list would include hiking, biking, fishing, sailing, waterskiing, jet skiing, rock climbing, hot-air ballooning, parasailing, horseback riding, and river rafting. Of course many of the more exotic adventures are pricey, but Tahoe is a great place to splurge. Your best printed matter on the possibilities is *Tahoe–Truckee Outdoors,* which gives trail maps, tips, and the latest news on biking, boating, hiking, and rafting, among other sports, as does *Tahoe Mountain News.* Tourist offices or the Forest Service (*see Basics, above*) have detailed information about all these sports. Barring droughts, white-water rafting on the American River is a

Going to the chapel? Then it might not surprise you to know that the wedding industry is second only to casinos in bringing the most business to the Tahoe area.

possibility—the Forest Service can point you in the right direction. If you're looking to rent equipment for just about any sport, **Don Cheepo's** (*see* Equipment Rental, in Skiing, *above*) carries everything from water skis to backpacks and other camping supplies. A good source of

There's One Born Every Minute . . .

Both the north and south shores offer opportunities to gamble away your last dollars, with very different attitudes and atmosphere on each side of the lake. On the south shore, which has more casinos and glitz, you'll find the big names, like Harrah's (tel. 702/588–6611), Harvey's (tel. 702/588–2411), and Caesar's (tel. 702/588–3515), all waiting to take your cash at blackjack and poker tables, slot machines, keno, and more, while distracting you with free drinks and tacky lounge acts. The cheapest and most declassé spot on this side—with a McDonald's, even—is Bill's Casino (tel. 702/588–2455), with round-the-clock $3 blackjack tables in a lurid, depressing atmosphere (funny how after a few free drinks, you don't seem to notice). Local motels and visitor centers often stock coupons for cheap casino buffets, not to mention free slot machine tokens and other free casino stuff.

The north shore's gambling scene is slightly more low-key. The atmosphere is friendlier, the dealers are laid-back, and the players seem to lack the frantic, nerve-racking energy that may drive you insane at south-shore casinos. Two of the best casinos to hit are in Crystal Bay—the Biltmore (tel. 916/831–0660) and the Crystal Bay Club (tel. 702/831–0512).

information and equipment for all sorts of outdoor sports in Tahoe City is **Alpenglow Sports** (415 North Lake Blvd., tel. 916/583–6917). **Gravity Works Rock Gym** in Truckee (10095 West River St., tel. 916/582–4510) is a good rock climbing resource.

HIKING Almost every acre in the Lake Tahoe Basin is protected by some national, state, or local agency. **Tahoe National Forest** lies to the northwest, **Eldorado National Forest** to the southwest, and **Toiyabe National Forest** to the east. What this means for visitors is a whole lot of hiking trails, from easy scenic walks to strenuous climbs over mountain passes. The Lake Tahoe Forest Service Visitor Center (*see* Basics, *above*) has a complete list of day hikes.

One of the more popular short walks is **Vikingsholm Trail,** a mile-long (one-way) paved path leading from the parking lot on the north side of Emerald Bay to the shoreline and the 38-room Vikingsholm Castle, a Scandinavian-style castle built in 1929. From the castle you can walk farther to **Eagle Falls,** the only waterfall that empties into the lake. For something a little more woodsy, try the **Mt. Tallac Trail,** ½ mile north of the Lake Tahoe Forest Service Visitor Center (follow the marked asphalt road opposite Baldwin Beach to the trailhead parking lot). A moderate hike takes you 2 miles through a beautiful pine forest to Cathedral Lake. For a serious day-long trek (with no potable water along the way), continue on the trail another 3 miles as it climbs past a series of boulder fields to the peak of Mt. Tallac, the highest point in the basin at 9,735 feet. At the top you'll find excellent views of the lake and Desolation Wilderness. The trip up and back should take seven to eight hours.

If you're looking to do extensive backcountry camping, you're going to have a hard time choosing where to go. Off the southwest corner of the lake, the 63,473-acre **Desolation Wilderness,** filled with granite peaks, glacial valleys, subalpine forests, and more than 80 lakes, is one of the most beautiful and popular backcountry destinations in the area. South of the lake, **Mokelumne Wilderness,** straddling the border of Eldorado and Stanislaus national forests, has terrain similar to Desolation without the crowds. Before you enter any wilderness area, either for a day or for an extended visit, it's crucial to pick up a wilderness permit from the Lake Tahoe Forest Service Visitor Center (*see* Basics, *above*)—if you don't you may actually be kicked off the trails.

BIKING Lake Tahoe has everything from mellow lakeshore trails to steep fire roads and tricky single-tracks. The Forest Service has detailed trail information, and the Tahoe North Visitors and Convention Bureau (*see* Basics, *above*) puts out an excellent brochure called "North Lake Tahoe Mountain Biking" that lists bike tours, trails, bike parks, and bike shops for rentals. Several paved, gently sloped paths skirt the lakeshore: Try the 3.4-mile **Pope Baldwin Bike Path** in South Lake Tahoe, at the Pope Baldwin Recreational Center or the **West Shore Bike Path,** which extends about 10 miles south from Tahoe City to Sugar Pine Point State Park near the town of Tahoma. Also worthwhile is the path along the **Truckee River** between Alpine Meadows and Tahoe City, and the **U.S. Forest Service Bike Trail,** an 8½-mile paved path (through pine forest and rare aspen groves) that starts at Emerald Bay Road just west of the South Lake Tahoe "Y" and ends at the lake.

Experienced riders should dare the famous **Flume Trail,** a 24-mile ride past several lakes and along a ridge with sweeping views of Lake Tahoe. The trail begins at the parking lot of Lake Tahoe–Nevada State Park, just north of Spooner Junction on the lake's eastern shore (take Hwy. 28 east from Tahoe City). A map is crucial, and the "**High Sierra Biking Map**" ($6) and its accompanying book ($9) offer a detailed description of the Flume Trail (including a way to cut the ride in half for people with two cars), along with several dozen other excellent rides in the area. If you like the idea of riding downhill all day, **Northstar-at-Tahoe, Donner Ranch, Kirkwood, Squaw Valley,** and **Sugar Bowl** (*see* Skiing, *above*) all open a number of ski runs for mountain biking June–September. All-day tickets run $15–$20 (bike rental $25–$35).

➤ **BIKE RENTALS** • Dozens of shops around Tahoe rent mountain bikes, generally for $4–$6 an hour or $15–$22 a day. On the south shore there's **Anderson's Bicycle Rental** (Hwy. 89, at 13th St., tel. 916/541–0500), conveniently located a half mile from the U.S. Forest Service Bike Trail. Slightly cheaper is **Don Cheepo's** (*see* Equipment Rental, in Skiing, *above*), near the east end of the Pope Baldwin Bike Path. On the north shore try **Porter's** (501 North Lake Blvd., tel. 916/583–2314), on Hwy. 28, east of the Tahoe City "Y."

BEACHES Dozens of beaches are scattered around the lake's shore, some charging $2–$5 for parking. Two of the best include **Chamber's Landing** south of Tahoe City, a favorite of young north-shore locals; and **Baldwin Beach,** a gorgeous and usually uncrowded sand beach between South Lake Tahoe and Emerald Bay. **Nevada Beach,** a more populated spot just across the Nevada border in Stateline, has great mountain views. **Sand Harbor,** a crescent-shaped beach off Hwy. 28 south of Incline Village, is ideal for sunsets.

WATER SPORTS Despite Lake Tahoe's often frigid waters, there's no lack of rental outfits specializing in sailing, waterskiing, jet skiing, windsurfing, kayaking, canoeing, and parasailing. Prices fluctuate a bit, but in general sailboats go for $30–$35 an hour, $85–$95 a day; Jet Skis run $50–$90 an hour; Windsurfers rent for $10–$15 an hour, $30–$40 a half day; and canoes go for $10–$15 an hour, $30–$40 a half day. Parasailing rides, which usually last about 15 minutes, range from $35 to $50.

On the south shore, the **Ski Run Boat Company** (tel. 916/544–0200), with motorboats, canoes, kayaks, and other toys, is one of several shops operating out of **Ski Run Marina,** off U.S. 50 about a half mile west of the California–Nevada border. On the north shore, you'll find rental outfits in the **Sunnyside Marina,** about 2 miles south of Tahoe City on Hwy. 89.

FISHING Like nearly everything in Tahoe, fishing options are abundant. Obviously, the most convenient spot is (can you guess?) **Lake Tahoe,** stocked occasionally with rainbow trout by the folks at the Fish and Wildlife Service (to find the section of the lake most recently stocked, call 916/355–7040 or 916/351–0832). Also popular is the stretch of the **Truckee River** between Truckee and Tahoe City—just pick a spot and cast your line. Wherever you fish, licenses ($9 a day, $24 a year) are required by law and available from most sporting-goods shops. For sport fishing on the lake, contact **Tahoe Sportfishing** (tel. 916/541–5448 or 800/696–7797) in the Ski Run Marina or **Let's Go Fishing** (tel. 916/541–5566) in South Lake Tahoe. Half-day trips generally start at $50–$55, full-day trips at $70–$75.

Yosemite National Park

Yosemite is the Disneyland of National Parks— it's crowded, expensive, and long lines prevail—but there is no other place in the world quite like it. Glacial sculpturing and prehistoric activity at the earth's mantle have formed a land so stunning that even the jaded contend it's not to be missed. Slightly smaller than the state of Rhode Island, Yosemite is packed with waterfalls, sheer granite cliffs, lush forests, and generous expanses of alpine meadows. **Yosemite Valley,** the central and most accessible portion of the park, stretches more than 20 miles from the Wawona Tunnel in the west to Curry Village in the east. The valley's major sites are **Half Dome** and **El Capitan**—two breathtaking but treacherous granite formations—as well as **Yosemite, Nevada,** and **Vernal falls.**

Because the valley is surrounded by so much hype, it can be hard to step back and let the beauty soak in. Most people never leave its congested confines—complete with tacky lodges and unsightly gift shops—to explore the rest of the park. That's a big mistake. While it's almost impossible to avoid the valley, consider it a departure point for hikes rather than a destination in itself. The other side of Yosemite—the undisturbed, forested backcountry with its massive granite formations and plunging waterfalls—is where you'll find the real soul of the park. Among the more spectacular non-valley sights are **Tuolumne Meadows** (say it: TWA-lo-mee), along Hwy. 120; the giant sequoias of **Mariposa Grove,** off Hwy. 41 in the southwest corner of the park; **Glacier Point,** near Badger Pass; and the **Hetch Hetchy Reservoir** (north of Big Oak Flat). These areas are most accessible to backpackers and horseback riders, though numerous turnouts and day-hike areas make them fairly easy to reach from the highway.

For centuries Yosemite was inhabited by the Ahwahneechee people who lived in settlements in the surrounding mountains. Unfortunately, the Mariposa Battalion, the first group of whites to enter the area (in 1851), saw Yosemite as a prime hunting and fur-trapping ground. By the late 19th century whites had settled (i.e., conquered) the Ahwahneechee and established a lucra-

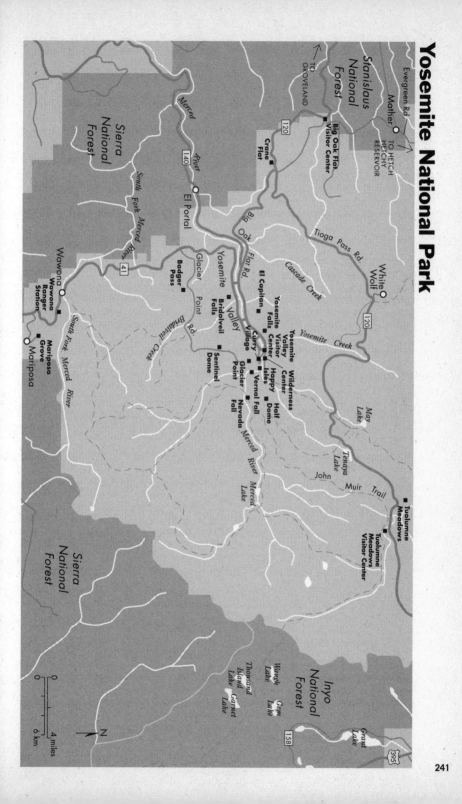

Yosemite National Park

Evergreen Rd.

Mather

TO HETCHY
RESERVOIR

TO
GROVELAND

*Stanislaus
National
Forest*

120

Big Oak Flat
Visitor Center

Crane
Flat

Merced

140

River

*Sierra
National
Forest*

El Portal

Big

Oak

Flat Rd.

Tioga Pass Rd.

Cascade Creek

White
Wolf

120

Yosemite Creek

El Capitan

Yosemite Falls
Center

Yosemite
Valley
Visitor
Center

Yosemite Wilderness
Center

May
Lake

Bridalveil
Falls

Glacier

Point

Rd.

Bridalveil Creek

Curry
Village

Isles

Happy
Dome

Half
Dome

Tenaya
Lake

Sentinel
Dome

Glacier
Point

Vernal Fall

Nevada
Fall

John

Merced River

Merced Lake

Muir

Trail

Tuolumne
Meadows

Tuolumne
Meadows
Visitor Center

South Fork Merced

River

41

Wawona

Wawona
Ranger
Station

Badger
Pass

South Fork Merced River

Mariposa
Grove

Mariposa

*Sierra
National
Forest*

*Inyo
National
Forest*

Waugh
Lake

Gem
Lake

Thousand
Island
Lake

Garnet
Lake

Grant
Lake

395

158

N

0

0

4 miles

6 km

tive lumber business and trading outpost. We have naturalists John Muir and Gaelen Clark to thank that today Yosemite Valley is more than a timber company parking lot. Clark lobbied extensively to get the Yosemite Grant enacted in 1864, creating the world's first state park. After Clark passed away in 1910, Muir took up the fight and played a vital role in having Yosemite declared a national park in 1890, when even then it was showing signs of wear and tear. He furthered his conservation efforts as the first president of the Sierra Club, formed in 1892, to secure federal protection for the Yosemite region.

BASICS

VISITOR INFORMATION For current events in Yosemite, check out the *Yosemite Guide*, available at all entrance stations. The visitor centers stock maps and brochures and distribute free wilderness permits (required for overnight camping in the backcountry; *see* Wilderness Permits, *below*). The **Yosemite Valley Visitor Center** (Shuttle Stops 6 and 9, tel. 209/372–0299) is 6 miles east of the Hwy. 140 entrance and open daily 8 AM–7 PM (June 17–Sept. 2), 9 AM–5 PM (Sept. 3–June 16). The **Tuolumne Meadows Visitor Center** (tel. 209/372–0263), open daily 8 AM–7:30 PM (summer only), is toward the east end of the park, 1 mile east of Tuolumne Meadows on Tioga Pass Road. It doesn't have much of a tourist desk, but the **Wawona Ranger Station** (tel. 209/375–9501), at the south end of Yosemite on Hwy. 41, does offer wilderness permits weekdays 8:30 AM–5 PM, summer only. The **Big Oak Flat Visitor Center** (tel. 209/372–0615), at the Hwy. 120 west entrance, is open daily 9 AM–5 PM from Memorial Day to Labor Day. If you're not actually in the park, the **Public Information Service** (Box 577, Yosemite National Park 95389, tel. 209/372–0264) is the place to begin your search for info on Yosemite, though getting through on the phone can be a task. Send a self-addressed, stamped envelope for free brochures and maps, or call weekdays between 9 and 5.

➤ **WILDERNESS PERMITS** • In 1972 Yosemite had to institute a permit system to limit the number of backpackers on the trails each day. Half the park's permits are reserved, while half are distributed on a first-come, first-served basis one day in advance. To make a reservation (available up to 24 weeks in advance), you'll need to pay a reservation fee of $3 per person, and send your dates of arrival and departure, specific trailheads of entry and exit, your main destination in the park, the number in your party, and alternative dates if your first choices aren't available to **Wilderness Reservations** (Wilderness Center, Box 545, Yosemite, CA 95389, tel. 209/372–0740). You may also call 209/372–0740 to reserve by phone.

For free first-come, first-served permits, head to the new **Wilderness Center** (tel. 209/372–0310; closed in winter), located two buildings east of the Yosemite Valley Visitor Center (*see above*). When the Wilderness Center is closed, you should go to the Wilderness Permit station nearest to your planned destination: Yosemite Valley Visitor Center (*see above*), Tuolumne Meadows (*see above*), Big Oak Flat Visitor Center (*see above*), Hetch Hetchy Entrance Station, and Wawona Ranger Station (*see above*). Free permits go quickly (some in just five minutes)—particularly for popular areas such as the valley and Tuolumne Meadows—so arrive early the day before your hike with a detailed itinerary, including trails and estimated overnight stops.

FEES The park fee for one week is $5 per car or $3 per hiker, bicyclist, or bus passenger. You can purchase annual passes for $15 that give you unlimited access to the park.

WHEN TO GO If possible, visit during spring or early fall, when crowds are less oppressive. Spring (late April–late May) is especially spectacular—the wildflowers are in bloom, and the waterfalls are at their peak of sound and fury as snowpack melts in the high country. Of the nearly four million people who visit each year, 70% arrive during summer (June–August), when temperatures reach a high of 85°F and a low of 40°F. Of those 70%, 90% will arrive on the same day you do. Can you say gridlock? To prevent congestion and overcrowding, automobile access to the park is occasionally restricted on spring weekends and busy holidays (Memorial Day, Independence Day, and Labor Day). At these times, those with lodging reservations are let in, so get a reservation or you'll be stuck tailgating. In winter (November–March), temperatures drop to a chilly 45°F by day and a downright frigid 15°F by night. You won't be able to explore the park as easily as you can during the summer—Tioga Pass and Glacier Point Road usually close by November due to inclement weather—but when dusted with a blanket of snow, Yosemite will definitely sneak its way into your heart.

WHAT TO PACK Rain gear is essential year-round. You may never have to battle one of Yosemite's sudden summertime tempests, but unless you want to be stuck sipping cocoa in a dreary coffee shop, it pays to be prepared. Water-repellent "shell" pants and a warm jacket with polar-fleece lining are a smart idea, and don't forget wool or wick-dry socks—they'll keep you warm even when it's wet. If you plan to camp in winter—you crazy thing, you—you'll need a sub-zero sleeping bag and a waterproof (or at least water-resistant), four-season tent. Broken-in hiking boots are a must for exploring the backcountry, and yes, snowshoes or crampons would be a good idea if you want to blaze your own trail.

GENERAL STORES If you're coming into the park from Hwy. 120, stop first at Oakdale's friendly, well-stocked **Newdeal Market** (888 Hwy. 120, Oakdale Plaza, tel. 209/847–5919), open daily 7 AM–10 PM. Otherwise you're stuck with the grocery and camping stores in pricey Yosemite Village, 5 miles east of Hwy. 41 in the middle of the park (at Shuttle Stops 3, 5, and 10). The **Village Sport Shop** (tel. 209/372–1286), open from spring to fall, has fishing and camping gear. Both the **Village Store** (tel. 209/372–1253), open daily 8 AM–10 PM, and the **Wawona Store** (Hwy. 41, near south end of park, tel. 209/375–6574), open daily 8 AM–8 PM, stock groceries and basic camping supplies.

Badger Pass Sport Shop (tel. 209/372–8430), open from December to April, has ski clothing and equipment, as well as picnic supplies. It's near Wawona and the Badger Pass ski slopes, off Hwy. 41 on the south side of the park. In Curry Village, at the far eastern end of Yosemite Valley (Shuttle Stop 14), you'll find a host of stores, including the **Curry Village Mountain Shop** (tel. 209/372–8396), where you can purchase overpriced rock-climbing supplies and topographic maps, and the **Yosemite Mountaineering School** (tel. 209/372–8344), where you can rent camping equipment including rock shoes, internal and external frame backpacks, daypacks, sleeping bags, bear canisters, gaitors, snowshoes, and foam pads at reasonable prices. Climbing shoes are rented to climbing students only.

MEDICAL AID The **Yosemite Medical Clinic** in Yosemite Village offers full medical service and 24-hour emergency care. *Btw visitor center and Ahwahnee Hotel, tel. 209/372–4637. Open weekdays 8–5, weekends 9–noon. Wheelchair access.*

COMING AND GOING

BY CAR You can reach Yosemite on three routes: **Highway 41** from the south, **Highway 140** from Merced in the west, and **Highway 120** from San Francisco. From San Francisco, take I-580 east to I-205 and connect to Hwy. 120 (4 hrs one-way). Hwys. 41 and 140 terminate in Yosemite Valley, and Hwy. 120 becomes Tioga Pass Road inside the park. In spring and winter the eastern portion of Hwy. 120 (from Crane Flat headed east to the Tioga Pass and into Inyo National Forest and Lee Vining) is closed until Memorial Day weekend. Be forewarned that summertime traffic is frequently bumper to bumper, especially around the Fourth of July and Memorial Day (*see* When To Go, *above*).

Your chances of being eaten by a bear are only slightly greater than that of finding a parking spot in the increasingly urban Yosemite Valley. Those in the know take the bus—you should too.

From late fall to early spring you should carry snow chains. The highways can get treacherous, and the California Highway Patrol often closes the roads to all traffic without snow gear. If you get stuck, you'll have to buy an expensive set of chains ($60) from a gas station (and boy do they love it when that happens). For current road and weather conditions, call 209/372–0200 or 800/427–ROAD within California (tel. 916/445–1534 outside California).

BY BUS AND TRAIN There is no direct bus service to Yosemite from San Francisco; all lines stop in either Fresno or Merced, where you have to change coaches. From Merced, a cheap option is **Via Adventures** (tel. 209/384–1315), which runs three buses a day (2½ hrs, $17 one-way) from Merced's Greyhound station on 16th and N streets. **Amtrak** (tel. 800/USA–RAIL) offers service in conjunction with Yosemite Sequoia Tours that takes you from San Francisco to the park and back for $53. The train stops in Emeryville and in Merced, where you board the bus to Yosemite. All buses stop at Yosemite Lodge, Ahwahnee Hotel, Curry Village, and Yosemite Village in the valley. From San Francisco, **Green Tortoise** (tel. 415/956–7500 or 800/867–8647) runs a three-day Yosemite and Eastern Sierras tour out of San Francisco that goes through much of the park and surrounding forest. The tour costs $99, plus $21 for food (for more info on Green Tortoise travel, *see* Getting In, Out, and Around, in Chapter 1). The friendly folks at **Incredible Adventures** (tel. 415/759–7071 or 800/777–8464) also lead four-day trips to Yosemite from San Francisco for $169 (everything included, even food and camping equipment) that feature camping, swimming, high-county hiking, and fireside cookouts.

GETTING AROUND

Curvy **Tioga Pass Road** (a.k.a. **Highway 120**) runs the entire 60-mile, east–west length of the park, climbing 8,000 feet in elevation. If you're on a bicycle (*see* Biking, *below*), you may want to limit yourself to the valley, since both Hwy. 41 and Tioga Pass Road are often narrow and have steep elevation gains.

BY PARK SHUTTLE Free shuttle buses operate throughout the year, though service hours vary according to season. The **Yosemite Valley Shuttle** travels every 20 minutes, year-round, between Curry Village, Yosemite Village, the Yosemite Lodge, and campgrounds and points of interest in between (*see* Where to Sleep, *below*). Starting in mid-April, the shuttle operates 7 AM–10 PM for most stops (excluding Happy Isles, the Mirror Lake Trail, and North Pines campground, when service stops at 7:30 PM). However, campers in North Pines can easily walk from Shuttle Stop 19 at Upper and Lower Pines after 7 PM. In winter, hours are reduced to 9 AM–10 PM, and some stops receive no service at all. Check the *Yosemite Guide* for a current schedule. During ski season a free shuttle leaves Yosemite Lodge for the **Badger Pass** ski area in the morning and returns in the afternoon. Another shuttle ($9.25 one-way, $17.75 round-trip) runs three times daily from mid-May to early October (weather permitting) between Yosemite Lodge and **Glacier Point** (*see* Scenic Drives and Views, *below*). Tickets can be purchased at a **Yosemite Travel Service** desk in all hotels. Stops are well marked; just look for the SHUTTLE BUS signs along the main roads. From July until Labor Day, an early-morning backpackers' shuttle (prices vary) runs once daily between Yosemite Lodge and Tuolumne Meadows with stops in between. It returns each day to Yosemite Valley. Call a visitor center for schedules. All shuttles are wheelchair accessible.

WHERE TO SLEEP

Close to the ground—that's the way to experience Yosemite, and camping and backpacking are the best ways to do it. After all, do you really want the sanitized experience of a tourist hotel,

Some Things to Bear in Mind

Yosemite is home to a good many healthy, curious, and hungry black bears. The good news is they have yet to devour a camper. The bad news is they have developed an appetite for your sunscreen, soap, toothpaste, hair spray, and any other scented articles you may have lugged along. This diet requires a high level of curiosity: Your tent, ice chest, backpack, and car are all fair game. Store all food and related supplies in the metal storage boxes provided at campsites, or rent or buy bear-proof containers for backcountry trips. Too much hassle? Consider this: If a bear decides to tear open your car doors like a refrigerator while searching for snacks, not only will this probably ruin your trip, your insurance probably won't cover it, and—to add insult to injury—you'll be fined for improperly storing food.

devoid of dirt and bugs? Even if you do, keep in mind that the privilege of four thin walls and a bed doesn't come cheap. Whatever you decide, reservations are highly—very, very, very highly—recommended: Beds and campsites go like hotcakes, especially in summer and fall.

One of the best kept secrets of Yosemite accommodations is the **Yosemite Lakes Hostel** (31191 Hardin Flat, Groveland, tel. 209/962–0121), found 5 miles west of the park on Hwy. 120. Here, you'll find all sorts of sleeping options: hostel rooms that sleep two ($29), cabins that sleep four ($28), fully equipped yurts (yes, yurts) that sleep up to eight ($74), and wooded tent sites ($16). Washing machines, TV, and microwaves are all found on the premises. And—best of all—they often have same day availability; take advantage of this deal before word gets out!

HOTELS AND CABINS Hotel reservations can be made up to 366 days in advance, and believe it or not, most places actually fill up that far ahead. Hotel, lodge, and cabin reservations are all handled through **Yosemite Concessions Services Corp.** (5410 E. Home Ave., Fresno 93727, tel. 209/252–4848). Because Yosemite is so mobbed, you probably won't have a choice when it comes to your hotel accommodations. If you can find a single vacancy, consider yourself lucky. If lady luck gives you the cold shoulder, check out the nearby towns of El Portal, Fishcamp, and Oakhurst, all of which have reasonably priced lodging.

This said, most people prefer the **Yosemite Lodge** (5 mi east of Hwy. 140 entrance, Yosemite Valley, tel. 209/372–1274), which has pleasant cabins for two starting at $57 (with shared bathroom) and $73 (with private bathroom). Each additional person costs an extra $8. Accommodations in **Curry Village** (tel. 209/372–1233) include canvas tent cabins (starting at $37) and simple wood cabins ($53 year-round, $72 with private bath). The fee for extra people in the tent cabins is $5, in the wood cabins $6. Otherwise, seek out the shantytown called **Housekeeping Camp** (tel. 209/252–4848). This site in the valley is for people who want to camp, but don't want to lug the equipment; here 282 identical cement-and-canvas "tent" units huddle close together, separated only by paper-thin walls. They're not particularly comfortable, but each bare-bones structure houses up to four people for only $39 per night (extra cots are $4 more). The camp is open from mid-March to late October. A grocery store, laundry, bathroom, and showers are nearby.

CAMPING Yosemite Valley's developed campgrounds share a number of characteristics: They're all large, flat, near a major road, and shaded by pine trees. Most have picnic tables, fire pits, flush toilets, piped water, and food-storage lockers, but none have direct access to showers (for that, you'll have to head to Housekeeping Camp or Curry Village). All but Tamerac, Yosemite Creek, and Porcupine have wheelchair access. Unfortunately, they're all extremely crowded, especially the ones in the valley. You may get lucky and find an open site during the off-season, but otherwise, reservations are a must. Campground reservations are available up to 12 weeks in advance through **Destinet** (tel. 800/436–PARK or 619/452–8787). If you're stuck, show up at one of the campground kiosks (at Curry Village, Big Oak Flat, and at Tuolumne Meadows), and put your name on the waiting list in case there's a cancellation. The campground kiosks usually call off names once or twice a day for cancellations and no-shows.

If you can't get a reservation at any of the major campgrounds, there are a few first-come, first-served sites you can try. In particular, check out the valley's only walk-in campground, **Sunnyside,** located near Yosemite Lodge in Yosemite Valley. In the '70s, Sunnyside was called Camp 4 and was known to host a particular kind of Bay Area crowd in between Dead shows. Today it's the favorite Yosemite campground of a new kind of subculture: the world's most hard-core rock climbers. Sunnyside has 35 sites ($3 per person) with running water and toilets. For walk-ins outside the valley, try **Tuolumne Meadows** (*see above*), where 25 sites are reserved for backpackers with Wilderness Permits—who may stay there or at Yosemite Valley Backpackers Camp (behind North Pines campground) the day before they head out and the day after they return—and visitors without vehicles. Tuolumne also reserves half its sites for same-day reservations; check the visitor center (either in the valley or in Tuolumne) for availability. Other first-come, first-served sites include **Wawona** (Hwy. 41, at south end of park) with 100 sites ($10), **White Wolf** (Tioga Pass Rd., about 10 mi east of Crane Flat) with 87 sites ($10), **Porcupine Flat** with

52 sites ($6), and **Yosemite Creek** with 75 sites ($6). The latter two are both off Tioga Pass Road east of White Wolf. Keep in mind that all the Tioga Pass Road campgrounds close in winter, usually mid-September or early October to early June. For info on backcountry camping, see Longer Hikes, *below*.

➤ **INSIDE YOSEMITE VALLEY** • **Upper Pines** is the biggest campground, with 238 tent and RV sites ($15) available March–November. It's conveniently located at Shuttle Stop 15, near trailheads to Mirror Lake and Vernal Fall. Misanthropes be warned: This place gets extremely crowded and the RVs pack together like sardines. Across the street at Shuttle Stop 19, **Lower Pines** is open year-round, with 172 tent and RV sites ($15) sandwiched between the Merced River and Storeman Meadow. Expect the same pack of RVs and families you see at Upper Pines. **North Pines Campground,** with 85 wheelchair accessible sites ($15) available April–October, is conveniently located at Shuttle Stop 18. Open to both tent campers and RV-owners, this campground sports spectacular views of Yosemite Falls and has many sites along the sandy shores of the Merced River. It is also a great starting point for the short hike to Mirror Lake. **Upper River Campground,** between Curry Village and Yosemite Valley at Shuttle Stop 2, is the only valley campground reserved for tents only. Open April–October, it's notably quieter than its counterparts. Some of the 124 sites ($15) lie near the Merced River. The nicest views (particularly of the Merced River and Yosemite Falls) can be found across the way at **Lower River Campground** with 126 sites ($15), but the views may not make up for the hordes of hyperactive youngsters who overrun the beach.

➤ **OUTSIDE YOSEMITE VALLEY** • Look for **Tuolumne Meadows,** an enormous creek-side campground perfect for exploring the eastern side of the park. Its 314 sites ($12) lie along Tioga Pass Road (Hwy. 120) and are usually open from July–October, depending on the weather. This campground, in some of the park's most beautiful country, attracts its share of day hikers, but it's still one of the last to fill up. **Hodgdon Meadow,** just past Hwy. 120 at the Big Oak Flat entrance on the west side of the park, allows you to escape the chaos of the valley and still remain within striking distance (30–40 minutes). It draws nature-loving car campers year-round, except when snow closes the road (sometimes until late spring).

FOOD

If you plan on camping, bring as much food as possible. Prices in Yosemite's stores (see General Stores, *above*) are predictably high. A dull variety of American eateries, from fast-food cafeterias to expensive sit-down restaurants, is the only other choice.

The **Yosemite Village** complex, 7 miles east of the Hwy. 140 entrance, has the largest selection of food in the park. The **Pasta Place** (Shuttle Stop 5, tel. 209/372–8381; closed in winter) is a cafeteria-style restaurant with basic pasta-with-sauce plates (from $4.60) to choose from. If you have the cash, you might want to stuff yourself with the dinner special ($9–$10): a full pasta plate, caesar salad, bread, and a large drink. Also in Yosemite Village, **Degnan's Deli** (tel. 209/372–8454), the healthiest place in the valley, has sandwiches ($4–$5), salads ($2–$4), and picnic supplies. Next door, **Degnan's Fast Foods** (tel. 209/372–8437) has pizza ($1.25 for a cheese slice) and ice cream ($1.25).

In **Curry Village** (tel. 209/372–8333), on the west side of the valley near Happy Isles, there's a cafeteria, a burger stand, and a small pizzeria adjoining a bar. While the cafeteria has cheap burgers, sandwiches, and breakfasts (under $5), a pizza, a pitcher, and a big TV might be just what you need after a long hike. Head to the pizzeria and Terrace Bar where a small pizza and a pitcher of beer both go for $7. It's open daily noon–9 PM.

EXPLORING YOSEMITE

It can take anywhere from a day to the rest of your life to familiarize yourself with Yosemite. Realistically, you'll need at least a few days to venture beyond the crowds. To get a good overview in summer, drive along **Tioga Pass Road** (Hwy. 120), stopping to take a walk or a hike wherever you're inclined. Scores of trails meander through the park, from relaxing strolls to highly demanding backcountry excursions. If you don't have a car, many trailheads are easily reached by shuttle bus (*see* Getting Around, *above*). In the winter, be sure to check trail conditions with the rangers before heading out. Not all trails and roads are open year-round; trails in Tuolomne Meadows and Glacier Point may be inaccessible. Those venturing off the beaten path will need serious snow gear in the winter months.

ORIENTATION AND TOURS The **Yosemite Valley Visitor Center** (*see* Basics, *above*) offers a worthwhile slide program on the park's geography and history. The free 20-minute show runs 10–3:30 Monday–Saturday and noon–3:30 Sunday. Check the *Yosemite Guide* for times. Also look for the center's documentaries about John Muir and Ansel Adams, shown in the late afternoon and evenings (call for schedules). Ranger programs like nature walks and storytelling last anywhere from one to three hours and are great ways to learn more about the park.

All kinds of guided bus tours originate in the valley, from two-hour excursions ($14) along the valley floor (every ½ hr daily 9–4) to a day-long grand tour ($40) of Mariposa Grove and Glacier Point (late spring to early fall). For reservations, contact the **Yosemite Lodge Tour Desk** (tel. 209/372–1240) or go to one of the tour booths at Curry Village, the Ahwahnee Hotel, or the Village Store in Yosemite Village.

SHORT HIKES **Yosemite Falls,** also known simply as "The Falls," is the highest waterfall in North America and the fifth highest in the world. It's divided into the upper falls (1,430 ft), the middle cascades (675 ft), and the lower falls (320 ft). From the parking lot, a ⅛-mile, wheelchair-accessible trail leads to the base. To reach the top, head to Sunnyside Campground and take the strenuous 3½-mile (one-way) **Yosemite Falls Trail,** which rises over 2,700 feet. The views from the top are breathtaking. If you're not up to the full trek (2–4 hrs round-trip), stop at **Columbia Rock** 1½ miles along the trail. You'll still get a good workout and dizzying vistas of Half Dome and the valley. Get off at Shuttle Stop 7 and follow signs.

The easy and popular 3-mile trail around **Mirror Lake** (Shuttle Stop 17), at the east end of the valley, offers some of the best photo opportunities in Yosemite. Expect a lot of camera-toting tourists here: The trail is the gentlest in the park, so nearly everyone takes it. From the Happy Isles Trailhead (Shuttle Stop 16), the difficult 6-mile round-trip trail to **Vernal Fall** (317 ft) and **Nevada Fall** (594 ft) takes two to three hours, but the view from the top is phenomenal. The first half of the trail (aptly named **Mist Trail**) is a great place to soak yourself on a hot day—bring a bathing suit or rain gear, and kiss your hairdo good-bye. A fantastic overnight hike continues past Nevada Fall to Half Dome (*see* Longer Hikes, *below*). If you arrive in Yosemite along Hwy. 41, your first view of the valley will be at **Bridalveil Falls,** a ragged 620-foot cascade that's often blown as much as 20 feet from side to side by the wind. The Ahwahneechee called it *Pohono* (Puffing Wind). An easy ⅛-mile trail leading to its base starts from the parking lot. For fabulous views of some of Yosemite's finest, follow the **Inspiration Point Trail.** The trek starts at Hwy. 41 at Wawona Tunnel and terminates at Glacier Point. If you start on the west side of the tunnel it's 1 mile to Inspiration Point where, looking eastward up the valley floor, you can bask in the shadow of El Capitan and Bridalveil Falls.

Numerous day hikes begin at **Tuolumne Meadows,** including an easy half-mile trail to **Soda Springs**—a potable, naturally carbonated spring. In 1863 William Brewer of the California Geologic Survey called its water "pungent and delightful," though a more recent visitor said, "It tastes like flat seltzer." A lovely but arduous (3 hrs, 5 mi round-trip) hike to emerald **Elizabeth Lake** wanders through mountain hemlock and lodgepole pine and across boisterous Unicorn Creek. These trails are less crowded than those originating in the valley.

LONGER HIKES There are hundreds of possible day hikes in Yosemite, but to beat the crowds you'll need to do some serious backpacking in the wilderness, miles away from the stench of civilization. All trails are limited to a certain number of backpackers to prevent overuse, and free wilderness permits are required for overnight stays (*see* Basics, Wilderness Permits, *above*). With a permit, you can take any of 70 trails (5–20 mi long) crisscrossing Yosemite's outback. These often involve strenuous climbs along jagged paths no more than a foot wide, and some trails take upward of a week to complete. Fire rings are interspersed along the way, but you'll need to bring your own tent and provisions, including a water filter or iodine tablets to treat water. You can rent special 3-pound bear-proof canisters for $3 at Yosemite Valley Sports Shop, Curry Village Mountain Shop, Crane Flat Grocery, Wawona Store, and

Tuolomne Meadows Sports Shop (*see box* Some Things to Bear in Mind, *above*). Order maps and a pamphlet of hiking suggestions from the **Yosemite Association Bookstore** (Box 230, Yosemite 95389, tel. 209/379–2648). At any of Yosemite's bookstores, you can buy topographic USGS maps ($2.50), but experienced backpackers swear by Trails Illustrated's waterproof topo map ($7.95), available at The Wilderness Center in Yosemite Village.

While that rushing water might look tempting, unless you want a bad case of the trots, you should treat all surface water or melted snow by boiling it for at least 3–5 minutes, using an iodine-based purifier, or using a giardia-rated water filter.

If you're in top physical condition, take the hike out of Yosemite Valley, following either the John Muir or Mist Trail to **Half Dome.** Follow the trail to Nevada Fall (*see* Short Hikes, *above*), and continue past Little Yosemite Campground to the Half Dome turnoff; then be prepared to climb and climb until you've risen nearly 5,000 feet. This trip (10–12 hrs, 17 mi round-trip) is not for those with vertigo or weak wills; indeed the last leg of the trip involves a steep area with guide-rail cables provided to help you keep your balance and pull yourself up. At the top, if you can stomach it, lie belly down and hang your chin over the precipice. You can make the trek an overnighter by camping at **Little Yosemite Campground,** but you'll need a wilderness permit (*see* Basics, Wilderness Permits, *above*). You can leave your pack at the campground and climb the last 4 miles without extra weight.

Hetch Hetchy, one of California's largest reservoirs, has irked conservationists since it was built early in the century. Environmentalists like John Muir fought actively against the damming of the Tuolumne River, which, they argued, would irreparably harm the region's wildlife. But politicians in San Francisco wanted mountain-fresh drinking water. Can you guess who won? Today, despite the massive Hetch Hetchy dam, the area still retains much of its beauty, and it contains the wonderfully isolated, moderately difficult **Rancheria Falls Trail** (13 mi round-trip), which leads to the eponymous lonely falls. You can do this trail in a day. If you have more time (five days) and excellent packing skills, go for the 52-mile **Rancheria Mountain and Bear Valley Loop,** a strenuous hike that offers a terrific view of the Grand Canyon of Tuolumne River, as well as secluded camping around Bear Valley Lake. To reach the Rancheria Falls Trailhead, exit the west side of the park on Tioga Pass Road (Hwy. 120), turn right on Evergreen Road after 1 mile, and continue for 8 miles (you'll see signs).

The area north of Tuolumne River is wild and untrammeled—a good place to get away from it all. The numerous trailheads near **Tuolumne Meadows** are great for backpackers who want to spend at least a few days in the wilderness. Serious hikers should consider the **Tuolumne Grand Canyon Trail** (accessed from either Tuolumne Meadows or White Wolf). It's a rough 29-mile hike to White Wolf, if you begin at Tuolumne Meadows. The first 4 miles follow the river along the forest and then drop down along a series of waterfalls and cascades, where the trail gets steeper as it descends through the Muir Gorge into Pate Valley. From there it's a really steep climb to White Wolf. This strenuous hike requires at least 3 full days. The climb out of

So You Want To Do A Little Hiking . . .

You can hook up with the Pacific Crest Trail out of Tuolumne Meadows and continue hiking for a few days, months, or a year by following the trail south all the way to Mexico, or back all the way to the Great White North of Canada. Routed in 1928 and first hiked in its entirety in 1972, the Pacific Crest Trail follows the crest of the Pacific's greatest ranges. Commencing on the California–Mexico border, the trail winds through three nations, 24 national forests, seven national parks, and 33 wilderness areas for a grand total of 2,638 miles of pure hiking satisfaction. It is the longest complete trail in America. For more info contact: The Pacific Crest Trail Association, 5325 Elkhorn Blvd., Suite 256, Sacramento, CA 95842. Or call 800/817–2243.

Pate Valley takes a full day for even the most experienced hiker. Another popular trip out of Tuolumne Meadows from the John Muir Trailhead is an excellent two- to three-day hike (about 30 mi round-trip) that leads to **Vogelsang Lake.** Hike up Lyell Fork on the **John Muir Trail** to the **Rafferty Creek Trail,** which becomes steep and difficult. This is a popular trip, so get your permits early (*see* Basics, Wilderness Permits, *above*).

If you're coming in on Route 41 at the southern end of the park, be sure to stop at the majestic Mariposa Grove of Giant Sequoias, the largest stand of giant Sequoias in Yosemite and home to the Grizzly Giant, the oldest tree in Mariposa Grove and one of the largest Sequoias in the world.

SCENIC DRIVES AND VIEWS During summer you can drive up to **Glacier Point** for a spectacular view of the valley and surrounding mountains. The 16-mile road starts at Chinquapin junction on Hwy. 41. Better yet, take a shuttle (*see* Getting Around, *above*) to the top and take Four Mile Trail back down into the valley (3 hrs), coming out on South Side Drive. **Tuolumne Meadows,** the largest subalpine meadow in the High Sierra and the site of several backcountry trailheads, is on Tioga Pass Road, 25 miles west of Lee Vining and U.S. 395. This is a gorgeous part of Yosemite, with delicate meadows surrounded by huge granite formations, and it's usually much less crowded than the valley. Tioga Pass Road is closed during winter and usually opens by late May, but harsh winters can force the road to remain closed into July.

PARK ACTIVITIES

For those who want to take it easy, the National Park Service rents binoculars ($3) for **birdwatching.** Free 1½-hour **photography walks,** which lead you to prime spots for shooting Yosemite, leave daily around 8:30 AM from the Yosemite Lodge or the Ahwahnee Hotel. **Horseback rides** originate at the stables next to North Pines Campground (*see above*); a four-hour trip to Vernal Fall is $44. In summer, you can take a leisurely 3-mile float (they call it "rafting") down the Merced for $13. Sign up at the **rafting** area in Curry Village, open daily 10–4. For more info on all these activities, consult the *Yosemite Guide* or check with the visitor center (tel. 209/372–0299).

BIKING Bikes are not permitted on any hiking trails, but Yosemite Valley has 8 miles of paved bike paths. Try the spectacular trail to Happy Isles and Mirror Lake, off the road to Curry Village; the easy 3-mile loop takes well under an hour unless you stop for a half-mile walk to Mirror Lake. Rent bikes ($5 per hour, $16 a day) from **Curry Village** (tel. 209/372–8333) or **Yosemite Lodge** (tel. 209/372–1274). Serious cyclists should consider the 15-mile round-trip trail from Tuolumne Meadows to Olmstead Point along Tioga Pass Road. The grades are difficult and the roads narrow, but the views are spine chilling.

ROCK CLIMBING Take a look around for two seconds and you'll understand why Yosemite is a mecca for world-class rock climbers. Basic and intermediate lessons ($120 for one person, $85 each for two) are available mid-April to mid-October with the **Yosemite Mountaineering School** (tel. 209/372–8344). They organize trips from Tuolumne Meadows. Unfortunately you can't rent climbing equipment in the park without enrolling in a class.

SKIING Yosemite's ski season usually lasts from late November or early December to March. Call 209/372–4605 for weather conditions.

➤ **DOWNHILL** • Yosemite has a small ski area, **Badger Pass** (tel. 209/372–8430 or 209/372–1000 for snow report), that won't pose much of a challenge to accomplished skiers. It's a good place to learn, however, and there are enough relatively uncrowded trails to keep intermediate skiers entertained. It's open daily 9–4:30 in winter. Lift tickets cost $25–$30, depending on the number of lifts open, which in turn depends on snowfall. They usually run three advanced lifts and six intermediate lifts. Ski rentals are $18 a day, snowboards $30 a day. Look for Badger Pass 6 miles east of Hwy. 41 on Glacier Point Road.

➤ **CROSS-COUNTRY** • Yosemite has 90 miles of cross-country trails through the Badger Pass ski area to Glacier Point. A free shuttle from the valley runs to Badger Pass, departing in the morning and returning in the afternoon. **Glacier Point Road** is a good place to start: Beginners will enjoy the groomed track, and advanced skiers will get a workout if they take the whole 21-mile round-trip. The **Cross-Country Ski School** (tel. 209/327–8444) offers two-hour lessons ($18) and four-hour lessons ($40, including rentals). A guided overnight trip—including meals and lodging—is $110 per person. Badger Pass (*see above*) has rentals ($9 half day, $13 full day). The **Tuolumne Grove of Giant Sequoias Trail** (3 mi round-trip), which starts at Crane Flat a few miles east of the Big Oak Flat entrance station, has a steep drop, but you get to ski among the largest living things on earth.

SNOWSHOEING National Park Service Ranger-naturalists conduct regular snowshoe walks from Badger Pass and Crane Flat. These easy walks ramble around the ski areas and the Tuolumne Grove of Giant Sequoias. The Yosemite Mountaineering School (tel. 209/372–8444 in winter) rents snowshoes at Badger Pass for $11 per day.

Santa Cruz
Originally founded in the late 18th century as a mission town, Santa Cruz has several identities. Old-time residents, many of Italian descent, still look askance at the liberal students and hippies who have been migrating to the town ever since the University of California opened its "alternative, no-stress" branch here in the 1960s. Back then, Santa Cruz was a city-size incarnation of the hippie. Of course that's no longer true, but people still call Santa Cruz a hippie town.

And though Santa Cruz's reputation as a happy-dappy beach town stretches far and wide, it has its fissure points, including the Loma Prieta fault, which runs through the mountains east of town. Bicycle riders spar with car drivers about bike lanes; small-business owners roll their eyes at the mangy folks clogging their cafés and panhandling on their sidewalks. Anti-immigration hysteria is taking its toll here, too, as migrant farm workers, mostly Mexicans and Mexican-Americans, move to Santa Cruz County in record numbers to work on nearby farmlands. Though they fit snugly into the local economy, these newest pieces of Santa Cruz's puzzle often find themselves made unwelcome by the largely homogeneous (i.e., white) community.

Most of downtown has been rebuilt since 1989's 7.1-magnitude Loma Prieta earthquake, and many say the squeaky-clean new buildings and chain stores symbolize a change toward conservatism. But even if the mall is blander than before, Santa Cruz's sloppy individuality is still very much in place.

Though subject to the conflicts of any sizable California community, Santa Cruz holds on to its idyllic beach-town atmosphere better than many. The carnival-like **Boardwalk** is Santa Cruz at its flashiest, drawing legions of hormone-crazed teenagers from Salinas and San Jose every weekend. The Boardwalk's most popular attraction is the **Giant Dipper,** one of the oldest wooden roller coasters in the world. The harrowing ride affords you a brief panorama of Monterey Bay before plunging you down toward the beach. If your stomach's not up to such antics, head to Santa Cruz's stunning coast. The rocks off the craggy shore are favored perches for seals, the beaches are thronged with surfers and their retinue, and the hills surrounding the town fade into idyllic redwood forests. You'll find $1.50 maps—and not much else—at the **Visitor Information Center** (701 Front St., tel. 408/425–1234). Gay and lesbian travelers can call the **Lesbian/Gay/Bisexual/Transgender Community Center Hotline** (tel. 408/425–LGCC) for listings of upcoming events and other resources.

COMING AND GOING

BY CAR The most scenic route from either San Francisco, 1½ hours north, or Monterey, an hour south, is along **Highway 1.** San Jose is about 45 minutes away on curvy **Highway 17,** which meets up with I–280, I–880, and U.S. 101, and is the faster drive to San Francisco and the East Bay. Avoid Hwy. 17 on weekend mornings, though, when the entire Silicon Valley seems to head for the beaches, and at night, when the sharp curves of the road are tricky.

BY BUS Green Tortoise (*see box* Getting In, Out, and Around, in Chapter 1) lumbers from San Francisco to Los Angeles, stopping in Santa Cruz once a week. From L.A., buses arrive in the

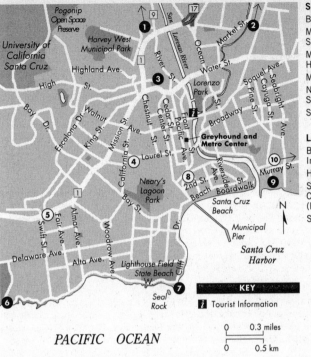

Sights ●

Brookdale Lodge, **1**
Mission
Santa Cruz, **3**
Museum of Natural
History, **9**
Mystery Spot, **2**
Natural Bridges
State Beach, **6**
Surfing Museum, **7**

Lodging ○

Babbling Brook
Inn, **4**
Harbor Inn, **10**
Santa Cruz
Carmelita Cottages
(HI), **8**
Sunset Inn, **5**

PACIFIC OCEAN

0   0.3 miles

0   0.5 km

Santa Cruz Safeway parking lot (2018 Mission St.) Monday mornings (9–12 hrs, $30); buses from San Francisco (3 hrs, $10) arrive in Santa Cruz Fridays at 11 PM. Reserve at least three days in advance, one week ahead in the summer. *Tel. 415/956–7500 in California or 800/867–8647.*

Greyhound (425 Front St., at Laurel St., tel. 408/423–1800) has direct service between Santa Cruz and San Francisco twice daily (½ hr, $14 one-way), and three times daily from Los Angeles (10 hrs, $50 one-way). **Highway 17 Express Bus** (tel. 408/425–8600) has hourly service (every 15 min during evening commute hours) and is the cheapest way to travel between San Jose and Santa Cruz ($2.25), but it only runs on weekdays. Buses stop in Santa Cruz at the junction of Soquel Drive and Hwy. 1, and in San Jose at the CalTrain station and at the corner of 3rd Street and San Fernando Avenue, one block from San Jose State University. On weekends, Amtrak buses (tel. 415/508–6455) roll between the San Jose CalTrain depot and the Santa Cruz Metro Center roughly every hour for $5 each way.

BY TRAIN While you can't get to Santa Cruz directly by train, **CalTrain** (tel. 800/660–4287) does offer daily train service between San Francisco and San Jose (1½ hrs, $4.50). Trains run at least once an hour between 8 AM and 3 PM, more frequently during commute hours. From the San Jose CalTrain station (Cahill and W. San Fernando Sts.), take the **Santa Cruz CalTrain Connector** (tel. 408/425–8600) to the Metro Center (*see* Getting Around by Bus, *below*) in Santa Cruz. The bus leaves every two hours on weekdays, less often on weekends; it takes an hour and costs $5.

HITCHING In town, hitching is a fairly reliable form of transportation. On the open road, however, be prepared to wait considerably longer, especially if you're grubby. Sooner or later a sympathetic student is sure to offer you a lift. As always, use good judgment when accepting a ride. To catch a ride north out of town, stand at the corner of Swift Street and Hwy. 1 (a.k.a. Mission St.) by the LITTER REMOVAL sign (no kidding). Hitching northeast along Hwy. 17 toward

San Jose or south along Hwy. 1 is trickier. Try the Ocean Street on-ramp to Hwy. 17. A less risky idea is the **UCSC rideboard** at Bay Tree Books (the college bookstore, in the center of campus). The availability of rides varies with the time of year, and some money to cover gas is appreciated, if not expected.

GETTING AROUND

Santa Cruz is insanity on a map and even more confusing in practice. On the edge of Monterey Bay and bisected by the San Lorenzo River, the town is full of crooked and puzzling streets, so keep a sharp eye on a map. Hwy. 1 becomes **Mission Street** when it enters Santa Cruz, and resumes its old identity on the way out of town. **Bay Street** and **High Street** both funnel into UCSC, which is on a hill 2 miles northeast of downtown, while the Boardwalk is on **Beach Street** just west of the river. The Boardwalk and downtown (which centers around **Pacific Avenue** and **Front Street**) are within comfortable walking distance of each other.

BY BUS Bus service is efficient and fairly easy to use. The Santa Cruz Metropolitan District Transit (SCMDT), also known as Metro, operates from the **Metro Center** adjoining the Greyhound Station. Any bus in town will eventually take you to the Metro Center, where you can pick up a copy of "Headways," a free pamphlet that lists all bus routes. The fare is $1, but you can purchase a special all-day pass for $3 on any bus or at the Metro Center. Exact change, in coins or one-dollar bills, is required; change machines are available at the Metro Center. *920 Pacific Ave., at Laurel St., tel. 408/425–8600. Open daily 7 AM–9 PM. Info booth in lobby open weekdays 8–5.*

BY BIKE Biking is the best way to get around Santa Cruz. Many streets have wide bike lanes, and the weather is quite moderate, especially in spring and summer. Bring wheels from home if you can, since renting can be expensive. **Pacific Avenue Cycles** (709 Pacific Avenue, at Laurel, tel. 408/423–1314), at the end of the Pacific Garden Mall, charges $23 per day.

HITCHING Within Santa Cruz, students without cars (or patience for the bus) hitch from bus stops along any main drag. Rides to the main campus are especially easy to catch at the corner of Bay and High streets or Bay and Mission streets. From campus, stick your thumb out by the bookstore to get downtown.

WHERE TO SLEEP

In the summer, especially on weekends, finding a budget room in Santa Cruz is next to impossible. During the rest of the year, hotels slash prices to rope in boarders. Year-round, the best deal is at the youth hostel if you can get a bed. Camping is popular in the area, evidenced by the saturated campgrounds in the summer. If the campgrounds listed below are full, make sure to call the headquarters after 5 PM, when Manresa and Sunset State Beaches open overflow sites. Failing that, Big Basin Redwoods State Park (*see* Near Santa Cruz, *below*) is 30–45 minutes away. The dorms at U.C. Santa Cruz (tel. 408/459–2611) accept guests from the end of June to the beginning of September, but the rooms are spartan, far from everything, and pricey. A single runs $50, $67 with full board; a double is $40 per person, $57 with full board. The dorms are limited to those on "official" business, so you may want to say you're considering enrolling and sign up for a campus tour.

HOTELS AND MOTELS Facing the Boardwalk on 2nd Street, 3rd Street, and Riverside Avenue are some scuzzy motels that lie in what some call a sketchy area, known as "The Flats." These places rarely fill up, but you'll find comparably priced places clustered on Mission and Ocean streets that are much more comfortable and equally convenient if you have a car. For a decadent treat, stay at one of several good B&Bs. At the downtown **Babbling Brook Inn** (1025 Laurel St., tel. 408/427–2437, fax 408/427–2457), rooms with country French–decor are surrounded by manicured gardens and a beautiful brook. Twelve rooms come complete with private bath and a fireplace or Jacuzzi. Double rooms, which include a full breakfast, range $85–$165 per night. In a residential neighborhood 10 minutes southeast of town, the **Harbor Inn** (645 7th Ave., tel. 408/479–9731) has doubles starting at $45 in summer, $35 in the off-season, with a hodgepodge of old furniture and wooden beds. Most rooms have kitchenettes, and groups of four can get a suite ($65–$85, depending on the season). The chain motel decor doesn't do much for the big rooms, but the **Sunset Inn** (2424 Mission St., at Swift St., tel. 408/423–3471) has some of the best rates in town. Weekdays, a double starts at $40, while a suite that sleeps six goes for $85.

HOSTELS **Santa Cruz Carmelita Cottages (HI).** The cottages are actually a cluster of houses made hosteler-friendly. Two blocks from the Boardwalk, on Beach Hill, these accommodations cost $12–$14 for members and $15–$17 for nonmembers. Travelers complain about the curfew and no-alcohol rule, but the cottages are quiet and conversational as a result. Private and "family" rooms (three to five people) cost $30–$40, depending on the number of beds. Cyclists can use the on-site repair and tune-up shop. You're almost sure to snag a spot as they leave most beds unreserved: Line-up for openings begins at 5 PM, but eager beavers show up around 3. Write (Box 1241, Santa Cruz 95061) or call ahead for reservations. *32 Main St., at 2nd St., tel. 408/423–8304. From Metro Center, Bus 7 to Main St. 25 beds. Curfew 11 PM, lockout 10–5. Reception open daily 7–9 AM and 5–10 PM. Lockers, sheet rental ($1). Wheelchair access.*

CAMPING **Henry Cowell Redwoods State Park.** Five miles north of Santa Cruz, this 113-site campground is buffered by a redwood forest and rests under madrone and mixed pine trees near several trailheads. In summer, RVs and screaming teens tend to overrun the place, but otherwise this is a fine spot. Bike campers share one large, shady site for $3 each. Reserve through Destinet (tel. 800/444–PARK). Both tent and RV sites are $17 weekdays, $18 weekends. *101 N. Big Trees Park Rd., Felton, tel. 408/335–4598 or 408/438–2396. From Hwy. 1, Hwy. 9 north; from Metro Center, Bus 35. Drinking water, flush toilets, showers. Closed Dec.–Feb.*

New Brighton State Beach. High above the ocean on a large cliff, this popular campground in Capitola, 5 miles southeast of Santa Cruz, offers an incredible view of the coast from a few of the 112 sites. A steep path leads downhill to the soft beach below. Neither the tent nor RV spaces have any privacy, however. Reservations—available through Destinet (tel. 800/444–PARK)—are a must between May and September, when the place is invariably filled. Sites go for $17 weekdays, $18 weekends. Follow signs from Hwy. 1. Otherwise, Bus 71 will take you to the corner of Soquel and Park avenues, but leaves you with a long walk. *1500 Park Ave., tel. 408/475–4850.*

Sunset State Beach and **Manresa State Beach.** Offering slightly more space and privacy than New Brighton, these two campgrounds, both about 10 minutes south of Santa Cruz, are short walks from wide, sandy beaches. Sunset has 90 campsites, all with fire rings, picnic tables, and hot showers. Spaces, reserved through Destinet (tel. 800/444–PARK), are $17 weekdays, $18 weekends. On the way to Sunset, you'll pass Manresa, which has 64 walk-in sites, 100 yards from the parking lot with the same facilities, prices, and reservation system as Sunset. Sites are on a plateau above the beach or set back in a sparse sprinkling of trees. Both campgrounds open overflow sites when they're all booked up; Manresa overflow accommodates RV's only, and Sunset puts tent campers in the picnic area. *San Andreas Rd. Sunset: tel. 408/724–1266. Manresa: tel. 408/761–1795. Hwy. 1 south to San Andreas Rd./Larkin Valley exit, right at bottom of ramp, right onto San Andreas Rd.*

ROUGHING IT Santa Cruz prohibits sleeping in public places, and police issue snoozers hefty citations both downtown and at the beach. If you need a place to crash, you're less likely to pick up a ticket in the hills. About 2 miles up Hwy. 9, past the railroad tracks but before Henry Cowell State Park, several turnouts lead to clearings where you could pitch a tent or bundle up in a blanket.

FOOD

Healthy cuisine and yummy yuppie vittles are the heir apparent of Santa Cruz's hippie legacy. For fresh produce, much of it organically grown, head to the **farmers' market,** held every Wednesday 2–6 on the corner of Pacific Avenue and Cathcart Street; then trot over to Lorenzo Park (River St., btw Water St. and Soquel Ave.) for a picnic. Also, look for the markets along Mission Street.

➤ **UNDER $5** • For a tasty slice of late-night pizza ($1.75 with drink), head to **Upper-crust Pizza** (2415 Mission St., tel. 408/423–9010), on the west side of town near the Hwy. 1 turnoff for Natural Bridges State Beach; it's open until 11 PM Sunday–Thursday, and midnight on Friday and Saturday. For heaping portions of Mexican food, hit **Taquería Vallarta** (608 Soquel Ave., 1 block east of Ocean St., tel. 408/457–8226). Enormous burritos ($3.25 vegetarian, $3.70 carnivore) are served up weekdays 10 AM–midnight, weekends 9 AM–midnight.

The Bagelry. This Santa Cruz institution specializes in hybrid bagel spreads like the Pink Flamingo (cream cheese with lox and dill; $2.65) and the Luna spread (pesto, ricotta, and almonds; $2.50). If you're short on cash, try the "three-seed slug"—a flat, wide bagel without the hole (55¢). *320A Cedar St., at Laurel St., tel. 408/429–8049. Other location: 4363 Soquel Dr., tel. 408/462–9888. Both open weekdays 6:30–5:30, Sat. 7:30–5:30, Sun. 7:30–4.*

Zachary's. The basic breakfast—two eggs, tasty home fries, and your choice of homemade breads—sells for a reasonable $4 here. On the more elaborate side, the huge stack of pancakes ($3.50) and the family-size omelets ($4.50 and up) are definitely worth the price. Usually crowded with students and locals alike, Zachary's outstanding food is worth the wait (except maybe on weekends, when it can take up to an hour to get a table). *819 Pacific Ave., btw Laurel and Maple Sts., tel. 408/427–0646. Open Tues.–Sun. 7–2:30. Wheelchair access.*

➤ **UNDER $10** • **Dolphin Restaurant.** Wade your way through tacky tourist traps to the end of Santa Cruz's municipal pier for crispy, fresh-caught fish and chips ($4.75). You could sit inside, but it's more expensive and the picnic tables adjacent to the Dolphin's serving window provide ample space to down a burger ($5.50). *End of pier, tel. 408/426–5830. Open summer, daily 8 AM–11 PM (Fri. and Sat. until midnight); winter hrs vary, so call ahead.*

Saturn Café. Something like a pizza parlor on acid, the interior of the Saturn features theme tables (*Charlie's Angels,* Richard Nixon, and Madonna, to name a few) and flying-saucer-like lamps. The mostly veggie menu offers stellar tomato-garlic pesto sauce over the pasta of the day and a small salad for $6.25, and soul-warming chili for $3.50. The Chocolate Madness ($4.50) frightens even the sweetest tooth with a mess of chocolate cookies, ice cream, mousse, and chocolate chips smothered in hot fudge. Let your wash tumble at the Laundromat behind the café while you get started on those zits. *1230 Mission St., near Laurel St., tel. 408/429–8505. Open noon–midnight. Wheelchair access. No credit cards.*

CAFES In a town with more than 15,000 college students, the absence of nighttime diversions for the under-21 set has fueled a serious café scene. In addition to being popular hangout spots for college students, cafés are also frequented by locals looking for a lively debate or a place to read a good book.

Caffè Pergolesi. In a big, rambling Victorian house blessed with a huge outdoor deck, the Perg has all of the trappings of a good café: good coffee that won't put a hole in your stomach ($1.25), espresso drinks that will ($1–$3), and several teas your gut will thank you for. Try *chai,* the milky Indian spice tea ($2) for a new caffeine vice. The limited menu offers veggie lasagna ($5) and quiche ($4.10), as well as bagels ($2) and pastries ($1.50–$2). The crowd ranges from UCSC earth muffins to Euro travelers. *418A Cedar St., at Elm St., tel. 408/426–1775. Open daily 8 AM–midnight.*

Herland Book-Café. Although men are allowed, this bookstore/café was conceived as a safe haven for women. The books, grouped in categories like "Women of the Wild West" or "Women Respond to the Men's Movement," are all (surprise) female-authored. The café serves coffee, tea, espresso drinks, and snacks. *902 Center St., at Locust St., tel. 408/42–WOMEN. Café open Mon.–Fri. 8 AM–6 PM, Sat.–Sun. 10 AM–6 PM; bookstore open daily 10 AM–6 PM.*

Jahva House. The Jahva House is found in a large, airy, comfortable warehouse, softened by big Oriental rugs and leafy ficus trees. The long coffee bar furnishes a multitude of coffees and teas, including organically grown varieties of both. Try a Mexican mocha (coffee, chocolate, and cinnamon; $2.60) or a slab of the banana bread ($3). *120 Union St., near Cedar St., tel. 408/459–9876. Open Mon.–Sat. 6 AM–midnight, Sun. 8–8. Wheelchair access.*

WORTH SEEING

Most of Santa Cruz's sights are downtown, within a walkable area. To explore the jagged coast, though, you'll definitely need a car or one hell of a mountain bike. Downtown, the **Pacific Garden Mall** is the center of the action, strewn with specialty stores, antique shops, restaurants, and cafés, and is an easy destination for an afternoon of window-shopping. **Bookshop Santa Cruz** (1520 Pacific Ave., at Locust St., tel. 408/423–0900) is a huge bookstore and café open until 11 PM that won't sweat you for nursing your coffee or perusing their stock for hours. **Logos** (1117 Pacific Ave., near Lincoln St., tel. 408/427–5100) is Santa Cruz's premier used-book and music store. If you're in the mood for a leisurely afternoon walk, the **Mission Santa Cruz** (126 High St.), built in 1791, destroyed by an earthquake in 1857, and rebuilt as a half-size replica in 1931, has grounds overrun with colorful gardens and fountains.

SANTA CRUZ BEACH BOARDWALK Thick with the smell of suntan oil and hair spray, the Boardwalk provides the stickiest, horniest, most commercialized sun-and-sand carnival west of Coney Island. The rows and rows of pinball machines are one of the best ways to lose a quarter. The Boardwalk is free, so pony up $2–$3 for only the rides you want and skip the overpriced unlimited ride passes. *400 Beach St., tel. 408/426–7433. From Front St. follow the signs to the ocean. Rides open weekends year-round, daily in summer. Wheelchair access.*

U.C. SANTA CRUZ UCSC boasts one of the most beautiful campuses in California. Like the environs, the bookstore at the center of campus is woody and natural, resembling a ski lodge more than a student union. The **admissions office** (tel. 408/459–4008) at the campus entrance is open weekdays 8–5 and has maps and tour schedules. Investigate the **limestone quarry** near the campus bookstore—it's a nice spot for a picnic—and take a self-guided tour of the organic growing system at the **Farm and Garden Project** (tel. 408/459–4140). If you park along Meder Avenue at the far west end of campus and catch the free shuttle at Bay and High streets, you can avoid the on-campus parking fee. Otherwise take Bus 41 from the Metro Center to the west entrance of campus.

SANTA CRUZ CITY MUSEUM OF NATURAL HISTORY You'll recognize this place by the huge stone statue of a whale out front. The museum is small, but full of info about the Ohlone Indians—who originally populated the area—and the seals and sea lions that still do. A slippery touch pool allows you to finger weird sea slugs and anemones. The museum is near Pleasure Point—a great place to watch local surfers. In January, the museum sponsors the **Fungus Fair,** celebrating the mushrooms that blanket the forest floor. *1305 East Cliff Dr., tel. 408/429–3773. From downtown, walk or drive east on Laurel St., cross river, turn right on San Lorenzo St. (which becomes East Cliff Dr.). Or take Bus 67 from Metro Center. Admission: $2 donation requested. Open Tues.–Sun. 10–5.*

SANTA CRUZ SURFING MUSEUM At Lighthouse Point on West Cliff Drive, there's a tiny exhibit on surfing—from its Hawaiian origins to the present. The museum is dedicated to the memory of an 18-year-old surfer who drowned in 1965. Also on display is a board bitten by a great white shark in 1987, testimony to the real danger posed by sharks along the coast from Santa Cruz to Pigeon Point. Plop down outside the lighthouse and watch the surfers on Steamer's Lane, one of the best surf spots in California. A little farther out you'll see Seal Rock, the summertime home of thousands of barking, shiny seals. *Mark Abbott Memorial Lighthouse, West Cliff Dr., tel. 408/429–3429. Bus 3A or 3B. Admission free. Open Mon., Wed.–Fri. noon–4, weekends noon–5.*

NATURAL BRIDGES STATE BEACH Two miles west of town, the secluded and spectacular Natural Bridges State Beach is the perfect place to escape the overwhelming sensory stimulation of Santa Cruz. As its name implies, the beach features a mudstone bridge-like formation, a nesting spot for pelicans, as well as excellent tidal pools, picnic tables,

At the bizarre Brookdale Lodge (9 mi from Santa Cruz on Hwy. 9, tel. 408/338–6433), an oasis of drink during Prohibition, a window behind the Mermaid bar once looked underwater into a swimming pool full of prostitutes. Men chose a date, met her in the secret passage behind the fireplace, and used a tunnel to get to the bordello across the street. Manager Terry offers free tours once a day.

barbecue pits, and plenty of soft, warm sand to stretch out on. Also on the grounds of the park is a **monarch butterfly colony,** where you can witness the amazing sight of thousands of brightly colored butterflies clustering in the trees from mid-October to February. Call ahead for the latest (and to make a reservation for guided walks). Park on Delaware Avenue just east of the park entrance to avoid the $6 parking fee. *West Cliff Dr., tel. 408/423–4609. From Boardwalk, follow West Cliff Dr. until you see signs. Or Bus 3B from Metro Center. Open daily 8 AM–sunset.*

MYSTERY SPOT This quirky little place lies in the redwoods 3 miles north of Santa Cruz and, in the minds of true believers, is at the center of a mysterious force that makes people taller and compels balls to roll uphill—basically, the spot is a life-size physics experiment. It's a tacky tourist trap, to be sure, but its gift shop is filled with one-of-a-kind souvenirs and kitschy knickknacks. Your $4 admission also buys you a Mystery Spot bumper sticker (that's why you see them everywhere). *465 Mystery Spot Rd., tel. 408/423–8897. From downtown, go east on Water St., left on Market St., go 2½ mi, then follow signs. Open summer daily 9–8:30, winter 9–4:30.*

CHEAP THRILLS

Hiding in the redwoods, **Felton, Ben Lomond,** and **Boulder Creek** are small towns in a grand setting, definitely worth a day trip. All three get a bit crowded on weekends, particularly in summer, but they manage to retain their mountain charm. It will take only 30–45 minutes to travel through all three. At first glance it seems as though these towns haven't changed in 50 years—until you notice the spiritual healers, chiropractors, and eco-conscious grocery stores lining the sidewalks. You won't find much to "do" in any of these towns—Boulder Creek is the most lively, which isn't saying much—but the beautiful drive alone is worth the trip. When you've soaked up enough of the small-town ambience, pack a picnic and head to Big Basin (*see Near Santa Cruz, below*), only 15 minutes farther from Boulder Creek. Weekends, Bus 35 travels through all three towns from the Metro Center; or drive north along Hwy. 9.

The oceanside town of **Capitola,** along the coast about 5 miles southeast of Santa Cruz, is popular with locals for its wide, quiet, sandy beach and rickety wooden pier, a welcome change from the sometimes frenetic pace of Santa Cruz. After you're done soaking up the sun, head straight to **Mr. Toot's** (221 Esplanade, tel. 408/475–3679), a café full of old wood tables, comfortable couches, and a deck overlooking the beach. Catch Bus 59 from Santa Cruz's Metro Center, or take Hwy. 1 south to the Capitola/Park Avenue exit and head toward the Pacific.

For a groovy Santa Cruz experience, go at sunset to **It's Beach,** immediately west of the lighthouse. Almost every summer evening, locals gather here to drum and dance as night falls. Also check out the numerous street performers on **Pacific Avenue** and the Boardwalk.

FESTIVALS

The **Cabrillo Music Festival,** usually held during the first week of August, has food, symphonic music, and other live entertainment. Call the Santa Cruz Civic Auditorium Box Office (tel. 408/429–3444) for more info. Tickets cost $6–$25 depending on the performance and seating. From mid-July to August, UCSC hosts **Shakespeare Santa Cruz** (tel. 408/459–2121): six weeks of the Bard's works set against a backdrop of beautiful redwoods. Tickets ($15–$21) should be reserved a few days in advance.

AFTER DARK

The dull nightlife offerings in Santa Cruz force most night crawlers to take up drinking—either in cafés or bars. If you want alcohol, be prepared to prove you're 21 since the bouncers card heavily. Only a few bars feature live music, listing upcoming shows in the weekly newspaper *Good Times.* Unless there's a big name playing, skip **The Catalyst** (1011 Pacific Ave., tel. 408/423–1336)—it has few redeeming qualities. The **Kuumbwa Jazz Center** (Cedar St., at

Laurel St., tel. 408/427–2227) hosts jazz and blues shows throughout the year. Call for tickets ($2–$14) and scheduling info. And if you like to shoot stick you're in luck—in Santa Cruz pool tables are ubiquitous.

If you've got a car, why not celebrate a dying American tradition at the **Skyview Drive-In Theater** (2260 Soquel Ave., at Thurber Ln., tel. 408/475–3405), where you can watch a double feature on the big screen for $5 a head. Two first-run films and two not-quite-on-video flicks play year-round starting around 7:30 in winter and 9 in the summer. Call first.

The Blue Lagoon. This is Santa Cruz's premier (read: only) gay and bisexual nighttime hangout. There's a $2 cover on weekends and Tuesdays, but it's worth it for some of the best DJ dance music in town; straight- and bi-friendly. *923 Pacific Ave., across from Metro Center, tel. 408/423–7117.*

Boulder Creek Brewing Company. Even though it's 25 minutes north of Santa Cruz, Boulder Creek combines great beer and the best live music in the area. Try their Ghost Rail Pale Ale ($3) and Redwood Ale ($3); for heartier appetites there's the Mudslide Stout ($2.75), billed "thick as a mudslide, twice as tasty." When live bands play there's usually a cover ($3 and up). Flamenco dancers, Middle Eastern musicians, and blues artists have all performed here. *13040 Hwy. 9, tel. 408/338–7882.*

The Red Room. This snazzy dive bar is a true UCSC institution, especially among the über-hip. Occasionally you can catch rockabilly and alternarock in the rear Crown room. Don't look for a sign out front; there isn't one. Some nights you pay a minimal cover. *1003 Cedar St., at Locust St., tel. 408/426–2994.*

Seabright Brewery. Despite the pastel-colored stucco building and bland interior, the Seabright is incredibly popular with locals, especially on Tuesday's "Neighborhood Night," when homeowners mingle with renting students on the concrete patio. Fridays bring live rock and blues from 6 to 10. Their award-winning brews go for $3 a pint; skip the food. *519 Seabright Ave., at Murray St., 7 blocks east of the river, tel. 408/426–BREW. Open daily 11:30 AM–11:30 PM. Wheelchair access.*

OUTDOOR ACTIVITIES

HIKING AND MOUNTAIN BIKING The redwood-filled hills surrounding Santa Cruz provide some of Northern California's best hiking and mountain-biking opportunities. Two or three times a week, the local chapter of the Sierra Club sponsors group outings—hikes, camping, and canoe trips. Stop by their office (903 Pacific Ave., tel. 408/426–HIKE) for a listing of upcoming wilderness forays. If you're more hip to the solo experience, head directly to **Big Basin Redwoods State Park** (*see* Near Santa Cruz, *below*). Closer to town, **Henry Cowell Redwoods State Park** (*see* Camping, *above*) has 20 miles of trails, many of which meander through virgin redwood forests. Bikes are allowed on designated fire and service roads, but not on hiking trails. For a beautiful, albeit crowded, stroll among some of the park's tallest trees, take the **Redwood Grove Trail**; you'll find the trailhead off Hwy. 9. For more of a workout, head 2 miles uphill to the observation deck for a beautiful view of the valley (walk up Pipeline Road from the nature center and turn left on Ridge Fire Road). To get here from downtown, follow Hwy. 9 toward Felton.

Hiking and biking locals adore the **Forest of Nisene Marks** (SW of Santa Cruz; exit Hwy. 1 at Seacliff, take Soquel Ave. ½ mile east to Aptos Creek Rd., tel. 408/761–3487) partly because most tourists ignore it. Amid the creeks, redwoods, and steep trails, you can view the ruins of a Chinese labor camp or walk 2 miles to the epicenter of the 1989 Loma Prieta earthquake; the trail is clearly marked from the end of the park's driveable road. There are also a few trails that mountain bikers are allowed to navigate—ask the friendly folks at the main gate to point the way. Bike rentals are available back in town (*see* Getting Around, *above*). Open 6 AM–sunset.

SURFING Santa Cruz is definitely the surf capital of Northern California. **Steamer's Lane,** between the Boardwalk and the lighthouse, always has a decent break and plays host to several competitions in the summer; consult the free quarterly *Ocean Life* for dates. The city's **Parks and Recreation Department** (tel. 408/429–3663) offers the best surf lesson deals: four hours of lessons over two days go for $64, board included. If you're already waveworthy but left your board at home, the **Beach 'n' Bikini Surf Shop** (cnr Beach and Front Sts., across from the wharf, tel. 408/427–2355) rents surfboards ($15) and wet suits ($10) by the day.

Near Santa Cruz

BIG BASIN REDWOODS STATE PARK

The first forest deemed a California State Park, Big Basin (23 mi NE of Santa Cruz off Hwy. 9) overwhelms you with thousands of acres of gigantic old-growth redwoods, lofty Douglas firs, rushing streams, and flowing waterfalls. All sorts of wildlife call Big Basin home, including black-tailed deer and an occasional fox, bobcat, coyote, or mountain lion. Worthy of at least a day's visit ($5 per car), and more if you groove on the outdoors, this is one park where you must get away from the main roads to fully appreciate nature's splendor. So lace up your hiking boots, and go commune with trees who've been here about 1,500 years longer than you have.

Just past the main entrance you'll come to the **park headquarters** (tel. 408/338–6132), where rangers can give you advice on which trails best suit your desires and energy level, or simply sell you a map ($1) and let you go to town. If you just have an hour or so, your best chance for drama is to head for the gorgeous **Silver Falls** and **Golden Falls**, about ¾ of a mile along the Skyline-to-the-Sea trail. Here, you can wade in the pools, shower in the falls themselves, or skip across the creek on redwood logs. For a less crowded hike, try the **Howard King Trail** from the parking lot to Mt. McAbee. Along the way you'll pass through several different ecosystems, from the redwoods to the chaparral, and be rewarded with an ocean view at the peak. You can return on Hammond Road for a round-trip of 5 miles in about two or three hours.

The truly fit should tackle the 12½-mile **Skyline-to-Sea Trail**—arguably the most scenic hike in the park—which travels over hill and dale all the way to the coast. This is the park's most popular trek, and those who've done it rave about how satisfying it is to reach the water after gazing at it from such a distance earlier in the trail. Leave a second car at the trail's endpoint at Waddell Beach, and either pay scrupulous attention to a map or accept the possibility of getting semi-lost, since several trailheads converge a few miles into the hike. Mountain biking is only allowed on fire roads in the park, and unfortunately there are few good loops: Your best bet is to follow North Escape Road a short distance from park headquarters to **Gazos Creek Road,** a 12-mile fire trail that stretches to the coast, and then return on Johansen Road via Middleridge Road.

➤ **COMING AND GOING** • To reach Big Basin from Santa Cruz, follow Hwy. 9 north for 12 miles, then follow the signs for another 9 miles from Boulder Creek. If you're coming from the north on I-280, take Hwy. 85 south from Cupertino to Hwy. 9 south, then pick up Hwy. 236 into the park. Bus 35 will take you 2½ miles short of the campgrounds. Hike or hitch the rest of the way.

➤ **WHERE TO SLEEP** • All of Big Basin's 110 drive-in camping sites have picnic tables, fire pits, food lockers, and access to toilets and showers. Most of the sites are spread out under the redwoods with lots of room to breathe, and many are situated on the banks of gentle streams. The sites, which fetch $17–$18, go quickly on weekends; make reservations through Destinet (tel. 800/444–PARK).

Even more lovely are the 24 primitive sites ($7) at Big Basin's trail camps. Though fires in the trail camps are strictly forbidden due to high fire danger, you'll be compensated by the seclusion and privacy of these sites, most along the major trails. Call the park headquarters to reserve a few weeks ahead of time, since these sites are also popular. If you can't tear yourself away from the beauty of the park but didn't bring a tent, rent a tent cabin—essentially a shack with a canvas cover and two cots and a wood stove inside—for about $40 for up to eight people. Call 800/874–TENT for more info.

Monterey

Monterey, with the possible exception of Carmel, is California's most unabashedly commercial seaside resort. John Steinbeck (1906–1968) immortalized the busy fishing port in *Cannery Row* and *Sweet Thursday,* describing it as "a poem, a stink, a grating noise, a quality of light, a tone, a habit, a nostalgia, a dream." By the 1950s, however, the sardines were gone, along with much that was poetic. Visitors will still find the fascinating Monterey Bay Aquarium a worthwhile stop, and historical conservation has preserved much of the city's past; Monterey was once the capital when Mexico ruled California from 1777 to 1846.

VISITOR INFORMATION The **Monterey Peninsula Chamber of Commerce** (380 Alvarado St., tel. 408/649–1770) offers free maps as well as information about the world-famous **Monterey Jazz Festival** (tel. 408/373–3366) in late September, and the **Monterey Blues Festival** (tel. 408/394–2652) in late June.

Jimi Hendrix made rock-and-roll history at the Monterey Fairgrounds in 1969 when he burned his guitar in front of awestruck fans. Later, horrified by the destruction, Indian sitarist Ravi Shankar, who considers instruments sacred objects, almost refused to perform.

COMING AND GOING Greyhound buses have regular service to Monterey from San Francisco (4 hrs, $19 one-way). The Monterey **Greyhound station** (42 Del Monte Ave., tel. 408/373–4735), in a gas station on the eastern end of town, is open daily 7:45 AM–9:50 PM.

Monterey-Salinas Transit (tel. 408/899–2555) has regular connections to Carmel, Big Sur, Santa Cruz, and Salinas from Monterey ($1–$3). All buses depart from the downtown **Monterey Transit Plaza** (cnr Tyler and Pearl Sts.). For Big Sur, take Bus 22; it will get you as far as the Nepenthe restaurant on Hwy. 1.

GETTING AROUND Getting around Monterey is not difficult. From Hwy. 1, the Pacific Grove/Del Monte Avenue exit will take you straight into downtown. The main drag is north–south **Alvarado Street,** with Fisherman's Wharf at the north end and Cannery Row (and the aquarium) 1½ miles further northwest. Once in town, your best bet for getting around is via **Wave** ($1, transfers free), a shuttle bus with frequent service and stops throughout the downtown/Cannery Row area. There is also a bike/pedestrian path (*see* Outdoor Activities, *below*) that parallels the shore from the historic downtown area to Fisherman's Wharf and Cannery Row. Because of summer tourism, both parking and crowds are a serious problem for drivers. The most reasonable parking garage downtown (btw Alvarado, Franklin, Washington, and Del Monte Sts.) charges $1 an hour.

WHERE TO SLEEP Monterey is almost devoid of cheap lodging—but if you're persistent (or if you have a tent) you may be able to scare up something reasonable. A slew of motels along North Fremont Street are close to downtown and accessible via Buses 9 and 10. Across from Del Monte Beach and one block east of the Greyhound station, **Del Monte Beach Inn** (1110 Del Monte Ave., tel. 408/649–4410, fax 408/375–3818) is a small B&B offering 18 rooms ($50–$60) decorated by a Martha Stewart disciple. Make sure to check in before 9 PM. A few rooms are wheelchair accessible. At the flawlessly clean (albeit dull) **Lone Oak Motel** (2221 Fremont St., tel. 408/372–4924) the price of a double—$48 weekdays, $80 (ouch!) weekends—includes unlimited access to a Jacuzzi and sauna room, a great way to unwind after a hard day's traveling. People who can't find (or afford) lodging have been known to sleep in their cars; they recommend pulling into a spot across the street from the cemetery by the Point Pinos Light Station.

Paramount Motel. Eight miles north of Monterey in the town of Marina, the Paramount looks shabby on the outside, but the proprietor is friendly and the rooms ($33 for a double) are secure, clean, and comfortable. No reservations are accepted so arrive early. *3298 Del Monte Blvd., tel. 408/384–8674. Hwy. 1 north to Del Monte Ave., 200 yards past the Beach St. intersection; or Bus 12 to Beach Ave. and walk up Del Monte Ave. 6 rooms, all with bath.*

➣ **CAMPING** • **Veteran's Memorial Park Campground.** Just five minutes from downtown, this first-come, first-served campground lies on a grassy knoll in a quiet valley. Although it's not exactly the great outdoors, its 40 tightly packed sites ($15) are well-maintained, some shadier and more secluded than others. Hikers and cyclists share one large site for $3 per person. Showers are available, but bring your own food. *Via del Rey, tel. 408/646–3865. From downtown, take Jefferson west, turn left on Pebble St., right on Johnson Ave.; or Bus 3 from Transit Plaza.*

FOOD On Tuesday afternoons, Alvarado Street downtown is closed off for a **farmers' market**; at all other times you can find a plethora of seafood and health-food restaurants here, but unfortunately most are overpriced. The **Bagel Bakery** (201 Lighthouse Blvd., at Reeside Ave., tel. 408/649–1714), open daily 6:30–6, has the best deal in town for breakfast or lunch: Tasty bagels are 40¢–50¢, and you can add whatever toppings suit your fancy. **Tillie Gort's Café** (111 Central Ave., Pacific Grove, tel. 408/373–0335) serves delicious Mexican and Mediterranean sandwiches with an emphasis on vegetarian dishes. A mushroom garden burger will set you back $6.25, and the turkey sandwich goes for $5.75. One of the best pasta and seafood restaurants on the peninsula, **Fishwife** (1996½ Sunset Dr., Pacific Grove, tel. 408/375–7107) is a favorite with locals and travelers in the know. Fish dishes start at $9, and pastas are all less than $9. For picnic supplies, head to **Joseph's Patisserie** (435 Alvarado St., at Bonifacio Pl., tel. 408/373–1108); sandwiches run $3–$5.

WORTH SEEING Monterey's main attraction is the justifiably world-famous **Monterey Bay Aquarium** (886 Cannery Row, tel. 408/648–4800), open daily 9–6 (10–6 in winter), where you'll find sharks and sea otters in convincingly natural habitats and a three-story kelp-forest aquarium. Admission is $13.75. Avoid hour-plus waits during the summer by purchasing your tickets in advance (tel. 800/756–3737 or 408/648–4888). AAA members can find $5-off coupons in *Motorland* magazine. From Hwy. 1 south, follow signs from the Pacific Grove/Del Monte Avenue exit.

Cannery Row lies along the waterfront south of the aquarium, ending at **Fisherman's Wharf.** Both places have seen better days. The Laida Café—an "institution of commercialized love" in Steinbeck's time—is now a bright-yellow ice cream parlor called **Kalisa's** (851 Cannery Row, tel. 408/372–3621); and the lab of Doc Ricketts, a Steinbeck character, is now a defunct nightclub (800 Cannery Row). To drown your sorrows over days gone by, head to **Bargetto Winery** (700 Cannery Row, tel. 408/373–4053), open daily 10:30–6, where you can sip their wares for free. Upstairs, **A Taste of Monterey** (700 Cannery Row, tel. 408/646–5446), also open daily 1–6, charges $2 for tasting—but think of it as a fee for the superlative bay views.

History buffs can pick up "The Path of History Walking Tour" brochure from the Chamber of Commerce (*see above*) or spend $2 on a guided tour organized by **Monterey State Historic Park** (20 Custom House Plaza, tel. 408/649–7118). Monterey's old buildings are fascinating and well preserved, and most tourists ignore them for the artificial flash of Cannery Row. Don't miss Colton Hall where the state constitution was written, the Cooper Molera Adobe, or the Custom House. Most buildings on the tour are free, but some charge $2 for a looksee. A $5 pass buys your admission to all of the houses and is good for two days.

When you've had it with quill pens and adobe walls, head for the water. The **Monterey State Beach** is nothing compared to fabulous **Asilomar State Beach** (tel. 408/372–4076), which features tide pools and enormous waves crashing on the rocky shore; look for it 2 miles west of Monterey in the quiet town of **Pacific Grove** (Bus 1 will get you within walking distance). Between October and March, glimpse thousands of monarch butterflies who make their winter homes in **Washington Park** (cnr Pine Ave. and Alder St.). Pacific Grove also houses the **Point Pinos Light Station** (Ocean View Blvd., at Point Pinos, tel. 408/648–3116), since 1855 the oldest continuously operating lighthouse on the West Coast (open Thurs., Sat., and Sun. 1 PM–4 PM).

AFTER DARK Monterey's night life around Cannery Row caters to tourists in search of gimmicky clubs and bizarre drink specials. There, you'll hear low-rent bands playing shoddy covers of "Brown Eyed Girl." Less than intrigued? Try the **Three Spirits Gallery** (361 Orange Ave., from Del Monte Blvd. north, turn west on Contra Costa St., first left is Orange Ave., or Bus 7 or 20, tel. 408/393–ARTS), a tiny art space in the middle of a warehouse district in Sand City 5 miles northeast of downtown Monterey. On some nights (make sure to call first) the gallery hosts solid go-go, surf, or indie rock bands for a $3–$5 cover. For more laid-back atmo-sphere—something like a café adorned with the walls of a medieval castle—**Morgan's Coffee & Tea** (498 Washington St., at Pearl St., tel. 408/373–5601) sometimes features local folk and jazz performers. Word has it microbrews are on the way. Business is slower since the Fort Ord military base shut down a few years ago, but gay men still get down on the dance floor at **After Dark** (214 Lighthouse Ave., at Reeside Ave., tel. 408/373–7828). Deep house on Thursday nights attracts straights who want to boogie as well.

OUTDOOR ACTIVITIES

➤ **BIKING AND MOPEDS** • Monterey Moped Adventures (1250 Del Monte Ave., at Sloat St., tel. 408/373–2696) rents beach cruisers ($15 a day) and mopeds ($20 for the first hour, then $10 an hour; $50 a day). Call ahead to reserve: A driver's license and deposit are required. For $20 a day you can rent a mountain bike from **Bay Bikes** (640 Wave St., 1 block inland from Cannery Row, tel. 408/646–9090) and make tracks for the paved path (4 mi) that stretches from the wharf past Cannery Row, and Lover's Point. Another great idea is to pedal down 17-Mile Drive (*see box, below*) into Carmel. Cyclists don't have to stop at the pay booth and can catch quite a few spectacular ocean views between the posh homes. Bay Bikes lets you return bikes to their Carmel location (near the south end of the drive) for an extra $2.50.

➤ **FISHING AND WHALE WATCHING** • For salmon- and tuna-related fun, contact **Chris's Fishing Trips** (tel. 408/375–5951) on Fisherman's Wharf for half-day sportfishing trips ($25–$40); you'll also pay $15 for a license and equipment. Chris's also offers two-hour whale-watching trips ($12–$15) between December and March, when Monterey Bay is filled with migrating gray whales.

➤ **KAYAKING** • Lover's Point in Pacific Grove, close to reefs, sea otters, harbor seals, and sea lions, is the best place to kayak. **Adventures by the Sea** (Lover's Point Beach, tel. 408/372–1807) can outfit you with a kayak, oars, wet suit, and a half-hour lesson for $25. Open summers 9–6; hours vary in winter.

➤ **SNORKELING AND SCUBA DIVING** • The bluffs and underwater caves off Ocean View Drive (between the aquarium and Asilomar Beach) are some of the best scuba and snorkeling spots in the area. Better yet, are the pristine waters of Whaler's Cove in Point Lobos (Hwy. 1, 4 mi south of Carmel). **Aquarius Dive Shop** (2040 Del Monte Ave., or 32 Cannery Row, tel. for both 408/375–1933) offers moderately priced equipment rentals for certified divers (about $70 the first day, $35 each additional day). A more feasible option for most people is snorkeling. Aquarius has gear for less than $34—not a high price, considering you'll need a wet suit, boots, gloves, and a hood to brave Monterey Bay's freezing waters. Snorkeling lessons and a tour will set you back $50 more.

The Poor Man's 17-Mile Drive

Probably the most notorious road on the Central Coast, 17-Mile Drive charges car own-ers an immensely annoying $6.50 toll to motor by chi-chi Pebble Beach's manicured golf courses and multimillion dollar mansions. If you'd rather lick asphalt than fork over your hard-earned cash to look at the homes of egotistical swells, there is another option. "The Poor Man's 17-Mile Drive," as locals like to call it, is really only 6 miles long, but it's as dramatic as the real thing (and gratis). From Monterey, head west on Ocean View Drive (just west of Cannery Row) and follow the road as it bends southward past spectacular Asilomar State Beach. Watch the sun set over wild sand dunes and the untamed Pacific; and look for Lover's Point, a grassy patch overlooking the ocean that's a popular picnic area.

Big Sur

Everyone defines Big Sur differently, but all agree that the region's precipitous cliffs, rocky beaches, and redwood forests make it one of the most dramatic stretches of coastline in the world. Henry Miller wrote of the land as "a region where extremes meet, a region where one is always conscious of weather, of space, of grandeur, of eloquent silence." The harsh geography, helped along by a core of adamantly protective locals, has precluded development; as a result the area is sparsely populated. The closest thing to a town is the group of stores surrounding the **River Inn,** 22 miles south of Carmel. Locals head over to the inn on Saturday nights to hear live jazz or drum music; and nearby, the **Big Sur Pub** (Hwy. 1, tel. 408/667–2355), open daily until 10 PM, sometimes hosts mariachi bands or guitarists.

Much of Big Sur lies within the 167,000-acre **Ventana Wilderness,** in Los Padres National Forest. Ventana's deep, wide valleys, waterfalls, hot springs, natural pools, perennial streams, and undisturbed wildlife (heaps of deer and a few bears) are enough to keep wilderness junkies on a perpetual high. **Big Sur Station** (Hwy. 1, just south of Pfeiffer Big Sur State Park, tel. 408/667–2315), open daily 8–6, is loaded with information on camping and exploring the surrounding wilderness. Of particular note, *El Sur Grande* offers a history lesson, a detailed map, and hiking tips in each issue. One tip hikers won't find, however, is a suggestion to park at one of Hwy. 1's turnouts and avoid paying $6 on state lots.

WHERE TO SLEEP   With more than 1,000 campsites up and down the coast, Big Sur is an ideal place to pitch a tent. You can camp for free in **Los Padres National Forest** as long as you hike 100 feet from a paved road and don't light a fire (*also see* Camping, in Chapter 1). Good access roads can be found all along Hwy. 1: If you've got four-wheel drive, try Willow Creek Road just north of Gorda, otherwise Nacimiento Road about 4 miles south of Lucia (*see* Camping *below*). The forest service also runs 11 designated campgrounds ($5) in the area, with fire pits and drinking water. For maps, fire permits, and info contact Big Sur Station (*see above*) or the **U.S. Forest Service District Headquarters** (406 S. Mildred St., King City 93930, tel. 408/385–5434).

If you want to sleep indoors, be prepared to pay handsomely for the privilege. Your best option is to rent one of the tent cabins available at private campgrounds for $30–$40. One of the nicest is **Big Sur Campground and Cabins** (tel. 408/667–2322), 3 miles south of Andrew Molera State Park (*see below*), where cabins sleeping two start at $44. **Riverside Campgrounds and Cabins** (Hwy. 1., tel. 408/667–2414), 25 miles south of Carmel, provides the cheapest indoor accommodations in all of Big Sur. Five excellent rooms graced with gorgeous redwood interiors start at $50. The two larger double cabins will set you back $80. You will find rustic, romantic cabins at **Deetjen's Big Sur Inn** (Hwy. 1, tel. 408/667–2377), secluded behind redwoods 3 miles south of Big Sur Station. Each of the 21 rooms ($85 and up) is decorated with homey, personal stuff and a down comforter (you'll need it). Both the atmosphere and the people who run the place are top-notch, and short walking trails lie behind the inn.

➤ **CAMPING** • If you want to escape from over-developed State Park campgrounds, head to the **Nacimiento Road Area.** One of the few access points to the interior of Big Sur, Nacimiento Road, 4 miles south of Lucia, twists and turns to eight $5 sites at **Nacimiento Campground** (11 miles from Hwy. 1) and 23 $10 sites at **Ponderosa Campground** (13½ miles from Hwy. 1). Both peaceful campgrounds, devoid of massive RVs year-round, lie on the bank of a babbling brook, but neither has showers and only Ponderosa has flush toilets; make sure to bring your own water or a purifier. Better yet, remember you can camp off any wide spot in the road (there are several great spots between Nacimiento and Ponderosa) for free as long as you walk 100 feet from your car and obtain a fire permit from the U.S. Forest Service (*see above*).

West of Hwy. 1, 10 miles south of Palo Colorado Road, **Andrew Molera State Park** has more than 4,000 largely undeveloped acres with beach access and camping. Campers pay $3 per person and $1 per dog. Don't try to get by without putting your money in the self-payment box—a ranger *will* come around at 8 AM to collect the cash and hand out $25 tickets to the weasels. The 50 tents-only sites are first-come, first-served, but they never turn anyone away, which means the park can become a beehive when overflow campers stack up on weekends. Call Big Sur Station (*see above*) for more info. If you want to soak up a view of a tremendous valley among the majestic madrones and oaks of the Ventana Wilderness, trek to the 11, first-come, first-served campsites ($12) in **Bottcher's Gap** (5 mi south of Garrapata State Beach, go east 8 mi on Palo Colorado Rd., tel. 408/625–5833). There's no phone and no showers, but you'll have running water; if you come on a weeknight, you'll have all the peace and solitude you could ever want. Hikers and tent campers vie for one of two secluded primitive sites ($17 weekdays, $18 on weekends), located in a cypress forest on bluffs overlooking the ocean at **Julia Pfeiffer Burns State Park.** Even without potable water or flush toilets, these spots book early. For info call or stop by Big Sur Station (*see above*). Reserve spots through Destinet (tel. 800/444–PARK).

FOOD Wise travelers will stock up at the supermarket in Carmel or San Luis Obispo. If you forget to pack the cooler, the **Center Deli** (Hwy. 1, next to Big Sur post office, tel. 408/667–2225) has groceries, a host of pasta salads, and the cheapest sandwiches around ($3–$5), as well as fruit smoothies ($3) in summer. The **Coast Gallery Café** (above Coast Art Gallery, Hwy. 1, 33 mi south of Carmel, tel. 408/667–2301) is a casual deli with hot sandwiches ($6–$7) and a great view of the coast. The **Big Sur Pub** (Hwy. 1, next to the River Inn, tel. 408/667–2355) has a filling veggie burrito ($5.25) and sandwiches for less than $5.

EXPLORING BIG SUR Eleven miles south of Carmel, Palo Colorado Road winds its way east from Hwy. 1 through the Ventana Wilderness for 8 serpentine miles until it ends at **Bottcher's Gap.** From the parking lot, **Skinner's Ridge Trail** climbs 4 miles (roughly 3 hrs) to Devil's Peak, which affords incredible views of Ventana's dramatic wooded peaks and valleys. South off Skinner's Ridge Trail, the 8-hour round-trip hike to **Pico Blanco**—a rugged, marble mountain peak that the Esselen Indians, Big Sur's earliest human inhabitants, thought of as the top of the world and the site of human creation—offers stunning views but winds through private property. The hike's not legal, but people do it anyway, trekking along the Boy Scout Service Road past the Boy Scout Camp and all the way up **Little Sur Trail.**

Double back ½ mile north from Andrew Molera to check out the **Point Sur Light Station** (tel. 408/625–4419), built in 1889 on a strange rock outcropping to prevent shipwrecks along this foggy and rocky stretch of coast. Tours of the lighthouse are available on weekends and Wednesdays May–October ($5). Call first for times and make sure to show up a half hour early so the docents can let you through the gate. Once the site of a Monterey Jack cheese factory and a dairy farm, **Andrew Molera State Park** offers more than 10 miles of hiking and mountain-biking trails. The strenuous hike on the **Ridge Trail** takes you through 4 miles of stunning coastal scenery to the top of a ridge. Take a deep breath and savor the spectacular view of the Pacific before you head down the **Panorama Trail** to the **Bluffs Trail,** which is especially striking in spring when the wildflowers bloom.

About 5 miles south of Andrew Molera State Park, **Pfeiffer Big Sur State Park** (east side of Hwy. 1, tel. 408/667–2315) is one of the most popular camping and hiking spots on the coast, especially during summer. Just south of Pfeiffer on the same side of the highway, Big Sur Sta-

Sykes Hot Springs

If you have two days and backpacking gear on your hands, think seriously about making the 10-mile trek to Sykes Hot Springs, one of the Central Coast's most enticing natural wonders. After a 6- to 7-hour hike up steep ridges and along a river valley crowded with redwoods, you can soak your bones in the thermal spring and sleep under the stars before heading back the next day or continuing on into the depths of the Ventana Wilderness. The largest of the spring's rock-dam tubs holds four people and on summer weekends you may have to vie for space—aim for the winter months, if possible. The trail begins at the Big Sur Station parking lot; register and get a fire permit from the rangers here before heading out.

tion (*see above*) is the starting point for the **Pine Ridge Trail,** a local favorite that leads into the Ventana Wilderness and **Sykes Hot Springs** (*see box, above*).

Sycamore Canyon Road, a mile south of Big Sur Station, is unmarked save for a stop sign. If you can find it, brave the road for 2 miles and you'll land at **Pfeiffer Beach,** a turbulent, windswept cove with huge rock formations and an angry ocean that's definitely not suited for swimming. About 2½ miles farther south lies **Nepenthe** (tel. 408/667–2345), an expensive restaurant with an extraordinary view (also the last stop of Bus 22 from Monterey).

Head ¼ mile south from Nepenthe to the **Henry Miller Library** (Hwy. 1, tel. 408/667–2574). More like a bookstore with a precise collection of literature, the tiny, one-room library displays the bohemian author's artifacts (sorry, no steamy letters to Miss Nin) and has rotating exhibits on artists and writers associated with Miller or Big Sur. The library is open daily 11–5 in summer; hours vary in the winter.

More spectacular than Pfeiffer Big Sur State Park, **Julia Pfeiffer Burns State Park** (12 mi south of Big Sur Station, tel. 408/667–2315) has excellent and often less crowded hiking trails. But most people pay the $6 entrance fee to see what was once the most spectacular sight in all of Big Sur, before parking lots, postcards, and crowds demystified some of its natural wonder: **McWay Falls,** which pours 70 feet down into the ocean. From the parking lot, a short half-mile wheelchair accessible path leads to a bluff with an incredible view of the creek at the head of the falls. Better, and far less crowded, the 6-mile **Ewoldsen Trail** loop is a fantastic rugged hike that offers one of the best vegetation samplings found on the Big Sur coast.

Three miles south of Julia Pfeiffer, a sign on the right side of the road reads: ESALEN INSTI-

Between 1 AM and 3:30 AM, you can relax naked in Esalen's natural hot springs, perched on a cliff overlooking the Pacific, for just $10—a pleasure that could run you 10 times that much during the day. Call the institute to make reservations.

TUTE–RESERVATIONS ONLY. At the end of the road you'll find the world-famous **Esalen Institute** (tel. 408/667–3000), a one-time wacked-out hippie colony that specializes in the "exploration of human value and potentials." Locals tend to scoff, but the institute was one of the first places to introduce Gestalt therapy in the late '60s. These days the grounds and natural hot springs are closed to the public during the day. Stop by anyway and the touchy-feely guard will hand you a catalog of the outrageously expensive workshops. Class titles and descriptions will keep you howling for miles down the road.

OUTDOOR ACTIVITIES The main activity in Big Sur is hiking (*see* Exploring Big Sur, *above*), but to the dismay of many drivers, lots of people also bicycle along Hwy. 1. Cyclists should be experienced and familiar with the narrowness of the highway and the lack of road shoulder. One benefit of pedaling the coast is that most of the state parks offer cheap campsites (usually $3) to those on two rather than four wheels.

Andrew Molera State Park is the only Big Sur park with single-track trails for mountain biking. Mountain bikers in tip-top shape can take on the steep, strenuous **Ridge Trail,** which is more than 2 miles long and has elevation gains of 1,200 feet. For a more relaxing ride, try the **River** and **Cottonwood trails** (2 mi), both of which wind through the park's meadows. Most trails start at the parking area or a half-mile away at the beach. Elsewhere in Big Sur, you'll have to stick to the fire and service roads, or risk a fine.

Index

A

Adelaide Inn, *176*
African American Historical
  Society Library and Archives,
  45
African American Museum (San
  Francisco), *55*
African American Museum and
  Library (Oakland), *72*
African-Americans, resources
  for, *14, 45*
Aida Hotel, *175*
Airport shuttles, *8*
Airports, *7–8*
Aladdin (restaurant), *110*
Albergo Verona (hotel), *175*
Alcatraz Island, *26–27*
Alexander Inn, *176*
Alpine Meadows ski resort, *237*
Alta Mira Continental Hotel, *189*
Amira (restaurant), *118*
Amsterdam (B&B), *177*
Amtrak, *6*
Amusement parks, *85, 255*
Ananda Fuara (restaurant),
  111
Andrew Molera State Park, *262,
  263, 264*
Angel Island State Park
  camping, *190*
  hiking and biking, *204–205*
  sightseeing, *76*
Ann's Soup Kitchen and
  Restaurant, *124*
Año Nuevo State Reserve, *89*
Ansel Adams Center, *55*
Anthony Chabot Regional Park,
  203
Apartment rentals, *185–186,
  188*
Aquariums, *55–56, 260*
Arawan (restaurant), *130–131*
Architectural tours, *42*
Art Center Bed and Breakfast,
  182
Art galleries and museums,
  55–58
  Berkeley, *67*
  downtown, *31, 58*
  Golden Gate Park, *30*
  Mission District, *58*
  Oakland, *72*

Palo Alto, *83*
SoMa, *52, 53, 58*
Asians/Pacific Islanders,
  resources for, *14*
Asian Art Museum, *55*
Asmara Restaurant, *128*
Auberge des Artistes (B&B),
  180
Audubon Canyon Ranch, *79*
Ayala Cove, *76*
AYH Hostel at Union Square,
  183–184

B

Bagdad Café, *108*
Baker Beach, *47, 54*
Balazo (restaurant), *114*
Bancroft Library, *63*
Bank of America, *31, 34*
Barbary Coast, *34*
Barbie Hall of Fame, *83*
Barney's Gourmet Hamburger
  (restaurant), *128*
Bars. *See also under areas*
  Berkeley, *155–156*
  Oakland, *156–157*
  San Francisco, *149–155*
BART subway, *5*
Baseball, *215*
Basketball, *196–197, 215,
  216*
Bay Model (Sausalito), *75*
Bay Wolf (restaurant), *130*
Beaches, *54–55*
  Lake Tahoe, *240*
  Marin County, *78–79*
  Monterrey, *260*
  Oakland, *72–73*
  Point Reyes National Seashore,
  81
  San Mateo County Coast, *85,
  86, 87*
  Santa Cruz, *253, 256–257*
Ben Lomond, *256*
Berkeley
  bars, *155–156*
  bus service, *4*
  cafés, *147–148*
  festivals, *62*
  free attractions, *67–68*
  gay and lesbian organizations,
  13–14

live music, *159–161*
lodging, *186–188*
markets and delis, *135–136*
medical services, *9*
museums, *66*
movie houses, *165–166*
nightclubs, *164*
outdoor activities, *197, 198,
  200–203*
parks and gardens, *65–66*
restaurants, *124–127*
shopping, *92–93, 94–95,
  96–97, 98–99, 100, 102,
  103, 104*
sightseeing, *60, 62–65*
theater, *168*
visitor information, *22*
weather, *21*
Berkeley Bowl Marketplace,
  135
Berkeley City Club (lodging),
  187
Berkeley Hills Fire Trail, *66*
Berkeley History Center and
  Museum, *67*
Berkeley Marina, *66, 214–215*
Berkeley Psychic Institute,
  67–68
Berkeley Rose Garden, *66*
Berkeley Thai House
  (restaurant), *125*
Bette's Oceanview Diner, *125*
Bicycling, *199–209*
  bikes on BART, *5–6*
  Big Sur, *264*
  bikes on buses, *6*
  East Bay, *200–203*
  information and maps, *5*
  Lake Tahoe area, *239*
  Marin County, *203–207*
  Monterrey, *261*
  rentals, *28, 197*
  San Francisco, *200*
  Santa Cruz, *252, 257*
  South Bay, *207–209*
  wine country, *220, 223*
  Yosemite, *249*
Big Basin Redwoods State Park,
  258
Big Sur, *262–264*
  camping and lodging, *262–263*
  food and dining, *263*

outdoor activities, *264*
sightseeing, *263–264*
Biltmore Hotel, *177*
Bird-watching, *80*
Black Stallion (B&B), *174*
Blondie's (restaurant), *124*
Blue and Gold Fleet, *7*
Blue Nile (restaurant), *125*
Boardwalk (Santa Cruz), *255*
Boat parties, *155*
Bocce Café, *120*
Bolinas, *80, 206*
Bongo Burger, *124*
Boogaloos (restaurant), *118*
Botanical gardens, *30, 66*
Bothe-Napa State Park, *224*
Boulder Creek, *256*
Brady Acres (hotel), *177*
Brewery tours, *59*
Brick Hut Café, *125*
Bridge tolls, *3*
Brother's Restaurant, *121*
Buena Vista Café, *113*
Buena Vista Park, *53–54*
Bus travel, *3–5*
Butano State Park
camping, *194*
hiking and biking, *208–209*
sightseeing, *89*

C

Cable Car Museum, *39*
Cable cars, *3*
Cabrillo Music Festival, *256*
Cactus Taquería (restaurant), *128*
Café Bastille, *113*
Café Claude, *113*
Café Intermezzo, *124*
Cafés. *See also under areas*
Berkeley, *147–148*
Oakland, *148*
San Francisco, *141–147*
Caffe Macaroni, *113*
Cal Adventures, *195–196*
California Academy of Sciences, *55–56*
California Historical Society, *53*
Calistoga, *224, 227*
CalTrain, *6*
Cameron's Inn, *193*
Campanile tower, *63*
Camping
Angel Island, *190*
Big Sur, *262–263*
Half Moon Bay, *193–194*
La Honda, *194*
Lake Tahoe, *234*
Monterrey, *259–260*
Mt. Tamalpais, *191*
Oakland, *189*
Pescadero, *194*
Point Reyes, *191–192*
San Rafael, *190*

Santa Cruz, *253*
Sausalito, *190*
wine country, *221, 224*
Yosemite, *245–246*
Camp Reynolds, *76*
Campus Motel, *187*
Camron-Stanford House, *71*
Cannery Row (Monterrey), *260*
Capitola, *256*
Capp Street Project, *52*
Carol Doda's Champagne and Lace Lingerie Boutique, *41*
Casa Sanchez (restaurant), *117*
Car travel, *1–3*
bridge tolls, *3*
parking, *2–3*
rentals, *2*
Castro district
bars, *150*
cafés, *142*
festivals, *18, 20, 46*
lodging, *174*
restaurants, *106–108*
sightseeing, *45–47*
Center for the Arts, *52–53, 56*
Cha Am (restaurant), *125*
Cha Cha Cha (restaurant), *115*
Cheese Board, *135–136*
Cheese Board Pizza Collective, *136*
Chef Jia's (restaurant), *109*
Chester's Cafe, *126*
Chez Panisse Café, *127*
Chez Sovan (restaurant), *133*
Chicanos, resources for, *14*
China Beach, *54*
China Camp State Park, *77, 190*
Chinatown (S.F.),
bars, *150*
lodging, *174–175*
restaurants, *109–110*
sightseeing, *36–38*
Chinese Historical Society of America, *56*
Chinese New Year, *17*
Chinese Telephone Exchange, *37*
Churches, *36, 39, 82*
Circle Gallery, *31*
City Hall (S.F.), *35*
City Lights Bookstore, *38, 95*
Civic Center district
bars, *150–151*
cafés, *142*
lodging, *175–176*
restaurants, *110–112*
sightseeing, *35–36*
Civic Center Lodge, *189*
Claremont Resort, Spa, and Tennis Club, *189*
Climate, *20–21*
Club Za Pizza, *122*
Codornices Park (Berkeley), *66*
Coit Tower, *28*

Coleman House, *42*
College sports, *216*
Colma, *83*
Cordon Bleu (restaurant), *111*
Cornell (hotel), *177*
Coronet Motel, *192*
Cowper Inn, *192*
Coyote Point Park, *215*
Creative Growth Art Center, *72*
Crêpes-A-Go-Go (restaurant), *124*
Crescent City Cafe, *114*
Crissy Field, *215*
Curtis Hotel, *183*

D

Dance, *171–172*
David's Hotel, *177*
Desolation Wilderness, *229*
Disabilities, resources for people with, *15–16*
Doe Library, *63*
Dolores Park Inn, *183*
Dolores Street (Mission District), *51–52*
Downtown district
bars, *150–151*
cafés, *142–143*
galleries, *58*
lodging, *176–177*
restaurants, *112–113*
sightseeing, *30–31, 34–35*
Drake's Beach, *81*
Duboce Park, *53*
Duxberry Reef, *80*

E

Ebisu (restaurant), *121–122*
Ebony Museum of Art, *72*
Elephant seals, *89*
El Farolito (restaurant), *108*
Elmwood District (Berkeley), *64*
El Toro (restaurant), *117*
El Trebol (restaurant), *117*
Embarcadero, *34*
Embarcadero Center, *34*
Emergencies, *8*
Yosemite, *243*
Empress Garden (restaurant), *121*
Eric's Hunan and Mandarin, *106*
Esalen Institute, *264*
Esperpento (restaurant), *119*
European Guest House, *184*
Exploratorium, *41, 56*

F

Farmers' markets, *77, 135*
Felton, *256*
Ferry Building, *34*
Ferry service, *7, 59*
to Alcatraz, *26–27*
to Angel Island, *76*

Festivals and street fairs, *16–20*
Berkeley, *62*
Castro District, *46*
Japantown, *42–43*
Marin County, *80*
Monterrey, *259*
San Jose, *84*
San Mateo County Coast, *86–87*
Santa Cruz, *256*
wine country, *228*
Financial district, *31, 34*
Firefly (restaurant), *108*
Fisherman's Wharf, *27, 113*
Fishing, *240, 261*
Flea markets, *100–101*
Flint's (restaurant), *128*
Flying Saucer (restaurant), *119*
Football, *215, 216*
Forest of Nisene Marks State Park, *257*
Fort Funston, *54*
Fort Mason, *40–41*
Ft. Mason International Hostel, *184*
Foundation for San Francisco's Architectural Heritage, *42*
425 Mission (hotel), *190*
Free attractions, *58–59*
Berkeley, *67–68*
Santa Cruz, *256*
French Hotel, *187*
Frisbee, *198*

G
Galleries, *57–58*
Garbage Museum, *84–85*
Gays and lesbians, *12–14*
AIDS support groups, *13*
neighborhoods, *45*
nightclubs, *163–164*
publications, *13*
Glen Canyon, *53*
Glide Memorial Church, *36*
Global Exchange, *50*
Globetrotter's Inn, *184*
Golden Bear Motel, *187*
Golden Boy Pizza, *119–120*
Golden Gate AYH-Hostel, *189–190*
Golden Gate Bridge, *3, 26*
Golden Gate Ferry, *7, 59*
Golden Gate Fortune Cookie Factory, *38*
Golden Gate Park, *28, 30*
Golf, *65*
Grace Cathedral, *39*
Gramma's Rose Garden Inn, *187*
Grand Central Hostel, *184*
Grant Avenue (Chinatown), *37*
Grant Plaza (hotel), *175*
Great America, *85*
Green Gulch Farm Zen Center, *78–79, 189*

Greens (restaurant), *116–117*
Green Tortoise buses, *4–5*
Green Tortoise Guest House, *184–185*
Greyhound, *4*
Grocery shopping, *134–136*
Grubstake (restaurant), *108*
Guaymas (restaurant), *131*
Gum Moon Women's Residence, *174*

H
Haas-Lilienthal House, *42*
Hahn's Hibachi (restaurant), *116*
Haight-Ashbury district
bars, *150–151*
cafés, *143*
lodging, *180*
restaurants, *114–115*
sightseeing, *43–44*
Half Dome, *248*
Half Moon Bay, *86–87, 193–194*
Hamburger Mary's (restaurant), *122*
Hamburgers (restaurant), *130*
Harvest Ranch Market, *134*
Harvey Milk Plaza, *46*
Heavenly ski resort, *237*
Henry Cowell Redwoods State Park, *253, 257*
Henry Miller Library, *264*
Herbert Hotel, *177*
Herbst Theatre, *35*
Hetch Hetchy Reservoir, *240*
Hidden Villa Hostel, *192*
Hiker's Hut (lodging), *194*
Hiking
Berkeley, *65, 66*
Big Sur, *264*
East Bay, *200–203*
Lake Tahoe, *239*
Marin County, *77, 78, 80, 81, 203–207*
San Francisco, *199–200*
San Mateo County Coast, *88, 89, 207–209*
Santa Cruz, *257*
wine country, *223, 228*
Yosemite, *247–249*
Hitchhiking, *251–252*
Hockey, *215–216*
Homemade Cafe, *126*
Homewood ski resort, *237*
Hoover Tower, *82–83*
Horseback riding, *208*
Hostels
Marin County, *188–189*
Palo Alto, *192–193*
San Francisco, *183–185*
San Mateo County Coast, *193, 194*
Hotel Astoria, *175*

Hotel Bohème, *183*
Hotel Durant, *187*
Hot 'n' Hunky (restaurant), *106*
Hot springs, *227–228, 263*
House O'Chicks (hotel), *182*
House of Bagels, *134*
House of Nanking (restaurant), *109–110*

I
Il Fornaio (restaurant), *112*
Il Pollaio (restaurant), *120*
Ina Coolbrith Park, *40*
Indian Rock Park (Berkeley), *66–67*
Inn on Castro (B&B), *174*
Inn San Francisco, *182*
Inspiration Point (Berkeley), *65*
Interclub Globe Hostel, *185*
Internet sites, *11*
Inverness, *81*
Isobune (restaurant), *115–116*
Izumiya (restaurant), *116*

J
Jack London Square (Oakland), *71*
Jackson Square Historical District, *34*
James V. Fitzgerald Marine Reserve, *86*
Japan Center, *42, 115*
Japanese Tea Garden, *30*
Japantown (S.F.), *42–43, 115–116*
Jazz clubs, *158–159, 160*
Jewish Museum, *56*
Jing Jing (restaurant), *132–133*
Josie's Cabaret and Juice Joint, *106–107*
Julia Pfeiffer Burns State Park, *264*
Juan's Place (restaurant), *126*
Juice Bar Collective (restaurant), *124*
Just Desserts (bakery), *123*
Justin Herman Plaza, *34–35*

K
Kabana (restaurant), *126*
Kabuki 8 Theaters, *43*
Kabuki Hot Springs, *43*
Kan Zaman (restaurant), *114*
Kate's Kitchen (restaurant), *114*
Kayaking, *211–212, 240, 261*
Khan Toke Thai House (restaurant), *122*
Kincaid's Bayhouse (restaurant), *130*
Kirala (restaurant), *127*
Kirkwood ski resort, *237*
Kowloon (restaurant), *109*

L

La Cumbre (restaurant), *117*
Lafayette Park, *42*
La Honda
camping, *194*
hiking and biking, *208*
sightseeing, *87–88*
Lake Anza, *65*
Lake Chabot Regional Park, *189*
Lake Merritt, *70–71*
Lake Tahoe, *229–240*
beaches, *240*
bicycling, *239*
camping and lodging,
232–234
fishing, *240*
food and dining, *234–236*
hiking, *239*
nightlife, *236*
skiing, *236–238*
transportation, *231–232*
visitor information, *229, 231*
water sports, *240*
weekly and weekend rentals,
234
La Méditerranée (restaurant),
107
Lands End, *54–55*
Larkspur Landing, *214*
La Rondalla (restaurant), *118*
Laserium, *30*
Latinos, resources for, *14*
Lawrence Hall of Science, *67*
Le Cheval (restaurant),
129–130
Legion of Honor Museum, *56*
Libraries
Berkeley, *63*
Big Sur, *264*
Civic Center, *35*
Oakland, *72*
Western Addition, *45*
Lighthouse Coffee Shop, *130*
Lighthouses, *81, 260*
Linda Mar Beach, *213*
Lodging, *173–194. See also
under cities and areas*
hostels, *183–185, 189–190*
longer-term stays, *185–186,
188*
Lois the Pie Queen (restaurant),
128
Lombard Plaza (hotel), *182*
Lombard Street (Russian Hill),
40
Long Haul, *65*
Long Life Vegi House, *126*
Los Cocos (restaurant), *128*
L'Osteria del Forno (restaurant),
120
**Lovejoy's Antiques and Tea
Room,** *123*
Lower Haight, *44*
Lucca Delicatessen, *134*

Lucky Creation (restaurant),
109
Lucy's Creole Kitchen, *128–129*
Lulu (restaurant), *123*

M

Maiden Lane, *31*
Mail, *10*
Main Squeeze (restaurant), *110*
Mama's Royal Café (Mill Valley),
131–132
Mama's Royal Café (Oakland),
129
Mango Café, *133*
Manora's Thai Cuisine, *122*
Manresa State Beach, *253*
Mansions Hotel, *182*
Marcello's (restaurant), *106*
Marina district
bars, *152*
lodging, *180, 182*
restaurants, *116–117*
sightseeing, *40–42*
Marin Civic Center, *77*
Marin County
bus service, *4*
lodging, *189–192*
medical services, *10*
outdoor activities, *203–207,
212, 213, 214*
restaurants, *130–132*
sightseeing, *73–81*
visitor information, *22*
weather, *21*
Marine Mammal Center, *74*
Marine View Motel, *193*
Marin Headlands
camping, *190*
hiking and biking, *203*
sightseeing, *73–74*
Mariposa Grove, *240*
Maritime Museum, *27*
Markets and delis, *134–136*
Maruwa (market), *115*
Massawa (restaurant), *114*
Mayflower Pub and Grill, *132*
Media, *10–12*
Medical services, *8–10, 243*
Memorial Church, *82*
Memorial County Park, *88, 194*
Meriwa (restaurant), *110*
Merry Pranksters, *88*
Metro Hotel, *180*
Mexicali Rose (restaurant), *129*
Mexican Museum, *57*
**M. H. de Young Memorial
Museum,** *56–57*
Mifune (restaurant), *116*
Mill Valley
restaurants, *131–132*
sightseeing, *76–77*
Mission Cultural Center, *58*
**Mission de Exaltación de la
Santa Cruz,** *255*

Mission district
bars, *152–153*
cafés, *144*
galleries, *58*
lodging, *182–183*
restaurants, *117–119*
sightseeing, *50–52*
Mission Dolores, *51–52*
Mission Dolores Park, *51,
53–54*
Mitchell's Ice Cream, *123*
Mission San Francisco Solano,
220–221
Miss Millie's (restaurant), *107*
Miss Pearl's Jam House
(restaurant), *111–112*
Miyake Sushi (restaurant),
133
Moishe's Pippic (restaurant),
110–111
Molinari Delicatessen, *134*
Montara, *85–86, 193*
Monterrey, *259–261*
camping and lodging,
259–260
food, *260*
nightlife, *260–261*
outdoor activities, *261*
sightseeing, *260*
transportation, *259*
visitor information, *259*
Morrison Planetarium, *55*
Mountain biking, *199–209. See
also Bicycling*
Mountain Theater (Mt.
Tamalpais), *79*
Mt. Tamalpais State Park
camping, *191*
hiking and biking, *205–206*
sightseeing, *79*
Movies, *17, 164–166*
Muir Beach, *78–79*
Muir Woods National Monument,
77–78, 205
MUNI buses, *3*
Museé Mécanique, *57*
Museo ItaloAmericano, *57*
Museums, *55–57. See also Art
galleries and museums*
Berkeley, *67, 68*
downtown, *34*
Fisherman's Wharf, *27*
Golden Gate Park, *30*
the Marina, *41*
Nob Hill, *39*
North Beach, *38*
Oakland, *70, 71, 72*
Presidio, *41*
San Jose, *84*
Santa Cruz, *255*
Sonoma, *221*
Music
blues, *159, 160*
classical, *169–171, 256*

folk, *161*
jazz, *158–159, 160*
rock, *157–158, 159–160*
world, *161*
Mystery Spot, *256*

N

NAMES Project Foundation,
46–47
Nan Yang (restaurant), *129*
Napa, *223, 224*
Napa Valley, *223–229*
NASA Ames Research Center,
83–84
Native Americans, resources for,
15
Natural Bridges State Beach,
255–256
Nature centers, *65, 66*
Neptune Society Columbarium,
59
New Brighton State Beach, *254*
New Dawn (restaurant), *117*
Newspapers, *10–11*
Nicaragua (restaurant), *118*
Nightclubs, *161–164*
Noah's Bagels, *124*
Nob Hill district
bars, *153*
sightseeing, *39–40*
Nob Hill Pensione, *176*
Noe Valley
restaurants, *106–108*
sightseeing, *47, 50*
No-Name (Nippon) Sushi, *107*
Nori Sushi (restaurant), *111*
North Beach district
bars, *153–154*
cafés, *144–145*
lodging, *183*
restaurants, *119–121*
sightseeing, *38–39*
North Beach Museum, *38*
North Beach Pizza (restaurant),
120
Northstar-at-Tahoe resort, *237*
Now and Zen (restaurant),
116

O

Oakland
ballet, *172*
bars, *156–157*
bus service, *4*
cafés, *148*
festivals, *71*
free attractions, *72–73*
live music, *160*
lodging and camping,
188–189
medical services, *9–10*
movie houses, *165–166*
nightclubs, *164*
outdoor activities, *200–203*

restaurants, *127–130*
shopping, *92, 94, 95, 97, 99,*
101
sightseeing, *69–71*
theater, *168*
visitor information, *22*
weather, *22*
Oakland Airport, *8*
Oakland Museum, *72*
Oasis Beer Garden, *133*
Ocean Beach, *55, 213*
Old St. Hilary's Historic
Preserve, *75*
Old Thyme Inn, *193*
101 Restaurant, *112*
On-line resources, *11*
Opera, *19, 170, 171*
Orphan Andy's (restaurant), *108*
Outdoor activities, *195–216.*
See also under cities and
areas
baseball, *215*
basketball, *196–197, 215*
bicycling, *199–209*
hiking, *199–209*
hockey, *215–216*
horseback riding, *208*
in-line skating, *209–210*
rock climbing, *210–211*
sailing, *211*
sea kayaking, *211–212*
soccer, *197–198, 216*
surfing, *212–213*
ultimate frisbee, *198*
volleyball, *198*
windsurfing, *213–215*
Outdoors Unlimited, *195*

P

Pacifica
hiking and biking, *207–208*
lodging, *193*
sightseeing, *85*
Pacific Heights, *42, 180, 182*
Pacific Heritage Museum, *57*
Pacific Tradewinds (hostel),
185
Painted Ladies, *45*
Palace of Fine Arts, *41*
Palo Alto
gay and lesbian organizations,
14
lodging, *192–193*
restaurants, *132–133*
sightseeing, *82–84*
Panama Hotel, *190*
Panchita's (restaurant), *118*
Pancho Villa (restaurant), *117*
Paramount Theatre, *69*
Parasailing, *240*
Parks and gardens, city, *53–54*
Berkeley, *65, 66*
Golden Gate Park, *28, 30*
North Beach, *39, 54*

Oakland, *71, 72*
Pacific Heights, *42*
Parks, state and county
Big Sur, *262, 263, 264*
East Bay area, *189, 201–204,*
210
Marin County, *76, 77, 78,*
190, 191–192, 204–206
San Mateo County, *86, 88, 89,*
193, 194, 208–209
Santa Cruz, *253, 255–256,*
258, 259
wine country, *221, 223, 224*
Pasand Madras Cuisine,
126–127
Pasta Pomodoro (restaurant),
107
Patio Café, *107*
Peace Plaza, *42*
People of color, resources for,
14–15
People's Park, *62*
Performance spaces, *168–169*
Pescadero, *88–89, 194*
Pescadero Creek County Park,
88, 194
Pfeiffer Big Sur State Park,
263–264
Phoebe Hearst Museum of
Anthropology, *67*
Phoenix Hotel, *175–176*
Phó' Lâm Viên (restaurant), *129*
Phuong Nam (restaurant), *133*
Picnic spots
Berkeley, *65*
Lands End, *54–55*
Marina, *40*
Marin County, *75, 76*
North Beach, *39, 54*
Oakland, *72*
Pigeon Point Lighthouse Youth
Hostel, *194*
P. J.'s Oyster Bed (restaurant),
122
Planetariums and observatories,
55–56
Plane travel, *7–8*
Pluto's (restaurant), *116*
Point Montara Lighthouse AYH-
Hostel, *193*
Point Reyes AYH-Hostel, *191*
Point Reyes National Seashore
camping and lodging,
191–192
hiking and biking, *206–207*
sightseeing, *80–81*
Polk Gulch, *36*
Pool halls, *152*
Pork Store Café, *114–115*
Portola Redwoods State Park,
88, 194
Portrero Hill, *52*
Precita Eyes Mural Arts Center,
51

Preservation Park (Oakland), 70
Presidio, The, 41, 200
Presidio Army Museum, 41
Public transportation
BART, 5
bicycles on, 5–6
buses, 3–5
ferry service, 7
information, 1
people with disabilities, 16
trains, 6
Puppet theater, 59

R

Racha Café, 111
Radio stations, 11–12
Rainbow Grocery, 134
R&G Lounge, 110
Real Foods (deli), 134–135
Red and White Fleet, 7
Red Rocks Beach, 79–80
Red Victorian (hotel), 180
Redwood Regional Park, 202–203
Redwood trees, 77–78, 87, 88
Rental cars, 2
Restaurants, 105–139. See also under cities and areas
dim sum, 109
late-night restaurants, 108
reference listings, 136–139
Richmond district, 43, 121–122
Rick and Ann's (restaurant), 126
Rincon Center, 35
Ristorante Ideale, 120
Robert Crown Memorial State Beach, 72–73
Rock climbing, 210–211, 249
Rock music, 157–158, 160–161
Rodin Sculpture Garden, 83
Roommate referral agencies, 186
Rose Pistola (restaurant), 121
Rosicrucian Egyptian Museum and Planetarium, 84
Royal Thai (restaurant), 132
Russian Hill district, 39–40, 120, 153

S

Sake sampling, 68
Sailing, 67, 211
St. Francis Soda Fountain and Candy Store, 50, 123
Sam McDonald County Park, 88
Sam's Anchor Cafe, 131
Samuel P. Taylor State Park, 191–192
San Benito House, 193

Sanborn Park Hostel, 192–193
San Francisco. See also specific districts
bars, 149–155
beaches, 54–55
cafés, 141–147
dance, 171–172
free attractions, 59
galleries, 57–58
live music, 157–159
lodging, 173–186
markets and delis, 134–135
movie houses, 164–165
museums, 55–57
nightclubs, 161–164
outdoor activities, 196, 197, 198, 199–200, 209–210
parks and gardens, 53–54
performance spaces, 168–169
restaurants, 105–123
shopping, 91–104
sightseeing, 26–53
theater, 166–168
visitor information, 21–22
San Francisco Airport, 7–8
San Francisco Art Institute Café, 120
San Francisco International Guest House, 185
San Francisco International Student Center, 185
San Francisco Museum of Modern Art, 53, 57
San Francisco Public Library, 35
San Francisco Residence Club, 177
San Francisco Zen Center, 176
San Gregorio, 87
San Jose
festivals, 84
restaurants, 133
sightseeing, 84–85
sports, 215–216
San Jose Airport, 8
San Rafael
lodging, 190
restaurants, 132
sightseeing, 77
San Rafael Station Café, 132
San Remo Hotel, 182
Santa Cruz, 250–258
beaches, 253, 255–256
bicycling, 257
cafés, 254
camping and lodging, 252–253
festivals, 256
food and dining, 253–254
free attractions, 256
hiking, 257
nightlife, 257
sightseeing, 255–256
surfing, 257
transportation, 250–252

Santa Cruz City Museum of Natural History, 255
Santa Cruz Surfing Museum, 255
Sather Gate, 63
Saul's (restaurant), 126
Sausalito
restaurants, 130–131
sightseeing, 75
Scavenging, 100
Scenic India (restaurant), 119
Scenic views, 47
Berkeley, 63, 65
Coit Tower, 28
Downtown, 34
Marina, 40
Mission District, 52, 53
Russian Hill, 40
Twin Peaks, 47
Scuba diving, 261
Seabreeze market, 135
Sea kayaking, 211–212, 261
Sea lions, 27
Semifreddi's (bread shop), 136
Shangri-La (restaurant), 121
Shopping, 91–104. See also under cities.
art and photography, 101–102
body decorations, 102
charitable causes, 102
flea markets, 100–101
games and toys, 102
hats and jewelry, 102
miscellaneous, 104
new clothing, 92–93
papers, cards, and stationery, 103
records, tapes, and CDs, 97–99
second-hand clothing, 93–95
sex accessories, 103
skateboards and motorcycles, 103
Silver (restaurant), 108
16th Street, 50
Skiing, 236–238, 249–250
Slanted Door (restaurant), 119
Smart Alec's (restaurant), 124
Snorkeling, 261
Snowshoeing, 250
Soccer, 197–198
Sonoma, 220–221
Sonoma Valley, 220–223
South Bay
bus service, 4
climate, 21
medical services, 10
visitor information, 22
Soups (restaurant), 111
South Lake Tahoe, 229
South of Market district (SoMa)
bars, 154–155
cafés, 145–146
galleries, 58

restaurants, *122–123*
sightseeing, *52–53*
South Park, *54*
South Park Café, *122–123*
Spaghetti Western (restaurant), *115*
Sparky's (restaurant), *108*
Specialty's (restaurant), *112*
Spectator sports, *215–216*
Spettro (restaurant), *129*
Spreckels Mansion, *42*
Sproul Plaza, *62–63*
Squat and Gobble Café, *115*
Squaw Valley ski resort, *237*
Stanford Linear Accelerator, *83*
Stanford University, *82–83*
Stanyan Park Hotel, *180*
Stateline, NV, *229*
Steam bath, *43*
Steep Ravine Campground and Cabins, *191*
Steinhart Aquarium, *55–56*
Stinson Beach, *79–80, 191*
Stinson Beach Motel, *191*
Stockton Street (Chinatown), *37–38*
Street fairs, *16–20.* See also Festivals and street fairs.
Strybing Arboretum and Botanical Gardens, *30*
Studio Café, *114*
Sugar Bowl ski resort, *237*
Sugarloaf State Park, *221*
Sunset district, *121–122*
Sunset State Beach, *253*
Supper clubs, *159*
Surfing, *212–213, 257–258*
Sushi Ya (restaurant), *133*
Sutro Forest, *54*
Swan Oyster Depot (restaurant), *111*
Sweden House Café, *131*
Swensen's (ice-cream parlor), *123*
Swimming, *65*
Sykes Hot Springs, *264*

T
Tahoe City, *229*
Tank Hill, *47*
Taquería Cancun (restaurant), *117–118*
Taqueria Morelia (restaurant), *127–128*
Taxis, *6–7*
Telegraph Avenue (Berkeley), *60, 62*
Temples, *38, 41*
Tenderloin District, *36*
Thai House (restaurant), *107*
Theater, *19, 79, 166–168*
Tiburon, *75, 131*
Ti Couz (restaurant), *118*

Tilden Regional Park, *65–66, 201–202*
Timo's (restaurant), *119*
Tom Peasant Pies (restaurant), *106*
Toy Boat (ice-cream parlor), *123*
Trader Joe's (market), *135*
Train travel, *6*
Transamerica Pyramid, *34*
Travel Inn, *187*
Travelodge (Berkeley), *187*
Travelodge (Marina), *182*
Treasure Island, *47*
Truckee, *229*
Truly Mediterranean (restaurant), *118*
Tu Lan (restaurant), *111*
Tuolomne Meadows, *240, 248, 249*
24 Henry (B&B), *174*
20 Tank Brewery (restaurant), *122*
Twin Peaks, *47*
Twin Peaks (motel), *174*

U
Ultimate frisbee, *198*
Union Square, *30–31*
Union Street, *41*
United Nations Plaza, *35*
University Art Museum, *67*
University Avenue (Berkeley), *64*
University of California
lodging, *187*
museums, *67*
sightseeing, *62–63*
University of California–Santa Cruz, *255*

V
Valencia Street (Mission District), *50–51*
Venezia (restaurant), *127*
Visitor information, *21–22*
Lake Tahoe, *229, 231*
Monterrey, *259*
wine country, *218–219*
Yosemite, *242*
Volleyball, *198*

W
Washington Square Park, *39, 54*
Wave Organ, *41–42*
Waverly Place (Chinatown), *38*
Weather information, *20–21*
Web sites, *11*
Wedding houses, *41*
Wells Fargo History Museum, *34*
Western Addition
bars, *150–151*
cafés, *143*

lodging, *180*
sightseeing, *44–45*
Whale watching, *261*
Wildcat Canyon Regional Park, *202*
Winchester Mystery House, *84*
Windsurfing, *213–215, 240*
Wine country, *217–229*
bicycling, *220*
camping and lodging, *221, 224*
food and dining, *221–222, 224–225*
free attractions, *223, 228*
hot springs, *227–228*
outdoor activities, *223, 228–229*
timing the visit, *219*
transportation, *219–220*
visitor information, *218–219*
Wineries, *222–223, 225–227*
Women, resources for, *15*
Women's Building, *63*
Wright, Frank Lloyd, *31, 77*

Y
Ya, Halla! (restaurant), *115*
Yank Sing (restaurant), *113*
Yerba Buena Gardens, *52–53*
YMCA (Berkeley), *186*
YMCA (Chinatown), *174–175*
YMCA (Civic Center), *175*
Yosemite National Park, *240–250*
bicycling, *249*
camping and lodging, *244–246*
fees, *242*
food, *246*
hiking, *247–248*
medical assistance, *243*
packing, *243*
rock climbing, *249*
scenic views, *249*
shopping, *243*
shuttle buses, *244*
sightseeing, *246–249*
skiing, *249–250*
snowshoeing, *250*
timing the visit, *242–243*
tours, *247*
transportation, *243–244*
visitor information, *242*
wilderness permits, *242*
Your Black Muslim Bakery, *136*
Yuet Lee (restaurant), *110*

Z
Zachary's Chicago Pizza Inc., *129*
Zarzuela (restaurant), *120–121*

Notes

Notes

TELL US WHAT YOU THINK

We're always trying to improve our books and would really appreciate any feedback on how to make them more useful. Thanks for taking a few minutes to fill out this survey. We'd also like to know about your latest find, a new scam, a budget deal, whatever . . . Please print your name and address clearly and send the completed survey to: The Berkeley Guides, 515 Eshelman Hall, U.C. Berkeley, CA 94720.

1. Your name _____

2. Your address _____

   _____ Zip _____

3. You are: Female   Male

4. Your age: under 17   17–22   23–30   31–40   41–55   over 55

5. If you're a student: Name of school _____ City & state _____

6. If you're employed: Occupation _____

7. Your yearly income: under $20,000 $21,000–$30,000 $31,000–$45,000
   $46,000–$60,000 $61,000–$100,000   over $100,000

8. Which of the following do you own? (Circle all that apply.)

   Computer   CD-ROM Drive   Modem

9. What speed (bps) is your modem?
   2400   4800   9600   14.4   19.2   28.8

10. Which on-line service(s) do you subscribe to apart from commercial services like AOL?

    _____

11. Do you have access to the World Wide Web? If so, is it through a university or a private service provider? _____

12. If you have a CD-ROM drive or plan to have one, would you purchase a Berkeley Guide CD-ROM? _____

13. Which Berkeley Guide(s) did you buy? _____

14. Where did you buy the book and when?   City _____ Month/Year _____

15. Why did you choose The Berkeley Guides? (Circle all that apply.)

    Budget focus   Design
    Outdoor emphasis   Attitude
    Off-the-beaten-track emphasis   Writing style
    Resources for gays and   Organization
      lesbians
                                          More maps
    Resources for people with
      disabilities   Accuracy
    Resources for women   Price
    Other _____

16. How did you hear about The Berkeley Guides? (Circle all that apply.)

Recommended by friend/acquaintance   Bookstore display   TV

Article in magazine/newspaper (which one?) _____

Ad in magazine/newspaper (which one?) _____

Radio program (which one?) _____

Other _____

17. Which other guides, if any, have you used before? (Circle all that apply.)

Fodor's	Let's Go	Rough Guides
Frommer's	Birnbaum	Lonely Planet

Other _____

18. When did you travel with this book?   Month/Year _____

19. Where did you travel? _____

20. What was the purpose of your trip?

Vacation	Business	Volunteer
Study abroad	Work	

21. About how much did you spend per day during your trip?

$0–$20	$31–$45	$61–$75	over $100
$21–$30	$46–$60	$76–$100	

22. After you arrived, how did you get around? (Circle all that apply.)

Rental car	Personal car	Plane	Bus
Train	Hiking	Bike	Hitching

23. Which features/sections did you use most? (Circle all that apply.)

Book Basics	City/region Basics	Coming and Going
Hitching	Getting Around	Where to Sleep
Camping	Roughing It	Food
Worth Seeing	Cheap Thrills	Festivals
Shopping	After Dark	Outdoor Activities

24. The information was (circle one):   V = very accurate   U = usually accurate

S = sometimes accurate   R = rarely accurate

Introductions	V U S R	Worth Seeing	V U S R
Basics	V U S R	After Dark	V U S R
Coming and Going	V U S R	Outdoor Activities	V U S R
Where to Sleep	V U S R	Maps	V U S R
Food	V U S R		

25. I would _____ would not _____ buy another Berkeley Guide.

26. Which of the following destinations are you planning to visit in the next five years?

The Americas
Chicago
Washington, D.C.
New Orleans
Los Angeles
Boston
Austin
The Midwest
The South
The Southwest
New England
The Pacific Northwest
Hawaii
Canada
South America

Middle East/Africa
Turkey
Israel
Egypt
Africa

Europe
Spain
Portugal
Greece
Russia
Scandinavia
Berlin
Prague
Rome

Australia/Asia
Australia
New Zealand
Vietnam
Philippines
Indonesia
Thailand
Singapore
Malaysia
Cambodia
India/Nepal